The Powered PARAGLIDING Bible³

Jeff Goin

Air Head Creations
www.FootFlyer.com

The Powered PARAGLIDING Bible³

Copyright © 2012 Jeff Goin All Rights Reserved
Published by
Airhead Creations dba FootFlyer.com

Third Edition
1st edition printed 2005
2nd edition printed 2008

ISBN: 978-0-9770966-3-3
Library of Congress Control Number: 2011961642

Edited by
Dennis Pagen
Tim Kaiser

Air Head Creations
Naperville, Illinois, USA

Email info@footflyer.com

Photographs by Jeff Goin except where noted.
For related materials, please visit **www.FootFlyer.com**.

The information is accurate to the best of our knowledge but errors may occur. This material is protected by U.S. and International copyright laws. No part may be reproduced or transmitted in any form or by any means, electronic or mechanical without written permission from the publisher.

The reader acknowledges that powered paragliding and related activities carry significant risk including dismemberment and death. You take this risk completely of your own volition and understand that the creators of this book assume no liability in connection with its contents.

Printed in Canada

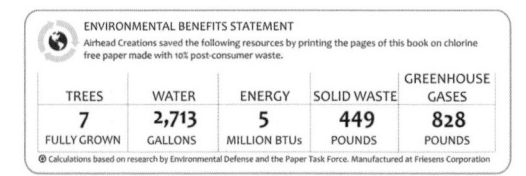

ENVIRONMENTAL BENEFITS STATEMENT
Airhead Creations saved the following resources by printing the pages of this book on chlorine free paper made with 10% post-consumer waste.

TREES	WATER	ENERGY	SOLID WASTE	GREENHOUSE GASES
7	2,713	5	449	828
FULLY GROWN	GALLONS	MILLION BTUs	POUNDS	POUNDS

Calculations based on research by Environmental Defense and the Paper Task Force. Manufactured by Friesens Corporation

Table of Contents

Foreword viii
How to Use This Book viii
Thanks To ix
Preface x

Section I: First Flight

    Ratings 2
    What it Takes Physically 2

Chapter 1 The Training Process
    Finding an Instructor 3
    The School 4
    Different Methods of Instructing 5
    Certification 7
    Training Aids 7
    Getting to that First Flight 10
    Progression 10

Chapter 2 Gearing Up
    The Wing 13
    The Risers 15
    The Harness 16
    The Motor 19
    Instruments 20
    Accessories 21

Chapter 3 Handling The Wing
    Deflating the Wing 24
    Brake Positions/Pressures 24
    Preparing Yourself 25
    Preparing the Wing 26
    Forward And Reverse Launch 26
    Light Winds (Forward Inflation) 26
    Wind Over 6 mph (Reverse Inflation) 29
    Storing the Wing 35

Chapter 4 Preparing For First Flight
    Adjusting the Motor 37
    Fueling 38
    Preflight Inspection 39
    Starting the Motor 41
    Have a Plan: Patterns, Areas and Altitudes 42
    Taking Instructions Via Radio 43
    Handling Emergencies 43

Chapter 5 The Flight
    Launch 51
    Climbout 56
    Flying Around 57
    Landing 59
    After Landing 62

Chapter 6 Adding Wheels
    Wheeled Types 64
    Setup 64
    Launch 65
    Flying 67
    Landing 68
    Risk Comparison 68
    Walk or Roll 68

Table of Contents

Section II: Spreading Your Wings

Chapter 7 Weather Basics
- The Perfect Day 71
- Thermals & The Daily Cycle 72
- Indications of Turbulence 72
- Thunderstorms 73
- Mountains 74
- Beach 74
- Whenever There's Wind 75
- Acquiring Aviation Weather 77
- Other Weather Sources 78

Chapter 8 Common Sense & The Law
- Regulations 80
- Case Law & Other Issues 81
- Commercial Use 83
- If I Violate the Rules? 84

Chapter 9 Airspace
- Airspace Types 86
- The ABC's of Airspace 86
- Reading The Charts 91
- The Airspace Test 94
- Other Uses for the charts 97

Chapter 10 Flying From Anywhere
- Choosing the site 100
- Site Permission 101
- High Elevation Fields 101
- Flying At or Near Airports 102
- Places to Look 105
- Safe Havens 106
- Telling Wind Direction From Flight Path 106

Chapter 11 Flying From Controlled Airports
- Telephone 107
- Aircraft Radio 108
- Letter of Agreement 112

Chapter 12 Setup & Maintenance
- Harness 113
- Motor 118
- Reduction Drive 119
- Clutch 120
- Propeller 120
- Propeller Repair 122
- The Wing 125
- Emergency Tool Kit 128
- Reserve 128

Chapter 13 Flying Cross Country
- Basic Tips 131
- Fuel & Range 133
- Getting Lost 133
- Navigation 133
- Pilotage 136
- Altitudes 137
- Using a GPS 138

Table of Contents

Chapter 14 Flying With Others
Courtesy 139
Risks 140
Rescuing a pilot 141
Communications 142
Formation Flying 142

Section III: Mastering The Sport

Chapter 15 Advanced Ground Handling
Upside down kiting to clean out cells. 145
Kiting Without a Harness. 146
High wind techniques 148
Light Wind Techniques 153
Inflation Issues 154

Chapter 16 Precision Flying
Brakes—The Feel Position 157
Straight Lines—Pendular Precision 158
Balance of Power 160
Low Flying 161
Hitting Suspended Targets 163
Formation 163
Active Flying in Turbulence 164
The Perfect Touchdown 165

Chapter 17 Challenging Sites
The Horror of Hot, High, and Humid 167
Tight Spaces 170

Chapter 18 Advanced Maneuvers
Weight Shift Turns 176
Speedbar Usage 177
Maneuvers Course 177
Descent Techniques 178
Wing Malfunctions 181
Pendular Control 183
Tip Line (Stabilo) Line Pull 184

Chapter 19 Risk Management
Probability and Severity 185
Energy and Injury 186
Getting Away With It 187
Where the Risk Is 187
Combining Risks 193
Handling Situational Emergencies 194

Chapter 20 Competition
How Good Do I Need To Be? 202
Ground Precision 202
Flight Precision (Navigation) 206
Fuel Limited Tasks 206
Endurance 207
Kiting 207

Chapter 21 Free Flight Transition
Transition to Thrust: Becoming a Power Pilot 209
Transition to Free Flight: Going Soaring 213

Table of Contents

Section IV: Theory & Understanding

Chapter 22 Aerodynamics
- Balance of Forces 219
- Stability 221
- Glide & Drag 222
- Center of Lift and Drag 223
- Sink Rate 223
- Speed 223
- Efficiency Under Power 224
- Wing 224

Chapter 23 Motor & Propeller
- Thrust & Horsepower 229
- 2 And 4-Stroke Motors 230
- Propeller & Reduction Drives 235
- Balance 238
- Twisting Forces At Work 239

Chapter 24 Weather & Wind
- Using Forecasts 243
- Principles 244
- Standard Atmosphere 244
- Daily Cycles 245
- Yearly Cycle 247
- All About Thermals 247
- Clouds 248
- Fronts 250
- Getting Weather Info 251
- Turbulence from Wind 251

Chapter 25 Roots: Our History
- Parasailing 253
- Hang Gliding & Ultralighting 253
- Sport Parachuting 254
- Lost Lineage 254
- Performance Improvements over time 256

Section V: Choosing Gear

Chapter 26 The Wing
- Ease of Launch 259
- Size 260
- Reflex 260
- Glide and Sink Rate 261
- Stability 261
- Handling 261
- Speed 262
- Center Cell Visibility 262
- Certification 262
- Risers 263
- Kiting Only Wing 264

Chapter 27 The Motor Unit
- Weight 266
- Comfort 266
- Thrust 266
- Quality 267
- Powerplant Considerations 267
- Ease of Launch 269
- Ease of Maintenance 270

Table of Contents

    Fuel Storage—Above, Below, or in the Frame ... 270
    Propeller Size and Style ... 270
    Attachment Points & Separation Bars ... 271
    Weight Shift ... 272
    Transportability ... 273
    Support—Parts and Expertise ... 273
    Safety ... 274

Chapter 28 Accessories
    Reserve ... 275
    Adding Wheels ... 276
    Tachometer ... 278
    Wind Indicators ... 278
    EGT, CHT ... 278
    Airspeed Indicator ... 279
    GPS ... 279
    Emergency Kit ... 280
    Cold Weather Gear ... 280

Chapter 29 Home Building
    Building Your Own Design ... 282
    Building From Plans (Scratch) ... 283
    Building From A Kit ... 283
    Testing & Changes ... 284

Section VI: Getting the Most Out of Powered Paragliding

Chapter 30 Other Uses
    Using PPG for Transportation ... 287
    Flags & Banners ... 288
    Cattle Herding ... 289
    Search and Rescue ... 290
    Finding Model Aircraft ... 290
    Public Relations & Exhibition ... 290

Chapter 31 Traveling With Gear
    Shipping ... 291
    Transporting via Road ... 293
    Customs ... 294

Chapter 32 Photography
    Still Photography Basics ... 295
    Video ... 299

Appendix - Checklists ... 301

Appendix - Resources ... 302
    Fuel/Oil Mix Chart ... 302
    Repair ... 302
    Instruction ... 302
    Welding ... 302

Appendix - FAR 103 ... 303

Glossary ... 305

Index ... 307

Foreword

The easy travel inherent in my "day job" has afforded me access to our sport's greatest pilots and teachers; people who have gone far beyond just succeeding. They have different styles, to be sure, and even different disciplines within the sport, but they have one thing in common: a desire for excellence. It is my desire to share that wealth of knowledge. The third edition incorporates new knowledge in many areas, including Reflex wings, which have gained broader acceptance. Plus it adds more illustrations and animation-based graphics.

Paramotor instructors remain our greatest resource; I hope that this material serves as an additional tool for them as well as for those coming into the sport and those aspiring to master it.

No book can instill a skill. What we hope to show is not only how to do a task, but what *practice* will turn the task into a skill along with ways to minimize risk in the process. There is no way to learn a kinematic "feel" from reading, but knowing which exercises develop what skills will go a long way towards gaining that feel.

Is it Risky?

No Risk, No Reward. Know Risk, Know Reward. Flight always involves risk. What limited statistics we have suggest that our odds for survival are slightly better than flying small airplanes or ultralights but at some higher prospects of minor injuries. Our primary advantage is low speed.

It's certainly not as safe as watching others experience life through TV but sure is a whole lot more fulfilling! As Wilbur Wright observed in response to his many naysayers: "If you are looking for perfect safety, you will do well to sit on a fence and watch the birds." But then, even that can be dangerous.

How to Use This Book

It is imperative that this book **not be used for self training!** That risky undertaking is fortunately no longer required given the presence of many qualified instructors. Absolutely nothing contained here should be tried without getting good instruction first.

Our craft is a wonder of simplicity—graceful and capable in the air but ungainly and challenging on the ground. It's impressive how much ungainliness can be overcome with a small investment in instruction.

Section I prepares you for initial training through first flight, including terminology. Later sections will be be more meaningful as you progress. It assumes that your instructor will take responsibility for determining appropriate gear, conditions, location and other minutia.

Section II covers the basic knowledge needed to head out on your own. Your instructor can help make the material more relevant to your particular location and situation. For example, if you live near a big city, ask about charts and airspace. If you live in mountainous terrain, dig more deeply into mountain weather.

Read Section III if you aspire to master the finer points of flying the craft accurately. The degree of control available to those who are willing to learn it is truly amazing. There are many nuances.

Every pilot should eventually read Section IV to build a more complete understanding of what's going on around them, especially the chapter on Aerodynamics. Among other things, it dispels myths that continue to circulate.

If you're an experienced pilot buying gear, read Section V first. New pilots should always choose an instructor rather then gear, but there is a lot of benefit to understanding the tradeoffs. It may help avoid shysters who would try to fit their round-pegged gear into your square-holed needs.

Section VI offers suggestions on "what now?" Some of it is just plain fun, but hey, that's what this sport is about.

Companion Web Site:

Updated and supplemental information to this book will be placed on **www.FootFlyer.com**. Videos and other material will also be placed there, too, organized under "Educational," just like the book's chapters.

Thanks To

Many have contributed to my earliest and fondest memories of this sport and my flying; I am thankful for them all. Here are just a few.

Mom: "It's a passing fad, you'll get over it." —Words that my 13 year old ears just wouldn't accept. Fortunately she not only relented, but eventually encouraged and even joined my quest for flight. And Dad, who tolerated all this with aplomb.

Eric Dufour: "Don't look at the wing—it won't tell you anything you can't feel." At my first fly-in, I watched this man really *control* the craft and found out what *could* be done with it.

Michelle Daniele: "It's a fly-in, if anyone gets mad at you for launching early, have them see me!" —After asking if it would be ok to launch at dawn during their first Balloon Fiesta fly-in.

Nick Scholtes: "I thought you weren't interested" —After introducing me to the sport, I disappeared. The next time we met I had gotten training, purchased gear and couldn't get enough. We proceeded to gorge ourselves on airtime over the next few years.

Mark Sorenson: "Power up to go up." —Words of my first PPG Instructor that I wish I would have heeded more. Sorry it took so long.

Jerry Daniele: "We fly at the pleasure of the people; tick them off and eventually we won't fly anymore." —Wisdom that has driven many of my early efforts and some current ones (including this book).

Chris Bowles: "Uh oh, it's on." Words that ended the first USPPA officer meeting after recognizing that soarable conditions had developed at his Moore Mountain home.

Alex Varv: "This is my baby, every now and then I like to come out and just admire it" —Referring to his newly updated machine equipped with more gauges then some airplanes. And he knew what they all meant.

Rob Sutter: "Jeff, you gotta check this out. You wanna to go in with me on one of these powered paraglider things?" —The fellow who enticed me into that first fateful look at powered paragliding. He never did get into it.

Alan Chuculate: "Just lean back and go for it!" —One of many admonishments from the instructor who *really* taught me kiting.

Jeff Williams: "You might even like the soaring." —My first paraglider instructor whose patient wisdom guided me beyond the basics to a love for free flight. Yes, Jeff, I understand now, you *can* soar the heights without a variometer.

The Brothers Casaudemecq, Jose & Javier: "It'll fly you just fine at that weight" —The two gentlemen who gave me advice on a used motor that would be my first and longest lasting. They were right on.

Elizabeth Guerin: "Oh, you were the one that was never on the ground." —After my first fly-in when we met up several months later.

Bruce Brown: "Wanna go play in the road?" —the enticement that preceded a remarkable low-level romp around the New Mexican desert floor at my first fly-in.

Phil Russman: "Is it over?" Gifted crafter of content who always challenged me to excel. Yes, it's over—again.

And also...

Mom—A wonderful human, a picky editor, an English Major, newspaper woman, flier of other things, creative wordsmith and *brutal*.
Dennis Pagen—For getting me to do it in the first place, refining it, tolerating all of my non-standardness and *more brutal*!
Tim Kaiser—Editing, continued pilot/photo victim and "Enterprise" captain whose many miles at the helm enabled many pages of work. And he survived being my first student. Thankfully, he was mercifully easy.

And to those who helped with material—you've improved this book *enormously*!

Mark Andrews	Maneuvers
Bob Armond	Carts, Setup, Emergencies
Chad Bastian	Maneuvers, Emergencies
Jeff Baumgartener	Homebuilding
Steve Boser	Propellers
Bill Briley	Maneuvers
Chris Bowles	History, Engines, Setup
Stu Caruk	Towing information, Airspace
Alan Chuculate	Wing Maintenance, Kiting, & Situational Emergencies
Francesco DeSantis	History, Homebuilding
Eric Dufour	History, Glossary
Betty Pfeiffer	Reserves
Bill Heaner	Glossary
Chris Lee	Aerial Photography
David McWhinnie	Shipping
Wayne Mitchler	Handling The Wing, Setup, Trikes
Mike Nowland	Cross Country, Motors, Wings
Dana Hague	Aerodynamics, Motors
Steve Mayer	My "Paraglider Encyclopedia"
Scott MacMurray	Line Tangles
Dennis Pagen	Everything
Phil Russman	Aerial Videography
Nick Scholtes	Motors, Trikes, Precision flying
Tom Scott	Composite Propeller Repair
Mo Sheldon	Carts, Glossary, Propellers
Geoff Soden	History
Alex Varv	Setup, Motor Maintenance

Preface

When my friend, Rob Sutter, first suggested this sport, I thought he was nuts. "You want to do what?" I asked. He knew that I was a flying freak. That wasn't hard—I lived on an airport, had a hangar in my back yard, owned an airplane, a helicopter, and flew for a living. Ridiculous. So he figured that I'd be an easy mark for yet *another* flying contraption, even one I'd never hear of. This paramotor reminded me of the guy who loosed himself over Los Angeles in a lawn chair with weather balloons. Not me. But Rob insisted, saying it was more refined and he wanted someone to share it with. So I went for a look.

What I found was astounding, revealing refinement and control that I never imagined. Before, I figured it must be more *influenced* than flown. But after much browsing, and many questions, it beame obvious that it *could* be finely controlled, and that it would not be subdueed a light wind's wily whirls. That got me fired up. It seeming too good to be true but within my reach. Being nearly free of rules was even more exciting. I've spent my aeronautical life adhering to those necessary limitations and this looked like a way out, a really cool way out at that.

My mind raced—thoughts of scooting around the surrounding fields at a whim ignited desire. You mean I could wander at my leisure, flitting from point to point, in any direction, exploring in three dimensions? "There's got to be a catch" I thought. The idea of running into the air was cooler still—stirring me like nothing else in aviation ever had. And I was already flying airplanes for work, airplanes for fun and, and had just earned my helicopter license. That was certainly all great but the paramotor seemed so much more intriguing. After all, I could take it *with* me.

I contacted Nick Scholtes who was already flying in the area. He was very welcoming and answered my many questions, even hanging me in his little DK motor unit from some contraption he had sitting around his shop (a tip of his iceberg, I eventually learned). We watched videos, talked endlessly and he allayed my fears. Yes, there is risk, but it appeared to be less than other risks I willingly accepted.

That visit sealed my fate. Unfortunately this all came about during Chicagoland's deep freeze—there would be no flying here and I wanted to start now! The recommended instructor, Alan Chuculate, was not available so I was steered towards another gem, Jeff Williams. After eight days, spanning two trips to California, I earned my USHGA P2 paraglider rating (for motorless flight), an experience that re-ignited a long-held fascination with soaring flight (I started flying gliders at 13). Then I went in search of propulsion. After a few calls, Aerolight in Miami satisfied my thirst for thrust as instructor Mark Sorenson sold me a little direct drive unit that he had modified. Aerolight's Jose & Javier had just taken over the Fly line and were extremely helpful. Mark agreed to include much-appreciated training.

A week later it was at my house: Wing, motor, helmet—everything was there. I was captivated. The prospect of trotting down to the end of my little road and launching from 50 feet of grass was amazing. In the summer of 1999 I flew every single day the weather cooperated, sometimes both morning and evening. First the local area, then on to more distant locales, then on to 15-plus mile cross-country jaunts in whatever direction suited me.

It was a freedom that I couldn't get enough of, a pent-up longing like nothing else I'd ever had. It so invigorated me that I started writing about it—something I'd never had any interest in doing. Ask any of my high school teachers to peg the writers and I wouldn't have even made the long list. But write I did, flights of fancy spilled into PPG newsgroups and eventually magazines, letting me relive these unbelievable experiences.

The passion exploded, filling many aspects of my life and revealing new ones. The simplicity, the freedom, the minimal regulation, it appealed like no other form of flight, including the helicopter. I wanted to help preserve it, to give our sport a voice, to help develop good training programs and to encourage others to embrace it in a sustainable way. This book is the culmination of that desire.

Now on edition 3, a lot had changed in the intervening years; incredible photos had been taken, wheeled launch flourished, reflex wings increased in popularity, I learned animation, learned more about paramotoring, and readers contributed more suggestions. So it became an opportunity for yet another overhaul. As before, I've had lots of help which is *greatly* appreciated. I hope you enjoy the results.

"If there's air there, it should be flown in."

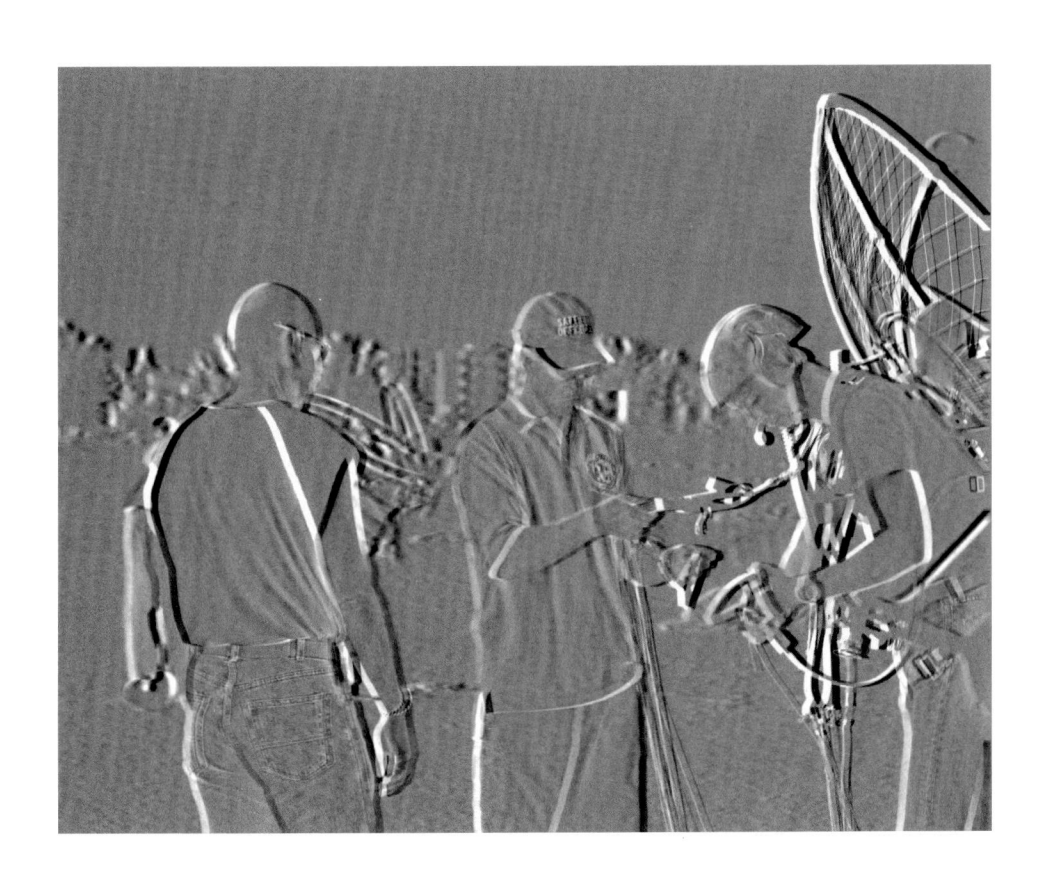

Section I
First Flight

Section I

For most who undertake it, powered paragliding is the apex of personal flying, offering unprecedented freedom, simplicity, controllable safety and low cost. There is no runway needed, no radio, no trailer, just pull up to a launch site, layout and go.

A dedicated student can learn the basics in as little as three days under the guidance of an experienced Instructor. However, to be a competent pilot, flying comfortably on your own, expect five to eight days of fairly intense training and practice. In about a year of fairly regular flying you'll build a confident autonomy. This section is intended to help with the knowledge required to solo—to achieve that first flight.

Ratings

Solo paramotor pilots in the U.S. do not require a license or rating but there *are* requirements for tandem (two seater) flying. See USPPA.org for the latest details. Some countries do require licenses or ratings and others don't even address the sport. Even if a rating is not required, achieving one is a meaningful way to measure personal accomplishment and progress. Ratings can also provide milestones during the learning process that will help assure thorough, methodical training.

We are blessed with the simplest path to flight of any aviation segment in the world, and it's up to us, as responsible citizens, *to keep it that way*.

What it Takes Physically

Physical requirements depend on whether you choose to launch on foot or wheels. Using a cart is much less demanding since you don't have to carry the motor or run. Even foot launching doesn't require athletic prowess although it will certainly extract some exertion—especially while learning. Flying itself is almost relaxing but the early stages of kiting and foot launching will produce some sweat.

Fortunately, as skills improve it gets *much* easier. Even after just a few sessions, newly recruited muscles adapt to their strange new use and brute force gives way to finesse. A skilled "kiter," for example, can go for an hour with minimal exertion whereas the neophyte will be winded in a few minutes.

Expect to be sore during the first few days but, fortunately, it diminishes quickly. This well-earned soreness is to be relished!

The Training Process

CHAPTER 1

No, a license is not required, but that doesn't mean *skill* is not required. Although powered paragliding may epitomize aerial simplicity, without proper training it can be a most vexing endeavor. A good instructor will guide you carefully through many milestones that will make it safer and far more enjoyable.

Skimping on training can easily cost more in equipment repair and/or medical expense than is saved on instruction—many just give up without proper training.

Additionally, flying in the national airspace system is not a trivial matter. Considering societal fears, heading aloft without knowing the legalities is irresponsible folly. Fortunately you've taken a huge step by using this book—let your instructor bring it to life.

Instructor Chris Bowles makes final checks before launching a student on his first powered paragliding flight.

Finding an Instructor

We do this because its fun—the training should be, too. Try to find an instructor you can get along with, who is thorough and has access to good flying sites. Be mindful that training is a lot of work for both of you; don't expect to be pampered, but do expect to be treated with respect. If you're willing to immerse yourself into the program then you will probably get along with just about anyone out there. Most instructors teach because they love the sport, certainly not for the fame and fortune! Even with decent profit margins on gear there is not enough volume to make it big business. Instructors are Powered Paragliding's (PPG's) national treasure.

The best resource for choosing a school is personal recommendation by a trusted pilot. Try to find someone in the community with nothing to sell who you can talk to. If possible, visit potential instructors, talk with them and watch them train—you'll learn a lot about their demeanor and style.

If you have no direct knowledge of an instructor or school, make sure they're certified for PPG as opposed to less relevant ultralight types like powered parachutes (PPC's). While government certification is not required (except for tandem), it does show that they have minimum demonstrated knowledge and skill. Not only do they meet standards established by a national organization (USPPA in the U.S.) but they enjoy the training resources of that organization.

Be wary of those who have only been flying for a year or so themselves—they won't be well versed on the intricacies of student issues. Just about any pilot can explain how it's done, but experience provides a depth of understanding to better recognize and correct student problems.

Students should get some air time in a tandem craft before going it alone. Wheeled tandems are ideal but the rules can make it difficult. In the U.S., for example, wheeled tandems must be done under the more restrictive Sport Pilot rules whereas foot launched tandems are allowed under less-involved exemptions granted to organizations such as the USPPA.

Ask your instructor to use the syllabus from a national organization to help insure that important information is covered.

Don't worry about equipment and be leery of sales pitches. There are some legends in their own minds out there. When you start hearing that this or that is the "best," step back and look around. Just because someone is vocal doesn't make them correct. Like all of aviation, there are trade-offs. Make sure you get matched up with appropriate gear for your size, weight and intended take-off elevation. Flying at Albuquerque's 5000 foot elevation requires different choices then flying at sea level. A reputable instructor will do this matching within the line of gear he is authorized to sell. It turns out that your success has far more to do with your attitude and choice of *instructor* rather than your choice of gear.

The School

A school is not better because it is bigger. Larger schools are almost always full-time which makes scheduling easier. You'll be able to spend three to five days in a row—a concentrated environment that allows rapid progression. You'll have to travel, though, and support will largely be by mail and phone.

Smaller schools, usually one-person affairs, can offer equally good training but it will probably spread out over more time. They may have to schedule you on weekends. Being local, though, helps since you'll enjoy close support for training, equipment, places to fly and probably a ready community of other pilots. If you have a local instructor and he's qualified, be thankful—most don't.

Some instructors will come to you, but find out what expenses you'll be paying, it could wind up being less of a value. Also consider how you'll get service after they leave. The benefit of having the instructor come to you is that they'll be able to help you pick out local sites, identify local weather patterns and airspace issues.

Any school should have access to a sufficiently open area to fly. They should also have a simulator, ground school materials, and examples of the various equipment available to buy. It is expected that they will prefer only a few types of wings and motors which is OK—they've figured out how to train on that gear and should be

> ⚠️ **Caution!**
> Never, ever have a non-instructor pull you up with a rope (even by hand) or tie yourself to a stationary object while hooked into your glider. There are dynamics that make this incredibly dangerous. Unsuspecting flyers have died trying these things since it looks so easy. One of several maladies can whip the wing off sideways and down, dragging you along for the whack. Once it gets started, the controls are insufficient to recover.

able to support it.

Schools that offer training on their equipment do so with the understanding that damage will be paid for by the student. They rightfully require a deposit. Some schools only train those who buy gear from them which is another reason to choose an instructor rather than gear.

If the school offers tandem introductory flights, try one to see if it's for you or not. You can also watch how the instructor and school operate with minimal commitment. Another good option is to find a school that will train you on their gear through first solo, then let you decide what to do. Be mindful that you are nowhere near ready to set out on your own after such an introduction.

Different Methods of Instructing

There are many different ways to learn and one size does not fit all. Some instructors are laid back, some are intense. Some are more aggressive and some are conservative. Drill sergeant types use the military approach and have a very serious demeanor but can still be very effective.

Schools in mountainous areas will frequently teach free-flying first. That is fun in its own right and will expose you to a different type of flying; it was the approach I took. But it takes more work in many ways since the weather must fit a narrower window. You will come to understand "parawaiting"—what pilots do while perched atop launch awaiting better winds.

Flatland schools tend to teach motor flying only. Their methods frequently incorporate towing or tandems although a few don't offer either—your first time aloft may be your first motor flight. That is not ideal but, with strong guidance, proper practice on the simulator, and a huge open field it can be done with reasonable safety. Doing so on a highly stable wheeled platform improves your chances for early success.

All methods can be effective although not all will be ideal for each student's learning style. The best instructors adapt somewhat to how each student learns but some adapting is left for the student, too.

There must be a balance in pacing your training. For example, if you (or the instructor) pushes too hard, its easy to skip necessary information or rehearsals, overlooking critical steps. On the other hand, training can bog down and require lessons to be relearned; it's easy to then become disenchanted—frustrated by the apparent lack of progress. There is a difference

1. Brad Weiss works with a student on high-wind kiting skills. Like many ocean beaches, this one serves up consistent on-shore breezes, ideal for learning to handle the wing. The bulging free-flight harness is for back protection—common on soaring harnesses.

2. Eric Dufour goes over last minute details before the student's first solo flight. Some schools start their students on wheels then transition them to foot launching.

Towing Types

Several tow methods are used. They all include a proper tow line, pilot's release mechanism, a way to control line tension by the tow operator, weak link and a way to cut the line (like a hook knife) in case of emergency. The pilot should rehearse using the release and hook knife. Towing requires *extreme* care—you must be ready to execute the instructor's commands regardless of what may be happening.

Special procedures make towing safer including visual signals and a well thought-out process. Radio communications are the norm, but pilot response usually comes from kicking his legs fore and aft to signal "yes" or waving them left and right to signal "no." Above all the tow operator must know how to operate the rig safely including emergencies.

Stationary *scooter towing* is common, especially for training. The scooter's rear wheel has been replaced by a drum containing tow line and the instructor adjusts reel-in pull with the twist-grip throttle. Electric winches are similar. They're relatively inexpensive and can be run by the instructor alone although it's best to have a separate tow operator who can chop the line quickly in case of emergency. These get pilots up to around 800 feet although higher tows are possible with more line and a stiffer breeze. A *turnaround pulley* (see below) may be used: the line goes out 1000' or so, through a pulley and back to the tow rig. This allows the student to start next to the instructor for better interaction and closer supervision of the launch. Low tows are commonly used and are somewhat safer if kept below 10 feet or so.

You may encounter *Step Towing* for highly experienced pilots. The towee is pulled up as usual, into the wind. At the normal release point, the winch clutch is released and the flyer turns downwind to fly *away* from the winch, pulling line out as he goes. Then he turns around back towards the winch as it powers up to pull again—"stepping" him up to higher altitude. Look out, though, if the line catches on something as the pilot is flying away it will be ugly. This is extremely dangerous!

Truck towing with a payout winch is used to reach higher altitudes (over 2000 feet depending on line and conditions). It requires a longer run and preferably another person, besides the driver, to be a winch operator. The truck starts off rolling, paying out line and pulling the pilot at a controlled tension. The truck may be moving 30 mph but the payout is letting line out at 15 mph so the effective pull is 15 mph. The line length increases as the truck progresses. If the glider is rocketing up at a steep angle (happens only with a breeze) then the payout may need to reel out so fast that the pilot is not even moving forward over the ground—just climbing like mad. This is where experienced tow operators must call on their expertise to prevent excess climb by metering payout rate and keeping line tension within limits. Gliders and tow bridles can be overstressed with these operations. Having some form of line release/cut is more important here because if the payout stops, the line suddenly starts moving at the same speed as the truck—a potential catastrophe.

Boat towing typically nets the highest tows—over 3000 feet in good conditions. Expect to pay more owing to the need for a powerful winch-equipped boat. It's normally reserved for getting pilots high enough to practice aerobatics or learn to handle wing malfunctions at *maneuvers clinics*. It is like truck towing except the pilot launches from shore and flies mostly over water. Extra precautions, such as flotation, must be in place for safety in case the pilot goes swimming.

Boat tows can be a bit bumpier if the water is rough since wave action gets transferred through the line.

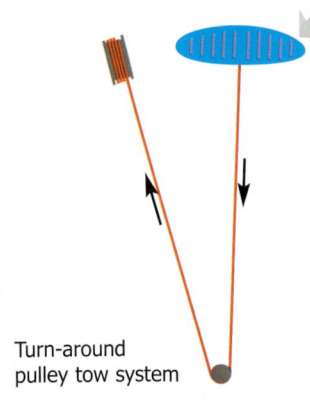

Turn-around pulley tow system

between rapidly paced and carelessly quick; with proper precautions, the quicker schedule can be reasonable safe. For example, there is benefit to working with higher wind in order to be prepared for it so, if it's windier, you ought to be learning how to deal with it within personal limits.

Your first flight is just a beginning; much more remains to be learned and practiced with the instructor's guidance. We are given much leeway in both regulation and training required. But those regs protect others, *not* pilots. So it's up to you to continue learning—not only for self preservation but also to understand the national airspace system in which we operate.

Like all freedoms, PPG flying requires responsibility—we either accept that responsibility, or lose the freedom.

Certification

Look for instructors certified by an organization with a thorough Powered Paraglider program. Anyone can hang a shingle out and call themselves an instructor but not everyone can demonstrate the skills and knowledge. While there may be good instructors who are *not* certified, the onus falls on the student to find out about them. Visit www.USPPA.org for a list of schools and their certification level.

Ask to use a recognized syllabus; it may not be required so it's up to you to request it and make sure everything gets covered.

Be aware that requirements for getting certified vary dramatically. Some organizations do little more than "stamp" instructors based on non-PPG skills. Check out what minimums apply and what skills have to be shown to become rated. If an instructor cannot demonstrate skills it sure will be hard for him to teach those skills.

No ratings program is perfect; they all rely on human instructors and, regardless of the organization, there will be variety. This same diversity bedevils even government certification programs, too.

Training Aids

Training aids for paramotoring are marvelously simple and surprisingly effective. All reputable schools use some form of simulator and most have other aids to grease the wheels of learning.

One invaluable aid is getting airborne and in control, even if for short unpowered flights, *before* your first powered solo. It can help alleviate first-flight anxieties and their attendant problems. If your school does not offer a method to do this (towing, hill launch or tandem), you should get at least one dual training flight in whatever craft is available. Even a powered parachute or other ultralight would be better than leaping aloft with no prior piloting experience. The fewer sensory firsts, the better.

Towing

Towing involves having an experienced operator pull you up like a kite—once airborne, you pull a release and glide down for landing. After a few low tows to get a basic feel for handling the glider, you may progress to higher flights, depending on the school.

Towing can also loft free flyers high enough to catch rising air currents (thermals) and soar without power. Very long lines offer releases well above 2000 feet. Under the right conditions, soaring pilots can then fly for hours. You need some advanced skills owing to the more turbulent conditions but it's risk allows a different sensory reward.

Tow operators must know what they are doing—preferably they are certified. Low tows are generally safer than high tows but still require extreme care since the pilot is continuously low to the ground.

With some breeze (5-10 mph), hand towing is possible with appropriate precautions. It gives some minimal feel for the wing, flying, and landing flare. Don't take it lightly, though—the puller must know

Towing in the right hands is a great training aid. Done casually or by inexperienced tow operators, it can be deadly.

1. Bill Briley controls a direct scooter tow using its throttle while talking to the student via radio. It's called that because it's built from a scooter whose rear wheel has been replaced by the line drum. It is anchored stationary as it reels in line.

2. Bruce Brown uses a turnaround pulley where the tow line goes out to a pulley and back to where both the student and tow operator can talk.

exactly what he's doing. Like other towing, it can quickly go awry if not done properly.

Hills

Bunny hills are small hills that allow ground-skimming free flight. You can practice launching, flying briefly and landing before ever strapping on the motor—a nice benefit. Lightweight harnesses mean trudging up the hill is easier. This is how most students learn to paraglide (without the motor)—launching from shallow hills at first then progressing up to bigger hills where soaring flights are possible.

The hill's slope should be about 4 to 1, where it drops 1 foot for every 4 feet forward, so that you can pull away from the hill once in flight. Your flight time (and height) can be metered by how far up the hill you start. Winds must be just right but most schools in hilly areas will have several sites to choose from.

Kyra Busque is getting an early start on wing handling. Her dad, Kyle, is showing her kiting without the risers. The wing is sized for him (larger) so she'll have to work pretty hard. There are no age limits for powered paragliding but parents must use good judgement. As a guide, student sailplane pilots can solo at age 14 in the U.S.

Tandems

Tandems allow you to get airborne with an experienced pilot at the helm of a two-place unit. Regulations change but generally it's not legal to do tandems on traditional wheeled units without more regulatory involvement. But going up dual offers a highly valuable opportunity to feel flight, gain a basic understanding of the craft's handling, and give the instructor an opportunity to gauge your reactions to flight.

In most countries, tandem pilots must adhere to extra equipment and pilot certification requirements since ultralights were intended for solo flight. In the U.S., Tandems must operate under an exemption from the solo limitation of the ultralight rules and are for training only (see USPPA.org).

Control feel on Tandem rigs is quite a bit heavier, and performance is sluggish, but the principles and directions are the same.

Tandem foot launched instruction is very demanding of the instructor since he must carry a motor powerful enough for both occupants.

1. Jarrod Bottonelli launches from 5000 feet elevation in Albuquerque, NM.
2. Francesco DeSantis and Dawn Pistocci cruise Florida's West Coast.

Wheels

Starting on wheels with a highly stable cart is another good method to learn. Some schools have students solo on wheels before moving on to foot launching. It will still take as much time to achieve the requisite skills, especially wing handling, but reduces the chance of equipment damage early on. Foot launching is, of course, quite different from wheel launching (see Chapter 6).

Simulator

The Simulator may well be the most important piece of equipment for learning: It provides a way for the pilot to sit in his motor unit by its intended hook-ins. It can be as simple as straps around a tree limb or an elaborate device with brake lines, bungees, and special riser spreaders.

Critical aspects of flying will be rehearsed from this simple setup. Besides certain normal flight drills, you will rehearse emergencies whose solution is not always obvious and must be practiced. Rehearsal is the only way to insure learned responses will be performed when required.

You will learn to react to instructor directives on the radio while coping with a flood of strange sensations. On that first flight, you'll be glad you paid attention in the simulator.

Throttle simulator

Handling the wing is challenging enough—adding a throttle to the mix can make it feel like you're all thumbs. A throttle simulator is a regular throttle, possibly with cable, that feels and behaves just like its connected cousin. You get used to wing handling *and* working the throttle before putting on a motor. Otherwise, your first time with a motor, and the unfamiliar stuff in your hands, will be far more difficult.

More advanced versions have a kill switch that beeps when pressed so the instructor knows you're pressing it—a critical reaction to learn. But even something as simple as practicing with a throttle-sized stick in your hand can help you acclimate to the feel of a throttle's extra complication.

Weighted Frame

You may use a motor frame (no motor) for early training then progressively add weight as you improve. This great technique lets you learn kiting with the bulky motor on but without the full burden of its weight.

Multimedia

You'll hopefully have some videos. *Risk and Reward* is a must-see followed by *Instability II* and the *Master Powered Paragliding* series among others. Keep in mind, these are just tools. Like this book, they are not intended to replace thorough instruction, but to supplement it.

Radios

Being a solo craft makes communication essential. Good radios allow the instructor to give directions while you learn launching, flying and landing. If something goes wrong, or conditions change, the instructor can provide guidance. You'll either have to purchase or be provided with a helmet that works with the radio that your instructor uses.

---

1. Airlines know the value of good training aids, too. This $16 Million dollar 737 simulator lets Southwest pilots master skills for situations that they will never likely encounter.
2. Bruce Brown has a student practice taking radio directions while experiencing the noise, vibration and feeling of full power. This invaluable rehearsal helps insure responses are swift and correct when it really counts. Emergency procedures should be rehearsed either with the motor running, or other distractions until the response is automatic.
3. Simulators that allow the pilot to manipulate risers and brakes are ideal.
4. Highly stable and well protected carts are perfect for early learning.

Getting to that First Flight

As with all training, your attitude will largely determine your success, enjoyment and safety. Listening to the instructor and reacting properly to his directives is paramount. It's not always easy; new pilots have difficulty processing the instructions during the noise and sensation overload of those first few flights. Having the right attitude and simulator rehearsal will help a lot—the instructor wants to see you succeed but must be able to work with you. Come to the lessons with that understanding. Even if the training seems almost harsh at times, it's because of the critical necessity of following directions properly. In all likelihood you will cement a relationship with your instructor that will be enjoyed for years.

How Long It Will Take

A must-see video is "Risk & Reward." It shows where the risk is and how to avoid it. Watch it with your instructor and Ask about anything that's not clear. But far more important than watching is rehearsing!

The video was commissioned by the USPPA and produced by paramotor pilot Phil Russman (pictured hanging.) Myself and others put countless hours into it.

William Shatner, who appears several times in the video, got 12 flights of instruction in California then, several years later, asked for help flying into a Chicagoland charity event.

As a certified airplane pilot he knew the importance of training, recency of experience and personal limitations. Nick Scholtes agreed to be the instructor and we all worked together to make it happen safely. The larger picture shows Mr. Shatner flying East over the Northern Illinois landscape, accompanied by Nick (on the right), myself (shooting the picture) and several other Illinois pilots. The mission was a success. Score one for the Federation.

Training time will vary a lot depending on weather, equipment, location and personal ability. If flyable conditions prevail, expect to solo in 2-5 days of solid training. A solo flight, with assistance, can be done quite early when extra precautions are taken but that's still early in the learning process.

You may rarely get an assisted solo on the first day, probably using wheels. Doing so increases risk slightly and you'll still be nowhere near ready to fly on your own.

Training time depends on your stamina, too. Being able to handle the wing on the ground (kiting) is your most important skill for launching—and it takes practice. Newly minted muscles will make their presence known after day one.

Learning is way more demanding than flying. Once equipped with the necessary skills, you'll only bear the motor's weight for a minute or so before launch transforms it into your magic chair. Expect to take at least 20 hours of "kiting" to gain enough skill for wing handling, but enjoy knowing that improvement will continue for years.

Getting to the pilot level (PPG2 in the U.S.), where you can reasonably go out on your own, will take at least 8 days of training and 25 flights. If you only get a few days, realize that you're not ready to be alone yet. Either fly with other experienced pilots or find another instructor.

Weather Dependent

We love still air for flying but it's not so great for early training where you want a 6 to 12 mph wind. And the gusty conditions of mid-day are as bad for learning as they are for flying. Beaches usually serve up the nicest conditions with a moderate "sea breeze" coming in almost every warm afternoon.

Winter weather is good if you can stand the cold. Low sun means the typically stronger winds are smoother—good for kiting, plus, it's mellow longer into the day.

Progression

If you must travel to a distant school try scheduling at least 3 consecutive days—5 is better—to have better odds of getting acceptable weather. Depending on the location and time of year, that can be a challenge. Count yourself lucky if the school is within daily driving range but be prepared to be cancelled due to weather—call first.

When you arrive on the first day, you'll be introduced to the people, the school, and yes, the paperwork. Have a full pen and strong glasses—the forms are many and the print is fine. Of course there's risk (see Chapter 19) but don't be put-off by the dreadful sounding waivers—the sport has proven safer than some of those would lead you to believe.

Depending on what the school provides, expect to buy a few things. This book, along with the video "Risk and Reward," were hopefully among them (kudos to your instructor.) A kiting harness and helmet are common first purchases. It is far better not to buy gear in advance unless requested to do so by the school—each instructor has reasons for using what they do. Frequently it is compatibility with their training style or gear. Hopefully you can decide on a motor and wing by the time training has completed. Most motors and wings are just as good for flying as they are for training—so your best bet is to purchase the gear on which you learn. Then after gaining a year or so of experience you are better equipped to judge other brands.

Expect to be kiting on your first day if conditions cooperate. You'll need to practice this essential skill on your own but get rudimentary training first to avoid picking up bad habits. Since mid-day conditions aren't good for flying (in most locations) expect to use that time for simulator, ground work and adjusting the harness.

After gaining proficiency with wing handling using just a small harness (15 - 25 hours is considered ideal), you'll graduate to doing it with the motor on, but not running. Then possibly more practice in the simulator with the instructor on radio, probably with the motor running.

The big day for your first flight will probably include some dress rehearsal and review of emergency procedures before actually going aloft. The solo may be "assisted," which can get you airborne earlier but in a less-prepared state. There is nothing wrong with that as long as you remain committed to further training.

For those able to do training in stages, learning to kite during an early visit is valuable so that you can then go home and practice. Mind the cautions given by your instructor—dangers lurk whenever you're hooked into the wing.

One common frustration is when you seem to reach a learning plateau or, worse yet, go backwards. It happens—one day everything is great and the next day you can't remember what a riser is. Maddening, but normal. Keep at it, success will come.

Regardless of past experience, treat this sport with great respect. Safety is almost entirely up to the pilot's attitude. A cocky approach is both obnoxious and dangerous.

Previous Experience

So you're an airline pilot (or helicopter pilot or sailplane pilot or hang glider pilot, etc)? That won't help you much here. Past knowledge *will* prove useful for airspace, general aerodynamics, and a few other relevant bits but the reactions required of paramotoring can make a mockery of prior experience.

We've found that previous experience in other flying machines has amazing irrelevance to learning powered paragliding. The critical maneuvering responses are vastly different than anything you've likely experienced. While not difficult, paramotoring responses deserve the same attention and respect as your first "V1 cuts" (or auto-rotations, or spot landings or hydraulic failures or whatever).

This warning is even more pertinent

The PPG Bible: A Complete Guide and Reference

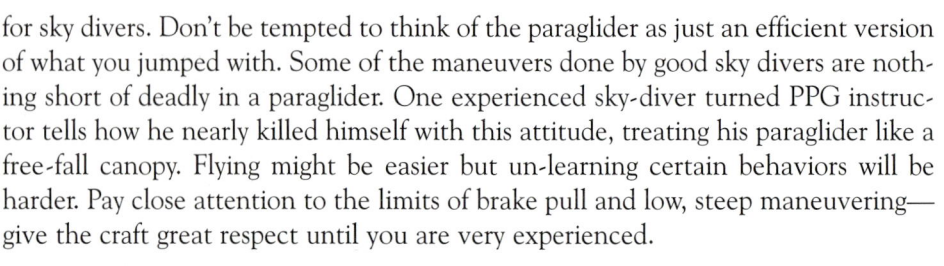

for sky divers. Don't be tempted to think of the paraglider as just an efficient version of what you jumped with. Some of the maneuvers done by good sky divers are nothing short of deadly in a paraglider. One experienced sky-diver turned PPG instructor tells how he nearly killed himself with this attitude, treating his paraglider like a free-fall canopy. Flying might be easier but un-learning certain behaviors will be harder. Pay close attention to the limits of brake pull and low, steep maneuvering—give the craft great respect until you are very experienced.

The worst thing you can do as a pilot of another craft is to short-change your training based on perceived existing capability. Such arrogance has preceded the demise of many who took this superior approach.

Training will be frustrating yet invigorating. It will have highs and lows but should provide an experience like none other, whose value will far exceed the effort.

Jonathan Tagle
Performance Designs
Factory Pilot
Photo: Chris Bazil

1. A skilled sky diver can expend his excess swooping energy over many yards after a long dive. But don't try this in a paraglider until you've mastered control and realize the limitations.

Pilots of other craft add enormous risk by short changing their paramotor training based on previous experience. Sky divers do enjoy some advantage by having similar controls, but the wings behave so differently that accidents are likely unless paragliding is treated with great respect.

2. Attending fly-ins is another way to learn and get help from a variety of experienced pilots. Safety officer Steve Boser (in yellow shirt) offers John Coulter advice on a challenging launch towards the inland buildings.

Eric Dufour (above, wearing hat) works with the History Channel's Josh Bernstien, an outdoor adventurist who learned powered paragliding for fun and to use on his show. At left is Josh enjoying the fruits of their combined labors.

Josh had the right attitude, he listened intently to his mentor and excelled. After five-days of training he had nearly 10 solo flights under his belt.

Page 12 Section I: First Flight

Gearing Up

CHAPTER 2

If only the Wright Brothers could see our stuff now. This overview covers the strange collection of gear that gets us airborne. A more thorough treatment of gear can be found in Chapter 12 and Section V covers adjustment, care and repair.

The Wing

The paraglider is, by far, your most important component. Although it may be able to suffer numerous individual failures and still fly—it degrades with time and use. When a wing wears out or fails an inspection, it must be repaired or replaced.

During flight, air is forced into the leading edge (front) openings, through internal holes, to create a very slight internal pressure that keeps the shape against tension in the lines.

We share almost identical technology with soaring (free flight) pilots who fly from hills or get towed up. Some models that are purpose-built for motoring may sacrifice varying amounts of efficiency for speed.

Standard and Reflex Gliders

Standard paragliders are optimized for efficiency and launch ease while reflex gliders are optimized for speed and collapse resistance, especially at their higher speeds. Reflex models are a bit more complicated, requiring pilots to avoid certain control combinations. They are also a bit harder to launch although technologies are improving and, once the technique is learned, launching is quite reliable.

Fabric

Most modern gliders use a coated ripstop nylon that is nearly airtight. Additional coatings improve longevity at some expense in weight and launch ease. With care, a wing will last 300-500 hours but abuse or neglect could halve that. Lightweight

The PPG Bible: A Complete Guide and Reference

models, or *mountain wings*, sacrifice durability for low weight and launch ease.

Wings don't like heat, sun, dampness, harsh chemicals or sharp objects. They easily succumb to craggy rocks, sticks, nails or other protrusions. "Ripstop" just means that tears don't spread easily but they will still spread.

Ultraviolet (UV) light causes nearly invisible degradation that weakens the fabric and makes it porous. Many manufacturers say that 300 hours of direct UV is the maximum recommended lifetime exposure. Limiting sun time to early morning or late afternoon lowers total UV so it may be possible to get more hours than that.

Lines

Suspension lines form a wing's primary airfoil shape by virtue of their position and length. The forward row of lines, the "A's", bear most of the weight, followed by the next row (the "B's") and so on. Reflex gliders are even more heavily loaded on their A lines. Some wings have 3 rows, some have 4 rows, and a very few competition soaring wings have only two rows of lines. Line *cascades* reduce the total number of lines and therefore drag.

Each line actually carries relatively little weight but must be strong enough to handle sudden "pops" in case part of the wing folds down then "pops" back to shape.

Most gliders have small loops sewn into the wing where the lines attach, making line replacement easier. A very few models have the lines sewn right into the wing—not a good arrangement when lines need to be replaced.

Main lines (*not* brake lines) are made with a strong bundle of finely spun material sheathed in a thin protective outer weave. This is very strong in the stretch direction (high tensile strength) but degrades quickly if bent sharply or heated too much. Avoid walking on or hooking lines in a way that could bend them sharply.

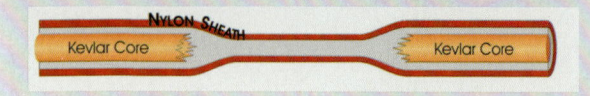

Brake and Tip Steering Lines:

Steering lines run from the trailing edge (back of wing), down through a brake pulley and into *toggles* held by the pilot. They are more flexible than main lines to better handle bending at the pulley and have less tensile strength since they carry no flight load.

Brakes work by pulling one side of the trailing edge down, slowing that side of the glider in order to affect a turn. The pilot swings in the opposite direction, pushing the wing into a bank.

Reflex gliders, when flown fast, are not intended to be steered with their regular brakes. So they come equipped with some form of tip steering which pulls only the tip's trailing edge or just pulls down the very tip to effect a turn.

Parts of the PARAGLIDER

⚠ **Caution!**
A line can break, undetected, inside its protective outer sheath. Sharp bending is the most likely cause, usually from yanking on a wing that's stuck on something.

To find such breaks run the line through your fingers, feeling for a "lip" where the Kevlar core has separated. If you find one, the line is unable to bear any significant load and must be changed. Brake lines are woven from a single material and have no kevlar core.

Higher performance gliders may have all or partially unsheathed lines. That reduces drag at some expense in durability.

The Risers

These critical strap-like assemblies transfer load from the carabineer to wing lines while providing several forms of control. Each riser has individual risers lettered A through D (or C for three riser systems). They spread the load out to individual rows of lines. Risers are usually color-coded but the color schemes vary by manufacturer—a red riser on one glider may be the green riser on another.

Wing lines are connected to the risers through *Quick Links* (also called *Maillons*). Risers can be separated easily from the lines, and therefore the glider, to allow easy change-out. Be careful: this changes the distance to each row of lines and therfore the wing's characteristics. Wings and risers are certified together so optional riser sets should only be installed after verifying compatibility. The most common reason to switch risers is to put motor risers on a free-flight wing. This adds trimmers and makes it easier to reach the brakes and lines when flying high hook-in machines.

Trimmers

Most wings intended for motoring have a strap-slider attached to each rear riser that, when extended in flight, increases airspeed. Letting the trimmers out raises the trailing edge for a 10% to 25% speed increase, even more for reflex models. It also increases the sink rate or, if flying level under power, requires more thrust. Reflex wings have a much longer trimmer range.

Split A's

Some wings have Split A's where the outermost A line has its own riser. That makes it easier to reach up and pull down just those outer lines which collapses the tips in a maneuver intended to increase descent rate called *big ears* (covered later).

Quick Links

It is never good to connect nylon to nylon (lines right through riser material) so metal fittings connect lines to their respective risers. A rubber O-Ring keeps the lines tightly together. When lines are replaced they are removed from this fitting on the riser and the wing.

Speed System

A speed system comes with most wings. It consists of a line on each riser that connects to a harness-mounted, foot-activated speed bar. Pushing the foot bar out pulls the A lines down which speeds up the wing. Interconnecting lines also pull the B's and C's down proportionally to keep the airfoil shape.

The wing portion of a speed system connects to the harness portion through "sister clips" that are made to be easily attached/detached.

A speed system works similar to trimmers (which raise the wing's rear instead of lowering its front) but is more effective on most wings. It also has the advantage that it can be released immediately by letting off the considerable foot pressure whereas trimmers stay set. On standard (non reflex) gliders it is best to avoid speedbar use with trimmers

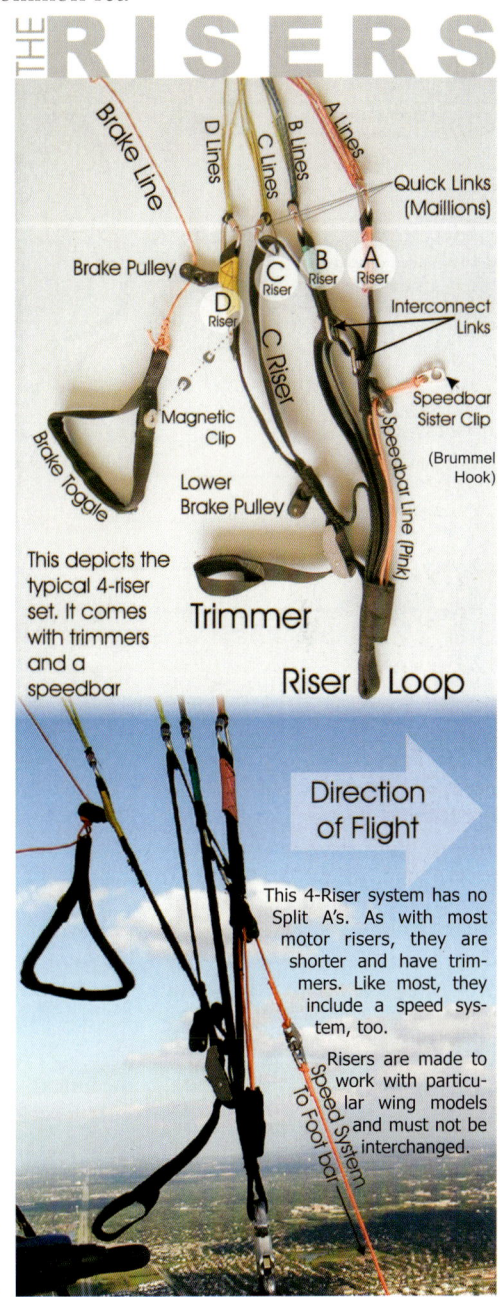

This depicts the typical 4-riser set. It comes with trimmers and a speedbar

This 4-Riser system has no Split A's. As with most motor risers, they are shorter and have trimmers. Like most, they include a speed system, too.

Risers are made to work with particular wing models and must not be interchanged.

The PPG Bible: A Complete Guide and Reference

1 Leading Edge, Line Cascades, Stabilo Tip & Lines
V-Rib design reduces lines while maintaining shape.
Trailing Edge
Rib with air equalization holes
Mylar Leading Edge Reinforcement

2 Direction Of Flight
A-Risers ("Split" A's Shown)
Brake Line
Brake Toggle

D Lines — Tip Steering Line (Recommended for flying fast (reflexed))
C Lines — Brake Steering Line (Recommended for flying slower (non-reflexed))
Upper Pulley (for low hookins)
Swivel — To keep brake line from twisting
Brake Toggle — Shown through upper pulley
Lower Pulley (for high hookins)
Trimmer Buckle
Trimmer Handle
Brake Toggle (when lower pulley used)
Trimmer Strap — reflex gliders have longer pull
Brake Keepers — Neodymium Magnets
Secondary Riser Loop
Primary Riser Loop

B Lines
A Lines — Tip A Line (for big ears), Main A Lines (for launching)
Torque Compensator Line (for use in cruise)
Torque Compensator Stop
Tip Steering Ball (sometimes it's a toggle)
Speed System Brummel Hook (Sister Clip)
Speed System Pulleys

Reflex Risers
Tip steering and a long trimmer range are the primary differences between standard and reflex glider risers.

nucleon
Courtesy Dudek Paragliders

1. **Structure**: Inner *ribs* hold the top surface's airfoil shape. Each space between ribs is a *cell*. More cells improve the airfoil shape but add weight, expense, and slightly different flight characteristics.
Air enters the leading edge openings and flows through internal holes which help the wing re-inflate quickly after a deflation (collapse or "fold").
V-Rib construction reduces the number of lines (lessen drag) and Mylar rib reinforcements (on the front most part of the rib) improve low-wind inflation characteristics. Higher performance wings typically have more cells.
2. **Split A Risers** make it easy to pull down the outer line (right one), useful for "pulling big ears."

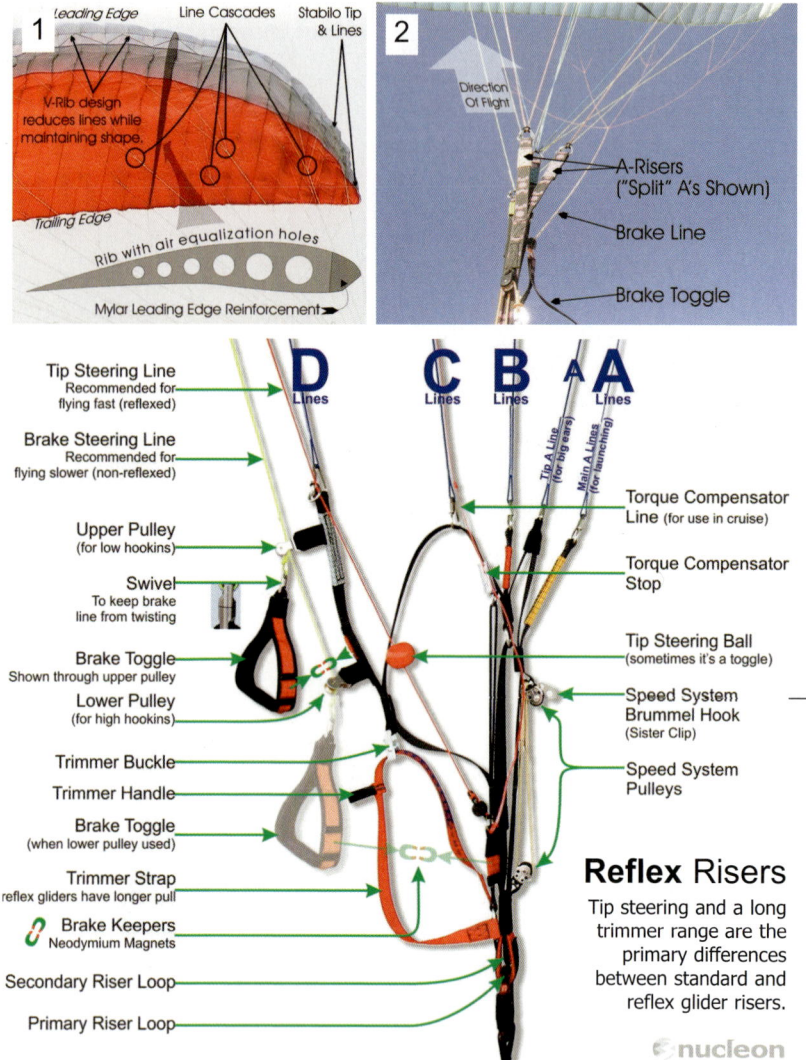

out (set for fast) or while in turbulence—doing so increases the chance for a "front tuck" (see Chapter 18). Reflex gliders can be flown trimmed fast and on speedbar. They are, in fact, *more* collapse resistant this way but should be steered using tip steering instead of brakes.

Most wings have 2 pulleys which are used like block and tackle to give mechanical leverage. It takes more speedbar travel than on one-pulley systems but is quite a bit easier to push.

Not all motor harnesses have the necessary footbar connection points and pulleys but they are easy to retrofit. Even if it is equipped, most schools will not have it hooked up for your early flights.

The Harness

The *harness* supports you and your motor in flight, making it the next most important piece after your wing. It's usually mated to a specific motor frame and has at least a seat with leg loops, waist belt, and a place to connect the motor and wing to. But there is a *lot* more than meets the eye.

Wheeled craft frequently have just a seat and belt, but offer multiple wing attachments to allow balancing; you want a slightly nose-high hang angle. Simple add-on carts may use the paramotor's harness but should provide additional support for ground operations.

Harnesses are usually overbuilt with webbing capable of supporting many times their rated loads. But steep turns or turbulence can push those limits, and UV exposure, chafing, chemical or other damage can reduce margins further.

During launch the wing first lifts the motor's weight then lifts you by the leg loops which are part of the harness. Once airborne, you wiggle, kick or push out a seat then sit back until ready for landing. The harness must be adjusted properly and be comfortable—not just for enjoyment but to avoid blocking leg circulation which could leave you numb for landing.

Numerous adjustments (see Chapter 12) are made on the harness to fit your weight, height, and desires so expect your instructor to spend some time getting you situated with it. Among other things, adjustments determine how your motor will hang, how it will handle torque, where the brakes will be and how to best get into the seat (not always a simple matter). These adjustments are critical—failure to do them properly could yield a dangerous or unflyable machine.

The PPG Bible: A Complete Guide and Reference

(Left) Not all motors have all features but these are common. It has high hook-in points and uses *underarm*, or *comfort* bars, to keep harness webbing away from the pilot's body.

Webbing is what we call the large load-bearing straps.

(Below) Most PPG carts connect to the wing with single-loop risers just like on foot launch units. But this cart uses multi line attachments. Lines connect to quick links that are mounted directly on the frame instead of being atop risers. See more in Chapter 6.

On a few brands you don the harness first, then the motor. The girl (preceding page) is wearing such a harness.

Diagonal Anti-Torque Strap

Propeller torque causes numerous turning evils so some harnesses add a strap that transfers pull from one side to the other to help even things out as depicted above.

Machines with *weight shift* (shifting one riser up and the other down to help turn) do not use this strap because it reduces weight shift. Plus, it only reduces one element of torque and with very limited authority, especially on leaned back machines. See chapter 23 for more on torque's various causes, cures and cautions.

Ground Handling Straps

Also known as *carry straps*, these are made to better carry the motor around on the ground. They bear no flying loads. Some ground handling straps include a chest strap (sternum strap) to keep them from falling off your shoulders. Most are designed to be loosened easily once airborne for more comfort in flight.

Over-The-Shoulder J-Bars

Nearly all machines have a *spreader system*, some way to keep the forward harness webbing from pushing against your chest while under thrust. Shoulder J-bars were an early solution and are still used, in a modified fashion, on some machines. They provide a metal piece over the pilot's shoulder into which the wing hooks. Two hang points, in front and behind the pilot, support all the weight through webbing. By having the wing hook-in up high it reduces turbulence-induced motion transferred to the pilot.

On many J-Bar units, the wing hooks up through a D shackle and then the J-bar attaches separately to a strap going down to the front of the seat. Since a failure of the bar or shackle could be catastrophic, a safety strap is frequently employed that connects the main harness to each riser in addition to the shackle.

Modern machines with J-Bars frequently have a "floating" variety that allows

Harness Styles & Spreader Systems

Spreaders transfer the motor's thrust forward to keep the pilot from being squeezed between the backrest and front harness webbing.

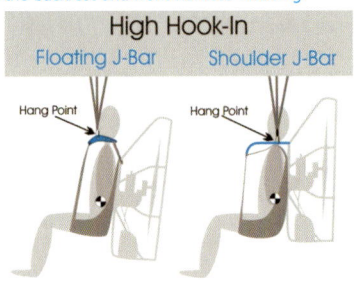

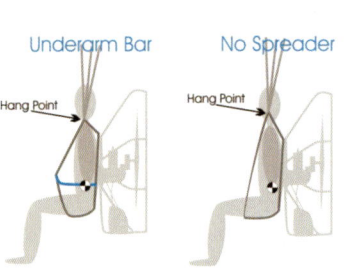

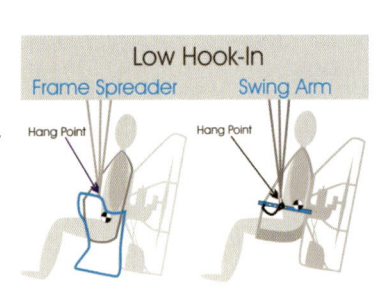

High Hook-In
Floating J-Bar Shoulder J-Bar

Underarm Bar No Spreader

Low Hook-In
Frame Spreader Swing Arm

Chapter 2: Gearing Up

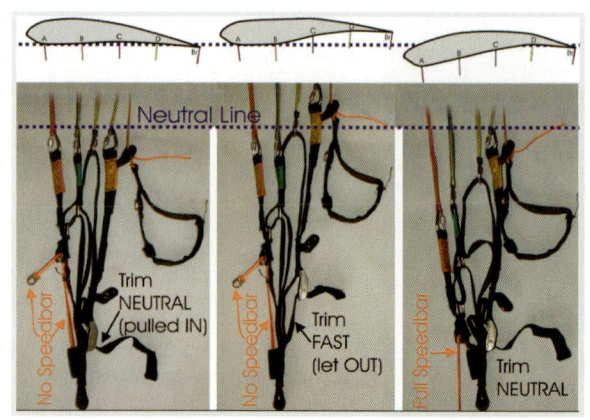

enough movement to give some feel for the wing. This keeps the pilot hanging in the same way as regular J-bars but without being as stiff. They can also allow varying amounts of weight shift steering (see Chapter 18).

J-Bar machines are considered high hook-in systems since the wing attaches above the pilot's shoulders.

Underarm or "Comfort" Bars

Underarm bars are another way to prevent motor thrust from pinching the pilot against the front straps. Like J-bars, they transfer force to the forward harness straps but are under the pilot's arms. On some machines they swivel up and down to provide weight shift steering. At least one brand allows them to swivel outward for easier ingress and egress but they must not be allowed to swivel *inward!*

On some systems, the carabiners attach right to the bar—usually to more closely mimic low hook-in free-flight harnesses and mate better with soaring wings which have longer risers. Machines with pivoting arms will have hook-in points that allow effective weight shift steering. Those without pivoting arms are *not* intended to have much weight shift capability.

Soft Harness

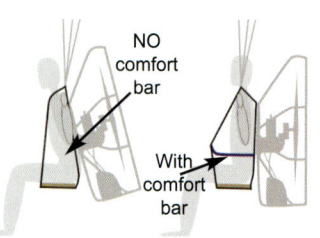

Only the simplest harnesses don't use separating bars at all, and they would only be suited for smaller pilots. They're mostly found on older, direct drive designs which have less thrust.

The Buckles

The vast majority of harnesses have quick release buckles with pinch buttons on the side. They are not designed to be release while under tension.

Some older harnesses have a pair of rectangular metal fittings that serve as buckles (shown on opposite page). The small rectangle goes through the larger one at an angle. Pulling it tight flattens the pieces together in a strong hold. They trade simplicity and light weight for convenience and safety since they're treacherously difficult to disconnect in an emergency.

The leg loops should always be buckled first and unbuckled last. This habit may be a life-saver if you start free flying where launching without the leg straps fastened can be fatal. Doing so with a motor is normally just embarrassing unless you try to

Trimmers and speedbar are two different ways of deforming the wing to speed it up. Speedbar lowers the leading edge while trimmers raise the trailing edge. Neutral trim is whatever puts the quick links all in a level line.

Trimmers are controlled through tabs on the back of the riser and the Speedbar is controlled through a foot bar whose line goes up to sister clips on each A riser.

Not all wings have both systems. Soaring wings tend to only have a speedbar-type system and motor wings tend to have both.

Standard gliders have 3 to 5 inches of trimmer range while reflex models may have twice that much. The reflex profile, as shown below, allows for increased speed *and* improved collapse resistance whereas standard gliders are more prone to collapse at their faster speeds.

Tip: Mountain climbing harnesses can work for kiting. They're lightweight and inexpensive but are less comfortable than dedicated models. In mountain climbing, there is only one connection point whereas we have two that are supposed to be separated. So connect the carabiners around the waste strap AND through the tool hoops. That should keep the risers separated, as shown, but still closer together than what would be ideal (about 15 inches).

High end dedicated kiting harnesses, like the one far right, are more expensive but are well worth it in comfort. They should include both low carabiner hook-ins for long-term kiting practice and high loops to prepare for high hook-in machines. Practice primarily with the lower loops to reduce back strain during long kiting sessions. Some pilots become expert wing handlers and find kiting to be as rewarding as flying.

Quick Release Buckle | **Simple Rectangle Buckle**

hang on and take off. Always buckle at least one leg loop, even when you're just wearing the motor, to avoid accidentally taking off with both leg loops unbuckled.

Make sure the buckles are properly fastened too—try to pull them apart. If they're not solidly fastened you could fall out after liftoff. The chest mustn't be forgotten, either, lest the motor falls backwards during launch (more likely during an abort).

A few brands are set up to help prevent forgetting the leg straps. These "diaper" styles (shown in right sidebar) make the chest strap fasten into a center piece that comes up from between your legs. If the chest portion is fastened then at least one leg is fastened too. Some may also use a central connection point where all the straps com together and fasten with one action. On those, make sure there is no way to accidentally unbuckle since you would fall out when getting out of the seat for landing. Their advantage is rapid escape in case of emergency (water or fire).

courtesy Alex Varv

Diaper Buckle

The Motor

The motor unit includes the engine, frame and a harness that can be detached, sometimes easily enough to use for kiting practice. Harnesses are nearly always designed with a particular frame in mind.

Any good school will match the pilot to the motor based on his size, weight and expected launch elevation. See chapter 27 for details on choosing motors. In all likelihood, it will have a 2-stroke engine with between 80 and 320 cc's (cubic centimeters of piston displacement).

Training success has little to do with brand as long as your instructor is familiar with it. If you bring your own gear then there may be a learning curve while the instructor figures out its nuances. If you bring unacceptable gear (too heavy, too little power, etc.) then the instructor may not be willing to train you on it.

Carabiners

Carabiners provide the connection from wing to motor/harness. They are nearly identical to what mountain climbers use with one important exception: paraglider 'biners use a locking gate to prevent accidental opening. Plus, most allow one-handed operation—quite convenient.

Almost none allow releasing under tension so as to "cut away" from the wing like sport skydiving canopies. Ours must be deliberately unclipped. In fact, releasing from the wing while it's under tension is nearly impossible. The need to insure staying connected while flying far outweighs the advantage of a quick disconnect. Even after a reserve deployment, the pilot does not "cut away" from the paraglider as they do in skydiving.

The strongest carabiners are made of steel but most pilots use lighter aluminum versions. Properly made, aluminum is quite sufficient. Strength is rated by how

The motor above has an uncommon feature that allows it to be jettisoned using Pull Rings.

Carry straps, or *ground-handling straps*, are common on many models. They make it more comfortable to wear and handle while on the ground.

This harness and fittings is called a *soft J-bar* system.

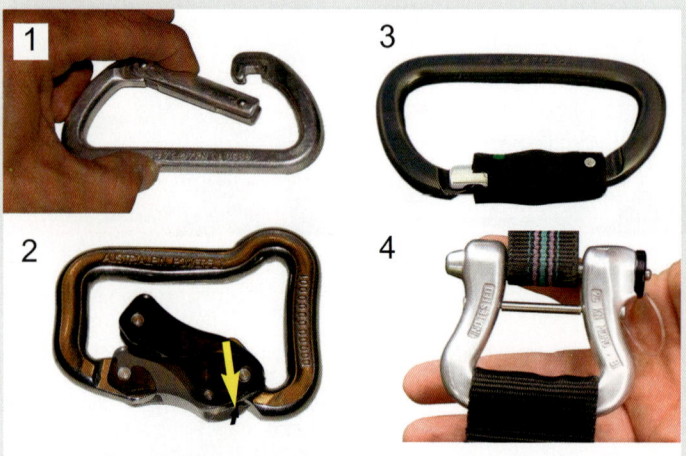

1. Non-locking carabiner. Use only for kiting practice since the gate can open easier by accident.

2. Press-gate carabiners, our most common type, have a self locking mechanism that can be operated by one hand. This one is steel—heavier but stronger. Pushing at the arrow both unlocks *and* opens the gate.

3. Another locking gate style where you push the green button and twist the gate to open. Requires 2 hands.

4. This uncommon style opens by pushing the small button in the load pin to remove it. Requires 2 hands.

Most carabiners are made of aluminum with a strength of at least 18 Kilonewtons (KN). Slightly heavier steel models go up to 28 KN.

This model can be released (opened) while loaded—great if you're getting dragged, not so great if it happens accidentally while flying. These are rarely used in powered paragliding.

much force they can bear without deforming while the gate is closed; it is measured in Kilonewtons (KNs). One KN is about 225 pounds. 18 to 22 KN is typical for aluminum whereas steel carabiners start at around 28 KN. They usually list the much lower strength rating for when the gate is open but should never be flown that way.

Nearly invisible scratches and cracks can dramatically degrade the carrying capability of carabiners, especially aluminum ones, so treat them with care. Some instructors recommend periodic replacement.

Kiting Harness

A kiting harness is important for learning so don't skimp—you'll spend a lot of time in it. Given the importance of kiting skills, it should be portable, convenient and comfortable.

Some motors have removable harnesses for use in kiting but, for most machines, it's a pain. Plus, harnesses with only high hook-in points will cause back strain after a short time.

The harness can be as simple as a strap tied in a special way or a full harness made for flying. Full sized free-flight harnesses do work but are expensive and bulky.

There are many good kiting harness options that are detailed in Chapter 3.

Instruments

Simplicity is the sport's hallmark but some instruments are useful. And human nature being what it is, if it can be carried, it eventually will. Start small, though; extra stuff adds risk. It 1) adds weight, 2) can foul moving parts and 3) fancies propellers. Anything that *can* fall off, *will* go through the prop.

Wrist altimeters are useful and surprisingly accurate (given their small size) and they're less likely to fall off or be forgotten. See more instruments in Chapter 28.

EGT and CHT

Exhaust Gas Temperature (EGT) is taken from the motor's exhaust stream (as opposed to the metal). It's nearly the hottest temperature inside the motor. Above-normal readings here are generally the first indication of a lean fuel-to-air mixture.

Cylinder Head Temperature (CHT) uses a probe at the spark plug to tell how hot the cylinder is. Since the metal has to heat up it does not respond quite as quickly as EGT but is useful for the same reason: Telling whether the engine is running too lean and if it is getting enough cooling air.

Tachometer

Motor RPM is the most common metric of power because it's easy to measure and highly relevant. Since our props are fixed pitch (meaning the blade angle never changes in flight), more RPM equals more thrust. Most tachometers work by counting the number of electronic pulses sent to the spark plug and displaying that as an RPM although some models work optically *(more on tachs in Chapter 28)*.

Altimeter

An altimeter reports altitude using atmospheric pressure (or *barometric pressure*). As you go up, the pressure decreases which registers as an altitude increase. Depending on how you set it, the displayed altitude is above mean sea level (MSL) or height above ground level (AGL).

Altimeter watches are generally accurate to within 20 feet, plenty good for powered paragliding. Every pilot should have some kind of altimeter, especially if they fly in areas where restricted airspace overlies their flying area. The altimeter should be set to launch elevation before takeoff.

Variometer

A Variometer gives vertical speed—how fast you're climbing or descending. Most models beep with increasing pitch in proportion to increasing climb rate and buzz with lowering pitch in proportion to increasing descent rate. They're most helpful for soaring and so are not terribly common with paramotor pilots.

1. A tachometer mounted on the throttle. The mirror is for viewing your fuel level—it doubles as a check to see how cool you look flying this thing.

2. Cylinder Head Temperature (CHT) uses a probe that mounts on the spark plug making it painless to install.

3. This wrist altimeter has a large display, with altimeter, vertical speed, compass and barometric pressure. It tells time, too.

4. A variometer shows climb or descent rate both visibly and audibly. Happy beeping indicates climb, sad buzzing indicates sinking.

Accessories

So many gadgets and so few places to put them. But remember that, if you bring it, you've got to launch with it (and muck with it in flight, and keep it out of the prop, etc.). Below are some of the basics with more in Chapter 28.

Helmet / Hearing Protection

Most schools will wisely require a helmet to protect your brain pan against head injury. It's beneficial, too, for kiting where you can get tossed around near the ground. Full face helmets protect you during "face plants"—the non-flattering result of falling forward.

Many PPG helmets have quality hearing protection with audio and a microphone. The quietest designs avoid having the chin strap going through the ear cups. A push-to-talk (PTT) switch will either be on a coil that goes out to your hand or, more likely, on the helmet itself, usually an ear cup.

Purpose-built PPG helmets usually come with a built-in PTT but other helmets can be modified by the mechanically inclined.

Radios

In the U.S., low quality FRS (Family Radio Service) radios are common for both training and pilot-to-pilot conversation. FRS radios frequently include some channels in the GMRS band and, on those channels, are more powerful but require an FCC license.

Some schools, clubs and pilots use 2-meter radios which are far more reliable. Unfortunately, they do cost more and require an amateur license (HAM) which can be had after two days of directed study and a two-hour multiple choice test. Morse code is no longer required in the U.S.

No standards are established so check with your instructor since helmets and radios rarely play well together (see Chapter 28).

Aviation radios can be used, especially if you plan to fly from airports. Regulations may require a Radio License or Pilot License, check your country's regulations. Mostly we use the air-to-air frequency of 122.75 MHz but check FAA AC 90-50D for aviation frequency allocation.

Boots

In most cases boots help prevent ankle injuries while running for launch or landing. They're more beneficial on rough surfaces and benefit free-flyers more since their launch sites are frequently strewn with nature's rockyrandomness. Choose boots that allow easy running—in light winds, you'll be thankful. Favor those with laces or loops instead of hooks which can catch paraglider lines during inflation.

Hook Knife

It's unlikely that a hook knife will be needed but, if you're getting dragged or pulled under water, it may be the only way out. It can quickly slice through lines and harness webbing with minimal risk to yourself.

Reserve

Reserve, or rescue, parachutes offer a last chance survival option for major wing malfunctions, midairs, or structural failures. While they can be a lifesaver, without proper installation and understanding, they can add more risk then benefit mostly due to the possibility of accidental or improper deployment.

Reserves go in a pouch which is attached to the motor's frame. Bridles (risers) then attach to the paramotor harness in such a way as to avoid entanglement during deployment. The bridles connect near the paramotor's normal carabiners to insure sufficient strength to endure opening shock while providing proper hang angle (tilt-back of the motor). Some motor harnesses have special reserve attachments, usually above the main carabiner hook-in. The reserve's pouch has a handle with pins that must be installed and inspected to prevent accidental deployment, a very serious situation (see Chapter 12).

1. This purpose-built helmet for motoring is made to work with FRS radios. Plugs are not standard; some can even look alike but wind up being slightly different and incompatible. Plugs can even be identical but not work due to different electronics. Your instructor should have compatible gear.

See FootFlyer.com to either build or purchase the *Hamann System* that can mount to any helmet and works with most 2-meter radios and some FRS radios.

2. It's hard to cut yourself with a hook knife but easy to cut through harness webbing or lines in an emergency. It should be mounted in a readily reachable area.

Left: This is the only time a pilot ever wants to see his reserve outside its container.

Inset: A reserve can be a lifesaver but it must be installed properly (see Chapter 12) and the pilot well versed in its use (See Chapter 19).

Your training rig may not have a reserve since some instructors prefer to avoid the possibility of new students deploying it accidentally.

Handling The Wing

CHAPTER 3

"But officer, I'm just flying my kite."

Ground handling the glider, or *kiting*, is getting the wing overhead and controlling it in a breeze. Fortunately it's fun, too, since ground handling is our sport's seminal skill. It's also the most challenging one to really master.

The goal of kiting is to keep the wing overhead while standing mostly in one place. To master kiting is to master launching. It will help you succeed, make you look good, and spare much costly aggravation.

Finesse and higher-wind skills come with practice which, thankfully, can be done in any open area having a smooth, steady breeze. Be careful, though, it is surprisingly risky without proper instruction.

Your site should be big, free of fabric-tearing, line snagging protrusions, and be upwind of buildings or other obstructions that would cause turbulence (a *wind shadow*). You also want smooth terrain downwind—space you're willing to get dragged through if the wind picks up. A wing's powerful pull in a gust can easily be overpowering.

Use your instructor. He can save enormous frustration with sometimes important and seemingly trivial tips. Once the basics are down and you understand the limitations of when to kite, doing it on your own will hasten the training process dramatically. Repetition greases the wheels of progress.

Few students will want to attempt kiting in more than about a 10 mph breeze and it takes at least a 7 mph to practice effectively. As skill develops you may be able to handle winds as light as 5 mph and as much as 14 mph.

A Kiting War puts kiting skills to the test against other pilots as each one tries to be the last one up.

Deflating the Wing

A wing in a wind has a mighty pull; before learning to control it, you must first learn how to deflate it. Here are some techniques. They work best while walking or running towards the wing but can also be used if you're being dragged. Your goal is to grab tip fabric then keep pulling it, hand over hand by the upper surface, until holding approximately the center cell.

> ⚠ **Caution!**
> In even moderate conditions, be ready to handle the wing as soon as you hook in. A sudden gust can quickly unravel your tenuous balance. Practice deflation methods and getting to your hook knife.

1. The normal method is to pull both brakes hard until the wing comes down. If it's windy, first release the brakes so the wing surges overhead then pull them hard so that it comes quickly down through the *power band* (highest pull force).
2. Reach up and pull the C risers (three rows back from the A's) down as far as possible. Hold them. They may be hard to find while being dragged so rehearse doing it under more controllable conditions.
3. Pull only *one* brake hard then keep pulling that brake line hand-over-hand if necessary, until you're holding tip fabric. The wing may flip over and swirl around, twisting the lines, but keep pulling.
4. Reach up to grab any center line and keep pulling until you get to fabric. This adds a high risk of line burns, especially without gloves.

Brake Positions/Pressures

We'll reference brake positions using a fractional position or a number from 0 to 5. Zero is hands up and five is the maximum brake pull possible without stalling the wing (flight stops, dropping begins). Note that forearms are kept vertical through 4.

Think of control inputs as *pressures* more than positions. If it takes 5 pounds of pressure to get position 3, remember the 5 pounds. Every wing is different too, and lower hookin motors will average lower hand positions than those with higher hookins. When trying a new model, be particularly careful about excessive brake pull. If possible, adjust your brake lines so the following positions work—they offer the most brake travel.

- Position 0: Hands up, no brake pull, the toggles are against the pulley.
- Position 1: Starting to feel brake pressure, around ½ pound.
- Position 2: Resting the weight of your arms. Your extended thumb would be about ear height on most configurations but see where it is by resting your arms.
- Position 3: Intermediate between 2 and 4.
- Position 4: About shoulder height. The forearm is kept vertical this position. It is the most brake pull that should ever be used for normal flight.
- Position 5: Anything beyond position 4 should only be used for landing flare or advanced maneuvering. Use with extreme care.

These positions will depend on your glider's brake-line length but it should be adjusted so that these positions generally work. Beware that a *glider can* stall well before reaching position 5 under the right (or wrong!) conditions.

---

1. Beaches are perfect for kiting with their smooth on-shore winds but still deserve great respect. If the wing gets into the surf, even shallow surf, disconnect! Pilots have drowned after being dragged into moving water or surf, unable to disconnect due to the wing's water-driven pull.

2. To regain control over a wind-whipped wing, either grab a wing tip or run around behind the wing and unclip.

Brake Positions/Pressures

References to hand positions use the descriptions below. However, you should learn to equate them to brake *pressure*, not position. They will vary by glider; one glider's position 2 may do very little, while on another it whips the glider into a spiral.

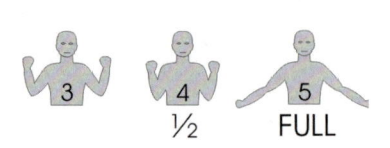

0 UP | 1 | 2 ¼
3 | 4 ½ | 5 FULL

Preparing Yourself

Besides the wing, you'll need a harness, helmet and gloves (recommended).

Strap-only harness (like for mountain climbing) can be difficult to put on. Make sure you understand how they work before trying to use one. Carabiners should fasten to the most structural part of the harness or the loops intended for them. Gliders have a recommended riser spread (see Chapter 12) which is why kiting harnesses, unless built for flying, should not be flown.

Carabiners should open toward the center, facing each other, to reduce the possibility for lines to snag on, or go through, the gates accidentally.

Lightweight gloves improve grip and prevent line burns in case a gust snatches part of the wing, pulling line through your fingers with skin searing force. Normally you only handle the risers but some more advanced moves do require pulling lines.

Before clipping into the wing, have a helmet on—the most likely time to need one is while kiting. Pilots have been seriously hurt while clipped into a wing that got caught by a big gust. The only exception should be if somebody is just showing how to handle the lines *and* there is no wind.

If possible, have something to simulate a throttle; it will help dramatically when transitioning to the motor. After learning basic kiting, start practicing with the throttle simulator in whatever hand you expect to use while motoring.

Keep the brake toggles snapped and store the risers separate from the rest of the wing to help prevent tangles.

Pull loops through

Rubbing the risers back and forth. See step 6.

This is a *line-over*. Go to the line and pull the wing through. See step 2.

Line overs can be difficult to see, check from behind.

Untangling Lines: Taming the Dips and Loops

Prevention is easier but, if tangles happen, these steps can help. Whatever you do, don't disconnect anything! Find a clear, open area to lay out the wing like a forward launch. If able, kiting it between steps may reveal a solution.

1. Snap the brakes into their retainers and separate the risers as much as possible. Pull the risers away from the trailing edge as far as the tangle allows and shake them to clear the easy stuff.
2. Make sure there are no *line overs* where a line goes under the trailing edge, behind and over the leading edge. If so, bring the rogue lines around (pull the wing through if necessary) so the lines are laying on top along with all the other lines.
3. Untwist the riser. It might be difficult to tell which way to do this in the early stages, but keep making sure they're untwisted as you proceed. Shake the riser and try teasing the lines apart as you go.
4. Remove sticks and make sure nothing is caught in the riser pulleys or brake handles.
5. Look for and remove loops. Clearing one loop (dip) may de-puzzle the whole mess.
6. While holding the risers up and outstretched, slide them back and forth so the lines rub on each other.
7. Hold the cleared A's up with some tension to help sort out remaining tangles. Then try tensioning and separating the individual B, C, and D risers.
8. If none of this works, start from the wing. Pull the innermost A through to its quick link at the riser. Have no lines above this A line—it should be clear to the wing. Hold the riser by this A line and let everything else drop below. Orient the A riser properly and, while holding some tension to the wing, it will be more obvious what needs to be done. In all likelihood you'll have to put the riser loops through some of the outstretched lines. You will sometimes have to twist the risers around to get it to work.

The PPG Bible: A Complete Guide and Reference

Preparing the Wing

Layout & Trimmer Setting

Pull the wing out of its bag while keeping the riser loops together but separate from everything else. Unclip them from each other (if clipped) then lay out the wing perpendicular to the wind as shown in figure 1 below. Don't let the riser loops go through any lines! Lay out the wing on its back so that the lines are on top, the riser loops are upwind and the cell openings (leading edge) are downwind. In light winds, doing this carefully is the most important part of a successful launch.

Hooking In for a Forward
(text on opposing page)

Right riser shown hanging down

Brake Lines
Brake Pulleys

The brakes lines should go straight through their pulleys with no twists or overlapping lines in the green areas.

Dan is pointing to the center cell, a dot near the trailing edge on this model. Most wings mark the center so you can easily make sure you're centered when getting ready.

A slight "U" or "V" shape (frame 9) helps the pilot center himself and helps the wing come up straighter. Most pilots find this is helpful but it may take a bit longer to inflate than a flatter layout.

Set the trimmers to halfway between their slowest (shortest) and fastest settings. Reflex wings should usually be set to neutral (0) but, as always, consult the wing's manual.

Clearing The Lines

Any line tangle whatsoever will prevent success. Pick up each riser and make sure the lines are clear to the wing, especially the A's. There should be no loops or lines draped over the A's when you hold up the A riser. While holding the riser with one hand, leave the brake toggle clipped in place and pull the brake *line* just enough to tug at the trailing edge. That helps verify the brake line is not snagged on anything and tugs out the trailing edge to insure it's not snagged on anything.

Forward and Reverse Launch

The terms *inflation* and *launch* are frequently used interchangeably although inflation is really just getting the wing overhead. A forward launch (or inflation) is where the pilot starts running with the wing behind him.

A *reverse* launch, used in winds over about 6 mph, is where the pilot faces the wing, pulls it up overhead, then turns around to launch. Technically it's a reverse inflation since, after turning around, there is no difference from a forward launch.

Light Winds (Forward Inflation)

Calm winds are great for PPG *flying* but a challenge for launching. Unless you're at a beach, most early flights will probably be in light or calm winds. That means lots of forward launch practice, a skill you'll be mighty thankful to have.

The basic technique is similar to what free flyers use and can be practiced at home with no motor. Other techniques use power to differing degrees.

The Gunslinger A-Grab
Brakes are omitted for clarity

"Turtling"

Section I: First Flight

Avoid forward launches in stronger winds. The breeze may topple you backwards as the wing catches air, snapping you back into the "turtle" position (lying on your back).

Hooking In

For this process, refer to the photo sequence beginning on the preceding page. Your wing should be laid out as shown (1) with the A risers up. Stand between the two risers facing away from the wing (2); if there's any breeze, it must be nearly direct on your face in this position or the wing will tend to come up crooked, turning into the wind. Step back towards the wing a few feet to prevent disturbing your layout during the process.

Pick up the left riser and hold it up with the riser loop down and A's forward (3). Think of how it will look in flight. Clip it to the carabiner and then let it fall forward and down (4) so the rear riser exposes its brake toggle for easy grabbing. Repeat for the other riser.

With your left hand, follow the left riser down and unclip its brake. Do the same on the right. You should be able to move the brake handle outward and see its line moving freely through the pulley (or ring) without any kinks (5). Keep hold of the brake handles through the remainder of the process.

Now refer to frames 5a through 5c—the brakes are omitted for clarity. Starting with your right hand, point your index finger down and thumb up like you're making a gun (5a). Bring the "gun" forward towards the risers/lines and beside your body, catching the A riser with your thumb as it comes up (5b). Bring it up so the A riser is between your thumb and index finger as the "gun" points up at about 45° angle (5c). The other risers/lines will be draped down over the top of your arm but the A-lines go cleanly back to the wing with nothing on top of them. Repeat for the left side. This will feel mighty awkward with the brake toggles and A-Lines but it does come together as shown in (6).

You're now standing there, facing away from the wing, with a brake toggle in each hand (7) and the A risers resting between their respective thumb and forefinger. If your wing has "split A's" then only use the center one in each thumb. Stay close enough to the wing so that you do not pull the leading edge over on itself which would make it harder to launch. After you gain proficiency, the instructor may have you start holding a throttle simulator to get used to it.

It is critical that you are centered on the wing and facing straight away. The instructor is invaluable here and will help with the nuances, of which there are several. To help insure being centered, look where the center of the wing is and position your body there, then walk carefully forward until you *barely* feel tension

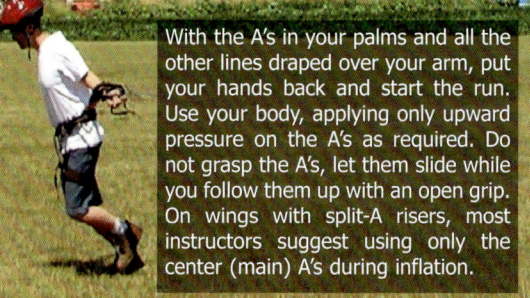

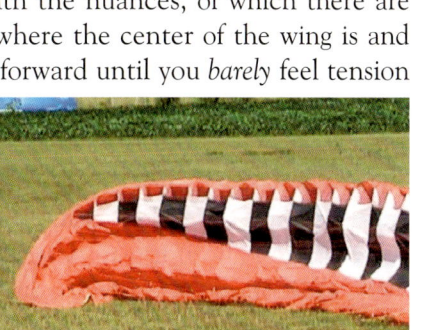

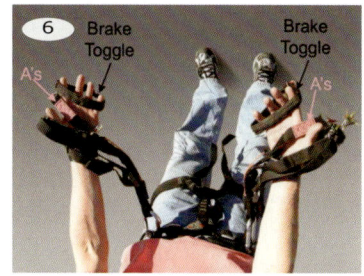

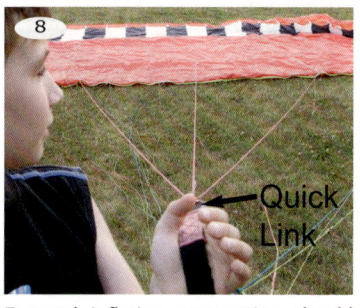

With the A's in your palms and all the other lines draped over your arm, put your hands back and start the run. Use your body, applying only upward pressure on the A's as required. Do not grasp the A's, let them slide while you follow them up with an open grip. On wings with split-A risers, most instructors suggest using only the center (main) A's during inflation.

Forward inflation preparation should leave you like frame (7). Looking back down the lines should reveal nothing draped over your A lines from the quick link to the wing (8).

It is important during the inflation that you do not *grasp* the A's, rather allow them to slide through your open palm as shown in the picture below left.

There are a very few exceptions (certain wings) where you must actually grasp and pull the A's but these will not generally be on beginner or solo wings. The instructor will let you know.

Below: "V" wing layout.

It takes a strong wind to do this. The pilot cannot move left/right so he must rely on brakes alone.

In a weaker wind you have to be able to move under the glider.

By David McWhinnie

By Tim Kaiser

Move with the wing. While reverse kiting, if the wing starts falling right: step right and pull right with your right hand like the pilot above. If the wing starts falling left, step left, pull left. If it tries to overfly you, pull both brakes. If it wants to sag downward, let up the brakes and walk backwards to give it more airflow.

While forward kiting, if the wing is falling to your right, step to the right while applying some left brake.

Get more airflow over the wing by walking into the wind. That provides more airspeed for better control unless, of course, it starts lifting you.

in the A's but with*out* curling the wing's leading edge. Move left or right so the tension is even—you're only feeling the weight of the lines to be centered here without actually pulling on them.

Take a step backwards toward the wing and plan the direction you'll start to run (directly away from the wing). Some pilots find an object to look at in that direction. You must be centered, perpendicular to the wing, and run straight in order for it to come up centered. And if there's any breeze at all, you must be headed into it. A very light crosswind component, up to 30°, is ok if it's less than about 2 mph. Don't try if there's *any* tailwind.

The Run

When you go for it, go hard! Lunge away from the wing, leading with your chest to quickly tension the lines. Pull hard through the resistance with your legs and body, hands back but exerting upward pressure on the A's with your open palms. Some wings need more A-pull than others and some will *front tuck* (leading edge folds downward) with even a small pull. Your instructor will let you know.

Keep forging forward with your body, speed is life. Arms back, A-pull as necessary, driving forward. If there's any wind, the wing will pull back fiercely as it arcs upward. When you think it's coming overhead, look up, or look left over your shoulder, to verify that the wing is centered but keep moving!

On some wings, especially reflex models, you may need to hold the A's for quite a while, at least until you've gathered some speed and the wing is fully overhead. These wings take more A-pull but are less likely to overfly you and front tuck.

You will learn to detect a subtle pull, left or right, from the tensioning lines. If the wing starts pulling you to the left, go left enough to keep under it while driving forward. Looking up at the wing too early can slow you down. Consider turning your head left or right, looking at the tip instead of looking straight up.

Later on, when doing this with a motor, you'll be leaning back into the thrust, For now, though, you'll need to lean forward to get enough oomph. In completely calm wind, the initial run will feel like you're pulling a limp rag with little resistance. Keep driving forward, speed=success.

With even a couple mph breeze, the wing will snap to attention much faster than in a dead calm. It will try to stop your forward momentum then come up quickly and want to overfly you; be ready to pull on the brakes *briefly* to slow it down while moving forward then let off the brakes. The vast majority of blown forward inflations can be traced to insufficient speed, releasing the A's too early, or pulling too much brake. Even a slightly crooked inflation can be managed if you'll get some speed and get under the wing while minimizing brake (usually none) pull.

Move Under the Wing

While running or forward kiting, you must move under the wing. If it leans right, you must go right; if it leans left, you must go left. Use no, or minimal brake pull while gathering speed, then use just enough brake pressure to steer and keep the wing from overflying you. This won't come easy, the wing will pull you to the left and you must go left even more to get under it. Fight hard the instinct to pull against the wing—it always wins.

Through inflation you should keep the A's in your hand, pushing them up and forward to help the wing come overhead. On some models, you must stay on the As (keep applying pressure) until it is fully overhead *and* your body is moving nicely forward. Then let off on the A's and pull just enough brakes to keep the wing from overflying you. Until you have some speed there is no point in doing much with the brakes, they will only make the wing fall back. *Once* you are moving forward, do what it takes to steer the wing. Right brake to turn right and left brake to turn left.

With forward momentum established and the wing centered, the goal is to keep enough speed (airflow) for control using brakes alone. More airflow equals better control. If the wing goes left or right move with it, but only as much as needed. Turning your body too much can thrust you to the other side and start a zig-zag oscillation that worsens as you get out of sync with the wing. You run right and the wing goes left in a series of increasing oscillations that end in a fall or worse. Use *small* direction changes and small brake inputs to the ease back into position. It's a fine dance that you'll just have to practice, but it's oh so fun when done right.

Remember that, when you're doing this with a motor you'll need to stand up straight and let the motor push.

Forward Kiting

Most wings need at least a 6 mph breeze to start being controllable and more is better, up to about 12 mph. If there is no wind then you must generate all 6 mph by running, a maximum effort for most people. The value of some breeze becomes painfully obvious after a few tries dragging twenty+ square meters of wing overhead. It's good that you *can* practice just by running as this is a very useful skill to master, but it's a lot of work in no wind.

Forward kiting reveals a critical behavior of the wing—if you move your body left, the wing goes right, and will continue to the right all the way to the ground. It reinforces why staying centered under the wing is so important. To move right by *your* choice you can first move slightly left to get the *wing* going right then follow it. Lead the wing a bit. If it's right but coming left overhead, apply right brake a couple seconds early to stop it. You want the *least* amount of input, though.

Wind Over 6 mph (Reverse Inflation)

Much of your early learning will involve reverse kiting. You'll need at least 7 mph wind to do so. Some schools may teach how to kite the wing without the harness, a useful skill covered in Chapter 15.

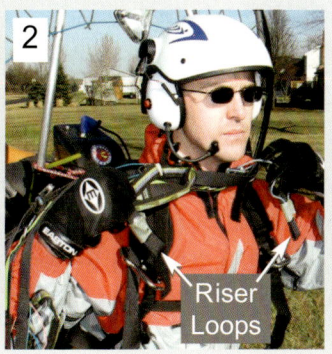

Tip: An alternate hook-in method for reverses is to treat it like the more obvious forward method. Free flyers transitioning to power may find this easier. Step up to the wing like a forward launch but stand *beside* the risers instead of between them (1). Pick up both risers while facing forward and lift them over your right shoulder (2). Remain facing away from the wing and hook the left riser to your left carabiner and the right riser to your right carabiner just like you do for a forward. Don't twist them. Envision how they will be in flight when the wing comes up.

(3) Once clipped in, the risers and lines are draped around your right side. Now turn right to face the wing—you're ready. After inflation, you'll turn to the left. Reverse the actions if you prefer turning right.

Reverse Hook-In: You should be facing the wing with its risers and lines laid out towards you (1), A-risers up. Pick up the risers and put them together (2), keeping the A's up. Flip them over counterclockwise a half-turn so that the A's are now facing the ground (3). Separate the risers and clip each one into the nearest carabiner (4,5). The carabiner should open inward. This will leave you hooked in with the risers crossed, brakes on top and a half twist in each riser. Move your right hand down the right riser and grab its brake. It may be covered by the other riser or its lines, just reach under them, grab the brake and bring it towards you. There should be no twist in the brake line; it will go from the pulley to your hand (6). Do the same with your left hand, reach down to the riser attached to the left carabiner and grab its brake from the holder (magnetic or snap).

6. Pull the brakes off their clip. They should be free and clear to the pulley. You now have the correct brake in each hand.

7. Cross the risers up near your body, then grab each "A" riser as shown. One brake line will cross over.

8. There should be no lines (including brake lines) draped over the A's when this is done properly.

Hooking In Reversed

Free flyers hook in forward then turn around while lifting one riser over their head. That's harder with a motor's cage so other techniques are normally used.

There are surprisingly many ways to hook in reversed but we cover the most common: hook in while facing the wing in such a way that everything is sorted out after turning around to launch as shown in **Reverse Hook-In**.

It seems complicated but, when you pull the wing to life and turn around (you'll turn to the left using these instructions), it all sorts out magically. Your right hand will control the right brake and left hand the left brake.

After you're hooked in, make the two risers cross each other right up near the carabiners then, while holding a brake in each hand, grab an A riser with each hand like shown. Alternatively, and for motor launches, you'll put both A's in your left hand. On wings with Split A's you may be holding four risers although it's usually best just to have the inner A's on those wings. Eventually you'll also have a throttle in that right hand (or left depending on the motor setup). This is confusing but repetition will fix that. There are many ways to teach this—go with what your instructor is most familiar. You're now ready to build a "wall."

Construction: Building the Wall

Having the wing partially inflated while it sits on the ground in a moderate breeze (it needs about 8 mph) is called "building a wall." Doing so helps control the wing while insuring that you're properly positioned so the wing comes up centered when you're ready to bring it overhead. Building a wall is the first thing to do after getting hooked in reversed as it improves the success rate for reverse launches. It is also a great exercise in handling the wing.

To build a wall, spread out the wing and hook in as described above. While holding the brakes, grab an A in each hand. Be prepared to pull brakes in case the wing tries to billow up before you're ready. Get some tension on the risers with your body, step forward once and then lurch backwards while applying some upward pressure on the A's. If there's enough wind, the wing will start to come up. Just as it leaves the ground, let go of the A's and pull the brakes to bring it back down but not too hard—you want to leave the wing standing there "at attention" with the leading edge a few feet above the ground. Do this several times—it will be confusing at first just finding the two A risers each time but practice really pays off.

Once the wall is built, you can modulate how tall it stands by stepping towards or away from it. Leveling the wall is done by stepping sideways toward the higher side. You can also practice holding both A's in your non-throttle hand to be ready for adding power. Get used to going for the A's, pulling the wing up mostly with your body, and then bringing it back down using brakes. Timing is a challenge, you want it to come just off the ground and then bring it right back down again—the trailing edge should never get more than a few feet high. Once you have gained some experience you can do this without the trailing edge even leaving the ground.

Use your body, not the A's. Only help it with the A's; if the leading edge deforms, you're pulling them too hard. The wing must see pressure more evenly on the lines, especially if there's barely enough wind. On some wings, you do not need any pull on the A's at all which improves your feel for the wing's pull.

Reverse Inflation

Once the wall is level and looking good (if there's enough breeze for a wall), step forward to lower it slightly then be prepared to lurch backwards. When ready, take several steps backwards, letting your body pull on the risers as your hands (or hand if using one hand) pulls *just enough* on the A's. This action should be more of a fast snatch than a walk. Otherwise you end up dragging the wing along the ground. Use your body, not just the A's.

As the wing comes up, keep some A pressure until it's nearly overhead then let off. Be prepared with some brakes—you may need to "check" the wing (pull brakes then reduce) if it's coming up fast. With much wind you'll get a rapid inflation and must be ready to release the A's earlier and jab in some brakes. Then reduce brake pull so it doesn't fall back.

If it's lumbering up limply then you'll need to hold the A's all the way up, waiting until it's nearly overhead before even thinking about pulling on the brakes. You'll be walking backwards to keep it coming overhead.

Which Way To Turn Around?

Plan to turn around opposite of your throttle hand. If your machine has a right hand throttle (as shown), plan to turn to the left. Later on you'll find it helpful since you can hold the A's longer during the turn-around as shown below.

Building a *wall* helps insure that you're square to the wing with lines clear. Move towards the high side to keep the wall level.

During initial inflation, it behaves like a wall--for the very first few feet of rise, stepping towards the high side will bring up the low side. But once the wing passes 45° that no longer works. It goes through this regime so fast that it's not useful for straightening a crooked inflation.

If the wing comes up crooked, set it back down and try again, starting from a level wall. Once it's up past 45° always step towards the center cell.

1. This is a common stance for reverse inflations with a motor. For a right-handed throttle, plan on turning around to the left.

Strap on the throttle, grab the brakes then get both A's in your non-throttle hand and throttle in the other. It feels awkward at first but does get easier.

2. The basic reverse kiting mantra is: one hand up, one hand down and move briskly. Always be moving towards the center cell until you're brake handling is good enough to keep the wing centered overhead with*out* moving your body. If the brakes aren't responding enough, step backwards a few steps to get more airflow over the wing.

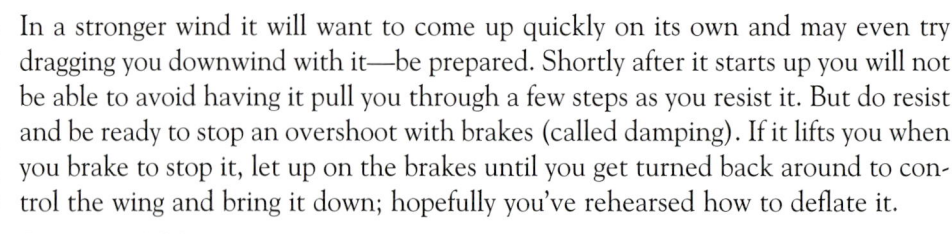

In a stronger wind it will want to come up quickly on its own and may even try dragging you downwind with it—be prepared. Shortly after it starts up you will not be able to avoid having it pull you through a few steps as you resist it. But do resist and be ready to stop an overshoot with brakes (called damping). If it lifts you when you brake to stop it, let up on the brakes until you get turned back around to control the wing and bring it down; hopefully you've rehearsed how to deflate it.

Reverse Kiting

Once the wing is happily overhead the fun is keeping it there. For the most part you will want to use as little brake pull as possible. We'll refine this process more later but, for now, the steps to successful reverse kiting are:

- Stay under the wing's center cell. If it moves left, walk left. If it moves right, immediately walk right.

- If the wing goes left, pull left (using the brake in your left hand), if it goes right, pull right (using the brake in your right hand). So if the wing drifts to the left, walk left, pull left. Pull only as much as you need. Walk as little as you can get away with but move aggressively at first.

- Be light on the brakes: you'll 1) avoid over-correcting, 2) be less likely to have the wing fall back down, and 3) work less. If it's sitting happily overhead, have little or no brake engaged at all. If the wing keeps falling back use less brake pull and walk backwards to increase airflow.

The goal is to stand there, in one place, using the least amount of brakes possible to kite it overhead. Move your body if needed, but shoot for being able to just stand there, kiting, without over controlling.

Another benefit of having minimum brake pull is that you're less likely to get lifted. If the wing is hanging back and you've got the trailing edge deflected (as you will with pulled brakes), you are vulnerable to gusts. It's like sticking your hand out the window of a fast moving car—if the hand is angled up, airflow pushes it up and backward, but if it's streamlined, there is less effect.

In a light wind you may need to walk backwards to keep decent airflow over the wing for good control. After all, if the wind isn't blowing enough, then *you* need to generate it. Airflow (airspeed over the wing) is life—the more the better for control.

If the wing tends to fly past you, apply both brakes, if it drops back ease up on the brakes and walk backwards (away from the wing). By modulating these inputs and movements you can become quite adept at making the wing stay where you want it, even in light winds. Wings that inflate easily tend to front tuck more.

Practice kiting until it's second nature. Besides being fun to master, good wing handling is the crux of being a good launcher. It is what will determine the conditions you can handle, especially stronger winds. More advanced techniques are covered later.

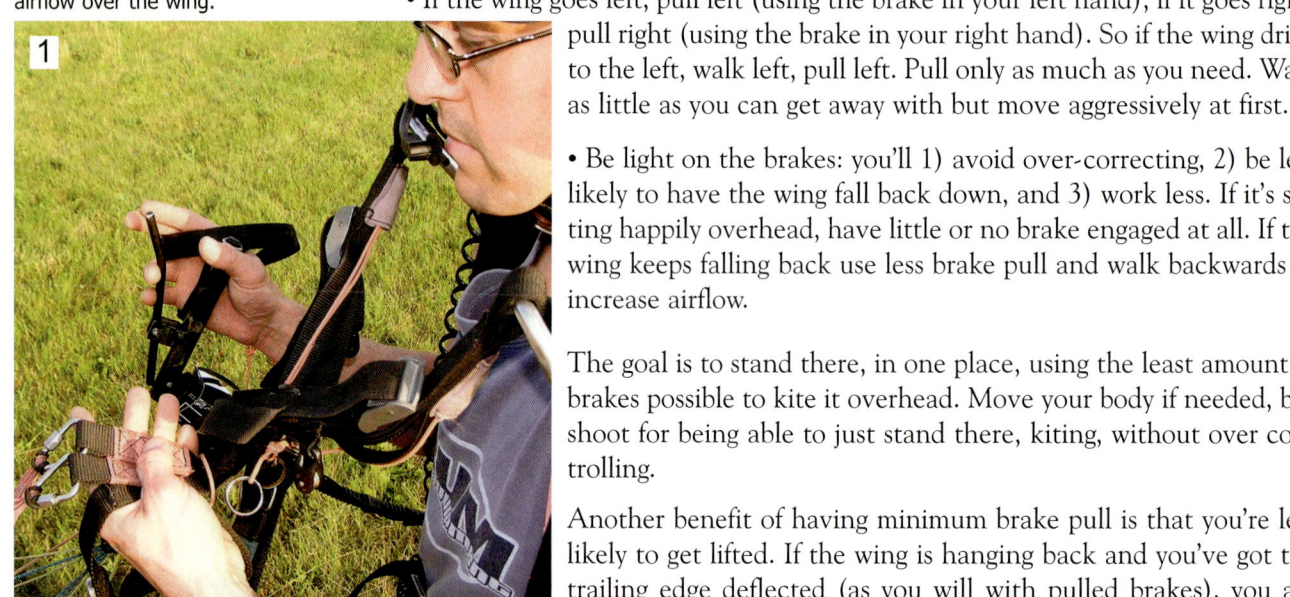

Alternative Training-Only Method: Straight Risers

The normal way of kiting while reversed can be confusing at first, so some instructors use a straight-riser method to quickly get the student kiting. But the regular method must eventually be learned so don't do this for long.

You forego a flight-ready hook-in for simplicity; the risers go straight out to the wing without crossing. The drawback is that brake input is backwards from what you'll eventually learn. It is quicker to master while still giving a good feel for the wing and how to stay centered under it.

It's simple: hook in without crossing the risers, A's face up. Grab the brake closest to each hand from the outside; there should be nothing crossed. With the brakes in your hands, reach up to hold the A's and inflate the wing as instructed above, using mostly your body but applying appropriate pressure to the A's.

As the wing comes overhead, be ready to dampen it with brakes so it doesn't overfly you. Then modulate the brakes to keep the wing there just like the other methods. In light winds you will generally have no brake pulled at all. If it wants to fall back, walk backwards to increase the wing's airflow. If the wing starts falling left, step left and pull some brake with the right hand and vice versa if it falls right. Only the brake pull is opposite to the flight-ready method (normally used and taught) of having the risers crossed.

Whether kiting with crossed (normal) or straight risers, **watch the trailing edge move** and visualize it slowing down that side of the wing which is exactly what's happening. This will make its behavior and response more clear.

Only do the straight riser method long enough to get a feel for the wing (if at all) since you will need to (re)learn the flight-ready method (walk left, pull left with the left hand) before adding power.

The Turn and Move

Once you are able to reliably kite the wing overhead, your next step is to turn around and kite it forward. You will turn left (counter-clockwise) if hooked in as described earlier.

While keeping the wing centered overhead, take a step backward (into the wind which is at your back) to get the wing moving, turn around quickly and *keep moving forward*. In light winds especially you must keep moving forward. Lean if necessary but remember that, with a motor on, you will stand up straight and throttle up to keep moving. If you'll be turning left, it's beneficial to have the wing lean slightly left before turning around so you're turning towards the wing.

You must turn and *move*. Speed is life since the wing needs airflow for the brakes to be effective. The most common failure is the wing falling back or sideways—moving faster usually prevents this. Once you've got the wing under control and moving forward, you're doing forward kiting as described earlier.

Bringing the Wing Down

You could just let it flop down in a heap but that is both messy and inconvenient. Far better is to let it down so that it is either easy to re-inflate or easy to put away.

Turn around to face the wing opposite to the direction you turned to kite forward.

Straight Riser Method

As a way to get students kiting quickly (as pictured), some instructors have them clip in directly, without any lines crossed. While this may get you kiting faster, don't do it for long since the control movements are backwards from what you'll need to launch.

Regardless of the kiting method used, always keep your body under the wing, and always be moving side to side until you get the feel for how much brake you can use without causing the wing to fall back.

The PPG Bible: A Complete Guide and Reference

You'll have the risers crossed as if to launch. Once you're facing the wing, pull the brakes hard enough so that it falls back evenly. You can turn the other way but it's easier to habitually use the same direction every time so you're ready to re-inflate in the familiar manner.

Just before the wing touches down, take a step towards it so the leading edge lays back nicely. This makes it somewhat easier to re-inflate or fold up.

If it's windy, you can bring the wing down on its side by pulling one brake more than the other; that reduces its tendency to re-inflate. A strong wind can make it difficult to bring the wing down at all (see also Chapter 15.) One solution is to get the wing way overhead, almost to the point of front-tucking, by simultaneously squatting down and letting off the brakes. Then, with one quick motion, pull the brakes hard as you stand up. It will yank hard briefly as it plunges through the power band (area of greatest pull).

A strong wind is also a good time to practice *C-Line deflations*. You can use the B's or D's too with somewhat less effectiveness. Reach up with both hands as high as possible, grab the C risers (not the lines) and pull as far down as you can. If it comes down and remains a few feet above the ground, "snaking" about in the breeze, you'll have to run towards it; when it hits the ground, get around behind it. Running towards it may be the only way to get it all the way down. Don't let go of those C's until you do run around it!

Adding the Motor

Before adding the motor, try kiting with a throttle simulator (a dummy throttle that's not hooked to anything). You'll be surprised at how confounding this simple addition is and will appreciate having practiced it.

The following description is for a right-handed throttle. If yours is left handed then you'll hold the A's in your right hand. Which side the throttle is on doesn't matter much but, if you have a reserve, its better for it to be opposite the throttle.

Learn where the kill switch is and practice pressing it. You want that reaction to be automatic for when things turn ugly. There will be times where the wind has its way with you and being quick on the switch will save many shekels. While kiting with the throttle simulator, practice hitting (and holding) the kill switch whenever the wing goes awry. At the first sign of trouble, press it!

After proficiency is gained with the throttle simulator (which happens quickly), put the motor on and practice kiting. This will be tiring but you won't do it for long. Some schools use frames with weights to help build up to the full motor weight, a useful tool.

Learn to "turn and run." That is, once the wing is mostly overhead and moving forward, you'll want to turn right away and start moving. Your instructor may pull or push you to simulate the

This *C-line deflation* disables the wing quickly. It is done by reaching up high on each C riser and pulling them down all the way. As the wing snakes onto the ground, let the C's go and pull the brakes far enough to keep it down.

On some wings it's more effective to use the rear risers (D's on a four riser wing).

In a strong wind, here's a tip: hold the D's (or C's) back as far as you can then put them in one hand while still pulled. With your other hand, grasp all the lines, including the pulled D's so that now you're holding them pulled. Bundle the wing normally. This keeps the D's pulled so wind is less likely to reinflate the wing.

> ⚠ **Caution!**
> More serious injuries come from getting body parts into a spinning prop than any other cause. Use extreme care when handling a motor and do not start it until given specific instructions.

motor's thrust. You must be able to control the wing with the motor pushing before even *considering* flight. The motor has a lot of inertia so when you turn around it will tend to continue twisting. It's just a matter of feel to turn fast without letting it swing you past forward.

With these skills reasonably in hand, you will start the motor (there are some significant "gotchyas" to know about) and go through these exercises with it running. Note that it is eminently possible for lines to go into the prop without due care.

Before hooking in, get used to the basic controls on the motor by running it up and feeling the range of power. Practice going for the kill switch.

Storing the Wing

Wings like it cool, dry and dark. Heat or chemicals can degrade the material strength while dampness and its moldy cousin can rot holes in the nylon. UV from sunlight weakens the fabric and makes it porous—all bad. With their 300-hour average lifetime measured mostly in UV exposure, and $3000 price, basking in sunshine costs about $10 per hour.

Before putting the wing away, try to make sure there are no bugs inside. That's best done by folding or stuffing it right away. If grasshoppers or other critters get trapped inside they'll make a hole one way or another; either by chewing to freedom or by leaving their acidic little remains. If you notice crawling things already inside, find a reasonably bugless place and shake the trailing edge so that they fall out the leading edge openings. This can be done inside but you'll be amazed at how big the wing is. It can be helpful to leave half of it folded while you attend to the other half. The ribs have big holes in them for the air to spread out but they also make fine bug highways.

Before putting the wing away, clip the riser ends together with a small carabiner or other clip. As you put it away, don't let the riser ends go through any lines. Keep them well separated to reduce the likelihood of tangles when pulling it out again. That's the purpose of a riser pouch if you have one.

Rosette

When finished with the wing, hold the riser pair with your left hand, grab all the lines with your right hand then slide the right hand out towards the wing. At full extension, coil the lines into your riser holding hand. Don't let the riser ends go through any lines! Slide your right hand out again and repeat until it reaches fabric, leaving you with a big, easy-to-carry, *rosette*. If there's a wind, turn around once so the fabric doesn't billow.

Stuffing

Stuffing the wing into a wide-opening *stuff sack* is quick and easy. Put it away the same way each time, with risers pointed down from the wing's center, so when you get it out again, you'll know which way it goes. A riser pouch is great, if available, or you can clip them to the sack's carry handle. Most importantly, make sure the risers are situated so that no lines will get mixed in.

Stuffing isn't better or worse than folding although stuffing will leave more wrinkles. Newer wings with special leading edge rib reinforcements benefit from an *accordion* (or concertina) fold where the leading edge cells are all kept flat.

1. A *rosette* is a good way to carry the wing—just throw it over your back. It's also what you do before putting it into a stuff sack.

2. Before stuffing, clip the risers together and make sure they remain clear of all other lines.

3. This light weight stuff sack comes with an integral riser bag. Put the risers in it to keep them separated which reduces tangles. Then, before launching, stuff the stuff sack into its riser bag and put the whole thing under your paramotor seat. Now if you land out, you've got a wing bag!

4. An *accordion,* or *concertina* fold keeps the leading edge rib reinforcements from getting creased or bent.

The PPG Bible: A Complete Guide and Reference

Folding

Folding takes a bit more time but allows for a much smaller package that's good for shipping and leaves fewer wrinkles. Methods abound but the one below is quick and easy even if you're alone.

First off, be loose with it. Tight folding stresses the stitching and weakens the seams if done repeatedly. Avoid crinkling the Mylar leading edges and reinforcements excessively so they stay crisp for better performance. These stiffeners help keep the cells open during light-wind inflations and hasten recovery from in-flight deflations (collapses).

Lay the wing out flat with the lines laid in the same position as for a forward launch (without any "V" of course). Pull the riser loops away from the trailing edge and lay them, A's up, on the ground then fold it as shown.

Folding:
1. Lay out like a forward.
2. Have the risers sticking out from the trailing edge to keep them separate. With two people, each one grabs a line while walking the tip.
3. Keep folding the tips to the center until it's about 1 foot wide then push the air out from the trailing edge towards the forward openings.
4. Roll or fold from the trailing edge. Loose folds are better for the wing especially the Mylar leading edge stiffener. Some pilots try to avoid getting folds in the Mylar to improve performance.

Section I: First Flight

Preparing For First Flight

CHAPTER 4

That first solo flight can be nearly overwhelming—a concoction of sensations and emotions that overpower normal reason. It is, for many, the zenith of their flight education and, with the steps described here and a good instructor, it won't become the nadir of that education.

Now that you can handle the wing, it's just a matter of adding power to become an aircraft under control. Expect it to feel awkward and tiring at first, but the results are well worth the effort.

The instructor will help insure that you're properly hooked up but it's a combined decision to launch—both you and the instructor must be ready.

Adjusting the Motor

You will start with a *hang check* in the simulator. Your instructor will adjust the motor (harness) so that it hangs properly in flight (see Chapter 12). The propeller, when aligned vertically, should be tilted back about 5° and no more than 15° (upper tip back). The harness must be comfortable, and without any straps or J-bars pushing excessively on any part of your body. If it has a kick-in strap you should be able to reach it while hanging there to get into the seat.

Getting into the seat is surprisingly critical. Harnesses are not designed for you to hang from the leg straps for more than a few minutes. Besides being uncomfortable, your legs may go numb, creating a dangerous situation on landing.

Practice getting into the seat while in the simulator and, if your equipment requires using a hand to do so, *Don't forget to let go of the brakes!* You don't want to make the potentially fatal mistake of holding the brakes while reaching down for your seat. Ideally, you can get in the seat by just lifting your legs and sliding back. The second best method is using a kick-in strap which should be heavy enough to hang down in the slipstream.

Nearly all harnesses have a way to move the hook-in position to accommodate differing pilot weights. A heavier pilot needs to move that point forward and lighter pilot needs to move it towards the motor. Results should be verified in a simulator.

Critical harness adjustments are covered more thoroughly in Chapter 12.

Siphoning Fuel

Siphon hoses use gravity to pull fuel up out of the source (gas can) and into your paramotor tank which must be *below* the source.

Here are two ways to start the siphon.

1. Submerge the hose in your source can until it fills completely with fuel. While keeping one end submerged, block the other end with your thumb, hold it, then lift that end out and into your paramotor tank. You now have a hose, full of fuel, running from the source can to your paramotor tank. Release your thumb and the fuel should flow.

2. Use a "wiggle pump" as shown above. Submerse the pump end into your gas can and the other end into your paramotor tank. Wiggle the pump end up and down for a few seconds to start the flow.

Once started, fuel will flow until the source tank empties or you pull it out.

Always put the cap back on your *motor's* tank right away after filling to avoid forgetting that important step. Otherwise, you *will* eventually forget and try to take off with fuel splashing everywhere, including the exhaust.

Fueling

Unless you're flying a four-stroke or electric, it will require a proper mix of gasoline and 2-stroke oil. You can mix it right in the motor's fuel tank, but most pilots use a different container for convenience and to insure that only mixed gas gets put in the motor's tank. Just a few minutes of non-mixed gas in a two-stroke motor is all it takes to seize up the piston. Put the oil in first to improve mixing.

Do your preflight inspection *after* refueling so as to catch a missing fuel cap, a common and dangerous mistake. Don't put much more fuel than you're planning on using since you have to lift it (mixed fuel weighs about 6.2 pounds per gallon).

When pouring premix (mixed fuel and oil) into your motor, a long skinny funnel (like a transmission funnel) or a siphon hose is handy (see left sidebar).

Fuel Selection and Storage

Fuel left exposed to the air for over a week can degrade and may not run properly. If stored in an airtight container (it hisses when you open the lid), fuel may last several months although some instructors recommend using fresh fuel (less than a few weeks old) regardless of storage.

Use what the manufacturer recommends but, absent that information, use mid or higher grade autogas. Higher octane ratings can prevent knocking, a premature rapid combustion that stresses the piston.

Aviation fuel (avgas) is recommended by some, but a few pilots have reported lead buildup. Although avgas is called "low lead," it's actually heavily leaded by automotive standards. Avgas does have a constant formulation throughout the year (auto gas varies), plus it doesn't stink and may run cooler. Avgas can be purchased at small airports where it is sold by Fixed Base Operators (FBO's) for about 30% more per gallon than auto gas. Tell them it's for your ultralight.

Mixtures

Two types of *mixtures* get discussed: fuel/oil mixture is how much oil you pour into a gallon of gas and fuel/*air* mixture is how much fuel is mixed with air in the carburetor. The proper fuel/air mixture is managed through carburetor jets, orifices and needle valves. When you hear the term *lean*, it means too little fuel in the fuel/air mix which can overheat the motor.

> ⚠ **Caution!**
>
> When filling your can at a gas station, always place it on the ground first. Doing so avoids an explosion risk caused by static electricity.

Oil Selection & Mixing

2-Stroke motors derive all their lubrication from what oil gets mixed into the gas and it must be mixed in the correct proportion.

Modern 2-cycle oils work well with a ratio of gas to oil around 40:1 which means there are 40 units of gas for each 1 unit of oil. Lower ratios (more oil) are frequently specified for the first few hours of a motor's life, the *break-in* period. A mix chart in the Appendix can be used to determine how much oil gets added to your fuel. Since many oils come in metric units (liters or milliliters), they are also included in the Appendix chart. Most 2-cycle oil has a chart printed on the container for other ratios as well.

You'll hear nearly religious fervor when seeking advice on oil selection and ratio—go with the manufacturer's recommendation, if available. Otherwise, make your selection based on the following priorities:

- Use two-cycle oil, never four-cycle oil such as that made for cars.
- Use two-cycle oil that is made for *air-cooled* motors. The marine stuff is made for cooler running outboards and may break down at our hotter temperatures.
- Use synthetics which are commonly recognized as having better characteristics at higher RPMs and hotter temperatures. They also leave fewer deposits.
- Use oil that is dyed so that you can tell whether a particular batch of fuel is mixed. If using clear oil, develop a fool-proof way to track what fuel is already mixed. The phrase "I thought it was mixed" commonly follows a piston seizure.

Avoid mixing synthetics and mineral oils. A very few brands may not mix well and could form gel-type clumps in the tank. This was more common years ago.

Preflight Inspection

A preflight inspection should be done before each flight. It has three important elements: (1) Consistency—always start from the same place, doing it the same way each time, (2) thoroughness—don't skip items; touching each item as you check it helps, and (3) don't let interruptions stop you. If they do, go back to the beginning.

Motor

There's little reason to skimp since preflighting a paramotor is so simple. On most machines, a sufficiently thorough inspection can be done in less than a minute. Resist the temptation to crank & go, and **never, *ever*** start it without insuring the throttle-carburetor linkage is at idle. That is your most important item.

Start the preflight by pulling at the carabiners. That will bring out the harness webbing to make potential problems easier to spot. Plus it allows better inspection of the very critical carabiners and harness. Check the webbing, fabric, straps and any attached connection hardware. They must be free of tears, cuts, badly worn sections or other damage that could affect integrity. Here are other items to check:

- Look for small cracks in the **carabiners;** such cracks could lead to a catastrophic in-flight failure, especially on some types of aluminum carabiners.
- Squeeze the **throttle** and watch the mechanism move at the carburetor. Besides ensuring proper function, it prevents the harrowing possibility of suddenly going to high power on startup. Skipping this check causes more serious (and sometimes debilitating) injury than any other cause.
- Walk around the machine, moving parts for security and looking for loose bolts or other parts. Loose prop bolts, even one or two, can set up a vibration that soon tears the prop completely off its mount. That's bad for the motor, prop, cage and your wallet.
- **Mufflers** cause many problems. Look for cracks, loose or broken mountings and general security. Safety wire is best used on anything that can loosen.
- Check **redrive** belts for proper tension and position.

1. Start your preflight from the front and do it the same way every time, uninterrupted. Avoid leaving the machine with anything unflyable (bolts loose, fuel cap off, etc).

2. This engine overheated and melted a hole in its piston, testimony to the value of thorough preflighting. You can catch problems before they make great sucking sounds on your wallet, not to mention how unwelcome an inflight motor failure is.

Anything that causes the mixture to run lean, from a clogged fuel vent to loose exhaust system bolts, can lead to overheating (see Chapter 12).

- Check **motor mounts and nuts** for security along with reduction drive bolts.

- **Spark plugs** loosen and fall off, especially on inverted engines. Check for general security.

- The **fuel system** needs a clear vent to allow air into the tank and a supply line running up to the carburetor. Check for tank security, line condition and turn on the appropriate valves. Some have an off valve for the vent—it must be open (on). If left closed, or the vent gets plugged, the engine will run for a while until diminishing fuel lowers the tank pressure, possibly collapsing the tank. Eventually the fuel pump can't suck any harder and the motor quits.

  Tighten the lid and vent (if removable).

- Check the **propeller** for condition. Small nicks are generally OK but long splits must be repaired. Fortunately many prop maladies can be repaired in the field without removal (see Chapter 12). Insure the blade bolts and center bolt (if equipped) are tight.

- Align the prop vertically then push the top tip fore and aft. It should have less than about 1/16th inch (1.5 millimeters) of play. Check the motor mounts when you do this to see that they flex but have no significant cracks.

- If the prop has been removed since its last flight, check that it's not on backwards. This embarrassing mistake will be felt when the motor produces about half of its normal thrust. The curved surface faces forward (towards the direction of flight). Another way to remember is that the fatter part of the prop, the leading edge, is more forward.

- Check the **cage** for security and complete assembly. If the motor has a clutch (the propeller spins freely without the motor running), spin the prop around to insure sufficient clearance from the hoop and cage parts.

- Ensure that accessories are secure and tuck loose straps out of harm's way. Nothing should be able to touch the exhaust or get into any moving parts. Close any zippered compartments.

- If equipped with a reserve, ensure the riser routing remains unobstructed, attached, and the reserve pins are secured properly without being pushed all the way through (see Chapter 12).

Wing

With a bit of breeze (6 mph), checking the wing is easier. The most minimal preflight is to kite the wing up for a look. Always check that:

- Lines are connected, kink-free and sheathed (outer covering intact).

- The fabric has no tears or holes.

- The risers have no visible damage, quick links are closed and tight, trimmers are set for takeoff, brakes are in their holders and the speedbar system is free. Check the brake lines where they go through the pulleys and that the pulleys are free spinning. A stuck pulley will wear the brake line quickly to failure.

A more thorough inspection should be done periodically (once every 25 flights or after any rough handling). Lay out the wing flat in a wind-shielded location and

---

1. The most important preflight action is to move the throttle while observing that the carburetor linkage returns to idle. The finger is pointing to the throttle arm on this unit. Float bowl carburetors hide the throttle mechanism inside a housing—on these machines, just make sure the throttle freely moves to idle.

2. This style of prop mount has a center bolt. If there is any play in the prop (wiggling fore and aft), this bolt may be loose.

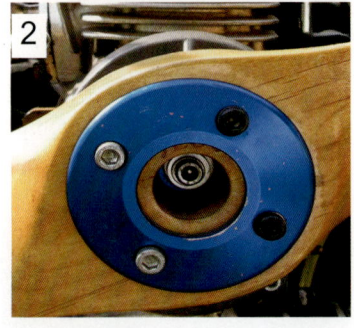

do the following:

- Field strength test; It should be done in several places on the most faded sections of the wing, which will usually be on the top surface. Pull the fabric taut with your hands about 3 inches apart then push your thumb into the spread as if trying to poke a hole. It should hold with about 5 pounds of pressure.

- Run each line between your fingers from the quick-link to the wing (or cascade). Feel for thin spots which would reveal the inside Kevlar is broken, rendering the line unusable. Having one line broken may not seem like a big deal, and usually isn't, but it stresses the remaining lines that much more. It's even more critical for inner A or B lines.

- Check overall condition of the risers, quick links, and brakes. Try to pull the risers apart at the stitching with about 20 pounds of pull.

Kiting the wing by hand is a good way to inspect it before committing to flight. There are many ways to do so, but holding the risers apart lets you look at it like it will be flying. Look for line problems, holes, unusual wrinkles or anything else that just doesn't look right.

If you leave something for later, you *will* forget it; maybe not this time, but eventually. A good example is the fuel cap. If you leave the machine, even for a moment, secure the cap. If you walk away from the motor, try to leave it in an airworthy condition. If unable to do so, use a reminder (like a wrench on the seat). Interruptions of routine contribute to many aviation accidents of all kinds.

Starting the Motor

Wait for your instructor to cover the vagaries of your particular brand before trying to start it.

Treat every start like it will go to full power, a too-common cause of tragic results. Cages primarily keep paraglider lines, not hands, out of the prop. Advise bystanders to stand clear and keep them away from the propeller arc, check the throttle at idle, and shout "CLEAR PROP" /engaging. Never start without a cage, a remarkably dangerous shortcut has caused nearly fatal injuries.

The motor and its prop require extreme care for both the operator and bystanders.

The safest way to start almost any machine is while wearing it. That's not always practical but, if possible, is preferred. This is where a good electric starter is valuable. If using a pull starter, have another pilot pull it for you unless you can pull it yourself with the motor on. The next safest way to start is by securing the motor to something firm like a tree or stand. The least desirable and, unfortunately, most common method is to start the motor by yourself while standing in front of it; be ready for unexpected thrust and be very careful.

Making it Go

Any gas motor requires fuel, air, spark and spin. An electric starter makes the spin easy but requires some extra care itself. Specific details of priming, choking, master switches and fuel/air valves will depend on your chosen model and will be described by your instructor or seller. If there's an owner's manual (be thankful), read it thoroughly.

If starting by yourself, put the throttle somewhere that it can't be activated acci-

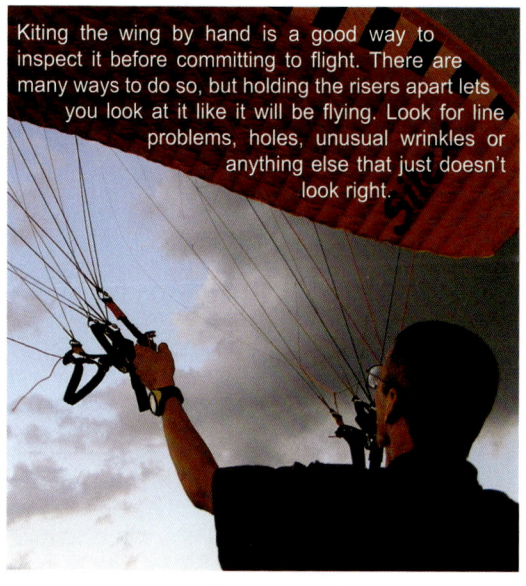

Setting Trimmers

Trimmers are used to make the wing fly slower (pull IN) or faster (let OUT). They will also affect launch so must be set properly before inflating.

As shown below, pull tabs shorten or lengthen the rear risers to change the wing's shape. You can also cause a turn by setting them differentially. If you speed up only the right side (let out the right trimmer) you'll turn left. If you speed up only the left side, you'll turn right.

Each wing is different and the manual should be consulted but, in general, set the trimmers to neutral which is the slow (IN) position on most wings and partway out on reflex wings.

If the wing is difficult to inflate (doesn't come overhead easily), set them to half-fast. If it comes up OK but you have to run forever before liftoff, set them slower.

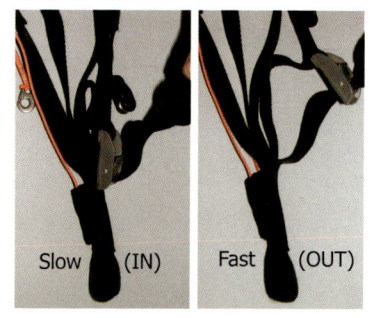

Slow (IN)   Fast (OUT)

Tip: Two Stroke Tuning:

There are many carburetors and many techniques for getting them to run just right. The owners manual, if available, is the best place to start. Chapter 12 contains a troubleshooting guide and chapter 27 explains adjusting the most common 2-stroke carburetors (*tuning*).

Tuning is frequently required after big changes in temperature or elevation. But if the motor ran fine the last time, and there has not been any big change in temperature or elevation, then tuning will not likely solve anything.

If you *have* to start the motor like this: Hold it so that you keep quick access to the kill button and the throttle cannot be actuated accidentally. A surprise burst of power could push your hand in a way that squeezes even more throttle.

Always verify the throttle linkage at the carburetor is at idle.

dentally by a thrusting motor, and make sure the kill button is accessible. One option is to hold the throttle stem, *not* the trigger; if the motor does power up, it won't push the throttle against your hand and you can still get to the kill button. Brace the motor with your free thumb hooked around a solid frame part and pretend that a gorilla is about to push against the propeller. They both have nasty bites. Position your body to be ready for the gorilla's push.

Make sure the ground area is clear of loose objects (rocks, diamonds, sticks, cell phones, etc.) that could get sucked into the prop. Loose straps or cords should not be able to reach the prop or exhaust. And be mindful of where the prop blast is going—even at idle it can disturb things nearby, especially paraglider wings.

Don't let the motor idle for too long, carbon builds up on the spark plug, cylinder head and other parts (called *loading up*). After idling for more than a few minutes, run it up to 50% power for about 10 seconds—that's called *clearing* the motor.

Have a Plan: Patterns, Areas and Altitudes.

Before soloing you must have a plan, including signals, to use in case of radio failure. The USPPA has adopted a set of common ones but your instructor's may differ. You will fly a rectangular *pattern* (see Chapter 5) that helps to judge landings, provides a known path that other pilots can easily search, and gives a way to describe location.

All patterns are based on taking off and landing into the wind. It is simply a rectangular path around the field to position yourself for landing. After reaching a safe altitude and getting into the seat you will turn left or right to go crosswind and continue climbing. The next turn is downwind and positions you for landing back at the launch site in case of a motor-out. Even if you're not landing right away this is a good path to fly before heading out of the immediate area. As a new solo student you will continue climbing so as to fly the entire flight within gliding distance of the launch area.

Your instructor will tell you where to fly and what maneuvers to practice. If you have not gotten into the seat then he will direct you to come in for a landing. You cannot keep flying while hanging from the leg straps—it's too uncomfortable and may cut off circulation to your legs, making them go numb. If everything is normal then you will just fly around and enjoy your accomplishment for a half hour or so. When you come back in, you will most likely enter the pattern for landing.

> ⚠ **Caution!**
>
> Most propeller injuries occur just after start. A working electric starter reduces this risk but must be disabled when not flying. If pull-starting, brace against the impending thrust. Re-rig any motor where the starter handle comes out the side—a dangerous design since unexpected thrust will quickly overpower your ability to stop it from falling forward. Hands can quickly dart into the propeller before realizing the extreme consequences.

Taking Instructions Via Radio

You'll be up there alone but the instructor's voice will be right there, suggesting appropriate responses, filling in the blanks or insisting on immediate corrections. It can be difficult to concentrate amidst all the new sensations, but concentrate you must. This is why simulator practice is so valuable, especially with the motor running and controls in hand. Some instructors may prefer not to run the motor in the simulator (which involves some risk of its own), but should have you go through the drills while causing other distractions. It could save your life: *Rehearsal is critical!*

You will be required to pull brakes, add power, reduce power, and kick your legs in response to your instructor's directives. A front/back kicking motion means "yes" and a left/right scissor motion means "no." Follow these instructions explicitly. You may not know why, but your instructor will. An immediate in-flight response will help reduce how dramatic the responses needs to be.

These are common hand signals used by many instructors and others. They supplement radio communications and can be effective in emergencies or when the radio fails.

Reaction and Overcontrol

Because you hang below the center of roll, your reaction to swings will be exactly opposite of what they should be. Plus, it is extremely common for new pilots to pull too much brakes. This combination can cause students to react very improperly and cause a serious oscillation or turn, especially on sportier or heavier loaded wings. It is critical that you use deliberate but smooth inputs then hold them for a couple seconds, resisting the urge to correct each swing. Listen and respond intently to the instructor, your life depends on it.

Rehearsing

If you have to think about a response, you can't count on it. Reactions must be rehearsed and automatic. For example, the reaction to a forward surging wing is applying some brake. The reaction to a wing falling back is to immediately reduce power and reduce brakes while preparing to "catch" the impending surge with brake pull. Throwing a reserve is another action that must be rehearsed—if it's needed, you won't be calmly contemplating your navel.

Mostly you must rehearse taking instructions for those early flights. Then, as experience is gained, add others. When hell is breaking loose, rehearsed reactions will most likely win the day.

Handling Emergencies

The vast majority of flights go without a hitch, but when "hitch" happens, you'll be glad you're prepared. These can be rehearsed in a simulator and some are best rehearsed with the motor running (or other artificial distractions). The flight environment is loud and foreign, but simulator practice will make it less so.

Distraction and reaction can be worse than its cause or consequence. So when something does go pop, take a deep breath and deal with it methodically.

Courtesy Jerry Starbuck and USPPA.org

Power-Loss & Surge

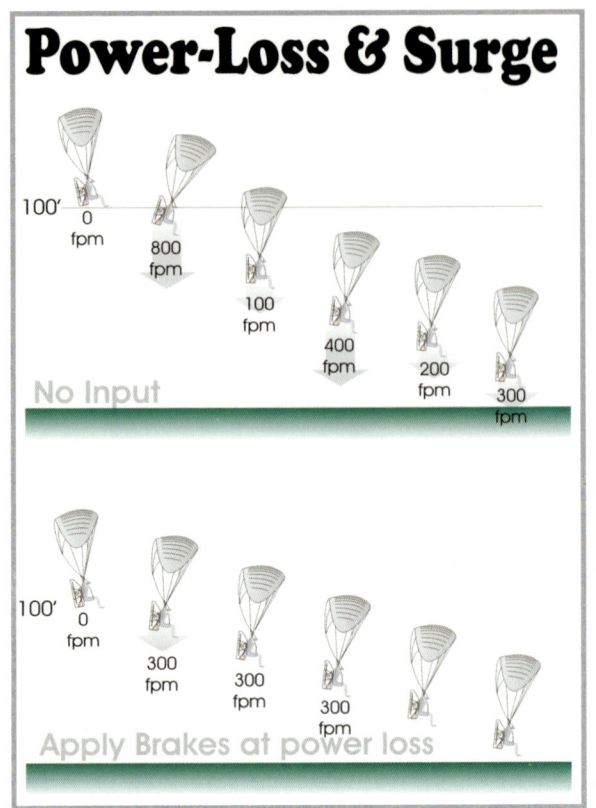

No Input: 100' / 0 fpm → 800 fpm → 100 fpm → 400 fpm → 200 fpm → 300 fpm

Apply Brakes at power loss: 100' / 0 fpm → 300 fpm → 300 fpm → 300 fpm

"What do you do when the engine quits?" It's a common question among the curious. "Not much" is pretty accurate if you're up high (200 feet or more). Applying brakes right when it quits helps reduce the surge, but even without doing so, the craft is entirely manageable. At low altitude, it's more critical to control the surge that follows a motor failure.

> ⚠️ **Caution!**
>
> Don't know what is happening?
>
> **"Reduce power, reduce brake, then steer."** Be smooth, be ready to dampen any surge but remember that too much brake is the most common cause of in-flight mishaps.
>
> After reducing brake pull, go back to, and hold, position/pressure 2 for a good feel of the wing. Do this unless you *know* a different action is correct.

Situational emergencies, where the pilot has time to analyze and react, are covered in Chapter 19 and include thought processes and options that should be considered.

Above All

Following your instructor's radio commands is paramount but a few common priorities apply to all emergencies:

• **Maintain Control**. Regardless of what happens, keep flying the craft. Remember "**reduce power, reduce brake, then steer**" in uncertain situations. Try to keep it flying essentially straight with the least control input possible. Avoid large movements—rash actions almost always do more harm then good. Panic destroys the reason that can extricate you from danger and the best way to reduce panic is preparation. Fortunately, very few situations require immediate action.

• To the extent possible, **get on a safe course and altitude**. When something happens, *look* towards a safe course, *steer* that way and climb slowly, if appropriate.

• Once control and flight path are established, **deal with the problem**. Look around at what you've got. Loud noises are rarely good. It's almost always better to kill the motor and land rather than trying to "limp" home.

• **Land Into the wind** and away from wind shadows (created by wind-blocking obstructions). Obviously there are exceptions: A downwind beach landing might be better than an upwind water landing. An upwind water landing might be better than a downwind landing in boulders. Hopefully you were thinking about this before the motor quit and have an obvious option. Regardless of landing direction, make sure you're nearly wing level before touchdown. Don't land in a turn.

If facing two undesirable outcomes, pick the least objectionable one. For example, pick a field of low scrub over a tree landing.

Throttle Cable Caught

If after launch you try to bring your hand back up and the throttle cable snags on something, your hand will be stuck. The throttle works but your hand is stuck.

Maintain control! This simple problem is a non-event *unless* you panic into an inappropriate reaction. Fly the craft using normal brake input of the other hand (make shallow turns in that direction), look forward and keep climbing; you may be in a shallow torque turn. Once at a safe height with a safe flight path, move the throttle back, away from the motor and up. Make turns to stay near the launch site. It will probably be a simple matter of looking down to see the obvious solution then executing it.

If it remains snagged, plan on a power-off landing. Get over the landing area with plenty of height and shut off the motor. Then pull your hand out of the throttle and do a regular power-off landing.

Radio Failure

Your instructor's presence on the radio is important but radios can quit; you must have a plan in mind. Usually you'll continue around the pattern, climb out above the field to get some feel for the machine then come in for a normal landing near the middle of the field. You'll hopefully have rehearsed this in the simulator and be able to recite it back to your instructor. It should be a detailed description of climbing up, getting into the seat (must be done properly!), pattern and landing.

Your instructor may have simple hand signals that you've worked out beforehand. If so, maneuver so as to see him and respond accordingly.

Brake Line Failure or Tangle

If a brake line fails, gets cut off by the prop, tangles, or becomes disconnected, there is plenty of steering authority available using the rear risers.

As with all emergency situations, *fly the aircraft first*. Use the available control to steer while climbing to a safe altitude.

Most likely it's a loop of brake line fouling the pulley. You may be able to undo this in flight but get up to a safe altitude first (at least 300). Remember, if the brake is stuck, it will still pull the rear riser albeit with much more force and much less effectiveness.

Like any abnormal situation, don't do anything rash; this problem is normally benign. If possible, climb up higher than usual, carefully get into the seat (if able) and establish level or slightly climbing flight. Once on a safe course with plenty of altitude you can look up to deal with the problem.

It's usually obvious what needs to be done—reach up and fix it. You can safely land without the brakes but it's obviously better to regain their use. If the brake line is missing then there is nothing to do but plan an approach and landing using the rear risers and throttle.

If the brake line is just stuck, you may be able to use it by reaching above the pulley, especially if you have shorter risers and/or a low hook-in machine.

If you cannot use normal brakes, plan on using the rear risers for steering and flare. Don't use one brake and one rear riser, use both rear risers. Do some practice turns and flares to get a feel for how much pull it takes to turn and slow down.

The rear risers can also be used for landing but won't be nearly as effective as the brakes. Allow for a longer, straight-in approach.

At the point where you would normally use the brakes to flare, pull harder on both rear risers and be ready for a harder touchdown. Landing power-off is generally preferable to avoid prop/cage damage but a fall is more likely without use of the brakes. With experience you can land power-on. That allows a softer, but still fast, touchdown at some

He's pulling the right rear riser (D) to turn. This wing uses a 4-riser set designed for motoring. A soaring wing will have longer risers and may require a longer reach to grab the quick-link - just grab as high as you can. On a 3-riser set you would be pulling the C's.

It takes a lot of pull to affect even a small turn. This technique is used in the event of a brake line failure.

Embarrassment Avoided

While kibitzing with another pilot about the flight we just had, a couple cops showed up. They were fascinated by the craft and started asking questions. "Let me just show you!" I said.

Right after liftoff, I discovered the right brake was stuck and there was no fixing it, either. Too bad I didn't catch that one on preflight. Not wanting to look bad in front of our new observers, I came back around, making a left turn of course, and landed using the D's (rear risers) to flare. They had no idea that anything was amiss and I wasn't about to tell them.

"Wasn't that cool?" I asked while quietly fixing my brake. "Here, I'll go again." And I took off uneventfully this time.

They probably wondered why that flight was so much longer.

Engine Failure
During Takeoff or At Low Altitude

Once airborne, the motor accelerates your body forward.

Motor Quits Here

Liftoff is usually with some brakes but reduce pressure for the climbout. If the motor quits before reaching about 30 feet, go immediately to 1/4 brake (position/pressure 3), hold it, and then flare just before touchdown. You may hit somewhat hard but should be able to remain standing.

Not doing anything after the motor quits will allow the wing to surge forward and dump you firmly during your swing back under it (as depicted with the faded flyer).

increased risk to your gear.

Avoid the temptation to pull the D's too hard since response is dramatically slower. Limit pull to just what you need to lessen the possibility of pulling into a parachutal stall.

Motor Failure

A motor failure is almost always a non-event; more of an inconvenience than an emergency unless you're over bad terrain. Our slow landing speed allows many options from all phases of flight *provided* you stay within gliding range of safe landing sites and remain aware of the wind direction so you can land into it.

The only time a quick response is needed to an engine failure is during the initial climb or while flying low (less than 100 feet). After a sudden power loss, especially during climb, you'll need a quick pull of the brakes to prevent the wing from surging way forward into a dive. The steeper the climb, the more pronounced the surge. A shallower climb reduces this risk.

> The proper action after a motor failure *during climb* is to immediately pull some brakes (about pressure 2) to control the surge then ease them up as the glide establishes, or flare as necessary.

Rehearse responding to a motor failure so that it is automatic. You are most vulnerable during the takeoff phase: If the surge is allowed to go unchecked, the wing will shoot forward and you could pendulum hard into the ground.

After that initial surge is controlled, the next action depends on altitude. If you're high enough, setting up for a normal flare is appropriate (brakes position 1 and then flare). But if you're less then 20 feet or so, the brakes should be held at position 2 or 3, with a flare at the normal height. A flare from that much brake won't be very effective but it's better than coming off the brakes completely and being swung into the ground.

A motor failure from more than a hundred feet or so gives plenty of time to turn into the wind and set up a normal flare and landing. Don't do any steep turns but always turn so as to land mostly into the wind. Only accept an off-wind landing if the terrain or obstructions for an into-the-wind landing are much worse. The stronger the wind, the more important landing directly into it is.

If you have enough time (more than a couple hundred feet), get established in a landing pattern, then try to restart. Always attend to piloting before dealing with the motor. Try different throttle settings when attempting the restart. If you do get it started, maintain the same power setting until reaching a point where a normal power-off landing pattern can be flown. Plan the landing with no power even if you let the motor idle. Concentrate on landing once you're below 200 feet.

Turbulence

If conditions turn bumpy, increase brake pressure to about level 2. *Pressure* is key. If a brake handle tries to yank upwards, let it, while maintaining the same pressure. Likewise, if a toggle goes limp, let it go down. When throttling off, increase brake pressure slightly, almost to 3. At low power settings, slowing down is generally better, but be careful—too much brake has proven way more dangerous than not enough. You'll be swinging around some but don't try to correct every motion.

Flying this way reduces the chance for various wing maladies including frontal collapses, where the leading edge tucks under causing a brief, but rapid descent.

If you must turn, use steady but minimal differential brake and hold it for 3 seconds. That will prevent getting into a left-right oscillation. You will get swung around a fair amount but don't try to counteract. In almost all cases, beginning pilots who try to counteract oscillations (active piloting) only make them worse. If you *do* start oscillating, ease up pressure, hold both arms steady, and ride it out!

Small Asymmetric Wing Collapse

Small wing collapses happen occasionally in turbulence and the wing usually snaps back before the pilot even knows it has occurred. Generally, just following the turbulence advice above will suffice. Small collapses that don't come out immediately can normally be cured with *gentle* pressure on that side's brake. Just do what it takes to steer straight and the wing will likely reform quickly.

Large Asymmetric Wing Collapse

A severe asymmetric collapse, covered in Chapter 18, is where more than half of the wing tucks under. It is rare enough in powered paragliding that most pilots have never experienced it. With a motor, lines *could* wrap around the prop or a frame part. That's why flying in *big air* (strong turbulence) is best avoided.

If you get a large collapse, the *initial* reaction should be to smoothly **reduce power, relax brake pressure, then steer**. That helps fight the tendency to over control which makes matters worse. Then carefully apply whatever brake input (and weight shift if your motor allows, see Chapter 18) is needed to steer straight. Use the amount of pressure you normally feel at position 1 on the collapsed side (it will be limp) while leaning away from the collapse. Be ready to let the brake come back up as its pressure builds. Nearly all PPG incidents that follow a collapse result from *too much* brake pulled by the pilot. If you're low to the ground or near an obstruction, do whatever it takes to steer clear even if that means a nearly immediate turn input.

Cravat

A cravat happens when part of the wing tip folds down and gets tangled in the lines, causing a turn. More fabric, more turn. A small cravat (3 on opposite page) isn't bad and, if you can steer easily, just come around to land. Sometimes a quick pump to

---

The malfunction below was induced by the pilot. As usual, the wing recovered nicely on its own. But it's easy to be surprised by the weather which is why you should know how to handle unusual situations.

Real turbulence-induced collapses, while incredibly rare, can easily be worse than what is done intentionally. Mostly because the leading edge can fold down, trapping fabric against the lines and inducing a turn.

Non reflex wings (or reflex wings trimmed slow) *are* more collapse resistant while holding brake pressure, but experience has shown that far more handling accidents arise from excessive brake rather than not enough.

pressure 2 will clear it. It could require quick action if a turn suddenly develops. Use minimum brakes at first, but *do what it takes to fly straight* (or as straight as you can).

Consider pulling the stabilo (tip) line on the cravated side. Doing so may free the fabric if it's a fairly small cravat. The line may be hard to find with so much going on which is why rehearsal in mellow conditions, or while kiting, is so valuable.

A large cravat, as covered in Chapter 18, is a *much* bigger deal.

Riser Twist

If you feel yourself starting to twist during launch, abort. Do so at the first sign of any uncontrollable turn. Before trying again, figure out why it happened and find a cure. Torque issues are covered in Chapter 23.

If a twist starts after launch, *immediately,* (but smoothly) **reduce power, reduce brake pressure, then steer**. Reducing brakes also helps keep them from getting stuck in the riser twist if you go all the way around. With the motor producing half thrust or less, you should swing back around and resume forward flight. The glider will actually fly just fine regardless of which way you're pointing as long as you minimize power and brakes. Once facing forward, throttle up only to what's necessary. An immediate landing into the wind may be your best option if terrain allows.

Riser twist almost always happens on launch. Trying to continue at full power can spin you around and result in a very hard hit. Even without going all the way around; if you point left, thrust will push you left which causes a right bank (motor induced lock out). The only solution is reducing power—trying to stop the twist with brakes alone can lead to spinning and dropping (see diagram below).

Kill Switch or Throttle Failure

Your runup should include a test of the kill switch but, if it fails in flight, you won't know it until landing. Just come in with the motor idling and have the instructor shut it off using other means. After touchdown, carefully turn around and bring the wing down to keep lines out of the prop. Another option is to climb up and run it out of gas; you'll need lots of room, time, and of course, a power-off landing.

Getting the throttle cable chopped off in the prop does two bad things. It can trap your throttle at a high setting *and* disable the kill switch (see more in Chapter 19). You may get stuck climbing. Hopefully, your motor has another pilot-accessible shutoff method such as a choke or primer bulb. Rehearse reaching for these in the simulator. What seems obvious while standing comfortably over the motor can become most perplexing in the noisy adrenaline-pumped aftermath of a chopped throttle.

Riser Twist & Spin

Riser twist right after liftoff is a serious threat to pilots who aren't properly prepared. The illustration below shows a belt-driven machine which yaws (twists) the pilot left. Gear driven models have the same forces but in opposite directions.

Remember, if you feel excessive yaw on your body: smoothly reduce power, reduce brakes, then steer.

1, 2. Just after liftoff, various forces conspire to cause some left pilot yaw. If the wing is slightly right as you lift, that left yaw is aggravated by *loaded riser twist*.

3. Once twisted, thrust now pushes your body left and the wing into a right bank.

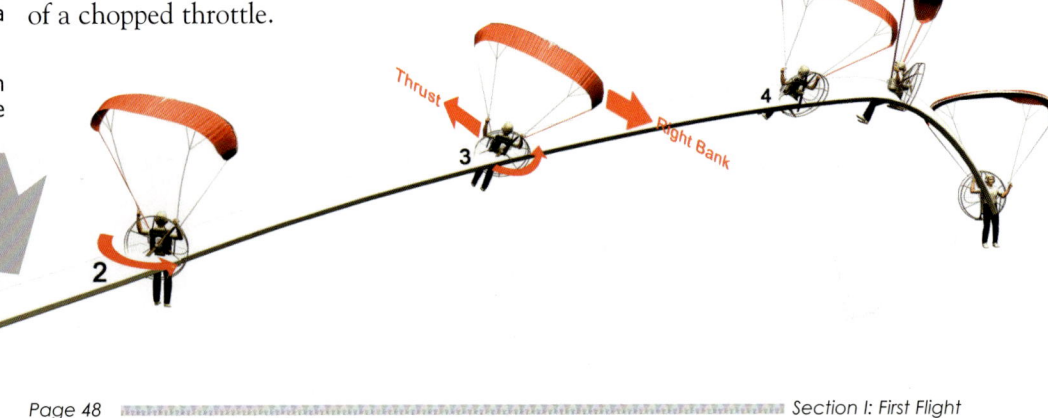

4. Pulling excessive left brake in an effort to stop turning right may cause a spin and rapid descent.

One hapless pilot on a first solo had this happen without knowing how to kill the motor. She wound up circling into the chilly heights above a large city, climbing through controlled airspace, until finally running out of fuel several thousand feet high. Fortunately her instructor guided her to a successful landing.

Unfastened Leg Straps

In free-flight paragliding, forgetting to buckle your leg straps can be tragic. It is equally dangerous for motor pilots if they try to hang on and "take care of it in the air." Plus, many motor pilots eventually wind up free-flying, so its helpful to get into the habit of buckling your legs first and *un*buckling them last. Use the checklist in the Appendix *every time* to prevent this problem.

If you do forget one (or both) leg straps you'll feel it quickly on launch as the motor tries to lift off without you. If that happens, let off the power smoothly and abort! Swallow your pride and quietly buckle up before another try.

Reserve Deployment

The need for a reserve parachute in motoring is rare but there have been some "saves," usually following botched aerobatics, strong thermal turbulence or huge changes in wind. Free flyers are far more likely to "toss the laundry" in their search for strong lift or aerobatic exuberance.

Situations that warrant deploying your reserve must involve nearly complete or impending loss of control: A mid-air collision, a serious collapse that won't recover (probably a cravat), and wing malfunctions are a few. If you start to spiral, act fast—G-forces can build so quickly as to make you un*able* to deploy the reserve. Very deliberately follow the steps below. You should be able to get the reserve out and tossed within 3 seconds.

1. Kill the motor. You don't want your "last chance" lines being chopped by the prop. You'll probably be getting tossed around and this must be automatic.

2. Look at the reserve handle—you'll avoid the wasted time of reaching endlessly for a handle that's not there. At least one pilot hit the ground while grasping wildly for the reserve handle on his right side—it was on the left.

3. Pull the handle out. The reserve sits at the end of a foot-long line. It can be difficult if you've never done it which is why simulator rehearsal is so valuable.

4. Clear. Find a clear direction that is free of wing lines and paramotor protrusions. Do be deliberate—but you want to get it out quickly.

5. Throw towards the clear air, outward and in the direction of turn if you're turning. It will be like tossing a 5 pound rock at the end of a foot long cord. Yank on the bridle to help open the parachute if it doesn't deploy immediately.

The actions above must be well rehearsed and performed with purpose. The procedure itself should be reviewed in advance and committed to memory: "Kill, Look, Pull, Clear and Throw." Say that line over and over until it's automatic.

Once the reserve opens your next action depends on the situation. The paraglider will probably fall below you and may reinflate then fly out to the side, pulling you somewhat in one direction. If everything is stable, leave it. If you start to rotate, or the glider is flailing, try to pull it in to disable it. Be careful since it can

1. This pilot is doing a reserve clinic and was surprised that his first "toss" barely moved the reserve. By the third try (pictured) he was getting good distance into what would have been clear air in a real emergency. Throwing a reserve is much like throwing a 5 pound weight from the end of a foot-long cord.

2. A Save. The pilot's reserve is shown sitting just left of his motor which is just left of the wing. After launching into rough air he took a major collapse. The reserve saved his bacon. It's never a guarantee, and the landing may be in a very bad location, but it sure beats the alternative.

⚠ **Caution!**

In any malady, do not accept an increasingly steep turn. After initially reducing brake pressure, use whatever input it takes to prevent a spiral dive.

3: Small Cravat — By Tim kaiser

Parachute Landing Fall

Landing under a reserve will probably be pretty hard. Depending on your weight and reserve size, the descent rate at touchdown will be the equivalent of jumping off about a 4-foot table. The bigger the reserve, the softer the arrival.

Many years ago, military paratroopers devised a way to get their soldiers down with fewer injuries—the Parachute Landing Fall (PLF). It works well for landings under reserve or any hard landing.

The idea is to transfer vertical energy into horizontal energy. For a motor pilot, the frame will usually intervene during the roll which is good. Some instructors advocate lifting your legs and letting the frame take the impact. While that may work, be very mindful of protecting your spine. Success depends on your motor's frame bottom. Consider that a broken leg beats a broken back.

Once you recognize the need for a PLF, put your legs together with knees slightly bent. At touchdown roll in whatever direction is natural, absorbing some with the knees, then hips then the frame should take the rest. Allow yourself to roll it out and end up on your back (or frame, more likely) as depicted.

If you remember nothing else, make sure your legs are together with knees slightly bent and toes slightly down.

yank powerfully out of your hands, causing burns.

When approaching the ground, look at the horizon and prepare for the *Parachute Landing Fall* (PLF), a tried and true method for absorbing high impact forces. Put your legs together with knees slightly bent. You'll hit hard but try to orient yourself such that you can roll to one side or the other. It should be feet, knee, hip then shoulder ending in a rolling motion. Use the motor to absorb some impact if the frame is below you. Protect your spine at all costs. Pulling your legs up to hit on the motor's frame may reduce the chance for leg injuries at the expense of your spine. Use the frame (lift your legs) only if you *know* it will give sufficient protection.

Parachutal Stall/Spin

A wing goes parachutal when it stops flying forward and starts descending vertically like an old round parachute. The wing, which remains fully inflated, may seem to fall back as forward airspeed slows. It usually involves several factors including too much brake, turbulence, power or a combination thereof. Many of these turn into spins, where the glider rotates due to one side having slightly more drag (from brakes or turbulence). See Chapter 19 for more details.

Parachutal stall is far more common under power because thrust keeps the paraglider stalled where it would otherwise recover on its own. Most PPG accidents involve the pilot impacting at full power under a fully inflated wing and frequently spinning. But it can also be caused by simply pulling too much brake such as when slowing down to make a landing spot.

Recovery is simple but must be done *immediately* and fully upon feeling the wing slow down or the airflow stop: "**Hands up, power off, prepare to dampen the surge.**" The normal emergency response of "Reduce Power, Reduce Brakes, Then Steer" is good but might not be enough in a parachutal situation.

In the *extremely* unlikely chance that it's *still* not flying, and you're above a hundred feet, then: reach for the A's, palms forward, thumbs down, and twist the A's down about 2 inches. this is called *tweaking the A's*. If you happen to have your feet on the speedbar (not likely), then push it. If a full vertical descent had established, recovery can be violent.

Be aware that, during recovery, the wing may surge violently forward, followed by you swinging below it. With too little altitude, that might be worse than landing from the parachutal stall. So if you're below about 60 feet, it's probably better to ride it down and prepare for the PLF.

The Flight

CHAPTER 5

Time to fly.

It's not always some momentous event, but rather a converging of skills and conditions that find you ready. You've learned essential kiting skills, rehearsed the flight and know what to expect. You've been practicing, waiting for the right conditions (see Chapter 7), and now they have arrived.

This day's flight adds new and significant elements into the mix: Sensation and adrenaline—don't underestimate them. That is why you've practiced so much. In the face of kinematic newness, you can't think things through. Anything not rehearsed will likely be done wrong. Like airline trainers, PPG instructors know of this human shortcoming and have found repetitive practice to be invaluable.

Launch

Variations in technique exist to accommodate different equipment, conditions, experience and simple preference; do what you've learned to minimize surprises. Listen intently to your instructor. Be prepared to abort quickly and nothing gets fed to the propeller.

Unlike other forms of flight, launch is literally and figuratively the biggest hurdle. You'll spend more time on this one area than all the others combined.

Lets begin. Carefully start and warm up your motor for a minute then shut it off; that insures it's ready. Go lay out your wing. A good layout is critical to launch success in light winds. Start the motor again and strap it on, fastening *all* the harness straps, starting with the leg straps. It's best to start with the legs because forgetting those has the worst consequence, especially if you ever go free flying. Get the

Below: Airlines use checklists for good reason: they work. Skipping the checklist for expediency or omitting items has proven deadly.

While it takes 32 items to safely get a Boeing 737 into the air, our checklist is mercifully brief. It is no less important though. An easy-to-use set of checklists is included in the Appendix.

Before launch, do a brief runup to insure the machine can smoothly develop full power and check that the kill switch works. Mind where the prop blast goes and keep the propeller plane away from bystanders in case it sheds pieces.

Ready for inflation: The A's and brakes are in each hand, the other risers are draped over your biceps or forearms and the throttle trigger is free. You must be able to get to the kill switch immediately if something goes awry. The A riser in your throttle hand is usually in *front* of the throttle stem but do whatever is most comfortable.

throttle situated comfortably in your hand then hook into the risers as you learned in Chapter 3. Grab the brakes, hold them out and make sure they're clear to the pulley with nothing crossed or twisted. With everything now connected, do a pre-launch checklist from memory to cover the basics (see Appendix - Checklists).

You'll do just as you've rehearsed but now, with the motor's throttle, thrust and weight, it will feel different. The difference is less if your kiting practice included using a throttle simulator (dummy throttle).

Just before launch, determine the wind direction (See Chapter 7). Your face is best suited for this if the prop isn't spinning (on clutched machines), otherwise use whatever wind indicators are available. If the wind has turned significantly, you'll either need to wait or move. When it's light and variable, waiting may be the better course. As the day wears on, thermals increasingly come through and can change the wind direction dramatically from minute to minute. About the time you get it laid out into a new direction, a thermal comes by, changing it again.

Inflation—Light or Nil Wind

Launching in zero wind is our toughest task. The following technique has proven quite successful although your instructor may use a different one. This *power forward* method starts with partial power from the outset to help develop and build the all-important forward speed. Some instructors suggest full power right away but that carries additional risk from torque, cage flexing and *face plant* (falling face-first.) On flexible cage machines you may need to lunge hard without power to get the wing almost overhead, then throttle up immediately as you stand up.

Start with your wing laid out as described in Chapter 3, lines cleared, and aligned directly into any hint of wind. Be poised as pictured at left with an A riser in the "V" of each thumb. On wings with split A's, hold only the centers.

Center yourself on the wing while holding the A's to *just* feel some line tension. Step left and right a few inches to feel the same line tension on each side but without pulling over the leading edge. Back up a couple steps and insure that your run direction will be exactly perpendicular to the wing. Make sure your shoulders are square to the wing. Pick a point straight ahead to look at—you're ready to go.

Power up to about 25% thrust (if your machine allows) then smoothly, but aggres-

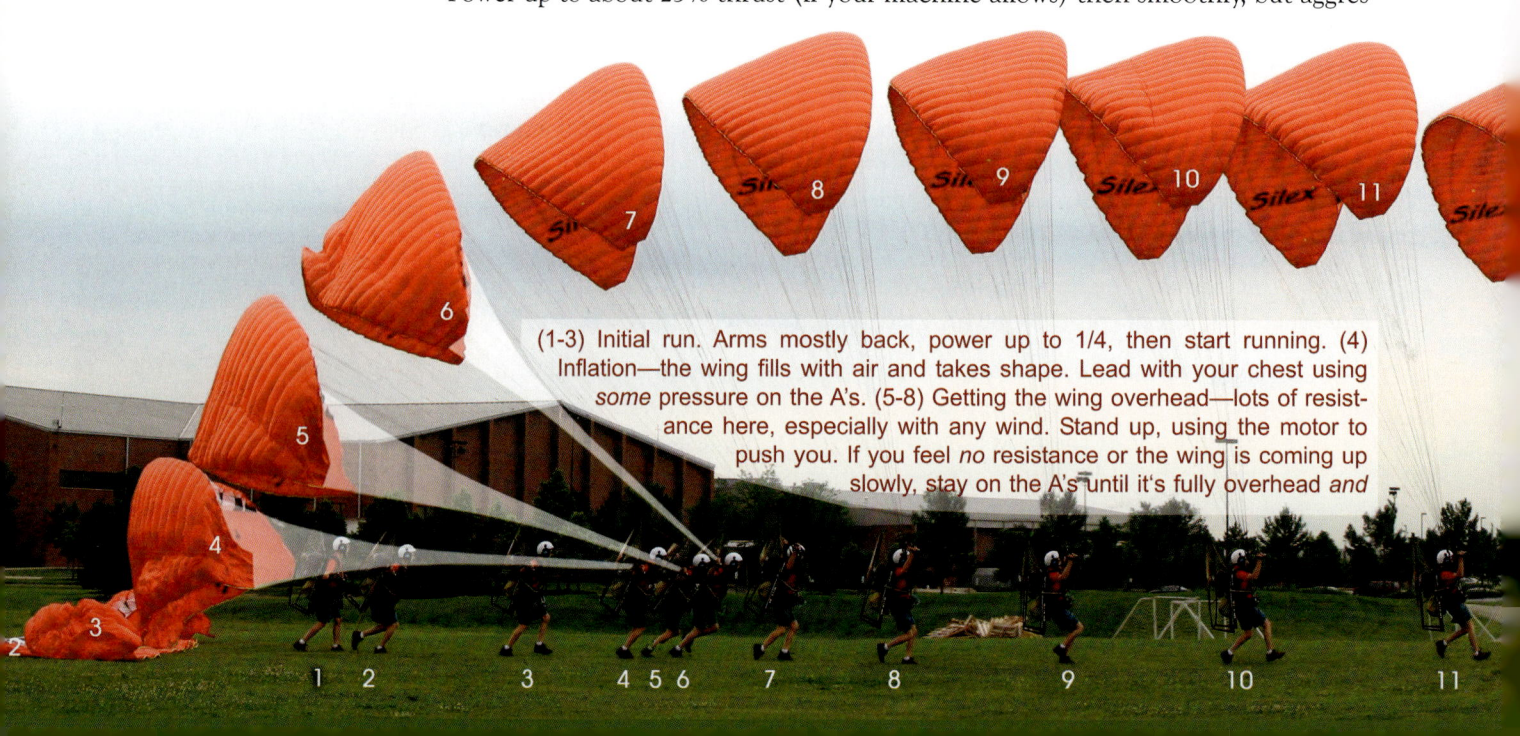

(1-3) Initial run. Arms mostly back, power up to 1/4, then start running. (4) Inflation—the wing fills with air and takes shape. Lead with your chest using *some* pressure on the A's. (5-8) Getting the wing overhead—lots of resistance here, especially with any wind. Stand up, using the motor to push you. If you feel *no* resistance or the wing is coming up slowly, stay on the A's until it's fully overhead *and*

Troubleshooting *Forward* Launch Problems

Some may seem contradictory but they address different problems. Follow your instructor's advice since he *sees* what's happening.

Symptom: Wing comes up crooked.
1. You're not starting or continuing the run exactly centered and perpendicular to the wing.
2. If the wing always comes up to the left, make a conscious effort to always point your body, and run, slightly to the right.
3. Start from a clean surface with a *perfect* U-shaped layout and be pointed *exactly* into whatever whiff of wind is present.
4. Be more aggressive to build speed faster. Speed improves control. This is easier with a relatively small wing.
5. Don't pull too much A's or pull them unevenly. Lead with your chest (arms back), then pull some A's, then power up.
6. Lines are catching on the cage (right photo). Install smooth tubing around the bottom halves of your cage hoop and insure there is nothing to snag on. Mounting line holders on the cage rim is not effective since lines easily fall off as you move around. You can also hold your arms up higher or wiggle the A's during the initial inflation but it's usually the rear (D) lines that catch.
7. A brake is tied too short or there is something caught in the lines.

Symptom: The wing doesn't come all the way overhead, especially when there's no wind.
1. Stay on the A's longer and delay going to the brakes. Some wings, especially reflex gliders, require lots of A pull during inflation and acceleration. Also, gather good forward speed before applying any brakes.
2. Make sure you're not pulling brakes inadvertently. Try this: After letting go of the A's, touch the risers before pulling any brake.
3. You're pulling *too much* A's and curling the leading edge. Have your arms back to start the inflation *then* apply A pressure.
4. Come up on the power earlier and use more of it.
5. Your initial run needs to be more aggressive. It's common to slow down when looking back at the wing—keep driving forward.
6. Let the trimmers out (faster setting) some. This will require a faster launch run, though.
7. Try looking back at the wing by turning your head sideways (instead of looking up) while keeping up the run.
8. Some pilots do better by looking up at the wing during power up. It forces them into a more correct upright posture.

Symptom: The wing tends to over-fly me then collapse.
1. Get off the A's earlier and dampen with brakes earlier. This is more common with more wind. Apply enough brakes to dampen then let off.
2. Make sure the trimmers are in their slowest setting (pulled in).
3. If using power, only establish 1/4 throttle before starting your inflation. The prop blast makes some wings shoot forward.

Symptom: I can't get airborne in spite of running my fastest.
1. After initial inflation, stand up straight as you go to full power. Concentrate on letting the motor push you as fast as your legs will go with long strides before easing in some brake. You may need some brake to take off but then ease them up to nearly pressure 0.
2. Make sure the trimmers are in, your motor is producing normal peak RPM and you're into the wind. If the motor is making full RPM but it's not pushing so hard, make sure the prop is mounted correctly. If its backwards, you'll get thrust, but not enough to fly.
3. Adjust your harness for the least amount of tilt-back possible so the wing's lift doesn't force you to run while tilted back.

Symptom: I tend to go side to side before lifting off.
1. Once you get the wing up overhead and moving, go to half power just to keep moving, steer the wing overhead straight, then go up to full power for lift off. Never takeoff in a pendulum swing.
2. Don't change running direction too much. Only correct half as much as you think.

Symptom: I tend to sink back down to the ground and land on my butt.
1. Keep running until you are churning air. Don't get in the seat until reaching at least 100 feet up.
2. Don't let off the brakes too quickly after liftoff. Ease them up slowly to accelerate into a climb.
3. Make sure the leg straps are somewhat loose to prevent the seat from kicking you into the air too early. Adjust the motor to be less tilted back.

Symptom: I tend to lose my balance just as the wing starts lifting and I fall down sometimes.
1. May be torque related. Stand straight up early in the launch run. If you're leaning forward when the wing lifts you, precession will impart a twist as you straighten up. Consider using less power for initial climb.
2. Adjust your harness to minimize torque affects (see Chapter 12), primarily decrease any tilt-back.
3. Make sure the wing is either exactly overhead or slightly left (right for geared machines) just as you lift off in order to prevent *loaded riser twist*.

sively, start to run, leading with your chest. Keep your hands back. Just *after* the wing has inflated, pull some on the A's but not enough to tuck the leading edge. If there's some wind, be less aggressive. If you run and feel nothing whatsoever, there you're moving at a good clip. Power up and accelerate (9-12). If the wing is rising quickly, get off the A's by 7 and brake so it doesn't overfly you. With some wind and/or lots of thrust, you'll lift off in just a few steps. With less wind, low power, smaller wing, higher elevation, and/o higher temperature, you'll need more run, possibly a lot. Gather speed then apply some brake to lift off. Too much brake will slow you down and may prevent takeoff. Once aloft, smoothly decrease brake pressure to 1 for the best climb rate.

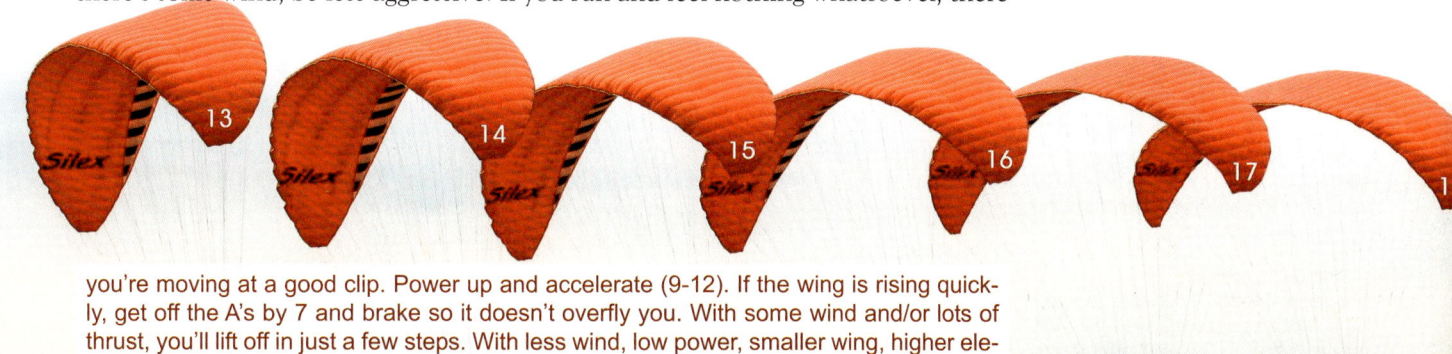

The PPG Bible: A Complete Guide and Reference

During inflation, if you must look at the wing, look the side. As the wing comes overhead, looking up is good as long as you don't slow down. In calm or light wind concentrate on getting speed quickly. Speed is life!

As the wing comes overhead, stand erect and let the motor push for quick acceleration.

Reflex gliders may require holding the A's well into the run. Since they are much less likely to front tuck than standard gliders you can hold the A's longer.

is probably a slight tailwind up where the wing is.

If the wing comes up slowly, keep driving hard with some forward pressure on the A's. Move under the wing if you feel it going to one side even if you must turn. Speed is success—keep moving. As the wing comes overhead, *and* you're moving, let go of the A's and pull just enough brakes to feel them. If the wing shoots overhead, falls to the side or back, abort! Reflex wings require more pull on the A's than others while easy-inflating wings will front tuck with just a bit too much pull.

If there is more than a couple mph of wind, the wing may shoot up quickly. You'll know because it pulls back hard as you try to run; be ready to let go of the A's early and dampen it (slow it down) with enough brakes to prevent it from overflying you. Only pull briefly *then let off* as you accelerate. Too little dampening and the wing may pass overhead, tucking expensively into your prop. Too much brake, especially before your body is moving, will make the wing fall back.

As the wing comes overhead, throttle up and stand up straight, letting the motor push you. Don't delay, there can be no hesitation and you may have to stay on the A's for some time in nil wind, especially on reflex wings. *Once you are moving* look up, or look sideways, at the wing which also forces you into an upright posture.

Move left or right to stay under the wing but don't over-correct into an oscillation. That is where you go too far left and the wing goes right then you go right in a worsening series of overcorrections that ends in a fall or worse. If you sense it beginning, reduce power and consciously straighten your run or just abort.

Once everything is stable, *smoothly* go to full power and accelerate. Once you're moving quickly, pull enough brake to lift off. Smaller wings require more brake.

When you feel the wing's lift, keep running! **Run until your feet are churning air**. A common mishap is feeling lift, trying to sit down early, then sinking back into the ground. At best this is hard on the prop and cage. Stay on the throttle, too—letting off early in the climb will cause you to swing into the ground.

Reverse Inflation—Stronger conditions

Anytime you can stand there and kite the wing, do a reverse inflation. With enough wind, build a wall as described in Chapter 3.

You'll be facing the wing holding everything as shown at left. With A's in one hand and throttle in the other, lean a bit towards the wing. When ready, snap back using your *body* to pull the wing up with just a *bit* of pull on the A's. Get it stable overhead and moving into the wind (walking backwards) before turning around. You want the wing to have some forward momentum before turning around. Then as soon as you are facing forward, *move forward*. Turn and move. Throttle up in the turn to help keep forward motion.

Some instructors will have you hold off throttling up until after you're walking forward with the wing stable. That reduces the chance of having the wing overfly you and collapsing into the prop. It's more difficult to walk forward without power but you'll only do it long enough to verify that the wing is under control.

Another approach is to go strictly by feel. You turn around and throttle up while

1. Pulling too much on the A's on a standard glider. The leading edge folds over (*frontals*) and prevents the wing from coming up.

2. Stance for reverse inflations with right hand throttle machines: the correct brake in each hand, A's in your left hand and throttle in your right hand. Plan to turn around to the left.

Troubleshooting *Reverse* Launch Problems

The reverse launch can vary from easy to frustrating depending on conditions. Here are some possible cures for your troubles.

Symptom: Wing doesn't come up even when the wind should be strong enough.
1. Take one step toward the wing before moving backwards to build momentum when you back up.
2. Only barely pull on the A's until most of the fabric is mostly inflated, then pull primarily with your body.
3. If there is enough wind, building a "wall" helps make sure it comes up straight and quickly.

Symptom: The wing falls back when I turn around.
1. With the wing overhead, step backwards to get it moving, go hands UP, turn around and start moving forward immediately.
2. Throttle up during the turn so there is less delay in getting forward momentum.
3. Try to turn around only when the wing has forward momentum (into the wind).
4. Do a forward inflation.

Symptom: The wing falls over sideways when I turn around.
1. Insure the brakes are up when you turn and the wing is tracking straight in the same direction as your movement.
2. Avoid stepping significantly sideways as you turn. If you step left, the wing will fall to the right.

1. Building a wall is best, but when winds are light, it may not be possible. Your back must be to the wind.

2. Snap back hard with your body, applying pressure to the A's as they allow. Keep walking backwards, if necessary.

3. Use no brakes as the wing comes up unless needed to slow it. Move left or right with the wing. Pull the A's as necessary.

4 & 5. Use minimum or no brakes while turning around and throttling up. A quick transition to forward motion is key.

looking forward and moving. Be sensitive to the small left or right tugs given by the wing and respond with brake and course change. Obviously this takes practice.

If the wing tends to fall back, you're applying too much brake or not moving enough. The wing needs airflow for control so you must keep it moving. As it comes overhead, reduce brake pressure but prevent it from overflying you.

During the turnaround, it's important that your hands go mostly up to avoid engaging any brake. Plus, you must move forward immediately after turning around. Don't just stand there, get moving: It is the only way you'll have any control. Once moving and under control, it's just like a forward launch.

In all situations, be quick to abort if things aren't going well—turn around and kill the motor. Trying again is better than "parablending" your wing.

While running, you must take off going straight (wing overhead) and into the wind as much as possible. Steering should be minimal with just enough input to keep yourself going in the correct direction. Insure that you are pointed in a good climbout direction and under the wing before committing to takeoff. If it gets squirrely, or you feel yourself running side-to-side, abort.

With abundant experience you can steer more while running. Capable pilots can steer to most any direction desired including around obstacles and crosswind—this is an important skill for conquering challenging sites.

When everything looks good and you're running in the right direction with the wing overhead, throttle up to full power and hold it. Stand up straight and let the motor push while taking increasingly larger strides. Upward glances at the wing are OK, but most attention should be focused on the run and steering. If the wing tries to pull right, steer it back to the left with *just enough* brake.

As the wing lifts but while you're still running, steer the wing slightly left (right for geared machines) to reduce torque twist effects. After liftoff reduce brake pressure.

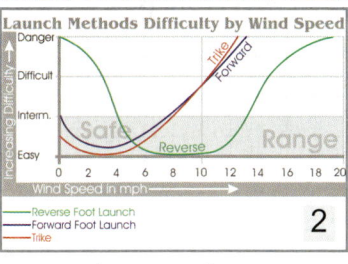

1. A typical reverse pull-up in stronger conditions—it's in the body, not the arms. He's pulling a bit of A's with his left hand (which also holds the left brake) while his right hand stays loose on its brake and keeps the kill switch available.

2. Here is how to select a launch method based on winds. Light wind reverses increase the chance for falling backwards while high wind forwards increase the chance for being pulled back into a "turtle" position. Trike flying is covered in the next chapter.

Kicking In

Rehearse getting seated in the simulator; it's not always easy and may require a particular technique that your instructor will cover. Regardless of how you do it: **Don't pull brakes while getting into the seat!** Students have stalled their wings and plummeted to the ground by doing that.

Also be careful letting go of the brakes, especially on machines with low hook-in points, since the toggles can get sucked into the prop with dire consequences.

The best kick-in system is an aluminum bar hanging by elastic down about 6 inches below the seat lip. It stretches out to 18 inches or so when needed, keeping it away from your legs while walking around but within easy foot reach after launch.

How The Seat Board Moves

Standing/Launch — Seated/Flight

Climbout

Use as little brake as possible while climbing out: "Hands up to go up." All motors *torque* (cause a turn) to one direction or another; use minimal brake to counteract it. If possible, let it turn in the direction it wants to go. If you feel any twisting in the risers, *ease* the power halfway back immediately even if your climb rate will suffer. If you *must* turn against the torque, do so gingerly. Too much brake will cause a *spin* (see Chapter 18).

If your body starts twisting one way but the wing is banking the other way, you are entering a *motor-induced lockout* and *must* reduce power.

Climb up to at least 300 ft above the ground while keeping your landing area within gliding range. Altitude is your friend, keeping your options open while avoiding obstacles. You can't hit something if you're above it.

Once up at a safe altitude, reduce power. Avoid long-term use of full power, whenever possible, for the motor's sake.

Getting Into the Seat

This action turns out to be surprisingly critical. After liftoff, you'll be hanging uncomfortably by the leg straps. If you cannot get into the seat easily, without letting go of the brakes, keep climbing. Tough it out until at least 50 feet high or advised by your instructor.

> ⚠ **Caution**
> If you must reach down for the seat, let go of the brake(s) first! Do it slowly, too. On some configurations it's possible for the brakes to flail into the prop.

If it's easy to do *without* letting go of the brakes (may require a kick-in strap), you may get in the seat as soon as a safe climb is established. Some machines, when adjusted properly, require just lifting the legs and a little wiggle to become seated.

If you *have* to reach down for the seat, be ready for a motor failure; new pilots sometimes hit the kill switch or get the throttle chopped off when it loops back towards the prop.

If the leg straps are too loose, it may be impossible to get into the seat.

Machines equipped with a *kick-in strap* or bar let you keep the brakes in your hands while using the kick-in strap (or bar) to push out the seat. If the bar is hard to reach with just a foot; carefully let go of the non-throttle brake toggle and reach down to position the strap for your foot. Then kick out the seat.

The next best way to get seated is by using one hand to push down on the back of the seatboard. Carefully release your non-throttle brake toggle or, if possible, put it in your throttle hand. Then reach down with your free hand to push down on the back of the seat board until it pops it out.

The least desirable way is *carefully* letting go of both brakes then using both hands to get into the seat. Make it two distinct steps: Palms open to release the brakes slowly, insuring they don't go in the prop, *then* go for the seat. Using your thumbs, grasp the forward outer part of the seatboard (where the front strap attaches) then push down and forward. On some motors, it's easier to push down on the *back* part of the seatboard to pop it "under center." Be careful not to press the kill switch.

Tightening the leg straps makes it easier to get into the seat on most machines but more difficult to run. Tighten them all the way, then loosen a couple inches. When setup properly, it's possible on some units to just lift your legs and wiggle into the seat. Get several successful launches under your belt before trying the wiggle, though, since its contortions can result in strange brake positions.

If it proves too difficult to get into the seat (this *can* happen on some equipment), return to land promptly so your landing gear doesn't goes numb.

Rehearse getting into the seat while hanging in a simulator, preferably with the motor running for realism. Do it until the action is automatic.

Flying Around

Now the reward: You're flying! Once up at altitude, everything gets much easier; its time to relax a bit and enjoy the view. Your instructor may have you try a few things after a while. Normally the flight should last no more than about a half hour to make sure you have no numb or tired parts (like arms).

Having an Out

Your first flight's flood of emotions will drown out many normal thought processes. That's why an instructor on the radio is so beneficial—but still there are some things you must think about.

1. Where would I land if the motor quit? Allow enough altitude to get back and set up a pattern. 500 feet is generally about right. Always have an out, the engine *will* eventually quit.

2. What is the wind doing? Where are the wind shadows and rotors (see Chapter 7)? Winds may change during your flight, possibly even reversing, and you must always plan on landing *into* it.

3. How much fuel/time do I have left. Noting your launch time and knowing your endurance is one way to avoid running out of gas. But it's also good to check the fuel level using a visual means such as a mirror. Even if you started with enough fuel, it is possible for a leak to dramatically reduce your flying time.

Turns

Before turning, use "Look, Lean, Pull then Power." That means **Look** where you're about to turn (called *clearing the turn*), **lean** if you are using weight shift, **pull** brake to turn then add **power** to hold altitude in the turn. Others will see your intentions, too, if your looking is deliberate. Start with a **shallow** turn, then look **up** and **down** in the direction of turn, and finally, turn.

Turns are made by raising one brake while pulling down the other. Pull brake in the turn direction *slowly* and *hold* it for three seconds or longer as needed. Start with position/pressure 1. Learn how much pressure it takes to get to position 1 and use that feeling (pressure) instead of position once you're familiar. When pulling the brake initially, you will swing out then swing back in to a stable shallow turn. Don't try to counteract that swing—hold the brake for 3 seconds minimum. Don't try to dampen oscillations yet, either; just use measured, steady pressure and wait

"Having an out" means having a good landing option. Always be assessing where you'll go when the motor quits.

Always have AN OUT!

The "Bump Scale:"

Here is a common reference to help when relating "bumpiness" to other pilots:

0 Completely smooth

1 Getting jostled, no real change in flight path.

2 Causes small changes in flight path. The most that new pilots should fly in.

3 Causes body swings of around 3 feet with no control input.

4 Causes moderate changes in flight path and body movements of around 5 ft. Causes significant surging/retreating and small tip collapses on high performance wings.

5 Very active air. Causes small tip collapses even on beginner wings.

6 Causes 50% collapses on high performance wings.

7 Causes 50% collapses even on beginner wings.

8-10 Increasing levels of dangerous air where 10 is completely uncontrollable.

for the turn to develop. Too much brake will spin the glider (see Chapter 18).

To level out of the turn, let up the brake *slowly* (about 3 seconds). It needs to be released slower than the natural tendency of the glider to swing back and forth (it's natural pendular period). Letting off too quickly can cause a left/right oscillation. Keeping your forearm vertical will naturally help prevent over-braking.

Wake Turbulence

Planes and paragliders fly by pushing air down as they move through it. A by-product is little vortices that swirl off of each wing tip, spreading slowly, drifting with the wind, and settling about 300 feet per minute (see Chapter 22).

If you do a medium to shallow 360° turn, you'll fly through your own wake, a potentially startling ripple in otherwise still air. It's not the prop blast, either, which is a disorganized burble of minimal effect.

Altitudes

Having altitude is having options; you stay out of obstacle's *reach*, have *time* to handle an engine-out and can reach more *landing sites*.

Pattern altitude is about 300 feet above ground level (AGL), high enough to easily make it back to the landing site and avoid obstacles, without being too high to judge ground track.

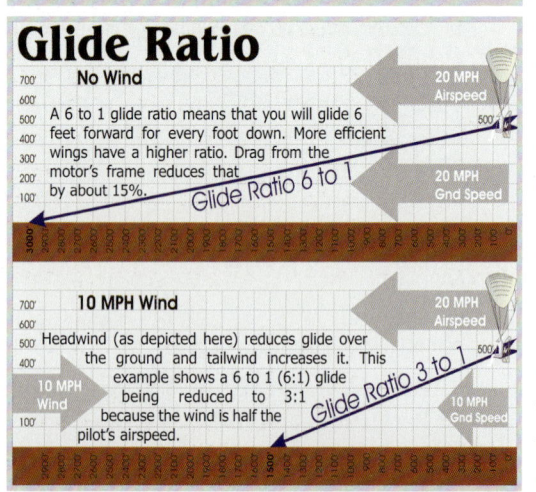

Cruising is best done between 200 and 500 feet which is below where most airplanes and helicopters fly, although a few aircraft fly that low (especially cropdusters and pipeline patrols). If you're flying near an airport, learn the patterns and altitudes where airplanes normally fly (Chapter 10); avoiding them is legally *our* obligation.

At higher altitudes more visibility is required (see Chapter 9) but, even down low, we can't ever fly with visibility less than 1 mile.

Glide Ratio & Wind

As part of always having an out (somewhere to land) you must know how far you can glide. This *glide ratio* is how far you'll travel per unit of altitude lost. Our craft typically achieve about a 6:1 glide ratio (pronounced "six to one") meaning that you go 6 feet forward for every foot down.

Wind has an important effect on glide. A 10 mph headwind cuts the glide in half for a craft that flies 20 mph. So you'd only glide 3 feet forward for every foot down or 3:1. Conversely, a tailwind helps your glide. That same 10 mph wind from behind means you're going 30 mph over the ground while still dropping at the same rate, yielding a glide ratio of 9:1 (9 feet forward for every foot down).

Think of your landing options as a cone spreading out below you (see page 198). Wind will move the cone of options downwind. As you go higher, the area of the cone at ground level gets bigger since you can glide farther. Of course you must allow room for maneuvering, too.

Energy & Injury

In an accident, energy and injury are powerfully intertwined. A fact of physics is that energy dissipated in a collision increases to the square of the speed: doubling the speed quadruples the energy (read damage).

Consider a mere 7 mph wind and a typical flying speed of 20 mph. Hitting something while flying into the wind is a 13 mph collision. Hitting it while flying downwind is a 27 mph whack: far more dramatic, having over twice the speed and more than four times the energy!

Glide Ratio

No Wind — A 6 to 1 glide ratio means that you will glide 6 feet forward for every foot down. More efficient wings have a higher ratio. Drag from the motor's frame reduces that by about 15%.

Glide Ratio 6 to 1 — 20 MPH Airspeed / 20 MPH Gnd Speed

10 MPH Wind — Headwind (as depicted here) reduces glide over the ground and tailwind increases it. This example shows a 6 to 1 (6:1) glide being reduced to 3:1 because the wind is half the pilot's airspeed.

Glide Ratio 3 to 1 — 20 MPH Airspeed / 10 MPH Gnd Speed

Ground Track

You may get aloft and notice that you're flying sideways after turning crosswind. That is because the wind is blowing you "downstream." Your wing is still flying through the air like it always does, but the air is moving over the ground and so you are, in fact, drifting with the wind.

Ground track is the line your flight path draws over the ground. If the goal is to be flying directly into the wind, as you will be on landing, then turn into the "current." So if you're drifting right (sliding sideways to the right), gently turn left. Don't just pull the brake and release it, but hold the gentle turn until drifting stops. Practice this input when you're up high so it doesn't surprise you on landing. You'll want to minimize sideways drift on landing.

Reflex Wings

If your first flights will be on a reflex wing, start with the trims set to neutral (0 on some wings) and leave them. Brake use and response will be essentially like any other glider. When trimmed fast, especially with speedbar applied, these gliders prefer to be flown using their tip steering system instead of the brakes.

Before adjusting the trimmers, practice using any provided tip steering controls (toggles or balls) while trimmed neutral. When you're comfortable with that, grab the tip steering controls in your hands, let go of the brakes (if necessary) *then* set the trims to fast. These gliders are most collapse resistant at their highest speeds (trimmers up and speedbar applied). As a beginner you will not likely be asked to do this.

Since tip steering does not work well, or at all, for fore/aft (pitch) control, when you're ready for landing, pull the trims back to neutral (0) and return to using the brakes for normal handling.

Landing

Beyond the mechanics and concepts, landing can't be simulated very well. That's why tow, hill or tandem training is so beneficial. But if you can manage to at least land into the wind with about quarter brake (position/pressure 2), you should do no worse than slide to your knees. And with just a bit of effort, landings can be reliably smooth and always on your feet (or wheels).

Always choose a specific landing spot to aim for; something the size of a Frisbee. It will take lots of practice to actually hit it, but always be trying. Don't try so hard, though, that you stall or spin. Chapter 16 and 17 have lots more on landing for when you're more experienced.

The Landing Pattern

Landing patterns provide for an orderly arrival with these benefits:

- Let you plan the approach by giving common reference points;
- Allows you to scope out the landing field for wind and obstructions;
- Keeps the flow of traffic in one direction and lets you know where to expect

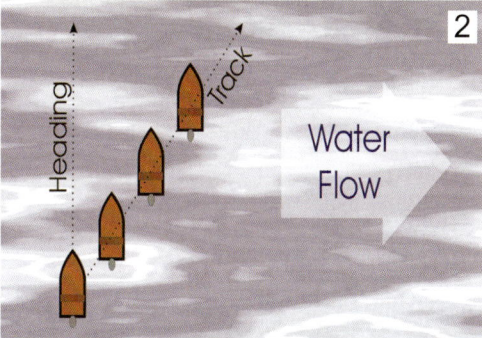

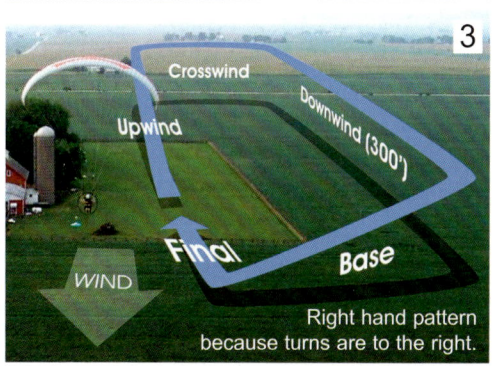

1. Reflex Wings have long trimmer travel to manage their wide speed range. But heed the maker's manual! This chart shows some typical trimmer usage scenarios. For example, under steering, use the brake toggles while trimmed slow and the tip steering when trimmed fast.

2. Ground Track: Picture the bottom of the river as ground, and the water is air. Relative to the water, you're just rowing straight forward. Relative to the river bottom, you're drifting downstream.

3. Landing patterns have proven to be a helpful staple of aviation for years. Almost all instructors will have their students fly some form of a pattern with variations based on location. Doing "S" turns on final is frequently done to lose altitude but should be straightened out and into the wind, by 50 feet Above Ground Level (AGL).

Landing: The Last 50 Feet No Wind

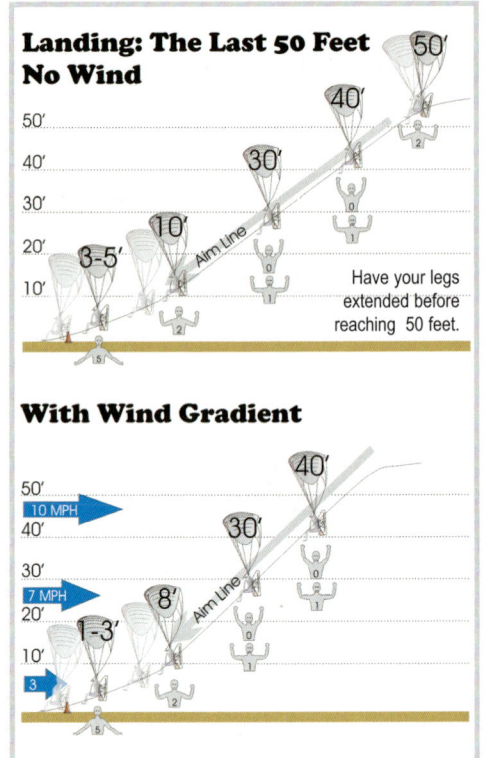

Have your legs extended before reaching 50 feet.

With Wind Gradient

With a calm or *steady* wind, the spot that you're going to hit will not be changing angle, just getting bigger. That is your "aim line" and hopefully it's also your target.

By 50 ft be out of your seat and shut off the motor—the wing will surge forward slightly as the thrust quits and you'll stabilize in a descent. Keep your hands mostly up, between pressure 0 and 1. At 10 feet, flare slightly. That will swing you out a bit (and the wing back), slowing both your forward speed and descent speed. At 3-5 feet do a full flare. Have one foot forward so you're ready to run. If there's a headwind, you can usually flare later and less. This technique varies somewhat by wing model and it's efficiencies.

If there's a wind then there's probably a wind gradient where wind speed slows near the ground. The descent angle is slightly steeper because the wing is losing airspeed in the descent and diving to compensate.

other pilots—very important for collision avoidance.

The initial pattern segments are named according to their relationship with the wind (see Landing Patterns graphic previous page). The downwind leg is about 300 feet away from the runway and 300 feet high. Leave the motor idling until the last 50 feet.

Patterns are either right or left according to the turn direction. A right pattern has all turns to the right and a left pattern to the left. Standard patterns are to the left but, for us, direction will more often be dictated by wind and terrain.

Enter the pattern on the downwind leg, flying level at about 300 feet AGL. Pass beside the desired landing point (abeam) and continue until it is about 45° behind you then ease off the power and turn onto base leg. Here is where you will want to judge whether you are high or low. If it looks like you're low and might not make the spot, turn towards it. If you're high, angle the base leg away from the spot.

Avoid doing a 360° in the pattern or turning completely away from the landing spot. You can quickly get too low or not make it back directly into the wind. Plus, losing eye contact with the desired spot can be disorienting for newer pilots.

For reflex wing flyers, set the trims to neutral or slow since you'll be using the brakes.

Final Approach

Turn final and point yourself towards the landing spot then extend your legs so that you're hanging by the leg loops. The seat folds back to where it was on launch. Make small corrections to keep aimed at the spot. Don't over control; make only *small* brake inputs, hold for 3 seconds, then ease up.

Once it's obvious that you'll make the landing area (not overshoot or undershoot), press and hold the kill switch until the motor stops completely. If you release it early, the motor will restart. You want the prop stopped by around 100 feet up and no later than 50 feet.

Be mindful of drift. If you're drifting to the left it means a wind from the right is pushing you. Ease in enough right brake to correct to the right and hold for a few seconds or until the drift is almost stopped then *ease* off the brake. Look at your wind streamers to verify wind direction.

> ⚠ **Caution!**
> Look at your desired flight path, **not** any nearby obstructions such as trees or buildings. A surprising number of accidents stem from *target fixation*, where a pilot looks at an obstruction that he wants to avoid, fixates on it, then flies into it.

Below 100 Feet

When you get within about 100 feet of the ground, disregard the chosen spot to concentrate on landing into the wind and making a good touchdown. Use minimum brakes. By 50 feet of altitude have your hands nearly all the way up (almost no brakes) in preparation for flare. You want to have maximum brake effectiveness (maximum speed) for the flare. Pulling brakes early will result in a hard landing!

If you start to swing left and right (like a pendulum) do *nothing*. At most, ease both brakes to position/pressure 1. Do *not* try to correct. Pendular dynamics are such

The PPG Bible: A Complete Guide and Reference

> **Troubleshooting Landing Problems**
> Landing is a given, style points are up for grabs. Here are some tips to improve on the second most demanding task of our sport. Remember, the point of flaring is to have your body swing forward. That makes the wing grab more air.
> **Symptom: My landings are consistently hard, making it difficult to stay on my feet.**
> 1. You have too much brake pull during the last 30 feet. Have your hands nearly full up (no brakes) below 50 feet AGL down through flare. Don't start pulling until you're below 10 feet.
> 2. If you consistently slow down then drop to the ground, you're flaring too early. Some wings, especially slow ones, do this more.
>
> **Symptom: My landings are fast and hard.**
> 1. You need to start the flare earlier. You must feel yourself swing out in front of the wing.
> 2. Make sure you're exactly into the wind.
> 3. Make sure you're landing with the trimmers in (slow), or neutral for reflex wings.
>
> **Symptom: I swing left/right a lot on final approach.**
> 1. Unless you have *mastered* dampening these oscillations, do *not* try to correct them below about 50 feet.
> 2. Practice oscillation damping at altitude.
>
> **Symptom: Sometimes I land drifting sideways.**
> 1. Insure you're lined up into the wind on final. For example, if you're drifting right, turn left gradually but be level by touchdown.
> 2. Avoid steering input during the last 20 feet or so.

that your attempts at correction all but guarantee a hard landing. Hold the brakes steady and let the wing sort itself out. It's much better to land in a small pendulum than to try correcting it until you've gained significant experience.

If you notice a drift while flaring, beware of a nearly irresistible urge to put out the downwind hand as if to protect yourself from the impending fall. That's exactly the *wrong* thing to do! Practice correcting for drift. Imagine yourself drifting left, pull a *bit* of right brake and hold for 3 seconds then ease up. Of course you cannot be aggressive on the brakes at this point but want to minimize drift, not pendulum—if it feels like a "swing" then don't do anything.

Flaring is the process of slowing your forward speed and sink rate as you reach the ground. It must be started from a nearly hands-up posture. It's not the brake application, but the pendular action that does the work.

At about 7 to 10 feet pull very slight brakes—only a couple inches for most wings to get your body swinging forward. That's what does the work. It angles the wing up and rounds out your descent. At about 2 to 4 feet start pulling more brake. If done properly you will arrive at the ground as you reach full brakes. Run a few steps forward then turn around and pull both brakes to quickly get the wing on the ground. If it's windy, walk towards the wing and grab a wingtip.

Before touchdown, your feet should be positioned for running—one slightly in front of the other. Touchdown with knees slightly bent, ready to absorb a potentially firm arrival. Fortunately our slow speeds and descent rates make this no big deal. In fact, going to your knees during the early landings is somewhat common.

Controlling Glide

The touchdown point can be predicted while gliding straight ahead. If it appears to be rising (you increasingly must look up) then you're going to land short. If it is falling below (you're increasingly looking lower) then you will pass over it. The stationary point is where you're gonna land. You've actually been doing this for years when walking or driving but in a horizontal direction: The stationary spot in your windshield or vision field is where you're headed, everything else slides by your periphery.

Gliding for spot 3, put your shoe up to the spot. If the spot rises as you descend, you'll land short. If the spot sinks below your shoe, you'll overfly it.

When trying to stretch glide *against* a wind, be hands up with trimmers out for more speed. Even with the higher sink rate, you'll cover more ground.

Glide is steeper (worse) when flying into a headwind and shallower with a tailwind. In a headwind you can steepen the descent by slowing down but don't use more than about a quarter brake (position/pressure 2) until you're *very* familiar with the wing. If you do slow down, ease up the brakes (take 3 seconds) to speed back up by 50 feet AGL so as to have enough speed left for an effective flare. As you let the brakes up, expect to drop 20 feet or so while regaining speed.

You can also do small S-turns to lose altitude and effectively shorten a glide. Keep them shallow, though, and get yourself steady back into the wind by 100 feet.

After Landing

Run out the landing enough to keep the wing from overflying you; it should come down behind you. As you stop, turn around quickly and apply brakes so that it falls on its top. This 1) makes bundling or folding easier, 2) offers less chance for the lines to become tangled, and 3) keeps lines out off the motor.

Unclip quickly to avoid letting a gust catch the wing and pull you off balance. Wearing a motor makes this both more likely and more expensive.

Postflight

Get the wing covered to reduce it's UV exposure, even with clouds. Either fold, bundle, or put it in the shade and away from sandy, dusty or gravel areas.

Check out the motor and harness just like a preflight inspection. It's far better to find problems now so you can fix them before your next session. Even if it was running fine when you landed, parts loosen and props get nicked.

Cleaning

Cleaning the machine after each flight allows detection of cracks and other problems that can hide under a cloak of grime. For example, if you see a large increase in the amount of black goo squirting onto the prop, suspect problems; that's hard to detect with a dirty machine.

Gasoline, WD 40 and mineral spirits are good for wiping down motor parts. Carburetor cleaner is great on un-painted surfaces but is brutal on paint. Avoid getting citrus-based cleaners on aluminum. Fabric sprays that offer other protection work well and help preserve the gear but don't use them on wing fabric. If possible, cover the motor during transport to prevent UV damage to the harness; it fades pretty quickly when exposed to sunlight.

Clean the wing by draping the trailing edge over a clothes line hung high enough to keep the leading edge off the ground. Spray clean water (no solvents) on the outside and up into the cells. Dirt and debris will run out. Let it air dry, preferably out of the sun. Dust and sand abrade the fabric, shortening its life.

1. Stowing equipment properly can be extremely important in some settings!

2 & 3. Covering the motors is best although they sometimes get relegated to exposed outside travel. Purpose built covers with cinch bottoms or zip-ups are convenient. The platforms can be found at most sporting goods or hardware stores and plug into standard trailer receivers.

Adding Wheels

CHAPTER 6

Wheels add a whole new dimension to Powered Paragliding, enabling more people to fly and providing another layer of fun. They can be anything from a simple add-on cart up to heavier, purpose-built machines with integrated motor and seat.

There will be more weight and drag so speeds are higher, climb rate is less and fuel burn is higher than the same foot-launched craft. Bigger motors are preferred since there's no help from your legs during initial inflation.

Carts do impose limitations, namely for weather and terrain. They don't like uneven ground or strong wind. They're more difficult in some respects—you can't step sideways during launch—but are overall easier, especially in nil winds or high elevations where groundspeed is higher.

Just like foot-launching, more skill means more capabilities. A good wheel pilot can handle nearly as much wind as a good foot flyer—it mostly depends on wing handling skill. About 10 mph is the practical wind limit for most pilots since reverse inflation is very difficult on wheels (see Chapter 15).

Tandem operations (See Chapter 8 for legalities) with wheels are easier and safer since little is required of the passenger/student. In foot launched tandems, the student must be active which is asking a lot for a first flight. Rolling aloft lets the student take it all in while only getting involved as the instructor sees fit.

Large, soft and slippery wheels are preferred since they act like shock absorbers and roll better on rough or soft surfaces. Being able to slide helps reduce the chance of flipping over since they don't grab in a sideways drift. Thinner wheels work OK on hard packed surfaces. A wide wheel base, with lower center of gravity (CG), and lower hook-in points reduces tippiness.

Elisabeth Guerin launches an add-on PPG trike that uses the paramotor and its harness. On most carts, like this one, your feet rest on steering pegs which are connected right to the axle.

Ground steering is opposite to how certified aircraft work but the transition is quick. Chapter 28 has a steering comparison diagram. Aircraft-style steering is overkill and it makes jumping into other PPG carts more difficult.

Brakes are rarely used because of our low speeds, but be careful, there is more mass than you think—it's just masked by the wheels. Heavier machines may have brakes.

Fresh Breeze's Xcitor is a hybrid PPC—heavy and powerful like a PPC but with hand controls and elliptical wing like a PPG. The wing has multiple-line wing attachments.

Paratour's "PPCg" is a lightweight hybrid PPC with a moderately powerful motor and hand-controls. Its paraglider-like wing uses multiple-line wing attachments.

Fly Products Flash Trike is a cable-braced, highly portable PPG trike. It uses regular riser attachments and you supply the paramotor with harness.

Paracruiser's PPG Quad uses paraglider wing attachments, foot-launch paramotor *and* harness (check legality in your country).

Paratoys' LowBoy quad has an integral seat but uses paraglider wing attachments and you supply the paramotor.

This TrikeBuggy.com unit has an integral seat but uses paraglider wing attachments and you supply the paramotor.

1. Chris Bowles pedals the Fresh Breeze Flyke—a roadable tricycle that doubles as a PPG cart. When launching, the pilot does no wheel-steering, rather it articulates about the mid section in response to pull from the wing.

He is dwarfed by the powered parachute (PPC) behind him.

2. This "Timber Trike" may be the simplest way to add wheels but you still have to know what you're doing. Proper balance, thrust line, and other aspects are critical.

Wheeled Types

Powered parachutes (PPC's) are high-powered craft with parachute style, draggy wings. They trade efficiency for ease of operation. High control forces necessitate foot steering—a primary difference from PPGs. PPC wings generally have very long risers or, on a few units, have *multiple line wing attachments* where lines attach at several points on each side.

The distinction between PPC's and wheeled PPG's have blurred but, if it's hand-flown using brake toggles and a hand throttle, then these techniques will work.

Hybrids are basically PPC's with hand controls—they are not intended to be foot launched, even without the wheels. Some of these have multiple-line wing attachments that don't unclip quickly. *Standard* wheeled PPG's use foot launchable paramotors and paragliders.

Wheeled PPG's have other distinctions such as the number of wheels. 3-wheel *trikes* are popular due to their simplicity while 4-wheel *Quads* are more stable. *Buggies* derive their name from kite buggies—low slung carts propelled by a paraglider-like kite. They usually have their own seat rather than use the paramotor's harness. *Collapsible cable-braced* carts are highly portable via fold-up structure. A very few carts are *jettisonable* but that's risky to others *and* the cart. Hook-in position, high or low, is another difference. High hook-in lessens in-flight wobbling of the cart while low hook-in resists tipping on the ground.

Setup

Weight distribution of a trike will affect how it hangs so you must do a hang check before flying. The rear wheels should be slightly lower than the nosewheel—a 5 to 15° nose-up angle is best. If the nosewheel hangs below the rear wheels it will wheelbarrow on takeoff or landing, making a rollover far more likely.

Adjusting clip-in position must be done for each different pilot weight to assure proper balance. A heavy pilot will be nose heavy (very bad) and a light pilot will tend to be tipped back (not *as* bad). All tandem and most solo carts allow moving the attachment points to get a good hang angle.

Set the motor angle so that, on the ground, thrust blows just *above* the wing. That minimizes ruffling the fabric at idle and lets the cart start rolling before wing inflation. If the wing inflates before you get moving, it can cause a tug-of-war where thrust pushes against the wing which pulls back on the cart and nothing moves.

Hook up the A-helpers, if installed (see photo next page). They pull the A's during the wing's first 70° of upward arc, then become slack.

Launch

The vast majority of cart launches use a forward inflation. See Chapter 15 for the advanced technique of doing revereses.

Layout is just like a forward foot launch. The wing and cart must be centered and directly into the wind. Lines should drape over the line holders, if installed, and be clear of the rear wheels (see image 3). Before starting, roll the cart forward, barely tensioning the lines to insure everything is centered. A slight tension helps keep the lines from getting sucked into the prop. Some instructors recommend rolling it back a few feet to allow some speed build up on launch, but not if the prop is likely to suck in lines.

The basic launch sequence is **Power** (partial or full as required), **A's** (if required), **Dampen** the wing as it gets overhead, **Reduce** Power, **Taxi**, then **Takeoff** if everything looks good. The order is critical.

1. Start the motor, get in and buckle up. Go through your pre-launch checklist. A little wing ruffling is OK as long as it doesn't ruin your layout. Strap the throttle onto your hand, grab the brakes then put the A's between your thumb and palm (if no A helpers). Put your feet on the steering pegs.

2. Look around to clear the area then, when ready, throttle up. How much throttle depends on your gear. Powerful units on smooth surfaces with small or easy inflating gliders do better with partial power.

How much A's you hold depends on the wing. Most require some A-pressure while a few larger models require a lot. It also depends on the trike's seating arrangement and whether you can get a good hold of the A's. Machines with *A helpers* pull the A's for you.

3. Look back at the wing—it's easiest to look left or right. A mirror can be helpful, too. As the wing comes overhead let off the A's and be ready to pull some brakes *briefly* to prevent the wing from overflying. Stay on the power until *after* dampening. Reducing power early or not dampening enough will cause the wing will overfly you and dive into the prop—an expensive blending of non-matching materials.

If the wing rockets upwards, get off the A's, dampening it sooner and with more vigor. Stay on the power, though—when the wing comes

1. These images illustrate two things well. Wing lift effectively raises the center of gravity (CG), making it surprisingly easy to topple a trike. Second, a natural human reaction is to put a hand out as if to brace against falling. That's bad since it pulls the wing over farther, aggravating the situation. The hand may get broken, too.

Rehearse your reaction to a rollover and practice keeping your hands inward and feet firmly on the pegs.

2. Adjust to keep the back wheels below the front wheel(s) in flight.

3. Wood planks let the cart get rolling in soft sand.

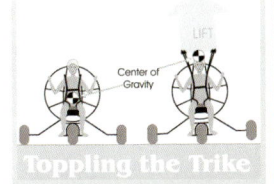

Throttle up to get rolling. When the wing catches air, pull some A's to help it rise (unless that's done by A helpers). As the wing comes overhead, dampen it with some brakes briefly. Allow the cart to gather some speed *then* reduce power. It's important to taxi first while insuring the wing is stable overhead, and tracking with you, before committing to flight.

1. *"A" helpers* (also called *A assist lines*) pull the A's during initial inflation. As the wing comes up, geometry is such that they go slack which is perfect since they're not needed anymore. Using A helpers frees the pilot from having to hold the A's during inflation.

2. A mirror can help to see the wing during initial inflation.

up quickly it usually stops the cart. Be just as quick to let *off* brake pressure as the wing comes overhead.

If the wing is hanging back or coming up slowly, you'll need to stay on the A's longer. Once the cart has accelerated to a good kiting speed, ease off the power enough to prevent further acceleration. Do not to take off yet.

If the wing comes overhead crooked, minimize brake pressure, keep up enough speed to kite, and turn *slightly* towards it. Don't overdo the turn lest an oscillation develop. If it gets more than about 20° off center, abort. As you build finesse—*lots* of finesse—you can redeem surprisingly crooked inflations.

4. Taxi the cart/wing combo mostly by steering the cart straight and keeping the wing overhead. Turn by first steering the wing in the desired direction then driving the cart below it. Keep enough airflow (rolling speed) over the wing to do this. It is imperative that the wing be tracking with the cart, centered and stabilized before accelerating for flight.

5. Once you and the wing are moving happily together, smoothly throttle up and hold it. Use minimum brake inputs and, if the wing gets very far off, abort.

On thick grass or soft surface you may have to add brake pressure to pop off but, once airborne, slowly ease off the brakes to accelerate. The best climb rate is almost always achieved with the least brake pressure. At high density altitudes you may be un*able* to climb if holding excessive brakes.

The worst carting sin is lifting off in an oscillation. If you feel the wing going side-to-side, slow down and get it straightened out or abort. Cart dynamics make matters worse; when the wing goes overhead in an oscillation, it unloads and the cart accelerates rapidly to the other side, pulling the wing into a bank the other way. You get airborne before flying speed is reached and return to earth with a mighty thwack.

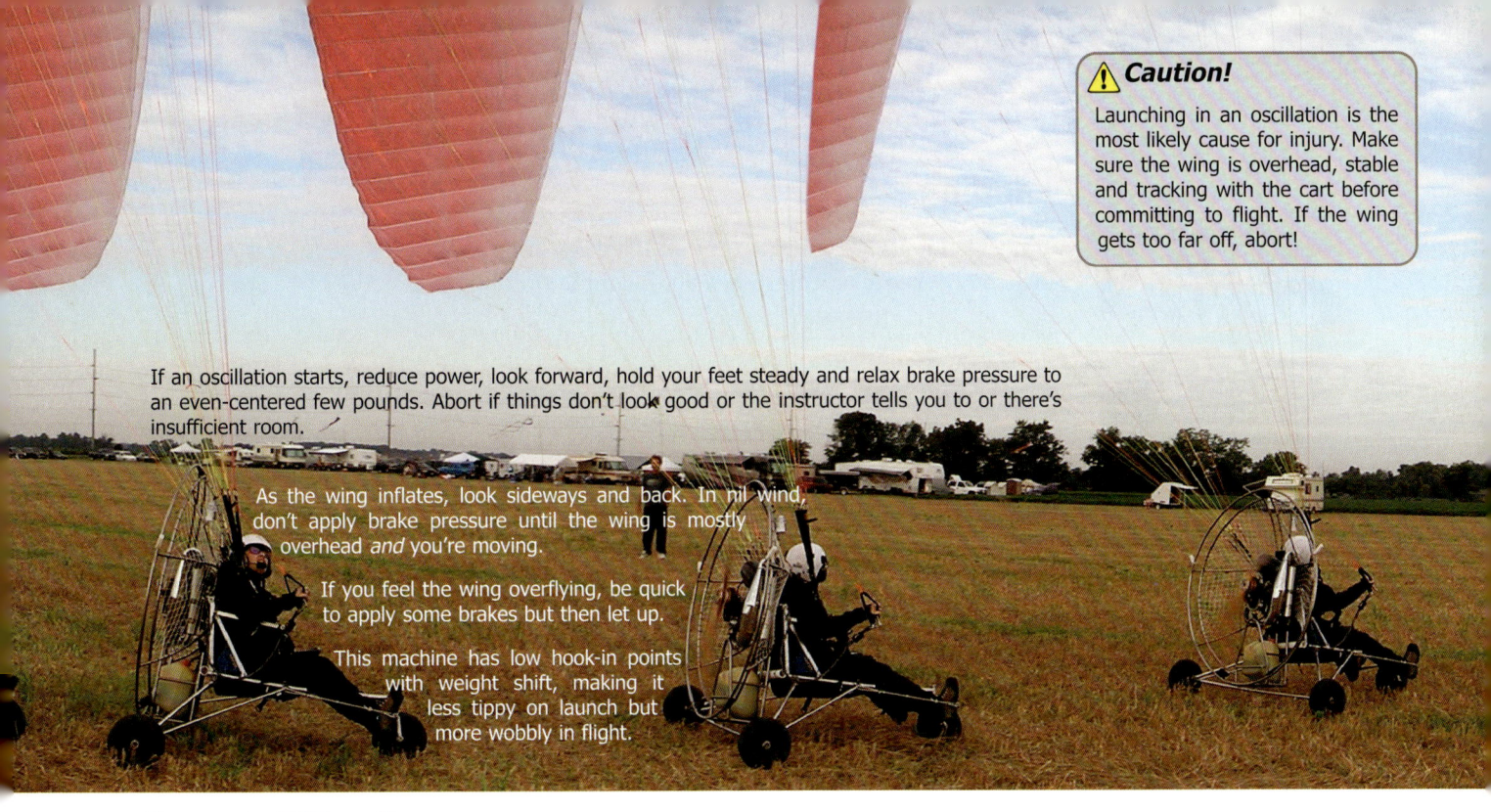

> **⚠ Caution!**
> Launching in an oscillation is the most likely cause for injury. Make sure the wing is overhead, stable and tracking with the cart before committing to flight. If the wing gets too far off, abort!

If an oscillation starts, reduce power, look forward, hold your feet steady and relax brake pressure to an even-centered few pounds. Abort if things don't look good or the instructor tells you to or there's insufficient room.

As the wing inflates, look sideways and back. In nil wind, don't apply brake pressure until the wing is mostly overhead *and* you're moving.

If you feel the wing overflying, be quick to apply some brakes but then let up.

This machine has low hook-in points with weight shift, making it less tippy on launch but more wobbly in flight.

Crosswind Takeoff

Taking off in a crosswind is tricky and is best saved for when you've gained lots of experience. It's useful anywhere that requires rolling in primarily one direction like a runway or road. Be careful, though, rollover risk is much higher.

Initial inflation should still be into whatever wind there is, if possible. Once the wing is overhead, you've dampened it, and are moving, turn *the wing* towards the runway then follow it with the cart. Your goal is to then keep the wing exactly overhead, pointed somewhat upwind (*crabbing*), as you do what it takes to track down the runway. More crosswind=more wing crab.

At liftoff the cart will twist to match the wing. It's a disconcerting and vulnerable transition that leaves you just over the ground, moving quickly and somewhat sideways, drifting with the wind. Touching back down like this is a sure flip or severe oscillation. So before liftoff, gather speed with minimal brakes, then apply enough brake to liftoff solidly and quickly, gaining a few feet right away. Don't overdo the brakes, though, lest you settle back to the ground.

Avoid inflating in a crosswind because the downwind part of the wing wants to catch air first and come up crooked. If a crosswind inflation is required, refer to the advice in Chapter 15.

Flying

The main difference in cart flying is a slightly higher airspeed and somewhat heavier control inputs. Carts bobble around a bit more due to having higher mass and having it spread out more. Torque is less noticeable because the center of gravity is lower and the motor is usually more vertical (not tilted back so far).

Low altitude maneuvering must be done with care and planning to account for a slower climb rate. Visibility is frequently slightly restricted by framework so you may have to move your head around somewhat to keep an eye out for traffic. Skimming the ground is fun since your eyeballs are so low.

Carts can be *turtled* too, usually in a breeze. It happens either during initial inflation or just after landing as the wing inflates or deflates. Thankfully, if you get to the kill switch quickly, as Michelle Daniele did here, it won't do any damage.

by Deb Ensery

In the U.S., wheeled solo craft are ultralights regulated under FAR 103 whereas tandem wheeled machines are considered Sport Pilot aircraft, requiring certification of both plane and pilot. See FootFlyer.com, Eductional, Chapter 8, for the latest rules.

In some countries even *solo* wheeled craft are regulated more than foot launchers; check your local regs.

Some pilots have a hard time leaving "man's best friend" behind (1). No tandem rating is required but be sure the pooch perch is secure—you never know when a stray cat could upset the cart. This particular canine, *Boots*, is rather at home here.

2 & 3. There's always someone at the extremes, in this case either too many, or too few wheels. The Author, Jeff Goin, roller blades aloft and Instructor Mo Sheldon, rides the world's only paramotor unicycle.

Landing

Wheel landings are easier than foot landings since you don't have to run it out. A little more speed, or a little heavier machine is no big deal.

Do a normal pattern then, if room permits, add some power to shallow the descent during the last 50 feet and *hold the power steady* to a touchdown. Use brakes like a normal landing then shut off the power. As always, if a left/right oscillation develops on final, ease up both brakes and *do not* try to correct it.

A power-off landing is the same as on foot but your eyeballs will be a bit closer to the ground. Glide will be slightly faster and steeper due to the extra weight and drag. Land into the wind to avoid a sideways touchdown which could flip you over.

While rolling out after landing, slow down then get the wing to fall over sideways. Turn slightly towards it to unload it and avoid dragging fabric. In breezy conditions, use minimal brake input as the wing comes down. You may need to pull one brake in, hand-over-hand, to disable it. If the wing falls straight back, you may get pulled backwards and end up flipping or tipping onto the cage and rear wheels—a *turtle* (*see previous page*). After landing with much wind, be ready to unbuckle, get out and secure the wing.

Risk Comparison

Flying with wheels does not appear to be any safer or riskier than foot launching. The risks are just different. Foot launchers have more minor mishaps related to falling on takeoff or landing while wheel pilots tend to roll over more often, usually during an oscillation on launch or landing. If the craft merely rolls over, injuries are rare unless the pilot sticks out a leg or hand.

The worst accidents involving carts happen when pilots expect too much performance, namely climb rate, and hit something. They end up in trees, power lines or water since exuberant hope never trumps lackluster performance.

The safest carts have rollover *resistance* (quads or a wide wheelbase), rollover *protection*, and enough shock absorption to handle vertical impacts. Other safety concerns are identical to foot launching. One nicety of wheels is that it's easier to carry a reserve parachute since you don't have to heft it.

Tandem operations are safer on wheels but may not be legal (check your country's regulations). Tandem foot launch includes the significant risk of the student/passenger sitting down early, imposing more weight than the pilot, who's still running, can probably bear. That usually means a face plant for the student and equipment damage. Thankfully, injuries are rare.

Walk or Roll

Besides making easy work of calm conditions, wheels add impressive capabilities, especially carrying capacity, for those wanting to explore them.

We'll all be rolling at some point if we want to keep flying into our sunset years. So, even for those who only plan on foot launching, take a good look at your wheeled options, they're pretty darn good.

Section II

Spreading Your Wings

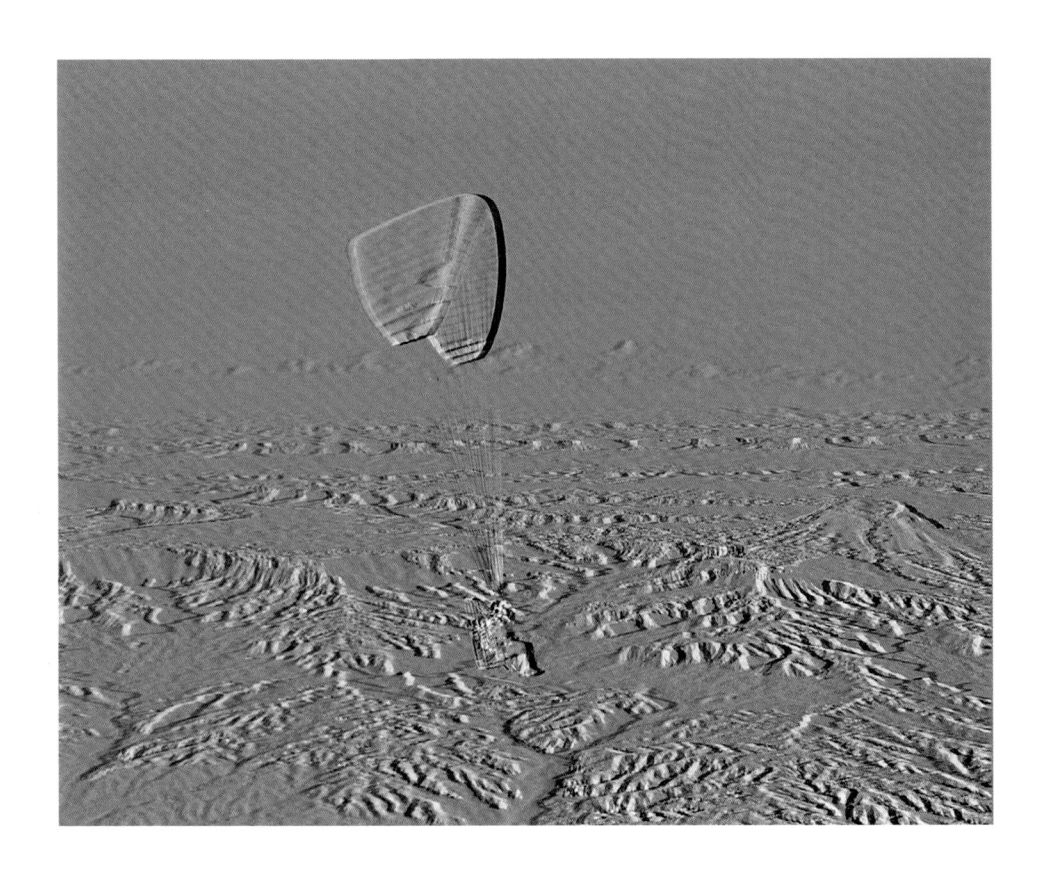

Section II
Spreading Your Wings

You've left training and plan to loose yourself on the world. Now what? Learning is far from over!

This Section covers what you'll need to know before heading out on your own. Remain under the instructor's watchful eye until these issues are well understood and, if at all possible, seek out other pilots whose brains you can pick. A willingness to learn from others is far more helpful than prideful distance. Be careful though, some input will be useful, some will be useless, and some may even be harmful. If something sounds fishy, ask your instructor or a trusted pilot before acting on it.

Ideally, you will practice on your own for a while then go back to your instructor who will excise bad habits and refresh proper techniques. By going back you can fix those shortcomings and introduce some more advanced techniques and refinements.

If ground schools or ratings clinics are held in your area, these are great ways to further your growth in the sport too.

If you haven't seen the USPPA's "Risk & Reward," you should. It covers some of this material in an entertaining, easy-to-understand format.

Weather Basics

CHAPTER 7

Most of the weather information we need for safe flying is available on local TV or the Internet. This chapter helps apply that information to your flying, especially for making the critical go/no-go decision. It's the bare minimum knowledge to have prior to setting out alone. A more thorough treatment is found in Chapter 24 and comprehensive coverage in Dennis Pagen's "Understanding the Sky."

One way to improve your understanding of local weather is by talking with other local ultralight pilots. They have probably formed some very useful observations on what to look out for.

It was good that he didn't fly. Soon after this picture was taken, a gust front blew through with 25+ mph winds.

The Perfect Day

In general, we want calm or steady light winds with little change expected during our time aloft. That means mornings and evenings during stable weather. Stable weather can be based on what the forecast says about clouds, wind and rain. Beaches can be flown all day but have their own risks.

Obviously rain is bad. It's uncomfortable, hard on vision, degrades the wing's collapse recovery ability and makes parachutal stall (parachute-like vertical descent) more likely. Heavier rain can cause pooling in the trailing edge which is even worse. The motor doesn't think much of it, either.

Rain *showers* are more ominous yet, portending cumulous clouds with significant vertical development and their associated dangerous gusts.

Pay particular attention to the wind forecast because changes there mean something is amiss. A forecast calling for calm in the morning followed by 5 to 10 mph in the afternoon and then calm in the evening is perfect. Having the same winds all day, provided they're light (less than 10 mph), is almost as good.

The wind normally increases during the day, a good reason to limit flying to the first and last three hours of daylight. Be leery of any wind forecast over 10 mph or a large change in speed or direction. Wait until after the change so that you can assess its strength before taking off. You do not want to be surprised while aloft.

Thermals & The Daily Cycle

Every day the sun comes up and starts heating the ground, churning up rising air currents that gather strength as the day heats up, peaking by around 2PM. These *thermals* are felt as turbulence when you're airborne and gusts while on the ground. In fact, a good indication of thermal strength is wind gusts: big gusts on the ground suggest big turbulence aloft. These gusts can be spread out by 15 to 30 minutes so don't be fooled by a few minutes of calm while standing in the field.

Under many conditions, thermal turbulence can become dangerous. Fortunately it builds predictably, making for nice mornings and evenings.

This daily cycle happens whether or not clouds are present but is diminished on overcast days. Sometimes, a sunny afternoon will sprout cumulus clouds (fluffy white with a piled-up look) that mark thermal tops.

Occasionally, on calm mornings, there can be a strong wind just a few hundred feet up (*see sidebar*). Thermals will soon mix with this fast-moving air causing strong, gusty surface winds. So if you launch early and encounter a strongish wind a few hundred feet high, expect strongish, turbulent conditions a few hours after sunrise.

Indications of Turbulence

Turbulence lurks in many places, but fortunately, with a little knowledge, can usually be predicted. Clouds are an important clue although dangerous atmospheric shenanigans take place in the clear, too.

Cumulus

Cumulus clouds, typical of warm, summer days, indicate a tumultuous atmosphere. Soaring pilots use them to mark rising air currents used to keep them aloft. Cumulus clouds that get tall (lots of vertical development) have strong turbulence and warrant a wide berth.

Dust Devils

Dust devils are miniature tornadoes swirling near the surface. Created by strong thermals, they are the visible evidence of very dangerous air. While some are wide, slow twirlers, most are quickly rotating funnels of air. Dry climates see them more frequently because thermal action is stronger and there is a source of visible matter to pick up. You don't even want be clipped into a wing, let alone flying, when one of these devils slice through.

Testing conditions

If you have any doubt about conditions, spend 10 to 15 minutes at your launch site feeling what the winds are doing and how much change is happening. Sudden shifts in direction or speed mean a bumpy ride aloft.

1. Cumulus Clouds.

2. Cumulus Clouds gone bad. We don't even mess with these (thunderstorms) in Boeings.

3. Dust devils, created by strong thermals, are deadly to paramotor pilots. Conditions strong enough to generate such turbulence are best avoided. Don't even be hooked in when these are likely.

4. It's nowhere near as strong as a real jetstream, but can be quite surprising. This occasional phenomena won't be found on aviation weather products.

Another tool for testing is to kite your wing. You can use a harness or just use your hands (one reason the technique can be beneficial). Only clip into a harness if you're certain the conditions will remain benign. If you can steadily kite your wing, or there is never enough wind to kite it, then conditions are probably OK.

Be careful though, it *can* still be bumpy even when the surface air seems mellow, so don't use this test alone. It may be that gusts are simply farther apart than a 15 minute wait would reveal. Like dust devils that are sparsely spaced, you could be out there all day and never feel one. That's why we typically avoid mid-day.

Thunderstorms

Thunderstorms are nature's most violent atmospheric production, especially when they spawn tornadoes.

Cumuli morph into cumulonimbus (rain producing cumulus) and get ugly in the process. Flying anywhere near them is almost suicidal. Pilots have died from getting sucked up to the heights and frozen. Even a small thunderhead is likely to go above 30,000 feet where the average temperature falls below -40°F (which also happens to be -40°C). Plus they can produce severe turbulence far beyond the capability of a paraglider to maneuver through.

Thunderstorms frequently produce gust fronts that precede the actual storm by up to 20 miles. The sudden wind change from such a gust front can be violent and impossible to outrun.

Mountain air, covered on the next page, demands great respect. Mo Sheldon (left) and Phil Russman (right) are enjoying a spectacular evening south of Phoenix, Arizona. Smooth, calm conditions prevail but, had the wind been from their right, cascading over these mountains, they would have been fighting a sinking, turbulent cauldron.

Downwind (lee side) of any large obstruction or terrain feature is no place to be in a paraglider.

With any wind at all, think of how air will flow around the terrain and where it will cause turbulence, lift and sink. A strong wind in mountainous areas (over about 12 MPH) can generate severe downstream turbulence.

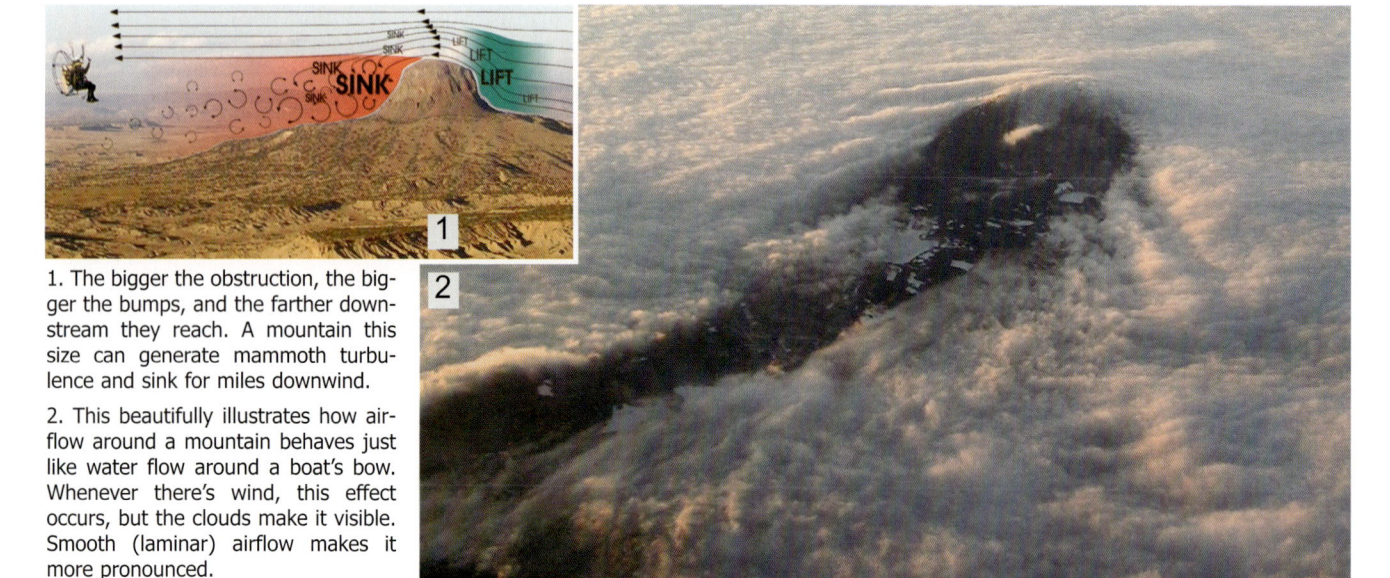

1. The bigger the obstruction, the bigger the bumps, and the farther downstream they reach. A mountain this size can generate mammoth turbulence and sink for miles downwind.

2. This beautifully illustrates how airflow around a mountain behaves just like water flow around a boat's bow. Whenever there's wind, this effect occurs, but the clouds make it visible. Smooth (laminar) airflow makes it more pronounced.

Soaring pilots will appreciate the rising portions of airflow well away from the source mountain. Motor pilots could save fuel by flying along the lines of rising air.

An inversion is present here where the air aloft is warmer than the air below which is why the stratus clouds have formed in the first place. When the turbulent flow behind the mountain mixes up the two layers, a clear area forms. It reveals the nastiness that can be found downwind of obstructions. This also shows how far away the effects of a large geographic shape can be felt.

Don't be tempted to fly immediately after storms pass, either. It seems innocuous at times—the thunderstorm rages through followed by a quiet calm with benign-looking clouds. Don't fall for it. Give time for the wind to shift and see what upwind stations are experiencing to insure there are no surprises. A localized, individual cell that is not associated with a front may leave flyable conditions but you should still wait at least an hour.

If there is severe weather behind one set of storms, even if it is many miles behind, don't fly. The danger is that while it *may* indeed remain mellow enough to fly, we can't tell. Going up is a dreadful gamble in such conditions.

Mountains

Wind in the mountains means turbulence in their lee (downwind). It can be completely calm at your launch site because of a wind shadow, but up a few hundred feet the air could be violent. A combination of local knowledge and forecasted winds aloft will help keep you out of such air.

For example, if you're launching at 4000 ft in an area surrounded by mountains, and the winds aloft at 6000 feet are forecast to be over 20 knots, then expect strong turbulence. If the winds are forecast to be westerly then make sure you're flying on the west side of the hills. If possible, it's hugely valuable to get to the top of a hill and see for yourself what the winds are doing up there.

Mountainous areas also have unique local conditions because of cool air flowing downhill and warmed air wicking up the sides (see Chapter 24). Even gradually sloping terrain can have local daily flow cycles from this effect.

Beach

Beach air is the best. On normal, sunny days, heated land sucks in the smooth sea breeze, lasting past sunset. Unfettered by thermal heating, this flow is normally steady and consistent—making for perfect flying. But if the forecast calls for wind blowing out to sea, look out: that is a *very* dangerous condition to fly in.

Check the weather inland and make sure there is no off-shore flow there. If an inland site predicts an off-shore breeze (land-breeze—from land to sea) and it is currently blowing from sea to land, that could be trouble. At some point these winds meet to form a *convergence zone*. At best it will produce uncomfortable turbulence, at worst, the outflow (away from land) could blow you out to sea. These conditions are hard to forecast and can quickly turn a benign wind around. The turbulence of that turnaround is bad enough, but getting blown out to sea could be disastrous (see Chapter 19).

Whenever conditions diverge from normal—winds seem different, clouds are forming too early, temperatures are unseasonal, etc.—be suspicious.

Whenever There's Wind

Here are some common, significant phenomena that show up whenever the wind blows. From the air, use flags, smoke, trees and other vegetation to reveal when the wind has picked up. Crops can be used to tell direction along with other methods shown at right and covered on the next page.

Mechanical Turbulence And Rotor

Just like a rock in a stream, whenever air blows past an obstruction it becomes turbulent (bumpy) downstream. More wind or bigger obstructions mean worse turbulence extending further past the obstruction and even *above* the obstruction. Rotor, wind shadow and mechanical turbulence all have specific meanings (covered in Chapter 24); the latter two are mistakenly referred to simply as rotor.

Wind Gradient

Friction slows airflow as it rubs against the ground. In the morning, when cool air sits at the surface, it can be calm while only a few hundred feet above it's blowing 20 MPH. As the ground heats up in the morning, the fast moving air aloft (if present) mixes with the still air below and a surface wind develops.

A strong wind aloft on a sunny morning can quickly yield a bumpy blow an hour or so later—be ready or be landed.

Wind Shear

A dramatic change in wind speed or direction from one altitude (or area) to another is wind shear. The transition is called a shear zone and will likely be quite turbulent. Wind shear associated with thunderstorms have brought down jet airplanes.

The forecast winds aloft give some indication of a shear's presence as do clouds moving in different directions at different altitudes. Days that are brewing thunderstorms can portend dramatic windshear in many directions, even without storms nearby.

Pilots experience it most often during climb; passing through some altitude you get strongly bounced around (hopefully that's all) and then notice that you're now drifting over the ground in a different direction, possibly even going backwards. Look for this when it's cooled a lot from the previous day's high temperature and the forecast winds aloft are strong (over about 15 mph).

---

1. Anything that sticks up into the wind will cause down stream turbulence—from mountains to trees and buildings to buses. Not only will there be turbulence on the lee (downwind) side, but there will be sink—descending air that may make it impossible to stay level.

2. While away from your windsock, still water is one of several ways to tell wind direction. It will be calmer next to the shore on the upwind side.

3. Smoke, steam and blowing dust also work well for wind indicators. But if you see blowing dust, be ready for a ride. And don't fly through smoke plumes—they may harbor horrendous turbulence depending on their source.

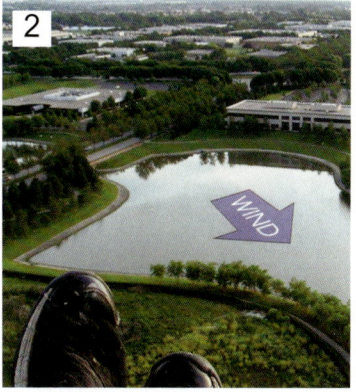

1. You can never have too many wind indicators. Especially when the wind is light and variable, it's nice to see what's happening at the LZ. Surveyors tape or similar material make great streamers (also called "telltales").

2. It took 13 - 15 MPH to get this big flag waving.

3. Marketing flags are great for adding a feel of excitement. They're even better for wind indicators. Landing pilots are another good indication but they don't last long.

Telling Wind Direction

A windsock or streamers at your launch site is best—both for launch and for when you come back. Wind direction frequently changes during your flight, sometimes dramatically, so it's good to keep tabs on it wind while you're up. Here are some clues to help:

- Lakes will be calm on the upwind side. Bigger waves overall mean more wind. Also, if boats are anchored off shore they will be pointing into the wind.

- Flags flap downwind of their pole but, be careful, big flags require a big wind to wave. What looks light on a big flag may be quite strong.

- Smoke is the most sensitive indicator. Plus it shows direction at different heights but, never, *ever*, fly in the updraft created by a large fire. The intensity, even up several thousand feet, can be extreme. Admittedly, the bumps given off by small fires are not that bad but large or particularly hot fires can create severe turbulence even many thousands of feet high.

- Crops and weeds can show direction, intensity and gusts. It's quite interesting to watch a gust form on wheat or beans and spread across the field.

- Moving cloud shadows work but can only tell the wind at cloud height.

- In desert areas, blowing sand and tumbleweed show wind but if there is visible blowing sand, a strong, bumpy wind is brewing.

- Ground track (direction of slowest groundspeed) will reveal the wind speed and direction at your altitude (see Chapter 10).

Lift & Sink

When air flows up over an obstruction it produces lift in front of the obstruction and sink behind it along with rotor and turbulence. The strength of each depends on the shape of the obstruction and strength of the wind. Soaring pilots make use of this lift (called ridge or

---

Universal Time: Converting to Zulu

Aviation and aviation weather use *Coordinated Universal Time,* abbreviated UTC and also known as *Zulu Time.* It's the time in Greenwich, England and does not recognize Daylight Saving Time (DST) so the conversion is different in summer and winter.

In the U.S. DST runs from the second Sunday of March to the first Sunday in November. In Europe it's called Summer Time where it runs from the last Sunday in March to the Last Sunday in October. ST is Standard time.

Convert to Zulu time by adding the following hours to your local time.

Zulu is:	Pacific	Mountain	Central	Eastern
In Summer (DST)	Local+7	Local+6	Local+5	Local+4
In Winter (ST)	Local+8	Local+7	Local+6	Local+5

The Flight Service Station (FSS) Briefing Made Easy

Here is a sample briefing for an early morning flight using 1-800-WX-BRIEF (U.S. only). Listen to the recording and select the appropriate menu options to get a human. It will go something like this.

Pilot:
"Hi, I'm ultralight pilot Fred Flyer," (Briefer write/types this down to record an activity). "I'll be flying from a field 8 miles northeast of Aurora Airport for a couple hours starting at about 7AM local and would like a standard briefing."

You can also ask for an *abbreviated* briefing which has only the main weather.

Briefer:
"How high will you be flying?" (Because you didn't mention that)

Pilot:
"No more than 1000 ft AGL (above ground level)."

Briefer:
"OK, You've got high pressure over the area with a cold front well to the north...(describes an overview)"

"Currently Aurora is reporting sky clear, visibility 6 miles in haze, winds are 220 at 7 knots, altimeter setting is 29.92 and the temperature is 22 with a dewpoint of 14." (temperatures are given in Celsius)."

"The Aurora forecast calls for clear skies, winds light and variable until 1400Z then becoming 230 at 10."

Pilot:
"What time is that local?" (If you don't know, ask, but it's better form to know the conversion before calling).

Briefer:
"That's 8am local. Then after that, calm."

"The winds aloft in your area, Joliet, should be 280 at 16, temperature +12 at 3000 feet."

"There is a NOTAM for taxiway closures at Aurora (in following a standard format they have to include information that may not be of much use) and the VASI to runway 26 is out of service"

Pilot:
OK, thank you very much, that will do it for me.

---

1. Wind direction is always given as the direction it is *from*. Nearly all aviation reports and forecasts use the 360 degrees of a compass rose relative to true north. Magnetic north is where a compass points and true north is what lines on a map are drawn with.

So a south wind would be given as 180° and a West wind would be 270°.

2. Flight Service personnel have access to many tools that give them a more complete picture of the weather, notices about airspace and other issues affecting flyers. They are not meteorologists but can provide a wealth of information.

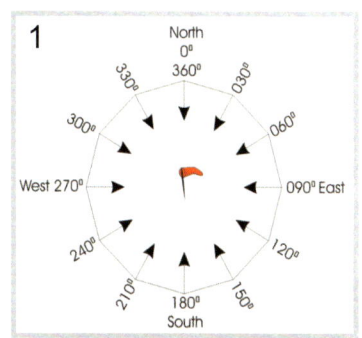

Orographic lift) to stay airborne but it must be given great respect—any lift powerful enough to keep a pilot aloft can also produce deadly turbulence if you end up in the wrong place.

Acquiring Aviation Weather

There is great value in *aviation* forecasts—they tell winds at altitude, estimated times for frontal passages, wind shifts and other useful info. The same call can be used for finding out about airspace restrictions, too (see Chapter 9).

In the U.S., our Federal Aviation Administration (FAA) funds a valuable resource through Flight Service Stations (FSS). These privately run facilities offer pilots a ready source for official aviation weather. Don't be daunted by the sound of that; it's not hard and they don't mind hearing from you (they helped edit this section).

To make it easier, have the following info on hand before calling:

- Launch location relative to an airport or VOR (if flying cross country.) The FSS folks primarily have airports and navigation aids charted. For example, if you're 10 miles south of your city's airport, tell them that.

- Approximate Launch time and how long you'll be flying. Although they work with the worldwide standard time, Universal Coordinated Time (UTC) they can translate to local; just be sure to say "local."

- Your planned maximum altitude above sea level (ASL). You can also use your height above ground level (AGL) but tell them that ("I'll be flying less than 500 ft AGL").

Air flows over the cool, wet ocean, gathering water vapor and condensing into a low cloud layer. It gets pushed up the mountains where moisture is spent making these clouds thicker. By the time it gets a few miles inland, there's little moisture left. So when the air starts descending back down the other side, it warms and immediately goes back into invisible water vapor again.

During the first major U.S. powered paraglider gathering, held in 2000, clues of a gust front went ignored. As pilots prepared to launch for a new record number of PPGs aloft, a line of cumulus clouds was massing upwind. Some didn't like the looks of it and stayed put.

One pilot offered to call Flight Service on his cell phone. He was rebuffed—the clouds just didn't look that bad. After the first launch, lemmings soon followed and, sure enough, ten minutes later, with 15 or so already airborne, a strong gust front came through.

Several didn't make it back to the field, landing in various places downwind. A few suffered minor injuries in the resulting high-wind fracas and only one made it back to the launch area. They were *all* quite lucky.

What they missed by skipping that call to Flight Service, was a newly formed and very local cold front. The forecast (we called afterwards to see what it said) cautioned that a 20 knot wind shift was expected. It was right.

Be wary of changing conditions or incorrect current weather. If the forecast for right now listed as winds south at 5 knots but the actual wind is northwest at 12, be suspicious of the entire forecast. See what's coming by checking upstream stations where the weather is coming from.

While on the phone, ask for another useful FSS product, the "VAD" (Velocity Azimuth Display) winds report. Winds are derived from special radar that uses airborne particulates to determine winds aloft over a wide area. VAD winds are helpful because they are actual winds given in thousand-foot increments (instead of 3000 feet for the regular winds aloft forecasts). Just ask if they have any VAD winds for your area.

Other Weather Sources

The Internet provides several great sources for weather information. Flight Service is good when you're out in the field (use a cell phone) or need to get NOTAMS, but consider looking at web sites that show surface winds throughout the day. Footflyer.com lists some good sources for both motor flying and soaring.

It is valuable to compare forecasts, though. Most of them get their data from the national weather service but may apply different interpretations. If one forecast calls for a big change in winds and another does not, one probably has old information. If there was no change in a forecast before, expect that the forecast containing the changes is probably newer.

Common Sense & The Law

CHAPTER 8

We operate at the pleasure of the people—a nervous and sensitive people. And unfortunately, it's all too easy for them to keep us grounded through laws on everything from noise to disturbing animals. Even if no prohibition exists, if you annoy enough of the right people, a law will be enacted.

It is expected of civilization to collectively establish and enforce such laws. For example, we may not like the neighbor running his chain saw every morning by our window so we collectively enact noise regulations to stop him.

Aggravating people is rarely beneficial—there are a lot more of them (non-flyers) than us. We must minimize aggravation, police ourselves and encourage others to behave for long-term survival. We have seen entire states ban flying on their beaches due to the inconsiderate actions of one pilot. Don't be that pilot. And when you see that pilot, let him know how much you despise his actions.

Keeping a Low Profile

Avoid over-using any one area if there are neighbors. Even if you have permission—launch and leave whenever possible. If confronted, try to work it out and don't flaunt our minimal regulation—it's the sport's crown jewel.

Animals have people and vice versa. Annoying either can be downright expensive. For example, if you spook someone's million-dollar horse into to an injurious rampage, expect a visit from the riled owner and/or his lawyer; the possible loss of that flying site may be the least of your concerns.

Fly quietly. Stay high, use minimal thrust in noise sensitive areas, and make your machine as quiet as it can be—air intake silencers, mufflers, and big props all help in this regard.

Like any human interaction, treating law enforcement with respect will smooth the encounter. You may be legal, but if they dislike your presence they'll find a way to make it difficult. They *may* just be curios about your strange flying machine.

In one case, an officer showed up at a pilot's flying site and the pilot got all defensive. Turns out the officer was a fellow pilot just checking out his launch technique.

Being able to show a copy of our regulations and the relevant air chart can let them know you're exercising due diligence to stay legal.

While the FAA (Federal Aviation Administration) governs U.S. Airspace, locals govern local launch sites. Many municipalities have laws that prohibit launching any type of human-carrying flying machine from within their jurisdiction except airports. Just as often the locals are unaware of those laws. Don't force them to figure it out!

Don't take the approach: "It's my land, I'll do what I want." That may be true but only to a point—neighbors don't always need to be right next door to cause problems—they just have to convince the right people that you're either violating some existing law or they will try to enact a new law. Numerous laws have blossomed for exactly this reason.

Regulations

In the U.S., a simple two-page Federal Aviation Regulation (FAR 103—see appendix) covers ultralights, defined as any powered single-occupant aircraft (termed vehicle) weighing under 254 pounds; that obviously includes us. The most recent version can be found at www.faa.gov. Its intent is that only participants incur risk, not others. So every interpretation of your flying must conclude that you weren't endangering anyone else.

The absence of specific training requirements is no excuse for ignorance of the law. Flying in any country's national airspace system is a privilege to be taken seriously. What a travesty it would be for someone to buy gear, train enough to get airborne, then crash into an airliner. Besides the obvious tragedy, public pressure to shut us down would be extreme. We must not only learn the rules and follow them, but must help our fellow flyers do the same.

Perception is important: If you look like you're doing something dangerous, you'll draw undesirable attention. Steer clear of the law by not getting reported. Avoid *looking* like you're doing something bad; that usually improves safety, too, and you won't disturb people or their animals. "Showing off," chasing critters, and flying close to gatherings are all ways to get noticed, possibly unfavorably. While we *can* fly close to objects, we must do so with discretion.

One common misconception is that we must maintain 500 ft away from anything on the ground. While that is a good conservative approach, it is not the law (as it is for fixed-wing aircraft). Being able to legally fly down a fence row at 5 feet is a fantastic freedom, allowing interaction with the land in amazing detail. Enjoy the freedom responsibly—don't endanger or annoy any humans.

Right of Way

All certified aircraft have the right of way. That means that if we see an airplane or helicopter, we have to stay clear or move, even if we're unpowered. Plus we must not create a collision hazard. Know where airplanes are likely to be and steer clear. Fortunately, we usually operate below their altitudes so it's easy, but near airports we have to be extra vigilant.

Among ultralights, the only rule is that powered craft must give way to unpowered ones. Common aviation practice, even though not regulatory, recommends:

- PPG's approaching head-on should each steer to the right.
- Overtake on the right.
- Landing pilots have the right of way although, when a field is crowded, landing pilots should let launchers go. Standing there while awaiting repeated touch-and-go's gets old quickly.
- The craft to the right has the right-of-way.

1. In the U.S., you can fly an additional 30 minutes before sunrise or beyond sunset by using a strobe that's visible for 3 miles and staying within class G airspace. Essentially that means staying below 700 ft AGL (1200 ft as charted).

2. Crossing fences and trespassing signs is bad enough, but crossing into this area would defy any definition of common sense. Not surprisingly, the area is near a military installation.

3. Even with the houses, ultralights have been flying out of this field for years and have had no complaint by any FAA officials. Those white hangars (yellow circle) belong to members of an ultralight club. Credit the responsible behavior of club pilots that it lasted well beyond the buildup of houses.

What is Congested?

It's the million dollar question. In the U.S., FAR 103.15 tells us "No person may operate an ultralight vehicle over any congested area of a city, town, or settlement, or over any open air assembly of persons." There is no altitude that allows overflight and no definition of congested—it's intentionally left to the eye of the enforcer. Some regional FAA offices consider even one house to constitute "congested," while others say that 6 houses qualifies, and others have no set number.

The rule makers crafted a simple but broad wording and the term, *congested area*, has many possible meanings. We will inject some practical experience into the interpretation that should be defensible by both the letter and intent of the law. Again, this is merely an interpretation, a *congested area* is:

- Any group of occupied buildings where there would not be enough room to easily launch or land. Remember, this defines the level of congestion, not the operational conduct. It should not be construed as suggesting flight over a congested area just because you have a good landing option nearby. You can never fly *over* a congested area at any altitude. But, if it is not sparse enough to easily land there, it should be considered congested even for overflight.

- An open-air assembly of people is any gathering of two or more people. That includes golfers, beachgoers, sporting events, parties, and spectators (even at *fly-ins!*) Again, flying high enough usually avoids the problem because you don't appear threatening and spread very little noise—nobody is likely to report you.

- One interesting situation is roads. There is much precedence that suggests overflight of roads is OK, but with caveats. There are fields with approved (by FAA control towers) ultralight flight patterns that go over major roads, even interstates like the OSH example at right. They usually specify some minimum altitude (300 feet is common). At major Fly-Ins there are ultralight flight patterns that go over well-traveled roads as well. But it requires reason: if you distract, annoy or endanger a motorist, then they may call the area congested. If there is enough traffic that something falling off your machine would likely hit a car and damage it, then it might be called congested. Your best bet is to climb to at least 300 feet AGL before crossing roads and do not operate in a manner that disturbs the groundlings or brings undue attention.

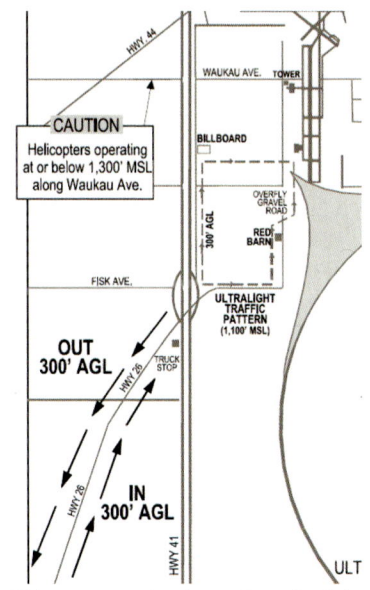

This excerpt is from the ultralight departure/arrival corridor at the world's largest airshow in Oshkosh, WI. It was in an FAA issued NOTAM (Notice to Airmen) and clearly shows a flight path over roads, including the well-traveled Highway 41. But pilots *have* been violated for flying over roads at times when they were considered "congested" so be careful.

Again, flying high makes you much less noticeable. It's not so much whether you are violating the law as it is whether you *look* like you are violating the law. Sad, but that's how it works.

Case Law & Other Issues

Verdicts handed down to pilots who ran afoul of the law warrant study. Even though U.S. flyers abide by Part 103, cases involving violations of other air regulations have been used as precedent for ultralight pilots—used to impose fines (or other sanctions) by virtue of their definitions.

In one case, a definition of congested was given by saying that: "30 to 40 homes, located on relatively small and adjoining lots, constitutes a 'congested area' within the meaning of the regulation." Unfortunately no dimensions were given but little is

Flying over congested areas is prohibited at any altitude. In this case, the pilot, David McWhinnie, and I took off from a clear area adjacent to the beach and kept the flight out over Lake Michigan. The zoom was used to bring Chicago much closer than it actually was.

needed; there's no doubting that most suburban developments would qualify.

Another case is even less encouraging. It is a bit more complicated because it involved an agricultural airplane that operates under different regulations but is not allowed over congested areas. The judge labeled the following as congested: An area 0.6 miles long and 0.3 miles wide (about 115 acres) with 60 houses—pretty sparse by most definitions. That would equate to lot sizes of just over an acre. This definition was used to say a PPG pilot was flying over a congested area.

An FAA web site offers some relief regarding congested. It says that an operation (this was given for aerobatic pilots) can be done over an area as small as an acre, even if surrounded by houses. That means flying along a right of way, beside railroad tracks or a path that keeps you away from buildings would be allowable. Just don't fly over the nearby houses and, above all, don't do anything that would make people complain to authorities. It is worth reading and heeding these rules; each violation carries a fine of $1000 or more and can get your equipment confiscated.

Endangerment & Dropping Objects

Anything you do that might endanger (or be perceived as endangering) another person would violate FAR 103.9(a), a catch-all regulation that says "No person may operate any ultralight vehicle in a manner that creates a hazard to other persons or property." Nearly every country has similar verbiage.

FAR 103.9(b) prohibits dropping things *if* they could be harmful. It says "No person may allow an object to be dropped from an ultralight vehicle if such action creates a hazard to other persons or property." That is why bean-bag dropping contests are legal.

What is "Flying Over?"

When are you "over" some prohibited area and how far away do you need to be? By one measure you must be *directly* over it. But if an observer thinks you are too close to something, then you will be labeled "flying over." For example, houses may be well to your right but, to an observer on your left, you may *appear* over them.

So here's a measure to use for keeping a reasonable distance horizontally from off-limits places: Use the distance you would travel in 5 seconds of flying time. In our 20 mph craft we go about 30 feet per second; that would be 150 ft. Up higher that should be increased to maybe 10 seconds at 300 ft. So if you're flying alongside a road that is busy enough to worry about, stay at least 5 seconds of flying time horizontally away from it. Also, don't let the trajectory of potential falling parts endanger people.

Like so many aspects of life, attitude can be the difference between a lip lashing and enforcement action. If local authorities question your operation, be respectful and explain how you were doing your best to follow the pertinent air regulation—they may not be aware of the specifics but don't assume that. And don't come off as arrogant—they may be quite knowledgeable. Offer to avoid the area and, if it seems appropriate, ask where a good alternative launch site might be.

1: He is not flying directly over any houses but certainly an observer might think otherwise. The best practice is to stay well away from anybody you consider hostile to your presence.

Either be up high or make sure than nobody can prove you were over their house. Being higher does not allow overflight, but sure reduces your likelihood of being accused.

2: You can drop things provided they don't endanger property or people on the surface.

Have a copy of the regulations, an altimeter, an air map excerpt of the area (sectional chart in the U.S.) and know how to read it. If confronted, and it feels appropriate, show them how you were staying within the law. It may be enough.

If you wind up being investigated or have to answer a letter of investigation, be prompt, be honest, but *be minimal!* It's quite possible that your response to that letter is the best thing they have against you. The vast majority of FAA folks that I have encountered are not "out to get" pilots. They are trying to do their job appropriately and with the least amount of effort. If you are belligerent, though, your prosecution may *become* their mission.

Commercial Use

Commercial use is prohibited in Part 103.

The FAA does not bother defining commercial use, rather it says our activity must be *only* for recreation or sport. This makes the stroke very broad and difficult to avoid. Don't confuse it with other rules such as those prohibiting private pilots from commercial activities—our rule is far more limiting. We are only allowed to fly for "recreation or sport." Flying for movies or photography missions is questionable even if no payment is made for the flying. A law judge must only decide that your flight was not for recreation or sport.

Regulators figured that, with no license given, there is little accountability and few safeguards to the public, so ultralight flying would not be inappropriate for commercial use.

Where the payment issue comes into play is when defending the "sport or recreational" nature of a flight. Getting paid makes it difficult to justify that purpose.

The most common question is about aerial photography. The temptation is to say that you are not getting paid to fly but rather are selling a service and just happened to have pictures from your PPG. If you were out flying for fun, taking pictures, and later discovered a really cool shot, it would technically be valid to sell it. If you flew solely to get pictures then it's not even the selling that is illegal, it's that the purpose of the flight was not for sport or recreation.

So the rule is quite limiting. The people most likely to report your activity are those who do aerial photography, aerial advertisers, and the like using certified aircraft and pilots. They have a lot to lose if someone drains away their business with inexpensive, unregulated capabilities.

Instructing

The only way to get paid to fly is by giving tandem instruction if allowed to do so in your country. Experienced pilots can go through an approved program that allows them to fly students using two-seat craft. Such flights are done under a special exemption for instruction only. In the U.S., approved programs are run by member organizations such as the U.S. Powered Paragliding Association (USPPA), and do not fall under the far more-involved Sport Pilot regulation which applies to heavier craft.

You can also get paid to teach PPG if you do not fly—there is no restriction on teaching someone from the ground. Of course there are many pitfalls to instructing which is why going through a thorough certification process is important.

Digging Deeper

FAA Advisory Circular AC 103-7, dated 1/30/84, spells out many details under which FAR 103 was concocted and gives some interesting background. It reveals the why of the regulation's restrictive stance. It is available at www.faa.gov.

Tandem instruction is one way to get paid for flying; teaching flying in this case. You can give introductory flights, too, but must have some form of certification in nearly all countries including the U.S.

In the U.S., wheeled two-seat operations fall under the Sport Pilot Rule which excludes foot launched PPG's. Tandem PPG operations are only allowed under an exemption from the single-occupant rule in FAR part 103. That exemption, administered by organizations such as the USPPA, must be renewed every other year. See FootFlyer.com or USPPA.org for the current status.

Our freedom is a double-edged sword that *can* cut deeply.

When one PPG pilot ran afoul of local law, police contacted FAA officials. The case went all the way to trial and FAA lawyers used prior rulings (below) to prosecute the pilot. Even though those jugglement weren't directly about FAR 103, they did include a reference to *congested*.

The pilot was fined over $1000 and had to pay his legal fees. There is, unfortunately, little recourse in such cases and one avenue, the National Transportation Safety Board (NTSB), is not likely to help.

Getting Someone Else to Pay

While you cannot get paid for flying, you can offset your flying costs by having a company buy your wing or motor for you. Their logo and text may be emblazoned all over it providing that they don't tell you when or where to fly it. It has nothing to do with getting paid—if you fly for the purpose of gaining exposure, it is a violation of the rule. If you're thinking that would be hard to enforce, you're right. But do something blatant where the purpose is obvious and you'll bring scrutiny.

If I Violate the Rules?

Professional pilots have the most to lose: FAA officials will go after their certificates because it's the easiest and most effective course. A good aviation attorney is a must in that situation.

Writing on the wing and having your sponsor buy the wing is about the only way to get someone else to help pay for your flying legally.

Generally the FAA is obliged to investigate any complaint and, once the wheels have started, there are many I's to dot and T's to cross; don't expect it to just go away. However, if handled amicably, the event may be settled with minimum fuss.

The first indication will usually be obvious: The police show up and take a report. They don't always contact the aviation authorities but will certainly do so if motivated. Be polite! And don't assume they're unaware of our rules. Be sensitive but it's possible they may accuse you of violating rules that don't apply. It can work in your favor if they cite you for a rule you don't fall under.

This is where flying with a copy of the regulations, air map and an altimeter can help show you're trying to be responsible. Don't be arrogant and only offer the rules if you think they may be swayed—otherwise, they may find something else to use. Offering to show them the chart may a better approach.

Exemptions

It is difficult but possible to get exemptions from the rules providing equivalent safety is maintained. For example, airshows commonly let pilots fly in ways that would otherwise be illegal but, by virtue of a waiver, are allowed under certain guidelines aimed at protecting the public.

Airspace

CHAPTER 9

"Can I launch here?" you ask. Probably, but there are some things you must know.

In the U.S. our freedom is inspiring; we can fly just about anywhere with few restrictions and no certification requirements. But, like all freedoms, that privilege carries great responsibility; namely, knowing the airspace and adhering to its limits. Launching into a sky full of airliners without knowing the rules is pure folly; a risk for you, others, and ultimately, the entire sport. You don't need to become an expert, either—this chapter provides the essentials.

Most local airports will be unfamiliar with ultralight rules but are a great resource for learning about local airspace. Explain that you're an ultralight pilot and ask if they would share advice on good areas to fly and areas to avoid.

Purchase and become familiar with the Aeronautical Sectional Chart for your flight area. These are packed with necessary airspace boundaries and much more. Bigger cities also have detailed VFR (Visual Flight Rules) Terminal Area Charts.

While describing airspace we will dispense with height limit descriptions, such as "up to but not including," and just use "above" or "below." The full U.S. air regulation, including cloud clearance minutia, is in the appendix.

There are two common sets of cloud clearance and visibility requirements that you should know. They are abbreviated here as follows:

- **5,1,2&3** means **500** feet below, **1000** feet above, **2000** feet horizontally away from the clouds with **3** miles visibility (most Class E airspace).

- **CoC&1** means "**Clear of Clouds**" and **1** mile vis. (most Class G airspace).

Sectional charts are available from most local airports (Fixed Base Operator or flight school), the Internet, and pilot shops. Charts come out every 6 months with the latest changes, although a call to Flight Service is the only way to be completely current.

You can also see current charts on some internet sites (Skyvector.com). These are not "official" but can be a great resource.

Airspace Types

Air Traffic: Airspace rules were implemented to control air traffic in busy areas. In 1993, the United States standardized on international airspace names with the letters from A through G (F isn't used in the U.S.) What used to be called "controlled airspace" is everything except G.

> **Altitude Abbreviations**
>
> Here are the common abbreviations when referring to airspace.
>
> **AGL** is Above Ground Level.
>
> **MSL** is above Mean Sea Level. It is used interchangeably with ASL, Above Sea Level.

Security airspace is those areas that keep air traffic away from nationally sensitive sites such as the Capitol, military installations, events with large crowds, politician's residences and others. They include Temporary Flight Restrictions (TFR's) that pop up whenever a dignitary swoops in, and can be issued with very little notice. Prohibited, Restricted and Alert areas are shown on charts but the temporary airspace information comes via Notices to Airmen (NOTAMs) which are accessed via computer or by calling a Flight Service Station (see Chapter 7).

Wilderness: Some national parks and other public areas have altitude minimums for overflight. Even if you fly legally according to air regulations, disturbing wildlife may run afoul of other rules. While it's true that the FAA governs airspace (in the U.S.), they don't define "disturbing" as it relates to animals.

Other: Special airspace restrictions can pop into being for a variety of reasons including tethered balloons, high powered rocket launches, and disaster areas.

The ABC's of Airspace

Airspace isn't as complex as it may seem. In the U.S., picture a 1200 foot thick blanket covering the whole country known as G airspace. Above that is E airspace reaching up to 18,000 feet MSL. In populated areas or near airports, the "blanket" of G airspace is only 700 feet thick. These *Transition Areas* are marked on charts by a shaded magenta (purplish-pink) line to accommodate air traffic descending

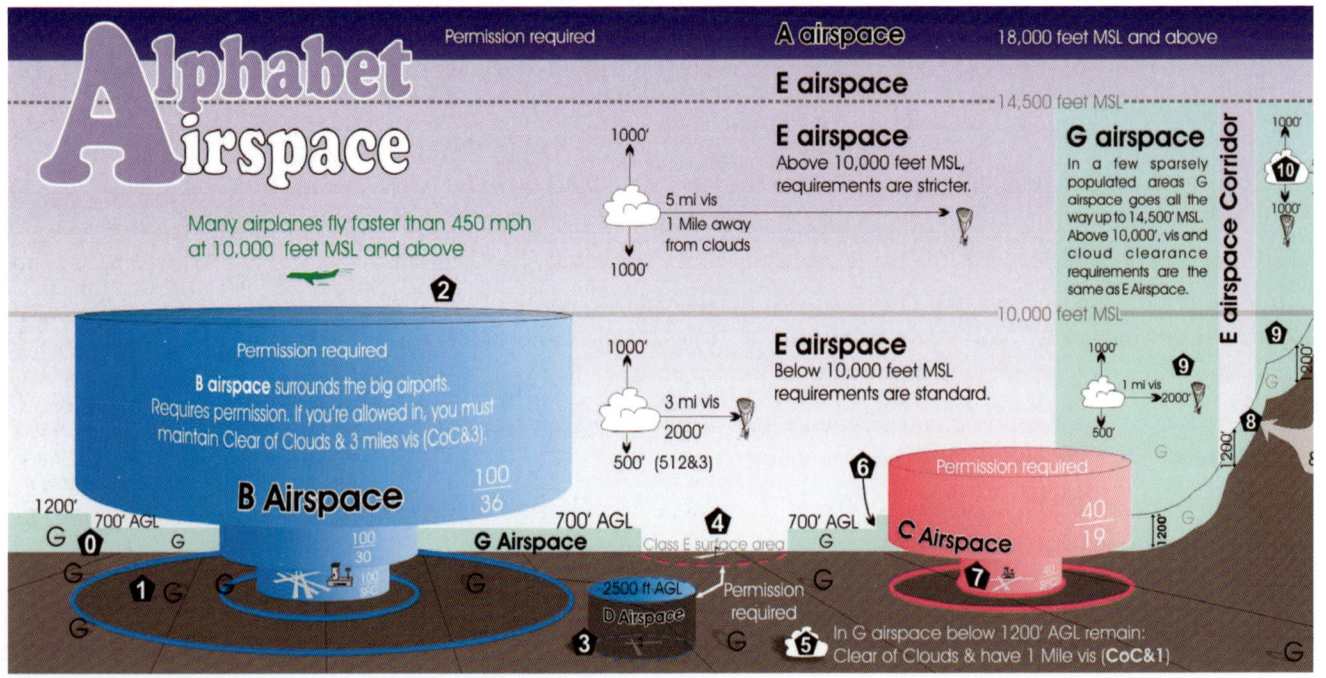

The diagram below shows most airspace types with their cloud clearance and visibility requirements.

You always need at least 1 mile of visibility and must stay clear of clouds. It gets more restrictive above 10,000 feet and we're not allowed above 18,000 feet.

Flying above 10,000 feet can be done with as little as 1 mile of visibility and clear of clouds provided you're within 1200 feet of the ground.

Positions 2 & 10, both above 10,000 feet, have identical minimums even with 2 in E and 10 in G airspace.

Positions 0, 6 & 8 have the lower Class G minimums, being below 1200 feet AGL.

You can fly below B and C airspace like position 1 and 7. You will probably launch in G and climb into E airspace until reaching the overlying B or C airspace.

You can fly at position 9 with only a mile visibility but need more cloud clearance. Position 10, being above 10,000 feet, requires much higher visibility. Position 6 points to a transition area where the floor of E drops from 1200 to 700 feet.

Alphabet Airspace

Many airplanes fly faster than 450 mph at 10,000 feet MSL and above

A airspace — Permission required — 18,000 feet MSL and above

E airspace — 14,500 feet MSL

E airspace — Above 10,000 feet MSL, requirements are stricter. — 5 mi vis, 1 Mile away from clouds, 1000', 1000'

G airspace — In a few sparsely populated areas G airspace goes all the way up to 14,500' MSL. Above 10,000', vis and cloud clearance requirements are the same as E Airspace.

E airspace Corridor

— 10,000 feet MSL —

B airspace surrounds the big airports. Requires permission. If you're allowed in, you must maintain Clear of Clouds & 3 miles vis (CoC&3). — Permission required

E airspace — Below 10,000 feet MSL requirements are standard. — 3 mi vis, 2000', 500' (512&3), 1000'

C Airspace — Permission required — 40/19

D Airspace — 2500 ft AGL — Permission required

B Airspace — 100/36, 100/30

1200' — 700' AGL — G — 700' AGL — **G Airspace** — Class E surface area — 700' AGL — G — 1200' — G

In G airspace below 1200' AGL remain: Clear of Clouds & have 1 Mile vis (CoC&1)

Positions: 0, 1, 2, 3, 4, 5, 6, 7, 8, 9, 10

Page 86 — Section II: Spreading Your Wings

lower to make approaches to nearby runways. We must either stay down lower (below the planes) or must have better visibility up higher (above 700 feet) so we can see and avoid them (covered shortly).

Paramotor pilots fly in class **G** (starts from the **G**round) and E airspace which is almost everywhere. The only difference is that E requires more visibility/cloud clearance to make "see and avoid" more effective up where air traffic flies faster.

If you live in a smaller city that has an airport but no control tower, there is probably no restriction on flying although it might be a good idea to talk with the airport manager about any special traffic flows nearby.

If you live near a city with more than about 50,000 people, there is probably a nearby airport with a control tower and its surrounding D airspace (requires permission). Bigger cities have bigger airports and more restrictions.

The Letter Meanings

Basic airspace definitions are recognized worldwide as shown on the "Alphabet Airspace" diagram (preceding page). The letters go down in severity of restriction as they go down the alphabet.

A airspace is above 18,000 feet MSL and is off limits to us. Aircraft must have special equipment, be on an instrument flight plan, and be talking to air traffic controllers.

- Coverage: Entire Country and up to 12 nm (nautical miles) from shore.
- On Chart: Not depicted.

B airspace is associated with the biggest airports. Layered like an upside down wedding cake, it is marked on charts with solid blue lines and has tops around 10,000 feet MSL. We can fly below the layers but so too can everyone else—expect a lot of traffic and fly *well* below the bottoms.

- Access: Authorization is required and is unlikely, even with an aircraft radio. You must maintain CoC (clear of Clouds) and 3 miles visibility.
- On Chart: Solid blue lines with numbered altitudes for segment floors and ceilings. The altitudes are in hundreds of feet MSL (the last 2 zeros are omitted.) On the Chicagoland excerpt ORD is the inner area of a class B airspace area whose top is 10,000 feet.

C airspace is a mini version of B with less traffic. Some major airlines and lots of commuter airlines fly into these airports along with business and private airplanes. The airspace typically extends 10 nm from the airport and goes up to about 4000 feet above the airport.

- Access: By permission only which is unlikely. You'll probably need an aircraft radio. Requires 5,1,2&3 (500 below, 1000 above, 2000 to the side of clouds and 3 miles visibility).
- On Chart: Similar to B airspace markings but with solid magenta lines. On the Chicagoland excerpt, MDW is the inner area of its class C airspace.

D airspace surrounds most airports with an operating control tower (see Chapter 11), typically extending 5 miles out and 2500 feet above the airport's center. If the control tower is not operating then it reverts to **E Surface Area** which still requires permission.

Although Class D airspace is normally associated with control towers, you

---

ORD is O'Hare International, Chicago's big airport with runways outlined in blue. It's rings of Class B airspace radiate outward with increasingly higher bottoms. The center ring (red shaded here for clarity) is off limits but you *can* legally fly below the outer layers. Under ring one, with the ground at 600 feet, you've got 1300 feet to play with. Finding enough uncongested area will be a far bigger problem.

Midway (MDW), Chicago's 2nd busiest airport, sports the smaller Class C airspace. Like O'Hare, you can't launch in the center but you can launch under the outer ring. It happens to be the same floor as O'hare's first ring, 1900 feet MSL.

However, these areas will be extremely congested with air traffic operating below the main airspace. If you do find a field, stay less than 500 feet AGL to avoid most air traffic (expect helicopters).

**Digging Deeper:
The Nautical Mile (nm)**

Aviation's standard measure of distance is the nautical mile (nm). It is one minute of one degree of the earth's circumference. There are 360 degrees, 60 minutes per degree, and 60 seconds per minute in the coordinate system.

Lines of latitude, also called parallels, run horizontally on a North-up earth. They don't converge at the poles like lines of longitude. On Sectional Charts, longitude lines have tic marks for each minute of latitude. These are one minute of latitude *and* one nautical mile. Don't use the tic markes on horizontal lines, they get closer together as you near the poles.

One nm equals 1.15 statute (regular) miles.

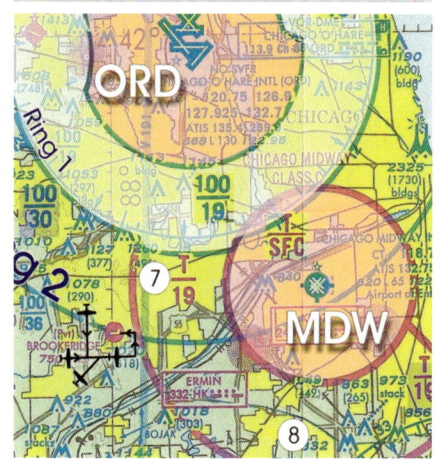

It's Almost all G Airspace
(Which is Where We Fly)

Nearly all the U.S., like all of this chart, is covered with class G airspace at the surface and E airspace above starting at 1200 (or 700) feet AGL. The 700 foot areas are inside the magenta circles (*Transition Areas*).

Transition areas give airplanes a safe descent to the airport—where anyone flying (including us) must have at least 3 miles of visibility. Below 700 feet we can have as little as 1 mile visibility.

Remember, airplanes (and all certified aircraft) always have the right of way over ultralights, even unpowered ultralights.

can have a tower with no Class D. Such an exception appears on this chapter's heading. Kissimee airport, southwest of Orlando International, has a control tower but no dashed lines, meaning no D airspace—you could legally launch right next to the field without talking to anybody (it has since added the D airspace).

    Access: By permission only and may require an aircraft radio. Requires 5,1,2&3.

    On Chart: Dashed blue lines around blue airport symbol. Its ceiling is in hundreds of feet MSL in the blue square. On the Chicagoland chart DPA, ORD and MDW are all control-towered airports.

E Surface Area is unusual. Only we ultralights are restricted. It's usually found as an extension from Class D airspace where E airspace goes to the surface instead of bottoming out at G airspace. Thousand Oaks (Position 2 below) is an example. Certified airplanes don't need to be talking with anyone but ultralights are not allowed in without permission. Strangely, that means we can legally fly over the airport (above its class D) but not over these extensions which top out at 14,500 feet MSL.

This is what FAR 103.17 calls the "surface area of Class E airspace designated for an airport."

    Access: By permission only, They may require an aircraft radio but usually not.

    On Chart: It is denoted on the charts by dashed magenta lines—just like the blue dashed lines around control tower airports, but magenta. On the

Can I Fly Here? Refer to the Thousand Oaks excerpt below.

1. Yes, you can fly here. It's G airspace with E starting at 700 feet AGL. You must remain CoC&1 (clear of clouds and 1 mile vis) until above 700 feet AGL (E airspace) when you must have 5,1,2&3 (500' below, 1000' above, 2000' beside the clouds and 3 mile visibility).

2. Requires Permission. It's Class E surface area. Must have 5,1,2&3 even if permission is granted.

3, 4, 5, 6. Requires permission. It's D airspace. Must have 5,1,2&3 even if permission is granted.

7. Yes, this ring denotes equipment required for airplanes. We don't need it (a Mode C Transponder allows the radar controllers to "see" airplanes better and know their altitude).

8. Yes, this is just like 1.

9. Yes, you'll launch in G airspace, climb into E at 700 feet AGL but must remain below 7000 feet MSL which is where this piece of LAX's class B airspace starts.

K. Same as 9 except that the class B airspace starts at 5000 feet MSL.

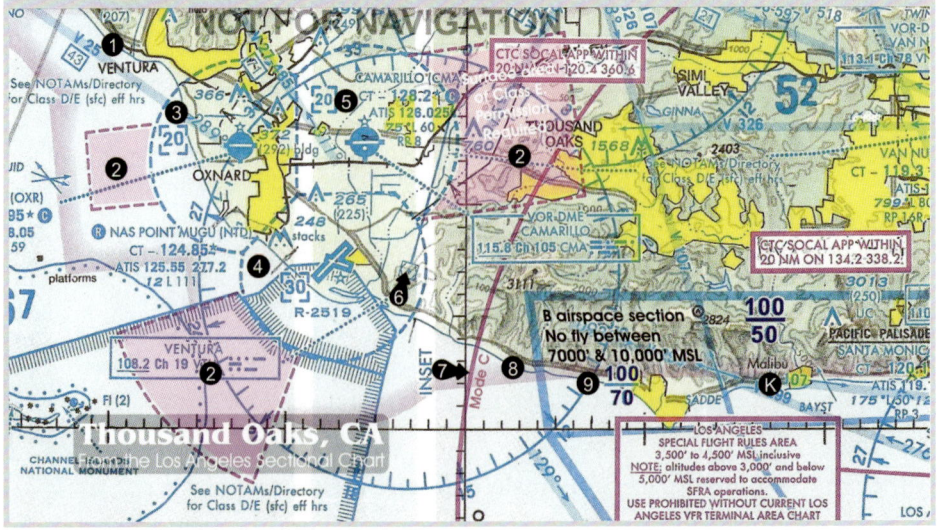

Chicagoland chart, number 4 (pg 93) is in such an extension (just squared-off extension, not the whole circle). The Danville excerpt has an unusual airport, number 5, where the entire space is class E at the surface.

E airspace overlies G airspace starting at 1200 feet AGL (or 700 feet in magenta shaded areas). It covers most of the country except some sparsely populated areas.

- Access: Access allowed. Requires 5,1,2&3 for cloud clearance and visibility while below 10,000 feet MSL.
- On Chart: No designation except in very sparse areas. A blue shaded line means no E airspace at all on the sharp side of the line—class G goes up to 14,500 feet. A shaded magenta line denotes the floor of E drops to 700 feet on the fuzzy side of the line. The entire area of both chart excerpts have E airspace overhead starting at either 700 or 1200 feet AGL.

G airspace is what's there if no other airspace is depicted. It's where we launch. Most of the country, including sparsely populated areas, are covered with G airspace. It goes from the surface up to the overlying E airspace or, in a few sparsely populated areas, all the way up to 14,500 feet MSL.

- Access: Access allowed, requires at least CoC&1 below 1200 AGL (clear of clouds and 1 mile visibility).
- On Chart: No specific designation. If there is nothing on the chart, G airspace is assumed.

Security Airspace

The many flavors of military airspace are mostly off-limits to us. Sometimes it's only closed during a specified time or altitude range and sometimes it's just advisory. "Military operating areas" (MOAs) are advisory—they don't use the airspace enough to close it but want to alert users about their possible presence.

Air Defense Identification Zones (ADIZ), previously surrounding only national borders, now keep traffic out of Capitol cities (including the U.S.) and a few other extremely sensitive sites. Flying in such a zone could get you shot at.

Visual and Instrument military routes (VR and IR) depict courses the military uses for practice and transit. While we're not prohibited, these thin, gray lines on sectional charts should encourage lively eyes. Aircraft frequently fly along them very low and very fast (up to 270 mph). Avoidance them would be wise.

Prohibited and Restricted areas keep airspace closed during certain published times as depicted on sectional charts. Times vary but you can call Flight Service to find out their "hot" (active) times. Chapter 7 addresses the call.

Alert areas, Controlled Firing areas and MOA's do not actually prohibit flight, rather they serve as a warning that military operations will be conducted and pilots should "look out." Keep in mind that some military training involves low-altitude flying (called "nap-of-the-earth") where they follow the terrain, staying below a couple hundred feet AGL, right in the middle of our favorite altitudes. We must avoid *them*. You can be sure these pilots won't be scanning for stray paramotorists!

Temporary Flight Restrictions (TFR's) are put up anywhere various government agencies deem them necessary. Some have been up for years while others pop up whenever the President or his people appear. Some pop up with no warning—don't be surprised when dignitaries soon show up. TFR's also appear during or after disasters.

5,1,2 & 3 means

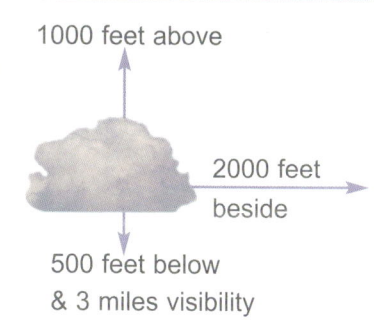

1000 feet above

2000 feet beside

500 feet below & 3 miles visibility

Several websites offer graphical depictions of current Temporary Flight Restrictions (TFR's). The most reliable way to get them is a briefing from flight service. These areas can pop up with little notice.

Many require special aircraft radio equipment (avionics) and a filed flight plan to fly into and out of the area.

Digging Deeper: What is "Mode C"

Around most class B airspace is a 30 mile ring that says "Mode C." It means that regular certified aircraft must have special equipment but does *not* apply to ultralights in the U.S.

These equipment requirements change as new technologies evolve. ADS-B, for example, is a satellite-based technology that will eventually supplant radar as the primary means for tracking aircraft.

Regulations prohibit flying near large events such as major sporting events, conventions and many other public gatherings. Some facilities that might be considered terrorist targets are off limits. Even when there are no specific restrictions, the regulation admonishes pilots not to "loiter" at sensitive sites. Doing so may garner a special reception, possibly by helicopter, at your return.

Knowing the rules is important but common sense is helpful too. If it looks like an area might be considered sensitive from the security eyes, either find out first or avoid it altogether.

Wilderness Areas

Many public parks, like the Grand Canyon, have areas preserved for their natural, quiet, separation from civilization. Some are protected by special rules prohibiting launch and even overflight. In most cases these areas are not strictly prohibited but pilots are admonished to avoid overflight below 2000 AGL.

Flying in national parks is prohibited. It's a big deal, too; violations could land you in jail with your gear confiscated and facing big fines.

Wilderness areas are indicated on charts by a blue dotted line. Some (like the Grand Canyon) have special restrictions outlined in Special Federal Aviation Regulations (SFARs) while other are covered in Notices To Airman (NOTAMs). Before flying in a popular park or famous site, contact the FSS and ask if they know of any restrictions. There may also be some local restrictions that apply—check with the Park administrators for that. Ask about overflight rules too.

NOTAMs

Whenever airspace is put off-limits, the FAA informs pilots through Notices to Airmen (NOTAMs). Adherence to these notices is critical; it may be for natural disasters, dignitaries, military needs, rocket launches or many other reasons. It could be a small area or, as on September 11, 2001, an entire country.

The NOTAM's location is usually referenced to a navigation station, such as a VOR, with direction (radial) and distance from the station. These are clearly marked on charts and have a convenient compass rose around them. Air traffic controllers have them on their radar maps, too.

NOTAM information can be obtained from FSS's in the same way as a weather briefing (see Chapter 7). If not offered, ask for any pertinent NOTAMs in the area.

Here's an example (reference "Digging Deeper" next page): A truck carrying propane explodes on the highway northeast of Vermillion, IL. The highway is closed as a rescue and firefighting operation gets underway complete with helicopters. FAA managers, at the behest of local officials, close the overlying airspace by issuing a NOTAM—prohibiting overflight below 2000 and within 2nm of the DNV 042 at 12.5nm. In this example, the closed TFR area is shaded red for clarity. It is expected that, once receiving this NOTAM, you will get your chart and plot it out. Locate the DNV VOR (Danville VOR, what #3 is pointing to) then follow its 042° radial (the line at #4) northeast out 12.5 nm.

The same or similar method will be used to alert pilots when a dignitary's presence closes off airspace. This is serious, with airborne and ground assets protecting the area.

Wilderness & Restricted Areas

Ocotillo airport is a popular ultralight field nestled amidst a charted wilderness area. The 2000 foot AGL minimum "request" applies there. Don't take this lightly, they can issue expensive fines for violating noise ordinances or disturbing habitat.

More important are Restricted areas just a few miles Southeast. The whole area with the blue hash marks is R-2510A. It goes from the surface to 15,000 feet. R-2510B sits atop the northern half of R-2510A, going from 15,000 feet up to 40,000.

The magenta Kane West MOA outlines a Military Operating Area that we can legally fly in but must understand the extra risk involved.

The details for all these areas are printed in the margin of the LAX sectional chart pictured above.

Visibility & Cloud Clearance

Besides knowing *if* we can fly in an area, we need to know what visibility and cloud clearance is required to fly there. The *least* we can ever have is 1 mile visibility and clear of clouds which applies only to G airspace.

As we fly higher (above 700 feet or more), the chance of mixing with airplanes increases and so do the minimums. This makes sense given that an airplane may be going 300 mph; that's 440 feet per *second*. At that speed, from a half-mile away, you're only 6 seconds from colliding—precious little time to recognize it, determine that it's on a collision course, do the right thing, and actually get out of the way in time. Realistically, it's too late. Better visibility provides more time for you or the airplane pilot to see and react.

Above 10,000 feet MSL airplanes go as fast as they want (they are limited to 250 knots below that) so visibility and cloud clearance minimums are higher yet. That makes sense—with jets commonly going over 400 mph, they need a lot of room to see and react to a PPG pilot. They punch through those innocuous looking cumulus clouds, too, which is why the horizontal cloud clearance requirement goes up to a mile and visibility goes up to 5 miles. Even then, a jet popping out of a cloud from a mile away has only 9 seconds to sort things out and maneuver away.

Reading The Charts

There is an information treasure trove in these charts. For example, airports show the runway orientation (paved only), enabling better prediction of where to expect airplane traffic. Runways are numbered in the direction of takeoff so that runway 27 means the pilot is taking off to the west (270° Magnetic). The chart's legend is an important resource that explains most of the symbology used.

The charts also reveal that relatively few areas are closed to us. In the Danville, IL excerpt (next page), the only off-limits places are shaded red: Spots 5, 10 and the TFR. Even those may be available with permission.

Danville, IL

Lets consider this chart excerpt with an eye to launching.

Position 1: Ignore the 0° radial; you want to launch from the arrow's tip.
  Launch?   Yes, you're in G airspace with E airspace starting at 1200 feet AGL.
  Need: CoC&1 (clear of clouds and 1 mile visibility) until climbing above 1200 feet AGL then it goes to 5,1,2&3 (500 below, 1000 above, 2000 horizontally from the clouds and 3 miles visibility).

The Danville VOR (what position 3 is pointing to): Notice it's just inside a shaded magenta line. That means the E Airspace floor dropped to 700 feet AGL as opposed to 1200 feet AGL outside that shaded line.
  Launch?   Yes, you're in G airspace with E starting at 700 feet (that's what the shaded magenta does—lower class E from 1200 to 700 feet AGL).
  Require: CoC&1 up to 700 feet AGL above which you must have 5,1,2&3.

Position 5 is just inside the "Surface area of Class E" which is off limits to us at any altitude without permission from air traffic control (ATC). The authority is usually an Approach Control or ARTCC facility ("Center") for that region.

Digging Deeper: VOR

The VHF Omnidirectional Range (VOR) is a special navigation transmitter for aviation. An airplane's receiver can tell the pilot what "radial" he is on from the VOR—i.e. what direction he is from the VOR. A radial is a magnetic direction from 0° to 360° where 0° or 360° is north and 180° is south. That's obviously useful for navigation although GPS has largely supplanted it for primary navigation.

Why do we care? Those stations are used as reference points for airspace and notices to airmen (NOTAMs). Their prominent placement on sectionals makes it easy to plot locations using a radial, distance and diameter.

The station name and its frequency is given in a blue box. In the excerpt above, the Danville VOR is on 111.0 Mhz (just left of spot 4 above).

Another reason they are of interest is that VOR's tend to concentrate airplane traffic overhead. It is best to avoid flying close to them, especially above about 800 feet. Most airplanes now use GPS's for navigation but still practice using VOR's.

Marking Position: VOR

This excerpt from the Chicago sectional chart shows how *radials* emanate from a VOR. A compass rose around the Danville VOR (position 3 points to the VOR) makes it easy to visualize them. A line (under position 4) is drawn out the 043° radial towards a temporary flight restriction (TFR) centered 12.5 nautical miles out. Cardinal degrees (0, 30, 60, 90, etc.) from the VOR are marked on the compass rose (positions 1, 2, and 7) so radials are easier to find. Position 7, for example, points to the 60° radial.

Hash marks going out the 043° radial line are nautical miles; they were added to show that they're the same as the marks going up lines of longitude (see position 11). That works because a nautical mile also happens to be 1/60th of one degree of latitude. Since lines of latitude are marked along each line of longitude (vertical line above the 87° at the chart's lower right), mileage is easy to figure, even without a special ruler. Mileage is also given along the bottom of each chart. Only use the hash marks on vertical lines, the marks on horizontal lines get closer together as you near the earth's poles.

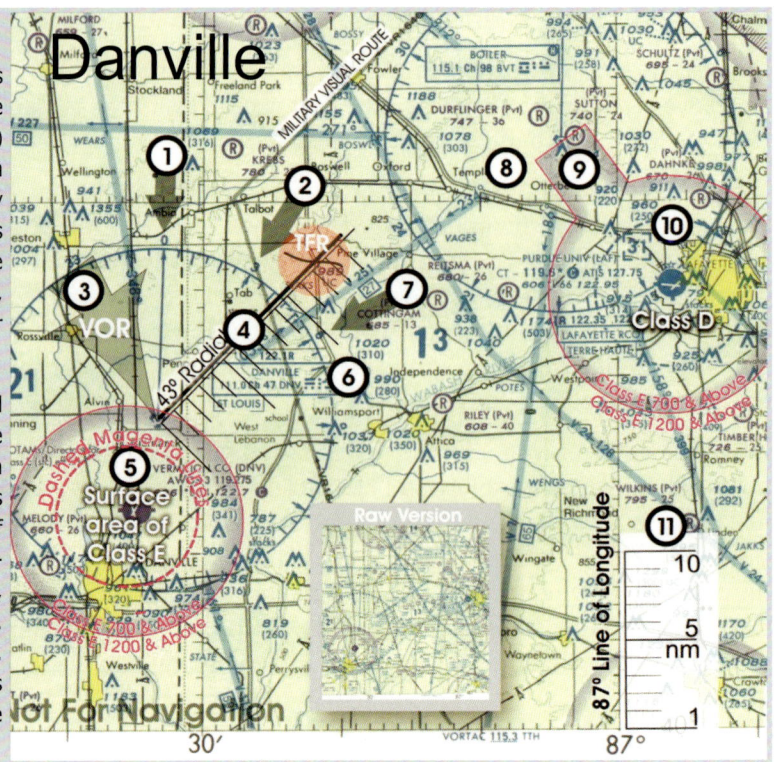

This VOR (VHF Omni Directional Range) in Southern Indiana also served as a turnpoint during the U.S. Nationals in 2004. Don't launch or land here—trespassing or affecting its operation is quite the federal sin.

Launch? No, unless you have permission. Call FSS for that since this is one of the few places in the country where an airport has class E at the surface that is not associated with a control tower airport.

Require: If you *do* get permission it would require 5,1,2&3.

TFR: The NOTAM that creates the TFR will give other information as to altitudes, restrictions and times of effectiveness.

Launch? No unless specified in the NOTAM verbiage.

Require: Specified in the NOTAM.

The Boiler VOR (a mile northwest of position 9): Purdue University, a control tower airport, is 8 nm southeast of here. We should be vigilant for airplanes flying instrument approaches from the VOR into Purdue airport—they may be down low.

Launch? Yes, you're in G airspace with E airspace starting at 700 feet AGL.

Require: CoC&1 up to 700 feet AGL above which you must have 5,1,2&3.

Position 10 is just inside a dashed blue line that represents the Purdue University airport's control tower airport.

Launch? No, unless you have permission. Have an aircraft radio but first call the control tower via telephone to explain your intentions. It's class D airspace.

Require: If you get permission, you must have 5,1,2&3.

Chicagoland, IL

Chicago's ORD and MDW airports are busy air hubs but all the same rules apply. Red shaded areas were added for clarity to show where you can*not* go without permission. Of course you can't climb up into the B (ORD) or C (MDW) airspace and there are many congested areas to avoid below. Certainly heading for open country is far wiser but this is done for illustration purposes.

Tip: Getting Permission

You can sometimes get permission to fly into control tower airports but only if the airport is reporting 3 miles visibility or more.

Position 1 is just outside the outer ring of ORD's class B airspace.

Launch? Yes, you're in G airspace with E airspace starting at 700 feet AGL. You can climb as high as you want legally. There is no shaded magenta line showing a transition from a 700 foot to a 1200 foot Class E floor. That's because the *entire area* has the Class E floor at 700 feet—common in heavily populated areas with a high concentration of airports.

Require: CoC&1 then 5,1,2&3 climbing above 700 feet AGL..

Position 2 is just inside the outer ring of ORD class B airspace. The label to its right shows the B airspace "shelf" goes from 4000 feet to 10,000 feet MSL and we can't fly there between those altitudes.

Launch: Yes, you're in G airspace with E airspace starting at 700 feet.

Require: CoC&1 then 5,1,2&3 if you climb above 700 feet AGL.

Concerns: Aircraft funnel through this area so they don't have to talk to O'hare. Expect heavy air traffic above about 600 feet AGL.

Position 3 This is just inside ring 2 of ORD class B airspace. The label to its right shows the B airspace "shelf" goes from 3000 feet to 10,000 feet MSL and we can't fly there between those altitudes.

Launch? Yes, you're in G airspace with E airspace starting at 700 feet AGL.

Require: CoC&1 then 5,1,2&3 above 700 feet AGL.

Position 4: This magenta dashed line, just beyond ARR's Class D airspace, outlines an extension that takes class E airspace to the surface. The blue dashed line outlines Aurora's Class D airspace associated with their control tower.

Launch? No, unless you have permission from Aurora tower. The tower frequency is 120.6 (you can only see the 0.6 on the excerpt).

Require: If you get permission, you need 5,1,2&3.

Position 5 is inside DPA's (DuPage) Class D airspace.

Launch? No, unless you have permission from DuPage tower. The tower frequency is 120.9 (that is on the airport information block above position 5.)

Require: If you get permission, you must have 5,1,2&3.

Notes: Airspace-wise you could fly above DPA's Class D (top at 3300 feet MSL) and below ORD's Class B (base at 4000 feet MSL) without talking to anybody. In the U.S., doing so would probably violate FAR 103.13(b) that forbids us from creating a "collision hazard with respect to any aircraft."

Position 6 is outside of the B airspace overlay and on the "Mode C" ring which doesn't apply to us. It is also just northeast of the Joliet VOR.

Chicagoland Excerpt

The 3D illustration is a visualization of Midway's Class C airspace, extruded from its solid magenta lines.

The 2D chart has shaded red areas added. These clarify the only 4 places, all surrounding airports, that we can *not* launch from.

Notice that airport symbols show the runway direction and relative length. That can help you know where to expect airplanes to fly when nearby. Landing patterns have been drawn in at certain airports like Brookeridge, just southwest of position 7. It's good to know where aircraft patterns are.

Note that a pilot could fly along the lake shore (position 9) from the surface up to 3000 feet MSL and remain below ORD's class B airspace. Be careful of Temporary Flight Restrictions, though, some big cities have them around prominent buildings.

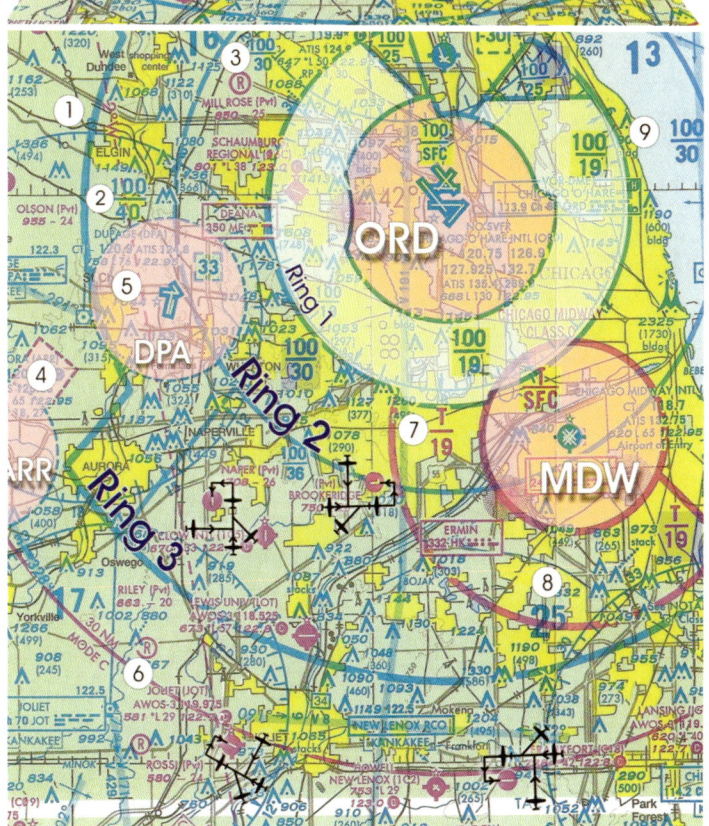

The PPG Bible: A Complete Guide and Reference

Launch?	Yes, you're in G airspace with E airspace 700 feet above.
Require:	You must have CoC&1 then 5,1,2&3 if climbing above 700 feet AGL.
Notes:	Expect more airplane traffic related to the Joliet VOR above about 800 feet AGL. You can climb as high as you want but there will be Jet and other traffic shuttling into the side of both ORD and MDW's airspace.

> **5,1,2&3** means cloud clearance of 500 feet below, 2000 feet horizontally, 1000 feet above and 3 miles visibility.
> **CoC&1** means Clear of Clouds and 1 mile visibility.

Positions 7 & 8 are below MDW's C airspace which starts at 1900 feet MSL and goes up into the overlying ORD B airspace (that's why the "T" for Top instead of an altitude). Obviously most of this airspace is off-limits due to being congested.

Launch?	Yes, you're in G airspace with E airspace 700 feet above.
Require:	You must have CoC&1 then 5,1,2&3 if climbing above 700 feet AGL.
Notes:	Expect high density airplane traffic to be skirting underneath and around MDW's airspace. This is a bad place to be more than about 500 hundred feet in a PPG. Helicopters are another threat and they operate close to our altitudes—they can be found cruising especially near the highways.

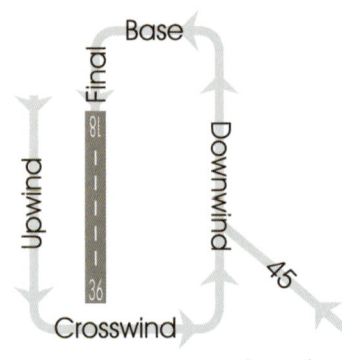

It's easier to anticipate where planes will be flying if you can visualize this pattern. Overlay it on the chart as done below according to what pattern is being flown.

All patterns are to the left unless "RP" is listed by beside a runway number. At Joliet, for example, it says RP 12. That means a right pattern is used for runway 12 (depicted below).

North of Joliet, at Naper Aero, there is no such verbiage and so all patterns are to the left. If planes are landing on runway 18 (landing to the south), then expect them to be flying the depicted pattern (shown above).

The Airspace Test

Think of this as a test. Look at the letters on the following pages and answer the questions yourself about launching from each point. What would you need to know and what are the concerns? To reduce page turning, the chart excerpts are split as PHX1 & PHX2.

First you have to know where you are on the chart. A GPS is great if you can translate the latitude and longitude (lat/long) coordinates. Sectional charts have lines of latitude (35° in the sample at left) and longitude (118°) clearly marked. The tick marks are *minutes* on lines of latitude and longitude. *Seconds* are 1/60th of a *minute*.

Point **A**: The 4$_9$ is a Maximum Elevation Figure (MEF) for that *quadrangle* (30 minutes of lat/long per side) meaning that the highest obstacle or terrain is 4900 feet MSL.

Launch?	Yes, It's G airspace with E airspace 700 feet above. Requires CoC&1 then 5,1,2&3 if you climb above 700 feet AGL. Stay below the B airspace which starts at 6000 feet MSL.
Notes:	This site sits on a Victor Airway (V95) which is the 185° *radial* from PHX VOR. You can expect increased airplane traffic above about 800 feet AGL.

Point **B** is also below the B airspace. The floor of the "upside down wedding cake" (B-airspace) is 4000 feet MSL and it goes up to 10,000. Point B is just south of some high obstructions (top at *3047*). Note that, except for MEF numbers, elevations above sea level are nearly always in italic.

Launch?	Yes, It's G airspace with E airspace 700 feet above. Requires CoC&1 then 5,1,2&3 if you climb above 700 feet AGL. Stay below 4000 feet ASL (B airspace).
Notes:	It's just west of the airway V95 so again, be vigilant for airplane traffic above 800 feet AGL or so.
	The little magenta flag to the north (above South Mountain) means that it is a *reporting point* for aircraft flying into PHX. Although they may fly right over it, more often they'll just report their position referencing it such as "2 miles west of South Mountain," but do watch for traffic near these.

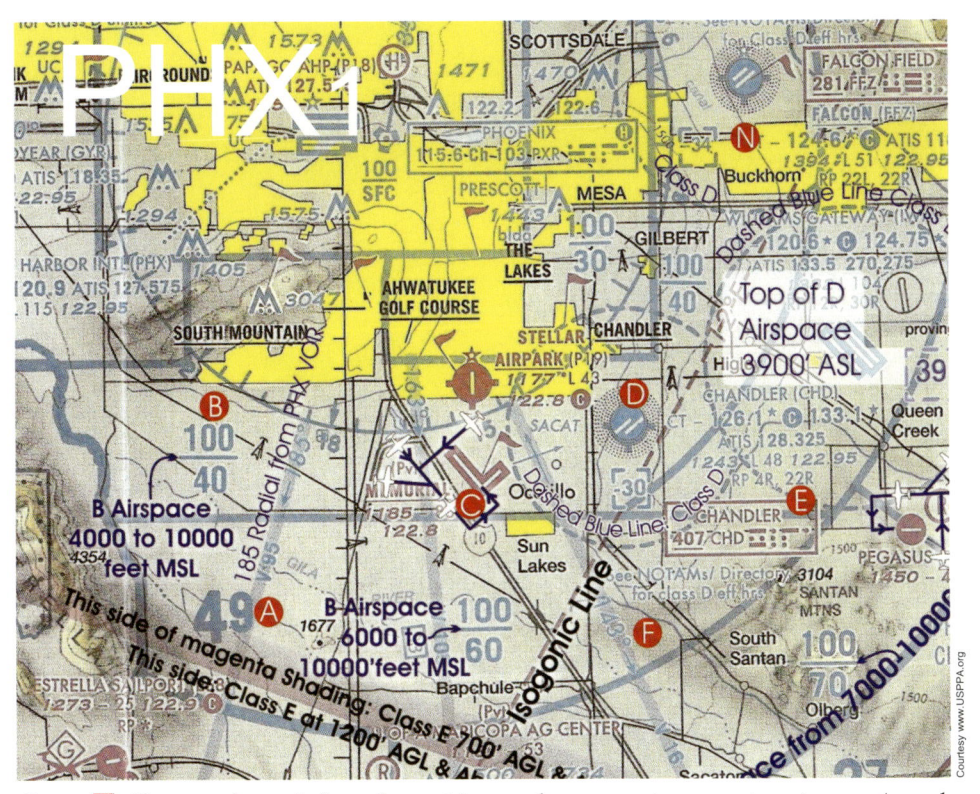

Point **C**: You can launch from here, it's got the same airspace situation as A and B but has an airport (Memorial) just northeast of it. You'll want to be familiar with that airport's traffic patterns to stay out the way and know where to look for airplanes. The depicted pattern, added for clarity, applies if airplanes are landing to the northwest. Since there's no "RP" in the airport information text, expect left-hand traffic patterns on runway 30 (headed 300° magnetic).

Launch?	Yes, It's G airspace with E airspace 700 feet above. Requires CoC&1 then 5,1,2&3 above 700 feet AGL. Stay below 4000 feet MSL to stay below Phoenix's B airspace.
Notes:	If you fly just a mile south, notice the B airspace floor goes up to 6000 feet MSL. If you have a hand-held aircraft radio, aircraft will be communicating on *122.8* Mhz as shown on the Memorial airport information text.

Point **D** is a control tower field, Chandler (CHD), with surrounding Class D airspace up to 3000 feet MSL—the last two 0's are dropped from the 3000.

Launch?	No, unless you have permission from Chandler tower. If you do get that permission, you'll need 5,1,2&3 and must stay below 4000 feet MSL to avoid the B airspace.

Point **E**: This line is the edge of Williams Gateway's Class D airspace. South of it you can launch without talking to anybody but if you want to fly north, you'll need permission. The magenta box with **407 CHD** is a navigation station that we can ignore. It is for a beacon that even airplanes don't use much anymore.

Launch?	Yes, if you are south of the dashed line which is G airspace with E airspace 700 feet above. Requires CoC&1 then 5,1,2&3 above 700 feet AGL.

Point **F**: This is well below the B airspace floor of 6000 feet MSL.

Launch?	Yes, It's G airspace with E airspace 700 feet above. Requires CoC&1 then 5,1,2&3 above 700 feet AGL.

Tip: Quick Weather

Some airports have Automatic Weather Observation Systems (AWOS) that broadcast their current weather continuously on the listed frequency which is always in the aviation band. For example, at Joliet (spot 6 on the Chicagoland excerpt), the AWOS is on 119.975.

They also usually have a telephone number where you can call and get their weather recording. Call the regular airport phone number to get its weather number.

The PPG Bible: A Complete Guide and Reference

South Mountain is a high point just south of Phoenix. Being festooned with towers makes it a great landmark and check on altitude. The chart shows the towers, depicted with the double blue teepees, to be *3047* MSL. You can set your altimeter to that. The magenta flag indicates that it is also a reporting point where airplanes radio their position to Phoenix approach control. The 100 over 40 means that Phoenix's B airspace starts at 4000 ft MSL and goes up to 10,000 ft MSL in that area. Expect heavy airplane traffic there.

Notes: The dashed magenta line to the left (running northeast to southwest) is an *isogonic* line showing there is 12° (the 12 is on PHX1) East variation between True North and Magnetic North (see Chapter 13). So if you are pointing True North, your compass will read 348°.

There's a Victor Airway (V16) that goes out the 143° radial from PHX VOR so you should expect heavier aircraft traffic above about 800 feet AGL.

Point **G** (reference PHX2) is well below the PHX B airspace who's floor is 7000 feet MSL here.

Launch? Yes, It's G airspace with E airspace above 1200 feet. Requires CoC&1 then 5,1,2&3 above 1200 feet AGL.

Notes: It's just east of an airway (V105) so expect more airplane traffic transiting the Stanfield VOR to the South. Airways present no restriction to us.

Point **H**: This little private airport, Ak Chin, has a paved runway, as indicated by the runway depiction, and might be a good site. It's elevation is *1210* feet MSL and the runway is 2900 feet long. Patterns would be left since there's no "RP" mentioned for any runway.

Launch? Yes, It's G airspace with E airspace 1200 feet above. Requires CoC&1 then 5,1,2&3 if you climb above 1200 feet AGL. You can climb as high as you want (up to 18,000 feet anyway).

Notes: If you have an aircraft radio, the airplanes will be using 122.9 Mhz to announce their position; that is the standard frequency for fields where no frequency is listed.

A few miles to the east is a high tower. The heights are shown just above the letter H. *1838* is the MSL elevation and (613) is its height above the ground. Expect some healthy guy wires spilling from its top.

Point **I**: This grass or gravel strip (as indicated by the open circle) is private but might be a good place to ask for permission.

Launch? Yes, It's G airspace with E airspace 1200 feet above. Requires CoC&1 then 5,1,2&3 if you climb above 1200 feet AGL.

Notes: If you have an aircraft radio, the airplanes will be using 122.9 Mhz.

Page 96 Section II: Spreading Your Wings

Point J is only a couple miles north of Casa Grande airport and warrants close attention to their airport pattern which is depicted for clarity (only runway 23).

- Launch?   Yes, It's G airspace with E airspace 700 feet above. Requires CoC&1 then 5,1,2&3 if you climb above 700 feet AGL.
- Notes: Notice the RP23 under Casa Grande's airport data block. That means that airplanes using runway 23 will be making right turns (shown) instead of the standard left turns. Stay well away from the pattern, especially the departure/arrival corridors. Typical aircraft pattern altitudes range from 800 to 1500 feet (lower for helicopters). The airport is at *1464* feet MSL (1500) so you would expect the pattern to be from 2300 to 3000 feet MSL.

  There's a tower just to the northeast (obscured a bit by the J) that tops out at *1794* MSL which is 265 feet tall.

Point K: This is an open area well clear of any airspace issues.

- Launch?   Yes, It's G airspace with E airspace 700 feet above. Requires CoC&1 then 5,1,2&3 if you climb above 700 feet AGL..
- Notes: If you fly towards Casa Grande and have an aircraft radio, the airplanes will be using Unicom on 122.7 Mhz and you can listen to their recorded *Automated Weather Observation System* (AWOS) on 132.175 Mhz.

Point L: This little sliver of airspace is different from Point J in that the floor of E airspace is 1200 feet. Owing to the vagaries of how transition areas (where the E floor lowers to 700 feet) are created, this area allows you to climb up to 1200 feet with only a mile visibility.

- Launch?   Yes, It's G airspace with E airspace 1200 feet above. Requires CoC&1 then 5,1,2&3 if you climb above 1200 feet AGL.
- Notes: The little mountains that stick up around there reach 2755 feet MSL just to the southeast.

Point N: (reference PHX1, there is no M) This is within the D Airspace surrounding a control towered airport.

- Launch?   No, unless you have permission. The airport info is not shown (it's off the excerpt). If you get permission, you'll need 5,1,2&3.
- Notes: The yellow area roughly equates to congested area but has no legal meaning and is usually derived from relatively old data.

Other Uses for the charts

What's available on the internet now eclipses what these charts present, but paper versions are still handier in most situations. And they're a lot easier to carry. Online versions (see www.FootFlyer.com) may be more current.

Topographical

One of the more useful elements is elevation. Not only do airports list elevation, but so do obstructions. Each tower gives the MSL top but also frequently the AGL height. Subtract the two for ground elevation. You can set your altimeter to that.

Contours give elevations in 500 foot (sometimes 250) increments—not terribly precise but good for general knowledge. You can generally estimate your height visually to within a couple hundred feet. Of course if you used the GPS to locate yourself on the chart then it will undoubtedly show your altitude within a few feet.

Always have fresh charts. The previous version of this one had Casa Grande as a non-paved airport. Plus, occasionally control towers are added with their surrounding D airspace—you do *not* want to go blundering into someone's newly minted controlled airspace.

An interesting aside: Some charted features can be quite inconspicuous on paper. The mine symbol just west of Casa Grande airport doesn't look like much on the chart, but the bottom picture reveals how "grande" it really is. Besides mountains, this abandoned copper mine is the most prominent landmark within 20 miles.

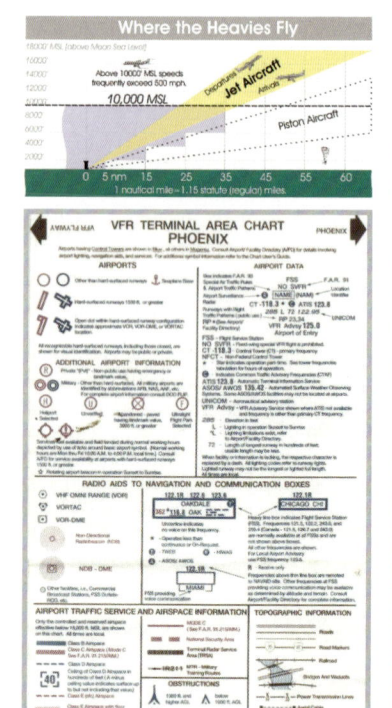

Finding Sites

Ultralight strips are usually friendly to us and occasionally soaring schools will tolerate us. Some private airports will let us to fly there so it may be worth asking. Small airports, especially grass ones, are pretty welcoming as are some sky diving airports. The latter is already used to seeing canopies although usually the canopies aren't going back up. Sky diving airports are marked by a little parachute symbol. On the chart, sailplane operations show a sailplane symbol with a G, hang glider sites show up with an H and ultralight strips use the letter U. Sorry, there's no symbol for paragliders.

Things Look Different Out West

Charts are colored by elevation which accounts for the browns on this highland excerpt. It's also far less populated out west so G airspace usually goes up to 1200 feet AGL and, in the sparsest areas, all the way up to 14,500 feet MSL like the area east of J (lower right of map).

Here are some other highlights.

Spot 1 is in G airspace with E at 1200 feet AGL. That's a pretty healthy ridge, be careful in any significant wind. Spot 2 is in an area where the G airspace only goes up to 700 feet AGL. You could launch from the gliderport. Spot 3 is pointing to an *airway* where airplanes are likely to be flying. Spot 4 is in G airspace with E starting 1200 feet above.

Spot 5 is the D airspace around Jackson Hole airport. You need permission from the control tower to fly in there. Spot 6 is inside the dashed blue lines that outline the D. The several spot 7's point to where the Class E floor goes from 700 feet AGL inside, to 1200 feet AGL outside the line.

Spot 8 points to a nature preserve of some sorts where you must stay above 2000 feet AGL while inside the area. Spot 9 is the DNW VOR, a navigational station used by airplanes.

The J's point to the edge of where classs E goes down to 1200 feet AGL with G airspace below. On the other side of that shaded blue line, where point L is, G airspace goes to up 14,500 with E above.

Spot K has G airspace at the surface and E airspace starting at 1200 feet AGL.

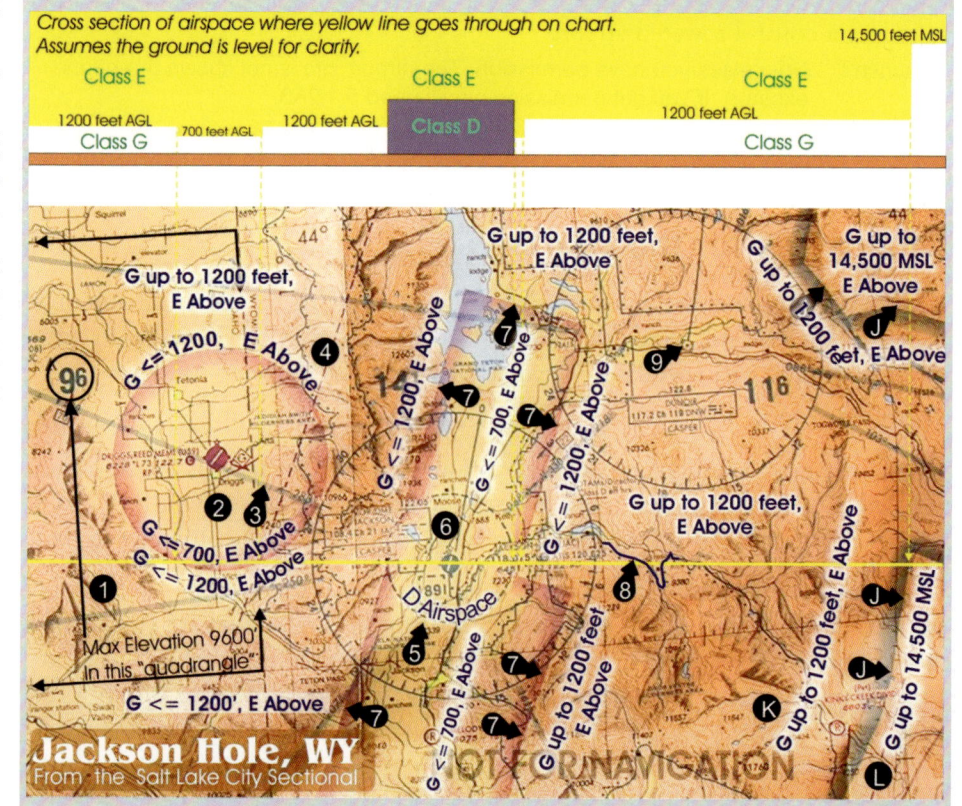

Top: Airplane traffic gets concentrated around predictable arrival and departure paths, both vertically and horizontally. Jets depart steeply and arrive at a shallower 300 feet per mile from the airport which is about 3 miles per 1000 feet of altitude loss.

Piston aircraft follow a shallower departure and arrival path.

So at 10 miles away from the airport you can expect jets to be about 3000' (10 * 300'). If you're flying at 10,000' MSL, expect jets to be about 30 to 40 miles away from their landing airport. Fast aircraft spend more time at 10,000' MSL than most other altitudes because they must slow down before going lower. Beware that controllers sometimes descend airplanes earlier or later than these figures. This is just a guide.

Above: Terminal Area Charts are more detailed than the more-common Sectional Charts which cover a far wider area.

We may not *need* airports to launch, but they sure are nice to use. Pay particular attention to traffic patterns though, airplane pilots and airport managers are not very forgiving of ignorance.

Flying From Anywhere

CHAPTER 10

What a treat—running aloft from the most unlikely locales and setting off for the where of our whim. Launching from almost anywhere is a fantastic capability, but it can bring enormous challenge and extra risk, too.

Choosing a suitable launch site is crucial to safety and success; heeding a few basic rules can prevent catastrophe whether the site is a wide-open prairie airport or a tight little mountain clearing.

Being *able* to launch from anywhere doesn't mean that you *should*. Both safety and permission can be show stoppers. There's nothing worse than being all suited up, your motor idling and wing laid out, only to have someone come up shaking their finger at you. Finding that perfect launch area is both a joy and a curse—in a country brimming with great sites, permission to use them can be elusive.

Any prospective site must first be in legal airspace, and second, must match your skill level. Additionally it should not require trampling through crops, climbing fences or ignoring "No Trespassing" signs. Public property, such as state or federal lands, frequently prohibit any kind of flying. Parks are notoriously difficult because they usually have specific prohibitions and the staff to enforce them.

Needing to maintain an emergency landing site puts many forested areas out of reach; same with swamps. Even in these areas, though, if you can find a sufficient clearing to launch from, it is fun to just climb up high over the landing zone (LZ) and check things out. Many otherwise boring views sprawl into gorgeous panoramas with a bit of altitude.

Choosing the site

Size Matters

Bigger is always better. Depending on your skills and the conditions, a congested site with trees or wires can be deadly. Your early unsupervised flights require more space. For one thing, you probably have little experience telling field size, knowing climb angle etc. Another factor that determines acceptability is your climb technique; a relatively new pilot should make sure the field allows a straight-out climb (requires no turns.)

The sizes shown at left seem large but, when launching in still air, distance goes by quickly. Don't launch anywhere that *requires* turning below 100 feet above ground level (AGL). Past incidents have shown that new pilots need more time after launch to get their bearings.

Don't be fooled by training experience where you got airborne in a hundred feet—launch distances can double or triple under hot, high or calm conditions and it's easy to underestimate distance requirements.

One way to size up a field is to pace it off. Find your stride's length by walking a known distance then dividing that by your footsteps.

Don't merely guess at a site's appropriateness when obstructions are involved. Wires, trees and buildings have all proven terribly unforgiving and the distance from them is hard to judge. Pace it off when in doubt.

A small field is OK providing the obstructions would let you plow through them harmlessly if things go awry (beans, wheat, tall grass, etc.) As experience gives you solid directional control during the run and after liftoff, then you can decrease the field size, especially the width (always minding mechanical turbulence, mentioned below).

A skilled pilot can launch from anywhere that's long enough to get airborne and circle over. That insures it's big enough to land in should the motor quit. But beware: wind can make a small, obstructed site dangerous at *any* skill level.

Mechanical Turbulence and Obstructions

As covered in Chapter 7, air burbling around obstructions creates *mechanical turbulence* downstream. This must be accounted for when choosing sites.

Some locations work well for certain wind directions only. For example, a big turbulence-causing building to the west is no problem in an easterly breeze (the wind is coming *from* the east). With less than about 5 mph wind, mechanical turbulence will be present but should be manageable. Look out, though, if the wind picks up—that light breeze at sunrise can turn nasty a couple hours later. Look at the forecasted wind direction and speed when considering a site.

In a 10 mph wind the turbulence will extend many times the obstruction's height, and it gets worse as wind increases. Be very leery of tall obstructions in moderate-

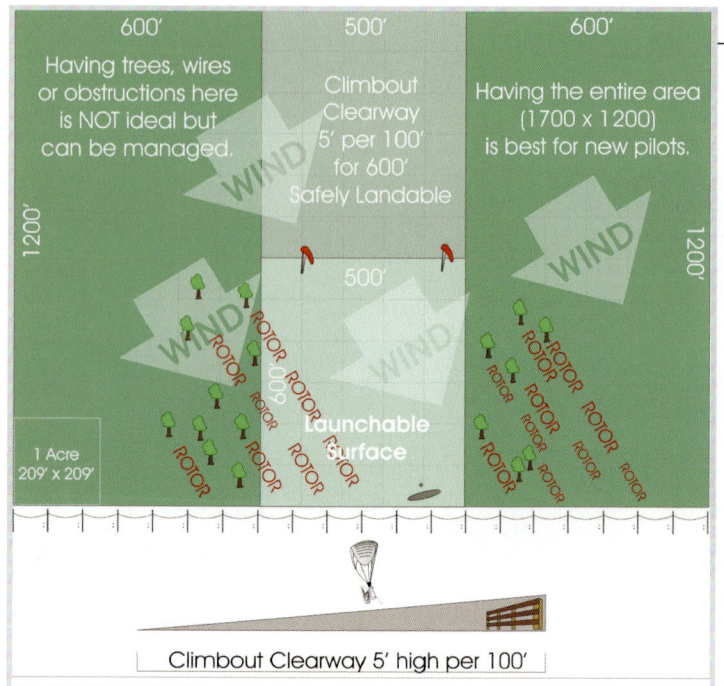

Choose a launch site with plenty of room that is appropriate for your skill level. Small sites have been the downfall of those who pushed it. Know your limits by measuring your regular field and comparing any new locations to that. Pacing the edges works well enough.

ly strong winds.

Mechanical turbulence can cause large collapses or altitude loss at the worst possible time (when you're down low). Wind shadow, the calm area just behind an obstruction, must also be avoided.

Slope And Surface

Launching downhill is always best for two reasons: (1) you can run faster and (2) the downhill component means the wing is already trying to lift you that much more. Downhill landings tend to be long because the ground is falling away as you descend towards it.

Landing uphill is dangerous and can yield a very hard impact due to both the slope and sinking air. If the wind is coming down the hill, try landing crosshill (and crosswind) to avoid flying into rising terrain.

Smooth surfaces are far better than rough ones. In fact, tall grass, soft sand, or a rutted surface can add so much leg drag (see Chapter 17) as to prevent a launch. They also make tripping and falling more likely.

Site Permission

"It's better to beg forgiveness than to ask for permission" is a well worn statement that can get us in trouble. Permission is always preferable! Even if you *think* a particular site is OK, at least mind these guidelines:

- Never climb a fence or cross a "No Trespassing" sign to get there. In some places doing so could get you shot.

- Never do any property damage in your effort to get to the site or while preparing. This is especially true for crops—destroying crops doesn't sit well with either the owner or his brother, the Sheriff.

- Never set up where somebody lives or has a presence. If there is somebody to ask, you must ask even at the risk of refusal.

- Never use a park or other facility where known rules prohibit flying. Almost all state and federal parks prohibit launching aircraft and ultralights except at airports. You can probably use the airport. Be mindful that many parks have a minimum altitude to fly over. Don't quibble over who controls the airspace (probably another agency), they can always get you for disturbing the animals.

- Avoid lingering. Launch then fly away to minimize attention from surrounding communities or neighbors.

High Elevation Fields

At higher elevations you'll need larger launch areas and better climbout options. More power and a bigger wing may be necessary to let you launch *at all*. Smaller or faster wings may require so much groundspeed (to get the necessary airspeed) as to exceed your ability to run, even with full thrust.

Chapter 17 offers details on procedures and techniques to improve your success rate. Make sure your site has an "out" that allows for an unexpectedly shallow climb over a route with neither obstructions nor hills. The worst case is having to

1. Learn your own takeoff distance by setting out four cones, 50 foot apart, in your launch direction. Then see how far it takes you to liftoff. Learn your circle radius by flying to a soccer field of known dimensions (they're not all the same) and seeing how far out of it you fly when circling. Google Earth is a good way to measure the soccer field size.

2. It looked good from the road but didn't measure up. The pilot nearly impaled himself on a fence post trying to launch from here. Pace off potential sites and be conservative about launch distance estimates.

3. Surfaces can be deceiving. Do a test walk without your motor on to make sure there is traction and support. This type of surface can hide quick sand.

climb over something; this is always a bad practice, but at higher elevations, is particularly dangerous. At least one climbout route must allow clawing your way to a safe altitude without having to traverse any obstructions, especially wires.

Unless there is some wind, the launch surface will need to be smooth. Ruts or tall growth can easily keep you from generating the requisite speed. Roads out in the boondocks are good as long they have no power lines. Beware of barbed wire fences which do surprising canopy damage. And don't park your car *on* the road.

Flying At or Near Airports

Uncontrolled airports (no control tower) can be a perfect PPG playground. Unfortunately, getting permission can be tough. Airports with control towers are usually too busy but *can* be used with the right equipment (see chapter 11).

General aviation (non-airline) un-controlled airports normally sit in G airspace with E airspace 700 feet above. Functionally that means you only need 1mile visibility to launch and must stay clear of clouds (CoC), with stricter requirements above that.

A popular misconception is that airports accepting federal funds have to let us use them. Unfortunately, that is not entirely true. They can, and frequently do, restrict or prohibit us based on perceived incompatibilities with other traffic. They can also impede access so much as to make it impractical for us.

Many licensed pilots and airport managers are quick to condemn any mixing with us; that's unfortunate since a knowledgeable, conscientious PPG pilot adds less risk than another general aviation airplane. Another reason for the occasional cold-shoulder (and probably a big one) is our lack of contribution. Airplanes based

It doesn't look like much but this dirt road got us airborne. We planned it so as to turn well before the highway. This entire area is landable leaving plentiful engine-out options.

Obviously roads must be nearly abandoned, have no wires and the pilot capable of steering during his run. That is an advanced skill that is well worth mastering.

> **Right of Way**
>
> Remember, we've got to stay out of *their* way. It's quite clear (in the U.S.):
>
> FAR 103.13 Operation near aircraft; right-of-way rules.
> (a) Each person operating an ultralight vehicle shall maintain vigilance so as to see and avoid aircraft and shall yield the right-of-way to all aircraft.
> (b) No person may operate an ultralight vehicle in a manner that creates a collision hazard with respect to any aircraft.
>
> That essentially means that we have to avoid putting ourselves in areas with heavy concentrations of airplanes in a way that could interfere. Airports are obviously the most common but most major cities also have jet routes published on charts. These must be avoided too. Fortunately they're high up, almost always 3000 feet or above. Check with local pilots in your area.

at the airport pay rent, buy fuel, charts, and other services; we generally don't.

It is simple for us to have little or no impact on airport operations, but we must work with management and other users. If possible, explain our capabilities (to those willing to listen) then follow through with consistently responsible flying. Launch away from airplane traffic and remain clear of their patterns.

The onus is on us to avoid becoming a collision hazard. Beyond complying with air regulations and local rules, we must not annoy people, create a hazard or even have the appearance of such.

If planning regular operations from an airport, contact the airport manager and find out the best places to operate. Explain how you plan to avoid conflicts with existing users. Ask what areas to avoid flying over. This will also reveal local requirements, noise sensitive areas and other location-specific needs.

About Runways & Patterns

You must know where the airplanes fly in order to avoid them. Fortunately their patterns are fairly well defined although they don't always follow them.

Understand runway numbers—they indicate the magnetic direction of aircraft taking off or landing with the ending "0" removed. So north is 0 or 360 (runway 36), east is 090 (runway 9), south is 180 (runway 18) and west is 270 (runway 27). So if the runway was aligned east/west then the *approach* end of the runway for aircraft landing west (270°) would be 27 whereas a pilot taking off or landing in the other direction (to the east) would be using runway 9.

Airplanes are flown from the left side and so standard traffic patterns for all runways are "left"—all turns are made to the left until final approach. Runway 27 in the diagram uses a left pattern. Runway 9, however, uses a right pattern.

Sometimes airport operators want certain runways to use a right pattern to keep noise away from a sensitive areas (called noise abatement). They may indicate pattern direction using a large, highly visible segmented circle near the runway complex. It has little "L"s oriented to the runways they depict. The short part of the leg represents the base leg and the long part of the L represents final approach to the runway. Looking at the letter L on a page would mean right traffic for runway 36 (top of the page is north or 360°). You fly the base leg then turn right (the long vertical part) to join final. The segmented circle quickly shows what pattern direction

It's best to remain well clear of aircraft patterns. But with concurrence of the airport operator, there are ways to safely co-exist.

One technique for crossing runways is to fly over the middle of the runway, maybe slightly closer to the beginning, at around 400' AGL The PPG is depicted below doing just that: He takes off into the wind then gains 400 feet in a left turn before heading across the runway.

Make sure the airport management approves of your plans. Otherwise, don't cross any runways at all—go around the ends, down low and at least a mile away.

On a standard glide slope, airplanes will be approximately 300 feet high for every mile away from the runway. Some airport managements ask us to be *above* pattern altitude before crossing the runways.

Watch out for aircraft wakes which descend at about 500 feet per minute (fpm) and can linger up to 2 minutes.

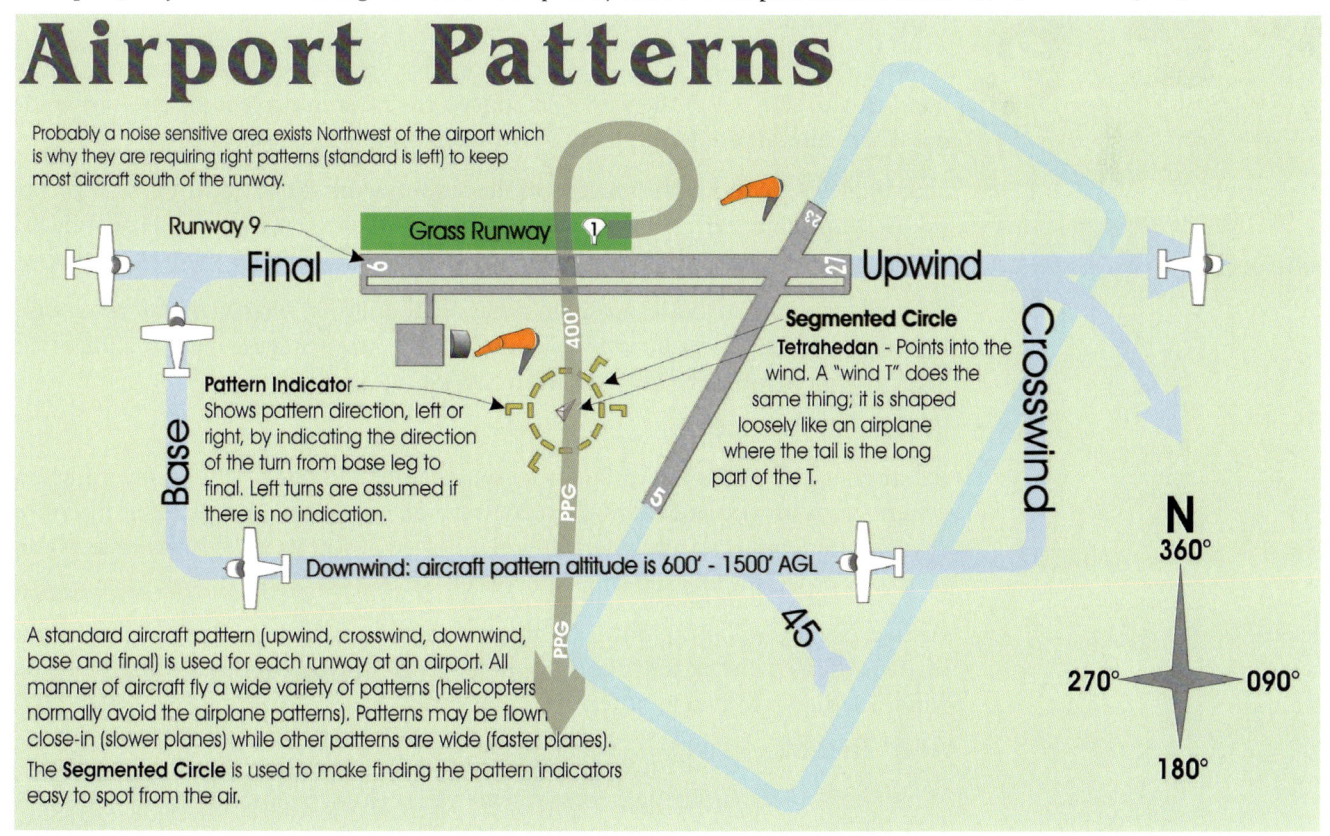

Airport Patterns

Probably a noise sensitive area exists Northwest of the airport which is why they are requiring right patterns (standard is left) to keep most aircraft south of the runway.

Runway 9
Grass Runway
Final
Upwind

Segmented Circle
Tetrahedan - Points into the wind. A "wind T" does the same thing; it is shaped loosely like an airplane where the tail is the long part of the T.

Pattern Indicator - Shows pattern direction, left or right, by indicating the direction of the turn from base leg to final. Left turns are assumed if there is no indication.

Base

Crosswind

Downwind: aircraft pattern altitude is 600' - 1500' AGL

N
360°
270° — 090°
180°

A standard aircraft pattern (upwind, crosswind, downwind, base and final) is used for each runway at an airport. All manner of aircraft fly a wide variety of patterns (helicopters normally avoid the airplane patterns). Patterns may be flown close-in (slower planes) while other patterns are wide (faster planes).
The **Segmented Circle** is used to make finding the pattern indicators easy to spot from the air.

The PPG Bible: A Complete Guide and Reference

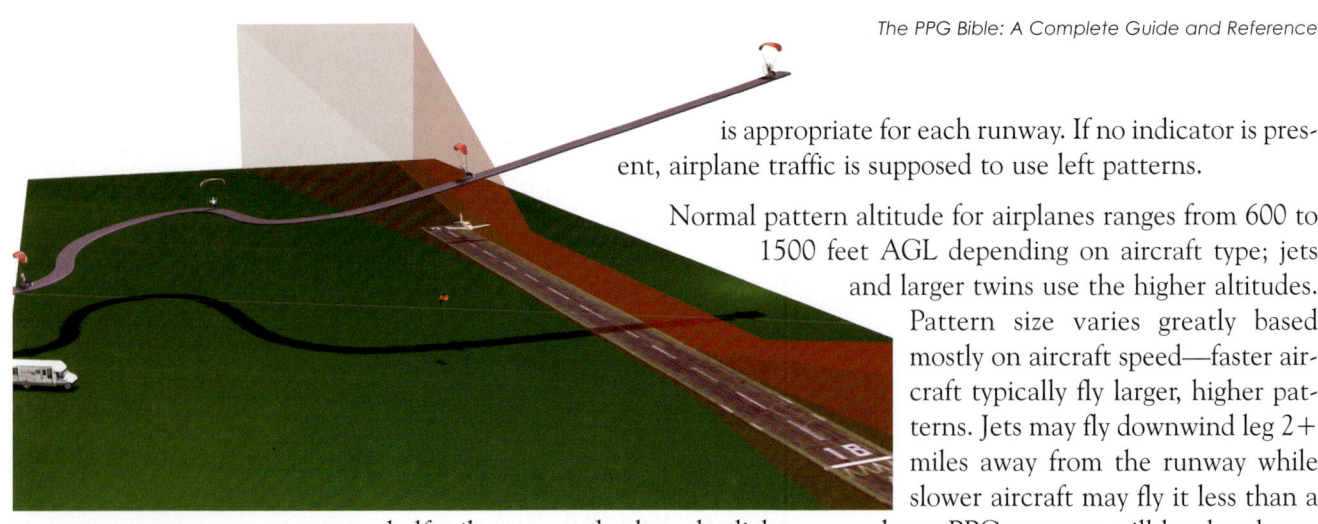

Above: The reddish shape shows typical corridors flown by aircraft landing or departing at an airport. It's our job to avoid them. This PPG pilot climbs while away from the runway then flies over the center at a sufficient height.

Below: Wingtip vortices are little tornadoes generated by any aircraft that's producing lift (flying). They are worse following heavy, slow, aerodynamically clean airplanes. Give such craft a wide berth; blundering through one would almost certainly cause a collapse. Between the vortices is sinking air.

is appropriate for each runway. If no indicator is present, airplane traffic is supposed to use left patterns.

Normal pattern altitude for airplanes ranges from 600 to 1500 feet AGL depending on aircraft type; jets and larger twins use the higher altitudes. Pattern size varies greatly based mostly on aircraft speed—faster aircraft typically fly larger, higher patterns. Jets may fly downwind leg 2+ miles away from the runway while slower aircraft may fly it less than a half mile away and other ultralights even closer. PPG patterns will be the closest to the runway (around 400 feet away and around 300-400 feet high).

Airport Status

You must know the airport's status—whether portions are closed, special operations are going on, or there are any other unique situations. Ask the airport manager if there is anything you should be aware of. If that's not possible, call Flight Service (See Chapter 7). Tell them your name, that you will be flying an ultralight at airport such-and-such, and that you would like the NOTAMS.

Airplane pilots normally choose the runway based on wind but not always. Sometimes they'll do a long, straight-in final approach to a different runway even if it has a tailwind (for convenience). PPGers must be on the lookout for this—5 knots of tailwind isn't as big a deal to an airplane.

How to Mesh

Now that you have the airport information and know where its patterns are, it is fairly easy to stay out of the way. And indeed the most important practice is avoiding where aircraft are likely to be. Fortunately that is pretty easy.

Your launch area should be away from the runways and their departure/arrival corridors. Your flight path should be planned so as to avoid runways, their extended centerlines, and any buildings.

Be vigilant to avoid noise sensitive areas: If the airport management gets noise complaints caused by you, your welcome may be brief. Staying clear of congested areas (required anyway) will frequently suffice.

Wake Turbulence

All aircraft produce wake turbulence (see chapter 22) but it can be severe when generated by an airplane. Slow-flying helicopters are worse. A helicopter in cruise is about the same as an airplane, but when slowed down, its wake turbulence could be worse, especially when it's flying between 20 and 55 mph.

Always plan your flight path to be above or well beside an airplane or helicopter flight path. Remember that the turbulence sinks, spreads out and drifts with the wind, lasting up to two minutes.

After Takeoff

When leaving the airport it is best to stay well below the aircraft traffic patterns; probably 400 ft. AGL or less (keep a safe landing option, though). If overflying a runway is absolutely necessary, go over the center, slightly closer to the beginning, at 400 ft. AGL. There is less likelihood an airplane will be flying there.

If climbout near the airport is necessary, do so opposite to any pattern in use. But realize that airplanes may overfly the airport from any direction, usually from pattern altitude up to 500 feet above pattern altitude. They do this to check things out before landing (a fairly common practice).

See and Be Seen

If you see an airplane that you suspect does not see you, *turn*. Not only will the motion make you more visible, but the changing aspect on the PPG wing will help as well.

The other obvious need is to keep a look out for others, especially when you're flying up where other air traffic may be. We have the best view in the world with nothing but a pair of risers between us and the visible planet—use it.

Be Heard

Aviation radios that can transmit and receive on the airport's frequency (called Unicom) are beneficial. Even a receive-only radio helps—you can hear where other radio-using traffic is. The airport frequency is found on air charts (122.8 pictured).

Keep any talk to a minimum but be listening for other traffic. When you're ready to go (if able to transmit), announce "Powered Paraglider launching from xyz and will be departing to the (state direction)."

Represent Us Well

We are the sport's ambassadors and, in the environment of an airport, a conscientious appearance does double duty. Our future access and acceptability will be based on our behavior. So, above all: Be polite, don't annoy anybody, fly quiet and, by all means, fly safely.

Places to Look

It's strange that you sometimes have to go near cities to find launch sites. We don't want to be in the city, but near its perimeter. Humanity is always building things, which is good since they tend to clear the land before building on it. Many industrial areas have a long way to go before build-out and, in the meantime, tend to keep it nicely mowed for potential customers. This can be perfect for us!

Private farms with a co-located home can be good too. They frequently have nice, launchable grass areas and agreeable owners.

While it's great that we can launch from so many places, always consider "what if." Besides the obvious engine-out concern, try to account for wind forecasts or trends. Launch sites that require an upslope wind, for example, may not allow a return if the wind shifts.

This site would only be feasible in a wind coming from the pilot's right.

Safe Havens

One beauty of our sport's uniqueness is that it's easy to make friends who share the passion. And the best places to fly are those that have already been pioneered by a local pilot. Locals will likely know where other pilots commonly fly. Most PPG schools have their own sites and will let others fly there providing they respect the site and its surroundings. Not surprisingly, these schools may require a membership or some form of payment from those who didn't train with them.

Almost any site where pilots fly regularly has rules which, among other things, help keep their neighbors happy. Follow them closely to maintain your welcome.

Also, every site has at least one unhappy, noise-hating neighbor. It doesn't matter that busy railroad tracks are in their back yard—they'll still call the cops on you. Stear clear for the sake of the site's regulars.

Telling Wind Direction From Flight Path

If you choose to alight somewhere that has no wind indicators, you'll need to know wind direction. Chapter 7 has tips on using ground features but, in the absence of those, here is one method to use while you're aloft. Descend to about 200 feet and do a slow 360° turn while watching the ground (or look at your GPS groundspeed). When you're moving the slowest over the ground, you're going directly into the wind. If there's much wind at all, you'll notice drift. If you're drifting left, the wind is from your right—turn into it until the drift stops and that's the wind direction.

The wind at the surface could possibly be completely different but this is a good start. In thermally conditions, of course, expect it to be variable and turbulent.

The owner of this palatial launch site discovered powered paragliding and shares it with friends. He keeps that lawn clear so that foot drags are possible for nearly the entire perimeter. Find out where the locals fly and respect their sites by adhering to any special requirements.

I've flown some unlikely lawns—you just never know until you ask.

Flying From Controlled Airports

CHAPTER 11

There are ultralight clubs that fly from controlled airports and their craft mix splendidly with others. Foot launching adds further challenge but can certainly be done with the same safety.

As learned in Chapter 9, airports with control towers have class D airspace around them and are off-limits without permission from the air traffic control (ATC) tower. It's not hard to get that approval but is generally easier if you have an aircraft radio; some towers may require it. See Chapter 10 for general information on flying from airports.

Telephone

If your launch site is within class D airspace, but not on the airport, you may be able to get permission via telephone. Even if you're using an aircraft radio, phoning first lets you to clearly explain your plans and accommodate any special needs they (ATC) may have. Explain what you are flying and your intentions.

Before calling, figure out where you'll launch relative to the airport. Using a sectional chart, plot out a bearing and distance in nautical miles. If there is a VOR (see Chapter 9) nearby, you can plot out a radial and distance from the VOR. Make sure you have an idea what the airport's elevation is and where the runways are (available on the sectional chart). They will obviously not let you get in anybody's way. Also, come up with a route that will let you quickly (as much as we can do "quickly") exit and re-enter their airspace.

In the U.S. you can look up the tower's number under Government, Department of Transportation, FAA Control tower. They are not always listed, in which case you can call Flight Service (800 WX-BRIEF) to get the number.

During my first summer flying PPG I wanted to fly it everywhere. As a professional pilot, I'd spent years of arriving on large airports' long ribbons of concrete with a 150+ mph chirp, now I wanted to land on one by foot. What a mesmerizing experience; running   down the first stripe then lifting back into the air.

Before taking off I had called the tower via telephone so they knew what to expect. That was exceedingly helpful. Of course I took my camera because it just seemed so unnatural.

A Note About Call Signs

You make up your own descriptive call sign for use with aviation radios, there is no need to register it with anyone. "Ultralight Papa Gulf" is one example.

Rules for aviation transceivers vary by country. Generally, if the equipment is used as intended there will be no legal problems but check your local rules.

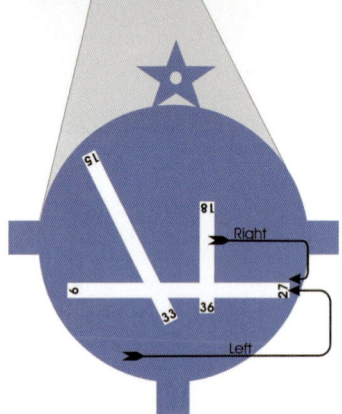

Call and ask for the *Tower Chief*—if unable to reach the chief, you may be out of luck. Arranging this a few days early may be wise. Explain that you:

1. Would like to launch your "ultralight, a powered paraglider" (that may take some explanation) from location x. Provide your direction and distance such as 3 nautical miles (nm) northeast of the airport. 1 nm = 1.15 statute miles.

2. Will stay below 500 feet AGL (or some acceptable altitude) as you exit or enter their class D airspace.

3. Have (or don't have) an aircraft transceiver and a transponder (used by radar controllers to identify specific aircraft.)

4. Will be flying between certain times.

Ask if that would be OK and if they have any special requests. This is one time where permission is *much* better than forgiveness!

If you do have a radio then find out what the tower frequency is (it's on the chart). If the airport has radar service they will likely still want you on the tower frequency, but ask to be sure.

Aircraft Radio

If you fly from the towered field itself then you will probably have to have an aircraft radio. These hand-held transceivers cost less than a top-line helmet but they require a special headset. Most helmets don't work with aviation radios although some can be modified to do so. You may be able to make inexpensive helmets work with aviation headsets by carving out a line of foam under the helmet's shell.

Flying into a controlled field safely requires a working knowledge of runways, how they're numbered and traffic patterns (see Chapter 10).

Call the tower via telephone to see if they'll allow the flight and, if so, what special requirements may be imposed. You need to work out a launch location, flight pattern and acceptable times.

You'll want to choose an easily understood, brief, and descriptive call sign. "Ultralight Papa Golf" is good because its easy to say, easy to understand, and conveys immediately that you're a low speed craft. You may want to describe yourself on the radio (or telephone) as being a "foot-launched powered parachute."

ATIS

Most controlled airports have a continuously repeating recording, **A**utomatic **T**erminal **I**nformation **S**ervice (ATIS), that is updated about every hour (but repeats continuously). It includes airport weather, runways in use and other relevant tidbits. To ensure pilots have the latest information, each update is labeled with a different letter. So the first hour's recording may be information "Alpha" (A) and the second hour's would be "information Bravo" (B) and so on. The tower wants to know that you've listened to this recording and will expect you to let them know on an initial call.

The ATIS frequency appears on sectional charts under the airport's name and control tower frequency (CT). Listen to this broadcast first then contact the tower via radio and mention it to them "…information Bravo" (if it's B).

Aurora airport's control tower is at 120.6 Mhz and the Automatic Terminal Information Service (ATIS) is broadcast on 125.85 Mhz.

The picture above was from a flight of three paramotor pilots who trekked into this Class D airport while one talked on the radio and the others followed.

We were instructed to make "Right Closed Traffic" for the grass North of runway 27 and remain east of runway 33. The enlarged airport above makes it clear what these instructions mean. We followed the right pattern, depicted above, meaning that our turns to final were to the right. Airplanes were using the standard left pattern.

Being instructed to remain East of 33 meant that we had to plan our climbout carefully to give that runway a wide berth. Airplane wake, just like our own wake, drifts with the wind and sinks. An encounter with that while down low could be messy.

Tower Talk: Launch

Communications is taken seriously, for good reason—woe to the pilot who hems and haws and gums up the frequency with slow, uncertain transmissions. Plan what you're going to say, press the transmit button and say it clearly and succinctly.

Your initial call to the tower should include the facility name, your call sign, the letter of the ATIS recording (if one is broadcast) and your request. When you're ready to launch, motor running, A's in hand then call the tower and radio that you're ready for launch. They will give you the winds, special instructions and clear you to launch. They will probably tell you to "proceed as requested" since technically you're not on any clearance.

When cleared, complete your launch and comply with any instructions. If you delay more than a half-minute or so they will probably cancel the clearance and ask you to call them back when you're ready. If the launch doesn't work out, explain that you needed to abort and will call back when ready in 8 minutes (or however long you need).

After you've launched and flown a few miles away the tower may offer a frequency change; just respond with your call sign and "roger". You are not required to ask for a frequency change when clear of their airspace.

Here is an example of ultralights playing well with aircraft. The tower controllers, airport management and club operators have agreed on this arrangement. It allows a very active ultralight pattern to be flown right next to the airport runway. Aviation radios are required but the ultralights aren't expected to mix with the regular traffic.

Tower Talk: Landing

Before returning to land, listen to the airport's ATIS and note the letter (Alpha for A, Bravo for B, etc.).

Call the tower by saying its name and tell them that you "have information such and such (ATIS letter)" followed by your request for a landing. They will give instructions regarding patterns and runways. If you're coming into the airport you will need to tell them exactly where on the field you want to land.

Example Communications

Here is a sample communication for a paramotor pilot flying from Aurora airport near Chicago, IL. It's in Class D airspace at 600 ft MSL elevation (above mean sea level). Ideally you will have already talked with the tower by phone to explain your craft, it's capabilities and speeds, and established where on the field you will launch from. Have a name for the place such as "in front of GF Aviation" where "GF

> **Tip: AWOS**
>
> Many non-tower airports also have recorded weather: Remote equipment that monitors conditions and broadcasts it continuously. It updates every few minutes, broadcasting current info on the listed frequency.
>
> These Automated Weather Observation Systems (AWOS) are noted on the sectional chart along with their frequency. They also sometimes have a phone number to allow retrieval that way.
>
> In the example below, Casa Grande airport's recorded weather can be picked up on an aviation band radio using 132.175 Mhz.

The PPG Bible: A Complete Guide and Reference

Aviation" is the name of a business on the field. Make sure you understand the airport's runway and taxiway layout along with its typical patterns.

In the examples, communications use this font and *ATC dialogue is italicized*.

Dial in the ATIS frequency—here is the sample ATIS:

"Aurora Tower information Charlie, time one four five three Zulu weather, wind 040 at 5, visibility 6 haze, scattered 35 hundred, broken at 250, temperature 24, dew point 18, runway 9 in use, runway 33/15 closed, caution for crane operating 600 feet east of the tower up to 150 feet, taxiway Charlie closed, tower and ground combined on 120.6, advise on initial contact you have information Charlie"

The above tells you that the wind is from the northeast at 5 knots and runway 9 is in use (airplanes will be taking off and landing towards the East). The weather observation was made at 1453 Zulu (the aviation standard time, see Chapter 7).

In our example, you are set up in the grass south of runway 9 near the GF Aviation building and plan to head south. Call the tower when you're ready to inflate.

"Aurora Tower, Ultralight Papa Golf by GF Aviation is ready to launch, would like south departure."

"Ultralight Papa Golf, remain clear of runway 9, southbound departure approved, proceed as requested, launch is at your own risk."

"Ultralight Papa Golf, will remain clear of runway 9"

After launch, turn south and head out. If the tower has, or knows about traffic in your vicinity, they may call it out. Positions are given relative to your ground track using clock directions where 9 O'clock is off your left, 12 O'clock is in front of your flight path and 3 O'clock is to the right.

"Ultralight Papa Golf, you have traffic at your 11 O'clock and a mile westbound at 1500 feet, he's on right downwind for runway 9"

Look for the traffic; it is given relative to sea level (not airport elevation) so 1500 feet means he's 900 feet above the ground. Stay below about 500 feet (airplane traffic patterns are nearly all 800 feet AGL or higher) and respond accordingly.

"Ultralight Papa Golf, traffic in sight" *or, if you don't see it,* "Ultralight Papa Golf, looking for Traffic."

After you've flown out of the tower's airspace you are legal to change frequencies (no permission required). They may, however, offer the change.

"Ultralight Papa Golf, clear of my area, frequency change approved."

"Ultralight Papa Golf, Roger."

When returning to land, listen to the ATIS again (note the letter it gives—X in this case) to make sure there are no changes. Call the tower with your position and request. Since this is an initial request, precede it with the facility name.

"Aurora Tower, Ultralight Papa Golf is 6 miles south, southeast, landing with 'X-Ray (the ATIS letter)'"

"Ultralight Papa Golf, approach the field from due South, remain below 1200 feet call 2 miles out."

When reaching 2 miles out, report your position.

"Ultralight Papa Golf is 2 miles out."

Tower controllers will not likely be familiar with our craft. It can help immensely to call them on the phone, introduce yourself, let them know what you want to do and describe the craft's limitations.

Ask when the slow periods are and how best to approach the field, if coming in from elsewhere.

Section II: Spreading Your Wings

If there's no traffic, it's fun to do a touch and go on a runway. If a runway is not being used, you may be able to get permission.

"Ultralight Papa Golf, if traffic permits, I'd like to do a touch and go on runway 36."

"Ultralight Papa Golf, roger, can you keep your pattern south of runway 27?"

If you are absolutely certain, beyond the slightest shadow of a doubt, that you can safely comply with this request then respond with "affirmative." In this case, however, it would be wise not to accept such a clearance (say "negative"). Look at the airport diagram 3 pages back; there is very little of runway 36 south of runway 27. It would be tough to stay clear of 27. For this exercise, however, we'll assume there is plenty of room and that the tower is well south of runway 27.

"Ultralight Papa Golf, keep your pattern south of runway 27, make right traffic for runway 36, report abeam the tower."

When abeam the tower (the tower passes by perpendicular to your flight path), report.

"Ultralight Papa Golf is abeam the tower."

"Ultralight Papa Golf, cleared for the option runway 9 then make right traffic."

This means you are cleared to land and stop, do a touch and go, or do a flyby of the runway. If you land and stop the clearance ends (you cannot takeoff again until cleared for takeoff) but if you touch and go or fly by then make your pattern turns to the right while staying south of runway 27.

"Ultralight Papa Golf, cleared for the option runway 9, will make right traffic."

When you are ready to land back at your launch site:

"Ultralight Papa Golf is ready to land back in front of GF Aviation"

"Ultralight Papa Golf, remain south of runway 9, landing is your own risk, proceed."

You will only be "cleared" to land or takeoff from a runway, not the adjoining grass or taxiways. Clearances, per se, are only issued when they involve the runway.

"Ultralight Papa Golf, roger."

Most instructions should be repeated (read back) to ensure you understand and will comply. All clearances relating to

This control tower was closed, leaving the surface area of E airspace. Permission is required and the pilots acquired it by contacting "Socal" (the Southern California Approach Control) by phone.

Digging Deeper: Phonetic Alphabet

Aviation radios are not known for high quality audio yet clear communications are obviously essential. So a special pronunciation alphabet was developed to reduce errors, especially with B's, C's, D's, T's and a few others. These words are used to represent each respective letter of the alphabet:

A	Alpha	B	Bravo	C	Charlie
D	Delta	E	Echo	F	—trot
G	Golf	H	Hotel	I	India
J	Juliet (See R, someone had a sense of humor!)				
K	Kilo	L	Lima	M	Mike
N	November	O	Oscar	P	Papa
Q	Quebec	R	Romeo	S	Sierra
T	Tango	U	Uniform	V	Victor
W	Whiskey (strange choice for aviation)				
X	X-Ray	Y	Yankee	Z	Zulu

These numbers carry different pronunciations to prevent confusion with words in some languages:

3	Tree	5	Fife	9	Niner

runways and taxiways *must* be read back. If you're only told to "proceed" then a full readback isn't really necessary; a simple "roger" will do. If you are asked to maintain an altitude it will be MSL so have a reasonably accurate altimeter available—most of the wrist altimeters are OK but make sure to set it to the field elevation before departure.

Letter of Agreement

If you fly frequently from one location that sits within D airspace then you may be able to work out an agreement with them. The controlling facility is almost always a control tower. Tower cab security is an issue so you'll usually need to call first.

Set up an appointment with the tower chief (or his appointed minion) and ready a map that shows where you fly along with a picture of your craft. If approved, then you will be issued a letter specifying boundaries, altitudes and times where you can fly without contacting them. It's easier if you represent an established club.

When you do fly out of an airport, represent us professionally. Those who follow in your footsteps will have an easier trail to tread.

A flight of five paramotorists (photographer and videographer not shown) flew right off the end of this airline airport runway. Sometimes all you have to do is ask. Another person on the ground monitored air traffic control via aviation radio and stayed in contact with the PPG pilots. They stayed well below the flight path of airplanes that were taking off and landing. Wake turbulence was a concern but moderately strong onshore winds reduced any chance for a turbulent encounter.

Setup & Maintenance

CHAPTER 12

Our flying machines look so simple and, in most regards, they are. But proper setup and maintenance is critical beyond appearances. Manufacturer information is best, when available, followed by guidance from an instructor or dealer who is experienced with your particular brand. Improper adjustments, especially to the harness, can render a paramotor unflyable or dangerous.

Harness

A paramotor harness includes the critical liftweb. Its webbing (the structural straps), fabric and padding connect you to the wing, provides a comfy seat, and supports the motor. It is also your most important item of adjustment since it determines hang angle, how torque is handled, comfort and just about every other aspect of flight. Avoid exposing it to damaging UV rays, extreme heat, cuts and harmful chemicals.

Riser Spread

The harness should provide a riser separation of 17 to 20 inches (42 – 50 cm) to keep most wings within certification. Your wing's manual may list other limits but few specify it. Be especially careful to avoid *less* than minimum separation which could accentuate *riser twist*, where the pilot spins around under the wing.

Setup

Setup *must* be done while hanging from the carabiners in a simulator (see Chapter 1). You can hang it from a tree limb, rafter, or anything high enough to get your feet off the ground. Use someone to help, preferably an instructor.

You want the thrust line to point slightly downward (between 0° and 15°) from

Below: The harness and frame mounting arrangement must keep the risers an appropriate distance apart. Being too wide hurts the wing's shape and being too close (2nd one pictured below) can allow a dangerous riser twist to develop.

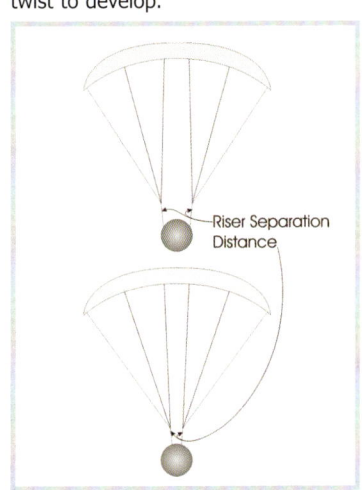

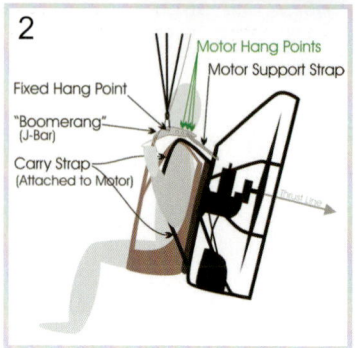

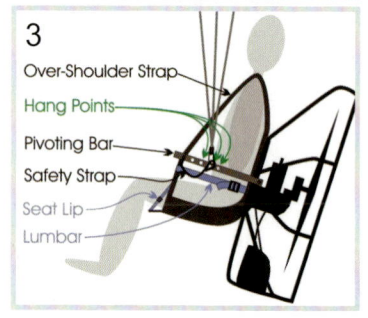

straight back (see diagrams at left). A leaned-back posture may be more comfortable but it makes takeoff and landing more difficult. Sitting bolt upright is less comfortable but minimizes the twisting effect of torque and makes launch easier.

Adjust the hang angle by moving the carabiner hook-in point. On many harnesses, like that pictured below, this is done by moving the carabiner loop along the upper front main web. Then adjust the upper rear main web (3) so that the motor or harness does not press against your body in flight. You should feel no (or very little) harness pressure on your body—the intent of distance/comfort bars is to transfer motor thrust to the forward harness straps while keeping them comfortably *away* from your chest and arms.

If the wing carabiners clip into a bar or frame and multiple holes are provided, selecting the appropriate hole is critical. Moving to a forward hole will make you tilt-back more. Light pilots typically use the most aft holes (those nearer the motor) to counteract the motor's weight. Its opposite if the *motor* clips into a bar—holes farther back make the motor tilt back farther.

Leg straps should be snugged up tightly then let out a couple inches. If they're too tight it's hard to run and, on most machines, if they're too loose it's difficult to get seated. A few models, however, are designed for the leg loops to be completely loose—check with the manufacturer.

The Anti-Torque strap, if equipped (see figure 1 at left), should be tightened until it's snug but without forcing the carabiners together. This reduces the effect of motor torque at some expense in weight shift. Machines *made* to weight shift won't likely have this strap since weight shift can counteract torque effects, too. This setup does not *prevent* torque turns, only reduces it somewhat.

On machines equipped with a seat lip adjustment strap, it should be left loose for launch and landing. Pull it tight while hanging in the simulator to get some feel for how much tightening it takes and then let it loose again.

The front chest web (figure 1 at left) keeps you from falling out forward and prevents the risers from spreading out too far. Being over-tight might bring the risers too close together and will also reduce weight shift authority (on machines so equipped). The chest strap should be just barely snug.

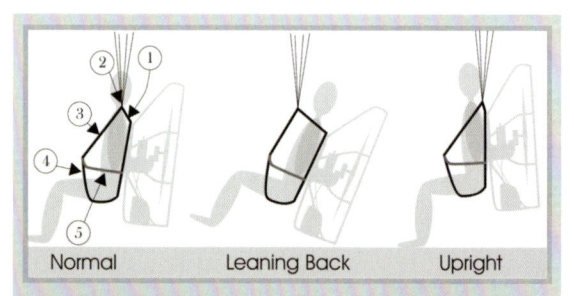

Ground Handling Straps

Ground Handling straps, or *carry straps* (see figure 2) help keep the motor "hiked up" while preparing for launch. On over-the-shoulder machines they keep the bars off your shoulder. And they make forward launch-

1. This excerpt from Chapter 2 shows the anti-torque strap, speedbar and kick-in bar which are not used on all machines.

2. This *soft j-bar* style adjusts the hang angle by changing which "boomerang" hole the motor hangs from. The last hole is typically used but moving to a more-forward hole gives a more upright hang position.

3. Low hook-in machines adjust the hang angle by choosing different holes in the weight shift bar (or rigid rail). Using a forward hole makes the motor hang back farther. Motors with no carry strap are normally launched with the main strap (over-shoulder) tight then it's loosened in flight for comfort.

Tightening the lumbar support (as equipped) moves the back of the harness forward. That moves the pilot, and therefore the CG, forward which tends to make the motor hang more upright.

Balancing the weight of the motor and pilot keeps the prop disk (area created by the spinning prop) nearly vertical or hanging back slightly. Many harness varieties exist; the example above shows a soft harness type where the high hook-in can be moved by lengthening the #1 distance. That moves the motor's weight farther aft causing the motor to tilt back more, vectoring (pointing) the thrust downward slightly. It may be more comfortable in flight but challenges the launch and landing. More tilt-back dramatically aggravates the twisting effect of torque.

A good compromise in comfort and safety is about a 5° tilt-back which means the thrust line is also correctly pointed about 5° down.

Repairs to the liftweb should be done by a certified parachute rigger or equally qualified professional. Other harness repairs can be made with any strong thread such as for leather or carpet. The hooked needle helps push through thick straps.

es easier by preventing the motor from wallowing around.

In flight, the ground handling straps can be loosened for comfort if needed. On harnesses where these straps pass through a buckle, tie a knot at the end so the strap can't come all they way out and wind up in the prop.

A sternum strap usually attaches to the ground handling straps to keep them from slipping off your shoulders.

Machines without carry straps should have their main over-shoulder webbing cinched up tightly. You can loosen them in flight for comfort. These machines may also provide a side strap lumbar tensioner that can be tightened for launch and loosened in flight if necessary.

Kick-In Bar

A kick-in bar or rope is used to aid getting into the seat on some machines. It should be heavy enough (like an aluminum bar) to hang down a bit and must not interfere with walking backwards (for reverse launches). Normally it should hang a little over halfway down to your foot while sitting in the simulator.

Speedbar

The speedbar is what your feet push to engage the speed system. More push = more change in wing shape to go faster. The bar should ride just above the kick-in strap or no lower than halfway down the back of your calf while seated. That's a good compromise between easy access and full travel. Having the bar closer (higher) allows more travel but makes it harder to get your feet up to. Some harnesses have handy loops where the foot bar can be stowed during takeoff and landing.

Speedbar adjustment in a simulator requires that you attach the wing's risers and hold them up like you're in flight with the sister clips connected. Make sure the speedbar line is not so tight that it pulls the A's with*out* the bar being pushed out—that could be deadly. When fully depressed, the two A-riser pulleys should almost touch each other as pictured at left.

One way to adjust the speedbar line length is to make it a bit longer than what the simulator suggests then go test fly it. While flying, pull the line up through it's rings (or pulleys, as equipped) until the bar almost touches the harness but you can still get to with your feet. Mark that spot then make adjustments after landing.

Some speedbars come with two straps (no bar). One strap attaches to the speed system and the other attaches to the seatboard as a kick-in strap. Another style uses two loops which allows for two-stage activation of the speedbar. Push out on the first loop to full leg extension then go to the closer loop for yet more travel.

Hard Point Hook-Ins

On machines with low hook-in points there are usually hard points that the carabiners attach too. Adjusting the hang angle is a compromise between keeping the

Speedbar Attachment

Almost all speedbar lines hook together with *brummel hooks*, commonly called *sister clips* (Shown below).

This is the simplest setup for a speedbar—a line goes from the foot bar, through one pulley (or ring) on each side of the harness and up to the wing's speed system.

The yellow bars are over-shoulder *floating J-bars*, considered a hard-point hook-in since the carabiner attaches to a J-bar. It is floating because the J-bars can move up and down. Motor tilt-back angle is affected by where on the J-bar the carabiner attaches to: Moving the carabiner back means you'll hang more upright.

J-bars spread the harness forward and away from your body while retaining a higher hook-in point. A back-up carabiner strap is frequently used in case the J-bar were to fail, retaining a load path through the harness's lift web. This type of J-Bars also forces a certain riser separation and prevents the motor from sliding around on the pilot's back. Fixed J-bar machines are typically only used on cart-launched machines.

HANG ANGLE
Adjusting your paramotor for safety, comfort and thrust

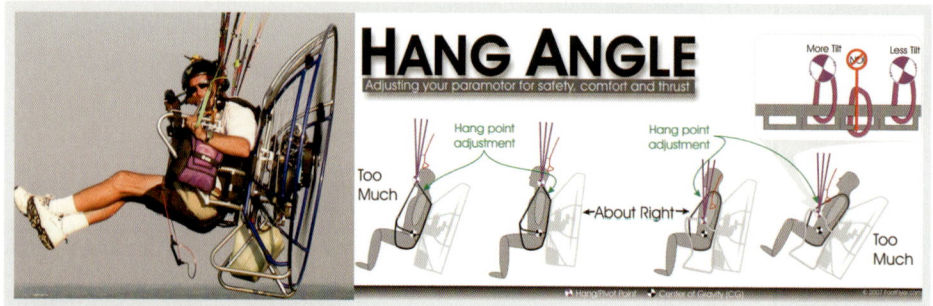

A lightweight pilot flying a heavier machine must hook the carabiners to the farthest point aft. The pilot can be reasonably well balanced with about 5° tilt-back.

The connection must be made through the frame holes intended for them on these machines. If they just go around the bars, they could slide forward, allowing the motor to tilt way back and cause a severe riser twist.

Torque Twist Fix

1. As the wing lifted, the motor moved to the pilots right shoulder causing a left twist and tilt back. Fortunately, he let off the throttle and aborted.

A temporary solution was to move the hook-in point aft. But then, at full power, the motor tilted up and forward which was solved by a short loop of rope (2) that kept the risers forward.

The real problem, it turns out, was that a new harness had been mounted but not attached properly. Once that was fixed, the torque was well managed. This was a great example of why proper motor setup is so critical.

risers forward enough for arm freedom and leaning back too far. These machines are designed to lean back farther to more closely mimic the free flight posture. Acceptable thrust line angles are between 5° and 20° but expect more twisting and more challenge on launch with more tilt angle.

Most over-the-shoulder J-Bar machines allow adjustment of the hang angle by providing different holes for the carabiners or D-shackles.

If the carabiners attach to a bar instead of the harness webbing, consider using a safety strap that goes from the riser loop to the harness. This is because a loose metal-to-metal contact point is slightly more susceptible to fatigue failure.

Reducing Torque

Chapter 23 has much more on torque and its twisty effects but the two main components are riser shift (weight shift) and yaw (left/right twisting). Yaw is worse since it redirects the thrust which can easily overpower your turn authority.

Here are some ways to mitigate or counter the effects of "torque turn."

- Reduce the hang-back angle. This is the most serious cause of riser twist due to the horizontal component of torque. It is even more important with smaller pilots flying powerful motors—they should limit the lean angle to 8° max.

- Make sure the motor cannot slide left or right on the harness which would cause offset thrust, the second most powerful twisting force. It's like having someone push on a shoulder blade with 100 or more pounds—you *will* twist. If you tend to twist right, (motor pushing on left shoulder) adjust the motor to push slightly on your *right* shoulder. Chapter 23, page 241 has a nice diagram of this. You could also move the hook-in point laterally (left or right) on one or both sides of the harness if your machine has fixed bars.

- Insure that there is sufficient riser separation and the motor is held rigidly in place. Left-right swinging arms must never swing inward (outward is ok).

- Create a differential carabiner hang height. In other words, if the motor torque tilts you to the right (pulls down the right riser), make the left carabiner lower. That will make it turn slightly left during power-off glides, fly straight at cruise power, and turn slightly right during climb. This works best on higher hang point motors because the motor's center of gravity (CG) is well below the hang points.

- Move the hook-in point aft on one side (easier on motors with hard point attachments). This angles the thrust slightly so as to oppose its natural tendency. So if you tend to twist left during climb (wing banks right), move the hook-in point on the left side back (aft) and/or move the right-side hook-in forward.

Two-Cycle Motor Troubleshooting Chart

Does the motor have compression when you pull/crank it

- **Yes** → Does the motor Start and continue to run?
- **Too Much** → Remove the spark plug. If there is still too much resistance to pulling then it could be:
  - Siezure (piston partially melts against cylinder wall).
  - Bad Pull or Electric Starter.
  - Other Internal Problem.

  Otherwise it could be:
  - Clogged decompression hole (if equipped) - clean it out.
  - Bad decompression valve (if equipped). Clean or replace.
- **No** → The following could be the problem:
  - Spark Plug is Loose - tighten.
  - The piston has a hole in it - replace.
  - If it has a decompression valve this is normal.

Does the motor Start and continue to run?

- **Yes** → Does it develop and keep full RPM?
- **No** → Does it fire at all? Make sure it is not flooded: remove the spark plug, pull it through, then replace the plug. A wet plug may indicate flooding.

Does it fire at all?

- **Yes** → (continues to RPM check)
- **No** → Is there spark? Set the connected plug on the cylinder and look for a spark while pulling/cranking the motor. Don't touch!

Is there spark?

- **Yes** → (continues)
- **No** → Either the spark is not being generated or it is being shorted. It could be:
  - Bad spark plug - Try a new one.
  - Kill switch is shorted - disconnect it and see if it fires or use an ohm meter to verify the kill circuit is an "open" when not pushed.
  - The coil or magneto (if equipped) is bad. Most use a magnet and coil to generate the high voltage required of the spark plug.

Does it develop and keep full RPM?

- **Yes** → If full RPM does not deliver full thrust then it could be:
  - The prop is on backwards - the curved side always faces forward (towards the motor).
  - The belt or clutch (if equipped) is slipping.
- **No** → Does it go to full RPM then fade or does the power vary without changing the throttle setting?

Does it go to full RPM then fade or does the power vary without changing the throttle setting?

- **Yes** → Is it overheating? A Cylinder Head Temp gauge is the best way to tell.
- **No** → Tune the Carburetor, Check the reed valve. Did that solve the problem?

Is it overheating?

- **Possibly** → Overheating has several possibilities: (see below)
- **No** → This common malady has many potential causes - some are not intuitive:
  - The prop is either too big or has too much pitch - "over propped".
  - The mixture may be changing as the motor heats up (even though it's not overheating. Tune Carb.
  - The cylinder and piston need to be de-carbonized.
  - Bad or broken tuned pipe. The damage is usually not visible. Try replacing the pipe if able.
  - There is an air leak into the cylinder or crankcase.
  - The throttle cable allows activation of the throttle without squeezing the trigger.

Tune the Carburetor, Check the reed valve. Did that solve the problem?

- **Yes** → (resolved)
- **No** → Is properly-mixed fuel getting to the carburetor? Try spraying starter fluid in the air intake. If it pops when cranked then fuel is *not* being delivered or is bad fuel.

Is properly-mixed fuel getting to the carburetor?

- **Yes** → Consider one of the following:
  - Hole in the piston.
  - Bad Reed Valve (if equipped).
  - Excess internal carbon deposits.
  - Bad ignition system. Even though it sparks the strength may be inadequate.
  - Exhaust is bad. Tuned pipes can make engines run rough if broken or improperly made.
- **No** → This may be caused by:
  - Air leak in a fuel line. Replace line. This can sometimes be seen as bubbles in the fuel line.
  - Blocked fuel filter.
  - Fuel tank air intake vent blocked. This will cause the motor to run for a while then become lean and quit.
  - Old fuel - it may last only a week if unsealed.
  - Improper fuel. Some machines don't like avgas or low octane fuel.

Overheating has several possibilities:
- The fuel/air mixture is (or gets) too lean.
- Not enough oil is mixed in with the fuel. This should not be a problem up to 50:1 Fuel/Oil ratio.
- Bearings have seized.
- The Cylinder is scored.
- The piston ring(s) are stuck.

Safety Wire, Tools and Bolts

Aircraft safety wire stays strong even after being twisted. Attach it so as to prevent the bolt or part from unscrewing or departing—they're always seeking freedom and this is good escape prevention. The muffler springs at right have been safetied so that, if they break, they stay out of the prop. Such projectiles can damage bystanders, the wing or cage on their way out.

Safety wire comes in various sizes; thicker is better given our machines' vibration. Use the thickest size your application allows. Few bolts are made to accept safety wire and must be drilled through the head.

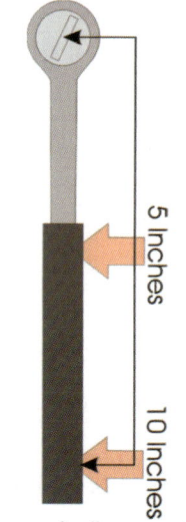

Torque

A torque wrench allows you to gauge how powerful you are twisting something. The farther out you push on the wrench, the more torque you exert. So 10 pounds of pressure at 10 inches produces the same torque that 20 pounds of pressure at 5 inches does— 100 inch-pounds.

Units

The standard international measure of torque is Newton Meters (N m). The U.S. uses Foot Pounds-force (ft·lbf) or just Foot Pounds. A less-often used measure is Kilogram-force meter (kgf m). 1 Ft Lbf = 1.36 N m = 0.14 kgf m.

Motor

Getting into this sport means, to some degree, becoming a mechanic. Precious few shops—motocross and cart racing shops mostly—can work on our gear and they may be reluctant once they know it's for flying (worried about liability). Local shops probably won't have parts so you'll need someone who specializes on your particular brand. In all likelihood, you'll need to ship your broken unit to a shop that knows the model. But if you want it fixed quickly, you better learn to do it yourself. There are, fortunately, some preventative measures that can keep little problems from blossoming into big ones that require repair.

Troubleshooting

All internal combustion motors need four elements in the right proportion and at the right time: spark, fuel, air and compression. Insure these are present and you'll likely solve the problem. Sometimes, just replacing the spark plug is all it takes. At other times you'll need full use of the preceding flowchart.

Start with the simple and cheap then progress to the more involved. If your dealer can't help, www.FootFlyer.com has a great troubleshooting section, and Internet discussion groups dedicated to your motor can also be a good resource.

Fortunately these machines are relatively simple, fairly reliable and easy to work on. Many "mechanically challenged" pilots, when faced with being grounded, have risen to the occasion.

The top two things to try whenever a problem eludes solution: 1) replace the spark plug and 2) if that doesn't work, replace the carburetor.

Bolt Tightening and Force

There is a universal way to describe how much force is used to tighten bolts: the Kilogram-Meter or Foot-Pound (imperial units list distance first). It is how much force and how far out on the handle to apply it. That describes torque.

If you hold a wrench way out on the handle, it doesn't take much force to get the bolt tight due to leverage. Torque is force times distance from the bolt's center.

Using the example at left, applying 10 pounds of pressure, 5 inches out on the wrench, is 50 inch-pounds of torque. Applying 5 pounds of force 10 inches out is also 50 inch-pounds of force. 1 Foot-Pound is 12 Inch-Pounds. Be careful with units: 50 foot-pounds is a *lot* more torque than 50 inch-pounds.

Over tightening bolts is worse than under tightening since you can easily strip out their threads, especially aluminum threads.

Preventative Maintenance

Spark Plugs may last as little as 10 hours before carbon deposits and other wear degrades performance. They should either be changed every 20 hours or at the first sign of trouble—primarily because they are so cheap, easy to change and are so commonly the problem. Tighten them to about 6 ft-pounds which is enough to flatten the washer that comes with most plugs. If you don't have a torque wrench, apply about 12 pounds of force 6 inches out on the handle (same as 6 pounds of force applied one foot out).

Fuel Lines harden over time, making them more likely to develop cracks or holes and should be replaced before becoming stiff. Tygon brand line is the gold standed. Don't route it around sharp corners or let it touch sharp objects lest chaffing causes holes. The primary symptom of holes is bubbles in the fuel line—that will make the motor run rough, lean or not at all. Don't secure fuel lines with wire ties.

Exhaust system bolts, rivets and springs are always trying to vibrate off—a serious problem if parts either deform or drop onto the fuel tank. Although a fire is still highly unlikely, this area deserves close scrutiny. Exhaust components, whenever possible, should be safety wired. Putting heat tolerant sealant into the springs helps prevent failure from vibration.

Head bolts should be checked with an *inch*-pound torque wrench, especially when the machine is new. They tend to loosen up along with many other fasteners.

Reduction Drive

Any mis-alignment of the pulleys will cause the belt to either come off or break well before its time. With proper adjustment and a light propeller, a belt should last 100 hours.

On average it should be tensioned so that there is about a 1/4" of play when pressed at spot 1 below.

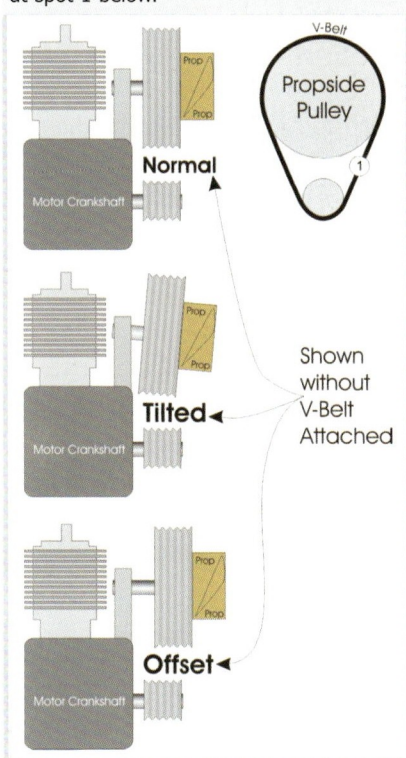

Most paramotors use a reduction drive to turn the motor's high-RPM into a propeller-friendly lower RPM. They either use a belt or gears.

Gear Drive

Most gear drives consist of 2 gears and 4 bearings in a sealed grease-laden aluminum housing. It's normally driven by the motor through a clutch bell.

Normal maintenance requires insuring sufficient grease (or gear oil depending on make) and good bearings. They generally require very little attention; however, on rare occasion little bits of metal can muck up the works. When that happens, the case must be split open and the debris removed.

If you feel play in the prop, and it's not due to prop bolts, the bearings may be failing. Replacement requires splitting the redrive (gearbox) which is fortunately easy. Unscrew the bolts part-way then tap on their heads with something that won't do damage. Once the halves are partway separated, use a gear puller or prying tool (chisel or something wide that won't scrape the metal) to finish the separation. If the gears are damaged you may need a gear puller. If the bearings are

This is a common belt-drive arrangement (2). One good way to check belt tension is determining how much torque it takes to make the belt slip. Put a torque wrench on the center nut as depicted, hold the prop still and try to tighten the nut. The nut should stay put but if the belt slips with less than 1.8 kg m (13 ft-lbs), then the belt is too loose. Tighten it and try again. The torque value will vary depending on the belt and motor.

Top picture (1): After installing new fasteners or parts, put a dab of fingernail polish on the juncture. You'll be able to quickly see, during preflight, if it has loosened.

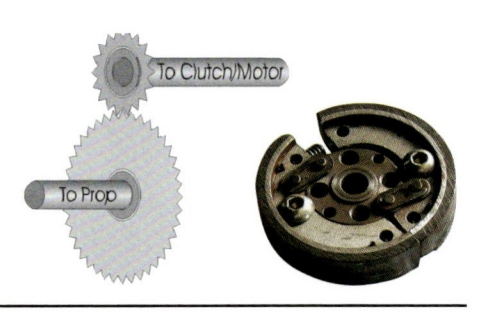

Gear reduction drive with clutch.

The motor spins the clutch fast enough for clutch "dogs" (like brake shoes to expand into the clutch bell which is connected to the redrive's small gear which then drives the much larger propside gear at a lower, more prop-friendly RPM.

At low RPM, springs keep the clutch dogs retracted so the prop does not turn.

The clutch pictured above, far right has one broken spring. So the two halves spread out against the clutch bell as soon as the motor is started causing the prop to spin even at idle (which it should not do).

bad, you'll probably have to heat the case to get them out. Be sure to replace any sealer around the edges to prevent leaks.

Belt Drive

The primary adjustment on belt-drive units is belt tension. Too loose and it slips—causing a "chirping" noise on each power stroke. Being too tight can bend the stand-off or stretch the belt. All motors have some way to adjust belt tension by changing the distance between pulleys You must tighten new belts a few times since they stretch in the first few flight hours.

The two pulleys must be aligned properly as shown on the previous page.

The belt should not squeak during power up, that's too loose. A heavy propeller (especially where the mass is out towards the tips) will aggravate slipping and may dramatically shorten belt or redrive bearing life.

Clutch

A clutch allows starting and idling the motor without spinning the prop. They are found mostly on smaller motors because larger motors need the prop's mass to act as a flywheel.

It's just like a mini-bike; at idle, springs hold the clutch shoes in. As you throttle up, the clutch shoes are thrown outward, rubbing against and grabbing the clutch bell. The prop is attached to that bell through either gears or a belt reduction drive. Make sure the prop is free-wheeling (no rubbing) with the motor off and that the clutch shoes are not too worn which would damage the bell.

If a clutch bell gets grooves worn in it or is pitted from rust, it will quickly eat up new clutch shoes and should be replaced.

Propeller

The propeller must be mounted with the curved side facing forward (direction of flight) and the bolts tightened evenly. The prop is held in place by friction with the plates, not the bolts. If there is torsional stress on the bolts, such as when they're too loose, they will break.

Do not drill extra holes in the prop hub to fit a different bolt pattern, the weakened wood could break, causing a catastrophic failure.

Use grade 8 bolts, or better, and check tightness periodically. They should be torqued to approximately 5 Foot-Pounds (0.7 kg m); the goal is not to deform the wood. Tighten each bolt partway in succession, one at a time, on opposite sides, until getting to the desired torque just like a car wheel. Composite props can be torqued up to 7 foot pounds (1.0 kg m).

Rotate the prop vertical and try to move the tip fore and aft while watching the engine mounts. A broken or nearly failed mount may allow enough flex for the prop to hit a frame/cage part and must be replaced. If the prop wiggles, check the center nut (on those motors that use it) and tighten if loose.

Balancing Act

Vibration is a paramotor's mortal enemy and props are big contributors. There are many methods for balancing, but the most common, and fortunately the easiest, is static balancing. Less obvious is balancing out various aerodynamic maladies that can cause equally bad vibration.

Static Balance

The prop should balance exactly at the center of the hub. Special balancers can be purchased that will quickly reveal if the prop is heavier either spanwise (tip to tip) or chordwise (leading edge to trailing edge). Most balancers have a cylinder plug sized to fit snugly in the prop's center hole. The prop is hung from a single point right in the middle. If one blade, or side, droops then it's too heavy. A lawnmower blade balancer works OK, too.

The cure is to put enough weight on the light side to bring it back to center. One method is to drill a hole opposite the heavy side and melt solder into it until balanced. Don't drill the hole all the way through so only one side has to be smoothed afterwards. Cover the hole with a glue and baking soda mix and sand to match the wood contour.

Carbon Fiber props are different since they're hollow. Drill a hole near the tip and add epoxy or, in more extreme cases, melt solder in it (usually only necessary after a significant repair on the opposite blade). Seal the solder with epoxy and sand to shape.

Minor corrections to fix an imbalance can be done by spraying clear varnish to the lighter side. Several coats will be necessary as much of the weight evaporates off.

Aerodynamic Balance

If one blade is pulling harder than the other blade, it will cause vibration; it is aerodynamically unbalanced. Possible causes are:
- The propeller has a chordwise offset (see diagram on page 123), probably one or two bolts on one side are over-tightened, compressing the prop unevenly.
- The propeller is warped. This is more likely if it has been significantly repaired.
- One blade is longer or fatter than the other. That's relatively easy to correct by shaving off some length. One way to tell is to set shelf paper on the floor, put the prop on it and carefully outline one half. Then put the other half over the outline and see if it's close. If not, reshape the larger half to match.

You can measure the angle of each blade by first setting it on a smooth, flat floor. Go 75% out towards the tip, hold a straight edge against the prop's flat bottom and measure its angle to the floor with a protractor.

Anytime a prop is worked on or reshaped, it should be statically balanced.

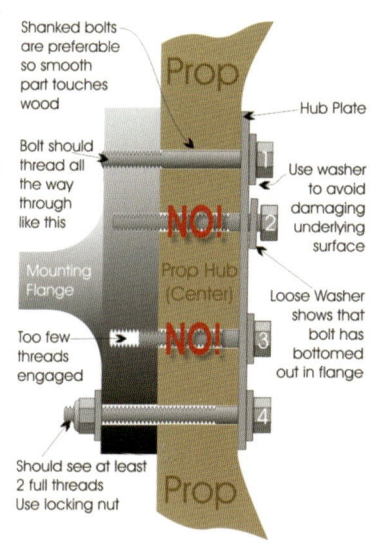

The curved surface mounts *towards* the motor so that it faces the direction of flight. Trying to launch with a backwards-mounted prop is embarrassing, at best. You'll have thrust but certainly not enough to fly. Looking at a paramotor from behind you should always see the prop's flat side.

The 4 bolt holes go through the *hub* which mounts to a *flange* on the motor—usually a redrive.

Tracking

If one blade tip passes by the same point in space at a different spot (either fore or aft) than the other blade, the tracking is off. The prop could be warped, improperly mounted (bolts unevenly tightened) or it could have an aerodynamic imbalance which would be more difficult to detect.

The tracking can be off by up to a ¼ inch with little effect. Any more than that, though, should be corrected by tightening the bolts evenly. If the prop is not causing vibration, leave it alone.

All propeller blades flex and twist a bit when under power—causing either more or less lift as they do. If one blade twists more than the other, it will cause a vibration even though the prop balances statically. A vibration that worsens faster than normal for a simple static imbalance may be caused by this. Poorly made, or thin, or props with large repairs are more likely to suffer from flexing.

Prop Tape

Special tape can be applied to the prop's leading edge to protect it from minor dings but it extracts some performance penalty. Also, if not adhering well, it can come off and cause an uncomfortable imbalance (it can generally be flown that way back to the destination).

Thin tape is better for going around the sometimes-difficult curves and tends not to hurt performance as much. Thick tape can sometimes be coaxed to work but may require small V-cuts or using a hair dryer to make it more malleable (see diagram at left).

Propeller Repair

Props will be sacrificed—to cages, to lines, to departing parts, and ground debris. Fortunately, many oops's are pretty easy to fix. Repairs must be done correctly to avoid pieces flying off with devastating consequences.

On all repairs, the surface should be cleaned first and sanded afterwards. If two-part epoxy is used, it should be allowed to fully cure before sanding; use a hard sanding block to prevent airflow-ruining bumps.

> ⚠ **Caution!**
>
> Poorly done repairs can leave props dangerously weakened. The repaired part could shoot off as a deadly missile.
>
> If uncertain about a damaged prop, send it to be professionally repaired. Be aware that even professionally repaired props shed parts occasionally.

If prop tape does not adhere well to the curves, cut V's out as depicted here.

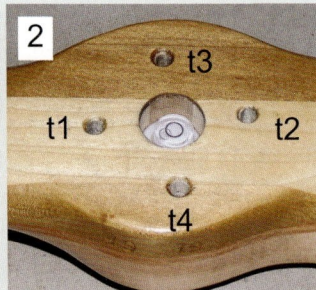

> **Cylinder Style Prop Balancing**
>
> Here is a cylinder-style prop balancer in use. It allows balancing both lengthwise and widthwise.
>
> The cylinder slides in the prop's center hole and then sits on the pointed stand. Any imbalance will cause the prop to tilt towards the heavy direction. On this prop, the bubble is down and left meaning that it's heavy to the right and up. Weight has to be added down and left.
>
> The t1 through t4 is what order the bolts should be tightened when re-mounting the prop. Barely tighten t1 then t2 then t3 then t4 then go around again until they are appropriately tightened.

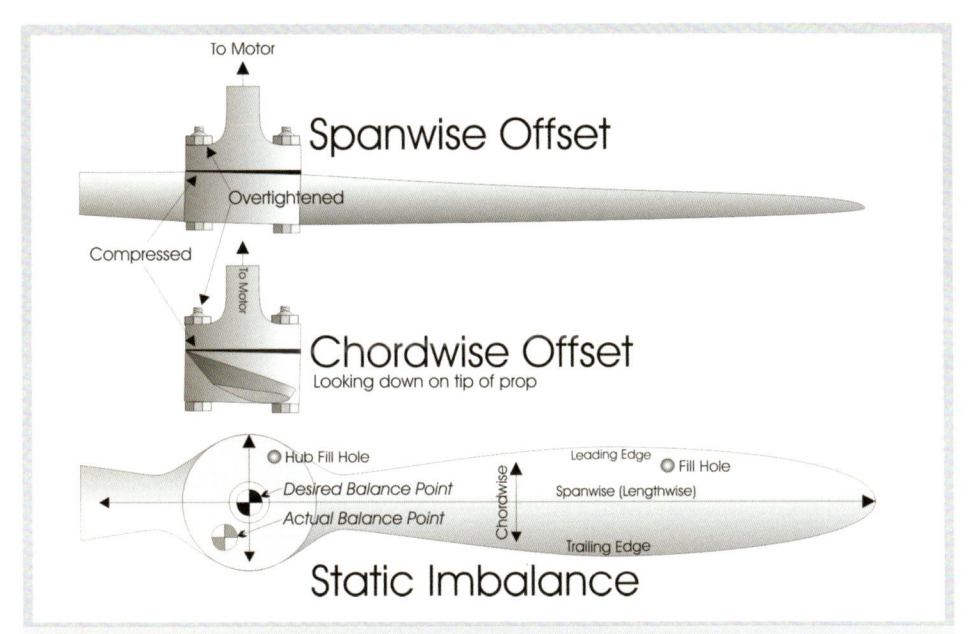

Spanwise Offset — Overtightened / Compressed
Chordwise Offset — Looking down on tip of prop
Static Imbalance — Hub Fill Hole, Desired Balance Point, Actual Balance Point, Leading Edge, Fill Hole, Spanwise (Lengthwise), Chordwise, Trailing Edge

If a prop is not flat on the flange, the offset will cause some vibration. A chordwise offset is far worse because one blade has a higher angle of attack than the other: It will pull harder as it goes around even though the prop is statically balanced.

Static balancing can be done by drilling a shallow hole where weight is needed and melting solder into it. Put a layer of epoxy on top to hold it in place then sand and varnish. The prop above (Static Imbalance) shows that weight needs to added at the "Fill Hole" to counteract an actual balance point low and to the left. Use a fill hole on the hub when it is mostly a chordwise imbalance.

Repairing Wood Props

The quickest repair for small divots is Super Glue™ (or equivalent) and baking soda. Micro balloons, available at hobby shops, can be used in place of baking soda—they are lighter and easier to sand. Layer on the glue and sprinkle in baking soda. In the right proportion the mix may smoke a bit but should harden quickly. Repeat until the damage is filled then sand to shape.

Somewhat bigger gouges can be filled with epoxy and baking soda (or micro balloons). Use tape to follow the prop's contour in a way that you can pour the mixed epoxy in. That reduces sanding. Use an equal amount of epoxy and baking soda (by volume) to help reduce weight and make it easier to sand.

After it hardens use a hard sanding block to reshape it. It must be well cured before sanding; 5-minute epoxy, for example, must harden for several hours first.

Larger repairs, up to 30% of the length or width of one blade can be done with a variety of methods, one of which is depicted on the next page.

Repairing Carbon Fiber Props

Carbon Fiber props are less forgiving of damage. Even after being repaired, they may harbor invisible degradation that could separate later, without notice, throwing shards. They should only be used when no risk to bystanders is present.

Carbon fiber props are usually hollow with a ½" thick or so foam core to keep the halves spaced appropriately. Lighter, but much more expensive than wooden props, they are also more challenging to repair. Don't expect them to look perfect after being repaired because the fiberglass used in the above method needs to cover part

Static Prop Balancers.

These balancers are accurate, reliable, and simple to use: The prop's heavy side droops down.

1. A stand balancer checks only for lengthwise imbalance, the cause of most vibration. Put the cylinder through the prop's center hole and place on the green stand. This one, modified by Alex Varv, uses razor blades mounted on the stand to improve sensitivity.

2. The Xplorer string balancer checks for both spanwise and chordwise imbalance. Put the cylinder through the prop and hang from its string.

Both of these commercial versions take the hassle out of balancing props. You can, of course, make your own but these are inexpensive and already fit almost all props.

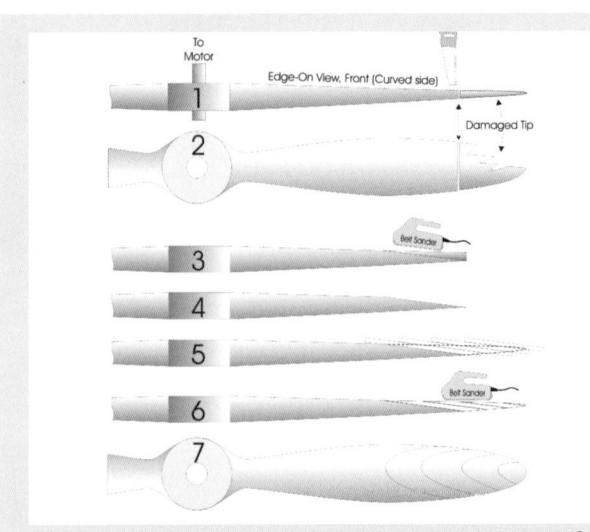

Surprisingly large repairs can be made on wooden props if done properly. A belt sander makes it easier but having a steady hand and some basic wood-working skill is a must.

Use a quality wood glue, spread evenly, on 1/4" thick slabs of poplar wood (step 5). Make sure they're completely flat against each other and clamp firmly for overnight drying before sanding.

Sand to shape then varnish, sand, varnish and balance.

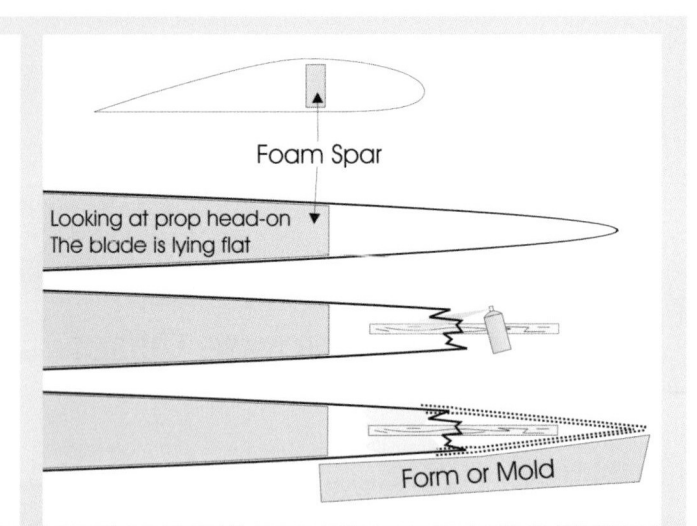

Small repairs can be filled without stiffening. Anything over about an inch across or deep needs more. Always wear a respirator and goggles whenever working with fiberglass resin or sanding the hardened result. Anything over 3 inches should be repaired professionally and some carbon fiber prop makers strongly recommend against trying to repair their products.

Fiberglass is heavier than carbon fiber so balancing after the repair is especially important.

of the top to have proper adhesion.

Simple cracks or holes aren't bad as they can be filled using epoxy. Force epoxy into the hole then use tape to form the prop's shape while the epoxy sets. Lay it so the epoxy puddles against the tape while curing. You can also use putty-type epoxy.

More severe damage, such as when more than about an inch of tip is missing, requires another technique. You'll need fiberglass cloth and resin (available at some hardware and most marine supply stores). See the diagram for clarification of these steps.

Clean and sand the area within two inches of the damage to have a good bonding surface for the resin.

Spray foam (insulating foam is sold at many hardware stores) into the tip void for support. With worse damage, embed some reinforcement material (wood or wire) into the foam such that it extends beyond the foam. That will help hold the repair (next steps) in place. Let the repair set up overnight.

Trim the foam so that so it does not protrude into the repair area.

Mix the resin according to its directions—a finicky step that warrants practicing elsewhere. The mix must be just right. Cut up pieces of cloth, mix them into the resin then work the saturated pieces into the tip and around the mold. Longer pieces should overlap the prop's top and bottom upper and lower surfaces for the best bond.

Once hardened completely, sand to shape. A belt sander really helps to speed up the process but don't sand away where the fiberglass overlaps the existing prop. It won't look perfect, but is necessary for strength.

Balance the prop and expect to add weight in the other tip.

The Wing

Paraglider wings require attention in proportion to how they are stored and used. Age and moisture exposure result in line shrinkage so lines must be stretched periodically. They can also get stretched due to overstress (aerobatics, B-Line Stalls, etc.) or weakened by heat or sharp bends (especially knots) and then must be replaced.

Fabric can tear, become porous, moldy or get chewed by insects and must be repaired. Most experienced pilots have found that beyond about 300 hours of strong UV time the wing has served its time. Here are some tips to help keep your wing airworthy and even extend its life.

Replacing Risers

Unless they get damaged, risers should outlast the rest of the wing; they are way over-built. When inspecting newly acquired risers, check general condition; especially check that the stitching is done correctly. At least one set was shipped with the riser loop only tack stitched—an incredibly dangerous flaw that will likely fail on the first flight.

Risers can be separated from the lines to accommodate either a different model or replacement. Mostly this is done to put *motor risers* (shorter) on soaring wings to use with motors having high attachment points. Otherwise the soaring wing's brake position can be too high. Risers on soaring wings are longer to go with typical free-flight harnesses which nearly always have low attachment points.

A different riser set can dramatically change the wing's flight characteristics and usually takes the wing out of certification. Only use riser sets recommended by the manufacturer. Even then the wing may be out of certification if it wasn't re-tested with those risers.

You can remove risers by taking the lines off at their *quick links*.

Complete one side before doing the other side, starting from the A's then proceeding back to the brakes. Put masking tape across a group of lines before detaching them and use a felt tip marker to note which side faces forward ("F" in the pictures) as well as what lines they are (A's, B's, etc.) including the split A, if equipped. Replacing the lines on one individual riser at a time is another good way to keep everything straight. Below is one method for replacing a riser in case you must do it all at once (such as sending a riser set away for replacement).

Start by marking the brake line knot location with a felt tip pen. Untie the brake toggle to pull its line through the brake pulley (or guide) then:

- If you have to cut away anything (like shrink wrap plastic) always cut *away* from the fabric. Be careful while using tools to avoid scratching the metal—that weakens it significantly.
- Pull the lines off and inspect any rubber O-rings that you remove. They keep the lines from misaligning or rubbing across the nut and threads. Replace old ones (plumbing supply outlets carry these) since they get brittle with age and break easily.
- If hard plastic shrink wrap was used, replace it with either electrical heat-

Don't change risers unless the manufacturer approves of the new set. Glider behavior and handling can differ dramatically with different risers. Picture 1 shows how risers affect relative line height, especially when the trimmers are up (fast).

2. Store the risers together either by clipping them to a small carabiner or by hooking them into each other like this.

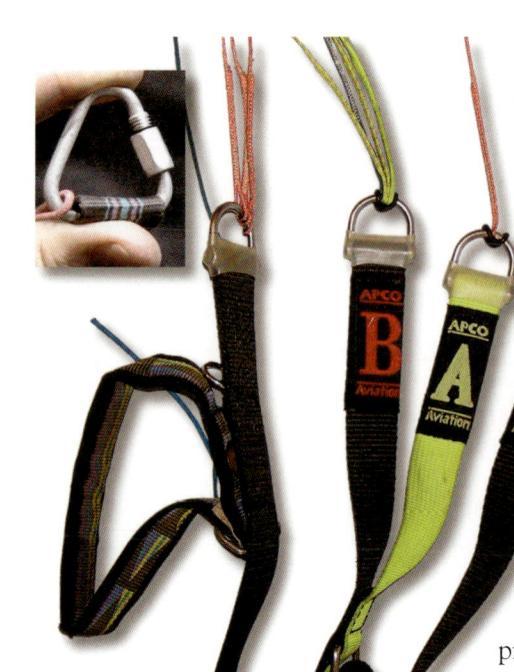

shrink tubing (from electronics supply stores) or electrical tape.

• Put the heat shrink tubing on the lines (if used), put the lines on the new riser, put the O-ring on with a figure 8 pattern (as shown) and then snug up the fastener.

• Snug to finger tight then go an 1/8th turn more with a tool.

When completed, kite the wing before flying to make sure everything appears in order and it handles as expected. Additionally, make sure the brake lines get adjusted before flying.

Adjusting Brake Lines

Brake line length is a critical dimension that should only be adjusted by, or under the guidance of, someone familiar with the procedure. Brake lines that are too short will deflect the trailing edge—a dangerous situation that could cause a parachutal stall (see Chapter 4). Excessively long brake lines might allow a toggle into the prop and also may limit flare authority for landing.

This riser set is ready to have it's lines removed.

On triangular quick-links (inset), if you have to use a tool to remove the connector, it's bent. Don't use pliers to force it on. You're better off replacing a bent one than flying with a compromised part. Over or under-tightening can cause structural failure under load.

The black rubber grommet is used to keep lines together and positioned properly on the quick link. It prevents them from snagging on an edge. These grommets should be replaced with new ones if cracked. On the riser set above, the C lines (rear risers on this wing) are missing the grommet.

When properly adjusted, with toggles at their pulley (flying hands-off), there should be some slack in the brake line with no trailing edge deflection. You'll see a slight arc in the line from its pulley up to the trailing edge. In flight, your hands should rest near position 2—that leaves enough flare authority while remaining comfortable. Having your arms hang lower may be more comfortable but sacrifices brake travel. Your bicep should be about horizontal when resting the weight of your arms in the brakes. A few inches can make a big difference in comfort.

Many free flyers set their toggles lower since they can take *wraps* (wrap the excess line around their hands) to have full authority. The throttle makes that difficult for motor pilots.

On those few wings that have two brake line pulleys to choose from, use the one that is most comfortable. Generally, with a low attachment motor, use the high pulley and for mid or high attachment motors use the low pulley.

Most wings come from the factory with the brakes set somewhat long to reduce the likelihood of a new pilot stalling. But that also limits control authority. To set the length, kite the wing and mark where the new knot should go. Untie the existing knot and retie it at the new location using the depicted brake line knot.

Brake Line Knots

The "8 Follow Through" is an ideal knot with low stress on the line. It is easy to tie since after looping through the brake toggle, it just follows itself back through the half-hitch.

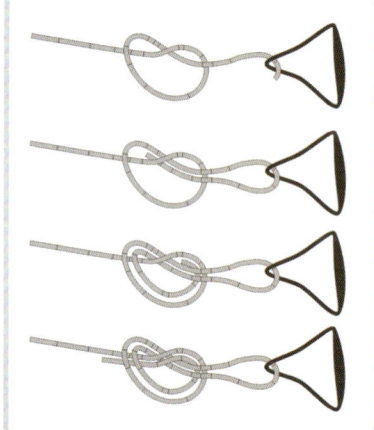

The Bowline (below) is commonly used for a quick tie but stresses the line more due to sharper bends and is not very secure.

Whichever you choose, keep the brake toggle and knot close together to prevent the toggle from flapping about in the breeze.

Repairing the Wing Fabric

Invariably you will tear the wing's fabric; either by pulling it too aggressively or mishandling. Sharp rocks and other protrusions are frequent culprits. Fortunately there is a lot of resilience and this doesn't always have to be a grounding item.

If the tear is structural then you'll have to bite the bullet and send it in for a full repair. Structural is where there is significant stress on the material at that point. The best example is just about any seam or anywhere lines attach to fabric. If the loop pulls out of the wing you'll have to send the wing to a shop for repairs.

Anytime wing meets spinning prop, the wing should be inspected. Even repair experts may not be able to put a torn mess back together but surprisingly excessive damage can be repaired by qualified shops. Small non-structural repairs can be done on the field. Obtain some self-adhesive repair material (repair tape) which comes in various colors and is similar to wing material. Cut it into an oval that covers the tear with about an inch of overlap. Make one for both sides of the fabric. Stretch the fabric out as much as possible, wipe it clean and dry then press the repair tape on top. Press hard. It is best to line the pattern of little squares up with the wing material's pattern. Repeat for the other side.

Inspection

After a couple years or 100 hours sun time on a new wing it should be professionally inspected. After that, annual inspections should be done for hard core flyers and biennual inspections for casual flyers (less than 20 hrs per year).

Don't be deluded by the high number of lines; a *cascade failure* is where one line breaks and transfers load to adjoining lines, which break in a cascade of many lines. It is rare but does happen, especially on wings that are "ridden hard and put away wet." That includes heavy maneuvering or aerobatics—such wings should see double the inspection interval.

Line Stretching

Don't tie a broken line together, it shortens the line and reduces its strength by half—replacement is required.

Lines shrink with time, especially if they get damp, losing up to a couple inches in length. Kevlar lines shrink less than Dyneema (or Spectra). Since the A's and B's

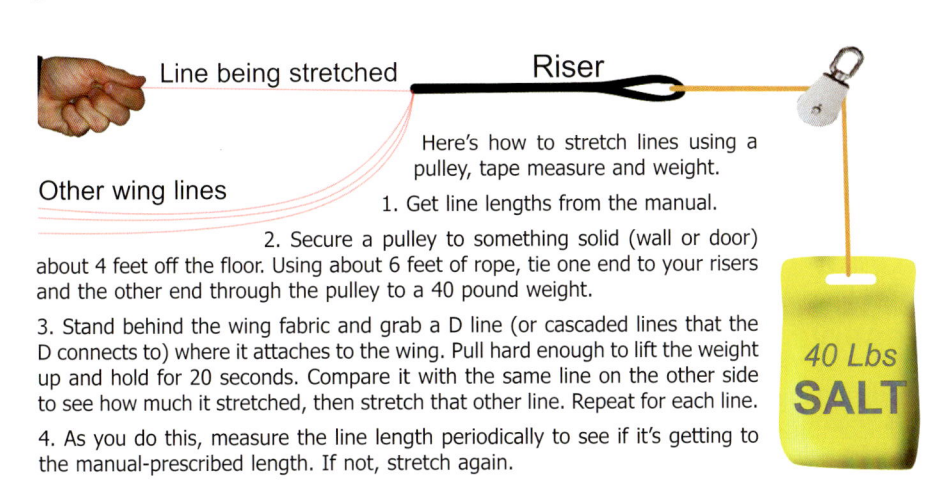

1. The hole.

2. The Patch.

3. The real fix. Here is a typical inspection shop where gliders are tested and repaired. The porosity meter (being used at left) measures how quickly air can seep through the fabric. Strength testing of lines is done with a scale and repairs are done with the sewing machine at right. There's more to it than meets the eye.

Here's how to stretch lines using a pulley, tape measure and weight.

1. Get line lengths from the manual.

2. Secure a pulley to something solid (wall or door) about 4 feet off the floor. Using about 6 feet of rope, tie one end to your risers and the other end through the pulley to a 40 pound weight.

3. Stand behind the wing fabric and grab a D line (or cascaded lines that the D connects to) where it attaches to the wing. Pull hard enough to lift the weight up and hold for 20 seconds. Compare it with the same line on the other side to see how much it stretched, then stretch that other line. Repeat for each line.

4. As you do this, measure the line length periodically to see if it's getting to the manual-prescribed length. If not, stretch again.

bear more load, they tend to stretch back to their proper length during flight leaving just the C's and D's shrunk.

Given that line length determines wing camber (curvature), they must be stretched back to their proper length as shown on the previous page. A wing that is getting hard to inflate may be suffering from line shrinkage and may benefit from stretching as shown on the previous page.

If you cannot get the lines to be within a 1/4 inch of their specified length, or they stretch too far, the offending lines need to be replaced. In all likelihood, that's a sign that all the lines should be replaced.

After An Ocean Dunking

It is universally accepted that dunking a wing in salt water is bad; finely abrasive salt crystals remain after the water evaporates, dramatically shortening the glider's life (both lines and fabric). But if you remove the salt water right away by hosing it down with fresh water, the damage can be avoided.

To rinse a wing after immersion, clip it along the trailing edge to a strong clothesline. Hoist it up high enough to get the cell openings above ground.

Spray it thoroughly with fresh water to clean out any remaining brine. Get up inside each cell opening to get it completely soaked. That should drain away or at least dilute the briny badness to a safe level. Then leave it on the line, out of direct sunlight, to dry.

At least hose the wing down wherever it lays. This may be preferable to waiting but then go through the above method as soon as you can.

Whether fresh or salt water, take care when extricating a submersed wing—it becomes extremely heavy and will tear easily if lifted with water in the cells. Pull it out *slowly* by the trailing edge.

Emergency Tool Kit

A lot can be fixed in the field with a few simple tools and parts that fit in your harness pouches. Mostly, you want to be able to tighten anything that can loosen, replace the belt (if applicable), adjust the carburetor and replace the spark plug.

- Allen wrenches. Almost all engines use metric sizes 3, 4, 5 and 6mm.
- Screw drivers. Make sure you can adjust the carburetor.
- Lightweight spark plug wrench. The type with just the round hex fitting and a hole is good—your screw driver can double as the leverage.
- Small Knife, small locking pliers, and small socket set (3, through 8mm sizes).
- Spark plug, wire ties, 2 feet of safety wire and super glue (for the prop).

Reserve

Reserves generally come from the factory ready to install and deploy; most come with containers that easily clip onto your motor frame and harness but this *must* be done correctly. Installing it wrong may be worse than not having it at all.

Alan Chuculate is repacking a reserve. It's not hard but must be done correctly. There's a lot more than just folding and stuffing. Some instructors give clinics and there are videos to teach repacking. Never rely on just a video though, do it with someone who knows how so they can make sure you're doing it right.

If you're not certain how, or haven't practiced, send it to a repacker. The manufacturer, your instructor, or FootFlyer.com can suggest a reputable shop.

⚠ Caution!
Never put the wing in a washing machine or dryer. The stress and heat would be very damaging. If it gets wet, dry it immediately in an open area, preferably out of direct sunlight.

There are several places where a reserve gets mounted: Behind the head, on the side, in front of the pilot or under the seat. Each has advantages and disadvantages but most are mounted beside the pilot because it's usually the easiest to install. Some motors come with a reserve mount in the seat bottom, a nice arrangement because it is out of the way. Same thing for reserves mounted above and behind the pilot's head. For a machine to have the reserve mounted anywhere but on the side or in front, it generally must be *designed* for it.

Setup

Mounting a reserve on your motor must be done with an eye on how it will deploy and how you will reach it. Make sure you can reach it quickly, have enough arm travel to pull it all the way out (over a foot of line pulls out before the reserve pouch itself), and be able to easily throw it in a clear direction.

Here are some considerations for mounting the reserve:

- Mount it opposite the throttle. Some suggest this to be your dominant hand but rehearsal can make either hand work. A front mount is acceptable but consider how the risers will pull on deployment. If your body gets between the risers and an inflating 'chute, it's *you that* will probably break.

- Change the throttle, if necessary, so you can mount it opposite the torque direction. If torque causes a left weight shift turn, mount the reserve on your right side.

- The reserve bridle should be routed along the harness or motor frame and remain clear of throttle cable, straps, speedbar or anything else that would get in the way during deployment. Use Velcro or very small wire ties that break loose with about 20 pounds of pull. This will prevent nuisance breaks during normal handling but allow the reserve to pull free when needed.

- Go through a deployment in your mind. Think about where the reserve will come out, catch air and where each reserve riser will be as it extends fully with you hanging below.

- Hook the reserve riser either to the same loops as the paraglider or as close as possible. Some consider it beneficial to come down leaning back so the motor absorbs impact. Most recommend being oriented upright so as to land on your feet for a parachute landing fall (PLF). That means the hang points for the reserve should be *higher* than for the paraglider. Of course if your harness comes equipped with reserve loops, use them—they will be designed for the opening shock.

1. On this installation, the pilot had two loops to choose from for his reserve bridle. The top ones would have been preferable but they were in use by the main carabiners. So he routed the reserve through the main carabiners to the lower "D" rings. When the reserve deploys, it will immediately scrunch these two carabiners together (should be ok but is not ideal).

2. This installation is preferred; the reserve risers go to the highest point on the harness meaning the pilot would land mostly upright after a deployment.

The wire ties/tape that keep the bridle (reserve risers) together must be able to break with only about 20 pounds of pull.

Insure the routing doesn't go through anything that would impede opening or cause injury.

Reserve Maintenance

Store the reserve as you would a paraglider—in a cool, dry place away from sunlight or chemicals. Of course, if it remains on your motor, be careful about where

The PPG Bible: A Complete Guide and Reference

Skydiving Reserves

Paraglider reserves differ structurally from sport parachuting reserves and the two must not be interchanged. A paraglider reserve is designed to open immediately while the sky diving version opens more gradually to avoid injuring the high-speed free-faller.

Terminal velocity (maximum fall speed) is over 120 MPH for a sky diver in free fall. Some paraglider reserves may not even hold together if thrown at that speed (a "terminal" open). A PPG reserve is more likely to be thrown below 50 MPH and a sky diving reserve might have difficulty opening at that lower speed.

the motor goes. For example, getting the motor wet is no big deal, getting the reserve wet scores a repack.

Repack your reserve once a year or, for those left in proper storage, every other year. It's necessary because the fabric will eventually tighten into shapes that don't open quickly; plus, rubber bands holding the bridle array in proper shape become brittle and break. Repacking is also great time to inspected the reserve.

The preferable way to repack is sending it to the factory that made it. They'll know it best and know what problems have come up on other similar models (fortunately they don't get tested a lot). You can also send it off to an experienced rigger who is familiar with the design. They will inspect it and replace anything as needed. Only repack it yourself if you're certain about the procedure and have the requisite parts. It's not that difficult to repack, but the steps must be done correctly.

If liquid spills on the container or it goes in the water, it should be inspected and repacked.

Always use the repack as an opportunity to practice tossing the reserve. Hanging from a simulator is ideal but, if that's not possible, just sit in your harness and practice throwing it. Do so several times while rehearsing the steps in Chapter 4.

1. This unit has a right-hand throttle so its reserve is on the pilot's left side. It must be secured both top and bottom so when the pilot pulls, he has full travel from the container. Some instructors recommend that the reserve be mounted on the side of your predominant hand so a right handed pilot would have a left-hand throttle.

Also note the hook-in style. Carabiners are attached to a strap that connects to the rails on either side of the pilot (what the reserve is mounted to). This is a fixed low hook-in style.

2. This one is made for an overhead mount. The two small metal carabiners on either side of the letter "C" (above the mains) are made for a reserve hook-in.

⚠️ **NO!**

A pilot pulling on the reserve at left would be unsuccessful. The red-circled pin is completely through its loops and wouldn't work. Make sure the hooks are through only halfway as shown in the green circles so they can pull out freely. Pulling the handle lets the flaps open to reveal a deployment bag.

Flying Cross Country

CHAPTER 13

Heading out on a cross-country is premier. Exploring new directions, going for miles to nowhere in particular, poking about the landscape from barely above—it is the freedom that many have only dreamt about.

Obviously there are limits. Don't plan on commuting to work, although it's been done, and beware of small changes in weather that can lay waste to plans. Don't get out somewhere and *need* to get back, that could pressure you to fly when you shouldn't. However, once armed with appropriate skills, gear and weather knowledge, cross country can be extremely rewarding. You launch from home, alight at some distant spot, relish the accomplishment, and then head back home via a different route.

The author found his mark. The pictured grass-runway airport was a target for the *Circle and 2 Lines* task of the U.S. Nationals in 2004. There were a lot of trees below which accounts for the high altitude.

Basic Tips

Whenever you fly farther than you're willing to walk, there are additional concerns. Some apply even to local flying but take on more importance with distance.

- Choose days with no weather changes anticipated near your flight times. You don't want to be away from your launch site when the weather turns sour.

- Let somebody know that you will be flying and take a cell phone if able.

- If the wind shifts, try changing altitudes to improve penetration (groundspeed into a headwind). Wind is normally stronger up high but occasionally you can climb into a *weaker* wind. A GPS is invaluable for maximizing groundspeed—as you climb, just watch the groundspeed readout and note the best altitude.

- Avoid flying low, but if you must, do so only while headed into the wind (see chapter 16). Staying above 200 feet AGL is dramatically safer since it keeps

The PPG Bible: A Complete Guide and Reference

Summer Escape

A warm summer afternoon beckoned and I rushed home. After gathering up my gear, I quickly slipped away before anyone could interfere: I had a mission. Fifteen miles south of my favorite launch site, a new racetrack had just opened up—I wanted to go see it. Plus, I wanted to fly to an airport just west of there. Quick calculations suggested nearly 3 hours of flight time—about my endurance—so I'd have to find thermals in order to loiter anywhere. True, I might not make the complete round trip, but this is the Midwest and landing options are plentiful.

Off I went, running into the sky, climbing on course, and making detours at interesting targets along the way. When something cool came into view I just went down and checked it out. A motocross track appeared. There was nobody on it so I went down and carved out it's hilly meanders, a few feet high, trying to stay over its curvy course; playing. *This* is the ultimate off-road vehicle!

Then back up I went, like a migrating bird, heading south towards a place I'd never been. Flight was so delicious. Earlier in that day I had flown over in a Boeing 737, working, but was now commanding nothing more than 28 square meters of nylon, searching for lift. Abundant thermals were well marked by cumulus clouds. I circled in the stronger updrafts, quickly getting above 3000 feet. Brrr. Sitting in my chair, overlooking the speckled sprawl of civilization was inspiring. Of course I've been that high thousands of times—three times just that day—but certainly never suspended by fabric and sitting in a little seat listening to my favorite music.

Finding the racetrack was brainless from that high. Nobody was on it so I went down for a closer look, cruising its outer perimeter from 100 feet, then again from 10 feet. Wow, that's a great way to experience a NASCAR track. After scouring the track, I pressed onward, westward, exploring. Landing at the Joliet airport let me really feel my new capability—actually *travelling* in the PPG. Here I was, many miles from home, having explored, gone to the heights, foot-dragged a speedway, and now just stood there at an airport, basking in the accomplishment. I doffed my motor to see how much gas remained. Lift had helped but it would be mightly close—there was maybe 45 minutes worth. After a few minutes I relaunched. Then a friend appeared below, waving wildly. It was Nick, my flyin' buddy—I *had* to stop. Of course that burned more fuel. Oh but how I enjoyed being able to do that—coming back around, alighting, and chatting. After a few minutes, I launched and beelined it for home. When I turned on the GPS it had bad news—with 15 miles to go, I was now making only 12 MPH. Nope, that won't work. Oh well—I figured I'd go as far as I could.

Sure enough, the GPS was right and it became obvious that I would, in fact, land short. Using thermals (slowing down in lift, speeding up in sink, circling in the stronger ones) helped, but alas, 4 miles or so shy of my starting point, Mr. Motor sputtered his last and I went on glide. Good fortune let me slip into a field where I could stash my gear and grab a ride back. What an incredible treat!

Road signs can be helpful to locate yourself but be extremely careful. Flying low is fun but risky. In this case the pilot found only the speed limit. *That* was useful!

Also, make sure there are no cars that could be distracted by your presence.

humanity's protrusions (especially wires) below you.

- Cross power lines at their supports (poles or towers), at least twice their height and at an angle. Judging wire height is surprisingly difficult unless you're over those supports. Cross them at an angle so you easily turn away if the motor quits.

- Check the airspace if it's a new area.

- After takeoff, look back and see what the launch area looks like for your return. Find a prominent landmark since the sun angle or clouds may change appearances. It can be hard to recognize your home site the first time out.

- Take a map or GPS if the area is not familiar or you plan on a long trip. It's value comes as much from the groundspeed readout as the distance and direction.

- Don't ever let yourself get squeezed into night time. Besides being illegal, finding your way safely to the ground can be tough. Do carry a small flashlight though. Even if you land before darkness settles, it would be handy to see what you're doing on the ground.

- Carry basic tools.

- Consider taking a small amount of two-stroke oil in case you wind up in someone's yard and they have only gas for their lawn mower. (Yes, I've benefited from this exact advice).

As with all flying, stay within gliding distance of safe landing areas, favoring those that are downwind of you since they'll be easier to reach. Stay close to roads so egress is easier (unless you don't mind walking).

Fuel & Range

When choosing a route, start off into the wind. It's no fun being airborne, trying to get back and fighting a headwind, especially when you're ready to be on the ground. Plus it makes fuel planning easier to go upwind for half of your endurance and then turn around. It's a conservative approach that is convenient and more fun. For one thing, when you've had enough, it's nice to get back more quickly.

If there is little or no wind, only fly 1/3 of your endurance before turning around just to leave some margin for error. If the route is a triangle, plan the flight's last leg to be going downwind.

You should have a very good idea of how long you can fly before setting out. Also have an in-flight way to check fuel remaining such as a mirror.

If you're carrying oil, sometimes it's possible to land near a gas station and refuel. It does feel funny—walking up to the pump with your weird looking tank, filling it and knowing you'll be using it to run off into the sky. Strange, but amazing.

Getting Lost

In most areas of the country, getting lost is merely an inconvenience and all but impossible if you're carrying a GPS. It may be embarrassing when you land to ask for directions but, given the ability to land about anywhere, there is little to really worry about unless you're out in the boondocks. But before getting to that dreadful state of affairs, there are ways to keep yourself oriented.

- After takeoff, look back towards your launch area. Do this first a mile out, then a few miles out. Remember what you saw so, on the way back, you will better recognize it.
- Climb up higher. As long as airspace and clouds allow, you may get a better perspective.
- Use Roads and other prominent landmarks. Think of major roads, rivers, or railroad tracks in your area and whether you've crossed them or not. For example, if a major highway runs northward and is west of your launch site, but you haven't yet crossed it, then you know you're east of it.
- Use road Signs. Find a nice, landable field along a road with signs and scoot down to read it. Only with a PPG! Don't get below wire height, though, and always maintain safe landing options. This could be quite risky if you're not careful and is only an option in the most open areas.

Navigation

The following tools are not *necessary* to enjoy cross-country flight but they can be fun to master. In fact, they are the basis for an entirely different skill set: *Pilotage* and *dead reckoning*. These have been (and continue to be) used in regular airplane pilot training.

Dead reckoning is using a plotted course, calculated groundspeed and heading, to navigate and predict your future whereabouts. Using forecast winds, a map and compass you can come up with the heading to fly that should keep you on course.

Is the airspace where you're going legal *today*?

Chicagoland pilots had this surprise one day when the President dropped into town. They closed airspace within 30 miles—including many popular PPG destinations.

When flying to or through new areas we must be especially vigilant about airspace issues.

Vector Diagram

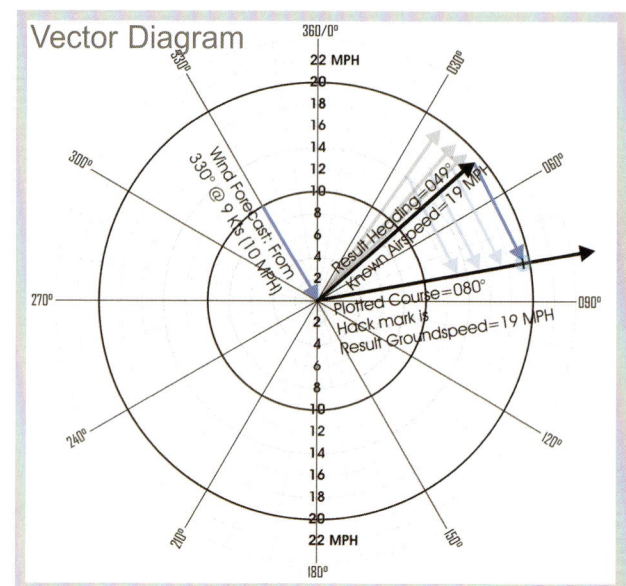

(Vector diagram showing: Wind Forecast: From 330° @ 9 Kts (10 MPH); Plotted Course = 080°; Result Heading = 049°; Known Airspeed = 19 MPH; Hack mark is Result Groundspeed = 19 MPH)

The latest blank version of this chart is provided at www.FootFlyer.com

Calculating Ground Track & Groundspeed

Once you know the desired ground track (plotted course) and your airspeed you can use this chart to derive heading and groundspeed:

1. Draw your plotted course (080°) from the center all the way outward.

2. Draw your forecast wind (blue line above) as the direction the wind is forecast from and long enough to represent the windspeed with the arrow head touching center.

3. You'll need two strips of paper. One should be marked as the wind arrow that represents the wind speed (mark an arrowhead to clarify wind direction) and mark the other piece's edge with your airspeed.

4. Keep the wind arrow parallel with the wind direction while sliding its arrowhead along the plotted course. At the same time, have the airspeed piece go from the center and stay in contact with the wind arrow. When the tail of the wind arrow touches the airspeed's marking, you've got a wind triangle. The airspeed arrow points to the heading-to-fly and the wind arrow is pointing at the groundspeed.

The example shows a plotted course of 080° (true course, without magnetic correction). The quartering tailwind turns out not to have any effect on groundspeed. The pilot will fly a 049° to maintain his 080° ground track.

Pilotage, covered later, is the process of reading the map in flight and adjusting heading to stay on the line. Manual navigation is a combination of these skills.

Even though we don't *need* all this, understanding it can be helpful. Mostly it can be a fun exercise—planning, then executing the plan accurately with just a map, compass and watch. International competition pilots must get good at this since it makes up to 33% of their score.

The purpose of all navigation is to fly a desired track over the ground and arrive at the destination at an estimated time. Using the navigation log below, do the following (details on each step are provided below):

- Draw a line on the map representing your desired ground track. Mark the line at easily identifiable checkpoints along the way and measure the distances between each mark. These get entered as checkpoints on your PPG navlog.

- Measure the true course of each straight segment, then apply *variation* to come up with a magnetic course for that segment.

- Calculate the magnetic heading that corrects for wind and tells what the

Magnetism, Truth & Courses

Aviation charts are laid out in grids of longitude and latitude with respect to true north. Compasses, however, point to magnetic north. The difference between true and magnetic north is shown on charts as lines of variation called Isogonic lines. For example, on this chart, the dashed line pointed to by #1 means that the difference is 14° east.

Magnetic course (MC) is derived by subtracting east ("east is least") variation and adding west variation to the true course (TC). So, in this case, the TC was 80°. After subtracting 14° of variation (use the closest isogonic line), you get a magnetic course of 66°. So if you used your compass to walk a 66° heading, you'd walk along the plotted line.

But air is usually moving, so we must account for wind drift. The result is magnetic heading (MH)—the compass heading you fly to stay on course.

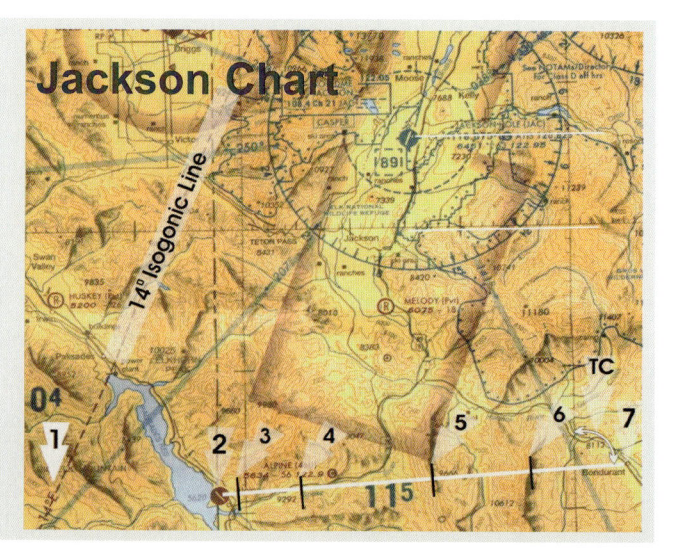

Jackson Chart

(Aeronautical chart showing the 14° Isogonic Line, with checkpoints numbered 1 through 7 along the TC line)

planned groundspeed will be (using the wind calculator described below)

- Build a navigation log to be used in flight or just for reference.
- Go fly the course using pilotage.

Plotting the Course and Heading

Chartmakers simplify matters by including vertical lines of longitude and horizontal lines of latitude on the charts. Point 1 on the Jackson Chart shows how it labels variation as E or W—in this case showing 14° east variation along the dashed *isogonic line* (a line that shows the magnetic variation in that area).

Remember this saying: "West is best, east is least." That means west variation is added to true course and east variation is subtracted from it. So if you want to go *true* east, (090°), subtracting 14° from 90° gives a magnetic course (MC) of 076°. Flying 76° in no wind would yield a 090° ground track.

Draw a course line on the chart representing your desired ground track from launch to landing and measure its degrees relative to true north. This can be done using a protractor and measuring from either a longitude or latitude line. With this true course in hand, add (for west) or subtract (for east) the variation to get a magnetic course. That is the magnetic heading you would fly with no wind. Add a correction for wind (covered below) to get the initial heading after launch.

Choose checkpoints along the route that will be easy to identify and easy to get a time measurement on. The best ones will be usable even if you're off-course. Rivers, power lines, highways or railroad tracks that cross perpendicular to your course are great. If they *angle* across your course, it is more difficult—you must know more accurately that you're on the course line when taking a time.

If you're writing out a navigation log, it can be filled in with the points, distances and magnetic courses. These are the most useful pieces of information along with the headings.

Wind Correction

Any wind will affect your groundspeed and track. Think of wind as a block of air with which you're drifting. When you're airborne, that motion is added to your own and must be accounted for to achieve a desired ground track. If you're trying to track due east and the wind is from the north (wind is always given in the direction it's *from*) then you'll need to hold a heading to the left—that is called *crabbing*. And with our slow speed, a little wind makes a lot of difference.

One way to figure this out is with a *vector diagram* as shown on the previous page—it represents speeds and directions visually. Vectors, in this case, are arrows, one for your in-flight speed and heading, and another for wind speed and direction. Follow the diagram's directions for "Calculating Ground Track & groundspeed."

If you're flying a round trip that ends up back at your launch site, any wind will *increase* your total flying time. Also, direct crosswinds slow you down. If any wind is present, it must have some tailwind component to keep groundspeed equal to or better than airspeed.

> **Digging Deeper:**
> **Earth's Moving Magnetic North**
>
> The Earth's magnetic north moves slowly over the years. In fact, the rate of drift is measurable and some charts show not only the current variation, but how fast it's drifting.
>
> The line of variation that shows where true and magnetic north are the same (lucky compass users there) is called the *Agonic Line*. In the U.S. this line goes through central Indiana—anywhere on that line and your compass reads both magnetic and true heading.
>
> The most significant difference between true and magnetic courses in the U.S. is on the northernmost coasts. Both east and west coasts have a difference of up to 20 degrees.
>
> Competition pilots may find that filling this out while flying is helpful. The latest blank version of this log is provided at www.FootFlyer.com

This is an example of *drift*. The wind from your right is causing a left drift. The resultant path over the ground is ground track.

You must angle into the wind so that ground track is taking you to the destination.

Pilotage

Pilotage is the process of flying your plan using a map, log, and visual cues to stay on course. It's the fun part and is amazingly easy in a PPG given our view.

Planning tells you what the ground track will be and offers an initial heading that corrects for wind (*crabbing* into the wind). It will be as accurate as the wind forecast. After launch, take up that heading until you can find some of the checkpoints and see what kind of correction it *really* takes to stay on track.

The goal is to maintain a ground track: if there's any crosswind, don't just point at the next checkpoint when it comes into view—you'll drift, have to re-aim, drift, re-aim, etc. That results in an inefficient curved path. You want a straight line *over the ground*. It's not necessarily intuitive since you're pointing upwind of the target, so make sure it is your *ground track* that is heading towards the target.

To see that you're tracking as desired, pick a nearby ground feature between you and the target then envision a line between the two; if you are drifting off of that line then adjust your heading accordingly.

Reading a map and associating ground features takes practice. Some things on the map are nearly worthless, small roads and populated areas, for example. The outlines of yellow that indicate populace (roughly equating to night illumination patterns) have little resemblance to what you'll see—they're usually too dated.

Obvious features, such as highways, railroad tracks, landmarks and the like are best. Using a long, straight feature (like railroad tracks) requires some way to tell where you are along that feature.

Telling distances is tricky too, more so in some areas than others. The U.S. Midwest has conveniently placed roads at one-mile intervals that run N/S and E/W which helps a lot. There is no such order in other areas, especially hilly ones.

The most useful tools on a navigation log are the mileage and estimated groundspeeds. You can either fill in the actual numbers or just use the log for reference. Some navlogs (or electronic calculators) have time in minutes; they must be converted to tenths—every 6 seconds is one tenth so 8 minutes and 12 seconds is 8.2 minutes.

Calculating Groundspeed

With a stopwatch and map you can calculate your groundspeed and, knowing that, you to can predict your position at any future point and time. If you also know your heading and airspeed you can even tell what the winds are although that starts getting complicated for someone piloting a paraglider.

Charts on the next page facilitate these calculations without any electronics. The charts can be taped to the same clipboard that you use for your navlog for easy reference. Competition is about the only time you would use these tools.

Altitudes

Choosing altitudes is critical for maximizing performance—climbing or descending can yield free additional groundspeed if more favorable winds are found. Start with the winds aloft information (see Chapter 7) to get an idea of what to expect, but improve your mental wind-image by trying different altitudes. Generally, the higher you go, the stronger the winds blow, but not always. Be quick to try different altitudes, especially if groundspeed dwindles appreciably.

Most airplanes cruise over 1000 feet AGL. Above 3000 feet they tend to fly in 500 foot increments with the eastbounders using odd altitudes (3000, 3500, 5000, 5500, etc.) and the westbounders using even altitudes (4000, 4500, 6000, 6500 etc.). Knowing that may help you know where to look out for them.

Lingering above 10,000 feet is a very bad idea since jets travel at their fastest speeds up there but this is more of a concern within 60 miles or so of larger cities.

Just because you *can* go direct doesn't mean it's always a good idea. And, besides safety, consider your retrieval options in case a landing becomes necessary.

Russman Flying the Panama Canal

Using a GPS

The Global Positioning System (GPS) provides incredibly useful information to hand-held *navigators*. The moving maps are simple to use but the most useful display is groundspeed and track. From that you can derive the winds aloft and plan what your groundspeeds will be.

If the GPS says you're tracking 120° (southeast) but you're pointed due east (090°) then you know the winds are out of the north, or have a significantly north component. If it says you're only going 15 mph and your normal airspeed is 25 mph then you have a 10 mph headwind component. If your route has a northerly pointed segment coming up, you may end up with too much headwind. The vector diagram at left can help.

The GPS time-to-destination or time-at-arrival is valuable, but mostly on the last straight segment of a journey. On routes with course changes it's better to know the winds aloft. Then choose the best altitude to cruise. You'll also have an idea of what the wind will do to your overall groundspeed.

GPS is a great tool when you have a group of pilots navigating to places that most aren't familiar with. Get GPS units that allow connecting to a computer so that waypoint files can be shared. It has proven quite handy to load those files beforehand.

Drawing a vector diagram can calculate winds aloft from your GPS ground track and groundspeed readouts. A full-sized version of the below graphic is available from FootFlyer.com.

One of many incredible scenes from Phil Russman's "Why We Fly" production.

Once you know the wind at your altitude, a vector diagram can help calculate your groundspeed for an upcoming route segment. For example, you may be able to follow a road that goes due east in a northerly wind of 30 mph, but you'll make no headway trying to go due north.

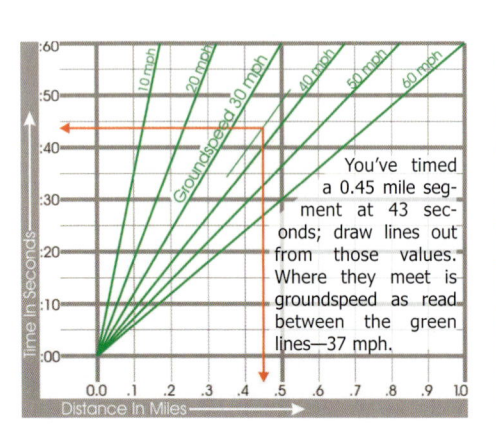

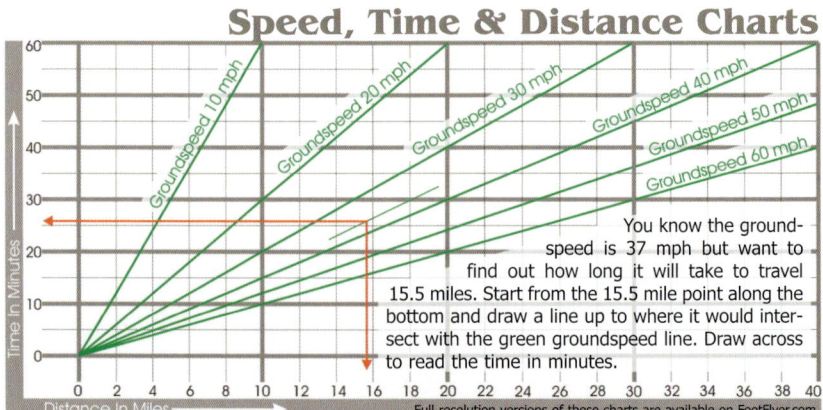

Mixing Units: As with all charts in this chapter, different units can be used as long as speed and distance are compatible. For example, knots are nautical miles per hour. So if distance is in nautical miles, then speed must be knots. If distance is regular (statute) miles, then speed must be in regular miles per hour. U.S. air maps (*sectionals*) are marked in nautical miles so knots and nautical miles are a convenient combination.

Speed, Time & Distance Charts

You've timed a 0.45 mile segment at 43 seconds; draw lines out from those values. Where they meet is groundspeed as read between the green lines—37 mph.

You know the groundspeed is 37 mph but want to find out how long it will take to travel 15.5 miles. Start from the 15.5 mile point along the bottom and draw a line up to where it would intersect with the green groundspeed line. Draw across to read the time in minutes.

Full resolution versions of these charts are available on FootFlyer.com.

Flying With Others

CHAPTER 14

These pilots are keeping an eye on each other in a side-by-side formation over Northern Illinois.

Techniques for formation flying are covered in Chapter 16. This chapter concentrates on the basics of surviving, and getting along, while flying with others.

Eventually, most pilots seek out like minded peers to share their passion with. It adds fun, education, and sometimes humor to the mix. But it can also complicate matters in unusual, possibly dangerous, ways; the more folks gather, the more complicated organization can get. Going to major events is the extreme case.

Courtesy

As with most issues of courtesy, a generous helping of common sense is essential. If an activity seems like it may be obnoxious, dangerous, or marginally safe—that's your better judgment whispering: "hmmm, maybe I should rethink this one." But since it's not always so clear cut here are some guidelines.

Where to Lay Out

If another pilot already has his wing laid out, avoid setting up in his way. Rather set up behind, or beside him. Even if you think you'll launch first, stay clear of his path in case you get delayed. It is bad form to lay out your glider in a way that requires another pilot to steer around it. If you think proximity is an issue, ask the affected pilot if it's OK or just move farther away. You'll make no friends by leaving your wing laid out for a long time, in a crowded field, taking up valuable space.

Look at where your run will take you and be sure that it's clear. Have a good climbout path that doesn't fly right over any spectators, campers or other pilots. Besides being is illegal, it's rude and dangerous. An inopportune motor failure would put the others in danger. Even at official gatherings be mindful of your noise during climbout; change locations, if necessary, to avoid getting too close to people.

While airborne, avoid buzzing about the launch area, especially in light winds. Your wake may linger for several minutes, making it even more difficult for those trying to takeoff. Plus, pilots in challenging conditions may be waiting for just the right puff of breeze and won't appreciate your annoying presence when it comes. Climb up at least 200 feet AGL after launch or go to another area so other pilots get their chance at clean air.

Prop Blast

Be mindful of your prop blast. Don't point it toward other people or their wings. Blowing someone's carefully positioned wing into a tangled mess will quickly sully your reputation. The same thing applies to fly-by's—be careful about where your prop blast goes. Even if nobody is preparing to launch, don't let wake or prop wash get to any laid-out wings. Flying near enough to roll up someone's wing is a sure sign of not being aware of your surroundings.

Keep the plane of the propeller clear so that if a prop were to come apart, the shards would miss those who might be in line with it.

Risks

We must manage additional risks when flying with others. First, be very vigilant about 1) your position, 2) the pattern and 3) keeping an active scan for other traffic. If you do not know where your flying buddies are, carefully look around, including above and blow. Do shallow turns to make sure they are not directly above you. Don't make sudden changes in altitude until you know it is clear in the desired altitude. Don't turn until satisfied there is nobody coming from that direction.

Follow the turning rule without fail: "Look, lean, turn." Besides weight shifting, the lean alerts other pilots of your impending turn. Even better is to **look**, start a **shallow** bank, look **up** and **down** in the turn direction, *then* start your **turn**.

Flying with one or two other pilots probably adds as much risk as flying with a hundred because we tend to drop our guard. A moment of distraction may be all it takes if your buddy comes up on you un-noticed.

Collision

One valuable tool for collision avoidance is your shadow. On sunny days you can find it quickly by noticing where the sun is and looking to where your shadow should be. The higher you are, the more blurry it is; the lower you are, the sharper it is. So even if you *do* see the shadow of another wing near yours, it's easy to tell whether its pilot is above or below you—a handy trick in crowded air. If you do not see any other wings near your shadow, you're alone. For now. If you see another wing shadow, and it's fuzzier than yours, then it's above you—descend while looking up towards the sun to find it.

Be leery of formation flying, especially with strangers but even with pilots you know (covered in Chapter 16).

Wake

Flying through a paramotor wake can be rough. At best it will be startling; at worst it can fold part of your wing, especially if combined with other factors such as

---

Flying with different types of aircraft adds complexity beyond what's obvious, even if they're slower than you. This animation, done for a real accident, shows how surprisingly insidious a balloon collision could be.

The PPG pilot was keeping track of a group of balloons to his left while a lone balloon, that had been on the ground for a while, launched without notice. It's relatively rapid ascent probably presented little relative motion and may have been partially obscured by the pilot's feet or trike frame.

When flying with others be vigilant in all directions, including down, to keep track of other craft especially with distractions such as photography.

A periodic turn of a few degrees will dramatically aid seeing another craft that may be coming up from below.

becoming unloaded (getting light in your seat). The motor, lines and wing produce turbulence, but the swirling wing tip vortices are the strongest (see Chapter 22).

Wing wake settles, spreads out slowly, drifts with the wind and is worse on heavier craft such as trikes, tandems, and even very heavy pilots. The wake of any craft, including your own, is much worse if it's in a steep turn.

The powerful wake of heavier machines, like PPC's, must be given a wide berth, even wider in smooth conditions where it can linger a lot longer.

Treat a wake encounter as you would any other turbulence—hold the brakes at pressure 2 and throttle for level flight. As always, if you feel the wing fall back, immediately "reduce power, reduce brakes, then steer."

Fly *above* the path of preceding aircraft to avoid their wakes. Flying between the vortices is another bad idea—there is sinking air there. You may not have enough thrust to out-climb it if you're low.

Rescuing a pilot

If you fly with other pilots long enough you'll probably be faced with the need to help extricate someone from one of trouble's many forms.

What a Drag

Kiting or flying in strong winds means that, eventually, somebody gets dragged along the ground. If you see this happening, don't lunge on the pilot or his motor—stop the *wing*. A wind-whipped wing can overpower even several burly helpers. Run around behind it so the wing drapes around your leg (see Chapter 3). Grabbing a wing tip and running it towards the pilot is also effective. Whatever you do, don't grab lines! They'll quickly leave painful burns.

Water

One of our biggest fears should be going in the water. Don't be fooled by stories of those who have survived dunkings—other pilots have not. And it doesn't take much water to be deadly, especially if it's moving. One pilot drowned after landing *beside* moving water—his wing went into a drainage culvert and dragged him under before he could unclip.

If faced with helping a pilot in the water, get flotation—*good* flotation. A boat is obviously best, but use whatever else can be found quickly such as a surfboard, inflatable mattress or life jacket. Don't jump in the water yourself since the lines may snag you when nearing the pilot's gear. The best response would be to give the pilot something to hold on to so he can unstrap and relax for a moment. If he is submersed then your options dwindle. Leaving your floatation could easily put you in the same tangled dilemma as the victim.

Power Lines

Voltage is to electricity what pressure is to water, and power lines have a *lot* of it. In the grip of such high voltage wires, your paraglider lines are conductive. They can make you a leak to ground (earth)—a small leak, to be sure, but with deadly pressure. The lowest voltage carried on poles is around 4000 and high-tension wires carry nearly half a million volts. While it may be current that kills, it's this voltage that drives it through our normally-resistant bodies and lines.

1. The higher you are, the more blurry your shadow is. Use this fact to tell whether someone is above or below you. Here the photographer is higher so his shadow is more blurry.

2. After crunching down through some branches, this lucky pilot was only a few feet above the helping hands of his rescuers. It's another example of why flying with others is a good idea.

3. Basic rules of courtesy apply when flying with others. Be aware of where your wake is going, don't prop blast others' wings, and help pilots setup after missing a launch (ask first).

So if a pilot lands in power lines and does not fall to the ground, leave him hanging! Do not reach up for him—that could complete the circuit that kills you both. Rather contact the power company and wait until they shut the lines down.

Trapped By A Thrusting Motor

It can happen that a pilot's motor will unexpectedly go to full thrust, pinning him in the process. This is risky for the pilot but even more so for a rescuer. Before jumping into the fray, have a plan. Make sure the plan keeps you out of the prop *and* that the pilot sees you coming so he doesn't swing the revving motor your way. Also, know how you're going to shut it off in case the regular kill switch has failed. Don't think this so uncommon—a severed throttle cable usually disables the kill switch too.

Alternative shutoff methods are covered in Chapter 19. They include pulling the choke or covering the air intake. Pulling the spark plug off works but be prepared for a startling shock. Shutting off the master switch, if there is one, may not kill the motor—it primarily prevents inadvertent starter activation.

If you're flying with a buddy know how to shut off each others motors.

Tim Kaiser (red), Phil Russman (blue) and Michael Purdy (yellow) pose in this formation flight just west of the Salton Sea in California.

A midair collision or entanglement would likely be catastrophic. There is more to formation flying than meets the eye, make sure you're up to the task. Two of these pilots had already worked together while taping parts of Risk & Reward before flying this close.

Communications

Flying with others gives added reason to have a radio (see Chapter 28), especially if it works through your helmet. Even if it doesn't, carry one so that if you go down, you can work out retrieval plans. Learn the *Bump Scale* (see Chapter 5) so you can communicate it to your flying friends.

Formation Flying

Formation flying requires precision handling (see Chapter 16) and should be avoided until you're experienced at precision flying. Specifically you should be able to actively keep the wing where you want it, even in turbulence, without really thinking about it. Until that point, avoid flying within 5 wing spans of other pilots and always keep your distance from someone who angles away when approached. They are obviously not comfortable with your proximity.

Never accept a visibly fast closure rate. It could quickly yield a collision or last-minute control inputs that cause you to spin or stall. If it looks like your approaching someone quickly, turn away before it's too late.

Section III

Mastering The Sport

There's nothing wrong with having merely adequate skill. You can safely enjoy this sport without ever needing to go beyond basic launch, landing and flying skills as long as you stay within your boundaries. Fly well-regarded, safe equipment from large fields and limit yourself to mellow weather. In fact, getting to a high level of mastery involves some extra risk since you must venture closer to control's edge in the process.

This section, however, is for those who want to go beyond flight's pure joy. It is for those who desire the thrill of surprisingly fine control, and who want to explore the limits of what our craft is capable of. It is, in fact, capable of a *lot*.

Section III is devoted to the endeavor of excellence. Here we will:

1. Show some of what's possible,
2. Explain the process to speed up learning,
3. Point out the risks, where appropriate and
4. Give methods to practice and to verify for yourself whether you've actually mastered the techniques involved.

Some of this practice is quite helpful to any pilot, but some must be left to the more risk-tolerant.

Section III

Mastering The Sport

*"It's not how many flights you have,
It's what you've done with the flights you've had"*

The Master Powered Paragliding video series, shown above, uses live action, animation, graphics, slow motion, and highly skilled pilots to make advanced topics crystal clear. They're intended for use with an experienced instructor who can coach you while reducing the likelihood of mishaps. This series will help anyone aspiring to mastery.

Advanced Ground Handling

CHAPTER 15

It's surprising what can be done with these wings when you know how. It's equally surprising how effortless the experts make it look, and how advancement can be so vexing! Fortunately, most skills can be practiced in the privacy of your own field.

Of course, if you see someone doing something that you want to learn, go talk to them about it; they'll probably be happy to share the knowledge. And the best pilots almost always have the best ground handling skills.

Upside down kiting to clean out cells.

All manner of detritus gets into a wing, acting like sandpaper and shortening its life; it must be removed. You *can* hold up the trailing edge and shake it out but that's boring compared with kiting the wing upside down.

Find a smooth, clean surface (preferably grass) with the wind blowing from 7 to 12 mph. You can do this in the sand but, unless you're real good, it's tough to avoid picking up more than is emptied. Gloves are nice because you'll be handling brake lines, not the toggles, which could cause line burns in a strong wind. First, shake the tips down since they don't have cell openings.

A harness makes it easier but you can use just the risers. You'll need good control to prevent the wing from slamming down onto its leading edge—potentially popping out cell stitching (yes, we've see it happen). Hook into your kiting harness just like you were going to fly, then:

- Get the wing laying on it's back with the leading edge upwind. If there's not enough wind, walk it into position. You can also flip the wing over while kiting.
- Grab the brake line closest to each hand above (beyond) the pulley as in pic-

Upside Down Kiting

1. Start from a regular reverse kiting position with the wing overhead. Or, build a wall and pull one tip A line just enough to get it turning over.

2. Keep pressure on the A line as the wing turns over. Walk with it until it turns but be prepared to pull on both brakes when it gets upside down.

3. As it comes over and down, pull on both brakes to cushion it's impact. Do *not* let it whack down hard on the leading edge which can blow out stitching.

4. With the wing laid out upside down (or towards you if flat on the ground), grab the brake lines above their pulleys to kite it upside down.

Here is another way to get debris out of your wing if you have two people. Lay it out on the ground with the leading edge downwind and the top up. With one person on each end, pick up the trailing edge and, while walking it into the wind, shake vigorously in a coordinated fashion as shown. The leading edge openings must be facing downward for this to work.

ture 4 above. Treat the brake lines like the A's of regular kiting. Pull them *just enough* to get the wing to come up while snatching your *body* backwards. Once up, pull the brake lines back and forth to shake stuff out. A satisfying show of falling debris means you did it right. Be careful to let the wing down gently on the leading edge.

If you're doing this in sand, dump the debris as described then, just before the leading edge touches down, lean (or run) towards the wing so that its cell openings lay down, face-up, with*out* scooping up more sand. You can try to kite the glider back over—but that usually just nets more sand. Instead, walk around it while holding the risers and bundle it up from downwind.

Kiting Without a Harness.

There are several reasons for kiting without a harness. It: (1) is a great way to get some feel for the air; 2) spreads out the wing nicely; 3) lets you quickly check for tangles; 4) makes repositioning the wing easy; and 5) is fun. Plus it looks cool. There are many techniques, each with different advantages, but we've picked a few that seem to work especially well.

Doing this with more than about 7 mph of wind is tiring and, in stronger winds, is dangerous if you let yourself get lifted. If that happens, let go of at least one riser immediately. That sounds ridiculous, but pilots have been injured when they held on too long and dropped 10 or more feet.

Regardless of the kiting method, you must move with the wing. If it goes left, go left with it. In fact, if you *want* it to go left, move right first, let the wing start falling left and follow it. To stop the wing, you must walk (run) beyond it. This works on all the kiting methods.

One Hand Per Riser—Good For Higher Winds

The value of this technique is that, with each hand holding a riser, it offers more weight bearing capability—good for higher winds. Those who do summersaults (need I mention risky?) while holding the risers usually do so with this method.

Face the wing and hold the risers as pictured (3 next page). Some wings may need you to inflate by first holding both the A's and B's in each hand. For most wings, hold the risers near where they split, the A's and B's go upwind with the C's and D's (if equipped) going out the back of your hand. If the wing doesn't want to come up, move your grip so as to pull more A's. If it wants to frontal or overfly you, then move the grip back so as to pull less on the A's.

Holding firmly, lurch backward as you would with a harness. When the wing comes overhead, decrease the pull or "rock" your hands back so as to pull the D's down. If the wing tries to overfly you, move backward while rocking your hands back. You have to be quick footed—moving quickly with the wing. Primary steering is done by pulling down one riser and letting up on the other. To go left, pull your left hand down and vice-versa with the right hand. To force the wing more overhead, or prevent it from falling back, tilt your hands so the A's are pulled down more.

You can re-grip but that's hard because of the wing's pull. If it is always trying to overfly you, let go of the risers briefly and grab them farther back. It's like letting go of a kite briefly while trying to catch the string in a different place.

There are several ways to bring the wing down: (1) walk towards it, steering it to the side so it falls over, 2) letting go of it (might make a mess though), 3) briefly letting go to re-grip back near the D riser or 4) put both risers in one hand and, with the free hand, reach back to pull the brake lines or rear risers.

A's and Brakes

This method offers the best control in light winds. Leave the brakes in their holders and grab both A's with your left hand and the brake lines (not the toggles) with your right hand as shown at right. Then:

- Inflate by pulling both A's *and* Brakes with just enough more A-pull to keep it coming up. It's important to feel pull in both the A's and brakes or else the leading edge will want to tuck over (frontal) and it won't come up as quick, if at all. You want it to initially inflate like a sailboat's spinnaker sail.

- This method makes inflation easy because you can modulate how much A's and brakes you pull. If the wing is jumping up quickly, pull more brakes with your right hand. If it's sluggish, walk backwards faster and let up on the brakes.

- Move left and right as necessary to keep under the wing. Steer with the brake hand, too—moving the hand right makes the wing fall left.

- If the wing wants to fall back, here are three ways to help bring it back up: (1) move backwards (into the wind), (2) pull more A's up to a point, and (3) ease both hands downward. After doing (3), when the wind picks back up, let your hands go up. Modulating like this can absorb small changes in wind speed that might otherwise require more moving around.

- If the wind increases and the wing wants to continually overfly you, either pull more brakes or walk downwind to reduce the relative airflow.

While you always want to move around as necessary, the *goal* is to control it well enough to stand still. That, of course, requires the finesse born of much practice.

To deflate the wing in a stronger wind, get it to fly overhead, almost to the point of front tucking. As it comes overhead, taking a step towards it can help. Then

No Harness Kiting

1. Using the **A's & Brakes** works very well in light winds. Pull just enough of *both* A's *and* brakes to hasten the initial inflation. Get the wing to billow first *then* add more A's.

Just being able to move your body in every direction while tweaking the brakes affords great control. If the wing wants to fall back, step backwards, lower the risers, and pull a bit more on the A's. This technique also allows your arms to absorb wind pulses by moving up and down.

2 & 3. One Hand Per Riser: Exactly where to hold the risers varies by wing. Experiment, but make sure you can rock your hands back and forth to pull more or less A's.

In light winds you may need to start out by holding both risers in one hand as shown in picture 2 so you can pull the A's with one hand to help it up. Once overhead, switch to the grip shown in picture 3 (the swap can take some practice).

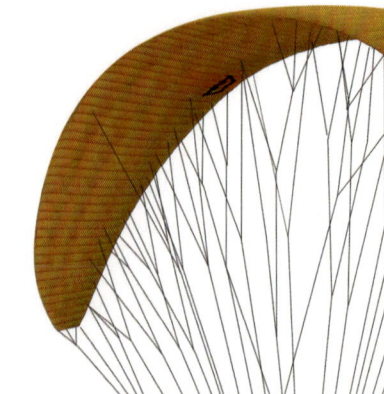

aggressively pull full brakes to snap it down through the power band (angle of highest pull) quickly. If you try to bring the wing down while it's hanging back, the effort will be far greater and you'll tend to get pulled quite a ways.

A's and D's (or C's)

This is essentially identical to A's and Brakes but, since the D's aren't as effective at steering, it is not as sensitive. Instead of holding the brake lines with your right hand, hold the D's with your right hand. It's like what you learned in emergency handling when a brake line fails—the glider can be steered and slowed this way.

Loops and Brakes

This is where you hold the risers by the very ends (the loops) with one hand and reach behind to pull on one or both brakes with the other hand. The pilot at left demonstrates steering the wing by pulling the necessary brake line.

To inflate the wing, hold both risers at the loops with your left hand and the A's with your right hand. Pull primarily on the loops but help it come up by pulling the A's as necessary. Once it nears the top, let go of the A's and be ready to go for one or both brakes with your right hand.

High wind techniques

This can hurt—be careful!

Extra site precautions are necessary to make sure there is nothing downwind that would hurt if you got blown into (or strained through). Start learning these techniques in less than a 15 mph wind and, even then, only with someone else present in case you lose control of the glider; brief them on how to handle the situation. Namely, they should know that if you're being dragged, they should grab a wing tip and run it upwind or get behind the wing and let it drape around them. They should not tackle you—the wing will potentially just pull the both of you.

Be prepared to deflate the wing as covered in Chapter 3 or later in this chapter.

Avoid doing this with the motor on—you are vulnerable to *turtling* onto the cage and getting dragged until you hit something. About the only way to stop such carnage is unbuckling from the harness, jumping out, and running after the remnants of your bouncing gear. It's much cheaper to master these skills with*out* the motor and in a harness with back protection.

Laying Out & Clipping In

Don't stretch the wing all the way out. Either leave it in a partial ball or lay it out 90° to the wind as described later in the chapter under "Smooth Surfaces." Only spread the wing out halfway with just the middle exposed.

Don't pull on the risers until you're ready to handle the wing. Initially, lay both risers within 10 feet of the wing's trailing edge. If you pull even a small bit on the risers a cell opening could catch the wing and start it inflating. Once that happens, it will want to inflate all the way with overwhelming power, dragging you along for the ride. So clip in close to the wing, get the correct brake in each hand and be ready to control it. Walk with it, if it starts getting blown downwind.

Loops & Brakes
Kiting with the loops requires holding both risers with one hand and using your free hand to control the brakes.

The Wall

1. Hold even brakes while pulling your body back against the wall to make it come up higher.

2. Step towards the wall to lower it and reduce it's tug.

3. If the tug gets too loose, wind may get under the trailing edge and cause it to flail upwards. If the tips want to come up, reach out to the brake lines and pull them in or get the wall high enough to prevent it in the first place.

4. This is Section III, so you probably already know that this pilot needs to step right to bring down the high right side.

Controlling the Wall

Be ready on the brakes when bringing your glider to "attention." Step back to tension the A's, giving them a small tug if necessary. As soon as it starts to inflate, pull back on the brakes; it may be necessary to pull them *way* back. But if you pull too far, air gets under the trailing edge and may cause the wing to snake up out of control. Some wings may not need any A-pull at all—just step back and it will lurch to life. Again, be ready on the brakes to keep it down.

Some pilots have found that holding the wall down using the C-risers works well, too. Get a hold of them before letting the wing catch air, though.

In stronger conditions, pulling brakes alone may not be enough to keep the tips down, especially with longer brake lines. If that's the case, reach to the rear risers and pull them back while keeping hold of the brakes. You can hold both brake lines in one hand, behind your back, to free up the other hand. Be careful wrapping the brake lines around your hand (taking wraps) which could cause line burns and cuts in this strong of a wind.

Once you have a well formed wall, it may be bucking up and down. As you've already learned, backing away from the wing will raise it while pulling the brakes more, or leaning towards the wall, will lower it. If you let the wall get too high, its pull may be overpowering. If you pull the brakes too hard, the trailing edge may flail up into the breeze; there is a balance.

Done correctly, you'll be standing there with *lots* of brake pulled, controlling the wall's height by leaning towards it to lower, or leaning back (away) to raise it.

If You Get Lifted Off Your Feet

If you're hooked in reversed (as you should be) and get airborne, you'll tend to untwist so you're facing forward then get deposited downwind somewhere. The *Alan Method*, described below, can prevent the unwanted turn-around—you'll come back down while still reversed and under control. Once you get the wing down, pack up and thank your lucky stars you didn't go flying in this wind.

One thing first: if you do get lifted, don't pull the brakes! Read that sentence again. Don't pull *any* brakes unless you're airborne and the wing is surging forward, then pull and release them. If you pull a bunch of brakes while facing forward, or with unsure footing, hang on for a

⚠ Caution!

High winds can be extremely dangerous with a paraglider. If it's blowing hard enough to use these techniques then understand the increased risk and be ready to act the minute you clip in. First work with an instructor who is familiar with high winds and can handle getting lifted or dragged himself.

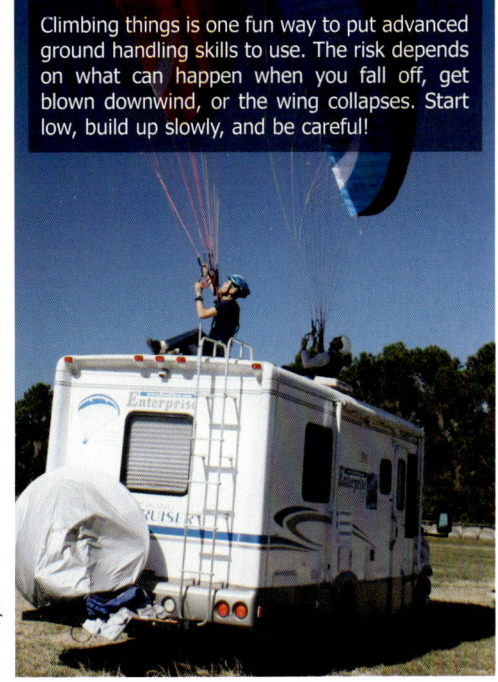

Climbing things is one fun way to put advanced ground handling skills to use. The risk depends on what can happen when you fall off, get blown downwind, or the wing collapses. Start low, build up slowly, and be careful!

High Winds

1. Don't take on strong winds until you're ready to get lifted and/or slide. Learn in moderate winds first, where you can run backwards and get airborne by pulling some brakes. Practice sliding on your feet during the inflation, too.

2. On higher performance wings, it's difficult to recover a dipping wing with brakes alone, especially if you can't move towards the low side. Try this: Let go of the dipping side's brake line and use some A's *and* brakes on the high side. Pull them at the same time.

3. If you get lifted way up, go hands up initially, then apply some brake pressure as you stop climbing. Look down and flare when appropriate.

1
By Brad Powell

2
He's pulling left brake and left A to get the wing to come back left.
By Tim Kaiser

3
By Eve Clarke

whoopin'. The wing will go back with vigor, first lifting then dragging you through whatever is downwind. Even just tapping the brakes in a strong blow can start this carnage; less brake is best.

Inflation

On a normal inflation you lean back, away from the wing, and pull just enough A's to help it come up. In high winds that may be difficult—the minute you reach for the A's, you reduce brake pull which may allow the wing to start inflating. Many wings will inflate at the tips which then come up and inward, leaving a mess. If that wants to happen, here are a some things to try.

- Pull the tips in. Start with the brake in your right hand which is going across to the opposite tip—pull it way back. Then reach out with your other hand and pull the tip in farther. Do the same for the other side so both tips are toward you. They may roll up a bit in the wind which is ok. Starting with the wing balled up, or horse-shoed slightly can prevent this from happening.

- Inflate the wing without pulling any A's at all. When ready, simultaneously reduce brake pull and step back. The wing will rocket upwards and pull you downwind—you'll need to run or slide towards it briefly. It can be tricky—the minute you let go of the brakes it will start coming up and want to yank you.

There is a balance in how much to resist the wing on its way up and how much to move with it. You must keep *some* resistance or it won't have any relative wind to work with. And you can't lock yourself in place (or try to) lest it shoot up and overfly you. That is why helpers, if used, must let you move with the wing some.

Sliding on your feet during inflation is perfect (and fun) albeit challenging. Done properly, you will slide (or run) about 5 to 10 feet, and stop the wing overhead. When you apply brakes to stop the wing it may lift you—be ready. By walking (or sliding) towards it while it's rising, there will be less chance of getting lifted. Once it stops overhead you *must* let up on the brakes

The Alan Method

One way to inflate and kite in high winds is to use the brake lines *above* their pulleys. Gloves are helpful since you'll be holding the brake *lines* (not the toggles) that could cause friction burns.

This gives deep control over the brake pull and, if you get lifted, allows you to remain reversed and in control which is hard while holding the brakes by their toggles. Once the risers start to un-cross, however, there is not enough leverage to prevent untwisting so keep yourself a little more twisted than exactly reversed.

- Hook in reversed as if you were going to fly but do not grab the brake toggles.

- Inflate the wing by stepping back with your body and pulling on the A's as necessary. As the wing nears overhead, let go of the A's, reach back around the outside of the risers to grab the brake lines above their pulleys. Pull them enough to prevent the wing from overflying—the challenge is getting to those brake lines quickly.

- Steering is backwards from the normal crossed method (where each hand controls the opposite trailing edge). That takes some practice. One way to visualize what you're doing is by watching the trailing edge react to your pull. Control the wing surges and left-right tendencies by modulating the brake lines.

• Keep the risers crossed and touching each other. That means you'll be turned slightly beyond 180° from facing forward. Doing so allows you to remain reversed if you get lifted off your feet.

• Lean way back if it wants to lift you—you'll have more rotational inertia. That means greater resistance to getting swung around if you get lifted off your feet.

If you do get lifted, keep yourself reversed by opposing the turn with the brake lines while maintaining wing direction. It is entirely possible to actually fly this way (without a motor, obviously), but it can be confusing too. Pulling with your left hand will initiate a turn to the right (as viewed by a spectator). It needs to be practiced a lot before actually putting yourself in a situation where you'll be very high and flying backwards like this.

If conditions are light, when the wing falls back, you'll need to periodically let go of the brakes and pull on the A's to help it come back up. Going back and forth quickly between the brakes and the A's is the greatest challenge. Practice it during mellower conditions first since you'll need to be pretty fast-acting in stronger winds.

Once mastered, this technique has other benefits. With very light winds it's a way to go quickly from kiting with the A's to using brakes. That's handy in light, switchy winds.

Kiting Control

Minimize brake use in strong winds. Move left or right instead. Lean way back so that getting lifted upwards a foot or so only angles your body up without losing traction. Keep your knees bent so that a quick gust only lifts you a few inches and will not scrap your balance.

While kiting reversed with crossed risers (the normal way), you can also control the wing using weight shift. Dip a hip toward the falling wing.

Kiting while facing forward lets you learn a "feel" for the wing without looking at it. There is no magic, you'll feel it go left or right and see the risers on your periphery move subtly left/right and forward/backward. Getting used to handling the wing like this is useful. A good test of your kiting skills is to be able to stand on the ground and kite while looking straight ahead at the horizon. It will take a fairly steady 8 mph wind or more to do so.

The Alan Method And Flying Backwards

Kiting with the Alan Method (see text) allows far more control in strong winds than using the toggles. It also lets you oppose the untwisting force so as to remain facing the wing even after getting lifted.

You can actually fly backwards (remain twisted) using this method. You'll be using the brake lines for two things: 1) to oppose the natural untwist tendency and 2) steering. Flying backwards is risky at any altitude higher than you're willing to crash. And don't try it with a motor!

Steering is easy, look at the trailing edge and imagine how the deflected brake will slow that side down causing a turn. Envision it that way and it will be obvious. Kiting practice will make it second nature.

Preventing the untwist isn't hard either. If the risers want to swing you left to face forward, use your hands on the brake lines to oppose it. Yes, you'll necessarily be pulling some brake pressure on both lines. For example, if the risers are trying to swing you left, move both hands left to counteract it.

The hard part is combining the two—modulating counter-twist force while also steering. This is a skill that highly experienced paraglider pilots learn for controlling launches in higher wind situations.

Once mastered, you'll also find it allows kiting up vehicles, poles and such just for the fun of it.

1. If you use a helper, tell him to let you move initially as the wing comes overhead so it doesn't overshoot you.

2. This risky activity is possible in a strong, steady breeze. Stick with soft sand and a height you're willing to fall from. Keep the wing loaded—a collapse could ruin your day.

Approach the object from just below (a few inches) then add some brake to swing up to it. Control via braking, flexing the knees and twisting the motor to redirect thrust opposite to an unwanted lean. Keep the power on and fly the wing while always maintaining some brake pressure. Master it first on level ground.

3. Here is one type of high wind layout where sand is used to anchor the upwind tip. Clip in and start pulling the wing into a normal wall or inflate the downwind tip fist straight to overhead.

Assisted Inflation

In strong winds, assisted motor launches are dangerous, mostly to the assistants, even if they're familiar with flying. They can get caught in parts of the harness and swung into the prop or get a hand into it. Consider that, if you require assistance, it's probably too strong for your skill level. In some ways, getting assistance makes it harder while adding risk to you *and* your helpers.

If you feel compelled to get help, make sure the helpers know to let you slide (on your feet hopefully) as the wing comes up. Do *not* have them try to hold you rigidly lest the wing dart up too quickly and overfly you. They should move with you as the wing comes up, resisting your motion with 30 or so pounds of pull. Doing so makes the inflation more manageable. It's important that your helper(s) not resist heavily until your motion has mostly stopped and *then* to try holding you in one place while allowing the left/right corrections necessary to kite. Instruct them that if you get lifted they should walk downwind while holding you. Emphatically instruct them to let go if they feel themselves start to get lifted (for their safety).

To further reduce risk, have the assistants use short ropes (not long enough to get into moving parts) tied to a sturdy part of the frame. The assistants pull on those ropes which are easy to let go of. Assistance is most often used when a large wing makes initial inflation difficult.

Handling smooth surfaces

High winds and smooth surfaces, like beaches, are a tough combination. The minute you lay the wing out it wants to go sliding away. To make the process easier, extract the wing so as to avoid the cell openings catching air. Here are two ways to get yourself clipped in.

1. If you normally stuff your wing, pull it out so that it's in a rosette but oriented properly to the wind. That's hard because some of the lines will be obscured, but if you always stow the wing in the same way, it's easier.

> **Tip: Testing the Technique**
>
> Test these techniques while kiting in a moderate breeze. From a normal reverse hook-in, tug on risers and lines to see how the wing behaves—it's a nice reinforcement.

2. Lay the wing out parallel with the wind and have someone hold the upwind tip. If you're alone, lay something heavy on the tip that won't damage the fabric. Sand works really well—just make sure it won't go in the cells. A slight tug on the downwind A's will bring the wing to life and it yank it around into position. Use brakes *immediately* to control the wall. You can use A riser pull *and* brake on the downwind tip to bring it around.

Regardless of the method used, be ready to get dragged! Have a plan and be somewhere with nothing nasty downwind to get strained through. And be ready to fly (get lifted) since, once the wing comes to life, it may be an ordeal to unclip.

The smooth surface will make the wing quicker to "snake" above the ground so you must hold the wall in a very narrow height range using the techniques described earlier. More than likely, you'll have to inflate it without using the A's—that's hard on some wings.

Reverse Inflation On A Cart

It is *possible* to do reverse inflations with a cart but requires high-end kiting skills.

The turn-around must be timed and steered to prevent the wing's pull from tipping you over. There's a huge risk for tipping over.

Layout like a foot-launch reverse with the cart facing the wing and risers crossed for the direction you'll turn. Hold yourself with either your feet or a brakes (if equipped). Bring the wing up, sliding/rolling a bit towards it as necessary. Steer the wing slightly in the direction you'll turn then use just enough power to steer the cart around towards the wing then into the wind. Use minimal brake pressure.

High Wind Landing

It's safer to leave the motor running if you'll be landing in strong wind because it leaves you with time and options. If you fall, there will be more damage but, with the motor running, it's easier to prevent a fall. There are two difficult steps after touchdown: (1) getting turned around to face the wing, and 2) bringing it down.

To get turned around, it's helpful to unload the wing some after landing. Keep the power on and hold some brake—as much as you can without getting lifted. When you're ready to turn, let off the brakes and squat down so the wing surges forward. As it unloads, turn around while standing up straight.

Once turned around, you'll use a similar technique to bring the wing down (deflate it). Apply brakes then let up as you bend down. That makes the wing surge forward and unload. Now pull *full* brakes. The wing comes down quickly through the power band with a brief, powerful yank on your body. Run towards a wingtip and grab fabric. The pull the wing towards you, hand over hand, by the top of the leading edge until you're holding about the middle cell. From here, it's easy to walk around holding the wing like this.

Light Wind Techniques

Normally, if it's too light to kite the wing overhead, a forward launch is easier and safer. But if you're ready to reverse when the wind dies, these are nice tools to have for launching without resetting your wing.

Any light wind reverse is easier with clutched motors because there's no thrust opposing your effort. One way to help using any motor is to get some air flowing over the wing just before you inflate. While you're standing there ready, move towards the wing and turn around so the thrust line is just over the wing. Run it up *just* above idle. Too much thrust blasts the air too quickly by the wing. Then, in one fluid motion, let off the throttle, turn around, back up and do your inflation.

Below: Long single-hold Method

Hold both A's with the hand opposite your throttle. You'll turn around in that direction like the pilot shown below. He has the throttle in his left hand and A's in his right so he turns to the right.

This allows you to hold (and pull) the A's while turning nearly all the way around and even during the initial acceleration—helpful in light winds.

Another help with light wind reverses is to step towards the wing, turn around and blow air over the wing at just above idle. Watch the lines, though. Throttle off then immediately turn and start the inflation.

Cross Armed Reverse

This method works in light winds by letting you impart energy to the wing as you turn around. With easy-inflating gliders and practice, this can be done in no wind (see the video at www.FootFlyer.com), not that you'd want to. Our description is for a pilot hooked in reversed who will turn to the *left* after inflating.

Clip in normally and grab the appropriate brakes as usual for a reverse. While holding the brake toggles, slide your right hand down the right riser to its A riser which will probably be to your left. Grab that A and continue left and up—that A should have a clear path to the wing (photo 1). With your left hand, reach *over* the other A and grab it as shown at left (photo 2).

Pull your hands back towards you (arms are now crossed) to see that both A's are clear to the wing. When ready, lunge backwards with your body, pulling both A's as necessary. You can help a lagging side by pulling more A on that side. When the wing gets to about 60° overhead, turn to the left and throttle up. As you turn, your arms will uncross and move forward which provides some pull to the A's during the turn—very helpful in light winds. This method doesn't work as well on wings that tend to front tuck easily.

Kiting with the A's

This technique allows kiting in light to moderate winds while keeping the wing only a few feet above the ground. It is almost useless by itself but the skill helps handle nearly all other inflations. It's handy, too, for kiting wars where the goal is to be the last one left kiting.

Set up for a regular reverse but, like the "Alan Method," do *not* grab the brake toggles. Grab the A risers beyond where they cross as shown in 4 at left.

Inflate the wing by stepping back and helping with the A's as usual. If the left side drops (as you're looking at it), pull more on the left A while stepping back. If the right side drops, pull the right A while stepping back. You may have to walk left and right to keep yourself centered as gusts come through.

When the wing is low to the ground your left/right motion is just like when building a wall—step towards the high side. Once the wing arcs above 45° go back to the normal movement of stepping towards the falling side. As always, the goal is to be able to kite with*out* having to move but do move when it's necessary.

Inflation Issues

In a perfect world, launch runs are always downhill, into a steady breeze, and the sign on the sod farm entrance reads "PARAMOTOR PILOTS WELCOME." However, the following tips will help in *our* world.

Fixing a Wall

An even layout is always best but sometimes the wing comes down in a heap after an abortive kiting effort. One side sits lifeless while the other has some form. Here's a way to rescue the mess quickly.

As long as some cells can get clear air, hold the A's going to those cells while holding their brake line in your other hand. Pull both sharply until they catch air. Done

Cross-Armed Inflation
It looks confusing but don't worry about those crossed brake lines, just do the procedure and it will sort itself out when you turn around.

3. Fixing a Wall: Your left hand holds the A line to an open part of the wing (the high side) while your right hand holds it's brake line. Get some air into the open cells so it blows out the mess to the left.

4. Kiting with the A's helps most in light winds. If one side sags, pull its A more as you back up. This works well with the "Alan Method" since you can quickly go from the A's to the brakes. In a strong wind, you'll want to walk towards the wing as it's coming up to reduce the relative wind and therefore the power of its pull.

properly and with enough wind, it will billow out nicely. Too much A's will be ineffective. If a whole side is clear (3 on previous page), use the riser to that side. Be careful when pulling only one or a few lines—it's easier to overstress the connection points or get line burns.

Salvaging Bad Inflations

In the beginning, an inflation that went this bad (see the series picture) had only two outcomes: Abort or crash. Aborting is always the safest option but, if you are intimately familiar with your wing and willing to take the extra risk, you can salvage many launches with these tips. Be forewarned that pushing too hard on launch risks having the prop munch your wing, lines or body parts.

- Keep forward motion. Powering up early, at least partially, makes doing so much easier.
- Turn towards the wing and keep pressure on the low side's A riser.
- Once you've got forward motion, use *just enough* brake pressure on the high side. The trick is using *just* enough—too much brake brings the entire wing back down.
- Do not accelerate or accept a liftoff until the wing is fully under control.

If things turn sour, be lightning fast on the kill switch.

Crooked Inflations

As learned in Section I, successful launches stem from a proper setups. Everything must be lined up, especially in light-wind forward inflations: lines clear, be centered on the wing, and be aligned straight into the wind.

The following factors can play havoc with your plans and lead to crooked inflations. Knowing crooked's cause will better enable its cure.

- The wing always tends to come up *into* the breeze. So a wind coming from your right will make the wing come up and turn to the right. The left cells catch the air more directly and come up first.
- Not running perpendicular to the wing will pull up the tip opposite to your run direction. So if you start your run facing slightly right of perpendicular, then the left cells get pulled up first. It doesn't take much before the wing is too crooked to recover. The left side shoots up first and the wing arcs over sideways.
- If you're left or right of the wing's center when starting your run, the far side will come up first. So if you're off-centered to the right, the left side will come

This started off badly. The pilot looked left to see the wing leaning heavily. He kept up the forward motion and turned towards it—you can see the prop blast off centered. He also kept slight pressure on the low A-riser and applied the slightest brake on the high side.

Thankfully, it worked, this time!

Turning slightly like this can counteract a natural tendency. If the wing always seems to come up to your right, angle yourself slightly left. The same is true for launching in a crosswind.

You can achieve the same result by slightly offsetting yourself from center. If the wing always seems to come up and go left, step a few inches to the right of centered.

up first. This is worse than scenario #2 since you're not running even slightly to the right. The left side would come up first and fall over to the right before you knew what happened.

So if the wing "always comes up to the right", then point yourself slightly to the left. If you've mastered the hip shifting, no hands kiting, you can use your hips as you inflate the wing to make corrections (with a weight shiftable harness). If you suspect there is a problem with the wing, try kiting it in a steady breeze or, better yet, have an experienced pilot kite the wing to get another opinion. Just ask them to report unusual behaviors. If it really does come up consistently crooked then there may be a problem with the wing and it should be sent in for inspection or repair.

Handling Crosswinds

Normally you always launch into the wind but, at some sites, especially long narrow ones, you may be forced to accept a crosswind (see Chapter 17). Also, the wind may shift after setting up. That's pretty common when thermals are budding.

The key is to use the previously mentioned inflation problems to your advantage. Use them intentionally to counter the crosswind effect by running or setting up off-center.

Lets say, for example, that you've set up pointing into a 1-2 mph breeze. But, just before launching, the wind shifts to be coming from your right. Simply driving hard may be enough but the wing will want to come up to the right—into the breeze. So point your launch run about 3° to the left to counter the crosswind that's trying to make it come up right. Done correctly, the effects will cancel each other out.

Excelling at ground handling is well worth the effort, not only for success in launching, but for its own sake. It's easy to see that the best ground handlers make the best launchers.

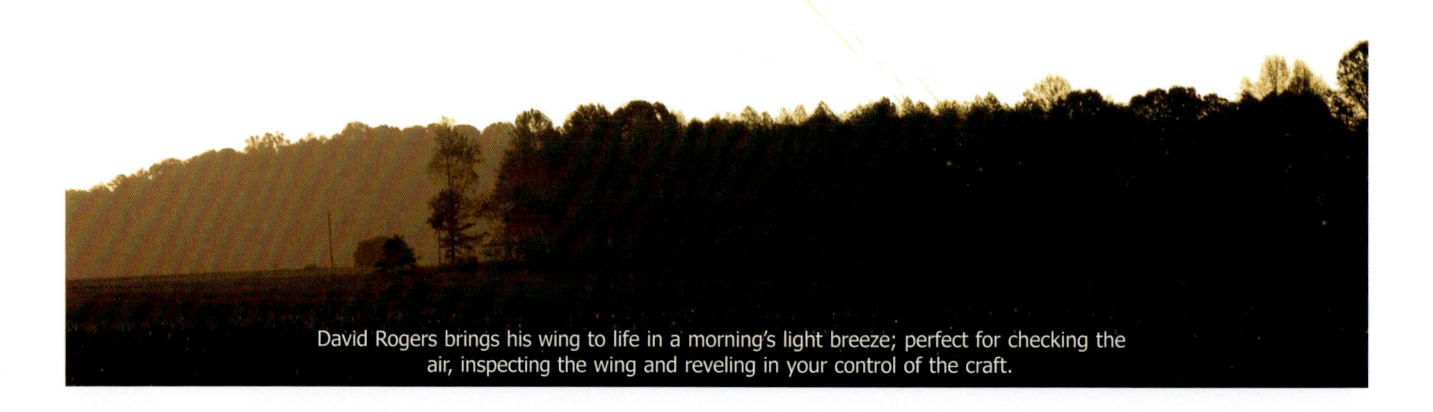

David Rogers brings his wing to life in a morning's light breeze; perfect for checking the air, inspecting the wing and reveling in your control of the craft.

Scott Johnson lays down a long foot drag along Oregon's smooth, wide beach.

Chapter 16 Precision Flying

Just *flying* a powered paraglider is all the enjoyment most pilots need and it can be enjoyed safely without ever becoming super precise—you just have to stay within your limits. While a skilled pilot will be better prepared for the unexpected, that advantage evaporates if it's spent taking on more challenging situations. Superior skill is easily overwhelmed by inferior judgement.

For those who aspire to really *master* the craft, for whatever reason, this chapter is for you. Don't think that a paraglider's soft nature means loose or imprecise control. The reality is blessedly more fun. In fact, *very* precise flight path control is available to those willing to work towards it.

Even in moderately bumpy air, a skilled pilot can carve a line within inches of his desired path. As you might imagine, such precision takes practice, especially since you hang so far below the wing. It requires learning anticipation and a sense for how long it takes your *body* to feel results from control inputs—both vertically and laterally. You must learn the feel of input and resultant motion. But oh how sweet it feels once mastered!

Brakes—The *Feel* Position

A lot of precision flight is done using minimum brake pull—not completely off, but just enough to affect minor corrections to the wing without giving up speed. This is the *feel* position, and is only about a pound of brake pressure on most wings which is about brake position/pressure 1. Hanging the weight of your arms is too much. That gives *great* control feel, but it also slows you down, sacrificing energy (speed) in the process. Find the feel position by pulling pressure, without looking at the wing, until you just *start* to notice a course or speed change.

In a regular turn, you apply brake (1) and hold it there (right brake depicted). The wing banks out to a maximum (2) then levels back to a lesser amount of bank (3). It stays at that reduced bank for as long as you hold the brake. The rate at which it goes out and back is the pendular rate for your particular motor/wing combination.

Remember to avoid pulling more brake while the wing is returning from it's farthest bank (2) since that so can cause a spin.

Coordinated Turn

The goal here is to minimize diving and slipping which is where the wing briefly moves sideways through the air. Do these steps about a second apart until you get a feel for it. Look for traffic first then:

1. Reduce power a bit, especially if turning against the motor's normal torque direction.

2. Weight shift (if able) to start the wing moving,

3. Apply inside brake towards the turn, then,

4. Just after the wing starts responding, prevent a dive by adding a bit of power and/or pulling slight outside brake. The resulting turn is smooth and level.

It should be paced like this (when spoken aloud at a normal pace): "Power, weight shift, one, brake inside, two, throttle up/add outside brake."

It will vary by wing since longer line lengths take longer to swing from side to side. Some gliders tend to have more level turns anyway.

Flying with *some* pressure is important when trying to fly super accurately, especially right next to the ground. Of course you *can* fly with a lot more brake pressure but that requires even more finesse in another area: Thrust control.

Always use brake Pressure not position

Wing moving back, hands up. Wing moving forward, pull pressure.

Straight Lines—Pendular Precision

Hanging below the wing means you swing—fore/aft and left/right. Like any pendulum, there is a natural frequency to the swing called its *period*. Controlling the left/right oscillations is most challenging because the brake input is not intuitive—in fact, on a small scale, it is backwards from what the body feels. The fore/aft motion is easier to learn but has its own quirks.

Being able to stop oscillations precisely is a prerequisite to nearly every other aspect of fine control; it's what gives us rule over the inches. A telling test of whether you have this skill is being able to fly a straight line, within 3 to 6 inches, both vertically and laterally. Of course the only place to even recognize such precision is while flying a few feet above the ground. Features such as corn rows, tracks in the sand, or lines in a field are good for this. Such lines can be found, in some form, on nearly every piece of the planet. They don't even need to be straight lines but, if you're using curves, they must be fairly smooth and gentle.

The boundary between corn and soybean fields is another perfect place to practice. When the corn is 8 feet and beans are 3 feet tall, fly a track just over the corn row. If you hit sink, throttle up a bit and turn towards the beans—you'll instantly have an extra 5 feet of clearance.

Only do this into the wind and realize that it requires extreme care.

Left/Right Pendular Control

You can feel the pendular action of a PPG by getting into a turn then letting up on the brakes. It will recover past level, swinging back and forth at its natural pendular rate, and in decreasing amounts until you are flying level again.

To fly precisely, these oscillations must be dampened. Wait until your body crests then, just as it *starts* to swing back the other way, pull a quarter brake in the direction you're about to swing. Hold it for *one* second then ease up. Done correctly, you will reach zero brake input just as the wing levels.

This works both for preventing oscillations and for damping them once begun. If you have already started a swing (by a gust or your own action), let it crest, then, as soon as your body reverses direction, pull brake in that direction for a second then release.

Timing is crucial—if turbulence swings you right, let it finish swinging then, just as it *starts* swinging to the left, pull a quarter *left* brake for a second and release. It may feel backwards at first—you start swinging left and have to pull a quarter left brake immediately. Don't hold it for too long or you'll make it worse. The amount of correction should be proportional to the swing's intensity. It may feel unnatural at first but will become automatic with practice. And practice you must.

The best way to rehearse this is by doing mild wingovers (see Chapter 18) and practicing returning to level flight with the least amount of oscillation. Fortunately, this skill can be mastered in the safety of altitude. You can also practice by getting into a bank, letting off the brakes, then dampening the resultant oscillation.

Flying a Line

Being able to closely follow a line on the ground requires mastery of the pendular tendency—you must catch it *before* you get swung. The previous explanation primarily covered how to stop it after it started—here is how to stop it before it even starts. This definitely takes practice. The problem is that you must feel even the slightest motions and modulate brake pull accordingly—stronger swing, more brake. Your reaction must be quick, too—any delay will only make it worse. The key to *preventing* oscillations is to apply brake in the direction of your body's movement *as soon as that movement starts* then let off.

For example, you're flying along a line (like a corn row) and feel your body start swinging left (body left, wing right). You must immediately pull left brake then let it up. If you catch it before you've moved more than a few inches, you will dampen the oscillation before it starts. If you wait too long, you'll be applying brake as you start swinging back which will make that swing bigger. Don't try to master this until you can dampen an established swing as described earlier.

Fore/Aft (Surge Control)

The wing always wants to maintain an equilibrium known as *trim speed*. That means if you pull some brakes to slow down, then release them, you'll dive a bit and accelerate back to your previous speed. Pulling trimmers sets a new, slower trim speed equilibrium.

A sudden increase of headwind (like a headwind gust) immediately increases your *air*speed—you'll swing forward (the wing falls back), climb and lose forward momentum (groundspeed). With no further wind change, the glider settles back to its trim speed and leaves you moving slower over the ground and a few feet higher. A sudden decrease in headwind (or increase in tailwind) would cause the opposite: airspeed drops, the wing dives a bit and you accelerate over the ground. Once it stabilizes, you wind up at the same trim airspeed but going faster over the ground and a bit lower.

A brief gust is worse than a one-time change because it's a really two changes. In a headwind gust, for example, the wing surges back and you climb as the wing seeks its previous airspeed. Groundspeed (momentum) decreases, too. Then, when the gust subsides, the wing suddenly feels less airflow (less airspeed) and dives to

You're flying along with brakes at position/pressure 1 when the wing suddenly surges forward. Quickly go to pressure 3 for a second, then back to pressure 1. As you gain experience, you'll do this naturally and time it properly.

It's just like the left/right pendulum: Give the input just as the wing *starts* to change direction. So if it goes forward, just as it *starts* to come back, let up on the pressure.

Controlling with pressure, not position, is critical in turbulence. Brake pressure 3 may happen at position 4 or more under some circumstances. Go to the pressure, not the position.

Digging Deeper

Pendular dampening *seems* backwards because we are not exactly pendulums. When the wing goes left, your body goes slightly right. Since we control the *wing* so we must translate that kinetic feel into what the wing is doing. Feel the body go right? *Immediately* jab a small bit of right brake then let up. When you felt your body start going right, the wing was going left and, if you reacted right away, you stopped it.

Higher performance wings react more intensely to turbulence so they require quicker pilot input and have stronger forward surges, with less provocation, than beginner wings.

get back to trim speed. This can be dramatic and cause large pitch changes where your body (and wing) angle upward or downward.

You can minimize all this with the brakes and power, keeping the wing overhead as much as possible—an essential skill to safely maintaining altitude within a few inches of the ground.

In the case of the wing surging forward, it will make you want to dive at the ground—you must quickly pull just enough brake to prevent the dive. So when you sense the wing *begin* to go forward, you must immediately add some brakes but be prepared to let them back up. As soon as you sense the surge has ended you must reduce brake pressure.

Hold somewhat more brake pressure (2) in turbulence while being mindful of keeping up forward speed. Airspeed means brake authority, especially in case you must stop a drop. That will need to be modulating thrust, too. So if you get lifted and tilted back, ease up the brakes immediately, reduce power and be ready to come back in with both. You must be quick—as soon as you *start* swinging back down (wing coming forward) you'll need to be adding power to maintain speed.

You must build skill through practice to really master the necessary reactions. This chapter may explain the principle but it's greatest contribution is describing what to practice and what to expect when you do.

Practice should start off in fairly smooth conditions, flying 10 feet over landable terrain, as always (sod farms, beaches or smooth desert floor are perfect. Try to hold altitude precisely. As you improve, go later in the morning (or earlier in the evening) when bumps appear but are not severe. You will build skill faster if practicing with *some* level of turbulence.

Balance of Power

In normal flight, you've learned that power controls altitude—power up to climb, power back to descend. But throttle changes take a second or two to act. To effect an *immediate* climb or descent use brakes. It's a limited and fleeting effect but, if you're cruising along at a few inches, that immediacy is key. You'll need to adjust the power soon afterwards to maintain your energy state.

Energy State

Energy state is a term, fancied by fighter pilots, that describes the trade-off between speed and altitude. It's like a roller coaster that accelerates going downhill, trading height (potential energy) for speed (kinetic energy). Climbing the next hill trades speed for height. Friction makes the cars gradually slow down (losing energy) but power overcomes it. A paraglider is no different. If you're going fast, you've got energy available to trade for height (briefly anyway) which is what a quick pull of brakes do. Reducing brakes will trade some height for an increase in airspeed. Thrust increases total energy.

When flying level, a few feet above the ground (or any altitude), power keeps the speed up, leaving brakes available for an immediate climb. If you start to sink, pull brakes to arrest it, then, before slowing down too far, add power to regain the lost speed (energy). That way, if you hit sinking air again, you can use the brakes.

1. Pilots feet have been saved by stout shoes or boots after getting a foot in the prop. Think twice before flying with this footware.

2 & 3. The accuracy available to a paramotor pilot is surprising given its minimal controls. Following the center of this gravel road or staying with a moving vehicle requires a careful dance between throttle and brakes—fine inputs that yields a flight path measured in inches.

Slow Flight

Slow flight puts you close to stalling or spinning. If you feel the wing start to slow unexpectedly, or a brake gets mushy, reduce brake pressure *immediately*.

To get into level slow flight, reduce power then pull enough brakes to prevent descending. Once the speed starts decreasing, you will need to add power to hold altitude, eventually requiring more power than before. You must be 100% sure where the wing will stall and what it feels like. Don't go beyond brake position/pressure 4.

In slow flight, the roles of brake pressure and power reverse. Since brakes are already pulled, you must control altitude almost exclusively with power. The good news is that, with so much brake applied, the wing responds quickly to increased power. And since you'll be carrying plenty of power, the motor should respond quickly to throttle changes. Flying at *minimum* speed requires holding the wing near stall while controlling height with power. Practice this either up very high (and with a reserve) or within a few inches of the ground.

The least amount of power is required when flying at the glider's minimum sink configuration: usually slight brake pressure, trimmers slow and speedbar off.

Turns

Turns require adding power to prevent altitude loss since some of the wing's lift is spent pulling you around the turn. More bank requires more thrust. Competition pilots doing steep low turns are almost always at full power as they swing around pylons then completely let off the power as they start to level out. They may even use speedbar to convert the turn energy into level speed.

When entering a turn, it can be helpful to reduce power briefly, start the turn, then come back in with power. That reduces the chance for spinning or stalling, especially if the turn is opposite your motor's natural torque turn direction.

Low Flying

For some, low flying is the single biggest reason they fly PPG—the ability to cruise about at any altitude while exploring a three dimensional realm. Be wary though, it's also where most of the risk lurks.

As always, stay within reach of a safe landing spot, climbing if necessary. When flying low that means remaining over landable terrain the whole time. Flying 3 feet over grass has minimal risk, flying 3 feet over deep water or trees is folly.

Start out by flying relatively high, 10 feet or so and do gentle maneuvering, remembering that any turn loses altitude and steep turns lose a lot. You must build up to learning how much. Never wind up deep in the brakes—they are your only control and, once pulled, there is nothing left to maneuver with. Like in the foot drag (covered below), if you notice that you're pulling high brake pressure, add power and ease your hands back up to recover back to cruise speed.

Foot Dragging

It's an amazing accomplishment to be flying with your feet on the ground, especially in mildly bumpy air (no more than 2 on the bump scale). You must first master precise control of altitude, within a few inches, while also minding power, ground

Eric Dufour picks up three cones in Albuquerque, NM.

⚠ Caution!

Doing steep maneuvers down low is incredibly dangerous. Don't do anything down low that you haven't mastered up high and don't ever let any kind of vertical velocity develop. Competition pilots minimize their risk because the rules discourage maneuvers with a big vertical component (big dives, for example).

Flying low and downwind sacrifices the inherent slow speed safety advantage of our craft. Higher speed makes it harder to detect/avoid an obstacle while increasing the consequence of a collision.

track and speed.

Always do this into the wind until you're extremely proficient—then doing it crosswind is possible. Crosswind foot-dragging is riskier since you'll be sliding somewhat sideways and will be far more susceptible to falling.

The safest stance for a foot-drag is with one foot out in front of the other so that you can be ready to run if necessary. Don't put much weight on the foot—drag can slow you down, forcing a run. Modulate the brakes and power to keep your cage from touching the ground. On wet, smooth ground you *can* get away with sliding the cage but that risks a prop strike.

Use brakes to control altitude and throttle to keep the speed up. If you lose a few inches, immediately add enough brake to regain it and then add power to accelerate back to speed. Use about brake pressure 1 so you'll have both up and down control. If you get gusted upwards you can immediately reduce brake pressure to avoid climbing and pull more brakes if you get dropped.

If you find yourself getting heavy in the brakes your airspeed is probably slowing down, too—get on the power immediately!

Picking Up Ground Objects

Start this slowly—first be able to do foot drags and control altitude within a few inches. Avoid descending towards an object but rather get down low and level well before reaching it. Otherwise, you're likely to hit the ground while concentrating on the object and not powering up in time.

Be flying level with no more than a quarter brake so that, when you close your feet to grab the object, a handful of brake will give an immediate climb. You want to simultaneously pull brake and add power. On approach, be stable so that you can concentrate on finesse and plan the snatch.

The best objects for this are medium sized exercise balls with low pressure. Hard or heavy items can be all but impossible to grasp with your feet. And be careful with anything you're unsure of. One pilot almost broke his foot when the kickball he was nabbing turned out to be a bowing ball. Ouch.

Having a Motor Failure

When the motor quits while flying low, the immediate loss of thrust will swing the wing forward into a descent. Unchecked, it could be quite the crash. But, if you're ready for the failure, and pull quarter brakes right away, the wing will not surge so far forward and you can minimize the effect.

If you're above about 50 feet you should be able to establish a normal glide (albeit very briefly) and have enough brake pull left for a normal flare.

Below about 30 feet you should only partially dampen the surge because you're probably too low to regain all the speed. Hold pressure 1 until needing to flare.

Below about 10 feet there may be no way around a hard landing after the motor quits. Pull the brakes immediately to pressure 2 and hold them until flaring fully at 2 to 3 feet. Unfortunately, there may be little flare authority left.

The main point is to be primed for a motor failure while flying down low, especially below 30 feet or so since there won't be enough altitude to turn around.

1. Eric Rys nabs a ball from an Illinois pasture. Before trying this, remind yourself to be extra vigilant about your surroundings—numerous pilots have hit their cages while trying this or lost track of nearby wires when concentrating on such tasks.

2. Foot draggin' Christy Damon squeezes the throttle and pulls brakes after settling too much. But the motor takes a second to spin up and if there's not enough energy (speed) in the wing, it may not be enough.

Hitting Suspended Targets

Trying to hit something floating or falling through the air is a fun challenge. A good way to practice it is by inflating a helium balloon just enough to be buoyant and taking it up with you (tie it off with a short string to the front of the harness webbing for launch). If the balloon is neutrally buoyant, you won't have to keep climbing as you try hitting it.

As you approach the balloon, try to put it on the horizon so that it's at your altitude. Head straight for it—if there is no relative motion of the object with the horizon then you are dead-on. Make *small* adjustments as necessary.

Formation

It's fun to fly in formation but there are some serious risks. To make it safer, insure that each pilot knows about the other and have no more than one inexperienced pilot in any formation. Use radios to actively coordinate the formation and follow these additional guidelines:

1. Never, ever accept a high closure rate. If things are converging quickly, break it off and re-form. Approach unknown pilots slowly, from the front side and very near their altitude. Don't get any closer than about 5 wingspans unless each pilot is looking at the other and the closure rate is slow. If another pilot starts turning away and you aren't sure of his desires, leave him be.

2. If you're closing on a pilot who doesn't know you're there, allow him room to maneuver unexpectedly so you can get out of his way.

3. Always keep both hands in the brake toggles. If taking pictures, have at least one hand in the brake toggle that would steer you clear.

4. The lead position is easy—fly steadily and don't do anything abrupt so your wingmen can react. It is better for the experienced pilots to follow.

5. Always have an out. Look at your formation and plan an escape in case one of the pilots maneuvers unexpectedly or takes a collapse.

6. Never get in someone's wake. Think of where your wing is relative to their wake and stay clear.

7. Avoid tip-to-tip formations or make them wide. Favor V formations where the following pilot keeps the preceding pilot in sight and is clear of his wake.

1. Randy Kester looks up at the one that got away. Only do this with something you're willing to get tangled in your lines and stay above 300 feet since you'll be distracted.

2. An Illinois gaggle heads for breakfast in loose formation at a couple hundred feet. Each pilot must be aware of the others so they don't get boxed in. Allow for an engine failure in a way that doesn't risk those flying around you.

Move carefully and look in all directions (up, down, right and left) before maneuvering. You can signal your intentions to other pilots by motioning a weight shift turn with your legs or pointing.

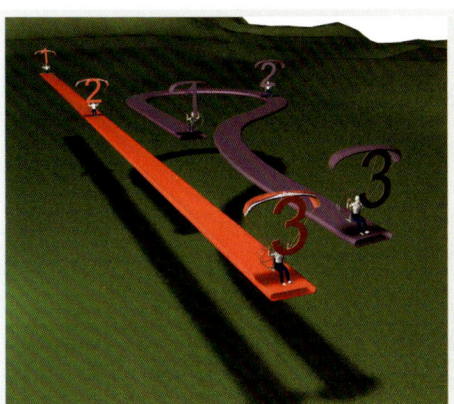

Intercepts: Forming Up On Someone

Forming up, or *intercepting*, another pilot presents challenges and risks, especially when done head-on. In this example the interceptor (purple) turns away from the interceptee's flight path which is safer than crossing flight paths as depicted on the next page. Notice how the interceptor must start his turn well before passing the interceptee.

When intercepting, it's better to start your turn early rather than late. If you wind up ahead of the interceptee, just S-turn to get back in position. But if you get behind, it will take time to catch up. In that case the Interceptee could fly a steady, shallow turn so the others can join up on the inside of the turn.

Consider being above the interceptee then descending down to his level once you're laterally in position. That way misjudgement can't cause a collision while also keeping you out of his wake. Do your maneuvering above the target's wake then descends back down into the desired formation.

Intercepting

See the **Intercepts** diagram (preceding page and at left). Joining up to fly alongside another pilot requires great care. It requires anticipation since speed is minimally adjustable. The most common error is not leading the intercept enough—you start late and wind up too far behind your target.

Turning

While turning in formation, the outside pilot must go faster than the inside pilot which may be impossible. A solution is, during the turn, climb up and cross over to get on the other side or climb up to get just behind and above the inside pilot. When leveling out, move back to the outside. Timed right, it looks good.

Other Considerations

Don't even think about "walking" on another pilot's wing. The walker's disruption in airflow can cause the walked-on wing to collapse dramatically and snare the walker. It's happened. A reserve may not even help with the resulting carnage.

Active Flying in Turbulence

Active flying is using the least amount of control necessary to keep the wing essentially overhead. Passive flying is just holding pressure while letting the wing to move around. The challenge is dampening oscillations (left-right) and surges (fore-aft) with correct input quickly with*out* overdoing it. And if you feel yourself slow down, reduce bakes and reduce power.

Use the *least* amount of input necessary; let the wing wander a bit rather than jabbing at every little twitch. As you get better, you'll be able to make very small corrections before the wing gets very far out of position. Until you've mastered that, it's better to let the wing wander within a range while mostly holding pressure.

For most wings, the best configuration in turbulence is: no speedbar, trimmers slow, brake pressure 2 or 3, and enough thrust to fly level. Lighter pilots on larger wings must be especially vigilant about parachutal stall (see Chapter 4) and be quick to reduce brake pressure and power at the first sign of slowing airspeed.

Becoming effective at active flying will take at least 50 flights and then only if you really work at it such as flying exactly straight lines within 100 feet of the ground in mildly bumpy air. While practicing, keep looking forward; use your kinetic sense to detect motion and then provide control inputs.

If at any time you start to "lose it" (not sure what to do), reduce brake pressure, reduce power for 5 seconds, let things settle down, *then* re-engage your corrections.

You must learn to interpret the small angular changes that get transferred to you through your harness as the wing moves around overhead. That takes practice. You'll need to apply the techniques covered earlier regarding pendular control. If your body swings left you apply *left* brake as soon as the swing *starts* then let up.

With repetition this becomes automatic. Don't try damping oscillations for landing until it is automatic since your attention is so focused on the flare that your steering inputs could easily devolve into pilot induced oscillations (PIO's).

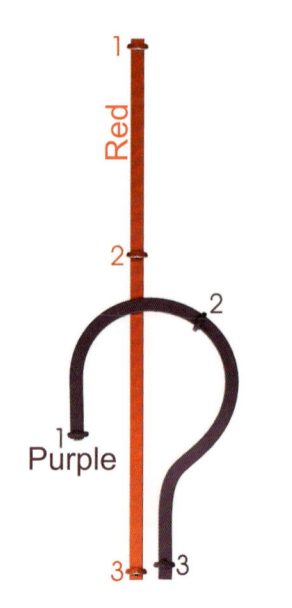

Overfly Intercept:

Here's another approach to intercepting. Purple is forming up on Red and must start his turn well before crossing abeam. After Purple gets going in the same direction, he descends and snuggles in just behind red.

As with the other intercept methods, Red must start his turn early so he doesn't wind up too far behind.

Purple *must* be higher than Red to avoid a collision risk where there flight paths cross even though, if done properly, Purple will be ahead of red when crossing.

The Perfect Touchdown

Among numerous landing styles, here are two ways to finesse touchdown. The *slider* landing is good for fast touchdowns on smooth surfaces while the *one step* helps to minimize run-out when terrain is rough. *Getting* to the target (spot landing) is covered in Chapter 17.

Sliding In, the *Scoop* Landing

Sliding in for a landing works better on smaller and/or higher performance wings (high glide ratio)—those that allow coming in for a power-off landing that have lots of flare authority in the brakes. You have such a wing if, on a power-off landing, you can flare and climb back up a few feet.

For a basic slider landing, also known as a *swoop* landing, start from a nearly hands-up glide at 50 feet. Reaching about 8 - 10 feet (wait until you're lower if there's more wind) pull enough brakes (position/pressure 1 - 2) to get your body swinging forward then ease up on the brakes briefly. That initial pull gets your body swinging forward which pitches the wing up, nearly stopping your descent. Time it so the level-off happens right as your feet reach the ground. Practice will reveal how much pull, when and how long to hold it. As you level off, speed will quickly start bleeding off—apply more brakes to keep weight off your feet as long as possible. Done properly, you'll skid to a stop with full brakes.

This is useful when ground speed is high on landing and the surface is smooth. Even if you don't skid to a stop, the slide bleeds off a lot of speed that you don't have to run off.

The *exaggerated* slider (see diagram) is a more aggressive swoop that's fun but has little practical value. Practice it up high to get a feel for how much dive you get by letting off the brakes. If you start it too high on landing, you'll level out too high on the recovery. If you start it too late (low) you'll hit the ground while diving before it has a chance to recover. *Be careful!*

Even with high-altitude practice, start it slowly, doing only a little dive at first then increasing it as you gain familiarity.

You can exaggerate the slide even more by doing it while rolling out of a bank. This dangerous maneuver is hard to judge and has very little margin for error. It's terribly unforgiving, too. Many sky divers have met their demise in an extreme version

A different type of touchdown.

It looks risky. Mo Sheldon threaded these goal posts at a vacant football field and, indeed, hooking a line would have been ruinous, but the zoom lens makes him look much closer. He was, in fact, just barely between the posts so there was virtually no risk of a line snag.

Pick your practice spots carefully and always allow for options should the engine quit. The tighter you squeeze your margins, the more certain you must be of your skills. Most accidents happen when the pilot pushes those margins just a bit too hard.

Slow, brakes=3   Hands up

Exaggerated Slider

This is diagramed on the next page but here is a real-life example of how far you can slide when the glider's energy is maximized. The engine was off from several hundred feet high.

The Exaggerated Slider or Swoop Landing

This uses the natural tendency of the glider to dive then recover after releasing the brakes from a slowed condition. Plan that natural recovery to happen right as you reach the ground.

Beware: mis-timing it can result in a dangerously hard landing. The key is using the natural swing without overdoing brake pull or starting too low.

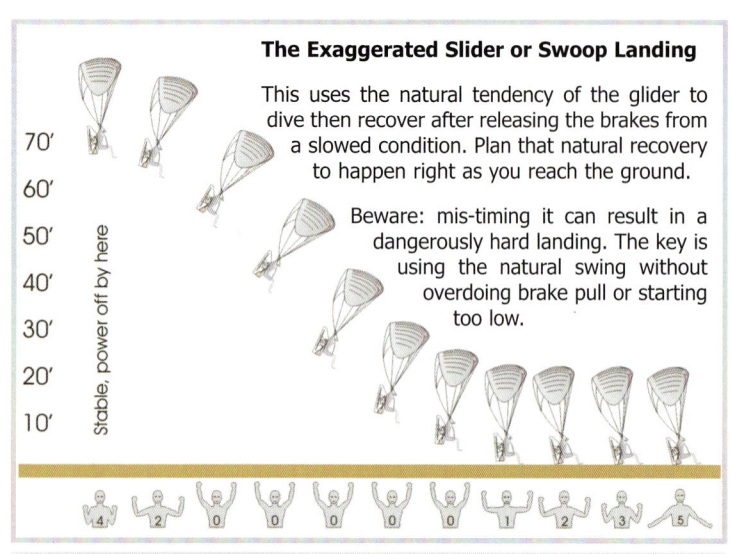

Power-On Landing

Landing with power can make you look good. Plus, in turbulent conditions it gives you more options in the event of getting dumped.

One good technique for power-on landing is to come in like any other approach but, during the last 30 feet or so, throttle up enough to shallow the descent rate by half. That enables better timing of the flare since you'll have more time to finesse out any errors.

Another technique that's fun and looks good, is to turn a foot-drag into a landing. While foot dragging, be prepared to bear all the weight in case of a gust—it's easy to fall if you're not ready for it.

of the same thing—what they call a *hook turn*. Carefully start out with shallow banks and know that the risk sky-rockets as they get steeper. Also, if you come out of a steepish bank you'll reach the ground with too much speed and climb back up. You must bleed off the speed by remaining in a turn (while skimming the ground) then leveling off as speed dissipates. It takes lots of practice, all of which is at the extreme end of any normally calibrated risk meter.

The One-Step

This is probably the most challenging type of landing to do well and the easiest one to get hurt on.

Everything is normal down to the last 50 feet. Hold about pressure 1 to 2, making steering inputs as necessary. Then at 4 to 8 feet, (depending on wing) pull enough brake so that you swing out a bit in front of the glider, climb slightly then drop the last foot or so. Go to full brakes just before touchdown.

Your starting speed must be such that you don't climb up more than a couple feet. That would hurt. Timing must be right on, too—start the final brake pull so as to exhaust all speed just as you touchdown. Some wings will require starting this from a no-brake position and maybe even swooping a bit to climb at the end.

Be extremely careful—if you wind up having pulled all the brake too early, you'll plummet the vertical distance to a *very* hard landing. A good place to practice this is soft sand. Like the exaggerated slider, errors are unforgiving.

One Step with Power

This shows one technique for landing on an elevated spot (motorhome here). Come in slightly below the top, pull some brakes to swing up and touch down, then reduce brakes as necessary to keep kiting the wing. Use power to avoid getting pulled back. Not quite one step, but close.

Although power was used, the idea of using the swing applies as you'll see in Chapter 17. A landing like this should only be attempted in a moderate, steady wind and with an understanding that errors would be most unforgiving!

Challenging Sites

CHAPTER 17

The fact that we *can* launch from so many places is incredible—and is a major draw to the sport. But some sites, under some conditions, and for some pilots may be impossible or dangerous to launch from. We must always make sure that our skills match the task and site at hand. The following tools will help manage some of those challenges and, more importantly, help recognize when to skip locations that are unsuitable.

The Horror of Hot, High, and Humid

The effect of high elevation on performance is dramatic. Gear that easily blasts you aloft at sea level may be downright doggy up at 5000 feet MSL. A machine that's weak at sea-level may not even get you airborne up there—it takes more thrust to launch than to simply fly.

Everything works against you at high elevations. Thinner air decreases thrust, makes you winded quicker, and requires faster running for the same lift. All told, launching from high elevations can be tricky, especially with no wind. Add in high temperatures or a weak motor and you may not have enough oomph to aviate.

If you've ever been to a high-altitude fly-in then you've likely witnessed (or fallen victim to) the struggle with still air where pilots sometimes simply can't get airborne. More thrust would be handy but there are possibilities.

- You may actually have a slight tailwind at 15 feet AGL up where the wing feels it but you don't. Try extending a telltale (small, very sensitive wind indicator) up high or just attempt launching the other way.
- The motor is not putting out full thrust for that altitude. A quick check of max

With no wind, the above patch of sand would be woefully inadequate. But in the steady 12 mph that was present on this day, it was easy. Beyond having enough room to launch, the pilot was able to maintain safe landing options during climbout by S-turning into the wind until gaining enough height to circle.

Tim Kaiser launching from near Kingman, Arizona. Moderately high elevation, nil winds and rough terrain sent us to this hard-packed road for launch. The wing must come up straight due to the unacceptable off-road terrain and the pilot must be able to steer his run.

RPM will confirm it. Thrust will, of course, be diminished but the RPM should be close to its sea-level value if everything is setup correctly. Chapter 27 has a chart that equates sea level thrust with what you'll get at altitude.

Leg Drag

A more insidious cause of launch woe is the design of our landing gear. Encumbered by *paraphernalia*, legs can only provide push up to a few mph. They're great for initial inflation but, beyond about 4 mph, represent only drag—thrust must do all the work. Leg drag can prevent launch and is aggravated by the following factors:

- High density altitudes (see margin) which require more ground speed.
- No wind which requires more groundspeed.
- Seatboard bottom sticking out, hitting your legs.
- Limited thrust.
- Angled-back motor styles. Adjust the motor so that you sit more erect in flight. A leaned-back motor means that you'll actually be pushing slightly with your legs as the wing lifts. It won't be as comfortable while airborne but at least you'll *get* airborne.
- Rough or soft surface.
- Short steps instead of long strides as the wing lifts. Also, make sure the seat board is flat so it doesn't interfere with your legs.

You must accelerate to get lift from the wing which then reduces leg drag. But if you can't accelerate enough to get that lift, takeoff may be impossible. You may just have to wait for some wind. One way to increase wing lift is with brakes, but, pulling too much, or too early, will also slow you down and may cause the wing to fall back. It's a fine line that requires experimentation while running.

Motors that force the pilot into a leaned-back posture in flight aggravate the prob-

---

Hot & High: Density Altitude

Density Altitude is elevation adjusted for atmospheric pressure and temperature. It's how high we and our equipment *feel* like we're operating.

Humidity has a small effect on performance but a larger effect on our bodies. Hot, humid air makes it harder to cool off—we sweat but it doesn't evaporate. The effect can make us feel like we're wearing concrete shoes. High humidity also reduces thrust.

Atmospheric pressure has a small effect—100 feet per 0.1 inches of mercury (Hg). So a real high pressure area will lower the density altitude by a few hundred feet.

The big bugaboo is temperature. As a rule of thumb, every 10°F warmer than standard (59°F at sea level) increases density altitude by about 600 feet.

In a standard atmosphere (see Chapter 24) it gets colder as you go up. At 5000 feet the standard temp is only 42°F. So a 72°F day (30° warmer than standard) at 5000 foot elevation is 6800 foot density altitude. You'll feel like you're launching at 6800 feet.

The effect is significant. At higher density altitudes you'll need to run faster and your motor won't push as hard.

lem. As the wing lifts, the motor tilts back. That's a difficult posture to run in and there may not be enough thrust to overcome resulting leg drag. Motor's that allow a vertical posture reduce the problem.

Hot and High Solutions

Here are some tips to help with high density altitude launches. Start with the smoothest surface available, downhill if possible. In a very light wind it may be better to launch crosswind from a smooth, firm surface then upwind through a soft or rutted surface. For example, soft sand can be impossible in still air whereas the nearby road, even if it is slightly crosswind, might be manageable. Never accept any downwind component. Here are some other preflight suggestions:

- If you have a choice of wings, pick the slowest one; usually that means the largest size. It must also be easy enough to inflate.
- If you have a choice of motors or propellers, go for the thrustiest.
- If you don't need all the fuel, tools, spare parts, camera gear, food and whatnot in your harness—leave them behind. Lighter is better.

Here are some tips for when you're ready to launch:

- Do a power forward inflation or go to full power as early as possible. Keep pressure on the A's until the wing is nicely overhead and you're moving briskly.
- Once you've got speed and are no longer worried about the wing falling back, concentrate on staying erect and running as fast as you can with your hands up. Pretend the wing is not there and use the smallest steering inputs possible. It may *feel* like it's not there.
- On soft surfaces, or if you've reached maximum speed, add enough brake pressure to get the wing lifting. That should relieve some weight from your legs. Don't add too much, though, and be ready to back off if you slow down. Add brake slowly to find the happy medium of wing lift and leg drag.
- Steer yourself to the smoothest, hardest surface possible or into the wind if you're not already.

If all goes well, this run will give way to long strides, then to slapping the ground with your feet and finally, to flight. Once airborne, ease up the brakes *slowly* to avoid settling back down to the ground. The best climb is typically achieved with no (or very little) brake pressure.

If you do settle back down, be prepared to run and start the process again.

> **High And Dry**
>
> The place I picked was just outside New Mexico's Sky City at a 6000 foot elevation. It wasn't much, especially considering my underpowered motor (for that altitude) and the rutted surface. Plus, on this particular morning, there was nary a whiff of wind. But I wasn't about to let that deter me. Or so I thought.
>
> After two tries, running my little legs off, I was exhausted. I simply could not generate enough speed in those ruts for the wing to lift the motor so that I could accelerate—leg drag held me back. More max efforts like that would have eventually led to a fall so I sat down to wait for a puff of headwind.
>
> Finally I felt it, and a smoke source confirmed it—the lightest little headwind, maybe 1 mph, was coming in. I stood up, setup, and went for it.
>
> The wing came up sluggishly as I lurched over deepish ruts. Thankfully it came up straight. Running my hardest with hands up and motor screaming, I slowly gathered speed. Finally, it felt fast enough to apply some brakes—too much, it seems—since I slowed down. So again I reduced brakes and concentrated on speed. By now I had reached a smoother surface which made a huge difference and pulling some brakes added enough lift to unload my legs to accelerate further. The pace quickened. More lift. More speed. Longer strides. And then finally—the magic smoothness of flight. I was skimming just inches high as I eased off the brakes, accelerated and settled into a *very* shallow climb. Oh sweet rise!
>
> Trials like these create an appreciation for *low* elevation launches. Admittedly, with more power and a bigger wing it would have been easier but the challenge sure made success taste sweet.

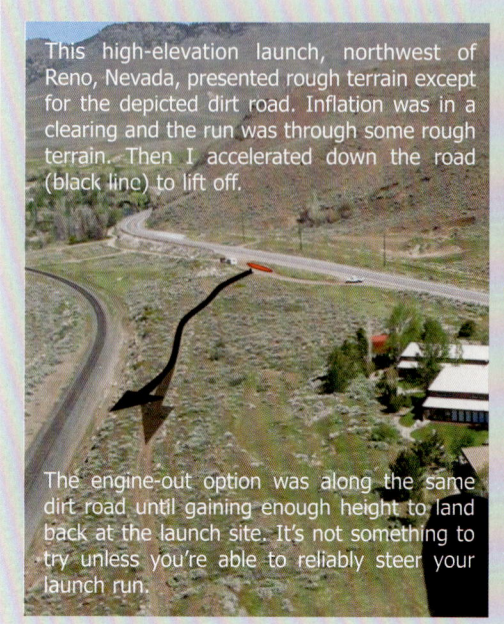

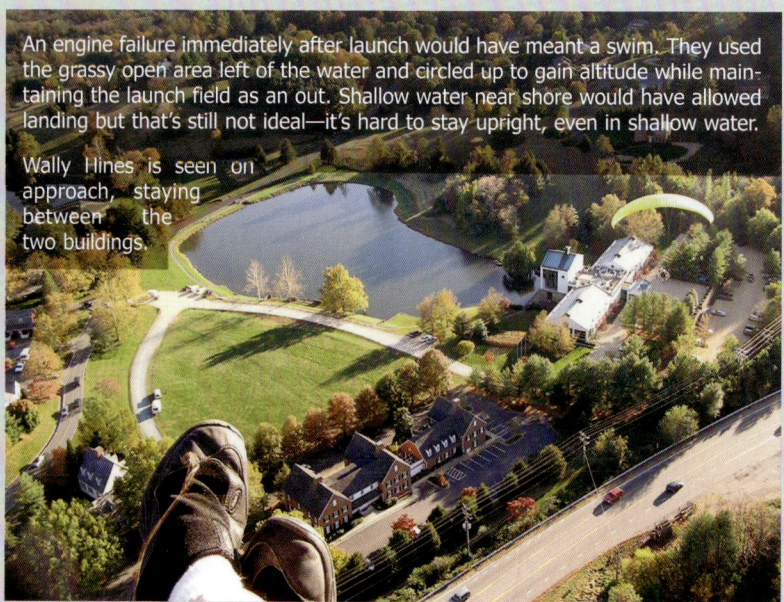

This high-elevation launch, northwest of Reno, Nevada, presented rough terrain except for the depicted dirt road. Inflation was in a clearing and the run was through some rough terrain. Then I accelerated down the road (black line) to lift off.

The engine-out option was along the same dirt road until gaining enough height to land back at the launch site. It's not something to try unless you're able to reliably steer your launch run.

An engine failure immediately after launch would have meant a swim. They used the grassy open area left of the water and circled up to gain altitude while maintaining the launch field as an out. Shallow water near shore would have allowed landing but that's still not ideal—it's hard to stay upright, even in shallow water.

Wally Hines is seen on approach, staying between the two buildings.

Tight Spaces

Make no mistake, it's always risky to shoehorn yourself into sub-optimal spaces. However, with skill, the right conditions and appropriate equipment, you *can* fly from surprisingly small areas.

Besides having sufficient room for running, a site must provide a clear path for climbout and departure. Make sure that if the motor quits at any point, you can either land safely along the departure, or be high enough to circle back.

Any site that doesn't allow inflating into the wind will be tougher (like roads) but it can be managed. The skills described in Chapter 15 will be valuable at such locations. Be incredibly leery of wind shadow—if the site is surrounded by high obstructions you'll be hard pressed to tell what the winds are doing up higher and powerful turbulence may lurk in the transition.

Steering the launch

Being able to steer while running or walking with the wing overhead is a seminal skill for success in tight locations. It allows launch from places that require a turn before liftoff such as an L shaped or obstructed field. This skill is useful elsewhere since it allows you to safely avoid obstacles, like another flyer and his gear, without having to abort. It can also allow you to inflate into the wind, which is easier, then turn and finish the takeoff in a different direction like a crosswind runway.

Steering with the wing overhead is easy to practice. Go out on a mildly breezy day and start to launch but don't actually take off. You'll be powering forward while keeping the wing overhead and walking briskly (or slowly in a stronger wind). The goal is learning how to steer the wing without looking up at it.

> **⚠ Caution!**
> Never choose a site that requires the motor's continued operation to clear obstacles. Always insure that if it quits at any point, you can land safely.

After mastering straight steering, try making the wing go right or left, off the wind direction somewhat. Start with just a few degrees. Use steering inputs to make the wing go where you want then follow under it. Remember, the wing has momentum, too. If you and the wing are angling to the right and *you* stop, the wing will keep going right. You must lead it—while walking right, pull left brake to stop the wing; take a few more steps then *you* can stop.

While facing forward, learn to *feel* where the wing is without looking. Only look at it when necessary, especially while figuring out the feel. Walk forward enough to keep sufficient airspeed—you should feel the lines tugging just a bit. When the glider drifts off to one side use just enough brakes to bring it back overhead.

Always lead with the wing. To go left, get the wing going left first then follow it. The amount of lead depends on how rapidly you want to change direction. When you want to stop going left and get back into the wind, pull right while still walking left. When the wing gets slightly to your right, stop — momentum will carry the wing a few more feet.

The goal is to steer with only the brakes. Move left or right if it's *necessary* to keep the wing up, but strive to use only the brakes. That improves mastery of where your feet go which is beneficial in tight spaces.

Another skill that improves feel is controlling the wing with *only* your body (*no* brakes). It's quite difficult but will help you understand how the wing reacts to being offset. Walk left to get it going right, but not far lest it quickly fall.

As the wind gets lighter, these exercises get more challenging but are certainly doable. You can even practice in no wind but it's mighty tiring. It takes a lot of running to keep air flow over the wing for control.

Water is bad, every launch should be planned so as to stay out of it if the engine fails at the worst possible time.

This launch from a private park near Vero Beach, FL, shows how the pilot kept his options open. The numbered paths are where he would have gone in case it quit.

Climbing out

The climbout should always allow a return to the field until you're high enough to circle back. If the field is surrounded by obstructions, climb out on the inside edge so that, if the motor quits, you can turn towards landable surface. Avoid high climb angles for the first 30 feet or so lest a motor failure swing you into the ground.

If possible, plan turns in the motor's normal torque-turn direction.

Landing Pattern

Tight spaces sometimes require different landing patterns. Fly it as standard as possible but realize that odd field shapes can dictate odd patterns. Plan it into the wind and away from rotor as much as possible.

An obstacle-lined field will require your final descent to follow the contour of obstacles. In the tree-lined field shown at right, you would plan your descent just inside the trees so as to end with a short final into the wind. Be careful not to snag a wingtip in the trees—a surprisingly easy, and dangerous, mistake to make.

This is obviously an emergency landing. Plan your approach to touch down as far as possible from rotor causing obstacles. You'll have to hug the edge of the field but don't get too close—hitting a tree up high is far worse than hitting rotor turbulence down low.

Dealing With Winds—Using Power

In turbulent conditions it is beneficial to keep the power on. Even if you need to get into a tight space, the value of having thrust available outweighs the chance of breaking a prop on landing. And it's not just to enable a go around—it can salvage what would otherwise be a very hard arrival.

Providing there is room, come up slightly on the power just before touchdown to shallow the descent. In a tight space, wait until you're within 10 feet of the ground or so. This will also "spool up" the motor enough to have instant throttle response if a sudden burst is necessary. That will leave you better prepared for a downward gust while landing.

If everything goes well and you do *not* get dumped, then do a normal flare and landing. In strong conditions, be quick to turn around and get the wing down while killing the motor.

This is something to practice long before it's needed. Become adept at making flawless power-on landings during smooth conditions then practice them when it's a bit rougher.

Without power, a gust that swings you forward (and possibly up) will make you bleed off speed followed by a drop into a possibly hard landing. Let off the brakes immediately if the wing goes back to minimize this possibility, but you'll still be swung out and have little speed with which to flare. Using a squirt of power just after the gust will regain the lost speed and preserve brake authority for a normal flare.

Spot Landing

Next to steering the launch, spot landing skill is what makes tight spaces manageable. You must be able to control your landing spot consistently—within 25 feet or so depending on the site. Practice and master it from a large area where there is no consequence to missing the target. Don't fly into a real confined space until you can consistently nail your target.

Come in with the motor idling but do *not* plan on using it. And don't fly over anything where a power loss would yield a crash—use turns if necessary to keep landable terrain available.

Fly a normal, but slightly tighter landing pattern, to stay oriented and aware of altitudes. Vary the pattern as necessary to maintain safe landing options. Your goal is hitting a 100 foot final approach where you can accurately judge the crucial final glide. Use S-turns on final, if necessary, to bleed off excess altitude but be level by about 50 feet.

If the touchdown area is small and obstructed, consider using heavier brake application (pressure 3) to slow down and steepen the glide. Be *extremely* careful though—you'll be closer to a stall and have very little extra speed to maneuver with. Once the wing is slowed down there is little more you can do with those brakes beyond letting them up. Practice this first where a spot landing is not required. Be ready with the power to catch a big drop. More importantly, be ready

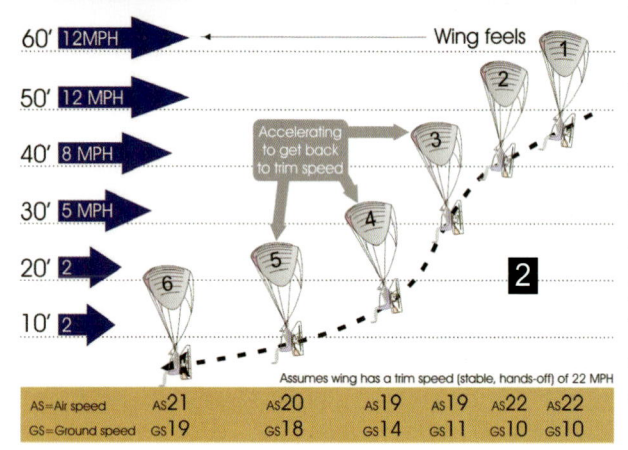

1. Bill heaner circles a field near Salt Lake City. Staying legal requires a clear path that avoids congested areas. In this case it was towards the mountains below and out of frame.

Launching required a well-planned run then a circling climb over the small field before heading out. With mountains behind, this site would be treacherous in strong winds blowing over them.

2. Chapter 5 introduced wind gradient effects during landing. To understand them better, this shows what would happen if no brake was applied. You can see why it's even more important to be hands nearly up by 50 feet so you have flare authority.

When dropping into a decreasing headwind, airspeed slows causing the wing to dive as it seeks trim speed. A high (200 foot or more), gradual gradient will let you glide farther from the decreased headwind while a small, strong gradient will dump you early and possibly hard as the wing dives aggressively.

to let up the brakes *immediately* if you feel yourself slowing down or the brakes getting limp—that could signal a stall or spin.

Judging glide is an important skill that must be mastered. Practice this judgment (or envision it) during your next approach in smooth air. Put a foot up so that it visually touches where you think your touchdown point will be. If your foot starts to pass over the spot then you're high, lift it up a bit to reflect the better glide. If your foot sinks below the spot then you're low and would land short. Move the foot down to reflect the steeper descent. Once the spot is no longer moving up or down, that is your aim line, it is where you'll touch down if nothing changes.

Glide is extended by letting the brakes up and steepened by pulling more brakes. If there's much headwind, you'll need to plan a much steeper approach. Be ever mindful of pulling too much brake—pilots have been seriously hurt when they were high and stalled or spun after pulling too much brake.

Once below about 50 feet avoid turns. Manage the aim line (glide angle) so that it stays on the target. Fortunately you can change your glide angle, but only so much.

Until you gain experience, forget the spot below about 30 feet and concentrate on touchdown quality, not location. Increase your speed (hands mostly up) to allow for a full flare. You'll briefly dive as the wing accelerates. Improving skill will let you concentrate longer on making the spot—staying on the brakes longer when necessary. That will, however, sacrifice flare authority and must be timed *very* precisely. Flaring from more than half-brake (pressure 3) is almost useless, you will just whack hard. There must be enough brake authority to cause *some* pendulum swing which is what actually slows your descent.

More headwind means worse glide—speed up to go farther (penetrate). Above 100 feet, go trimmers fast or push on the speedbar. You'll drop initially then glide

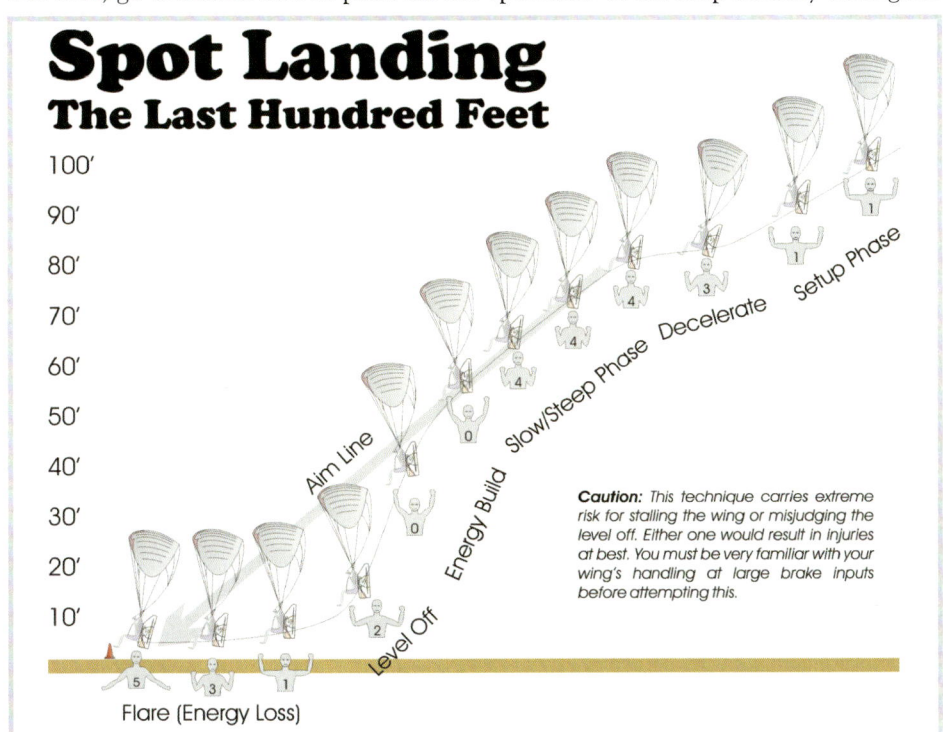

Spot Landing Pattern

The pattern is flown tighter to reduce the affect of changing winds and thermals.

Go to brake position/pressure 3 after turning base leg. That way you can extend glide by reducing brakes. By 20 feet you must be concentrating on the flare, regardless of the spot. Land wings level even if you're not going right into the wind.

Spot Landing Last 100'

This technique is for hitting an exact spot such as a frisbee—it's riskier than a normal landing so be careful. To make it safer, allow more room for error and avoid brake extremes.

If it's bumpy, don't use any more than brake pressure 3 or you'll risk hitting sink and having too little brake authority to arrest the drop.

The basic steps are:

1. Use a normal power-off landing pattern that is slightly high.

2. S-Turn on final to bleed off any excess height but start the final glide with brakes around pressure 3.

3. Hands up to extend the glide if you get low, brakes to pressure 4 if you get high.

4. At about 30 feet, forget the spot and reduce brake pressure to regain speed for a normal flare and touchdown.

will improve. Avoid letting off the speedbar at the same time you let off the brakes which makes a front tuck more likely.

In calm air or a headwind, slowing down steepens glide. So holding a lot of brake (don't stall it!) steepens glide after you initially apply the brakes. Leave enough altitude to re-build airspeed for the flare—a landing from this slowed condition is less predictable and may be painfully hard.

Flapping is another technique for descending steeply without stalling. The pilot repeatedly snatches heavy brakes then releases them in a "flapping" motion. It doesn't *prevent* a stall, it just insures that the wing sees some time without brake input while creating enormous drag. Regardless of technique, pulling heavy brakes like this adds extra risk for stall or spin.

Power-On Spot Landing Over an Obstruction

If you're trying to make it into a really confined area, like the boxing ring below, here's how. Come in with power, be level or slightly below the obstruction (ropes), holding moderate brake pressure (about 3). A second or two before crossing the obstruction, pull more brake to swing your body forward and slightly up. Once past the obstruction, throttle off and increase brake pressure to keep the wing behind you as you plunk down onto the target.

You want to come in moderately slow, using a combination of power and brakes to hold altitude. Leave *some* brake authority while staying slow. The reason for braking just before the obstruction is so that your body swings out front then, after crossing the obstruction, brakes keep the wing behind you while the swinging back allows for an even slower speed at touchdown.

Mis-timing this would be painful so practice with imaginary fences on soft targets. Beaches are perfect. You want to be proficient before trying it somewhere hard or important. A motor with rapid response time is helpful, too, because you'll be modulating the power a lot since the brakes will be of little value for height control.

Choose the slowest wing possible to improve your odds and be careful!

Top: Don't launch where you'll cross a road unless you've got someone stopping traffic. In the heat of launching it would be easy to miss an approaching vehicle from the side.

Above: This beautiful slice of New Mexico sits over 6000 feet high, giving these para-campers a challenging launch. Off the road, scrub brush and general roughness make it difficult.

A small crosswind on a smooth surface may beat into-the-wind through difficult terrain.

Red means more power, white means no power, so pink means some power is being held. Wind helps this effort dramatically as long as it's not too bumpy.

Advanced Maneuvers

CHAPTER 18

Maneuvers serve various purposes in flight: losing altitude, changing flight path, skill enhancement, demonstration and just plain fun. But there's huge risk: the more extreme, the more risk. Before doing anything steep, we strongly recommend a special *maneuvers clinic*, sometimes called an *SIV* course (Simulation d'Incident en Vol - simulated incidence in flight). Don't try them on your own since they can become un-recoverable. You can do the course as soon as you're comfortable with basic launching and landing skills but it will mean more if you have at least 100 flights. You'll learn the latest methods for recovering from unusual situations and, more importantly, get to practice them in a safer environment.

Techniques do change with technology. What you read here, or even learn in a clinic, may become dated as knowledge and gear improve. Experts acknowledge that they are always learning better methods to fly and train. Ask instructors and respected pilots about the latest wrinkles.

Don't induce wing malfunctions outside of a clinic. Whenever doing maneuvers beyond normal flight or flying in turbulence, make sure you have a suitable reserve and know how to use it (see Chapter 12).

Aerobatics such as loops, rolls, helicopters, SAT's and such are maneuvers intended for show. Only the most risk-tolerant souls should consider attempting them and then only with the highest level of training—be ready for reserve rides!

Any advanced maneuver is best done first in a free flight harness to reduce the chance for getting lines tangled in the cage. A motor complicates matters by adding twisting mass (possibly causing severe riser twists). If the extreme risk of a motor is to be accepted, at least have the propeller stopped before trying anything.

> ⚠ **Caution!**
> Trying these maneuvers has resulted in serious accidents. It is essential that pilots seek proper guidance from a qualified, experienced instructor before attempting any maneuver.

1. It's in the hips. The whole point of weight shift is to lower one riser while the other goes up. Low hook-in machines designed for weight shift (like this one) get results by the pilot throwing his body (and harness and motor) over to one side, similar to how it's done in free-flight harnesses. The pivoting bar actually moves for only a portion of the riser travel, tilting does the rest.

2. Machines with high hook-ins are weight-shifted by lowering one leg on the turn side. That pulls the harness webbing down which lowers the attached riser. On some units, pushing against the ground handling strap with one shoulder adds leverage and increases riser movement.

Weight Shift Turns

This isn't an advanced maneuver but is included here because it's not intuitive on all machines. Weight shift steering is helpful in precision flying but is not necessary.

Motors with weight shift let you shift in the harness such that one riser is lowered relative to the other causing a small amount of turn towards the lowered riser. More importantly, it gets the wing moving in the desired direction so brake input can be more effective. The whole goal is riser shift. Body contorting and leg swinging may look impressive, but if the risers don't shift, the wing will not be impressed.

Use weight shift to begin a turn *then* apply brake. As the bank increases, pull slight outside brake pressure to reduce diving tendency and prevent collapse of the outside tip. This *coordinated turn* allows faster entry into banks since less total brake is required (more valuable if you're soaring or competing). Combining weight shift with medium brakes will induce a turn as quickly as heavy brakes alone but with less risk for spinning.

High Hook-Ins

Low hook-in models with pivoting arms have the best weight shift but machines with high hook-ins can have it, too, if they use a moving bar or sliding straps in front of the J-bar. Pilot technique varies but the effect is the same: pulling one riser down while the other goes up.

On high hook-in systems, the pilot pushes one leg down to push that side of the seat down which lowers its attached webbing and riser—right leg down to turn right. On units with ground handling (shoulder) straps even more weight shift may be possible by pushing your shoulder against the strap while pushing down the leg: right leg down, right shoulder up. The ground handling straps must be tighter for this to work. Do whatever works to maximize riser shift.

Your harness's chest strap and anti-torque strap (if equipped) should be fairly loose for the best weight shift.

Low Hook-Ins

Units with low hang points use a different method of weight shift—the pilot tilts the entire machine left or right, more like a free flight harness. Pivoting bars provide about half the riser movement, tilting does the rest. On these machines, you lean, shift your hips, and throw your weight over to one side. This is made easier because the center of gravity is so close to the attachment points.

If the low hook-in machine has no pivoting bars then it's not designed for significant weight shifting. These machines depend on having the center of mass very near the hook-in point. Even just a few inches lower sacrifices weight shift ability. So just because a machine has low hook-ins does not mean it readily weight-shifts. Check with the maker or an experienced pilot who knows the model.

Some pilots of low hook-in motors cross their legs when turning. They put the high-side leg over the low-side leg which makes it easier to hold for a longer time, but it doesn't improve the turn. It can also serve as a signal to nearby pilots that you are about to turn which adds value to the "lean" in "look, lean, then turn".

Speedbar Usage

Although our craft is mostly a slow, one-speed affair, we can hasten it up with the speed system, especially on reflex wings. It must be used carefully, though, since engaging it leaves the wing more susceptible to a front collapse (covered later) on standard gliders and must be used only as directed on reflex gliders. Apply it slowly and steadily while holding constant power. If combining speedbar with trimmers let out the trimmers first, wait a second, then apply speedbar—that avoids collapse and keeps your hands on the brakes while accelerating.

Most maneuvers have a far more severe reaction to wing maladies and recoveries at higher speed (trimmers fast, speedbar engaged). Sporty handling, highly loaded wings can have eye-popping results. On non-reflex wings, avoid speedbar use in bumpy air or less than about 100 feet AGL. On most reflex wings, speedbar should only be used while trimmed fast and without using the main brakes.

It takes significant leg-push to keep the speedbar engaged. That's good on standard gliders because it can be released quickly, restoring the wing to normal flight if rough air is encountered. Trimmers, however, take longer to get to and require that your hands release brake pressure in the process—not good in turbulence.

Maneuvers Course

Well coached maneuvers clinics will help you learn how your glider behaves in extreme situations and how to recover. Flights are almost always done over water, in good air, after getting towed up a couple thousand feet by boat. The tow operator and helpers must be extremely competent. Take this very seriously, a water impact at high speed can be fatal. Clinics won't make you an expert—they merely give you some tools. Pilots have died after going home then trying the maneuvers on their own, over land and without coaching. Weather conditions play a big part, too; a recovery learned in smooth air may go much differently in turbulence.

Proper and rapid recovery from many maladies requires correct, decisive reactions that, if done at the wrong time, can make matters worse. Keep in mind that acci-

---

1. Getting ready to engage the speedbar from its retracted position.

The green line shows a better pulley position and routing. The pull force should be in line with the risers with pulleys mounted to the frame, if possible, to reduce squeezing the seat upwards when pushing the speedbar.

2. Fully accelerated. It also shows another possible pulley arrangement that may be more comfortable (green line and pulleys).

3. Pilot's-eye view of extended speedbar.

Having the pulley closer to your hips and secured to the frame will likely be more comfortable.

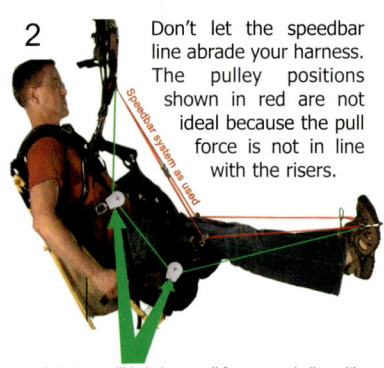

Don't let the speedbar line abrade your harness. The pulley positions shown in red are not ideal because the pull force is not in line with the risers.

TWO Pulleys will help keep pull force more in line with the risers but they will want to squeeze together.

dent reports show most control-related mishaps in paramotors result from *too much brake*. If in doubt, reduce brake input. Certified gliders are designed to return to normal flight with *no* input from the pilot in most cases, spiral dives being an important exception. More on that shortly.

Descent Techniques

As with all maneuvers, do these under the guidance of an instructor first!

Start the following descent methods with trimmers neutral, usually full slow, unless told otherwise. Power should be off with the propeller stopped or windmilling. Build up gradually, starting out shallow and increasing very, very slowly.

This adds stress to individual sets of lines. If done repeatedly, your glider may wear out faster and should be inspected more frequently (at least once per year).

Big Ears

Big Ears is a fairly benign technique that roughly doubles your normal descent rate. Combining big ears with speedbar (pull ears first, though), adds about 25% to that rate. Steer using weight shift, if available, and avoid adding power or brakes which increase the chance of entering parachutal stall. Stress increases on the center lines which must support everything once the tips are pulled down. Forward speed stays about the same because, while wing area is reduced, drag is increased.

Descent rate: Up to 800 FPM (4 m/s).

Entry: Reach up with palms facing outward (thumbs down) and pull the outermost A lines down. Twist the hand inward so that your palm faces you. It is easier if the wing is equipped with split A's like the one shown below.

Recovery: Let go of the A lines and do not pull any brake—see if the tips open on their own. Higher aspect ratio wings tend to recover slower and may even need a brief brake pull to pressure 1 or 2.

"**Big Ears**" is the most common canopy reduction method in use. Pull down the outer A line on each wingtip (1). The faster and farther you pull it, the more dramatic is the tip fold. Make sure to grab only the outer line lest you pull down the entire leading edge of the wing (frontal).

Since the angle of attack goes up (descending faster with the same forward speed), this slightly increases your chance of entering parachutal stall. Many instructors advise against doing big ears close to the ground.

Note: The outer A line is being pulled. Don't confuse that with the Stabilo line which, on this wing (and most), is the outer B line.

Glider with Split A's shown

BIG EARS

B-Line Stall

A B-Line stall stops the wing's forward motion while leaving it fully inflated. Air spills equally around the leading and trailing edges as you descend vertically. There's added stress on the B line attachment points so use it sparingly, especially heavily loaded. And it's far more dramatic than big ears with possible complications. For example, excessive pull may cause a front horseshoe and cravat on exit.

Descent rate: Up to 1600 FPM (8 m/s).

Entry: Reach up high on the B lines (quick links if possible) and pull them down to your shoulders with forearms upright. It will initially take a lot of force which decreases once established. The wing falls back abruptly (you swing forward) then settles overhead in a vertical descent. How far you pull the B's down depends on the wing and where you grabbed them.

More pull gives more descent but too much pull may cause a front horseshoe where the tips fly forward into a U shape. If that happens, immediately let your hands up slightly.

Recovery: Let up on the B lines *quickly* and *evenly*. Some instructors recommend Letting up slowly but that may cause a parachutal stall and letting up unevenly may cause a spin. Also, let the wing get fully flying before applying any brakes—it will typically surge less than 45°. Don't just let go.

Steep Turns

In a normal turn, you pull a brake to about pressure 2 and hold it there. The glider arcs into a bank then shallows out a bit, remaining in the turn as long as you hold that brake pressure. Sporty gliders respond quicker but have similar behavior.

> ⚠ **Caution!**
> When initiating a turn, if pulling more brake does not cause more turn, don't pull more brake—you may spin the glider. Also, once you start coming out of a steep turn, don't try to go back into it; let it fully recover first.

A steep turn is different. You pull a bit harder on the brake and hold it there until reaching the desired bank angle. But as long as you hold that pressure, the bank *continues to steepen* (not coming back towards level). You'll feel pressed into your seat, G-forces building, as the bank increases. Brake responsiveness and pressure increase as the bank steepens. So a steep turn is where, once at the desired bank angle, you must reduce brake input to prevent careening into a spiral dive, the dangerous extreme of steep turns. Remember, start out slowly!

Any turn causes altitude loss (or requires more power) and gets dramatic at steeper angles. A 60° bank is pretty steep—you'll experience 2 times the pull of gravity (2 G's) and require probably half-again more thrust. Much steeper than that puts you in the spiral dive category.

Descent rate: Up to 2000 FPM (10 m/s).

Entry: Initiate a turn and hold enough brake so that it gradually steepens to about 60° then modulate the brakes to hold it there. It looks about like frame 2 at right. Enter into the turn gradually to avoid pulling the wing into a spin.

Recovery: Enormous energy builds up during a steep turn and must be managed. Remove the turn input and the bank should start leveling out. Once it *starts* doing so, be ready to re-apply a bit of inside brake to slow the recovery. Much of the risk comes during this level-out—your body and motor are travelling far faster than the wing and want to swing up into a steep climb, possibly followed by the lines going slack. That could result in severe collapses, cravats, or lines wrapping around the cage.

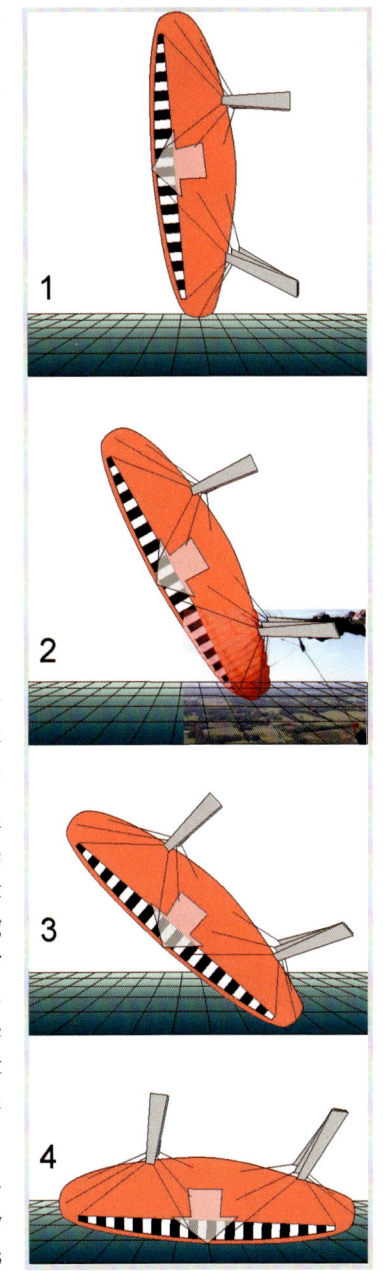

Banks 1 & 2 are steep turns, 3 would be considered a spiral dive. By the time a bank reaches 4, it may not be possible to recover. This "over-the-nose" spiral may inflict G-forces that prevent the pilot from even getting to his reserve.

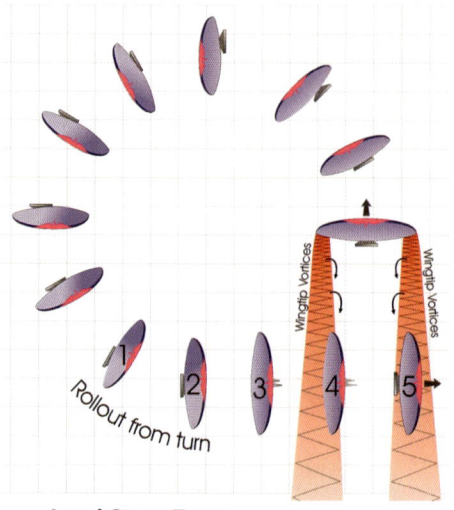

The PPG Bible: A Complete Guide and Reference

Spiral Dive

Spiral Dives are steep turns with a very rapid descent (steeper than frame 2 on the preceding page) where letting up on the brakes may not initiate a recovery. They are dangerous beyond appearances. Even beginner wings may not recover from the steepest spirals. You can wind up "locked in" such that it takes strong opposite brake pressure to start the recover (possibly two hands).

Once established, the highly loaded wing is hyper-sensitive to brake input. You'll quickly get to 4 G's—enough to possibly cause a black out. It has happened numerous times where a pilot blacks out and spirals into the ground. Vertigo, where the pilot gets disoriented to the point of not knowing what brake to pull, is also a possibility. Proper recovery, as with the steep turn, is critical.

An **Asymmetric Spiral** is where one side of the circle is higher than the other. It is generally considered safer than a regular spiral because the chance of "locking in" is lessened. The G-load decreases on the high side and increases on the low side. This type of spiral requires high-end active piloting skills since the high-G's on the bottom makes it very sensitive to improper inputs and the pilot can quickly get slack lines on the high side if not careful.

The most vertical spirals may not be recoverable. For one, this *over the nose* spiral is enormously disorienting. Your body is going to the left and the wing right (or vice-versa), possibly confusing which brake to pull. Plus, high G's can prevent deploying your reserve. Fatalities have resulted from these maladies, even on beginner wings.

Descent rate: Up to 5000 FPM (25 m/s).

Entry: Weight shift (if able), then pull enough brake (probably will require pressure 3) to enter a turn and keep the bank increasing. Build slowly, taking an entire 360° turn to get into the spiral—too much brake can cause a spin.

Recovery: Remove any weight shift, put both hands up and let it start rolling out. If it doesn't start right away, pull both brakes some then opposite brake. As soon as it *starts* recovering, let up. If it's leveling off quickly, ease in some inside brake (in the direction you're turning) to dampen the recovery.

The steepest spirals may require weight shift and *heavy* opposite brake to start the recovery.

Think about the spiral in advance. Once banked up, with your body whistling earthward at breakneck speed and G's building, the recovery may not be obvious. In a right spiral, for example, you will have used right brake to enter, then very little or no brake to stay in it and may need left brake to initiate the recovery. Although most modern beginner-type wings will roll out on their own, some may not.

Level Steep Turns

Be cafeful when doing steep turns through your own wake. Don't unload the wing by rolling out too quickly (see Chapter 19). Hitting the wake at that point would probably cause a collapse.

A moderate level out and climb while using inside brake (left in the diagram) *and* some outside brake is best. Add power as the wing comes overhead. When the wing surges forward, use appropriate brake pressure to dampen it. Here are the steps:

1) Initiate rollout by reducing left brake. Once it starts leveling out, reduce power and reapply some left brake pressure to slow the rollout.

2) As you reach the top of any climb, around point 4, add some brakes and power. They must be added when the glider *starts* surging forward.

During the rollout always keep some pressure (2 to 3) on both brakes in anticipation of going through the wake.

Staying in the bank is another way to keep the wing more heavily loaded and therefore collapse resistant. Consider climbing to avoid the wake altogether.

During a symmetrical, steep, level turn, the wing vortices should remain outside your flight path.

---

1. Richard Good does a B-Line stall.

2. This is why full stalls should be left to SIV courses! Richard is thrown on his back violently and, although he controls this one, a line snagged on the cage, or many other maladies, could render the glider unflyable.

3. B-line stalls, frontal collapses and others can wind up with a frontal horseshoe. Pulling brake to pressure 3 normally brings order quickly. It is important to recover quickly to avoid the possibility of a cravat.

Wing Malfunctions

Bad stuff happens, especially to those who push weather limits, their skills, or both. A maneuvers clinic is good but avoiding nasty conditions is even better. And inducing any of these on your own can prove fatal without proper training and, even then, is risky.

Parachutal Stall is covered in Chapter 4 under Emergencies.

The standard response to unknow situations is: smoothly "**reduce power, reduce brakes, then steer.**" If you're near terrain use *just* enough brake to steer away. Look up at the wing to see what has happened then look back at the horizon to stay oriented. Again, *too much* brake causes more problems for motor pilots than not enough. For sure do what it takes, but be mindful of over controlling.

Turbulence can play havoc on recovery so, even if you've practiced, don't expect it to always go the same way in rough air.

Cravat

Chapter 4 covered small, relatively benign cravats. Don't be fooled, large cravats can be dramatically worse. While it takes a 60 to 70% wing fold to do much, a mere 30% fold, when tucked against the lines in a cravat, can be deadly. The same is true if a wing half folds down against the lines but doesn't get stuck. It presents a huge resistance, pushing that side of the wing into an abrupt, plunging, vertical spiral dive. Reserve or not, this is bad.

Cravats are frequently complications of collapses from turbulence or botched maneuvers. Once in the spiral, G-forces build rapidly, making recovery difficult or impossible. Tossing your reserve may be all that's left—but do it quickly, especially down low. Otherwise do what you can to stop the spiral. If you can find the stabilo line, pull it hard, hand over hand if necessary. If you can*not* find it, use whatever opposite brake it takes.

Spin

Spins are another malady caused by excessive brake pull. If it's uneven pull, especially against the motor's torque turn direction, part of the wing stalls while the rest keeps flying. The glider slows then rotates nearly overhead as you descend. A riser twist is possible as the pilot tries to catch up to the spinning wing, potentially locking the brakes in place and preventing recovery.

If you feel any unusual slowing or turning, reduce power and brakes immediately! Most pilots won't detect the spin until it's already spun half way around; that's why prevention is so important.

> **Descent rate:** Around 1200 FPM (6 m/s).
> **Cause:** Uneven heavy breaking, especially against the torque. Turbulence can aggravate it but you must be pulling brake.
> **Recovery:** Reduce power, reduce brakes immediately, and prepare to dampen the surge. If you get a riser twist, and

Full Stall

Full stalls are violent, unpredictable maneuvers. Fortunately, the wing must be really provoked with heavy brakes to get into it.

The biggest danger is getting cocooned in your wing but there could also be complications on recovery. It's one maneuver where "reduce power, reduce brakes" may *not* be the appropriate reaction. If you are being heavy handed and then suddenly feel dumped on your back—welcome to a stall.

In most cases, if you merely think you're getting into a stall, then indeed immediately reduce brake pressure and power to let the glider fly again. But in an honest-to-goodness full stall there's a *lot* more to it.

If you *know* it's a full stall, you must then hold the brakes down for several seconds to let the glider stabilize overhead before recovering. Do not let up on the brakes with the wing back! It will shoot forward and down, possibly pulling your flailing body into it.

Entry: Pull the brakes all the way down and lock your hands below your thighs. The wing slows, then falls back as you get yanked hard onto your back and drop. Hold the brakes until the wing stabilizes overhead. It may be "bucking" about wildly but hold on for a couple seconds!

You'll be dropping at over 2000 FPM (10 m/s).

Recovery: Once the glider is reasonably overhead, let up the brakes smoothly, evenly and quickly to about halfway (position 4). Hold them there for a few seconds while the glider sorts itself out. Then let your hands up to pressure one. Let the glider surge, do *not* dampen it aggressively during recovery and do not try to control the surges unless you're certain of what you're doing.

A full stall's only practical value is as a last resort "paraglider reset." If you have an unrecoverable malfunction, lots of altitude (1000 feet plus), no reserve and a crash is otherwise inevitable, then consider a full stall. This is strictly a last ditch effort with no guarantees.

For a pilot who has never done one at a coached SIV clinic, the outcome is even less certain (see Cravat).

you're in a low hook-in machine, you may be able to reach above the twist and pull outward to help untwist yourself. Be aware of altitude and know where the reserve is—be ready to toss it.

Asymmetric Collapse

Remember that what nature doles out can be far worse than what you induce. A big asymmetric collapse can cause a violent bank, dropping you towards the collapsed side as it erupts into a turn (more collapse, more turn). Don't just start yanking on things but carefully do what it takes to prevent a spiral.

Descent rate: From 600 FPM (3 m/s) to 1000 FPM (5 m/s).

Cause: Turbulence. It can be simulated by reaching up high on one A riser (or both parts of a split A) and pulling down slowly. A faster (harder) pull will collapse more wing—be careful, a fast pull can cause a big (70%+) fold.

This has also happened to students who inadvertently grabbed a riser while trying to get in the seat.

Recovery: If possible, steer using weight shift and *careful* brake pressure on the open side. As always, too much brake risks a stall or spin. The deflated side will probably be limp but, as soon as pressure builds (the collapse starts coming out), let that hand come up while keeping some pressure (about pressure 2). Consider "pumping" the deflated side by using long brake pulls. "Accelerate briefly, steer, *then* clear" (by pumping) the collapse.

Pilots usually make matters worse by pulling too much brakes; be careful.

Asymmetric Collapse

Pulling the right A riser down hard caused this 60% collapse but it's completely controllable. Only a little left brake on the inflated side and some weight shift is required. Don't pull too hard lest it spin or stall. You'll normally only require position/pressure 2 to go straight. In this case, the right hand will be limp; let it go down until it feels about pressure 1. Long pumps of the deflated side *may* help after you've got some speed.

A full stall into soft sand. Entry and recovery varies by wing but it should never be done outside an SIV course. Full stall differs from parachutal stall by virtue of the wing deforming during a full stall.

You can see why it's so important to recover *before* it fully develops. If you feel the brakes get "mushy" or forward speed deteriorate, *immediately* reduce brake pressure, but if the wing has already fallen back, execute the full-stall recovery.

Frontal Collapse

A *frontal*, or *front tuck*, results from the leading edge being forced downward, closing off the cells. You drop and the wing falls back, normally followed by a quick recovery with no pilot input.

Descent rate: Up to 1000 FPM (5 m/s).

Cause: A sudden and severe forward surge of the wing which can happen from a bad maneuver recovery, pilot action or turbulence, especially a strong downward gust.

Aggressively applying speedbar while at fast trim *and* letting off the throttle can also cause the wing to rocket forward enough to frontal. It is more likely when trimmed fast.

Recovery: Release the speedbar, if engaged, and "tap" the brakes if needed (to about pressure 2). Let it surge forward to get the glider flying before adding more brake which could cause a parachutal stall (also called constant stall). If it does go into parachutal stall, "reduce power, reduce brakes, then steer" and be ready to "tweak" the A's—where you grab each A riser, palms forward and twist them downward to lower the A's a couple inches.

Pendular Control

Wingovers and surges are foundational maneuvers for anyone wanting to move into acro. But they are extremely risky if you get aggressive beyond your skill and should be done first with an advanced instructor on the radio.

Start off gently and without power. Rehearse the reserve deployment sequence in your mind just in case things go awry.

Stay up high and never get so steep that the wing unloads (you feel light in the seat). Also, keep *some* brake pressure on to reduce the likelihood of a front tuck or collapse. Once you've really mastered this level of control it will help you handle turbulence, too. As always, fly by brake pressure, not position. Let the brakes "float" at a given pressure instead of holding them rigidly. Your hands may move a fair amount (lots of brake *travel*) even though the pressure is relatively low.

Wingovers

Wingovers are left and right turns done at the glider's natural pendular rate. Enter a wingover by first applying left turn input (weight shift, if able, then brake to about pressure 2) for one second, then let up. As your body crests and *starts* coming back, apply right turn input and hold for two seconds, then release. The idea is to time each weight shift/brake pull so that the swings get a bit bigger. Just like a swing set, you don't need *much* input, it just has to be at the right *time*. Gliders with longer lines will take longer to go from side to side since they have a longer pendular period.

Recover to level by using the opposite actions. This is a great exercise to grow skill in pendular control but don't let it get too steep which can happen quickly. You'll need a bit of outside brake at the end of each swing and be prepared for the wing to twist you slighty outward, too.

Finesse requires using both brakes at times to prevent the tips from curling up or collapsing. Always keep some brake pressure on throughout to minimize the

Big Wingovers tend to look like figure eights with the ends raised. Your heading changes a lot while continually adjusting the turn using fine inputs. If you get tip collapses, you're not using enough outside brake at the top of each turn, or inside brake to keep the glider square with the direction of flight (being coordinated, not slipping).

Another characteristic of wingovers is a little twist at the steepest bank. The wing turns quicker than you because of your rotational inertia and propeller forces. Heavy motors or carts make this more noticeable.

Wing briefly turns faster than you do here.

By Mathieu Roanet

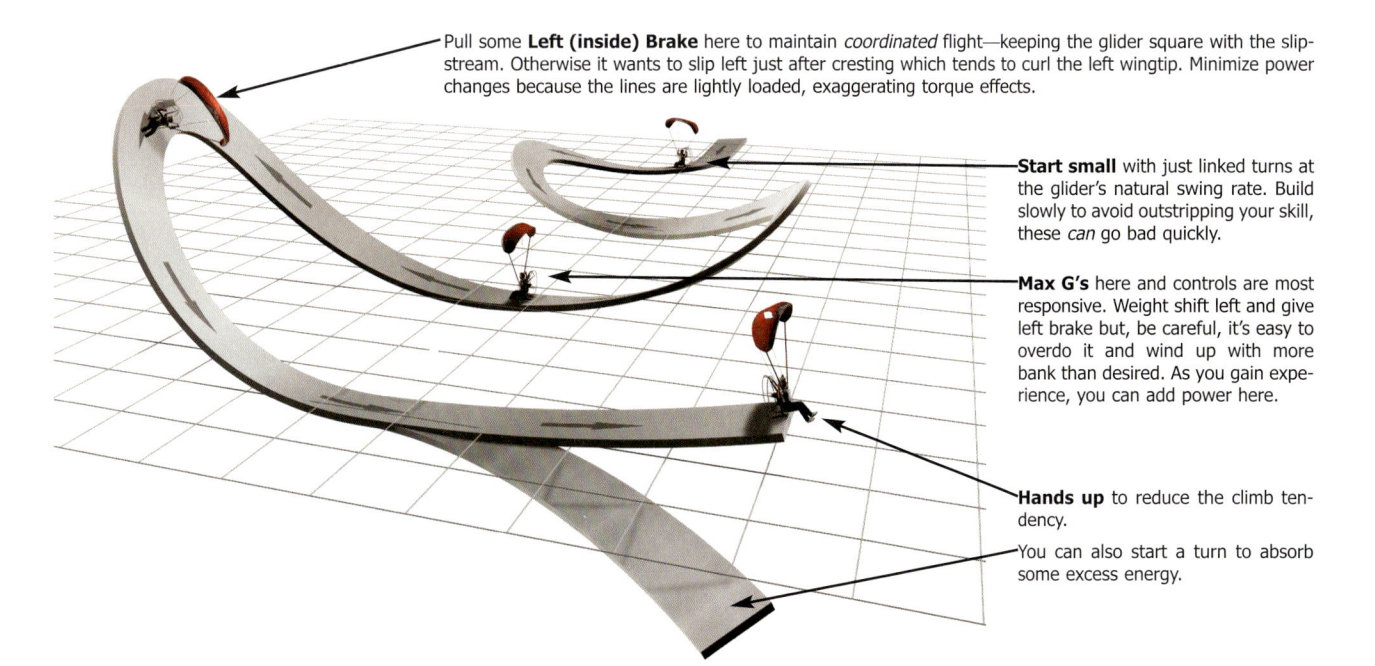

Pull some **Left (inside) Brake** here to maintain *coordinated* flight—keeping the glider square with the slipstream. Otherwise it wants to slip left just after cresting which tends to curl the left wingtip. Minimize power changes because the lines are lightly loaded, exaggerating torque effects.

Start small with just linked turns at the glider's natural swing rate. Build slowly to avoid outstripping your skill, these *can* go bad quickly.

Max G's here and controls are most responsive. Weight shift left and give left brake but, be careful, it's easy to overdo it and wind up with more bank than desired. As you gain experience, you can add power here.

Hands up to reduce the climb tendency.

You can also start a turn to absorb some excess energy.

Tip Line (Stabilo)

chance of getting a collapse, especially on the ends where the wing is less loaded. And don't let the glider get too far ahead of you.

Fore/Aft Pendulums (Surge and Retreats)

Add power or pull brakes to pressure 2 for two seconds then let off. You'll swing out forward as the wing falls back. Then you'll swing back under the wing. When your body starts swinging forward again, gingerly add power or pull brake for a second then let off. Like on a swing set, you'll gradually get steeper and steeper. *Build slowly!* Practice stopping the maneuver quickly. Like the swing, you want to build instinct for how to dampen these pendular actions.

Like any maneuver, as the wing surges farther forward, it gets closer to front tucking, possibly on only one side. To reduce this possibility, be mellow and always keep *some* pressure on the brakes to ensure there is fore/aft tension on the wing fabric.

Also, never get so steep that you feel near weightless in your seat. That puts you perilously close to unloading the lines and taking a major collapse. Also, avoid using both power *and* brakes until you're very experienced.

Tip Line (Stabilo) Line Pull

The stabilo line is the outermost B or C line that goes to the tip and is often a different color. Its importance lies in clearing cravats, discussed earlier.

While kiting, practice finding the stabilo line after inducing a tip collapse—it can be hard to locate with other lines draped around it. Then do the same in flight by pulling an outer A line down slowly (makes one "big ear") and watching what happens with the stabilo line so you'll know where it is when you need to use it.

1. Surge and retreats can be fun and build skill but don't let them get too steep. Practice dampening them quickly. Be careful not to unload the glider which increases vulnerability to collapses.

You can also use power or a combination of power and brakes but build slowly.

2. This moderately steep wingover shows why it's so important to use brake *pressure,* not position. The wing is unloaded and surging forward. Heavy trailing edge deflection shows lots of brake *travel,* a necessity here, but not much *pressure.* Without this input, the wing would likely take a collapse (frontal or asymmetric).

As soon as the wing starts loading up, the brakes will want to come back up. Let them! Keep the brake pressure on and your hands will return to a nearly full-up position. Holding them against an increasing pressure may lead to a stall or spin.

3. A frontal collapse is induced by pulling down both A's. Recovery is normally quick when the A's are released. Most wings come out on their own but some may require a tug (position/pressure 2) on the brakes. On some wings this can result in a front horseshoe where the wing tips come forward.

Risk Management

CHAPTER 19

We're fortunate that most mistakes in paramotoring have already been made. And even more fortunate that we know how to prevent their recurrence.

A lot can be learned from the airlines which have achieved remarkable safety by applying the lessons from accidents to develop better hardware and procedures. Success has turned an inherently dangerous operation (flying jet airplanes at ridiculous speeds) into the safest form of transportation ever devised. This chapter and, in fact, much of the book, aims to do the same for powered paragliding.

The familiar saying, "It's as safe as you make it," is especially true for us since nearly all risk comes from pilot action, not equipment failures or other peoples' actions. Enormous risk can be avoided through behavior changes through an intelligent application of knowledge. It's sad enough when tragedy hits known risk takers, but what a wasteful shame when it blunders in from ignorance.

During a demonstration flight, Russian pilot Igor Potapkin got his wing tip within grabbing distance of organizers. Getting to this point takes skill, experience, risk tolerance, and frequently, numerous crashes.

Unlike other segments of microlight aviation, a catastrophic equipment failure is incredibly rare, far less than even general aviation. Pilot behavior and questionable weather conditions are where most risk comes from.

Probability and Severity

Some behaviors increase the *probability* of an accident and some increase the *severity*. For example, foregoing maintenance on your gear, using really old fuel, or ignoring fuel quantity, all increase the *probability* of a motor failure. Flying beyond reach of a safe landing site increases the *severity* if it does happen. Each probability has a related severity which changes throughout a flight.

Another good example is flying without a helmet. The probability of a mishap is no higher but the severity sure is. Just like seat belts in a car — they don't prevent the accident, they just lessen its horrific consequence.

Some actions increase both probability and severity. Doing foot drags in deep water

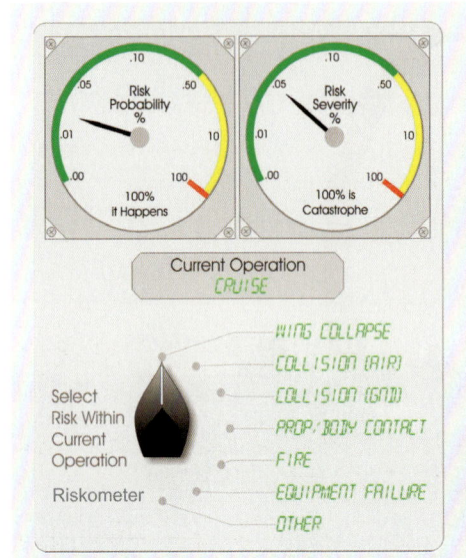

If we had risk gauges they might look like these—one reading for probability and another for severity. They would know the current operation (starting, takeoff, climb, cruise, etc.) and let you select the risk type for that operation then display its severity.

For example, the *probability* of a mishap while cruising along at 2000 feet AGL is miniscule. Select FIRE and the probability gauge would be near zero but with a high severity. Fire is extremely *unlikely* but it would be severe given the longish descent time.

Sitting next to your paramotor, the current operation would read PRE-FLIGHT and both needles would be 0. Starting the motor while standing in front of it moves both probability *and* severity needles way up since starting has proven so risky. Once the motor is running and strapped on your back, both needles go back down to near zero—almost nobody gets hurt at this point.

Doing foot drags is interesting. Of course bad things can happen but the pilot doesn't have very far to fall. So, while the probability of a mishap is quite high (falling), the severity is low provided they're done into the wind. Doing them downwind or over rough surface increases probability slightly but the severity goes way up.

Both needles would frequently move in unison. For example, flying downwind, in the mechanical turbulence of large buildings or mountains increases both the probability and severity of a mishap. Stronger winds give higher readings.

Flying out of a tight field with surrounding corn yields a high probability of hitting the corn, but fairly low severity. But flying out of a tight *tree*-lined field is another matter given the severity of hitting a tree. Flying over water, beyond gliding range of land does not increase the *probability* of an engine failure, but the *severity* skyrockets (drowning) if you don't have floatation.

One common practice is to keep the severity reading low while letting the probability fluctuate. Maneuvers clinics (SIV courses) are this way. You'll induce serious things (like wing collapses) to learn proper reactions but, through careful preparation (rescue boat, pilot floatation, radio instructions, etc.) organizers keep the severity reasonably low. Frontal collapses, spins, asymmetric collapses and so forth are all induced over water, with a boat and safeguards in place to handle the worst.

is a good example—the chance of a motor failure increases due to water spray fouling the ignition and the severity increases due to the likelihood of drowning. Shallow water (less than 6 inches) carries the same increased probability but without the severity.

Energy and Injury

Our sport's overall safety comes mostly from its very low speed. Increasing the speed dramatically increases the injury potential, especially considering how exposed we are. Energy dissipated in a collision increases by the square of the speed, so doubling the speed quadruples the energy (and injury). For example, hitting something at 30 mph carries four times more energy than hitting it at 15 mph. The slow collision will hurt whereas the fast one may be lethal.

Anything that puts you in a high-energy state, especially near hard, immovable objects ramps up the severity of a mishap. That's why flying low and downwind or doing steep, low turns is so treacherous.

Getting Away With It

Why do I need to use a helmet anyway? Personal choice is a valued freedom but *know* what you risk. The same is true of standard aviation safety practices that are eschewed by a few—helmets, patterns, footgear, preflights, reserves, checklists, etc.—are all layers that reduce the likelihood and/or severity of a mishap. Never accept the argument "such and such has never happened to me or anyone I know."

The helmet is a big one. It reduces injury from impacts to the cage or ground and protects against exploding props. How often does it happen? Not often, but it *does* happen and has yielded fatal results. Quality footwear reduces the chance of injury from rough ground or prop strikes. At least one pilot avoided a prop-mangled foot by virtue of his stout boots.

This sport is replete with examples of those who ignored common safety practices and it caught up with them. New people come in, forego collective wisdom or never learn it, succeed for a time and then consider the risk acceptable. Then it gets them. The worst thing we can do is assume that past success will continue in the face of bad practice. Fortunately, accidents are rare, but when they do happen it's usually to those taking chances most often. Do relish the freedom to risk, but wield that freedom carefully.

Where the Risk Is

Here is where the risk is along with ways to minimize it. Always evaluate whether a planned activity is worth the possible consequence. What is the likelihood? How bad would it hurt and is the reward worth it?

The top fatality risks are: 1) going into water and drowning, 2) steep maneuvering low to the ground, especially spiral dives and extreme wingovers, 3) the learning process, including training, 4) weather-related collapses. Notice that the top 3 risks involve flying perfectly good gear into something other than a landing zone.

Starting and Handling the Motor

It's the most dangerous part of our sport—starting and handling the motor. Serious and permanent injuries have disfigured those who lost sight of this fact.

It happens, even to conscientious pilots who, in a brief moment of inattentiveness, let the motor get away from them. Then whack! The U.S. Powered Paragliding Association (see the www.USPPA.org Incident Database) labels these "Body contact with spinning propeller" and they are rarely forgiving.

> *Always* inspect the throttle linkage before starting. *Do it every time*, insuring that the carburetor is at idle and throttle can't be increased accidentally.

Training

Inadequate training contributes enormous risk; unfortunately, they won't even know it. To have read these words and still skimp on instruction is to dramatically *and knowingly* increase both probability and severity of risk.

Even *with* training, the early stages are risky. Improve your odds by going tandem; you'll get an important feel for flying *before* soloing. Also, make sure the school uses a very benign handling beginner wing to start and has you practice emergencies in

1. Good training with appropriate training aids, such as this riser-equipped simulator, helps prepare for both normal flight and in-flight emergencies. In the hands of an good instructor, it's invaluable.

2. Just because you've succeeded at a risky endeavor before doesn't make it safe. For example, you may fly low over wires all the time. But if a problem, such as misjudgment or motor failure does happen, it will have potentially dire consequences.

Nobody launches expecting to crash. Analyze the operation: is it late? Is there questionable weather? Has someone suggested not flying? Am I going to fly low? Am I wearing appropriate safety gear?

Testing New Gear

Trying or testing new equipment is risky; here are some ways to make it less so. Before flying, review the gear while hanging from a simulator with the owner or instructor present.

1. Note the attachment points. Low hook-ins will have a lower average brake position than higher hook-ins, possibly by a lot.

2. Find out where the harness adjustments are and how they should be set for takeoff, cruise and landing. Having this wrong could render an otherwise fine machine, unsafe.

3. Operate the throttle, starter, and kill switch, especially if the throttle is in a different hand than you're used to. Locate the master switch and think of other ways to shut off the motor.

4. Prepare for the torque effect which may differ in both amount and direction. Belt driven machines twist left, causing a right bank, which is opposite of gear driven machines.

5. Find out about any special instructions for getting into the seat. On some low attachment machines, brake toggles can get in the prop if released, especially while you're still hanging in the harness.

6. Find out what the wing's trimmer settings are for cruising, turbulence, launch and landing. Learn what special handling or procedures apply to the wing, especially if you plan to use the speed system.

This is the single most likely time to be seriously injured with a paramotor. Make sure the throttle is at idle and it can't be accidentally squeezed.

What Is The Risk?

Foot or cart launching a PPG is about the same risk as moderately aggressive skiing. You may get a twisted ankle or similar type of injury during your flying career but it won't likely be fatal. The safety appears close to motorcycle riding based on the number of participants in both activities and the number of fatalities which, for paramotoring, is quite small even for the low number of participants.

Unlike motorcycles, we control more of our own risk. Good choices can eliminate much of our risk whereas motorcyclists depend on the choices of less-than-attentive car drivers.

a riser-equipped simulator.

Tow (if used) is also risky but can be made much safer with a good instructor who uses appropriate precautions. Overall, instruction risk is reduced with the use of a thorough, standardized syllabus, simulator work, a methodical approach, and appropriate location. Simulator rehearsal of emergency procedures helps you be prepared.

Intermediate Syndrome

Guard against Intermediate Syndrome, a common haunt of moderately experienced pilots. As skills improve they start taking on challenges that are beyond their ability. Losing hurts.

Excelling at anything *will* put your skills to the test, but choose situations where the results of failure are tolerable. For example, take on higher winds to improve your skills, but choose places where getting dragged won't hurt.

Inappropriate Gear

Inappropriate gear or improper technique for that gear adds risk. Most equipment trade-offs are covered in Section VI but here are some common risks related to having inappropriate equipment.

- Excessive power for your weight increases the risk of riser twist and, to a lesser degree, makes falling more likely due to weight and torque. It can also increase the chance for a "face-plant."

- Insufficient power increases your risk of tripping during the extended run and will not allow a quick climb over surprise obstructions. Plus, the slow climb adds vulnerability to even small downdrafts after takeoff.

- Flying an advanced wing without a mastery of active piloting increases risk, especially if flown in conditions other than calm.

- Unduly small wing area increases speed which makes any accident worse. It also lengthens the takeoff run. Sportier handling can lead to a loss of control.

- Unduly large wing area increases the chance for parachutal stall, collapse and, being slower, may not allow penetration into a strong wind.

- Poor design (structurally weak, dangerous attributes, etc.) is always inappropriate. Seek out models that embrace safety features over those using older, less-safe technology. It's always a trade off—sometimes safety features get traded for other attributes. Talking to respected, experienced pilots who are familiar with various models. See "A Better Paramotor" on www.Footflyer.com.

Steep Maneuvering & Aerobatics

Steep maneuvers at low altitude, especially those with a vertical component, produce the sport's greatest lethality. While a prop strike is the most common serious injury, this is among the most deadly. Of the few fatalities in paramotoring, this single category represents over a quarter of them, up there with landing in water.

It's happens easily—after gaining some experience pilots get "braver," trying maneuvers beyond their skill and without instruction. Little banks graduate to steeper banks that become spiral dives. Little pendulums morph into wingovers, etc. Given the need for our soft wing to always be loaded, these maneuvers can get ugly quickly. Plus, when the wing is heavily loaded (as in a steep turn), the controls become extremely sensitive—surprised pilots wind up with large excursions following small inputs. Steep maneuvering also adds enormous speed, too.

Allowing yourself to become weightless, or nearly so, is *really* asking for it—consider what happens when lines have no pressure with which to hold the glider into its gliderly shape. Worse yet, those loose lines can now find things to wrap around (including pilot parts) only to reload with a bang.

If done without instruction or low to the ground, aerobatics are a terrible risk. Doing this stuff close to the ground has been the final ingredient in a dangerous cocktail of risk for pilots who pushed it too far.

Low Flying

You can't hit something if you're above it. Almost all the airborne injuries happen while cruising or maneuvering down low. Not only is mechanical turbulence more likely at low altitude, but there is less time to recover. Climbing to at least 200 feet eliminates most risk.

Simple misjudgment in turns are aggravated by low flying. The distraction of nearby ground objects contributes to this, especially with any downwind component.

Wire strikes, even at slow speeds, are a big risk. Most injury comes from the ensuing fall although electrocution is certainly possible. In most cases, the area was familiar to the pilot, but he either forgot about, or just didn't see, the lines—they can be essentially invisible.

Don't think wires will be stand out like they do from the ground. From below they are set against a plain sky, having contrast and uniqueness. But seen from above, they can blend completely into the background.

If you can't resist the allure of low, here are a few tips to mitigate *some* of the risk:

- Avoid flying *downwind* while low. With higher ground speed, any miscalculation, unexpected obstruction, or motor failure will be far worse. The speed difference between a collision going downwind and one going into the wind is dramatic. Plus, higher ground speed leaves less time to notice and react to obstructions.

- Fly into an area above 200 feet AGL and scout for obstructions before descending into the danger zone. Look for poles or their shadows and be suspicious of any straight lines (road edges, field edges, etc.).

- As always, stay over landable terrain. This is even more important when flying down low because you won't have time to maneuver after a power failure.

- Respect power lines and other obstructions. Don't ever plan a climb over something if a power loss would leave you without options.

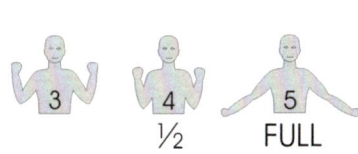

For convenience, the brake positions (pressures) are included here. Remember, positions are just a reference to calm air use—always use the equivalent pressure. If the brake line wants to pull back, let it do so while holding the same pressure.

There's almost never any reason to go beyond position/pressure 4 except for landing.

In any situation that you do not know what is happening, reduce brake input first then steer carefully.

Think of position 0 and 1 as the "Green zone," Position 2 and 3 as the "Yellow caution zone," and position 4 or more as the "Red danger Zone."

Always approach wires at an angle so that you can quickly veer away if necessary. Fly over the poles since the wires are difficult to judge height over. Fly straight across only when clearly more than twice the pole height.

Downwind Operations, The "Demon"

To the paraglider itself, flying downwind is no different than flying upwind. The same for turning from upwind to downwind—it's no different. But talk to enough pilots and you'll eventually hear of the dreaded "downwind demon," a myth incorrectly suggesting that, when turning downwind, the air "hits the back of the wing, causing it to sink." It simply isn't so. Like a boat in a wide river, our craft operates in a fluid-like environment (the air) that is moving along over the ground. The best evidence is to go up high and do your turn. You'll see there is no difference whatsoever; in fact, it's hard to even know what the wind is doing up high. Look at the wake of a boat doing a nice, round 360° turn in the middle of a river—the whole circle is moving downstream but no part of the turn feels different to the boat driver.

There are, however, some powerful *illusions*, and one real effect, that happen when turning from upwind to downwind—and they can easily fool us into pulling too much brake. They are the real "downwind demons" and only happen down low.

Much of this stems from the fact that pulling brakes makes you go up in a fleeting sacrifice of speed for altitude, training the subconscious mind, incorrectly, that you "pull brakes to climb."

The Climb Illusion: You take off into a 10 mph headwind, flying 20 mph and climb at 200 fpm. The groundspeed is only 10 mph so that climb looks impressively steep. Now you turn downwind. The *angle* decreases a lot even though the *rate* of climb remains unchanged. Earth is zinging by at 30 mph while you continue climbing at 200 fpm. The subconscious inclination is to pull more brake so that the climb looks the same as before, relative to the ground below.

Wind Gradient: This effect is no illusion. If you climb into an increasing headwind (wind gradient), the wing "sees" a bigger headwind and really does climb better as it seeks to get back to its trim airspeed. Your groundspeed is slowing down in the process. The reverse is true during a downwind climb in that gradient. You'll encounter an increasing tailwind that reduces climb as the wing *accelerates* to maintain airspeed. The stronger the gradient, the stronger the effect and it is usually most dramatic down low. Climbing upwind for the first 200 feet usually gets you above the gradient.

The Turn Illusion is usually a mild effect that, like most, can become psychologically overpowering in moderately strong winds and lower altitudes.

Rate of turn depends only on bank angle and *air*speed. If it takes you 2 minutes to turn all the way around when it's calm, it will take you 2 minutes to go all the way around in a strong wind. And the rate of turn is exactly the same whether going upwind or downwind. However, if you're looking at the *ground* track, the upwind portion describes a tight arc while the downwind portion has a shallow arc. If you're low, that shallow arc can *feel* like you're hardly turning.

A pilot in the throes of this illusion will subconsciously add more inside brake to steepen the turn so it looks the same as a

---

Tip:

Remember, our wing flies in reference to the air, not the ground. All "downwind demon" illusions happen when pilots look at the ground while maneuvering down low. It causes them to pull too much brake in certain situations. Use minimum brake and practice ignoring the illusions.

You can avoid *all* the "downwind demon" risk by climbing up to 200 feet, into the wind, before turning.

The Climb Illusion. Into the wind, your climb *angle* looks great since the ground speed is low. Turn downwind and, even though the climb *rate* is the same, the shallow angle can fool you into pulling more brake.

The Turn Illusion: When turning from upwind to downwind the turn rate is the same all the way around (number of degrees per second). But the ground speed picks up and the ground track shallows as you get pointed downwind. The inexperienced may succumb to the illusion and pull more brakes, potentially causing a stall.

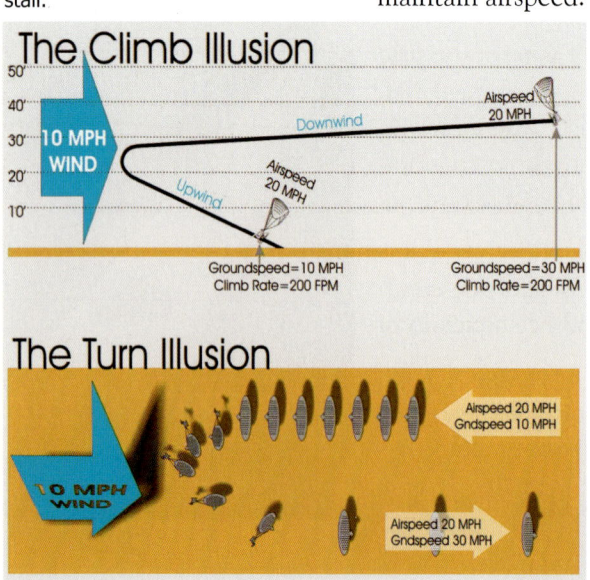

no-wind or upwind turn. Bank angle can steepen dangerously before the pilot realizes it. Once banked up, the pilot dives into the ground, usually at high speed because it happens during the downwind portion.

You can avoid all these effects by climbing *into* the wind to 200 feet before turning.

Distractions

Taking pictures, flying formation, and listening to or fiddling with music are among the many distractions that increase risk. They divert attention from the primary task of maintaining a safe flight path. Additionally, items can easily slip from your grasp and head for the prop.

Stuff hung around your neck holds the potential to slide back and catch on a moving motor part—not necessarily the propeller. Its strap could get pulled into the motor, bringing whatever it is connected to along. One pilot almost got decapitated when his camera strap went into the pull-start mechanism. Fortunately, the strap broke before his neck did.

Cinch neck straps so they cannot slide backwards into the motor area.

Formation

Flying near others adds a serious risk of collision or wing collapse due to wake turbulence. There are many nuances to formation flying (see Chapter 16) that should be learned gradually and first learned with large margins.

Before flying close formation, both pilots should be skilled with active flying and understand the severity of any mishap. What carnage remains after two wings get tangled up may not even allow tossing a reserve.

Watch This!

An interesting observation is that nearly half of all serious flying accidents have occurred with spectators watching or cameras rolling. Resist the urge to push it under such conditions, it's very tempting. The term "Kodak Courage" is an apt epitaph for many pilots whose demise goes before a crowd and its cameras.

Note that professional airshow pilots practice their routines over and over again at high altitudes in order to perfect them. They also frequently practice them in the same locale where the airshow will take place. Then when they perform they do the exact same thing without exceeding their usual limits. "Show-Offs," however, tend to *exceed* their limits in front of eyes or lenses.

If you find yourself doing something steeper, lower, or wilder when folks are watching, consciously mellow out.

Mid-air collisions are rare but disastrous. Formation flight must be done with extreme care. Collisions happen quickly and with surprisingly few people in the air at once. In fact, having just a few people aloft can foster a deadly complacency. Keep an eye out.

When flying with others, use the admonition to "look, shallow, up, down, turn". That is **Look** in the planned direction, start a **shallow** bank, look **up** and **down** then begin your **turn**. Another variant is "Look, Lean, Up/Down, Turn" for those who use weight shift to initiate a bank.

Planned formations, such as the one shown above, should only be done by experienced pilots with a plan and good communications to minimize risk.

Camera Encounter

At a major PPG event, an experienced pilot was doing close flybys while a cameraman filmed. The experienced cameraman left it up to the experienced pilot to avoid contact. But the pilot wasn't so experienced with the higher elevation and slightly misjudged his pull-up. He wound up hitting the camera, leaving its operator with a walloping black eye. The cameraman was lucky.

Cameras and flying continue to prove their dysfunctional relationship—be extra vigilant when the two are together.

You don't expect new equipment to have problems but look out—brand new gear still deserves a close inspection. The above quick link on the right was discovered *after* the pilot landed from a high G flight. It was the glider's first time out of its bag.

Quick links should look like the left one. This wing arrived from the factory like that—all the screw gates were open, cutting their strength by more than half.

Terrain

Flying from flat land, with its more benign weather patterns and forgiving sites, adds safety. We give up a lot of that safety in mountainous terrain or by flying from confined sites. Other risky terrain features include water and congestion.

Flying mountainous regions also increases opportunity for weather related jams. Local knowledge is a good way to avoid surprises here.

Equipment Condition

Wings get porous, lines break, motors wear out, harnesses weaken, carabiners get scratched and other critical flight components degrade with time and use. These must be maintained properly and inspected regularly, especially the wing.

Carabiners are possibly the sport's only single-point where a failure would be catastrophic. Steel carabiners are stronger, but regardless of the material, make sure they have no scratches and the gates close properly.

The wing should command most of our attention as its degradation is most likely to cause problems. Having porous fabric or shortened or stretched lines dramatically increases the possibility of parachutal stall. Add some other factor, such as being too light for your wing or flying in turbulence, and a stall may be inevitable.

Don't neglect the motor—some failure modes involve the prop coming off and slicing into the tank. An engine failure, while relatively benign, can put you somewhere undesirable depending on where it happens.

Disintegrating props can send shards flying in all directions. Most of the time this mishap occurs when some piece of the machine vibrates loose and goes through the prop. Anything that can work loose should have lock nuts, safety wire, or other means to prevent ejection. Improperly repaired propellers, especially composites, are more susceptible to failure even with no prop strike.

Weather

A large accident category is weather related—pilots ignore weather warnings and fly anyway. One deception is that you can frequently get away with it—a success that leads to falsely thinking that the risk is small.

For example, and this is one of many, most thunderstorms don't actually cause problems until they're fairly close, but *occasionally* they cause horrendous winds from some distance—a gust front—and there's no warning.

Competition

This pursuit involves maneuvering low to the ground, sometimes at high speed, at the limits of pilot control and with distracting goals—obviously a riskier combination than regular flying.

A lot of risk, however, is mitigated by keeping pilots from getting high enough to develop dangerous *vertical* speed. They may fly low and fast but are rarely pointed at the ground. That's probably why competition has enjoyed a good safety record both in the U.S. and even Europe, where it's done a lot.

The way to minimize competition's higher risk is to be ever mindful of the fact that an injury will, at best, end an event with a low score. Fly within your ability and improve gradually instead of trying to do it all at once. A middling performer who

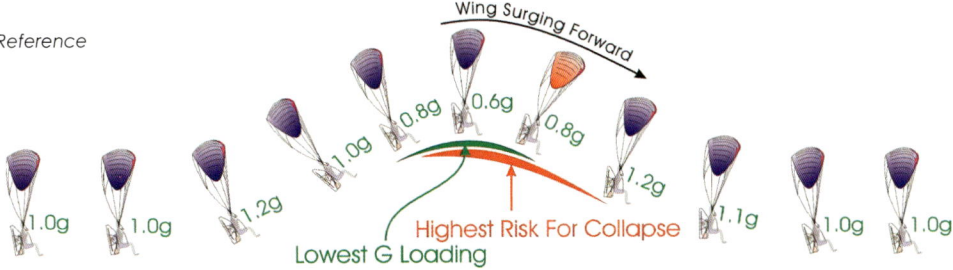

Wing Surging Forward
1.0g 1.0g 1.2g 1.0g 0.8g 0.6g 0.8g 1.2g 1.1g 1.0g 1.0g
Highest Risk For Collapse
Lowest G Loading

safely completes all the tasks will beat the aggressive pilot who crashes in pursuit of perfection.

Unloading The Wing

Minimize low G conditions—where you unload the wing, even partially. That is where you feel lighter in your seat like at the top of a roller coaster. You're dramatically more vulnerable to wing collapse from even small downward gusts, especially if the wing is allowed to surge past the overhead point.

Turbulence or pilot action that rocks you back and causes a momentary climb can cause it. Improper recovery from a steep turn is another common culprit, especially if you fly through your own wake made stronger by a steep turn.

Adding Safety Equipment

Our choice of safety equipment depends on flying style and locale. If you fly over forests, a tree extraction kit is essential. If you fly over water then "Spare Air" (see Chapter 28) and floatation would be prudent. Certain items will help regardless of locale and style—a cell phone and hook knife are good examples.

Some safety gear reduces the odds of a mishap while some reduces the severity of it. Some, like tree rescue kits and floatation, help in the aftermath. Reserve parachutes are severity reducers. They won't decrease the probability of a malfunction but sure may improve the results. Flying in rowdy air makes a reserve that much more beneficial. Of course, it must be installed properly and its use rehearsed. There is some slight risk of accidental deployment.

Gloves are important for operating in windy conditions since ground handling the glider is where you're most likely to get line burns.

Boots can prevent ankle injuries and other foot-related maladies. Rough or rocky surfaces makes them even more valuable.

The helmet is probably the single most important safety element because, although unlikely, head injuries are so dire. They are essential for ground handling in strong conditions, too.

Combining Risks

Combining risks can increase the chance of a mishap exponentially—way more then just adding them together. A perfect example is doing steep maneuvers down low. Both the *odds* of calamity and *severity of its outcome* skyrocket. The chances are far higher than just adding the two risks together.

Another example is doing just about anything in rowdy air. It increases the overall probability of an accident, especially during takeoff or landing.

By knowing what operations carry what risk, you can carefully pick and choose only those operations rewarding enough to justify that risk. Knowing the risk will also help direct extra attention to where it is needed most.

If you get into the situation above, apply brake pressure at the beginning of the green band. Apply some power, too, just as the wing starts coming forward. This will both reduce unloading the wing and preventing it from getting ahead of you.

Some safety equipment will only help after the fact. See chapter 28 for tree self-rescue kits.

Gusted

After a week of unflyable, lousy weather I was anxious to get airborne. The receding rumble of thunderstorms had quieted and outside was a quiet calm.

Hmmm...

A mellow sky beckoned. It was strangely calm but I gathered my gear and headed out. A half-mile away, past my nicely open field, I could see to the horizon and noted darkness in the distance.

Hmmm...

I waited 5 minutes. Sure enough, through the silence of that calm it was clear—a muted rumble. More storms lurked. Thinking this wasn't such a good Idea, I packed up and headed home. It wouldn't be fun anyway, knowing that this thing was bearing down on me.

Shortly after settling back at home into my project du jour, I heard it. Even before thunder signaled the storm's arrival was the unmistakable howl of a strong wind. The gust front had arrived. Within minutes, a destructive wind blew that would have been horrendous to anyone flying anything, let alone with a 15 pound wing. I was thankful to be inside.

Handling Situational Emergencies

Dangerous situations may confront you while leaving time to make choices. These cannot be rehearsed in a simulator but rather require a cool, thinking head. Most are incredibly unlikely, especially during early training where the instructor keeps closer tabs on you. All of these can be avoided, but we're all human.

Each situation will normally have several options, not all will be included here. They should be considered with your particular skills and situation. What may be appropriate with one pilot in one situation may be a disaster for another. Weigh your choices and pick the least objectionable.

Be wary of absolutes and analyze your options before acting. Sometimes the first action that pops in your head isn't the best one. Having thought about options in advance (like reading this) can be helpful, but anything that requires a quick response must be rehearsed. The airlines have learned that reactionary physical skills, if not rehearsed, will likely be done wrong when they are really needed.

Landing In Water (Ditching)

To make the best of this very bad situation, undo your leg, chest and sternum straps. Time permitting, dispose of anything hanging around your neck (camera, radio, etc.), remove your shoes, if possible, and prepare to jump out of the seat but not yet. Grab and extract your hook knife or at least practice reaching for it.

Approach with about brake 1 or 2 and don't flare unless you're absolutely certain of your height above the water—that can be deceptively difficult. In calm conditions, plan for the wing to overfly you, going hands up at touchdown. The wing should land on its leading edge, trapping air in the cells. In a wind over about 5 mph, land into it, going to full brakes at touchdown so the wing falls backwards and lines drape behind you.

Take a full breath of air just before impact. As soon as your feet touch the water, exit and swim away from the gear. The motor, especially carts, may sink quickly. Also, carts may flip forward, leaving you upside down. Do *not* try to estimate height and jump early—at least one pilot died from such mis-judgment. Once clear, do not swim back to your gear lest it entangle you, especially in moving water. The wing will probably float but the motor will sink once its cavities fill. The wing may hold the motor up for some time.

If you start getting entangled in lines, *immediately* start cutting them with your hook knife as much as necessary to swim away.

If you end up on land but your wing goes into ocean surf or a stream, *immediately* unclip as you walk toward it to prevent the wing from pulling you in. If it does start pulling, it will be nigh impossible to unclip; your only option may be to start cutting with the hook knife. Pilots have landed on dry ground and then drowned

Options Trading

If water is your only power-off landing option, the outcome is far from guaranteed. Pilots have drowned even after doing all the right things. These suggestions merely improve your odds.

Floatation

If you must tempt wet fate, an auto-inflating device, such as the Agama (2), may save your life. It mounts to the paramotor and inflates upon immersion. That keeps the paramotor from sinking but you'll need floatation, too. Consider a ski-type life vest like the pilot pictured in (1). That will provide floatation after leaving the paramotor. See also Chapter 28.

At least one pilot, a strong swimmer, drowned after landing in a pond. He successfully got away from the motor but became exhausted while swimming with clothing on.

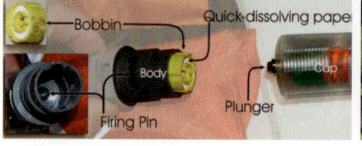

when their wing fell into moving water. It seems so benign, but quickly becomes overpowering due to the waters incredible pull on the wing.

If landing in very shallow water (less than 3 feet) you will obviously not want to jump out. Unclip as described above but consider landing seated, with one or both legs forward, especially if there is no wind (high groundspeed). This will prevent you from "face planting" since it is impossible to run out a landing in even a foot of water.

Gust Front and Landing Backwards

Gust fronts occur on many scales, the worst being thunderstorms. Cold air plummets earthward, spreading rapidly at the surface in a deadly cauldron of turbulence. Gust fronts may be preceded by virga, a wall of dust, or debris, but not always. Your first indication may be nasty bumps or negative groundspeed—you are flying into the wind but moving backwards over the ground.

If you get caught in such a front, expect the ride to be wild with occasional wing collapses and extreme oscillations. Follow the turbulence penetration guidance in Chapter 4. Here are some things to consider regarding gust fronts:

- If you can land before it hits, do so, but only if you *know* it won't catch up with you during landing.

- If you don't think you can land before it reaches you, make a downwind dash to get as far from the source as possible. Even if you can't outrun it, getting farther away may let the front expend itself into a weaker state. Consider going crosswind if that will keep you out of an advancing storm.

After the gust front passes and you are already in it, consider these options:

- If you are over a lake consider landing on the opposite shore before exhausting your fuel.

- If you suspect the wind will worsen, power off and land immediately. Accept a backward landing even if it means that you may get dragged. Aim for an area offering the most forgiving blowback zone and least mechanical turbulence (which will be wicked).

- Some gust fronts are short lived. If you can safely control the wing and expect the wind to subside quickly (i.e. it's not associated with major weather such as an approaching thunderstorm) you may be better off waiting it out. The same is true if landing options are unsatisfactory—consider riding it out.

- Typically, there is a gradient where winds diminish close to the ground. Going lower may allow upwind penetration but, be careful, it will also be more turbulent, possibly too much. Don't ever put yourself behind an obstruction that could cause severe rotor. Also consider that gust fronts can be limited, low-level affairs and climbing may help.

If you become committed to a high wind landing while drifting backward:

- Be thankful you thought to wear gloves!

- If it's smooth enough that you can momentarily let go of a brake or maybe hold both brakes in one hand, unclip from all but one leg strap to enable a rapid exit after landing. That will help if you are getting dragged and choose to try exit-

To ease your exodus from a machine with old style buckles (normally done like 1), fasten them as shown in picture 2. Simply pulling on the end will release it immediately.

ing the harness. Mentally rehearse going for that remaining buckle.

- Locate your hook knife and be prepared to use it.
- While still airborne, find the C risers and prepare to pull them hard at touchdown. Even if you fall, keep pulling until you are able to get up and run around the wing. Unclip as soon as you're able.
- Kill the wing using one of the methods in Chapter 3. If you are getting dragged and cannot do so, use the hook knife to cut through the A risers or lines.

Consider finding a site where getting dragged back will be less injurious. Landing in front of a solid tree line, for example, will stop the wing when you get dragged to the trees. Be leery of small ridge-shaped obstructions, though, as the wing can pull you right up over the top.

Motor Stuck at Full or Partial Power

The most likely cause of this situation is having the throttle cable, and enclosed kill wire, go into the prop. There are several options available that depend on your situation. If conditions permit, you may be able to simply run it out of gas. Pulling big ears (with speedbar, if you've got it) or doing spirals will help prevent a climb. *Don't* do B-Line stalls since the recovery may not be possible with the motor at power. See Chapter 18 for information on these maneuvers.

If you decide to reach back and kill the motor, understand the extreme risk. On most units, you *can* get your hand into the prop. Hopefully you've rehearsed this in a simulator. Use the method requiring the least amount of reach. For example, if the air vent is right by your head, then plugging it is safer than reaching farther back for the spark plug.

After making sure you're over landable terrain, here are some ways to shut off the motor. Pick the easiest, most accessible one:

- If you have an alternate kill switch, relish your forethought and use it.
- If there's enough of the throttle left, try to work it down to idle.
- If you have a remote choke, pull it.
- If you can reach the fuel line, pinch it hard until it quits. This will take up to 20 seconds.
- If you can reach the air intake easily, cover it—it takes about 5 seconds for the motor to quit.
- If you have a primer bulb (or knob), squeeze it to flood out the motor.
- If you can yank the plug wire out or pry the spark plug cap off without touching it (you'll get shocked) then do so.
- If you can plug the fuel vent, do so. It may take several minutes until a vacuum forms from the fuel getting sucked out. With enough vacuum, the motor will die from a lean mixture. There's a chance this could seize the motor.
- If you cannot kill the motor safely, you'll have to run it out of gas.

1. After landing in a strong and increasing wind, the pilot got lifted, dragged, and turtled but got it under control with the help of some fellow pilots.

2. This throttle got damaged by the prop. The most common cause of a stuck throttle is either debris in the cable or damage when the cable gets hit by the prop. That usually happens when reaching down to get into the seat using your throttle-holding hand.

Landing in a Tree

Trees only look soft from above. If there is no better option and you're going to wind up in a tree, go for its middle near the top and, as always, land into the wind. Grazing the branches may simply collapse the wing, sending you free-falling to the ground. Do a normal flare and keep your feet together, knees bent, and in front. Once motion stops, your ride may not be over. Grab a stout branch and hang on.

Getting Out of a Tree

If you fly where tree landing are a possibility then carry a tree rescue kit. It includes a roll of dental floss (or similar strong, light line) and a fishing weight. The weighted line is lowered down to a rescuer so that a strong rope can be pulled up.

Most injuries come from falling out of the tree after landing so remain in your harness while waiting for help. The wing may be the only thing preventing you from falling. If help is not likely or your status is precarious, try using the wing's lines to secure your harness to a solid part of the tree. Do that before trying to climb down.

If help comes with an adequate rope, lower a line to the rescuer. Pull the rope up and loop it over a strong branch. Secure the rope around your waist and have the rescuer wrap the rope around a strong, low branch for friction so he can lower you gently to the ground. If you're 50 feet up, you'll need probably 110 feet of rope.

If you have no rescue kit and time is critical (impending cold, weather, darkness, etc), consider using your reserve or glider lines to help lower yourself.

Getting Out of Power Lines

Paraglider lines can conduct current from even low voltage power lines. Power lines on poles are not insulated and carry a minimum of 4000 Volts. High tension lines have over 100,000 Volts. Do not allow yourself or rescuers to touch any part of the gear *and* the ground—they have been electrocuted just by getting close to a hung-up glider. Wait until the power company is alerted and the power removed. They will also have equipment that can reach up to allow for easy retrieval.

If you're low enough, jumping is an option but it's easy to misjudge height and get hurt. Awaiting rescue is still the best bet.

Cloud Suck

Taller cumulus clouds (over 500 ft thick) can have powerful lift just below the bases. This *cloud suck* can be dramatic in bigger clouds, with violent updrafts and downdrafts exceeding 3000 feet per minute (fpm). Pilots have died from hypothermia and/or hypoxia after being sucked into the upper atmosphere by these behemoths.

If you start getting lifted, act quickly, using one of the descent techniques in Chapter 18. Realize that *big ears*, while benign, will not likely be enough.

A quick spiral may work if done right away but do *not* use it after being enveloped in cloud—you risk vertigo or blacking out from G forces. That would be a spiral to a splat. The B-line stall is reasonably effective, and is stable, but can have exit problems. The full stall, which plummets nicely, is even more risky in recovery unless you've done them enough to be comfortable. One thing, do *not* toss your reserve since that would eliminate all control of descent rate.

1. Obviously, staying out of the wires is best. But if this happens, don't let yourself or anyone else touch the ground and gear simultaneously until you know the power is off. High voltage has a way of finding ground and both humans and lines work just fine if given the chance.

Chapter 14, page 142 addresses power lines for rescuers.

Cone of Range

With no wind, your glide options are the same in all directions. With wind, you have more options downwind than upwind.

The bottom frame illustrates a wind that's blowing as fast as you're flying. Groundspeed is 0 if you're pointed directly into this wind meaning that *all* your options are downwind.

STRETCHING GLIDE

Extended Glide

If forced to a field far away, make your ground track straight for it using every means available to extend glide. Pick a spot where you can arrive with some altitude to spare. That cushions against un-planned headwind or sink while giving room to inspect and fine tune the landing location.

When it's obvious you've made it, plan at least an abbreviated pattern with base leg and final. That will improve your odds of nailing the spot. Never turn completely away from the target unless you're *real* high—rather make all turns *toward* the spot.

Motor Failure and Out Landing

The specifics of spot landings are covered in Chapter 17, but when the motor quits away from your field, there are some other considerations.

If the motor is just running poorly, try to find a throttle range that improves power ("milking the throttle"). You may be able to hobble back or at least reach a more favorable landing site.

An unusual vibration usually means that something bad is about to get worse—landing is highly recommended. Pressing on may result in motor separation or prop shards shooting through the wing.

Once an out-landing is inevitable, here are some priorities. Remember that there is no hard and fast rule—choose the best option for the situation.

- You'll glide farther headed downwind but make sure you're pointed back into the wind by touchdown.

- **Land into clean wind!** All things being equal, it's almost hard to get hurt if you follow this rule. Land crosswind or downwind only if it's much better. For example, if the upwind option puts you in water or power lines and the downwind or crosswind option is smooth grass, choose the grass. Even then, try to get turned into the wind as much as possible while making sure to be level by touchdown.

- Choose a rotor-free location with no upslope. Avoid landing in a wind shadow or rotor.

- When presented with multiple safe, landing options, consider retrieval difficulty or whether you can re-launch.

- Scout for wires on the way down. Any straight-line features or poles should raise suspicions that wires may be present. Plan your approach accordingly.

- Look for animals. A single cow in a field may be a bull.

- Consider where the wing will go if landing near water. Don't let it get into any moving water, including surf. If a water landing is inevitable, prepare for it.

Here are ways to **stretch** your **glide** depending on the situation. If trying to *penetrate* (reach a spot that is upwind), fly faster. More headwind means more speed. Anything over about a 12 mph headwind will call for maximum speed on most gliders, but only do that if it's fairly smooth or your glider is stable flying fast.

With a tailwind, slow to minimum sink speed for best glide. That's trimmers slow and brake pressure 1 or 2 on most gliders.

Regardless of wind, maximize glide by minimizing drag. Lift your legs and bring your arms in to present the smallest frontal area possible. Do turns using weight shift instead of brakes, if possible.

Fogged In

Besides being illegal, it's extremely dangerous to fly without ground reference. Even though the craft is stable, fog conceals wires or other surprises. So if you see fog forming or rolling in, *land while there is still enough visibility*, even if away from your launch site. Failing that, climb up above it, but do *not* put yourself in busy airspace. A PPG should be landed in the fog before risking heavy airplane traffic. If you can fly to a fog-free location, do so.

Here are considerations if you're faced with a landing in the fog:

- Note or recall the wind direction; you may need that later.
- Having a GPS in this situation is obviously helpful. Hopefully you've stored the launch site as a waypoint. If not, mark your current location and stay nearby. On many units you may be able to follow a plotted ground track back to your site.
- Consider circling above and waiting if you think the fog may move through or burn off. Use this option only if you're certain that wind drift won't take you somewhere undesirable.

If you must land in the fog, use whatever means are available (compass, GPS, sunlight) to stay pointed into the wind. Leaving the motor run is probably best since it reduces the descent rate and allows going around if something unpleasant emerges. There is, however, some benefit to having the prop stopped in case you hit something while blundering through the muck.

On final descent, go to quarter brake (pressure 2) and be ready for impact. Keep your feet angled down and forward, knees together, bent, and ready to absorb the energy of a collision or to run. Even in thick fog you should have enough visibility to flare—but beware of illusions that could spur a reactionary and inappropriate pull on the brakes.

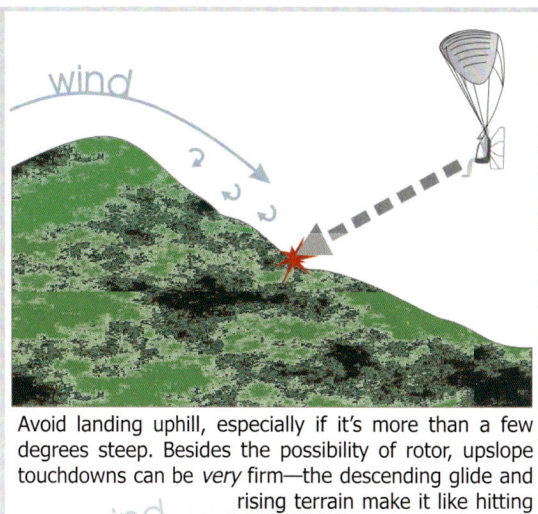

Avoid landing uphill, especially if it's more than a few degrees steep. Besides the possibility of rotor, upslope touchdowns can be *very* firm—the descending glide and rising terrain make it like hitting a wall with your feet.

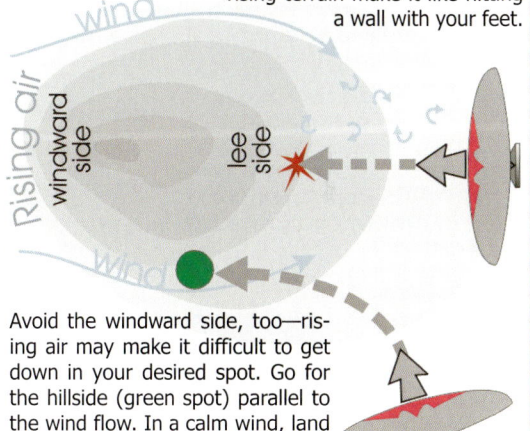

Avoid the windward side, too—rising air may make it difficult to get down in your desired spot. Go for the hillside (green spot) parallel to the wind flow. In a calm wind, land parallel to the slope.

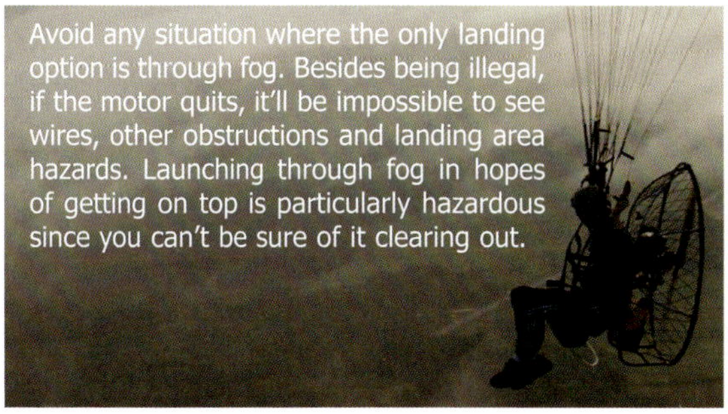

Avoid any situation where the only landing option is through fog. Besides being illegal, if the motor quits, it'll be impossible to see wires, other obstructions and landing area hazards. Launching through fog in hopes of getting on top is particularly hazardous since you can't be sure of it clearing out.

Impending Aerial Collision

If you see a threatening aircraft, watch it for *just* long enough to know that it's really on a collision course, and then act decisively. If it's stationary relative to the horizon (not moving left/right/up/down) then it's on a collision course. For example, an airplane may be just above you but descending quickly. An aggressive descending spiral could put you in its path whereas doing nothing may let it pass.

If you're sure a collision is imminent, quickly enter as steep a spiral as you're comfortable with. Since you're so slow, this makes you more visible while also getting out of the way. If the other pilot suddenly sees you he will also see your downward motion and should pull up in response. Don't yank the glider into a spin and create another emergency.

Kite Lines

A child's kite line can destroy your wing. Be careful when flying along the beach since kites are common and their lines nearly invisible. Even the cheap ones can destroy a paraglider—the line slides through, slicing as it goes.

If you're up fairly high and do contact a line, consider circling down to a landing so the string is not able to cut all the way through your wing. Once the kite is de-tensioned from its mooring (the child below), the damage may be reduced.

The Jolly Roger paraglider, pictured above, was no match for a $4 kid's kite line which sliced it asunder. Amazingly, the pilot was able to safely land the remains.

Failure of Wing, Line, Riser, or Connection

Be thankful you carry a reserve, this would not likely be survivable. You'll probably be thrust into a spiral with only a few seconds to get the reserve out before rapidly building G-forces prevent it. With no reserve, you'll be riding half the wing down in a high-speed spiral. Pulling brake may only worsen the spiral since most brakes act more towards the tip. The brake on the failed side will probably have ripped out of your hand but, if not, hold onto it as long as you're able.

Consider reaching up (if able) and trying to pull the inside rear riser line to oppose the turn direction. Pull just one line. Given the angle that you'll be dangling from, reaching it would be a long shot, actually pulling it even longer.

Quality carabiners and a back-up strap that goes from your harness webbing into the riser loop nearly eliminates the dreadful results of this extremely rare failure.

Accidental Reserve Deployment

Shut off the motor. Realistically, that's all you'll probably have time for. As long as the reserve comes out properly, ride it down as described in Chapter 4. Only if it looks like you'll be set down somewhere really unpleasant, *and your wing is still inflated*, consider cutting away the reserve bridles with your hook knife or disabling it with your hands by pulling in some reserve lines (extremely difficult).

Grabbing the reserve on its way out is probably only possible if it gets snagged or malfunctions. Even then, having a hand full of reserve lines when its fabric catches air may cause severe line burns as it snaps open.

Fire

Fire is extremely rare and even more rare in flight. There's little to do besides shut off the motor and land immediately. It's so rare that no established procedure has come forward but here are some recommendations:

- Spiral down to minimize your time aloft. Consider leaning forward to keep your body farther from the fire and reducing the swirl of wind around your back.
- If the motor has an ejection feature, this is the time to use it! Grab those tabs and pull outward just like you've rehearsed.
- Unclip from all but one leg strap and be ready to get away from the machine quickly. Rehearse going for that remaining strap.
- Consider landing next to, or in, shallow water so you can immerse yourself after getting free of the machine. Only land *in* water you know is very shallow.
- Roll in dirt, a blanket, tarp, or water as available to put out any remaining fire.
- Approach the motor with great caution. Although it's unlikely, certain failure modes can allow the tank to burst, spewing flaming fuel.

Reading this chapter is like reading a medical book—lots of maladies, but they're mercifully rare. The sport has proven safer than it's appearance would indicate but, being aviation, it still requires extreme vigilance to keep that way.

Competition

CHAPTER 20

Eric Dufour puts his best foot forward during a practice run of the *cloverleaf*. Even while kicking the center stick he must be planning his next turn.

It is human nature to see what we're capable of. Like all competition, with the right attitude, it's a healthy motivator to excellence.

Competing is riskier than just flying around, primarily the low-level tasks. Risk is reduced, however, by (1) avoiding tasks where pilots dive towards the ground, 2) minimum experience requirements and 3) rules that penalize dangerous maneuvers.

Those steep and low turns flown by competition pilots look riskier than they are. As long as the pilot knows how to keep them level (no diving), even touching the ground doesn't guarantee damage or injury. Of course it does mean zero points. A common question is "what happens if the motor quits during those turns?" Surprisingly, for an experienced pilot, the answer is: nothing. There's enough energy that the pilot can level off land on his feet—it has occurred a number of times.

Rules try to 1) recognize skill in a fair manner, 2) minimize risk, 3) limit arbitrary factors, and 4) keep the event flowing. Rarely is the simplest solution the most fair. Rules must be understood, too—knowing how a task is scored can be just as important as being talented. More than one loser's last words were "I didn't know you could do that!"

Different sanctioning bodies have different flavors of the same basic tasks, so check the ules closely. The Fédération Aéronautique Internationale (FAI) is the worldwide governing body for all competition and their International Microlight Commission (CIMA) handles microlight activities, including PPG. Most countries have national organizations that govern national competition and work with the FAI. Some countries have national organizations whose competition is run independently.

> **Equipment Selection**
>
> What equipment you select depends on the type of competition. Low-level precision tasks benefit from powerful motors whereas cross country type tasks need efficiency. That's why four stroke, and small two stroke motors are popular at navigation-heavy competitions. Where both types of tasks are flown, it's tougher to choose. If you're really good at precision tasks, you should lean towards more thrust. If you excel at navigation tasks, lean towards efficiency. Most rules require using the same equipment for an entire event so choose wisely.
>
> Small, fast wings are good for most low-level precision tasks but not necessarily so for navigation because of their higher fuel burn. Reflex wings are ideal for competition because of their large speed *range* which is helpful for both cross country and precision tasks.
>
> The reflex wing's speed range must be employed carefully since using brakes while fully accelerated can be risky. Check with the wing's maker about how best to steer in different combinations of speedbar and trimmer settings.

How Good Do I Need To Be?

Everybody has to start somewhere. If you have 50 flights, can reliably launch and land within 100 feet of a target, then you have what it takes to compete. Other minimums may be imposed but these qualifications are usually enough.

Being competitive is another matter but, if you've got the basic gear and a place to practice, you may be surprised at how well you do. Simply entering these events will improve and focus your skills.

If you've been refining your finesse, even just for the fun of it, then you're probably already competitive. To win, you must indeed be a master of the craft, able to control your path within inches on a calm day and within a few feet in level 2 turbulence (see Chapter 5 for the Bump Scale). You should be able to prevent pendulum swings and generally keep yourself locked under the wing even with some bumps. Having the skills as described in Chapter 16 (Precision Flying) should be enough to earn a top 25 percent ranking.

Whether you're new to competition or a veteran, be ever mindful of personal limitations; it's easy to get carried away and damage yourself or your gear. Many pilots have done well by consistenttly just *finishing* each task, even with average points.

A common pitfall is when a good pilot pushes too hard and hits the ground, zeroing his points for a task. That really hurts in a close contest. Plus, the damage may prevent scoring on the next few tasks while repairs are affected.

Ground Precision

For many pilots, ground precision is the fun stuff. It can be intimidating, though—the key is to stay within your ability and build skill slowly.

The Cloverleaf

This is the mother of all precision flying tasks (see diagram for description). It mixes a number of skills: Turning, power management, spatial orientation, adjusting constantly for the wind and planning ahead. Don't minimize spatial orientation—it is not as obvious as it seems. When you're down low, corning hard and looking to the center, can make everything appear the same, allowing confusion to cause a wrong turn, especially with wind playing havoc on your flight path.

Competition adds several elements to the basic foot drag. Rules may not allow the cage to touch and you must steer through the gates while trying to be as *fast* as possible.

1. Tim Kaiser turning and dragging at a Chicago competition.

2. Bill Heaner speeds through a "slow-fast" gate in Phoenix, Arizona.

It's typically only flown in light wind, less than 10 mph, to avoid fast, downwind ground speeds.

Here are some practice tips:

- Be able to kick the center stick. You cannot win without doing this perfectly. So go out, find some small bush or other safe target, and practice kicking it from an approach in all directions. Of course, if you can set up a regulation-height stick, that's better.

- Practice level, fairly steep turns that require modulating power as you roll in and out. Pick a distant spot on the horizon and practice rolling out towards it.

- Make sure you know the order. Go out and fly the course from a couple hundred feet while looking down on it. Then do it at 50 feet, then at 30 feet, etc. Don't worry about time until you've got the turn directions nailed.

- Before entering the course, mentally go over it. Look at the center then the left-far stick (1st one), look back to the center and across to the opposite stick, etc. until visualizing the last stick and finish. Great pilots have given up great times by turning the wrong direction, earning a great big zero.

- After you're consistently making make all the sticks, work on time. Being fast on the wing helps but it's most important to minimize distance. Only your body must needs to round the corners (all the rules require) and being wide takes more time. In the same vein, always plan your turns so as to finish with the least distance to the center *and* next stick. If the course uses large pylons then obviously you must go wide enough to avoid them.

Power management is critical—as you go into each turn, throttle up enough to prevent settling (red in the illustration above). Steep banks may require full power. As soon as you *start* rolling out from the turn, relax the power—from a steep bank you will go completely to idle and still climb a bit. If you're using a speedbar, start applying it as you level out and modulate the power to keep from settling. Be careful using a speedbar on this task, it is difficult and makes it harder to kick the center stick since your feet are on the speedbar (or stirrup).

Being fast is good, to a point. Load up with fuel and (if permitted) ballast but it's certainly not worth being so heavy as to blow a launch. Setting the trimmers to fast seems most beneficial in spite of adding slightly to turn times.

Wind changes how the cloverleaf is flown quite a bit (see diagram). With wind, the basic idea is to always go upwind of the upwind sticks before turning. That minimizes the turn required to get back to the center and aim for the next stick. When flying downwind, anticipate the need to start turning earlier. Finish all turns with a crab into the wind so as to further minimize distance flown.

> ⚠ **Caution!** Using the speedbar leaves you vulnerable to a collapse, especially while flying through your own wake or other turbulence.

Cloverleaf At Home

Make your own course by laying out 5 sticks like the 5 die, with 71 meter (233 feet) sides. The center should be springy enough to be easily kicked without getting in your prop. Two meter tall (6 feet) fiberglass poles with a pointy end ground into it works well. Put foam material on top like they use in pool "noodles" for best visibility along with ribbons on the center stick to see wind direction.

Fly the course by entering upwind, kicking the center stick first, then turning left and following the pattern above. Time starts on the first center kick and ends on the last. Some contests may begin timing when the pilot is told to launch. Don't climb too high since it wastes time and some organizer impose a maximum height.

Dark red equates to max power and white equates idle power assuming you use moderately steep banks in the turns. Do only what you're comfortable with, though, since crashing scores no points.

Cloverleaf With Wind

In general, if there's some wind, you must move your flight track to be upwind of the sticks. More wind, more change.

Foot Drag Course

The foot drag course does not involve a lot of turning but it's still a challenge when attending to everything else. The pilot is timed from start to finish and must drag at least one foot through the course. He can lift a foot or run but it costs points. Don't hit the poles or fall—both are bad for points.

The foot-drag is not typically done in European competitions.

1. Going through the *slow* course requires lots of brakes, lots of power, finesse, and hopefully smooth air. If it gets bumpy, don't go too slow since you can't just pop up with the brakes which are already pulled. And adding power may take too much time.

In this picture, the author is deep in the brakes, "hanging on the prop" during a Florida competition. Don't touch that cage!

2. Going fast is tough, too, in bumpy air. You must remain below the minimum altitude or be able to kick the sticks and, at that speed, it's easy to get popped up. Tim Kaiser is pictured on full speedbar with trimmers out during a Chicago competition.

Foot Drag

Once you've mastered the foot-drag basics described in Chapter 16, you can apply them to competition. Mostly you must learn how to do it fast (trimmers out), with some crosswind, and how to turn while dragging.

The course is a simple slalom of three gates where the center gate is offset. You drag at least one foot the whole distance through each of the gates. Faster is better and speed counts for about a fourth of the points. Passing all the gates with a foot on the ground is most important because lifting a foot or running reduces points significantly. Don't try too hard, though, falling scores a 0.

The best stance is one foot out in front of the other so that you can be ready to run if necessary. Don't put much weight on the foot—drag will slow you down and leaves you vulnerable to a point-sapping run. But do run, if necessary, to avoid losing so much speed that the wing falls back—that's another 0.

Minimizing brake use is good for both points and options: If you slow down too much, the brakes will no longer be effective at quickly adding lift. If you wind up heavy in the brakes it means your airspeed is slowing down—add power immediately!

To be competitive, you'll need to fly with the trimmers out (fast) but only if you're willing to be dumped going fast. Dumping happens whenever you get a sudden tailwind or downward gust, thus losing lift and forcing a run or possibly a fall. Using the speedbar (one foot pushing the bar, the other dragging) is nearly impossible and, since touching any frame part on the ground zeros all points, it wouldn't be worth the risk of trying. Tying off the speed system so that it remains engaged is too risky—the wing is so much more susceptible to frontal collapse since the wing gets partially unloaded during the foot drag.

Slow/Fast

This simple task is surprisingly difficult to do well. You fly a straight course as slow as possible then do it again as fast as possible. To be competitive, though, you must be comfortable on full speedbar, trimmers (fast), while only a few feet high. In a calm wind, that's fast! Contestants must stay in a 5-meter wide lane or kick three 2-meter tall sticks in a row.

If you're on a reflex wing, its manual may recommend against using brakes while fully accelerated. If so, consider using tip steering for directional control and speedbar for height. That's tough, though—if you drop, you must *immediately* let up on the speedbar then get back on it as you climb, a reaction that must be automatic while down low.

The slow part requires heavy brake pressure but, be careful, that will leave you vulnerable to getting dumped by sink or lifted above the height maximum. Altitude is controlled mostly by power since the brakes are already pulled about as far as they can go—adding more brake will just stall the wing.

The fast part should be flown with the trimmers out and, turbulence permitting, on full speedbar. You'll need to use brakes for finessing altitude but use them minimally. This is partially an equipment challenge given how some wings are faster, and have a broader speed range, than others.

Touch and Go

Spot landing with power is easy so a challenge was added. After touching the spot, you throttle up, take exactly 10 steps then lift off again (touchdown plus 9). There is no need to put full weight on your legs during the run but the steps must be completed in a fairly short distance to preclude a fly-by with 10 foot ground taps.

Probably the best technique is to keep nearly flying speed so that your feet do not carry *much* weight. That way you can be ready to lift off quickly but within the limited distance. You'll still be fairly heavy in the brakes and need to power up on about step 7. At high elevations or with low power machines, you may need to be powering up much earlier..

Spot Landing

Power-off spot landings are covered in Chapter 17 but here are some tips for competition. Normally, you climb to 300 feet or so, power off, then glide down to land on a Frisbee-sized target *and stop*. Where you first touch counts most.

It's a great task to master given that every flight ends with a landing. But it's risky, especially if you're high and pulling fistfuls of brake to steepen glide. That can easily lead to stalling and falling—a painful, expensive way to score zero points. Some pilots prefer *flapping* (see Chapter 17) to steepen their glide. But let up in time to accelerate and flare so you don't fall or touch the cage which may be disqualifying (a rule that discourages trying too hard).

With practice, many pilots can touch the spot nearly every time, but arriving with minimum speed is another matter. Some tasks reward energy management (the USPPA's, for example) by also scoring how far you travel after touchdown. Less is better. Regardless of scoring, though, it's most important to hit the target: don't miss or fall because you're worrying about traveled distance.

If the scoring does *not* incorporate stopping distance then the *swoop* landing (Chapter 16), where you come in fast and just touch the spot, is best.

One way to minimize excessive run-out is to use moderate brakes (pressure 2 - 3) nearly all the way down. Have just enough speed to flare hard and swing forward slightly, stopping just as you touch. With too-little flare authority, this technique risks a point-sapping cage-touch or fall.

Another variation is where they have 5 cones lined up 10 feet apart. Your goal is to kick cone 1, then as many of the other cones as you can before touching down. It's a lot tougher because you must land in the exact direction as dictated by the cone row. Small wings are better at this because they allow a much bigger dive and higher speed during the bottom swoop.

On all spot landings, especially in windy conditions, it's generally better to have your trims set to fast, so as to have more control over energy management.

Kick sticks 1, 2, 3; come back to slalom around 1, 2, 3, then come back to kick 1, 4, 3. Time is from the first to the last kick.

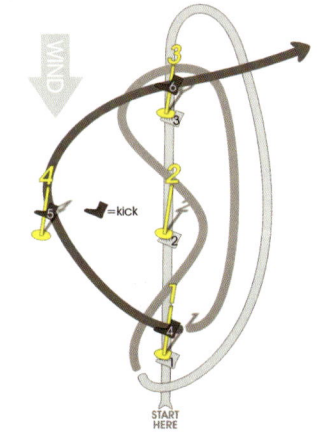

1. Michel Carnet wrings out the last few mph with full speedbar. This does trade some safety for speed but, given the smooth air, added minimal risk.

2. The Japanese Slalom is an FAI task like the slow/fast and cloverleaf. They all involve the same basic skills but employ different ways to express them. U.S. rules allow the course to be flown with a mirror image layout to accomdate different field restrictions.

Flight Precision (Navigation)

These tasks challenge a completely different type of piloting skill. You must be adept at planning, reading maps, pilotage and know your machine's fuel burn characteristics. Scoring involves flying with a covered GPS (so it can't be used for navigation) that will later be read by a computer to see what points you actually flew over and at what time. Other methods can be used for scoring where the pilot is given photographs that are used to identify (and write in a log) locations on the ground.

Competition directors will provide maps, pictures (if used) and instructions after which, pilots are given some time to do planning. This is where competition organizers spend a lot of time, getting all these things together. For the competitors, though, it can provide many hours of enjoyable flying. It is, in many ways, the relaxing part of competition. Of course that depends on your intensity—there is always *something* that motivated flyers can do to improve their odds or awareness—verifying position, studying the map for coming waypoints, determining wind, checking fuel, strategizing, etc.

Finding Points on a Map

One key skill is being able to correlate what is on the map or photograph with what you see on the ground—not necessarily an easy task. Some of the tasks require familiarity with your machine's fuel burn in various configurations.

Flying with a speedbar is a must since some of the tasks are almost pure speed. They'll give you unlimited fuel and limited time to go find as many points possible.

Planning

You must have some idea of the winds aloft and apply that to your planning (see Chapter 13) for flights. Understand the effect of wind gradient and try to maximize it. For example, if the winds at 1000 feet are south at 15 mph but at 500 feet they are west at 12 mph, plan accordingly.

Don't count on trying to do much writing in flight; organize the map and pictures to minimize moving things around. Some contestants have a larger map display on a kneeboard that is several pages wide so they don't have to flip pages.

Fuel Limited Tasks

A variety of fuel-limited tasks can be called that require optimization based on conditions. The idea is usually to cover the most amount of ground with the least amount of fuel burned. In no wind, fly at your glider's best L/D speed (usually trim

---

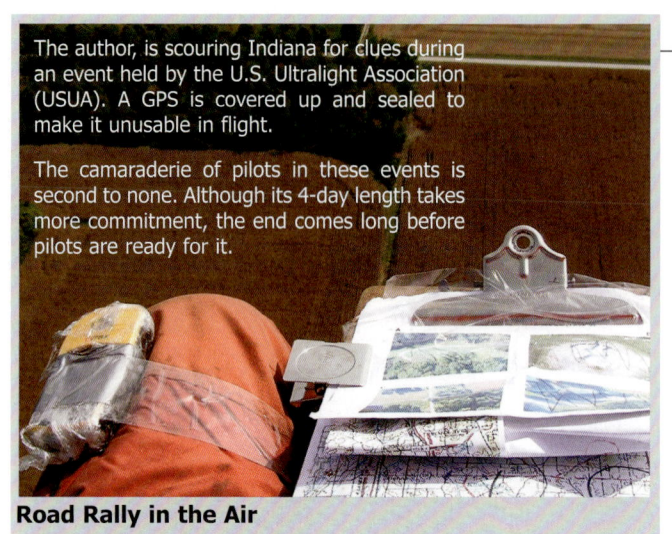

The author, is scouring Indiana for clues during an event held by the U.S. Ultralight Association (USUA). A GPS is covered up and sealed to make it unusable in flight.

The camaraderie of pilots in these events is second to none. Although its 4-day length takes more commitment, the end comes long before pilots are ready for it.

Road Rally in the Air

European style competitions involve a wide variety of navigation tasks. One good example is the fun-to-fly *Circle and Two Lines*.

The objective (from the FAI Rulebook) is: "To follow a circular track in the direction briefed, finding markers or identifying ground features from photographs and locating their positions on a map. It may be required to distinguish between on-track and off-track markers and ground features. Four markers or ground features will identify the points from which lines must be drawn. The task ends with an out landing at the point outside the circle where these lines intersect. Any route may be chosen from the airfield to the circle or from the circle to the out landing site."

Implementation is challenging and entertaining for both the flyer and the organizer (see diagram on next page).

The pilot gets a map with a circle drawn on it and a bunch of pictures. His mission is to fly the circle and put a hack mark each time he identifies one of the pictured points. Pictured points are sometimes a bit off the circle but the mark goes on the circle abeam where it is seen. Once all four marks have been made the pilot draws two lines that intersect those points. Where those two lines cross is the new destination. A judge awaits at that location for those who figure this out (while flying, I might add.)

It doesn't have to be a circle either—the same task is flown with other shapes using the same concept. If a possibility for ambiguity exists, the instructions will indicate the outlanding site's general direction.

Since it would be possible to fly the circle, miss only one point and therefore not be able to complete the task, an option is given. Just before takeoff, each pilot is given a sealed envelope. It contains the out landing site plotted on a map, just open the envelope and go find it. Of course, opening the envelope entails an enormous penalty but it's still better than not finding the site at all.

speed). Fly faster in a headwind and slower in a tailwind but never below minimum sink speed (see Chapter 22).

When flying between thermals, speed up in sink and slow down (or circle) in lift. That feels counter-intuitive since, in sink, you're already plummeting and speeding up seems to make it worse—but more importantly, speeding up gets you out of the sink faster and you'll end up higher. Depending on how the scoring is weighted, it may be beneficial to circle in thermals when going downwind and slow down in thermals when going upwind. The more that time counts, the less circling you want to do.

The FAI "Circle and Two Lines" navigation task is a fun challenge. Don't miss a point though, it forces you to open your sealed pre-launch envelope containing the destination.

Endurance

Endurance, also called *economy*, is a fuel-limited task that rewards those with soaring skills and efficient gear (motor and wing). It is normally flown just as thermals start heating up or later on when they're diminishing, but still present. Cloudy days, where little thermal action is available, primarily rewards the lightest pilots flying the smallest motors on the most efficient wings.

Pilots meet in a common area to ensure that tanks are empty (motors run out) and each one gets exactly 2 liters of fuel (or some other agreed-on amount) in their tank. They all must launch within a given time window and the longest one up, in minutes, wins.

One proven method is to climb to a couple hundred feet then throttle back just enough to hold altitude or climb slowly. Keep that power until you find a thermal then reduce power to about half of what it took to fly level. Circle in the thermal's lift, building a mental picture of where the strongest updraft is and trying to make that your circle's center. If lift is strong you may be able to shut off the motor (providing you can reliably restart it in flight). In weak lift, use *some* power to help you stay in the thermal.

Kiting

This simple competition is unique to the U.S. for scoring. It is a colorful spectator favorite too, evidenced by the many images of wings billowing to life that end up on videos and publications.

Competitors start off in the field, arrayed evenly within a boundary. When the judge calls "GO," they bring up their wings together and begin the battle. Kiters

This is, by far, the most physically demanding task of the competition. It is frequently brief for many pilots, but for those who stay up, it is very tiring. The winners deserve every point they get, especially since it's not worth that many points.

must stay within the designated area and keep their wing up for at least 2 minutes to score anything. They are allowed to maneuver so as to bring other wings down but cannot touch other competitors with their bodies. The last 3 wings up get 1st, 2nd and 3rd place according to who stays up the longest.

Tactically, the best way to bring down someone else's wing is to block their airflow with your wing. Advanced kiting skills are obviously a must, especially kiting with the A's, but even then it's difficult. If a couple of wings get upwind of yours, it might be impossible to keep it up, especially if your route to clear air is blocked.

You don't need to wear a harness (can hold the risers with just your hands) but, if there's much wind, your arms will tire quickly. Kiting with your arms only (no harness) may work better in a very light wind since you have more finesse—it's a judgement call based on conditions and your ability to riser-only kite.

Here are some points of strategy.

- Pick the right location. In a stronger wind, be as upwind as possible. In a really light wind, where you'll have to move just to keep the wing up, pick a downwind location.
- Avoid battles, if possible, but when it becomes inevitable, try to always stay upwind. You can turn and run forward but the lost time in turning may be too much and remember that you can't go out of bounds.
- If your wing gets down low, grab the A's to kite it just above the ground.
- If rules allow grabbing other pilots' lines, use that more as a threat than actually doing it since you usually pull their wing into yours.

This task is worth only a few points but can make a difference in a close match.

As with all tasks, you must use the same wing you started with but are allowed to choose any kiting harness. In most permutations, it is acceptable to pull other pilots' *lines* as long as you don't touch the pilot. That, in itself is hard because it tends to bring their glider down on *yours*. The judges have a hard time telling who's wing hit first in that situation.

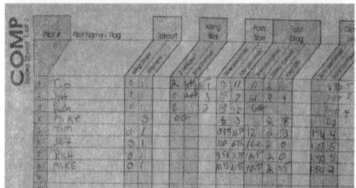

1. Pilots preparing for the real deal at a large gathering near Orlando, Florida.

2. Scoring is done on a computer but the judges (marshals) only write down times, distances and other raw data. They do no actual scoring on the field.

Each organization has a process to help insure fairness. They know it must be fair but also recognize that nobody is perfect and sometimes bad calls get made. Don't take it out on the volunteer judges, it probably won't do you any good and will make finding these valuable volunteers harder yet.

Unintended Consequences: Scoring buffoonery

At first it seemed simple. You get more points for touching down within the rings closest to a bullseye and none for landing beyond the outer ring. Then at one competition, an unexpected wind forced even the best pilots to land beyond the outer ring. Nobody got any points. That's not fair since the closest pilot was a lot closer than the farthest.

So the scoring was changed to reward pilots with distance points in addition to the ring points. Ahhh, that was better—it would make a portion of the score based on the farthest pilot getting 0 and the closest getting 100 points (plus any ring points he got).

Then at another competition, one pilot nailed the center and all but one of the other pilots landed close to the center. The one that who landed out was a *long* way out. By having him so far out it skewed the score; he got 0 but everyone else got over 95% of the available distance points, wiping out much of the close-landing pilot's advantage. Back to the score-designing drawing board.

Even the best scoring system will not always seem completely fair.

Free Flight Transition

CHAPTER 21

Free flying a paraglider is an adventure worthy of its own pursuit, an enjoyable use of many skills that you've already learned. Paragliding first was my chosen path to PPG and soaring became an enjoyable staple. It is worthy of much respect, too, mastering conditions strong enough to keep you aloft is a serious undertaking.

Many free flyers find that power flying opens a gratifying addition to their sport. Be ready to learn, though, there's a lot more to it than just adding another launch skill.

When launching a free flight harness you lean forward with your hands back. When launching with a motor you must stand up straight to let the motor push.

Transition to Thrust: Becoming a Power Pilot

With power, the world becomes your playsky, allowing exploration of new launches, soaring sites and lift bands that were previously beyond reach. For example, rising air that coalesces well above its source becomes accessible, offering power-off soaring for hours. You can climb through the air to better understand it or use partial thrust to mimic high performance gliders. But what fires up most most motor pilots is the ability to go almost anywhere.

Exploring terrain in smooth air becomes a purpose unto its own. Portability and launch flexibility find their ultimate expression in this craft.

It's a completely different challenge, of course. Where soaring pilots strategize to fleece the air of its lift, motor pilots seek precision control of flight path; control that is measured in inches. Of course you don't *have* to master it to that degree, but it's possible, and the best motor flyers do it effortlessly. A pilot can be excellent at soaring without needing such precision, just as a skilled motor pilot can be masterfully precise with little clue about coring thermals. Fortunately the sports go wonderfully hand in hand.

If you're an accomplished paraglider pilot who is willing to adapt, then motor flying will come quickly. A very few points must be closely minded but then the transition will be easy. It's the same wing and behaves essentially the same but thrust adds some potentially dangerous differences. Don't minimize them.

Seek out an experienced, certified power instructor. His best service will be to set up your equipment properly and instruct you on its nuances.

Launch Differences

Below: Eric Dufour set up for the typical power reverse with one hand on the A's and the other hand working power.

Bottom: Jose Casaudemecq leans back into the power during a forward launch.

Hefting the motor will seem awkward at first. A lightweight motor, adjusted properly, speeds the process.

Reverse Inflation: Getting ready will be quite different. The normal method in paragliding is to hook in while facing forward then turn around as you pass one riser overhead. The motor's cage makes that difficult so you'll want to learn a different technique. One practice that may be easier is the alternate hook-in method described in Chapter 3, where you stand next to the risers facing forward.

Walking backwards is harder, especially with a paramotor whose cage hits your legs. Avoid doing reverses in winds too light to kite the wing.

Another difference is the riser hold. You'll have the correct brake in each hand, as usual, with the risers crossed and one hand holding the throttle, lets say the right hand. You'll hold both A's in the left hand. If the wing comes up crooked to the right (throttle side), then you can just pull the brake in the right (throttle) hand. But if it comes up crooked to the left, you can't just pull the brake in your left hand can't since it's holding the A's. Instead, reach up with the throttle hand and pull the brake line *above* its pulley. This definitely takes some practice. Initially you're better off to abandon a crooked inflation and try again.

Forward Inflation: Hook-in is the same but the launch itself has one glaring difference: As the power comes up, you *must* stand up straight and lean back against the motor's push. The initial inflation is mostly the same, lean forward, but not as much as you would free flying. Dig into it with your hands back, pressing upwards on the A's, but once you start applying thrust, stand up straight. If you start with thrust right away, be standing up right away so that the thrust doesn't drive you into the ground (a "face plant"). Remember: "Stand up at throttle up." More than one free flyer has learned this lesson after tasting a mouthful of launch dirt.

The *power forward*, coming up to 30% power prior to starting your run, gives the most consistent low-wind success. On reverse inflations, since you can't lean, you must be ready to throttle up as soon as you turn around. Turn and *move forward* with some power, then, when everything looks good, add power and launch.

The most common cause for failed motor launches by free-flight pilots is leaning forward. Thankfully, that's easy to fix.

All Launches: Learn to be quick on the motor's kill button; if the launch goes bad you must act fast to prevent parablending the lines or glider. If the wing gets nearly all the way up but you need to abort, quickly turn around to face it. Step backwards, if needed, to make sure the wing comes down away from the prop.

Some motors make it hard to see the wing because your helmet hits the cage. Get used to looking left or right to tell what the wing is doing.

Be mindful to stay on the power after lifting off. A common malady for free flyers is letting off the power after liftoff and settling back to the ground.

Climbout

Torque will be your next surprise: the more power, the more torque—a surprising array of forces that conspire to cause a turn (see Chapter 23). These can be dramatically reduced by proper setup (see Chapter 12) which is why a capable motor instructor will quickly earn his keep.

Depending on your motor model, the turning tendency can be so powerful that trying to counteract it with brakes alone (most machines have only limited weight shift capability) can cause a spin. If it wants to turn, let it. If it's still turning too much or in a bad direction, ease off on the power *then* correct the flight path. It is entirely possible for a powerful machine to spin you around into a riser twist—that won't have a happy ending. Reduce the power *smoothly*.

Maneuvering Differences

By virtue of adding weight and pushing so far below the wing, motor thrust tends to reduce the chance for collapses (slightly). And when they do happen they're typically shorter lived. The trade-off is that there is the potential to get lines wrapped around the motor or its propeller in wild air—a good reason to avoid such air while powered. Plus, the motor adds a lot of twisting mass and offers less weight shift (very little on many units) so recovery from malfunctions can be more difficult.

Also, be sensitive to the wing falling back. Thrust can hold a glider into parachutal stall, a phenomenon that is almost unheard of in free-flight but *far* more common in motoring. It frequently ends in a spin.

If you do feel the wing go back, or your speed suddenly slows down, *immediately* reduce power, reduce brake pull and be prepared to dampen the surge. Rehearse that action in normal flight so that it's automatic. Of course, if it feels like a full stall (*very* unlikely unless you were holding heavy brakes) then react accordingly.

Landing

Once you're experienced at landing with the motor (power off), it can be helpful to land power-on in turbulent conditions. Having some thrust (maybe 10% power) reduces your descent rate and may prevent an otherwise firm arrival if you hit a downdraft. You must be quick to add throttle when needed—if you get that sinking feeling, quickly squeeze on some thrust to regain airspeed for the flare. If things look really bad, go around and try again. New pilots (including recently transitioned free-flyers) should land power-off since the chance of falling is higher with the motor's extra weight and complexity.

Be ready for the extra weight after landing. Have your knees slightly bent, one foot forward, and be ready to run. A fast, smooth arrival can be slid out. Most motors will allow sliding on the cage bottom (curved base skids) but that risks damage, it's always best to try landing on your feet.

Kiting

A good kiter will do well but there are some differences, especially since you can't lean forward as easily (lines go awkwardly around the cage hoop). The only way to

Torque and it's related effects can quickly derail the best launch. Be prepared to reduce throttle if you feel yourself twisting. You can twist all the way around into a spectacular crash.

Tip: Handling The Unknown

If something unusual is happening, remember: Hands up, power off, and prepare to dampen the surge. There are certainly times where a skilled pilot can get better results by actively controlling the wing, but experience shows that far more damage is done by pulling too much brake rather than not enough. Also, be smooth on all power changes—abruptness makes matters worse.

safely kite while facing forward is with the motor pushing you. Trying to kite forward with*out* the motor's thrust is a bad idea—a gust can pull you back into the decidedly awkward *turtle* position (on your back with arms and legs flailing).

Reverse kiting is tougher on units with high hook-in points—you wind up using back muscles instead of body weight and it is quickly tiring. Plus, if you get lifted in a strong gust, the motor's inertia can make getting turned back forward difficult at best. If that happens, remember to keep flying the wing!

New Capabilities

The motor offers more options—keep them in mind as you fly. Primarily, if the wind picks up you may be able to reach a more favorable landing site, maybe even your original site. Consider going higher or lower to find less wind—normally it's weaker near the ground but expect more the mechanical turbulence. At least there's no reason to let yourself get blown into a bad rotor situation.

Landing in turbulence is easier with a motor. Once you're accustomed to the throttle and how it interacts with surges, you can essentially make every landing far more predictable. However, as a beginner, it is far better to land power off until you gain skill at managing power.

If you're doing power-off soaring with the ability to restart in the air, you can let yourself get out of gliding distance from launch but always stay in range of a safe landing option. This is a great way to explore an area's thermalscape—you can launch from nearly anywhere and land back there when you're ready.

Added Vulnerabilities

It's easy to get complacent about motor failure. Resist. If you fly long enough, it *will* fail! Always be mindful of available options when it does, including while you're at full power right after takeoff. Be leery of steep climbouts. Having said that, be aware that an even bigger risk for newly transitioned free flyers is letting off the power abruptly just after takeoff and swinging into the ground. Until you're experienced, and as long as you're not twisting under the risers, keep nearly full power until you've reached at least 100 feet. Then, as always, reduce it *gradually*.

Spinning propellers represent the sport's single most common cause of severe injuries. Most of them happen while starting or running up the motor when it is *not* on your back. A few have also resulted from pilots reaching back during launch or in flight. Respect the prop anytime its powered.

Wires and obstructions become greater risks now that you can spend more time down low. Flying low *and* downwind is a dreadful risk because of increased ground speed—illusions cause misjudgment, escape time plummets, and results worsen.

Soaring

You lose efficiency with the motor, a full point or more off your glide ratio, but you can still soar. The windmilling prop of a clutched unit creates more drag then a stopped prop. Prop protection is draggy but obviously well worth it. Going cageless is nearly suicidal—pilots have been nearly beheaded when trying such folly.

Soaring with the motor running at some constant thrust lets you simulate a high performance glider. Just pick a throttle setting that yields some lowered sink rate.

You can soar with the motor but glide performance suffers by up to 20% due to the frame's draginess. Below, Thad Spencer powers up to cross a low spot on the ridge; weak lift would have otherwise dumped him to the beach.

Quiet beauty brings many pilots into free-flight. There is also the challenge to match wits with nature, to stay aloft, and even go cross country. Eric Rys is pictured here enjoying smooth, easy ridge lift off the Pacific Ocean in Baja, California, Mexico. Lift continued well past sunset—he stayed airborne into evening with no worry whatsoever.

Basic Right-Of-Way

Free flight, especially on a ridge with limited lift, can concentrate traffic in a small area. So a few simple rules have been adopted to minimize conflict.

First and foremost is see and avoid. Use the rules below in conjunction with common sense. When turning, remember "Look, lean then brake."

For **thermaling** it's pretty easy—if there's already a pilot circling, go in the same direction. If another glider is below you, give way to him—he can't see you as well.

On the **ridge**:

1. Always turn away from the ridge. Always. This is a survival rule.

2. Overtake other gliders between them and the ridge. This allows them to turn away from you and be turning away from the ridge.

3. When head-on, the pilot with the ridge to his right has the right of way. "Ridge on your right, you're alright, stay in tight." If not head-on, give way to whoever is closer to the ridge.

So if you're flying along with the ridge on your left, move away from it to let oncoming traffic pass (the ridge is on their right). Exceptions to 3 are:

a. With the ridge on your left, when you turn around it could be confusing. Do what makes sense.

b. A lower pilot has the right of way—he's probably trying to "scratch" back up and needs to stay close to the ridge.

Ridge on the right, you're alright.

Noise

Possibly the biggest drawback to motoring is noise. The quickest way to lose sites or gain the ire of authorities is to buzz around the same locale. If people complain, you will get undesirable notice. People complain the loudest about noise. Altitude is a wonderful buffer and distance is even better. Climb up and get away—adopt the philosophy "launch and leave." When returning, do so with minimal power.

Transition to Free Flight: Going Soaring

Free flight is a quiet realm that warrants preserving. Sites are limited with some teetering on extinction—they must be avoided with motors to keep the area quiet for both free flyers and the surrounding property owners. Always respect the local's requests regarding where motoring is to be avoided.

The view alone from many launch sites is invigorating; it can be intimidating too. Running into the air from cliffs and mountains can be a thrill on its own right.

Your wing handling and flying skills will serve you well; a talented motor pilot will do fine flying a paraglider—the challenge will be soaring. Additionally, there are some skills that must be learned to handle potentially perilous sites that are far from flat and grassy. And thermal flying means conquering the turbulent air that comes with stronger conditions. Your early flights should be in relatively still air with less emphasis on soaring and more emphasis on getting used to the differences in feel and technique.

Free-flying adds risk in some areas while reducing it in others; most soaring risk comes from strong conditions and challenging sites. Even ridge soaring, which looks benign, requires significant skills and knowledge to do *safely*.

The best money you'll ever spend is to take a course from a free-flight instructor that offers transition training. Seek out material on paragliding since what's covered here only scratches the surface. Dennis Pagen's "The Art of Paragliding" covers this subject in depth.

Free-flying in mellow mornings and evenings is not much different then motoring other than the requisite power-off landing. Conversely, flying in air buoyant enough to remain aloft requires far more attention. You must have, or develop, active flying skills (see Chapter 16) that let you keep the wing overhead without thinking about it. The adage "less brake and let it fly" applies here too. Just like in motoring, more pilots get into trouble by pulling too much brake rather than not enough. However, active flying is a far more important skill than in motoring. If you haven't mastered how to keep the wing overhead in rough air, avoid excessively turbulent conditions (thermally or gusty) like the plague.

An experienced motor pilot should devote from 1 to 3 full days of free-flight instruction before going on his own. Plus, many sites require ratings (such as those from the USHPA in the U.S.) and, in some countries, licenses to fly.

Weather at the typical mountain site is often unique; even rated pilots should seek out local expertise before flying a new site. Locals will have knowledge gained from sometimes bad experience—it's worth not repeating the experience.

Equipment

You'll love the harness. After being so nearly upright as with many motor models, the laid-back position of a soaring rig will feel downright dreamy. Almost all harnesses come with a reserve mount, speedbar accommodations and low hook-in points for comfort and weight shift authority.

Most include some form of back protection. Learn how that protection works because it may require proper setup. Airbag harnesses, for example, *must* be zipped properly (using the correct compartment) in order to have any effectiveness. Other styles have their own specifics.

Your motor helmet would work but, since you don't need the ear protection, a lightweight model is far more comfortable. Many free-flight sites use a different radio (2-meter FM in the U.S.) than what motor pilots use. They're more expensive but far more reliable (see Chapter 28).

Your motoring wing should work just fine as long as you follow the common practice of being heavy on the wing while motoring. If the wing was specifically made for motoring, than it may not be as efficient as those specifically made for soaring. A wing that takes a lot of power to fly level will take a lot of lift to stay up.

You'll want a reserve parachute even more so than with the motor. They have scored many saves for free-flyers who ran afoul of mean-spirited air. Good boots are helpful, too, especially in the mountains or other challenging terrain.

Launch Differences

Being able to deal with rough surfaces and a brisk wind is part and parcel of paragliding. Whether thermals are cranking up the hillside or stiff winds are making a ridge lifty, it is quite common to be launching in winds over 12 mph.

Bone-up on the high-wind techniques covered Chapter 15 and practice them in safe areas. You'll quickly warm up to kiting with a light-weight free-flight harness. Since free flying requires lift to stay aloft, pilots typically seek out wind blowing up hills. Although thermals thrive in a no-wind condition, they get good starts when forced up a mountain or some other land perturbation. The vast majority of sites are found atop ridges or mountains, facing the prevailing wind. Expect to deal with small obstructions (plants, rocks, etc) that are put there to snag wings and lines. They're usually very good at it.

1. Tammy Bowles departing Moore Mountain, North Carolina. It's common to need a *lot* of brakes when inflating on a slope. Not only are the hook-in points lower, but you actually do need more brake to keep the glider from overflying.

2. Most free flight harnesses have excellent back protection and some, like this one, are made to reduce wind resistance.

As for technique, the main difference on launch is that, once committed, you must lean forward to run since there is no motor pushing. Whether the initial inflation was reversed or forward, once facing forward, lean over while putting your hands back and up to prevent engaging the brakes. Then run hard until you get lifted off the hill.

Doing no-wind forward launches is easier in some ways since the downward slope helps with your run and getting the wing to come to overhead. Be quick to damp it though, it will probably want to overfly you.

One situation that commands respect is launching from a cliff. Air carries great momentum and a vertical cliff will direct it up right in front of launch, leaving you in a difficult rotor. You may have to move back away from the edge just to get your wing in clear enough air.

Be mindful of the preflight check—forgetting to hook up properly can be disastrous when launching from a hill. Pilots have died after forgetting to buckle their leg loops—they wound up hanging by their arm pits for a time before falling out. Getting into the harness is nigh impossible from that situation although it *can* be done with some physical dexterity and the proper technique (covered in Pagen's "The Art of Paragliding"). One technique is to *never* unhook your leg straps without also unhooking the chest strap too. When it happens, it's usually after the pilot un-did his leg straps to walk. Modern harnesses incorporate buckle systems that reduce this possibility—buy one of those, if able.

Phil Russman tries out a small "mountain" glider near Salt Lake City, Utah. These lightweight wings are for hiking up mountains and flying down. Good ground handling skill is especially important for succeeding in strong winds.

The risers are almost always farther apart in free flight harnesses to allow more weight shift into the turn. Plus with low hang points, the pilot is essentially tilting on the balance point.

"Turbo" Bob Ryan swings back to head south on this Pacific Coast ridge.

Maneuvering Differences

The brakes behave the same, of course, but free flight harnesses add significant weight-shift capability. That becomes more important for several reasons:

- It's way more effective—the typical harness allows over 14 inches of up and down riser travel.
- It is more efficient than using brakes alone. When soaring, the goal is to minimize drag while staying in lift. That means flying near the minimum sink speed of the glider—usually only a few inches of brake pull, any more hurts sink rate.
- Recoveries from asymmetric wing malfunctions or spirals are enhanced.

Weight shifting is done differently in paragliding. Instead of shifting the whole motor or moving the thigh and shoulder, you use your hips. It's not what you do with your body, it's in the hips. Lower your right hip to turn right and left hip to turn left. Some pilots cross the high leg over the low one but do whatever it takes to maximize riser movement. Use the same coordinated turn technique as described in Chapter 16.

Big ears are easier to pull since the risers, and thus their A lines, are easier to reach. Plus, with better weight shift authority you can steer more effectively while holding big ears.

Free flying means you're usually seeking out lifting conditions and it's entirely possible to get into so much lift (on a mountain or ridge, especially) that you cannot come down at a desired location. Big ears is one way to do that but there are other, more effective ways to consider (see Chapter 18).

Kiting

There is little difference in basic kiting although, absent the motor, you can get lifted easier. Plus, many mountain sites will be steep and bringing a wing up in strong, mountain conditions must only be done if you're ready to fly. Learning, and becoming proficient, at one of the advanced methods mentioned in Chapter 15 will be invaluable since you will stay reversed and maintain better control if you do get lifted.

New Capabilities

The best new capability is to fly soaring locations where motors are not allowed (soaring sites that are sensitive to noise). These treasured spots are gained by and maintained by dedicated volunteers and should be respected.

To realize these capabilities, most sites require free-flight ratings to ensure some minimum skill level. Working towards these ratings will further advance your skills and is fun to boot.

Added Vulnerabilities

Without the motor there are some new concerns to deal with. The obvious lack of go-around capability must keep you even more focused on your landing options. Plus, unless you're willing to land away from your landing zone (and the ride home), you must keep getting closer to it as you descend. Pilots do frequently head out on cross-country adventures but they usually have a ride arranged.

You're far more likely to need a spot landing somewhere strange. Make sure your skills are up to par.

You will be inclined to fly in more turbulent conditions since, by nature, you need enough thermal strength or ridge lift to remain aloft. Most of the increased risk in free flying comes from this fact. Thermal turbulence in some areas, at some times of the day, and some locations can be disastrously strong, especially for pilots not adept at active piloting.

The wing is slightly more susceptible to collapse since it will be loaded lighter. It should also be less violent in the recovery but be ready to handle it or avoid stronger conditions altogether. You'll want to use more brakes in turbulence, about position/pressure 3.

For those who plan on venturing into the "biggest" (most turbulent) air, a maneuvers clinic is highly recommended (see Chapter 18). You will learn recovery and descent techniques that may be extremely beneficial, if not life saving.

1. A group of pilots paramotored over to this beach and set up camp. They pulled out alpine soaring harnesses and proceeded to soar all day long.

2. A tandem paragliding lesson is great for a site introduction. Choose your instructor carefully—this is not easy. The pilot must manage a huge wing in usually strongish conditions. When available, help is beneficial. Good tandem pilots know how to use helpers and aren't afraid to ask.

Above, Phil Russman is helping Alan Chuculate launch a tandem during strong conditions on the western Baja peninsula of Mexico.

If you get recruited as a helper: Never let yourself get lifted all the way off the ground while hanging on—let go *immediately*.

Section IV

Theory & Understanding

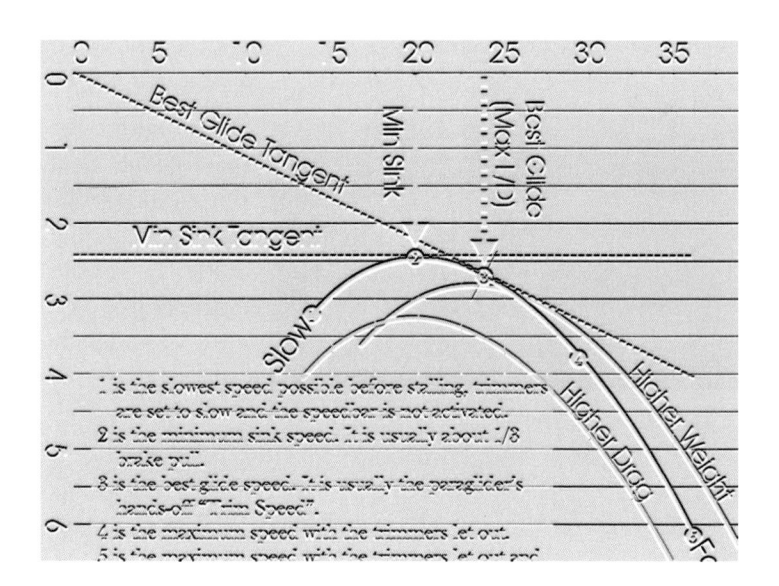

Section IV

Theory & Understanding

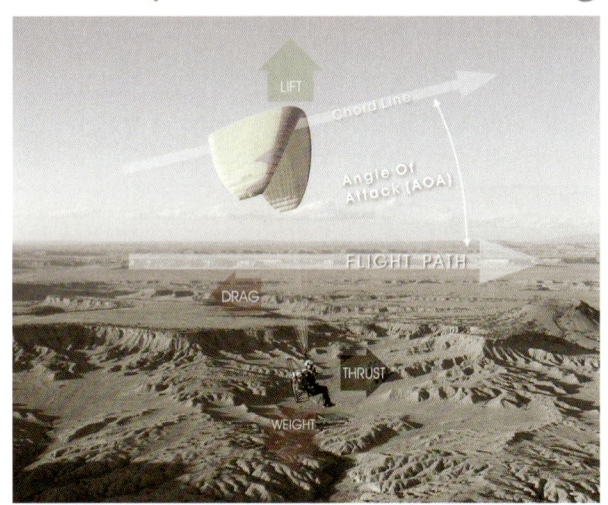

Section IV builds an important foundation of understanding about what's going on around you; knowledge that will improve decision making and make you a safer pilot. Besides, it's just plain interesting to know how things work. And for anyone aspiring to design the next generation of gear, it represents a good start at knowing what's involved. The simple PPG turns out not to be as simple as it looks.

Pilots would be well served to learn this material gradually by reading, asking questions and learning through experience. After gaining some flight time, it would be enlightening to revisit the information. There's nothing like actual air time to grease the gears of understanding.

Aerodynamics

CHAPTER 22

Flight is a fine dance of forces that must remain in step for you to stay aloft and in control. We follow the same aerodynamic rules as our fixed wing brethren, but with a few important differences.

- Thrust, weight, and drag all hang well below the wing. That gives great stability but imparts some different behavior, too.

- There is no tail which means very limited control of pitch and yaw (covered later).

- The soft wing and lines must always be under tension so weightlessness or negative G (like the top of a really big roller coaster) maneuvering is verboten.

Balance of Forces

You can learn most of what you need to know by sticking your hand out the window of a moving car. If it's flat and level with the air stream (or *relative wind*), there is no lift but it still gets pushed back a bit (drag). Angle the hand up slightly (increase the *angle of attack*) and it generates lift. Angle it up more and it gets more lift while pushing backwards more too—more drag. Angle it up too much and the lift stops altogether while drag skyrockets—that's a *stall*. If you keep the slight angle that produces lift, but drive faster, then lift and drag both go up.

Some dynamics of our pilot-on-a-string craft can be understood by imagining a small rock tied to a foot-long line hanging from your finger. Moving the finger around approximates how a pilot/motor will behave when the wing moves around in response to control inputs or turbulence.

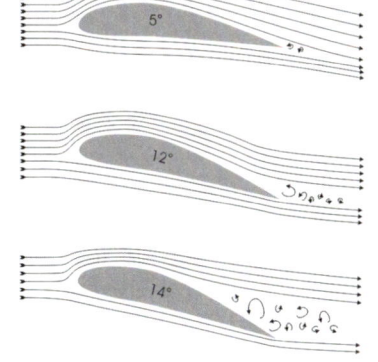

The air can only "stick" so much. Beyond a certain angle (the *critical angle of attack*), it separates causing lift to plummet and drag to skyrocket: A stall.

Sum of Forces

All forces in kg

- Lift = 100 kg
- Deck Angle = 10°
- Chord Line
- AOA: Angle of Attack = 10°
- Relative Wind / FLIGHT PATH
- Drag = 20
- Horizontal component of Thrust = 20 kg
- Weight 100 kg

Component Forces

- Lift = 98 kg
- Wing Force = 99 kg
- Induced Drag = 1 kg
- LIFT from motor = 2 kg
- Parasite Drag = 19 kg
- Total Motor Thrust = 21 kg
- Weight 100 kg

Steady Climb

All forces in kg

- Lift = 99 kg
- Chord Line
- AOA: Angle of Attack = 11°
- Deck Angle = 15°
- Relative Wind / FLIGHT PATH
- Thrust = 30
- Drag = 20
- Weight 100 kg

Climb comes from thrust in excess of what's required to maintain level flight. Airspeed slows down slightly in a powered climb.

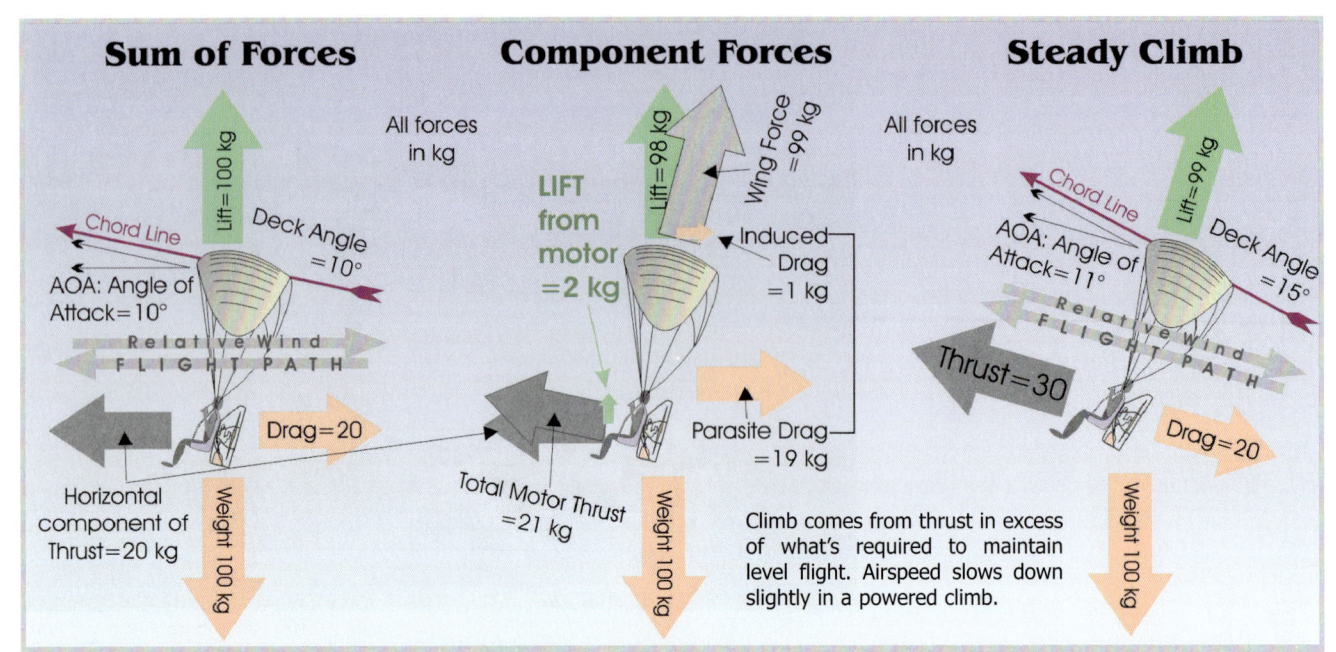

It's really kind of messy. The 4 forces are always described relative to flight path for simplicity, but they aren't actually lined up that way. Leaned-back motors, for example, make thrust contribute slightly to lift. Even the wing force is tilted back, adding *induced drag* to parasite drag (from you and all the lines). Each force can be represented as an arrow (vector), with direction and magnitude. In steady flight, they must all balance each other out as shown in the **Sum of Forces**.

Throttling up changes everything. After swinging forward then settling back into a steady climb, the flight path tilts up and the angle of attack (AoA) increases only slightly while lift decreases slightly due to engine thrust lifting some weight. Speed slows down slightly and induced drag goes up a bit. Since weight is always pulling down to earth, thrust must keep air you moving speed *and* overcome gravity (just like going uphill). In powered flight the wing is slightly more likely to enter a parachutal stall and far less likely to recover from it.

Lift

There is no magic here, we fly by pushing air downward—just like your hand does when angled out the car window. A wing's carefully curved surfaces just do it more efficiently. Motor thrust provides forward speed while the wing redirects air downward. It's pure Newton: push enough air down and up we go.

To generate lift, any flat surface will work, even a plywood board. Surface curving helps keep even the top airflow sticking enough to get redirected downward whereas the board's sharp angles makes airflow separate readily from its top surface into useless, draggy eddies. That would leave only lift from the bottom, and boatloads of drag from the top. Lift is our superhero, drag is the villian.

Drag

PPG's, with all those lines, frame, and a distinctly un-aerodynamic pilot, have lots of drag. Shape has a lot to do with it—round tubes are terrible while the familiar teardrop shape is quite clean.

Drag comes in two forms: parasitic and induced. Parasitic drag is basic air resistance. Induced drag is a result of the wing's lifting force angling backwards from the flight path—it is a by-product of lift. Wingtip vortices contribute to it, also.

Put a symmetrical wing (curved the same on top and bottom) parallel with the slipstream and it produces no lift, only parasitic or *form* drag. Angle it up, like your hand out the car window, and it comes to life with lift. Induced drag goes up too

G Loads

Flying along in level flight, you feel your body weight in the seat; that's 1 G (force of Gravity). In a bank, as you swing around, it forces you against the seat and makes you feel heavier. When you steepen the bank to 60° it feels like you weigh twice your weight—2 G's.

Just like swinging a rock around on a string, the faster you swing it, the higher the G's.

since you had to angle it back slightly and part of the total wing lift is rearward.

The *Center of Drag* is where drag appears to act—for our craft it falls about halfway between the pilot and wing.

Speeding up increases drag dramatically; a doubling of speed quadruples the parasitic drag. That's why our abundant drag is less of a problem—we go so slow.

Thrust

Thrust overcomes drag. Whenever thrust exceeds drag, we get acceleration. In our case, having the thrust hang so low also causes the pilot and motor to swing out in front of the wing. That in turn pitches the wing up, increasing the flight path and slightly increasing the angle of attack.

In level flight these forces are balanced; just enough lift counteracts the total weight and just enough thrust overcomes the total drag. Climbing flight obviously requires more thrust since the motor must overcome gravity *and* keep the airspeed.

Thrust is vectored—it will always push in the direction it's pointed and that is not necessarily the same as the direction you're flying. Serious problems can occur when the thrust line (which way the push is pointed) gets too far off kilter. Point the thrust to the right and the pilot will be pushed left—with potentially unpleasant consequences.

Weight

Weight is what lift overcomes—gravity pulling down on a mass. The center of mass is where an object theoretically balances—for a PPG, that's near the pilot's neck since there is so little mass (in spite of all the area up there) in the wing.

Stability

Stability is resistance to upset and the tendency to return to a previous steady state. By virtue of having the center of gravity (CG) so far below the center of lift our craft is inherently very stable. Unlike almost any other type of aircraft, if the pilot does nothing at all, it will tend to fly straight at it's *trim* speed (see below).

Sometimes *stability* is erroneously invoked to describe a wing that resists collapses or recovers from them quickly. More accurately, it describes a wing/pilot that resists fore/aft movements and returns quickly to steady flight. For example, a vertical gust of air will make the wing surge forward, then back, and continue back and forth in decreasing amounts. A stable wing will not surge as far forward, will not fall as far back, and will settle into a steady state more quickly.

Motor units that mask wing movements to the pilot are frequently called "stable." This is a misnomer because they do not affect stability, but rather the *sensation* of stability. The higher the hookin points are above the CG, the less the wing's bouncing around will wiggle the motor unit around. Whereas a motor with very low hook-in points will move more, and feels "busier" in flight, it is not less stable.

Axis of Motion

Motion occurs around various axes as shown below. Pulling brakes makes you pitch around the lower (motor) latitudinal axis. Changing power makes you pitch around the upper (wing) latitudinal axis. Yaw is left-right twisting around the vertical axis and happens initially when pulling a brake. Roll happens around the longitudinal axis whenever you enter a bank.

Pulling one brake does attempt to cause some opposite roll due increased lift on that side, but it is easily overcome by the pendular stability of a low-slung pilot and motor.

Stability is like a rock hanging from a finger. Move the finger and the rock swings in diminishing amounts until it's still again.

Glide & Drag

Without power we glide, going downhill at a steepness defined by our *glide ratio*—the forward distance divided by the distance dropped. This primary measure of efficiency is also known as the Lift/Drag (L/D) ratio—how much lift versus how much drag is produced at any given speed. Lowering drag (friction) is the easiest way to improve glide since the wing planform and shape is fixed. Changes to the wing, such as adding brakes, trimmers, speedbar, or big ears, change the glide ratio.

A 6 to 1 glide ratio (or L/D) is just stated as 6. That means it will go 6 feet forward for every foot dropped so higher numbers are better. An 8 to 1 (8:1) wing will go further from the same altitude than a 6 to 1 wing.

Glide ratio varies with speed and configuration. Each wing and motor combination will have a speed at which it is most efficient, the *best L/D speed*. Going faster *or* slower will steepen the glide (worsen it). For most wings, the speed for best glide occurs at *trim speed*, which is hands up, no speedbar, and trimmers neutral (usually the slowest setting). However, check your manual—there are exceptions.

Adding drag always hurts glide. Hanging a flag from your wing lines, for example, adds a lot of drag. In this case, speed stays the same while sink rate increases. Going faster with the extra drag dramatically increases sink rate.

Wing manufacturers advertise their glide ratio with*out* a motor to get the best number possible. They shoehorn a skinny pilot into a minimal free-flight harness with his hands and feet tucked in. But a paramotor, with its hoop, netting and frame, make that number a distant dream.

A windmilling prop has dramatically more drag than a stationary one. That is because the spinning keeps the blade's angle of a attack low enough for the air to stick to the back. A stopped prop, on the other hand, only represents the drag of its frontal area. A gyrocopter is a good example, it creates lift by having the air flow past it's spinning rotors. Stop the rotors and the area represented by the blades is woefully inadequate to stop its plummet. Expect a 10-20% decrease in glide performance with a windmilling prop (clutched units), 2 to 4% decrease with a stopped prop and no change for an idling prop (no clutch).

Good glide performance comes from:

- Large span wings. They reduce inefficiencies due to the tendency of air to flow spanwise around the tips rather than back and downward. The reason that soaring wings are long and skinny is to keep the total area the same but reduce these tip losses.

- Fewer and skinnier lines to reduce drag. The highest performance competition wings take this to an extreme—leaving off the protective sheath from lines to reduce their radius. They'll also have fewer lines by employing more cascades where one line goes up then splits into two which then splits and so on.

- A flatter profile—longer lines allow a flatter wing which improves efficiency but this factor must be weighed carefully against the increased line drag.

- More cells. More ribs mean a more precise airfoil shape. Closer spacing prevents each cell from billowing so far out of shape.

Measuring Your Glide

You need to have a GPS and variometer. An altimeter and watch works in place of the variometer.

Set up the GPS to display speed (it only measures groundspeed). Climb 1000' up into a smooth atmosphere and align yourself exactly into the wind, watching the ground to do so. Throttle off slowly and watch the ground speed as you keep yourself pointed into the wind. Note the sink rate (or calculate).

Do that for a half minute then climb back up to 1000' and turn exactly downwind. Throttle off and again watch the ground speed and sink rate. Average the two groundspeeds and sink rates. A 10 mph upwind speed and 30 mph downwind speed means your airspeed is 20 mph. Sink rate should be the same both ways.

Convert sink rate in feet per minute to miles per hour (fpm x 0.011) and divide the average airspeed by sink rate to get glide ratio.

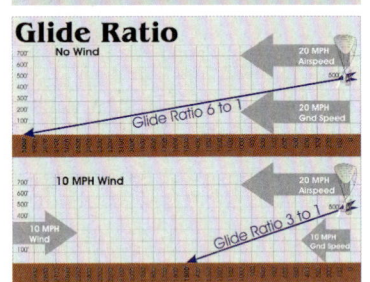

Glide Ratio

No Wind — Glide Ratio 6 to 1 — 20 MPH Airspeed / 20 MPH Gnd Speed

10 MPH Wind — Glide Ratio 3 to 1 — 20 MPH Airspeed / 10 MPH Gnd Speed

With a craft as slow as ours, glide ratio will be dramatically affected by wind. When trying to stretch glide into the wind, it is always best to speed up even though the overall sink rate is higher. You want to get through the sink faster. Picture the extreme: You're flying 20 mph in a 20 mph headwind. The glide ratio is 0, you're sinking over one spot on the ground. Speeding up makes you move forward although only by a few mph, but that's infinitely better than 0!

Interestingly, increasing the weight doesn't change the glide performance, it just increases the speed at which it occurs. *Sink Rate* will be higher, but the maximum glide ratio stays the same. This effect can be useful and, in fact, competition soaring pilots sometimes carry ballast to increase their cross country speeds. For example: A 150 pound pilot on an 8:1 glider may have a best glide speed of 20 mph. With a 200 pound pilot, that same glider still has a maximum 8:1 glide ratio but it will occur at 22 mph and will sink proportionally faster, too.

Center of Lift and Drag

The center of lift is an imaginary point on the wing where lift is said to act. The entire wing provides some lift but it is concentrated in the first 30% of the chord (front to back measurement) and the inside 60% of span. If you could attach a rope to this point the glider/pilot combination would balance from it.

The center of drag is the point where drag is said to act. It will be somewhere between the pilot and wing. If you could attach a line to tow the glider/pilot from this point it would have no tendency to pitch or twist due to drag.

Sink Rate

How fast you descend is *sink rate*, commonly measured in meters per second (m/s) or feet per minute (fpm). Minimum sink rate is the lowest descent rate the glider is capable of. Minimum sink *speed* is how fast you must fly to get that minimum rate. Going faster or slower will always increase the descent rate. Unlike glide ratio, increasing weight always increases sink rate.

Wings with a good glide ratio will have a lower sink rate at the same speed as gliders with a worse glide ratio.

Wing area, usually measured in square meters, is hugely important. More wing area means a better (lower) sink rate but at a slower speed. A small, efficient (good glide ratio) wing will be fast and cover ground nicely, but will sink faster.

The *Polar Curve* (at the end of this chapter) shows these relationships. At each weight there is a speed that produces the minimum sink. For most gliders, that speed comes with about brake pressure 2 (one quarter).

Speed

Adding power does not add speed—it causes a climb along with a slight slow down. If you could move the motor thrust up to the center of drag then throttling up would indeed make you go faster.

There *are* other ways to go faster, and they *do* always require more power. Anytime the speed goes up, more thrust is required to overcome the increased drag—and these craft have *lots* of drag. Here are some ways to go faster with a PPG:

1. Design. Some wings are made for speed. Reflex wings, in particular, effectively decrease wing area with trims full up (fast).

Digging Deeper: Angle of Attack

Does adding power increase the AoA? Some say that only the flight path changes while other pilots argue that the AoA increases a fair amount. The truth appears to be in the middle. Experiments have shown that adding power mostly affects the flight path, but also *does* increase the angle of attack a small amount.

Parachutal stall has proven nettlesome for powered flyers far more than non-powered flyers. It nearly always happens at full or nearly full power, too. The thrust can help get the AoA to its critical stall value but, more importantly, will hold it there once stalled. Without power, most wings recover immediately on their own.

At extremely steep climb angles, the wing's weight will be trying to pull it back farther. Imagine a nearly vertical climb where line tension would be less. Line drag, wing drag, and wing weight would make the wing fall below the pilot—most undesirable.

In level flight, deck angle is the same as angle of attack. Powering up will only push the pilot into a climb, not increase speed.

Digging Deeper: Ground Effect

Ground effect happens when a wing gets within about a half wingspan of the ground. Lift increases and drag decreases because the tip vortices are reduced. Air is prevented from circling around the wing tip.

Paraglider wings benefit very little, if at all, from ground effect since the wing is too high above the ground. Plus, paragliders by design of their anhedral tips (downward curved), reduce the amount of lift lost to tip vortices.

2. Higher weight or a smaller wing. You'll take more space to launch and will, of course, require more thrust.

3. Trimmer adjustments can increase speed by about 15%.

4. Speedbar activation increases speed by about 25%. Even more than trimmers, it increases the possibility of frontal collapse in turbulence on most wings.

5. Angling the thrust line upward (thrust vector downward) is like adding weight. You're leaning forward and down which isn't terribly comfortable but it slightly increases the speed just like adding weight does.

Efficiency Under Power

Thrust results from the propeller accelerating a mass of air from some speed to some new faster speed—pushing us in the opposite direction. How much thrust depends on how much air and how quickly it's accelerated. We can either accelerate a little bit of air a lot, or a lot of air a little. Jet engines burn copious amounts of fuel to accelerate a little bit of air (relatively) a lot. That's great for going hundreds of mph, but is terribly inefficient at low speeds. It's noisy, too. For slow craft—and we're about as slow as it gets—higher efficiency comes from accelerating a lot of air a little; i.e. using a big prop. That is, fortunately, also the quietest arrangement.

Efficiency can be spent either on improved fuel consumption or more thrust. In general, the larger the prop, the quieter and more "thrusty" the machine. Even jet engine makers have taken the large mass route, designing *high bypass* motors with huge fans that are quieter and more powerful.

Wing

The airfoil shape is chosen by designers to optimize performance. Although, in principle, airfoil design is identical to rigid wings, softness dictates some special requirements.

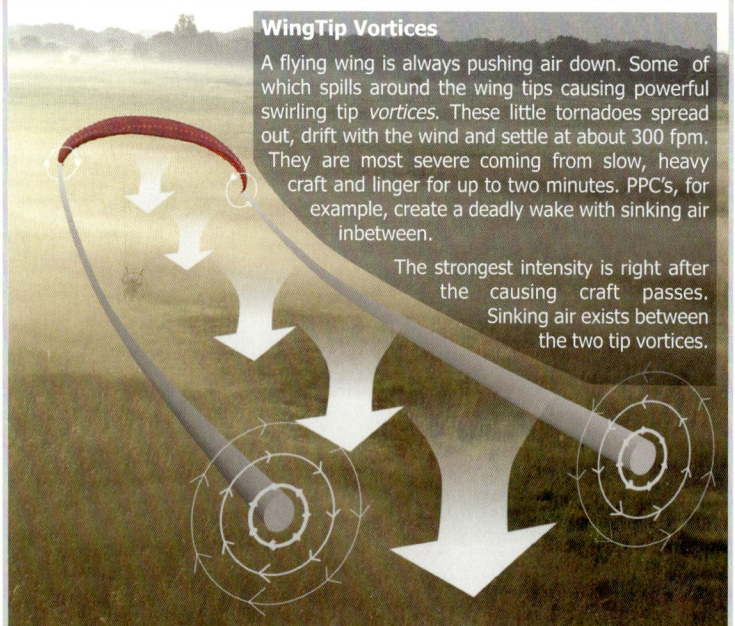

Anhedral Curvature

That graceful arc carved by the wing's drooping tips is *anhedral curvature*, a concession to a support structure that can only pull. It must keep perpendicular pressure on the lines. Without that 90 degree pull angle, the fabric would deform. Higher performance wings minimize the curvature using longer lines at some expense in drag.

Tip Tornadoes

Tip vortices are a pair of surprisingly strong airflow spirals attached to the tips of any lifting wing. They represent the most dangerous element of wake turbulence which is left by an aircraft, like a boat leaves a wake in water. Prop blast also stirs up the air but that is just turbu-

WingTip Vortices

A flying wing is always pushing air down. Some of which spills around the wing tips causing powerful swirling tip *vortices*. These little tornadoes spread out, drift with the wind and settle at about 300 fpm. They are most severe coming from slow, heavy craft and linger for up to two minutes. PPC's, for example, create a deadly wake with sinking air inbetween.

The strongest intensity is right after the causing craft passes. Sinking air exists between the two tip vortices.

lence and doesn't linger for long.

Wake turbulence is worse when it's generated by craft that are heavy, slow and clean. Powered paraglider tandems and powered parachutes, for example, meet two of the criteria and can make vicious turbulence that must be avoided for at least 2 minutes.

Doing tighter turns loads the wing more which generates commensurately more powerful wake turbulence. If you pull a 2-G turn, the wake turbulence will behave like it came from a craft weighing twice as much.

Aspect Ratio

Aspect ratio is wingspan divided by the chord (leading edge to trailing edge distance). A 32 foot wingspan with an 8 foot average chord means the aspect ratio is 4:1. Without knowing the average chord, you can also derive the aspect ratio using $Span^2$ divided by Area. Flat aspect ratio is measured with the wing laying flat, while inflated aspect ratio is measured from an inflated wing's shadow.

Long, skinny wings are more efficient (better L/D) than short fat ones because they minimize tip vortices but there are trade-offs. On a paraglider, the only way to have long, skinny wings is to put them on long lines which increases line drag. Long, skinny wings (high aspect ratio) also tend to suffer deflations easier and don't recover as well as short fat ones—that is why beginner wings frequently have low aspect ratios.

Airfoil Shape and Bernoulli

A plank will create lift. But shaping it like an airfoil will dramatically increase its lift while decreasing its drag. Bernoulli's law, which describes conservation of energy in fluid mediums, helps explain how air behaves around airfoils. It doesn't explain lift in the way old textbooks say it does, but that's only because the law was misused.

Our soft wings give up some performance due to their puffed-up cells. Builders employ many tricks to minimize this through line cascades, internal bracing and different types of reinforcement, but losses are unavoidable. Higher performance wings typically have more cells and fewer lines to reduce this effect.

Shapes have trade-offs too. Some sacrifice stability for performance and vice-versa.

Angle of the Dangle

Air flowing past the pilot/wing combination is called the relative wind or slipstream. Angle of attack is the angle between the wing chord line and this relative wind. The climb or descent angle is the angle that your flight path makes to the ground. *Angle of incidence* is the angle the chord line makes to the B lines.

Deck angle is the angle made between the chord line and the Earth.

Increasing the angle of attack increases lift up to a point. That point is called the *critical angle of attack* beyond which airflow breaks off the wing's top causing lift to plummet while drag soars—it is called a *stall*.

When you add power, three things happen as thrust pushes you out in front of the wing: (1) the angle of attack (AoA) goes up, momentarily increasing lift and drag,

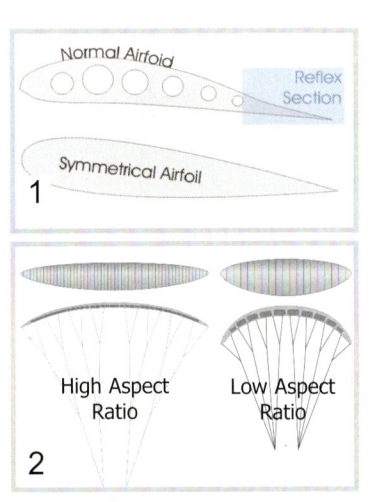

1. A normal paraglider airfoil has more curve on the top than the bottom. A symmetrical airfoil is the same on both sides and is used for aircraft designed to fly upside down. They are not as efficient, but are way more efficient while upside down than a regular airfoil would be if *it* was flown upside down.

Given our craft's unlikely time in inverted flight, symmetrical airfoils are never used.

Reflex airfoils have an upward tilt near the trailing edge that conveys collapse resistance at higher speed. Primarily because it moves the center of lift forward. See also Chapter 26 on reflexed wings.

2. High aspect ratios are commonly found on high performance soaring wings. Beginner models usually have a lower aspect ratio.

A lot happens when you throttle up. This pilot went to full power starting at 2; here's the result:

AoA increases as your body swings forward, increasing lift and accelerating you upwards into a steep climb briefly. The AoA peaks (4). Then the wing surges forward, causing AoA to decrease as the wing catches up (6).

Finally, you settle into a steady state climb (7) with the AoA only slightly higher than when you started. You'll keep this condition as long as the power lasts.

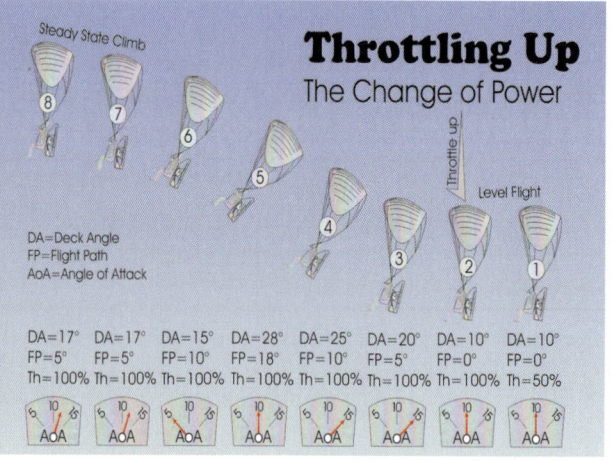

Throttling Up
The Change of Power

DA = Deck Angle
FP = Flight Path
AoA = Angle of Attack

DA=17°	DA=17°	DA=15°	DA=28°	DA=25°	DA=20°	DA=10°	DA=10°
FP=5°	FP=5°	FP=10°	FP=18°	FP=10°	FP=5°	FP=0°	FP=0°
Th=100%	Th=100%	Th=100%	Th=100%	Th=100%	Th=100%	Th=100%	Th=50%

2) the deck angle increases by the same amount, and 3) the climb angle goes up. Once you're in a climb, the AoA decreases to be just slightly higher than before.

Adding power increases AoA which increases lift, drag, and causes a climb (or decreases descent) with minimal airspeed change. What little change does occur is a slow down.

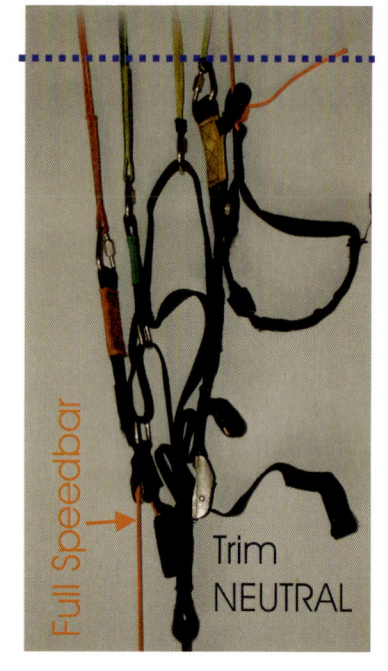

Angle of Incidence (AoI)

Angle of Incidence (AoI), the angle between the chord line and B-line, is a design characteristic fixed by the the paraglider's line lengths.

You can adjust it to some degree while flying by applying speedbar or letting the trimmers out, both of which reduces AoI to go faster. Speedbar action primarily lowers the leading edge while trimmer action primarily raises the trailing edge. Each one deforms the wing differently with trimmers acting more like they are decreasing wing area.

Changing Angle of Attack (AoA)

Lift is a function of speed and Angle of Attack (AoA). More speed, more lift. More AoA, more lift. So changing the AoA will have a big effect. Adding or subtracting power gives a small change to AoA. It feels like a bigger change because the flight path also changes.

Pulling brakes increases the AoA by lowering the trailing edge which immediately tilts the chord line. Brakes also add drag by making the airfoil shape less efficient.

Reflex Airfoils

Reflex airfoils have been used for many years on tailless aircraft to increase pitch stability. On paragliders they allow greater speed while increasing collapse resistance whereas normal paragliders are *more* prone to collapse at their higher speeds.

By raising the aft portion of the airfoil (fast trimmer setting), the center of pressure moves forward and tuck (collapse) resistance improves. You can see this when kiting a reflex wing by pulling down hard on the A lines: the whole wing tends to come down without tucking the leading edge under. This comes at some small penalty in efficiency—the more reflex is employed, the less efficient the airfoil is.

Pulling brakes while trimmed fast is particularly bad because it moves the center of pressure aft and makes the wing far more susceptible to front tuck, which is why tip steering is almost always included on full reflex wings.

Turning

When you pull a brake, the trailing edge deflects downward, increasing lift and drag on that side. You might think the wing would bank opposite to brake pull since there is more lift on the braked side—much like how airplanes bank their

Angle of Incidence

These risers show the speedbar applied, pulling the forward risers down which lowers the Angle of Incidence.

Don't confuse this with Angle of Attack (AoA) which is the angle between the wing's chord line and the *slipstream* (relative wind).

wings with a downward deflected aileron. But, due to pendular stability, a paraglider acts more on the drag, slowing down that side and causing a turn. As the wing changes direction, you swing outward, causing a bank. That bank is what actually does the work by redirecting the wing's overall lift to pull you around the turn.

On many designs, the brake also pulls the wing sideways a bit which improves handling. Any brake input slows down the overall airspeed which will either require more power or, if gliding, will worsen glide performance.

A turn always increases sink rate since some of the wing's lift is now being spent pulling you around the turn.

Thrust Vectoring

Normally the thrust should be nearly perpendicular to the C line of the wing, pushing nearly straight backwards while in flight.

If the thrust line is angled upwards (thrust vector pushing you down slightly) then increasing power will increase down force on the wing, increasing speed slightly. If the thrust line is pointed downward (motor tilted back) it will have the opposite effect. This small effect can generally be ignored.

If the thrust line is offset relative to the risers' center, you'll twist which will cause a bank in the opposite direction. A motor pushing your body left will cause a bank to the right.

In a very few cases, the wing and motor can interact in a way that causes a "wallowing" action back and forth while under power. This is due to *loaded riser twist*: as the wing reaches a bank limit and starts coming back, uneven riser load causes the motor to twist the pilot slightly, redirecting thrust which pushes him in the other direction. It's more pronounced on smaller wings.

How a wing Collapses

A *collapse*, also called deflation, is where part of the wing folds under (it can't fold upwards) after getting pushed down by a vertical or horizontal gust. Usually it recovers before the pilot even knows it happened. A frontal collapse is where the leading edge tucks under while the rest of the wing remains mostly inflated or forms a "horseshoe" shape. There are two basic causes, **atmospheric turbulence** and **pilot inducement** (*see chapter 18*).

Atmospheric turbulence is what most pilots fear, the proverbial "hand of God" swatting them out of the sky, and it is surprisingly rare unless you seek out lively air. Usually it comes from flying through a vortex or swirl that hits the wing, blowing it down and out of shape. The slipstream pushes the now-loose fabric (with probably closed cells) back for a few seconds until internal pressure and line geometry sort things out. Pressure to stay inflated (or "open") comes both from the leading edge openings and from the exterior surface tensioning its lines.

One way to get a turbulence-induced collapse is to fly into a rapidly changing wind such as a thermal. If you fly into a horizontal shear, it can "curl up" a tip as air tries to push the fabric in a different direction. Low G's, such as from a wingover where you feel light in the seat (unloading), makes a collapse far more likely.

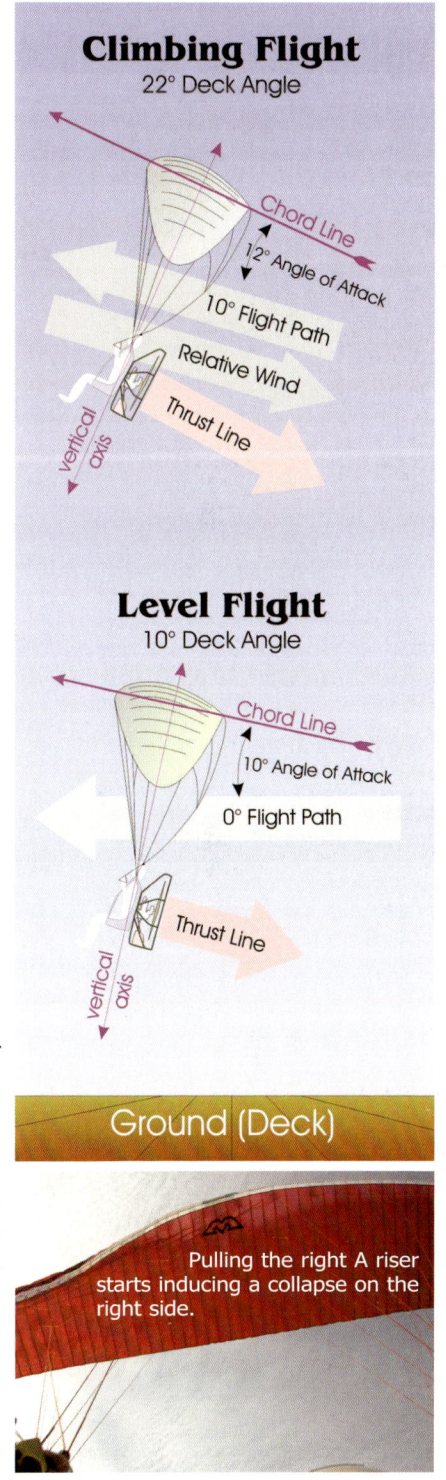

Climbing Flight
22° Deck Angle
Chord Line
12° Angle of Attack
10° Flight Path
Relative Wind
Thrust Line
vertical axis

Level Flight
10° Deck Angle
Chord Line
10° Angle of Attack
0° Flight Path
Thrust Line
vertical axis

Ground (Deck)

Pulling the right A riser starts inducing a collapse on the right side.

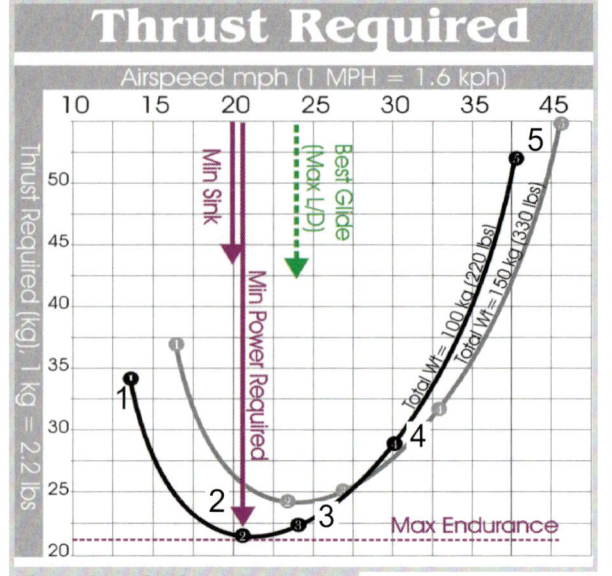

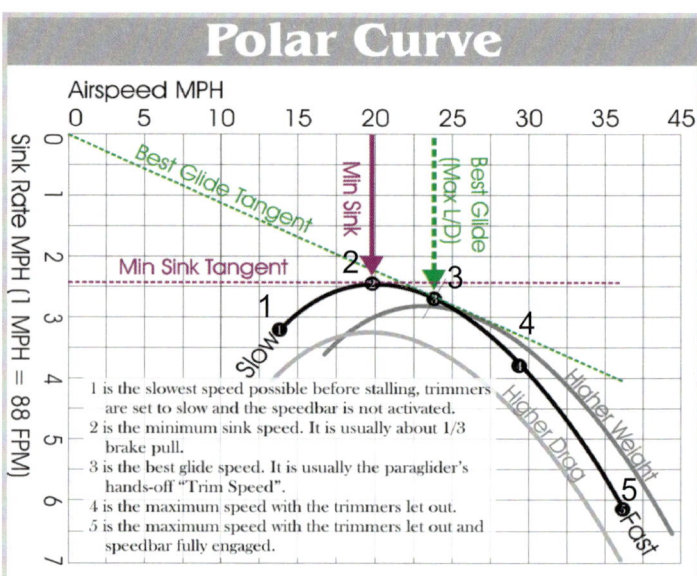

Thrust Required

This graph shows how much thrust is required to hold level flight at various airspeeds. Each labeled point has some significance. The gray line represents thrust required for a heavier pilot flying the same wing. You can see that a weak motor, with trimmers fast and on full speedbar may not have enough thrust to keep him level with trimmers out and full speedbar.

The Points' Significance

1: The slowest speed possible before stalling, trimmers are set to slow and the speedbar is not activated.

2: Mminimum thrust required. On most wings it is the slowest trimmer setting and about brake pressure 1.

3: Trimmers slow (or neutral) and no brakes, which is normally very close to the best L/D speed.

4: Trimmers fast but no speedbar.

5: Trimmers fast and full speedbar.

Stalling

A wing stalls when airflow over the top separates into a turbulent, random flow. That happens when the *critical angle of attack* is exceeded and, although technically not related to speed, high angles of attack result from heavy brakes and flying slow. If you're already flying slowly, it doesn't take much of a gust to cause a stall. A spin happens when only half of the wing stalls and the other half keeps flying, causing a rotation around the vertical axis.

What is frequently called a full stall, when the pilot stuffs the brakes below his seat, is really more of an aerodynamic aberration than a stall—and far more violent, too. The wing does indeed whip through the stall AoA but then essentially becomes a luffing sail—flapping wildly in a hurricane force wind as you plummet. Raising the brakes lets it re-inflate, returning normal aerodynamics with an unpredictable bang and surge (*see Chapter 18*).

The Polar Curve

Polar curves (shown above) graph a glider's sink rate and flying speed. It is a great way to understand many relationships between control settings, speed, sink rate, glide ratio and endurance. The next chapter has a discussion of power vs thrust but know that *power* must take into account airspeed.

The polar curve shows sink rate as speed changes. At your slowest speed, just before stalling, the sink rate is quite high. As you speed up the sink rate improves until reaching the "Min Sink" speed. Then sink rate increases again as you speed up. The tangent line to the curve from 0,0 is the best L/D (glide). Where it touches the curve is the speed and its slope is the best glide ratio itself. Being heavy doesn't worsen the glide *ratio*; it just increases the speed and descent rate where it occurs. Sadly, paraglider wing manufacturers don't go to the trouble of producing these charts.

Combining aerodynamics with shenanigans, Phil Russman surfs Glammis Dunes' sea of sand in California.

Motor & Propeller

CHAPTER 23

Thrust comes from pushing air. Rockets would work but the fuel is hard to come by and smells bad. Jet engines have lots of thrust but burn too much gas, plus they're expensive and loud. Electric motors await improved batteries. Fuel cells will be perfect if they become affordable. And four strokes are quiet, clean and efficient but are heavy for their power.

So that leaves the venerable 2-stroke, powerplant of choice for chain sawmen, go-cart racers and nearly all foot-launch powered paraglider pilots. Wheeled-launch craft have more 4-stroke options since legs don't have to carry the extra weight.

Thrust & Horsepower

The only measure of power that we really care about is thrust—how hard will it push. The industry has never settled on a thrust testing standard and claims are frequently exaggerated. Independent tests, occasionally done at fly-ins, are valuable since they use the same tester, under similar conditions, and with stakeholders mothering over the process. You can all but ignore the *absolute* thrust numbers since they vary due to external conditions and tester calibration, but they are great for *comparison*.

Horsepower (HP) is commonly used to measure power, but it's not as useful for our purposes. A 30 HP motor is powerful for PPG, but mated to the wrong prop, it's worthless. Spinning a plank, for example, still takes 30 HP but provides no thrust. Mostly, horsepower tells what a motor is capable of, given the right propeller and reduction ratio. It does have value since manufacturers will always try to extract the most thrust possible and therefore wind up with similar efficiencies. Thrust rating is still the more useful information since it incorporates all factors.

Expect a lot of variability. One motor that tests at 100 lbs. on one day may do 105 lbs. on the next day, even using the same tester. Plus, there are surprising variations within brand and propeller. Manufacturing vagaries will easily cause a 10% difference from the same model of paramotor and propeller. Wooden props can account for rpm differences up to 5%. Molded props, usually made from carbon fiber, have less of this effect.

2 And 4-Stroke Motors

"Suck, squeeze, bang, and blow" is the mantra of all internal combustion engines. The term "Two-Cycle" (or "Two-Stroke") means that a complete cycle of the piston takes only two strokes, up and down. It fires every time the piston reaches the top whereas a four stroke motor fires every *other* time. That's why 2-stroke motors get more power per pound than 4-strokes and why they run hotter.

Four-stroke motors have valves and cams so they require better lubrication, ergo crankcase oil, whereas two-stroke engines get lubricated from a gas/oil mix.

Four Strokes

The four-cycle (4-stroke) motor, common in cars, lawnmowers, snowblowers, etc., is more complicated. It has intake and exhaust valves in each cylinder's head (the uppermost part) that open and close in conjunction with the piston's travel. They control how fuel/air flows and exhaust gasses flow in four distinct strokes or *cycles*.

The valves, piston, camshaft, oil pump and other moving parts add weight and complexity. Some small 4-strokes get by with just splashing the crankcase oil to needy parts.

Understanding the 2-Stroke

Two stroke motors have come a long way since appearing over 50 years ago. Accumulated tweaks, such as reed valves and tuned pipes, are the big improvements, but geometrics, electronics and materials have helped as well.

During one revolution the motor doubles up on tasks so that, while the piston is being pushed down by burning fuel on top, it's also compressing the next fuel/air charge in the crankcase below.

A *tuned pipe*, common on modern 2-strokes, optimizes performance but only works through a narrow rpm range called the *power band*. The improved efficiency can be spent on either reduced fuel consumption or more power.

With a two-stroke motor, all the interesting stuff happens during the piston's bottom half of travel; and a lot is happening.

- As the piston rises, it sucks a new fuel/air charge through the carburetor and reed valve, into the crankcase below (**suck**).
- Above the rising piston, a fuel/air charge is being compressed (**squeeze**).
- When the piston nears its peak a spark ignites the mixture, powering the piston downward (**bang**).
- On its way down, the piston's bottom compresses a new fuel/air charge in the crankcase (**minor squeeze**).

This Bailey 4-stroke motor is one of few to make it commercially as a paramotor powerplant. Although it is heavier for the power, its efficiency allows carrying less fuel which partially offsets the extra weight.

Horse Power

In the 1800's, James Watt (yes, *that* Watt) was trying to sell his new steam engines but needed a way to compare their output with the standard powerplant of the day: horses.

Mr. Watt determined that, on average, a horse could sustain 180 pounds of pull at 181 feet per minute—a pretty common workload in factories that used horses.

So the horsepower, 33,000 ft-lbs. per minute, was born. Like all measures of power, HP = work for some period of time. In this case, the power is measured as rpm x torque where torque is measured in ft-lbs.

Ironically, some engine makers measure power in Watts, the common measure of electrical power. 746 Watts=1 Horsepower.

- About halfway down the exhaust port is exposed, squirting the burned, high pressure gas out (**blow**). Some of the incoming fuel/air charge can escape out the exhaust, too, but a tuned pipe uses pressure waves to push it back in.
- As the piston continues down, a transfer port is exposed allowing the newly compressed crankcase fuel/air charge to rush up around the piston and into the cylinder starting a new cycle.

Besides producing power, the piston doubles as intake and exhaust valves. Fewer moving parts on a two-cycle makes it lighter and helps reliability. Unfortunately, minimal lubrication and heat (twice as many power strokes as a 4-stroke) sap some of that reliability which is why two-strokes tend to need more attention than four-strokes. Plus, lubrication relies on the proper type and amount of oil being mixed in with the fuel. Any malady that increases heat or decreases cooling can cause piston seizure, an unwelcome welding of piston to cylinder wall.

Longevity is better when rpm is kept relatively low.

Wear increases significantly near a motor's maximum power output—you'll get more hours from a motor lightly tasked than one that screams through life near maximum rpm.

Carburetors

The carburetor feeds an appropriate mix of fuel and air to the motor according to throttle setting. Piston action is always sucking air through the carburetor during intake pulses.

The primary structure of a carburetor is some sort of throttle valve that operates in a venturi, a constriction that lowers pressure to help suck fuel in as a fine mist,

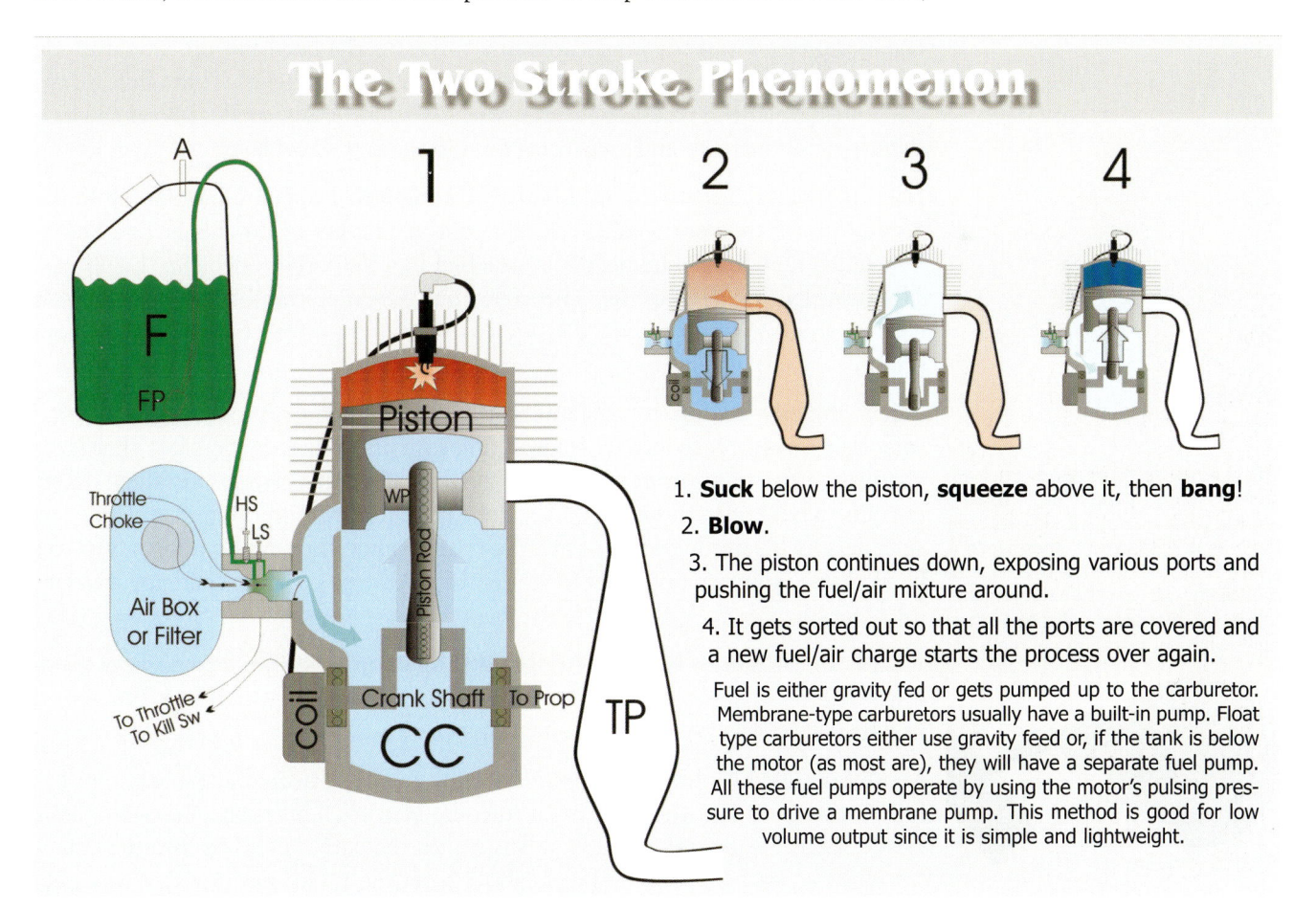

The Two Stroke Phenomenon

1. **Suck** below the piston, **squeeze** above it, then **bang**!
2. **Blow**.
3. The piston continues down, exposing various ports and pushing the fuel/air mixture around.
4. It gets sorted out so that all the ports are covered and a new fuel/air charge starts the process over again.

Fuel is either gravity fed or gets pumped up to the carburetor. Membrane-type carburetors usually have a built-in pump. Float type carburetors either use gravity feed or, if the tank is below the motor (as most are), they will have a separate fuel pump. All these fuel pumps operate by using the motor's pulsing pressure to drive a membrane pump. This method is good for low volume output since it is simple and lightweight.

The PPG Bible: A Complete Guide and Reference

Left: The back of a Top 80 motor reveals some common features employed on re-drive equipped machines. The clutch, in this case has 3 *shoes* that move out to engage the clutch bell with the centripetal force of increased engine rpm. The prop is attached through gears to the clutch.

Right: The other side, showing some basic parts of a fan-cooled motor with the cooling shroud removed. The fan wheel blows air upwards where the cooling shroud redirects it over the motor's cooling fins. If the fan breaks, the motor will overheat in just a few minutes.

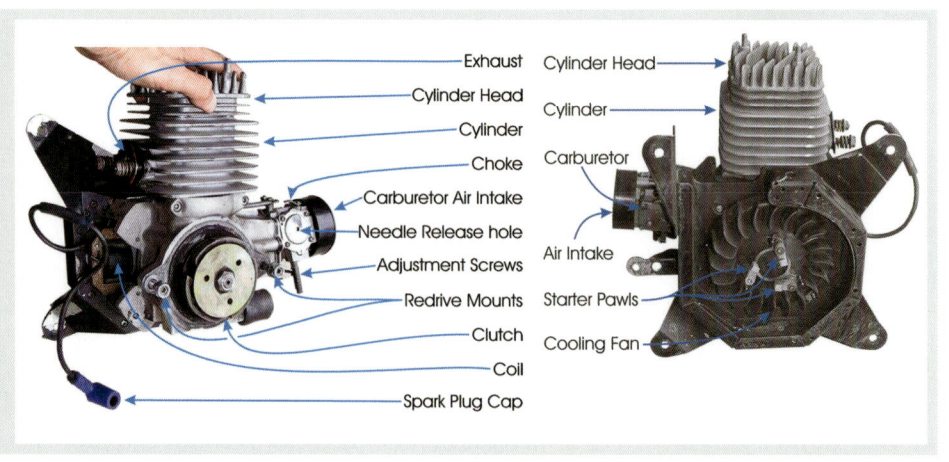

This pull starter assembly is what the starter pawls (see motor above) engage when you pull it. Springs hold them against the teeth, then when it starts, they ride over the back side of the teeth. At idle rpm, centripetal force pulls the pawls outward so they don't wear out riding on the teeth.

atomizing it. As the throttle valve is opened, more air gets sucked in, thus pulling in more fuel that gets mixed in to speed up the motor. All carbs have various adjustments and/or interchangeable parts designed to optimize operation based on elevation and temperature.

Two types of carburetors are commonly used that differ in how they deliver fuel to the venturi: *Float bowls* and *diaphragms*. As you can expect, each has advantages and disadvantages.

Float bowl carbs use a bowl and float just like those found in float bowl toilets. Fuel is delivered into the bowl through a valve. As the bowl fills up, a float inside rises to shut off incoming fuel which maintains a constant level. That offers a constant pressure at the pickup near the bowl's bottom. A higher float bowl causes a slightly richer mixture and vice-versa for a lower float bowl level.

Fuel is sucked up from the bowl's bottom through the *main jet* (an orifice) into the venturi past a tapered needle. How far that needle goes into the jet determines how much fuel flows. The needle is attached to a *slider* that opens up the air passageway, exposing more of the venturi opening. Opening the throttle opens the air passage and, by lifting the needle, increases fuel flow. More fuel/air makes more power.

Once properly set up, float bowl carburetors generally provide a somewhat smoother throttle response with fewer adjustments. Their drawback is that large changes in elevation (more than a few thousand feet) necessitate installing different jets. Thankfully that's a painless job. Higher elevations require smaller jets since less fuel is needed to mix with the thinner air. Other minor adjustments can be available either by raising or lowering the needle position or changing fixed air inlets for idle.

Float bowl carbs must be oriented right side up in order for the float to work properly. They must always maintain positive G-Loading, too, which isn't much of a problem given that your wing needs the same.

Membrane (or Diaphragm) carburetors work by filling a small expandable *metering chamber* with fuel then pulsing it into the venturi. This process uses changing crank case pressure and one-way valves within the carb. Fuel runs into the chamber when crank case pressure builds above a certain point, pushing against a needle valve held closed by spring pressure.

The design, originally intended for machines like chain saws, works at any orientation. The membrane expands as fuel comes in through the inlet needle so it matters little whether the carburetor is right side up or sideways. Their drawback is being finicky. Small particles have myriad nooks to lodge in and the membranes, springs and other small parts can get worn or damaged without being visibly obvious.

Most of these carbs include a *high speed* and a *low speed needle* valve to allow fine mixture adjustments for their respective realm. These needle valves alter how much fuel passes by—unscrew the needle and it opens up for a richer mixture.

Tuning a Membrane Carburetor

If you can get a hold of your motor's manual, use it. That's your best source for information. Barring that, this advice may help. If your motor strays too far from the recommended initial settings then there is probably a problem that tuning won't help. Consult the troubleshooting chart in chapter 12.

These basic guidelines apply to machines with membrane-type carbs having a low and a high mixture screw. The high screw primarily affects the mixture at high rpm while the low screw primarily affects the mixture at low rpm although they each have some affect throughout the throttle range.

First, a note about tuning. When a two-stroke motor is rich, it runs rough and sometimes fires every other stroke, that's called *4-cycling*. As you lean the mixture, it runs smoother and faster, eventually peaking then decreasing while remaining smooth. Further leaning makes it die. Whenever a needle valve controls fuel (as most do on membrane carburetors), screwing it in (turning clockwise) makes the fuel/air mixture leaner and unscrewing it makes the mixture richer.

Set the motor to its initial factory settings, strap it to something solid (tree, stout fence, stout friend, etc.) and start it. *Remember, more serious injuries occur from prop strikes than from flying.* It will start off lean and get richer as it warms up. After a minute or so, you're ready to begin the adjustments. Use increments of about an 1/8th of a turn when making changes.

Start by adjusting the low screw. Adjust it so the rpm peaks, then unscrew it (richen) slowly until the rpm drops a bit. It should remain smooth. If the motor quits when throttle is applied, richen the low screw further. If it coughs or runs rough when throttle is applied, then lean it a bit.

Now to the high screw. Throttle up to full power. Just like before—you want to adjust the high screw until the rpm peaks, then back off (richen) a bit, about 50 rpm. This is called being slightly "rich of peak." It sacrifices higher fuel flow for cooler running—a good trade since a lean mixture frequently overheats and seizes the motor. An excessively rich mixture makes carbon deposits on the cylinder head and spark plug. Unlike human health, motors are better rich than lean.

With the high screw adjusted we need to recheck the throttle response. Try adding power quickly—if it runs rough, lean the high screw just a bit. If it dies, richen the high screw slightly. You may need to repeat this whole process once or twice.

Higher elevations, above 3000 feet MSL, require leaning the mixtures. Once set, however, you should not have to adjust them until you change elevations again. Be especially careful to re-adjust them after going to a lower elevation because the

Float Bowl Carb

The float-bowl carburetor doesn't need much tuning. But when you go to a significantly different altitude, you may have to screw in a different *jet*, an orifice that the needle (inset) slides into. A bigger jet lets in more fuel which richens the overall mixture. At higher altitudes, a smaller jet is required.

On this carb, the barrel slides up and down which also regulates the amount of air that flows through. The tapered needle, which is attached to the barrel, lets more fuel in as the barrel lets more air through. This generally gives a smoother throttle response since it provides a gradual but immediate increase in both fuel and air as the throttle opens. Besides changing jets, the only adjustments are for idle—a large screw (1) sets the idle stop up or down and a small screw (2) can change the amount of air let in; screwing it in decreases airflow, making the mixture richer.

Fuel comes up from the bowl that stays about 3/4 full to provide constant pressure to the orifice. A float valve keeps the level just like a float-bowl toilet keeps the tank at a constant level.

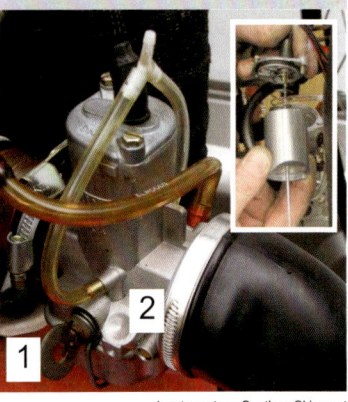

Inset courtesy SouthernSkies.net

Membrane carburetors (left) are the most common type on paramotors. They're lightweight and cheap.

A Walbro WG8 model is shown at left with its throttle and choke wide open. The choke is normally open but closed for starting since a cold motor needs more fuel than air.

The basic operating theory is that, as the throttle butterfly valve opens, airflow increases. That sucks more fuel out of the jets (openings). As the throttle opens more, airflow increases, sucking out more fuel and exposing extra jets, all in an effort to provide the motor's ideal mixture through its throttle range.

Most membrane carburetors have two circuits that control the fuel/air mixture for high and low power. On the one shown here, there is only one circuit—for idle (1). Screwing it in leans the idle mixture. The other rod (2) is a throttle stop that controls how far open the throttle is at idle. Screwing it in increases idle rpm by moving the throttle arm away.

The **reed valve** below, from a Black Devil motor, is simply a one-way valve that opens every time the piston draws in a new fuel/air charge. It's just like a heart valve.

The pointy part faces the cylinder and its reeds allow only inward airflow—they close if it tries to blow the other way.

The curved metal parts are strain relief—they make the reeds open around the curve thus preventing extra stress at the attachment points.

mixture will be lean which risks overheating.

Anytime a nettlesome problem eludes you, consider replacing the carburetor whole. They are inexpensive, install easily, and can save many, many hours of headache. If that's not the problem, then you've got a spare carburetor on hand.

Pop-off Pressure and Other Membrane Carburetor Issues

The membrane carb's metering chamber is like a float bowl. An inlet needle reacts to incoming fuel pressure and vacuum in the venturi to keep the chamber nearly full of fuel, ready to deliver it to the various throttle circuits. *Pop off pressure* is how many pounds of pressure it takes to lift the inlet needle against its spring. When fuel pressure pushes the needle off its seat, fuel flows into the fuel manifold (its "bowl").

If the inlet needle can't pop off the seat easily enough, fuel doesn't fill the chamber and the mixture will be too lean. If the spring is weak and the needle pops off too easily, excess fuel will make the motor run rich. Cutting the inlet needle's spring a bit shorter decreases the pop-off pressure and stretching it increases pop-off pressure. Only do this if you know exactly what you're doing, though.

Other little details can muck up the works too. Have a good fuel filter to keep unwanted debris from gumming things up. Carburetor rebuild kits are cheap and relatively easy to install. They usually replace the spring that determines pop-off pressure although that's rarely the problem. Rebuild kits will also replace the fuel pump membrane and a miscellany of gaskets and springs.

Reed Valves

Most modern two stroke motors employ reed valves (see sidebar above left) which increase efficiency. These stout one-way valves mount between the carburetor and motor. As the piston moves to compress the fuel/air mixture, the reed valve prevents that mixture from trying to go back into the carburetor. They do eventually wear out but are blessedly easy to replace.

Compression Release

Some motors come with a *compression release* (decompression) valve that makes pull starting easier. It works by venting the cylinder during compression. As soon as the motor fires, the valve closes. Manual versions must be reset after each start but are less prone to sticking open which renders the motor unable to start. Some motors use just a small internal hole that goes from the cylinder head to the crankcase—these must be cleaned out about every 10 to 20 hours.

Propeller & Reduction Drives

A propeller is a rotating wing, pitched steeply at the center and flattening out to a skinny tip. Since the tip is moving very fast, it's made to have a shallow angle to the air. Strangely, the most efficient propeller would have only one blade since that blade would have the least amount of interference from the other blade's wake. The extreme imbalance would, of course, be problematic.

Propeller choice dramatically effects a motor's performance—it's a case study in compromise. Matching the right prop to a particular motor is critical for harnessing the motor's full potential. Here are some of the trades:

- Long, skinny blades are better for thrust but are harder to make strong. Plus the tips must not be allowed to go near supersonic due to noise and drag.
- Lighter is better for rpm acceleration but doesn't wear well in the presence of abrasives (beach sand and gravel roadway are good examples).
- Fewer blades are more efficient but more blades allow bigger motors to have a smaller prop diameter.

Tip Speed, Noise and Performance

The only things that moves fast on a paramotor are its propeller tips—and they move over 350 mph. That's more than half the speed of sound, or Mach 0.5, where Mach 1.0 is the speed of sound. Any faster than that and loud, thrust-robbing supersonic shock waves start to form. Above Mach 0.6, (60% the speed of sound) the noise and drag increases dramatically with Mach 0.8 being a practical limit.

High rpm is doubly bad for noise since, besides creating stronger sound waves, their high pitch is more annoying. Given the same tip speed, a small prop at high rpm will sound louder than a large prop at low rpm.

The quietest combination for any motor is to spin the largest possible diameter prop (45 inches or more) at the slowest possible rpm. The large prop disk helps by having more clean air since it extends outward farther beyond the pilot's body.

Getting the RPM Right

Most two stroke motors get their best power at high rpm. A reduction drive lets designers extract maximum HP while keeping the prop at a more desirable (lower) rpm. Using gears or pulleys, a reduction drive lowers the output rpm by some ratio. If the input gear has three times as many teeth as the output gear then the ratio would be 3:1 (three to one). The motor would be spinning the small gear at 9000 rpm but the propeller, mounted to the large gear, would be going 3000 rpm. The extra weight and complexity of a reduction drive is well worth it.

Direct drive motors, where the prop is bolted to the crankshaft, are saddled with trying to balance the slower rpm needs of the prop with higher rpm needs of the motor. This noisy compromise provides small size in exchange for minimal thrust.

Since larger pistons typically get their horsepower at lower rpm, larger displace-

Reduction drives come in many ratios. The same housing is frequently used with different gears to give the user a choice. A larger ratio means the motor's high rpm will be converted to a lower prop rpm. The lower the prop rpm, the larger the prop can be.

The gears bathe continuously in gear oil or grease. The prop is connected to the large gear in a ratio determined by the relative tooth count of each gear. This reduction drive utilizes four bearings, two for each gear, to keep things running smoothly.

ment motors have a better chance of working as direct drives but would give up enormous thrust potential. Larger pistons are heavier, though, so most engines use a small piston that goes up and down *real* fast (high rpm). Small piston motors are lightweight but can't spin large props without a reduction drive.

For example, the Solo 210, a relatively large displacement motor (210 cc's), gets it's peak HP at around 6500 rpm. The Top 80, a small displacement motor (80 cc's), hits peak power at about 9500 rpm. The much-lighter Top 80, by virtue of its high rpm, can generate about 90% of the Solo's HP but there's no way the Top 80 could work as a direct drive.

Even for the slower spinning Solo 210, a direct drive arrangement doesn't work well. If you bolted a 48 inch prop directly to the solo and tried to get the motor running at 6500 rpm, the tip speed would be an impossible Mach 1.2. To get the tip speed manageable, a smaller prop must be used. Even with a 30 inch prop, the motor only achieves 5500 rpm—a noisy Mach .65 (noisy at that high an rpm). And it only gets about 80 pounds of thrust. That same motor, spinning a big prop through a reduction drive can easily put out a much-quieter 105 pounds of thrust.

One major prop maker recommends that wooden PPG propeller tips never exceed Mach 0.75 and should remain under Mach 0.6 for quietness. Mach 0.6 at 3000 rpm will sound quieter than Mach 0.6 at 5000 rpm (smaller prop). And the quietest motors spin large props (48 inches or more) with tip speeds of less than Mach 0.5. On those machines the prop will likely be quieter then the motor, intake, redrive or exhaust.

Where the Thrust Is

Most thrust comes from the outer half of the prop since it's moving the fastest and has the cleanest air. The blade gets thinner near it's tip which also makes it flex—mostly fore/aft but also some twist. Flexing forward does not affect thrust but could allow the prop to flex into the cage. A long prop will flex up to 2 inches (towards the cage) at full power. Twisting can reduce thrust and, if one blade twists more than the other, cause vibration since it will be pushing differently than the other blade(s).

Pitch – A Bite of Air

A higher pitch equates to a higher angle of attack on the blades. Pitch is commonly described as how far the propeller would travel forward during one revolution in a frictionless fluid. Propellers normally give two dimensions—length and pitch. So "48 by 23" means the prop is 48 inches long and would travel 23 inches forward during one revolution in that magic fluid. Since the outer portions of the propeller travel a greater distance, the blade angle steadily decreases towards the tip but the *pitch* is the same. For various reasons, props are made with pitch that varies along the blade, but it's commonly measured 75% out towards the tip.

Like a wing, more pitch means more lift (thrust) *up to a point*. Beyond that point it produces less thrust since the airflow separates early. But if the propeller is moving quickly forward, like on a fast airplane, then the angle of attack decreases. Some airplanes use *cruise* propellers which sacrifice slow speed thrust for more high-speed thrust. At paramotor speeds this effect is negligible—the difference between static thrust (no forward airspeed) and cruise thrust is too small to matter.

Calculating Tip Speed

If you're considering a different sized prop then you must take into account the ideal rpm and tip speed with respect to the speed of sound. Besides being loud, a lot of power is given up at high tip speeds.

Mach 1 is the speed of sound. It varies only by temperature and is faster in warmer air. At the standard temperature of 15°C (59°F) it is 761 mph.

To calculate tip speed as a mach number, use the following formula:

Tip Speed Mach = Prop rpm x prop diameter (in inches) / 256000. So a 48 inch prop spinning at 3000 rpm would have a tip speed of 0.56 Mach (56% the speed of sound).

Prop angle of attack is highest when the pilot is just standing there. As he accelerates forward, the angle of attack decreases because now the air is hitting the prop with some speed. Props can be designed with this in mind so that they actually produce slightly more thrust at 20 mph than they do with no speed although, for us, this difference is very small. In reality, our props are designed to maximize static thrust, especially since that's what gets measured in thrust comparisons.

Some propellers have special hubs that let the pilot set the pitch to better match the motor. They have mechanisms for insuring that each blade gets the same angle. The greatest benefit of this variable-pitch arrangement is to determine the best prop pitch for a particular motor and reduction drive combo.

Like wings, long skinny prop blades are generally more efficient but require more strength. That is why the more-expensive composite props enjoy some thrust advantage—they can be made skinnier while maintaining sufficient strength.

Designing For Thrust and Quietness

When putting together design goals there are many options regarding propeller and redrive selection. The **Lowest noise** means low tip speeds and low rpm. **Maximum thrust** means the most powerful motor you're willing to lift and the largest prop you can fit without having the tips exceed about Mach 0.75. That's still noisy but doesn't have too much sonic drag. The pitch can't be too high lest it lose efficiency. If you have more power than your maximum-radius two-blade prop can handle without over revving then you'll have to add more blades. More blades can be quieter since the smaller diameter means lower tip speeds.

Lets say, for example, that your motor turns out 25 hp at 8000 rpm and you can fit a 48 inch propeller. For maximum thrust, you want the prop rpm to get the blade tips to hit Mach 0.75. Calculations (download the spreadsheet from www.FootFlyer.com | Educational) show that the prop should spin at 3900 rpm which requires a reduction drive of about 2. At these tip speeds, it will be a screamer. Next you need to find a prop whose pitch allows the motor to accelerate to 8000. Too much pitch or too much prop area will bog down the motor without ever

Tip shape affects noise—curves are quieter. Even the flat end should be rounded. Makers of higher speed props sometimes angle back (rake) the tips to reduce noise. Our props aren't fast enough to benefit from the technique.

Left: These PPG props are getting ready for their final treatment by hand. Wood is well suited to this application although there is more variation in shape and strength than with carbon fiber props.

Chart: A lightweight prop is desirable because it spins up quicker. Weight towards the tips should be minimized the most.

> **Horsepower Revisited**
>
> Your motor's horsepower turns torque into propulsion through the prop. In level flight, the resulting push can itself be measured as horsepower using the airspeed. HP = Thrust (lbs) x Airspeed (mph) / 375.
>
> For example, cruising at 30 mph with your motor pushing out 100 pounds of thrust, is 8 HP. The motor is probably putting 14 HP into the prop to achieve that. The difference is due to propeller inefficiency. Normally, cruise thrust is far lower but, with the trimmers out and speedbar engaged, it could easily require that much push.

hitting 8000—that is called *being over-propped*. Too little pitch and it would *over-rev*, probably causing internal motor damage. If you find that the pitch must be over about 26 inches, then you'll want more or bigger blades. Two-blade props are more efficient than 3 bladers which are more efficient than 4 but more blades are better than having too much pitch.

Fatter, thicker blades can increase the effective push of a prop, and it may be quieter, but there's some cost in efficiency.

Materials: Rigidity and Strength

Propellers should be lightweight while being strong enough to handle normal loads. That means they break easily when striking something other than air such as poorly designed cages or careless human parts; it's far better to sacrifice the propeller. That is why most PPG props are made of lightweight wood or carbon fiber material that shatters relatively easily. Although the damage will *still* be severe, it will be *less* than if the prop were made of super strong, heavy material.

Frangible props also help prevent motor damage since they transfer less impact energy to the crankshaft and other rotating parts. In certified aircraft, a prop strike requires an engine teardown and inspection.

Being lightweight also helps the prop spin up faster, especially if the weight is concentrated close to the hub. Rotational inertia is based on both weight and its distance from the center. Five pounds, centrally concentrated, will accelerate quicker than that same weight spread out near the tips.

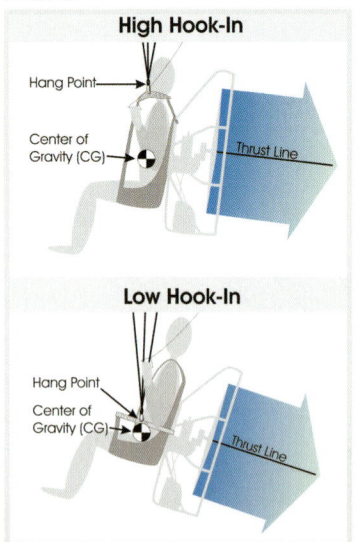

Balance

CG, Hang Point and Thrust Line

The pilot/motor center of gravity (CG) is the balance point. It's what determines how far it leans back in level flight. Machines with a heavy engine, set far aft, will have an aft CG that tends to tilt the pilot/motor back. A heavy pilot will offset the aft CG somewhat whereas a lightweight pilot would lean back even more.

Hang point is where the carabiners, or their extensions, connect to the harness (see Center of Gravity at left) or motor frame. It is also the point around which fore/aft motor swings occur—the *Pivot Point*. A thrust line above that point will mean that throttling up causes a forward tilt. Ideally, the thrust line will be on or below the pivot point. With the CG well below the pivot point there will be less swinging around in turbulence. Hang point has no effect on *wing* stability, it just affects how "busy" the ride feels.

Center of Gravity is the center of mass for the motor and pilot combined. Additionally, the motor pivots fore/aft around its hang points. If thrust acts above those hang points then you will tilt forward.

Although thrust always acts forward, you'll sometimes hear that "your thrust line is angled down" meaning that the air is blowing downward some amount.

Twisting Forces At Work

Several things conspire to cause turning when under power, most are by-products of torque but other powerful forces exist. Techniques for overcoming these are covered elsewhere (mostly in Chapter 12, page 116) but the easiest operational cure is decreasing power. That lessens (or eliminates) most problems induced or aggravated by torque and its cousins.

Effects of Torque

Spin a prop one way and the attached motor/pilot tries to spin the other way. It's just like drilling into wood where your hand is the pilot/motor and the prop is the drill bit. This basic torque effect causes one riser to lower and the other to rise which induces a weight-shift type turn force towards the lowered riser. But there are other, more significant, forces at work trying to turn you while under power.

Twisting effects are always more pronounced with more thrust. This incontrovertible physical relationship is one reason why more power is not always better. Two forces act around two axes: weight shift effects act around the propeller axis and riser twist forces act around the vertical axis, also known as yawing.

Weight shift turn. This would more accurately be called riser shift and gets wrongly blamed for most problems but it's actually relatively benign. Even a full weight-shift effect due to power will move the risers less than 2 inches (4 inch differential). That's counteracted rather easily with medium brake. This force does *not* try to twist the pilot left/right (yaw) in the risers.

Vertical axis twist is any force that tries to yaw the pilot's heading left or right. Offset thrust is one pronounced cause and, although not a product of torque directly, it happens when the motor's thrustline slides into an offset position, pushing on a shoulder. As you twist, the redirected thrust now pushes sideways, decreasing climb and causing a bank. That makes correction difficult since the only cure is to reduce thrust—very unintuitive at low altitude with minimal climb. We've seen pilots twist all the way around while clinging to full, or nearly full, throttle, inevitably ending with an expensive and painful crunch.

The most common torque related accident comes from vertical axis twist. The pilot launches and starts twisting to the left (to the right on geared redrives). Sideways thrust pushes him left, putting the wing in a right bank. Not wanting to go right he pulls left brake. As the twist increases, side force increases and resistance to twist decreases. With the thrust pushing leftward, climb suffers. He keeps the throttle mashed and pulls more left brake but can't overcome the sideways push. It's a confusing situation: he's pointing well left but in steepening right bank. Soon, increasing left brake spins the glider left. We call this *motor-induced lock-out* owing to its resemblance of the lock out that can happen while towing. There, a

Torque Causing Offset Thrust

Off-Center Thrust

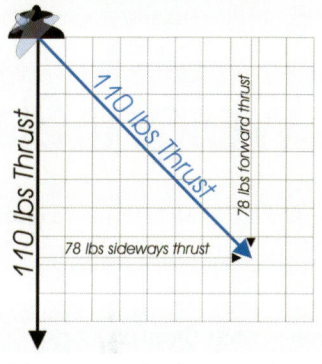

1. Torque can twist the motor into an offset position. It then pushes on your shoulder, causing you to twist in the risers and re-direct the thrust line.

2. Once twisted, the thrust is no longer helping but rather spends itself pushing sideways into an ever-increasing bank. The only immediate cure is reducing power. This is one of the strongest and most common causes of power-related crashes. Chapter 12 covers adjustments that can nearly eliminate the problem.

Torque's most obvious effect is the prop spinning in one direction trying to twist you in the other direction. A far more insidious effect is how it also causes a yaw (heading change). Riser tension is what opposes that. As you get into a steep climb, line tension decreases and you become more susceptible to riser twist. The only solution is immediately reducing power.

Many other factors, including wing selection, play a part in allowing torque to cause problems. In almost all cases, an experienced pilot or instructor can adjust out most twisting tendencies.

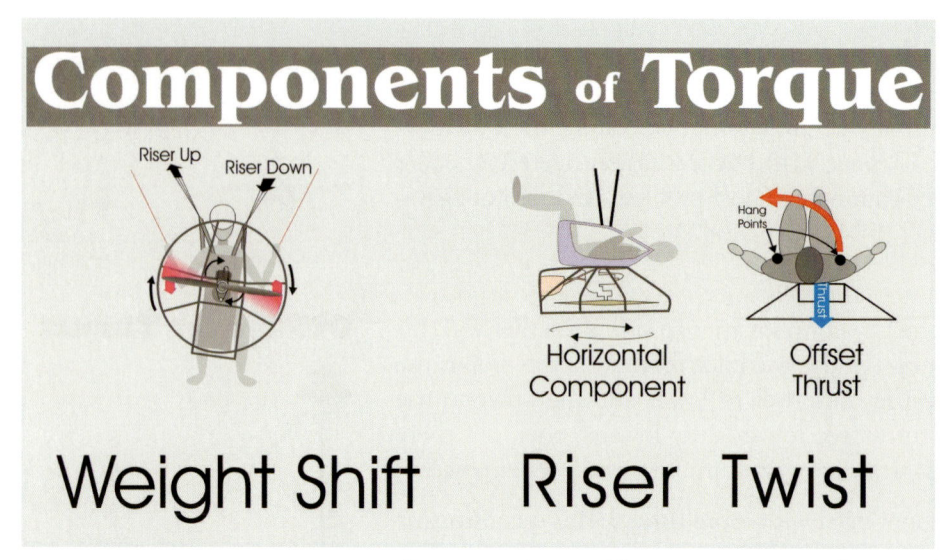

Components of Torque

Weight Shift
Riser Up / Riser Down

Riser Twist
Horizontal Component / Offset Thrust

These are the two basic ways a motor tries to turn you: Around the propeller axis (weight shift) or around the vertical axis (riser twist).

Weight Shift (Propeller Axis)

Any force that tries to make one riser go up and the other riser go down is causing a weight shift (riser shift) effect. It's what basic torque causes because the force acts around the propeller shaft (axis).

Vertical Axis Torque (Riser Twist)

This is the most powerful and dangerous aspect of torque. It's the sum of forces trying to twist you left or right under the risers.

The two primary causes are horizontal component of propeller torque and offset thrust.

Making matters worse is that, as the bank steepens, the lines get less loaded. As the lines unload there is less resistance to riser twist. Trying to stop the bank with brakes usually spins the glider.

The only solution when this happens in flight is reducing power.

pilot who turns away from the towline doesn't have enough brake pressure to counteract the towline's sideways pull. The only cure for this, once in flight, is to reduce power and, if necessary, land.

Horizontal Component of Torque is another cause of twist and it affects motors that are leaned back a lot. Picture the motor leaned all the way back like in the illustration above-left where the thrust line is pointing straight down. Throttling up in that scenario would create an immediate and powerful twisting in the risers. Obviously that's extreme but illustrates what's happening and why more lean-back makes the effect stronger. If the pilot is sitting entirely erect (thrust line horizontal) then this force doesn't exist at all.

Angled Thrust. If the motor hangs off the harness angled left or right then it will push sideways.

Unfortunately, once in flight, the *only* solution for this is reducing power which will almost undoubtedly result in a landing since you'll already have given up power by being twisted. But landing under control is a lot better than crashing from a spin.

Gyroscopic Precession

Spinning objects tends to remain in their plane of rotation. More spin, or more mass, or more spread-out mass, and the more they want to stay put. Also, force applied to a spinning object, perpendicular to its plane of rotation, will act 90° away in the direction of spin (See Experiment below). This effect can be a factor during launch when you try to change the plane of the spinning prop, such as when you lean back at liftoff. Leaning back is the same as pushing backwards at the top of the prop plane; it will try to twist you left on a belt drive machine.

This force isn't a big factor for us but it does happen at the worst time during takeoff. Try this sometime: with the motor on your back, run it up while leaned forward then quickly stand up straight. On a belt-drive machine you'll feel a momentary left twist (right twist on a gear drive). Once you've stopped moving, the force goes away.

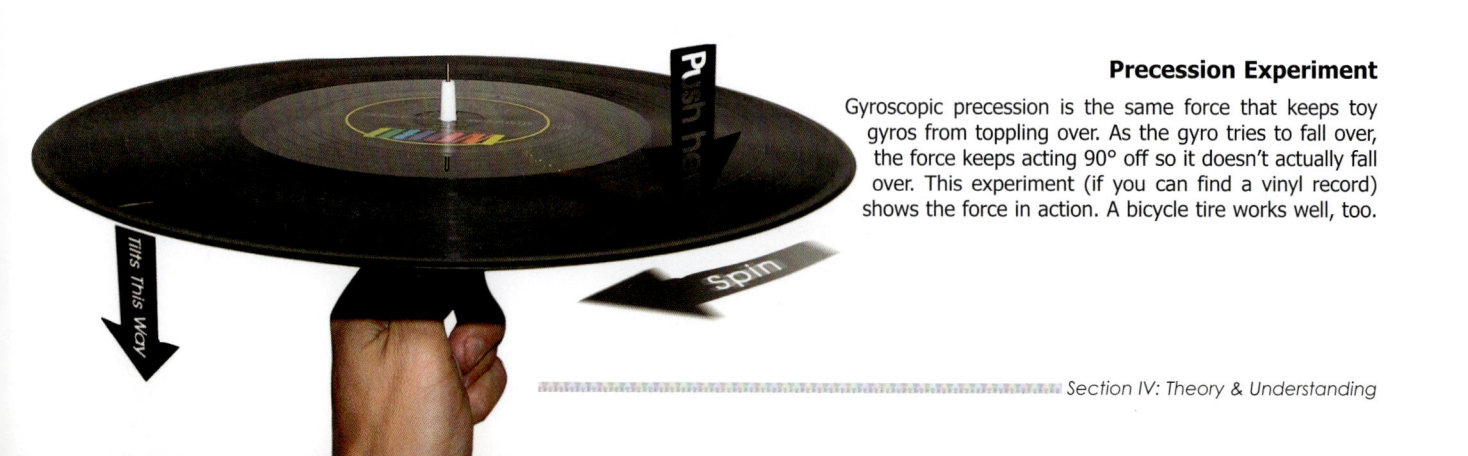

Precession Experiment

Gyroscopic precession is the same force that keeps toy gyros from toppling over. As the gyro tries to fall over, the force keeps acting 90° off so it doesn't actually fall over. This experiment (if you can find a vinyl record) shows the force in action. A bicycle tire works well, too.

Rotational Mass Acceleration

If you've felt your car tilt when stomping on the gas while parked then you've noticed rotational mass acceleration. Any motor has a rotating mass—the crankshaft, flywheel, belts, propeller, etc. When that mass is accelerated, it wants to twist whatever is causing the acceleration in the opposite direction. However, the effect goes completely away once the motor is up to speed. It is only present during rpm *acceleration*. On belt-driven machines, the propeller spins in the same direction as the motor. On geared machines, the prop spins opposite to the motor's rotating mass so the effect is muted. Even then, the prop has far greater rotational inertia than the motor's rotating parts.

Sales people who claim that gear-reduction machines eliminate torque are engaged in subterfuge or ignorance. The torque difference between the two is *only* present during spin-up. In other words, that brief period when accelerating from idle to take-off power. Otherwise torque is *identical* in force albeit opposite in direction. At most there is some negligible difference in gyroscopic effects between the two types.

Gyroscopic Precession happens only when the pilot tries to tilt. That's usually when he leans for launch or goes back to vertical. Quickly tilting forward, for example, is like a force is pushing forward on the cage top (1). Precession causes that push to appear (be felt) 90° away (2), which would twist him to the right. It is brief and the strength depends on rpm, prop mass, and amount/rate of tilt change.

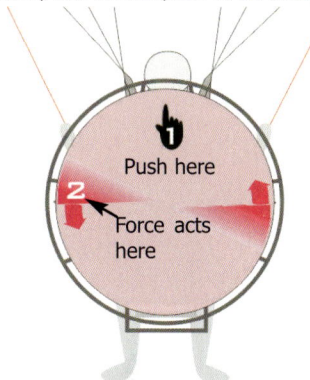

Countering Offset Thrust

(Red) Other torque forces causing some left twist.

Offset thrust aggravating the existing torque turn tendency.

Offset thrust (green) cancelling out existing torque turn tendency.

This illustrates one method to counteract offset thrust. Adjust your harness so the motor is pushing on the *other* shoulder. If you always twist to the left, move your motor so that it's trying to twist you right. The two tendencies will cancel each other out to some degree.

Transverse Flow or Uneven Thrust

Having part of the airflow blocked by the pilot/motor may induce a slight force left or right at the prop (up or down too but that would be less likely). The farther the prop disk is away from the hang points, the more pronounced the effect. Gyroscopic precession can aggravate this force by making thrust at the top act on the side, causing a twisting force.

Loaded Riser Twist

If the wing goes right while you're running, the left riser gets more heavily loaded, partially unloading the right riser which now doesn't hold back the motor as well. You twist around the loaded left riser.

This is the same force that causes a left-right swinging back and forth during cruise on some machines, primarily high hook-in models under smaller wings.

Wing-Enabled Riser Twist

Wing shape and lines play a large part in allowing or preventing riser twist. While the motor always *causes* the twisting force, the wing and lines work to prevent it. Short fat wings do better than others in this regard than long skinny ones.

Loaded Riser Twist

On launch, when the wing goes right, the left riser loads up, making the motor try to push you around to the left. While flying this left yaw increases a right bank.

On belt drive machines it aggravates other left yawing forces and may be enough to spin the pilot all the way around. So avoid lifting off with the wing to your right. *After* liftoff, a shallow right turn is fine, even preferable.

It is quite simple: Angle the lines away from the pilot more and the wing will be more resistant to riser twist. Skinny wings (high aspect ratio) and long lines aggravate the problem. That leaves high-performance wings most susceptible since they are usually long and skinny with longer lines.

P-Factor

P-Factor, also called *Asymmetric Blade Thrust*, is what happens whenever the propeller disk is not hitting the air head-on. It results from one blade having more angle than the other due to the tilted relative wind. With the motor angled back (as is normal), the descending blade takes a bigger bite of air and pulls slightly harder.

Its effect is minor since it depends on the difference between forward airspeed (not much for us) and blade rpm. Plus, it acts opposite to most other twisting forces but we're just too slow for it to be noticed.

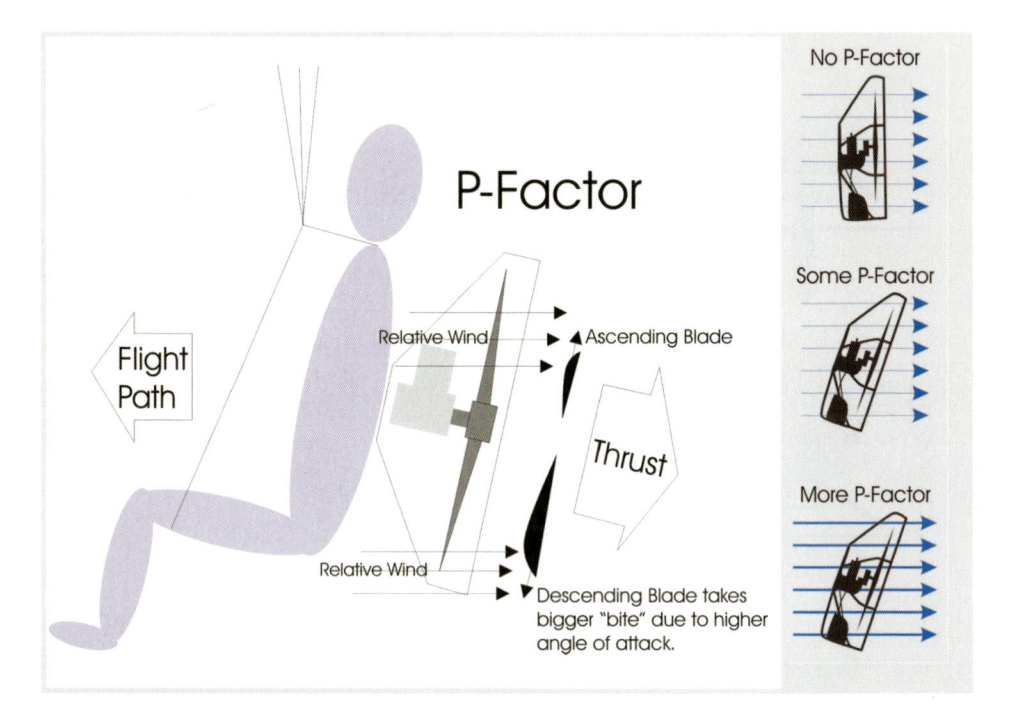

Weather & Wind

CHAPTER 24

You don't have to be a meteorologist to manage a useful understanding of weather. Grasping *micro*meteorology, however, is quite helpful and that is our focus. Entire books are devoted to atmospheric lore, a complicated puzzle that academia is piecing together. This chapter covers what's more useful to a paramotor pilot.

Most weather predictions revolve around the "big picture," stuff that can be left for the pros—frontal passage, strong winds, precipitation, etc. We're not interested in taking on such violence with our uniquely susceptible wings. However, on days where basically benign weather is forecast, knowledge of the little stuff will be invaluable. Some basics on the big stuff are provided for completeness. Dennis Pagen's "Understanding the Sky" covers this topic in far more detail.

Using Forecasts

You've learned the basics in Chapter 7 and should know how to get the forecasts and make basic decisions on when it's appropriate to fly. These extra details will help you interpret them and better understand what's going on. We can now delve deeper into the details: What happens around this one cumulus cloud? How does air behave in the presence of hills? What happens from the surface up to 100 feet, and so on. Use professional weather people for the big picture and this knowledge for applying it to our smaller scale.

A forecast can be trusted more if what they expected earlier is becoming reality *right now*. That shows the weather service grasps what's going on atmospherically. If the current weather doesn't match what was forecast to be the current weather, their model is no longer valid—watch out. Did they expect a south wind and its actually from the northwest? If so, be suspicious of their remaining predictions.

Sensing Weather

While out west one time, I was motoring along a 20 foot ridge that ran parallel to, and below, a bigger mountain. I saw a chance to experiment; to see if my understanding was accurate.

Waning sunlight meant the ground was cooling, which in turn was cooling the adjacent air. Indeed, the bottom few feet was now 4° to 5°F cooler than at 50 feet. The ridge had channels carved out where water drained to the lower level. I wondered—shouldn't the cool air try to drain down those channels, too, and spill out at the bottom of the ridge? It was otherwise calm so I decided to find out.

I flew parallel along the ridge's bottom where the culverts drained and, sure enough, as I passed along each culvert, felt a noticeable spill of air. It worked just as published!

Principles

Peeling back the onion of atmospheric understanding can water the eyes. Deep physics underpin the rules but here are some fundamentals to help understand our most important micrometeorology.

- Hot air rises, cool air sinks and then flows downhill to the lowest point, just like water seeks its lowest point.
- Air gets thinner with altitude and its pressure drops about 1 inch of mercury per 1000 feet. Sea level is the deepest reach in an ocean of air where, just like in deep water, pressure is greatest.
- *Radiant cooling* is where the earth looses heat into space just like a radiant heater can make your hands warm without warming the air. Solar heating is the warming part, where sunlight heats the land.
- *Conduction* is when terrain warms (or cools) the overlying air and *convection* is when heat is transferred by warm air moving into an area of cold air (or vice versa).
- The earth is always radiating heat, day and night; more with clear skies since clouds reflect infrared energy back down. During the day, sunlight adds more heat than radiant cooling subtracts. Heating starts at sunrise and quickly (in about a half hour) overcomes radiant cooling. Sun-facing hills or dark, dry spots warm up first.
- In a standard atmosphere (see below), air at higher altitudes is colder than at lower altitudes. The rate that it gets cooler is the *lapse rate*.
- If you expand a parcel of air (increase its volume), without adding or removing heat, its pressure and temperature drops. That's called *adiabatic* cooling because there's no external exchange of heat. The reverse happens when you compress air such as when it descends. So, rising air cools at the *Adiabatic Lapse Rate*. Moisture complicates matters. The condensing process releases heat so air, rising as clouds, will be condensing out its moisture and releasing heat. That slows the rate at which the parcel cools as it rises. It's the *Wet Adiabatic Lapse Rate*.
- Warm air can hold more water vapor (an invisible gas) then cold air. Cooling the air beyond what it can hold forces its load of water vapor to change state (condense) into very fine droplets (liquid) better known as clouds or fog. The temperature where this occurs is the *dew point*.

Standard Atmosphere

A standard atmosphere is meteorology's common point of reference. It is also used by aircraft makers (and others) to base performance numbers on.

The International Standard Atmosphere (ISA) is 0% humidity, 59°F (15°C) and has a pressure of 29.92 inches of mercury (Hg) at sea level. For every 1000 feet of height, the temperature decreases by 3.5°F (2°C) which is the standard *lapse rate,* and the pressure falls by about 1 inch of mercury (Hg). So at 3000 feet, you would expect the pressure to be 26.92 inches Hg and the temperature to be 10.5°F cooler or 48.5°F.

Daily Cycles

Depending on your local terrain, there is an underlying daily cycle that represents the norm. Experienced local pilots know it best which is why they can provide such valuable input. This cycle can be as powerful as it is predictable. Some locations have very specific places and times when flying is very dangerous owing to these daily cycles.

Since the cycle is driven by sunlight, clouds usually reduce its intensity. But clouds and pressure systems may point to some greater atmospheric change that will overpower the daily cycle. Be extra leery at such times.

Radiation Cycle

Overnight, the ground radiates heat into space, cooling off the land. The land in turn, cools the air just above. That increasingly chilled (and therefore heavier) air tries to sink, finding its way into low spots. The cooling ground is like an ice cube—it just keeps cooling the air nearby. If the air cools enough, some of its water vapor condenses into fog or onto the cold surfaces as dew. This is why low spots get foggy first—cool air flows downhill. All this cooling inverts the normal atmospheric temperature gradient. Instead of being cooler aloft, a cooler layer along the ground forms, so by morning the coldest air is at the surface. At some point up higher (maybe only a few hundred feet) there is a significant increase in temperature called an *inversion*. Above that, the normal temperature gradient of cooling with altitude resumes.

Sunrise is typically a very stable time—cool air sits in low places, with no desire to go anywhere. The sun starts heating the land right away while heat loss from radiation continues. Soon, around a half-hour past sunrise, the sun's heating wins out and temperatures begin to rise. Dry, dark spots heat up first and the air above them tries to rise. Hills that face sunward will heat up even more in the direct rays. Soon these warmer areas become the day's nascent thermals. They are joined by many others as the day wears on, mixing and warming the atmosphere.

At sunrise, there is typically an inversion—warmer air sits above cool surface air. Sunrise starts warming the ground which starts warming the air just above. Morning thermals start rising but stop when they hit the inversion air.

As the sun continues heating up the surface, thermals get hotter until they are warmer than even the overlying inversion air.

By mid-day, a more normal lapse rate exists: warm at the surface, cooling with altitude. If enough moisture is present, cumulus clouds will form atop thermals as the rising air cools to its dewpoint.

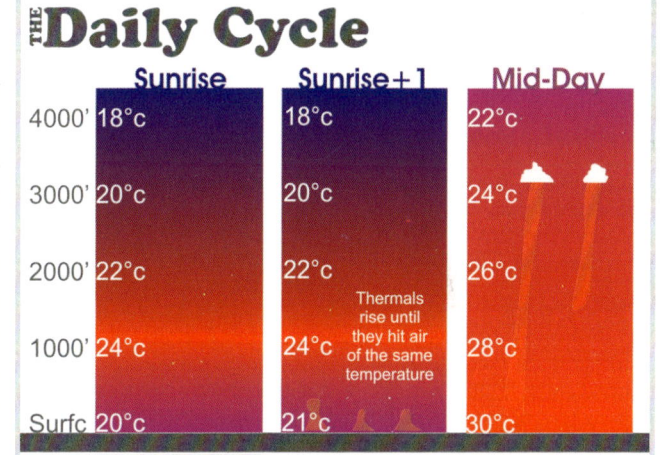

The Daily Cycle

Altitude	Sunrise	Sunrise + 1	Mid-Day
4000'	18°c	18°c	22°c
3000'	20°c	20°c	24°c
2000'	22°c	22°c	26°c
1000'	24°c	24°c	28°c
Surfc	20°c	21°c	30°c

Thermals rise until they hit air of the same temperature.

As air rises, it expands and cools. As long as it stays warmer than the surrounding air, it will rise. Eventually the cooling due to expansion exceeds the atmosphere's normal lapse rate and the upward movement stops. With enough moisture present, it will form clouds when cooled to the dew point.

As the day wears on, thermals get stronger and go higher. Cloud bases go up too. Solar heating peaks at noon but this process peaks a couple hours later. Late afternoon's decreasing sun angle finally takes its toll and the process wanes although cloud bases keep rising. Thermal strength can easily be dangerous up to within a couple hours of sunset depending on location.

Flatland

In flat areas there is little beyond the daily cycle and large scale changes. Afternoons can be dangerously turbulent during periods of instability so stick with the first and last 3 hours of sunlight, especially in the summer.

Typical days start out smooth with nearly calm winds in the morning. These can be wonderful times to fly—smooth and pristine. The "dog days of summer" describe the flatlander's heyday—calm mornings and evenings with sultry afternoons of light breezes.

If the wind aloft is very strong, expect it to get bumpy quickly. Wind and thermals don't mix well. You'll know soon after launch what the wind is doing. In fact, it's not difficult to climb up into a perfectly smooth wind that matches or exceeds your airspeed. You wind up parked over one location (or moving backwards) while facing into the wind. It's strange and can happen pretty low. This is a wind gradient and the smoothness will be short lived once sunlight churns up the air.

Hilly

Surprisingly intense micro meteorology happens when air interacts with hills—even before the sun comes up. That's why flying in mountainous areas warrants so much attention. As air cools it tries to flow downhill, sometimes becoming a torrent. Like an avalanche, it gathers speed, causing rapid wind changes. Mountain passes, or anywhere that geographic constrictions squeeze the flow, intensity increases. Its just like a wide, mellow river that narrows to rapids in tight places.

Hills also interfere with larger scale movements and mask winds. If the air is forced to go up or around a geographic protrusion you can expect turbulence in the lee (downwind of it). Be careful if launching in a valley with calm air but a known wind aloft—up near the level of the mountain tops could be a wild ride. And that turbulence *can* come down well below the peak's height.

Coastal

The beauty of a beach is in its smooth predictability. Usually by 11 AM the warming land is sucking air in a steady *sea breeze* (on shore) that makes launching painless. Free of thermal turbulence, this airflow from the water is usually very smooth. Most of the time the wind continues well past sunset. The cycle reverses at night when the land cools and a *land breeze* (off-shore) sets in with wind blowing out to sea.

One risk is when a prevailing off-shore wind gets overcome by the sea breeze. A few miles inland the wind is blowing out to sea but, on the beach, it's coming on shore. Somewhere in the middle these two airflows meet in a potentially turbulent *convergence zone*. Besides turbulence, if you're flying beachside when the prevailing off-shore breeze wins the pushing contest, you could be blown out to sea.

Digging Deeper: State Change

A significant impact on weather is the *state* change of water—going from ice to liquid to gas. Its lowest energy level is ice. If you add heat (energy) to ice it will warm up at a constant rate until it gets to the melting point (32°F). It will remain at that temperature while absorbing the heat until changing to the new state at which point it continues warming.

For example, put a 10°F block of ice in a 300°F oven and stick a thermometer in the ice. The ice will warm gradually until hits the melting point (32°F) where it momentarily stops warming as it changes from ice to water. The difference in energy between the two states is called *latent heat*. So immediately after changing from 32°F ice to 32°F water it is said to have gained some latent heat energy. The water will now continue warming at a steady rate until it reaches the boiling point (212°F) where it will again stop warming to change state from a liquid to a gas. Then the water vapor will continue warming.

Sublimation is where water vapor comes directly from ice. Evaporation is where liquid water changes to gas even though it's below the boiling point. As it evaporates, it cools the surface from which it evaporated. All evaporative coolant systems rely on this principal. The higher the temperatures, the more sublimation or evaporation happens.

The reverse happens during cooling. As water vapor cools, it does so evenly until becoming a liquid (like cloud). As it makes the change, it resists further cooling for a period of time until the state has fully changed.

These physics drive the formation of severe weather—giving teeth to a process that would otherwise peter out. It helps thunderstorms reach momentous heights and powers a hurricane's horrendous winds. If lifted air is cooled quickly, it would soon become the same temperature as the surrounding air and lose its buoyancy. The process would die out. But water vapor will hold it's temperature while rising because it needs to make that state change. Its buoyancy will remain as it slowly changes state from a vapor to liquid. This phenomenon happens on smaller scales, too, and pilots call it *cloud suck*, where the cloud formation itself is driving the lift instead of the original thermal. Air mixing with the cooler surrounding air is what prevents it from shooting out of control.

Desert

Deserts are beautiful in their own dry, rugged way. And they spawn the strongest, meanest thermals in the country—making for a wild daily cycle that can be much more dramatic than in wetter areas. It happens because the sun's rays don't get used up in evaporation—they go right into heating the ground.

One indicator of thermal strength is the difference in temperature from morning low to afternoon high—something deserts have to extreme.

These factors combine to make mid-day desert flying a spin of the roulette wheel.

Dust devils are the visible manifestation of a violent phenomenon that causes a rapid swirl of air as thermals surge upwards. These little tornadoes may also be occurring up high but would be invisible.

Flying the desert is beautiful in the mornings and evenings, but deserves great respect during mid-day.

Yearly Cycle

Many yearly cycles exist besides the obvious temperature swings: The monsoons of Tucson and Phoenix, the dry period of Portland, hurricane season, Santa Ana winds, etc. Some of these involve winds erupting with little warning. Long term local knowledge can be a life saver—if you don't know a local pilot, seek one out from the nearest airport. Most are happy to answer such questions as "I'm gonna be flying an ultralight in the local area, is there any significant seasonal weather I should know about?"

The most prevalent and relevant cycle, though, is thermal intensity. It follows the length of day where thermals are strongest in summer and weakest in winter. That makes sense—their driving force is sunshine and summer solstice packs many more heating hours and at a more direct angle than winter's shortest day.

The difference can be a dramatic. Long hours of direct sunlight heat up the ground, boiling its atmospheric soup into a sporty cauldron. The short days of winter get only a few hours of low-angle light leaving many smooth but chilly days to fly. Winter even tames the deserts enormously.

All About Thermals

A lot has been written on this topic but anyone who has watched a 1970's lava lamp (pictured at right) knows the process: sun-warmed patches of ground heat the air immediately above, making it want to rise. At some point this warm air blob punches through the overlying cooler air to begin ascending. Air rushes in below to fill the vacated, rising mass. Free flyers ride these updrafts to sometimes great heights. Most motor pilots avoid them and their related turbulence. Some motor pilots use them for soaring and simply accept the increased risk of collapses.

Thriving thermals need the right type of atmosphere. Primarily that means a steady decrease in temperature with altitude (lapse rate), direct sunlight and a heatable surface. An overcast will douse the process dramatically which is why you can frequently fly safely all day long on cloudy days (as long as no rain is expected) even in the middle of summer.

> **⚠ Caution!**
> If a dust devil is present, don't even be hooked into your glider. Kiting is equally dangerous under such conditions.

1. If you see this coming your way, unclip! Then pack up. If you're airborne, stay well away but land when your LZ is clear.

2. Brian Smith is chasing the swirling cauldron of a moderately strong but long-lasting dust devil in Albuquerque, NM with an anemometer. The overall winds that day were light but, even after several minutes, this was likely spinning air at over 30 MPH.

3. A lava lamp demonstrates thermal action nicely.

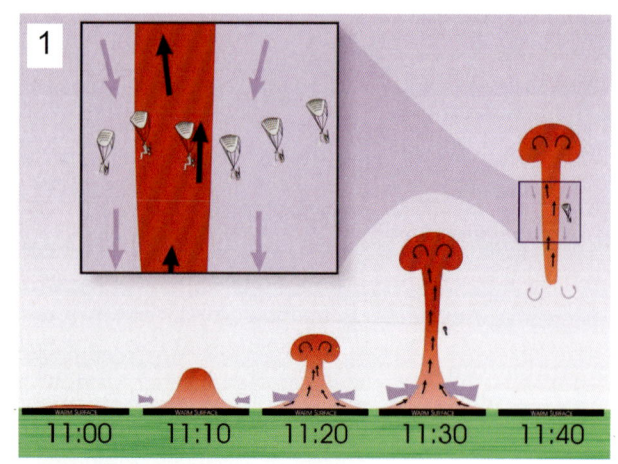

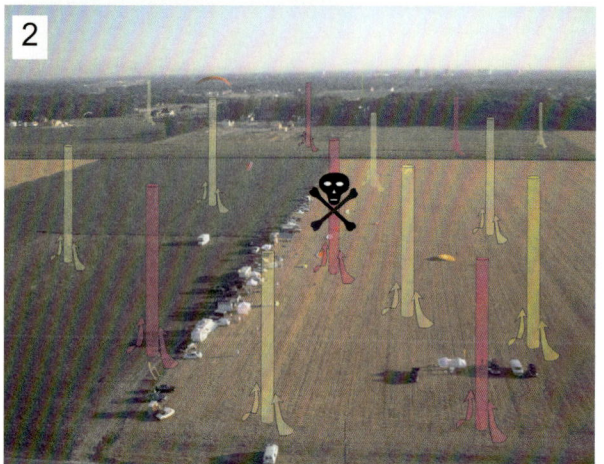

Telling Thermal Intensity from the Ground

A good way to predict thermal turbulence from the ground is by wind gusts. Stand in one place or just be observant while setting up. Calm conditions on the ground portend calm air above while gusty conditions suggest lumpy air aloft. Sharp gusts, where the wind speed or direction changes rapidly, indicate sharper, more dangerous thermals.

Flying on a day with rapid gusts from 5-12 mph could be deadly whereas soft changes of the same magnitude might be manageable. Direction must be watched too—if it goes from east at 12 mph (the wind is coming *from* the east) and suddenly switches to west at 5—that's bad.

Thermals and strong winds don't mix. Gusts from mechanical turbulence add to energetic thermals to make potentially dangerous air.

Dust devils show that, even away from the swirl itself, the atmosphere is particularly turbulent. Any day brewing sufficiently vigorous turbulence to trigger dust devils is brewing nasty conditions.

Where Thermals Thrive

Cross country soaring pilots know where to find the "biggest air"—a description for powerful thermals that can carry pilots skyward at well over a 1000 fpm. Associated turbulence can play havoc on a paraglider, causing collapses. The immediate spiral that spurts from such a collapse may require immediate and correct action or a reserve toss. Every year, it seems, at least one experienced free flyer succumbs to an unpleasant fate in "big air."

Dryer air breeds more dramatic thermals. Arid regions consistently give soaring pilots the highest altitude gains and longest soaring flights.

The *lifted index* is an atmospheric measurement that tells whether a parcel of lifted air will be warmer or colder than its surroundings after reaching a certain height. Negative numbers mean the parcel is warmer—it wants to accelerate upwards. That's unstable. It has to do with the atmosphere's lapse rate and moisture content. In an atmosphere that gets cold quickly as you climb, a lifted parcel of air would tend to remain warmer and therefore keep rising. Moist air rises more readily because water vapor is lighter than dry air. Lifted index charts can be found on the Internet although you'll need additional study to really know how to use them.

1. Here is a fairly typical thermal and what it can do when a paraglider flies through it. As the pilot exits, downward moving air makes him susceptible to a frontal collapse (see Chapter 18).

2. This illustrates the distribution of thermals on a bright, sunny day, especially in the summer. Yellow represents moderate thermals, red represents strong ones, and the skull represents dangerous versions that would make bad shapes of your paraglider. How many of these dangerous thermals exist depend on many factors, but the distribution is such that you could fly for a long time in mid-day and simply be lucky enough to miss them all. Or you could hit one the first time out on such a day.

Summer afternoon's invisible fury should not to be treated lightly.

Clouds

The highest clouds, *cirrus* (or *cirriform*), are wispy affairs comprised of ice crystals. They form above 25,000 feet and can sometimes spread out from jet contrails. Mid-level clouds live between about 8000 and 25,000 feet. They're usually prefaced with the word *alto* (e.g. *altocumulus* and *altostratus*) and mostly only concern our micro view for their value in blocking out thermal-producing sunshine.

Stratiform

Stratus clouds are the flat, boring, frequently drizzly, clouds that form mostly on weekends. Their flat, gray appearance generally indicates stable conditions with little vertical movement. When they drop rain, they're called nimbostratus.

Smooth and frequently layered, stratus clouds are usually associated with fairly benign weather although they *can* conceal significant ugliness. They frequently follow fronts and occupy large swaths of low pressure areas. The two worst worries of flying under stratus clouds are rain and imbedded thunderstorms. However, if neither is forecast, then all-day flying may be possible. By blocking the sun's most direct heating rays, they block most of the thermal-induced turbulence, leaving good, but bleak, motoring conditions (and lousy soaring conditions).

Stratus clouds must not be ignored when the forecast includes rain showers. It's hard to tell where the rain showers are and, with thicker clouds, it's easy to get rained on by surprise. If you see a darkening in the sky then it's most likely because of embedded cumulus clouds which indicate coming trouble.

Stratus clouds that form around severe weather are particularly dangerous in that they conceal where the really bad weather is. That is why its important to know the forecast and only fly on forecasted dry days.

Cumuliform

When vertical development gets involved the term *cumulo* (having a heaped on appearance) gets appended or preppended to cloud names. Cumulus clouds that form mostly on nice summer afternoons cap thermals and indicate bumpy conditions. Any cloud with more then about 3000 feet of vertical development can produce rain. Once a cloud produces rain it earns the *nimbus* moniker: Cumulonimbus is the most violent example and is what thunderstorms come from.

The wispy beginnings of cumulus clouds typically form about 3 hours after sunrise and a few thousand feet high. If a steady breeze has picked up within a couple hours of sunrise *and* cumulus start popping, expect sporty air. Dry air could be just as sporty but without the cumulus clouds.

You must pay very careful attention to cumuliform clouds. What goes up must come down and big cumulus clouds can bring them down with vigor, cause strong downdrafts that spread well away from the ground in a *gust front (see below)*. Little ones are felt all the time, both from popping thermals sucking in air, and from sinking air spreading out. But bigger cumulus clouds or, even worse, lines of them can cause gust fronts tens of miles away.

Be leery of wandering too close to large cumulus clouds. The cloud formation process itself generates extra lift which increases as you near the base. This *cloud suck* can easily overpower a paraglider pilot's ability to descend. Getting caught in such lift is a chilling experience that some pilots have not survived. Depending on the cloud's size, it can easily take you to heights where the temperature is

Stratiform clouds usually indicate benign conditions. Be sure you can see everything though, they sometimes hide cumulus clouds.

Christine Doughty is flying over a low scattered to broken layer in smooth air. She had good ground contact, good visibility and was able to stay clear of clouds. Had she been above 1200' AGL, she would have needed more cloud clearance (see Chapter 9 for all the airspace details).

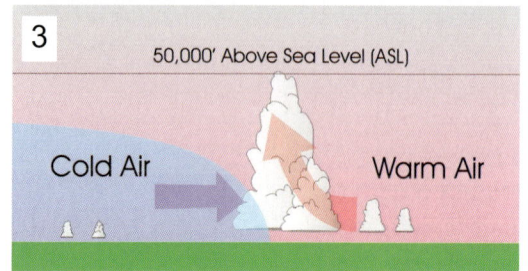

well below freezing and the air is too thin to keep you conscious. And, of course, it's extremely violent.

Thunderstorms

Nature's fury is unleashed in the majestic and deadly thunderstorm. These mammoth storms, covered in Chapter 7, play havoc with winds over a broad area.

They come in two types: Airmass and frontal. Airmass thunderstorms are usually scattered buildups on otherwise nice but muggy summer afternoons. They are typically not as severe. Normally airmass storms germinate in aging high pressure areas with lots of moisture and some instability in the air.

Frontal storms come in lines and are associated with fronts, usually cold fronts. They produce the worst weather including tornadoes.

When an atmosphere is unstable enough to produce thunderstorms it is no place for a paramotor. In most cases, two hours after a storm passes is enough to consider flying as long as there are no more storms (or cumulonimbus clouds) anticipated. First, find out what the weather is doing elsewhere before taking off.

Gust fronts are probably the thunderstorm's most dangerous fallout. Rain pulls cold air downward until it hits the ground and spreads out in a fast-moving, turbulent boil that can extend many miles from the storm. Although technically related only to thunderstorms, gust fronts happen in different degrees from other causes, too.

1. An old but appropriate axiom.
2. The zoom makes this menacing storm appear much closer then it actually is. However, thunderstorm wrath can extend tens of miles beyond the cloud itself.
3. A cold front spawning thunderstorms.

Fronts

These really belong to *macro*meteorology which we don't cover in great detail. Fronts are the boundaries between air masses of different temperatures. They get moved around by high level winds, frequently swirling around low pressure areas. Low pressure areas arise from many causes including high level winds, called *jet streams*, which can suck air upwards under some conditions. Low-level air tries to flow inward to fill the low pressure and gets turned by Coriolis effect (the result of a spinning world)—thus the low spins, dragging fronts along with it.

Cold fronts are the most violent. Cold air wedges under a warm air mass ahead, lifting it quickly and creating lines of cumulonastiness. These fronts spawn the worst of all thunderstorms because they combine several powerful forces. Fortunately, they are usually fast moving—doing their damage and moving on.

Warm fronts ride over retreating cooler air and are more typically wet and mellow. Be careful for they do sometimes harbor thunderstorms in the stratiform mass of clouds. Unfortunately, they tend to linger and can muck up the weather for quite some time.

Lots of bad weather happens near fronts. If there is a forecast for frontal passage, even if no rain or clouds are present, be very wary of flying. Check out the wind forecast—there can easily be a dangerous and dry wind shift planned that you should avoid. If you're out on the field, unusual, especially sudden, temperature changes should lead to suspicion. For example, a day that gets to 80°F by noon but then forecasts a temperature drop to 70°F by afternoon would likely have a wind shift. That is a dry cold front—you would want to avoid flying until after the wind shifted since it could easily be violent.

Getting Weather Info

Chapter 7 covers acquiring weather through Flight Service. But a good way to improve your awareness of what's happening aloft is get the weather at locations around your site, especially upwind of it. It's not foolproof, and it doesn't work as well in mountainous regions, but it's a good start.

Be aware that the surface wind is not a good indication of where the weather is coming from. Look at the clouds and see which way they're moving. Different cloud layers may well be moving different directions; you're most interested in the low to mid-level layers (between 3000 and 10,000 feet).

TV is a reasonable source for weather information but the internet is much better; you can customize what you're looking for and probably get more detail on your particular area. Sites come and go but you can find links to good ones on www.FootFlyer.com.

Turbulence from Wind

There are some important differences in what pilots frequently lump into the term *rotor*. Knowing what those differences could be a lifesaver.

Mechanical turbulence is the general bumpiness that extends downwind from anything that sticks up into a wind, up to 20 times the obstacle's height. The resultant eddies drift with the wind and spread upward above the height of the causing obstacle. Turbulence extends further downstream as wind speed picks up. So, too, does intensity and quite dramatically—a 15 mph wind will have over double the intensity of a 10 mph wind.

Rotor itself is a stationary swirl of air that spins immediately downwind of the causing obstruction. It can be very powerful and produce incredibly strong shear since it's so well organized. Rotors don't always form—it depends on the obstruction's shape, wind speed and wind gradients.

Wind shadow is the calm that exists just downwind, and usually at the bottom, of an obstruction. It's what you feel when seeking shelter from the wind behind a building (or other obstruction). It extends about to the height of the obstruction. Picture your paraglider moving from that stillness out into the free airstream. That would be bumpy.

In a light wind, less than about 5 mph, mechanical turbulence and rotor are almost non existent—flying next to obstructions poses little problem.

1. A localized front near Phoenix, AZ. Fortunately, the dust makes it quite visible. These happen on various scales from a few miles to over a hundred miles and the results are always dangerous.

2. Another type of localized front that was spawned by a line of cumulus clouds. Virga (rain that evaporates before reaching the ground) was an early indication of dangerous gusts that were soon to hit the ground.

Also, avoid dark bottomed clouds, they indicate there's a lot of vertical development above with potential turbulence.

Testing It Out

One summer afternoon, thunderstorms were coming through like waves. It had been a while since my last flight and I felt the need for air. So, just after a nasty storm passed by, I drove to my nearest field to see what conditions were like.

The air was perfectly still.

Unfortunately, there on the horizon was an early darkening of the western sky. Oh but it was so calm—and quiet. Alas, my sensible side prevailed and I decided against it.

By the time I got back inside, only 15 minutes later, an enormous gust front erupted—trees swayed and the house groaned.

It would not have been a good time to be aloft.

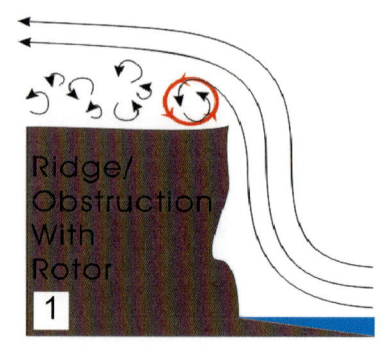

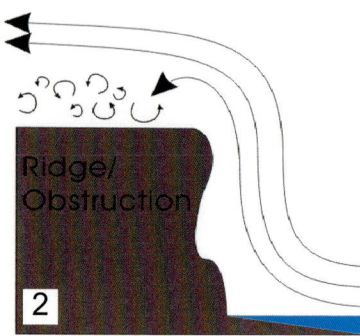

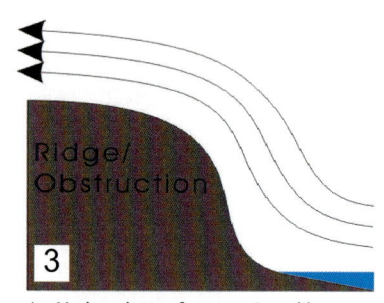

Mountain Waves

When strong wind blows perpendicular to a mountain range, there may be mountain wave downwind of the range. It can extend many thousands of feet above the mountain but our real concern is what happens below the wave action—rotor. Besides the main rotor, powerful eddies cause turbulence that even sailplanes try to avoid. It's no place for a paraglider. Rotor extends from just below the mountain's crest down to a few hundred feet AGL, sometimes to the surface.

Terrain and Flow

Whenever air is squeezed between two hills, its speed will pick up. Just like where a river narrows and the water speeds up. In a craft as slow as ours, that could stop all forward motion. Fortunately for power pilots, we can throttle up and climb away from this *venturi effect*.

When air is forced up over obstructions it causes lift just upwind of the obstruction. Ridge lift, as its called, remains fairly smooth as long as there are no thermals in it and the pilot stays upwind or over the causing obstruction. The obstruction's shape determines the strength of the lift—a smooth, steep rise in the face of a steady wind creates the most lift. Terrain can also act like an airfoil where the air goes over the top then back down the back side, sticking to the surface and creating sink. For example, flying just downwind of a tree line can create enough sink to make climbing difficult or impossible.

1. Air has lots of mass. Just like over an airfoil, it won't make sharp bends. So when you envision the airflow past obstructions, expect turbulence and dramatic changes in the area of those bends. This shows that the air cannot stick and creates a standing rotor.

2. The lip of this ridge is sharp enough to create turbulence but not enough to create a standing rotor.

3. This smooth ridge would be perfect for soaring. If you stand near the lip of a sharp edge, you'll feel very little wind on your face. Setting up to launch there would be difficult at best. But on a curvy ridge, like #3, the wind flows steadily along the smoother surface—a much easier launch proposition.

> **Digging Deeper: Highs And Lows**
>
> Areas of high and low pressure resemble swells on the ocean but on a very, very large scale, spanning hundreds of miles. The troughs are low pressure and the peaks are high pressure. Air moves, in some ways, like a big slinky; piling up both vertically and horizontally. For example, it's possible to have the air pile up high in the atmosphere. It will, of course, start falling down but air has a lot of mass and that will take time.
>
> Other forces act to lift air and pile it up in different ways. For example, the jet stream has influence. It can start moving air upwards into the jet, creating a low pressure area.
>
> A hurricane is a good example of another force that forms a low pressure area. Warm water feeds a group of thunderstorms that create enormous lifting force. They're like a bunch of vacuum cleaners, accelerating air upwards and spitting it out the top. Air flows into this continuous low pressure and gets turned by the Coriolis effect (like the marble that you roll inward on a rotating record). Rotation keeps pressure low because the air can't fill in the center low. That's why hurricanes cannot form on the equator—there's nothing that causes them to rotate. You get low pressure areas at the equator, but air is able to fill them in fairly quickly since it's not deflected into a spin.
>
> Why do lows get the bad rap? Almost by definition, the air in a low is being sucked (or lifted) upwards, frequently by jetstream action. The motion is too slow to feel from the ground or even in flight, but is enough to cool the air which tends to form clouds. Air in a low pressure area gets concentrated since it's flowing inward and upward. Conservation of energy means that when the air is deflected inward, toward the low, it wants to speed up. Just like the ballerina that tucks her body in to speed up. But high pressure air is generally descending and heading outward. The ballerina is spreading out, sinking and slowing down.

Roots: Our History

CHAPTER 25

It's a short history. Powered paragliding grew from paragliding which itself started in the early 1980's. Paramotors have several other interesting roots, not all contributing to the same tree, but rather growing in an underbrush of ultralight flying that prospered simultaneously.

Frenchman Didier Eymin has done photo work using a paramotor all over the world. He is pictured here taking off with one his first machines in the early 1990's.

Below: Phil Russman takes wing on one of the earliest hang gliders, before motors were being added.

Parasailing

You will soon tire of hearing your sport called parasailing. After all, you *ride* under a parasail, you *pilot* a PPG. Not that there's anything wrong with parasailing; it's a fun activity to be sure, but is essentially a brainless amusement for the parasailer. A necessarily stable platform gives the rider almost no control which is why they can whisk unsuspecting tourists up in reasonable safety. Don't try that with a powered paraglider!

Our sport has no origins in parasailing, a sport that branched off from the round canopies of sport parachuting. They still use modified rounds for stability's sake.

Hang Gliding & Ultralighting

Development of hang gliders started in earnest during the mid 1970's after a few enterprising individuals adopted Francis Rogallo's design, dreamt up way back in 1948. Rogallo was scheming to safely return spacecraft through the atmosphere while enterprising 1970's earthmen applied his designs to create bamboo gliders. Eventually, professional manufacturers entered the fray with real soaring craft. Efficiency and safety drove improvements into fixed wing variants that eventually sported motors. Strangely (and fortunately), the FAA did little about this grass roots effort as the pilots stayed mostly away from populated areas and only carried one person who bore the brunt of their then-significant risk. They remained, literally and figuratively, "below the radar."

As weight increased, wheels were added and Ultralighting was born. Flex wing Rogallos got longer, skinnier wings and became capable soaring craft. The proliferating rigid wing configurations all but took over the powered segment.

Sport Parachuting

Pilots first used cloth to soften their intentional falls in the late 1700's when balloons and buildings were the only way up. But until 1961 there was no control of the canopy—it just broke the fall and sometimes the legs. Then the *Paracommander* came along with holes in the back that streamed enough air backwards to gain minimal forward speed. At last the parachutist could influence his destiny. At about the same time, a Rogallo shaped parachute was devised but never really explored.

The big development came in 1964 with the square Ram-Air parachute. This design formed the underpinnings of modern paragliding.

These sport parachutists could fly almost like a glider but with very limited glide performance. French mountain climbers learned to launch their canopies from the slopes, a much quicker way down from scaled heights. Others saw an opportunity and began to improve the wings, getting the sport well established in Europe by 1986. Modern paragliding came to Joe Public when manufacturers actually started producing wings for the masses by about 1988.

Efficiency gains earned it the name paragliding and enterprising European pilots started adding power. Large motors were required to overcome the drag penalty of early wings. These had necessarily high hang points to balance the heavy motors.

As wings became more efficient, the motors got smaller and lighter, requiring less thrust. By 1989 the Pagojet, using a 3-cylinder radial engine, became the first production unit available to the public. Not that the masses flocked to it, but at least they had the opportunity. By 1991 a number of European manufacturers were building machines and the US market was soon to follow.

Lost Lineage

An evolutionary aside to the paraglider story is that of David Barish, an airline pilot turned aeronautical engineer turned parachute designer. Like Rogallo, he was striving for a spacecraft re-entry method as mankind raced moonward in 1965. He and Rogallo only met once at NASA but their designs both shared some commonality—both sported about a 4 to 1 glide ratio and both were abandoned by the space agency.

But Barish, an avid and accomplished skier, took his single-surface paraglider to the slopes – scooting/flying down the hills at no more than about 30 feet high. He toured the country's finest ski sites in the summer of 1966, demonstrating his new-fangled version of "downhill" with an apparently cool reception; it seems the pub-

Alan Chuculate is braving the -20°F Alaskan air to try his 11-cell Harley. It was an English parascending canopy built in about 1987 to carry two people.

Efficiency has come a long way; it took Alan 500 feet of altitude loss to do one 360° turn.

The shape was not very distant from it's sport parachuting origins although it did have unsheathed lines that are now common on competition wings. But it had a *lot* of lines, far more than on modern gliders.

Mike Byrne about to launch on a 5 minute flight with his home-grown, Konig-powered early paramotor in 1980. He could only fly for 5 minutes because the 100-pound motor hung from him, not the harness. That got uncomfortable in a hurry!

The rightmost picture was him flying the same wing but with wheels.

lic just wasn't ready yet.

He even tried using a motor with his creation but must not have found an adequate power system that he could lift; there is no record of any motorized flights with his wing.

Powering Up

Englishman Mike Byrne should probably be credited as the first to foot launch a paramotor. He first flew in the fall of 1979 and, by the summer of 1980, was intriguing airshow and television audiences around England. The 95-pound home-built unit used a 3-cylinder Konig motor and hung from his back. It had no seat and probably limited appeal. Flights lasted about 5 minutes since the motor's weight hung from his back and he hung from the harness. Ouch. He was also probably the first to name the craft, along with his brother Johnny, calling it a paramotor.

It obviously didn't catch on and Mike moved to bigger, faster craft, mostly with wheels. No more hanging from a harness: the privates could only stand so much.

Digging Deeper: Fan Man

James Miller had a passion for both flight and for freedom—paragliding gave his desire wings. He took to it quickly, learning from a friend before instruction was widely available. Residents of Juneau, Alaska spotted him frequently flying from Mt. Roberts near his home. He knew the value of training, though, and sought out advanced instruction in flying and towing, from Alan Chuculate, one of the sport's early instructors and certainly one of very few in Alaska.

Alan noted that besides "Having a lot of energy," James was enthusiastic, motivated, and his previous experience made him an easy student. James earned his USHPA (then USHGA) P2 paraglider and tow ratings in the fall of 1990 but he wanted to add the additional freedom of power. For that he would have to leave Alaska.

James' date with fate and fame was set when he traveled to Las Vegas in 1992. He hooked up with Patrick Sugrue who had recently started importing the LaMouette paramotor. After a few days of instruction he set out on his own flying with power.

Having flown for some time in Alaska, he found the desert conditions quite different. The dry, high-powered thermals caused frequent wing collapses and other maladies. Alan remembers getting a call from James with two questions: "How do I recover from collapses?" and "How do I thermal to stay up?"

The night before his famous flight, James called his brother Eric: "I'm going to do something big tomorrow," he said. Sure enough, On Nov 6, 1993, two minutes into round 7 of the Evander Holyfield-Riddick Bowe heavyweight championship, James Miller landed his PPG in the ring. His mark was etched in history. It cost him a beating to unconsciousness by the crowd, 4 days in jail and a $4000 fine. A year later he made headlines again by landing on the roof of Buckingham Palace, naked.

His irreverence and free spirit bubbled up in English court just before being deported. On hearing the judge ban him permanently from England, he asked "How about my ashes, can they come back?" She said no.

He eventually gave his life back to the mountains he loved so much and had flown over. Health problems made the strapping 37 year old James Jarrett Miller unable to care for himself; in 2002 he took his own life in a wilderness area near his home.

Thanks to Mike Coppock of the Anchorage Press for information used in this story.

The PPG Bible: A Complete Guide and Reference

Barndt Bartig was another pioneer, foot launching from level ground in 1981. But he kept it secret until the first commercial paramotor, the German-built PagoJet, came out in 1987. It too, had a 3-cylinder Konig engine. Right behind him was Jet Pocket (also known as Air Plum), the first French company to manufacture and commercialize a foot launched paramotor starting in 1988, quickly followed by the Propulsar whose owner then joined up with Guy Leon Dufour of Adventure. There are several pilots in Italy who also started making personal units as early as 1987, including the past owner of Vitorazzi and Diego of Miniplane.

The U.S. saw its first paramotor when Patrick Sugrue flew one in 1988. He imported the LaMouette brand and his most notorious customer was James Miller.

Unfortunately, the real introduction of paramotoring to America came during a boxing re-match in November, 1993. Evander Holyfield was avenging his prior year loss to Riddick Bowe under an open-air arena in Las Vegas. Punches weren't the only thing flying. In the 7th round, James Miller descended with his paramotor into the ring, stopping the flight and then getting pummeled by an angry crowd.

Performance Improvements over time

Most of the technology has matured quite a bit, slowing the rate of improvement in both wings and motors. Gear gets better, knowledge improves, and training generally gets more available—all good progressions.

Advances frequently in spurts when some new development lifts the entire sector. Hopefully electric motors will be next. Manufactures employ various innovations and the good ones propagate. Copying is rampant because the sport's small size makes patent efforts unduly expensive and difficult to enforce.

Motor technology mostly comes from go-cart racing and motor scooters although purpose built motors have started to evolve. Economies of scale mean that development in other areas is more likely to drive innovation in our sport since paramotor production runs are way too small compared to the thousands built for larger industries. A few manufacturers do specialize in paramotors but improvements are incremental. Power to weight ratio, which measures power per pound, is the best measure of a new motor's performance.

It's hard for a company to invest heavily into an endeavor with so little payoff. Fortunately, enthusiasts come along periodically and pour themselves into a project without need for large profits. We all benefit from their vision.

Our future is bright, with weight coming down, performance improving, and, even more importantly, with knowledge increasing. We have a lot to look forward to.

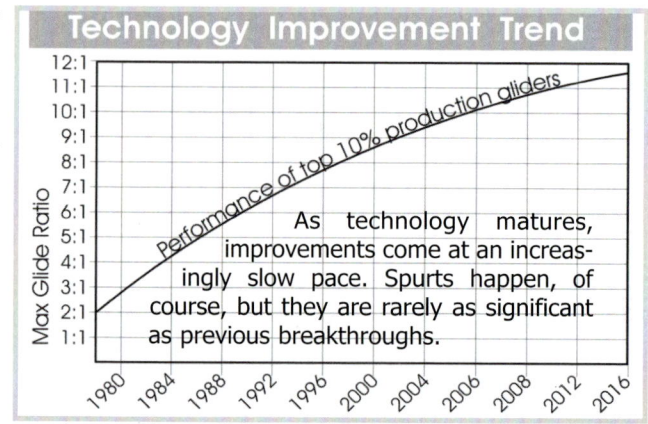

1. The powered parachute (PPC) came first. It isn't really part of our lineage but is related.

In the beginning, wings were glorified air-plows and motors were heavy—they needed to be on wheels. As wings grew more efficient, resourceful pilots strapped tiny engines upon their backs. The paramotor was born.

The difference between PPC's and PPG's is mostly weight. A PPG trike is, by definition, a PPG. Functionally, the biggest distinguishing factor is that a PPG has hand controls and PPC's have foot controls.

Anything over about 120 pounds (trike and motor) was probably designed from the outset to be wheel launched. Some definitions try to dig into attachments and other minutia but the essence is that it was intended to be foot launched.

Most PPC's are *way* heavier (over 200 lbs) and have proportionally more power.

2. The Electric PPG will be an ideal solution when batteries and/or fuel cells get better. Fortunately, improvements continue apace. Ecliptic cars will hopefully drive battery technology in both performance and price, eventually trickling their benefits down to us.

Technology Improvement Trend — Performance of top 10% production gliders. As technology matures, improvements come at an increasingly slow pace. Spurts happen, of course, but they are rarely as significant as previous breakthroughs.

Section V

Choosing Gear

Section V

Choosing Gear

Other Ultralight Types

Weight Shift / Hang Glider Trike

Powered Parachute

3-Axis Control

If you're just starting out, review Chapter 1 before even thinking about gear. Use your instructor's guidance to select the right wing and motor. If nobody is distributing your prospective purchase, you may be asking for trouble. Exceptions exist, mostly for newly introduced products by reputable companies, but those models must be purchased with extreme care and only by experienced, risk tolerant types with mechanical acumen.

Who to Talk to

The fact that you're reading this book is a great sign; you want to be informed. Hopefully these words get to you before some shady salesman does. The Internet is rife with them.

Your best resource is a trusted instructor or, absent that, experienced pilots who have nothing to sell. Seek out pilots who have flown a variety of wings and motors. A great approach is going to a fly-in to see what's out there. Not only will you *see* the various offerings, but you'll also see what people like and find out why. There will be a broad group of folks to talk with and pilots love talking about their gear!

Sales pitches are just that, pitches, and a few of them are out in left field. There is no perfect machine or wing, but rather many trade-offs.

Appearances

We all want stuff that looks good, but remember that your life depends on your choice—prioritize accordingly. The best looking gear on the ground pales next to the ugly duckling that will get you airborne. If you can't fly it, looks won't count for much.

Cost

No, it's not cheap. While this is one of the least expensive ways into the air, it's still aviation. Requirements for lightweight reliability drive up the cost as does low sales volume. It's necessary that sellers and instructors make profits; their success is good for all of us, and for the sport in general.

Cost will certainly be a factor for most people and you should know what you're getting into. Always price gear with any training packages that might be included.

If avoiding the middleman means skipping the local instructor or school, that's usually a bad trade-off. In the long run, local support can be well worth paying a bit extra to your local dealer.

Realize, too, that costs will continue. Breaking a prop is not terribly uncommon and costs 3% to 6% of your motor's new purchase price. Wings wear out, too; after about 300-500 hours of sun time they should be replaced.

Test Flying

Be extremely careful when trying out new gear—it can be dangerously different. Have an instructor present who teaches on that equipment to sort out its idiosyncrasies. They *all* have idiosyncrasies. See Chapter 19 for how to make the process safer.

The Wing

CHAPTER 26

The correct choice of a wing will have a profound effect on your safety, success and enjoyment of powered paragliding. It's not the place to skimp or buy on a whim. Like cars, there is no "best" car, and there is a huge selection with lots of good choices. Be extremely leery of aggressive "mine is the best!" pitchmen. The more aggressive they are, the less likely they will have your best interests at heart.

Ease of Launch

A wing should be easy to launch in the conditions you expect to fly. After all, if you can't get it airborne, it's useless. This is even more true for infrequent flyers who won't have opportunity to master different techniques. Our toughest condition is, by far, the no-wind footlaunch, especially in soft sand, high density altitude, or rough surface. It's a situation that screams for an easy inflating wing.

Lightweight wings excel at inflating easily but there's more to it than weight. Design is at least as important. The downside is that they are a bit less durable, tend to overfly the pilot easier, and get blown around easier on smooth surfaces. If you always fly in a steady breeze then inflation characteristics are less important. Smaller wings inflate quite a bit easier because there's less pull-back. Of course you must run faster after getting them up.

If you're accomplished at launching, or don't mind the steeper learning curve, then a more difficult wing should be a trade-off for some other redeeming quality such as speed or soarability. Some launch-challenged wings may actually be reasonably easy with the right technique, but you should find out before buying.

Wings with a high aspect ratio, usually higher performance soaring models, are more challenging because they tend to fall off to one side more often during slug-

Wing Loading

Calculate placard wing loadings by dividing the maximum weight into the wing's flat area. Compare the different models to see which ones are already planned to be flown heavy.

The models below represent three different wing loadings. The Compra would probably be a high-performance glider (possibly not certified) and the Super Floater more geared to soaring. You wouldn't want to fly the Compra overweight since it's high wing loading suggests it will already be heavily loaded. Nor would you want to fly the Supra Floater anywhere near its minimum weight.

Wing Model	Flat Area	Placard Max Wt.	Wing Loading /m²
Compra (uncert)	20 m²	100kg/220#	5.0kg/11.0#
Sportifly II	25 m²	100kg/220#	4.0kg/ 8.8#
SuperFloater	28 m²	100kg/220#	3.5kg/ 7.8#

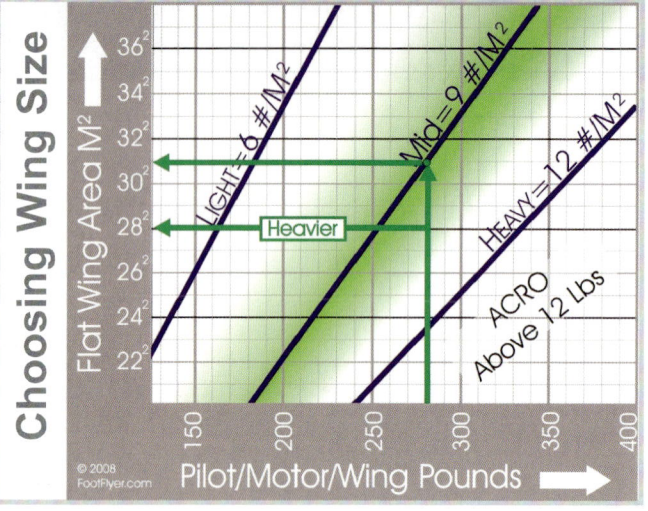

In the example above, a 200 pound pilot has a 60 pound motor and allows 20 pounds for the wing's weight. So he enters the chart at 280 pounds, going up to the "Mid" line of 9 Lbs per m² then left to the wing size shown. That's a good starting point, 31 m². Going down to a 28 m² wing would still be in the green range but would be sportier and faster since it's a heavier wing loading.

gish inflations. And their longer lines take more time to get overhead. They tend to over-fly you during windy inflations or gusts, and are "slippery" while kiting. Once they start sliding off to the side or yawing, it takes more effort to get them centered again. Reflex wings also tend to be a bit more sluggish on inflation. If you're on a firm, level surface these are manageable, but will be less so on a hot, soft sand beach with nary a dribble of breeze.

Don't forget that age slows down even the best inflaters due to line shrinkage and increasing porosity.

Size

Heavier pilot/motor combinations need bigger wings. Every wing has a recommended weight range (*placard weight*) and, except on higher elevation launches, it's generally better to be on the heavy side. Most instructors consider being up to 10% overweight to be OK; it will be 1) sportier, 2) faster, 3) easier to inflate, 4) less likely to enter Parachutal Stall, and 5) more resistant to collapses. On the down side it will: 1) take slightly more power to fly level, 2) sink faster, 3) require more running during takeoff and landing and, 4) be more dramatic if a collapse does happen.

Size is listed two ways: Flat and projected. Flat is the more common measure—the wing stretched out flat on the ground. Projected is the area made by an inflated wing's shadow and averages about 15% smaller than flat area.

An important measurement is wing loading. Certified gliders are tested through their placarded weight ranges but some are more heavily loaded than others. Divide the placarded maximum weight of your wing by its flat area then compare with the chart at left. Being overweight on an already-heavy range may be excessive. Aerobatic wings are normally very heavily loaded.

Using the Wing Loading chart, look at the Compra's wing loading. At 220 Lbs (placard max weight) it's 11 Lbs/m²; that's a lot. Be leery of loadings past about 12 Lbs/m²—speeds are high and handling can be extremely sensitive. The Choosing Wing Size graph gives a good idea of desirable wing sizes but, as always, go with your instructor's recommendation.

Reflex

Reflex airfoils allow higher speeds with greater safety than regular paragliders (see Chapter 22 for more on the airfoil), but they must be flown properly. For example, using brakes while accelerated decreases collapse resistance and, while trimmed slow, the speedbar must be avoided—a common practice on regular wings.

Regardless of wing type, collapses at higher speed will be more dramatic.

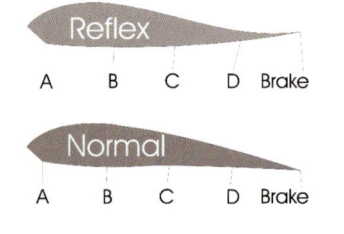

Some wings come with varying amounts of reflex. More reflex means more speed and collapse resistance in trade for efficiency, inflation ease and handling although improvements continue to lessen these penalties. For example, lightweight fabric makes inflation easier (as it does on any wing) at some sacrifice in durability.

Full reflex models offer an enormous usable speed range—usable because of solid collapse resistance at those higher speeds. That also makes them ideal for many types of competition.

Although they'll require more fuel per hour they typically don't burn any more fuel per *mile*. So if you're going cross country, especially with a headwind, reflex wings shine.

These technologies are always improving so pay close attention to the wing's manual which condenses test pilot experience nicely. The march from early reflex models with horrible handling and slothful inflation has made dramatic strides.

Glide and Sink Rate

The lower the sink rate, the less power you'll need to stay up. The higher the glide ratio the farther you'll go on a gallon of gas. And because the speed range is so small, wings with a low sink rate will likely have a good glide ratio.

Overall, wings with a better glide ratio will be easier to land because you'll have more flare authority after the initial pull for landing. The glide ratio given on specifications should be taken with a grain of salt—there seems to be some fudging on those numbers, especially on wings intended for motoring.

Stability

Stability, described in Chapter 22, usually refers to collapse resistance when talking about wings as opposed to its more technical meaning of resistance to upset.

Beginner-type certified wings are generally more collapse resistant, and recover more predictably, than advanced wings. Of course they must be flown within their placarded weight range to maintain that benefit. The tradeoff is that "stable" models can be boring for pilots later on. But for new students with uncertain responses, these "boring" wings are *dramatically* safer.

Beginner gliders tend to have fewer cells which helps expedite recovery from upsets and longer brake travel to reduce the likelihood of pilot-induced-oscillation.

Handling

Responsiveness to brake input is the biggest element of handling. Being heavy on a wing makes it more responsive. Here are other items that affect handling:

- **Brakes**. The brakes should be in a comfortable position and tug the trailing edge within a few inches of pull. Besides feistier control response, it insures full brake travel for landing. When brake application crumples the tip slightly, it confers more responsiveness and dive tendency which some pilots like.
- **Linearity**. The response should be incremental throughout the range with no significant dead spots or unexpected reactions. A little pull does a little and more pull does proportionally more.

Reflex Steering

For most reflex gliders, using brakes when fully reflexed (speedbar applied and trimmers fast) is undesirable. So designers employ various steering methods to get around this problem including the two methods shown below.

1. This approach uses a double action "2D" brake system where the pilot can engage either the center trailing edge, the tip trailing edge, or both based on how he pulls the brakes.

2. This method uses two toggles, one inside the other, where the smaller toggle controls the tips while the main toggle controls all the brake lines as usual. Pulling the main handle pulls the small one as well.

Nearly all reflex gliders employ some form of tip steering, frequently with separate toggles, as shown here in orange.

Each style will have its own advantages and disadvantages but one reigning truth is that pilots must first become extremely comfortable with any steering variant before doing aggressive maneuvering, especially down low.

- **Dive**. All wings descend faster when banked, but some tend to enter a dive easier than others. Having short lines makes this more noticeable. It can be a dangerous characteristic for the ham-fisted but a joy to the master. All wings can be turned flat, but some models require more pilot finesse to do so (see Chapter 16 on coordinated turns).

- **Heaviness** is how hard you must pull to achieve the result. Tandem wings flown with two people are going to feel heavy. Small wings will tend to have higher pressure, but are more responsive, reacting quickly to even short pulls.

Some wings are "twitchy," meaning they move around a lot in turbulence. If you're into active flying this may be okay. These tend to also have sporty handling.

Speed

Some wings advertise a high speed but that will depend hugely on weight. Maximum speeds will be given at the maximum certified weight so check to see how heavily loaded that would be. Fortunately, the makers of certified wings all do it the same way. Reflex models reign supreme for speed on a same-size comparison.

When comparing wings of about the same efficiency, fast models tend to require more fuel burn per hour than slow ones. You won't stay up as long on a fast wing but will go the same distance and in less time. If you fly with others having slower wings, though, you'll give up that advantage circling to wait for them.

Speedbar

The speedbar is an arrangement of pulleys and lines that, when activated through a foot bar, lowers the forward rows of lines and speeds up the wing. Most motor pilots don't regularly hook it up. Almost all free-flight wings have a speed system so they can speed through sink faster and fight strong winds.

Different arrangements exist that trade off foot pressure for travel. Since the speedbar pulls down the highly loaded A's and B's, using pulleys provides mechanical advantage. Having only one pulley means the pilot does not have to press very *far* to get full travel, but must push *hard*. Having two pulleys lowers the foot pressure but increases the foot travel required.

Trimmers

You'll want trimmers. Fortunately, most motor wings have them. These adjustments can be let out to raise the C and D lines, which makes the wing go a bit faster. Trimmer range for reflex wings is huge, reflecting their large speed range.

Center Cell Visibility

It's generally helpful to see the wing's center cell easily. First to know that you're centered on it for takeoff and then to see if it is centered overhead.

If you use the technique of looking sideways on launch to check the wing then being able to see the center cell is less important except for being centered before inflation.

1. Some reflex wings have a flatter arc but many other models are essentially the same. Their big deal is speed with safety, relatively speaking, since you can fly a reflex wing trimmed fast and on full speedbar with much less worry about a collapse than on standard wings.

2. Lettering and graphics make it immediately clear where this glider's center cell is. Such marking is more common on beginner-type wings but is useful on all types.

Certification

Certification by a recognized body suggests how a wing will behave in certain defined circumstances. Most commonly, flight and strength tests are done to European Normalization (EN) standards that assign a letter A through D where A has the most passive safety and D the least. You'll also see DHV and other certifications that numbers where 1 has the most passive safety and 3 the least.

Wing's rarely get tested with a motor because there's little demand. Behavior is essentially the same with a motor. And, more importantly, the much larger free-flight market wants testing geared towards their use.

Gliders may hide bad behaviors that testing frequently reveals and can be corrected by the maker. That's why it's so important and why new pilots should stick with certified wings.

Reflex gliders usually only test with trimmers closed (slow) because these gliders concentrate on collapse *resistance* in their accelerated condition. Small wings are almost never certified because they are so dynamic during deflations. Certification is expensive so it's common that only the popular sizes of a glider get certified.

You'll know a wing is certified only if it has a label detailing the make, model, size, weight range (frequently in kilograms: 2.2 pounds per Kg) and certification level. Never buy a wing with*out* this label unless you're an expert who can verify its behavior. The label is usually located on the wing tip or center cell and its absence likely means it has no certification.

Testing involves putting the glider into various maneuvers and collapses, then letting it recover on its own with no pilot input. Time to recover is measured, and fast recoveries get better grades (or a lower number). Those that take a long time or require pilot input to recover get the worst grades (or higher number). Gliders certified with trimmers must be tested at their slowest and fastest settings with and without speedbar. Wings with trimmers are usually only certified in one setting, usually slow or neutral; you have to look at the test report to know.

EN A (DHV 1, AFNOR Standard) paragliders are what we recommend for new pilots. They are less likely to collapse and generally recover quickly on their own. You can still get into trouble, of course, but it takes more turbulence or pilot buffoonery to do so.

EN B (DHV 1-2, AFNOR Standard) gliders still have good passive safety and are considered suitable for students although they won't recover from collapses quite as quickly as the A's.

EN C (DHV 2, AFNOR Performance) gliders have moderate passive safety but could be a handful during turbulence, requiring high level active flying skills.

EN D (DHV 3, AFNOR Competition) gliders have are the most demanding and dangerous without appropriate skill. Pilots must be expert active flyers and even they can expect to work at controlling these wings during a collapse. They are more prone to collapse and require more expertise to recover. They are mostly flown by competition soaring pilots wanting to maximize performance at some increased risk.

The wing above is certified in the EN B category—suitable as a beginner wing. Some manufacturers have the placards filled in with magic markers at the factory, an unfortunate practice that can be hard to read after a few years.

Placards can usually be found on a center cell rib or near one of the inside tips.

Some modern "beginner" wings have the same performance as competition wings from 10 years ago but with greater safety.

Risers

Make sure the wing you're considering has its original risers, or that you know how the new risers will behave. Soaring wings are sometimes fitted with motor risers to accommodate higher hang points and add trimmers—a change that usually takes it out of certification and should only be done with the wing manufacturer's approval or your acceptance of the risk.

Split A's

A lot of wings come with split A's, pictured left, to ease the application of *big ears*, a descent technique (see Chapter 18). Rarely is big ears required in motoring since pilots don't fly in the lifty, rowdy conditions that require them. If your wing doesn't have split A's, you can add a handle on the tip A-line with a short length of clear tubing (see Big Ear Line at left) to make "ears" easier to pull. The hose acts as a stand-off for leverage. Always be careful when adding something that can pull on a wing line.

Brake Holders

This may seem like a small issue but, if you fly an area with lots of iron in the sand or soil, it can render button-type magnetic brake holders useless since they fill with iron-laced sand. And cleaning them is almost impossible. Possibly the best solution is powerful covered magnets, usually neodymium. These do tend to snap to the wrong riser but that's far easier to deal with than extracting iron ore deposits.

It may sound trivial but it's a real pain. Without the brakes in their holders, a tangle is all but guaranteed.

Old fashioned snaps, velcro or covered magnets also solve the problem nicely but have their own issues.

Kiting Only Wing

There are many good deals to be had if you're just learning and want a wing for kiting only. Plus, you spare your main wing all that UV exposure.

Smaller wings are better because they'll take less effort to kite and can safely handle a higher wind range. Try to find one with good inflation, although such a glider will be more challenging to buy on the cheap. It can't be in too bad a shape, either, because you don't want it coming apart if you simply get lifted in a gust.

Don't be tempted to fly it; structural failure could easily be dire.

Some companies sell wings intended for kiting only and these are wonderful for that purpose. Unfortunately, they're also expensive. But can be used for practice in higher winds because they're normally less than half the size of a regular wing.

If you're buying a kiting-only wing, try to get the smallest size possible. Preferably it will handle like the wing you'll be flying but that's not necessary unless you're learning on a difficult wing.

The Motor Unit

CHAPTER 27

The perfect machine for one person may be another's nightmare. It depends on desires and dimensions; petit Patti will struggle with heavy motors as much as a big Al will struggle with being underpowered. There is no "best" machine, they are all compromises. Anyone telling you otherwise is probably selling snake oil—steer clear.

Trying new gear can be risky, especially for new pilots. Check out Chapter 19 for tips on minimizing that risk.

Some relics *should* be relegated to leaf blowing, having long been supplanted by better designs, but they're still shamelessly hawked to unwitting marks. Always dig beyond the slick brochures, websites and fast talkers. For example, for solo foot launching, only the most powerful machines should weigh much over 70 pounds.

Be careful thinking you're going to buy a powerful machine and take passengers up. In the U.S. and other countries that is either limited to instructors or regulated more closely than solo flying. It's harder, too. Foot-launched tandem is probably the sport's most demanding skill. Carts are much easier and safer for tandem but may not be legal in your country or may require special certification.

Be suspicious of advertised weights. Some companies don't include the weight of the prop, harness or other necessary parts and may not say so in advertisements. It's true that different harnesses and props can be used but, when comparing, find out what's included and how much it *all* weighs.

These considerations are for choosing your *second* motor. Your first machine should come from your instructor unless you have very specific circumstances (like you inherited your mother's motor, for example).

This aesthetic design gives up the practicality of straight bars which are easier to replace and easier to assemble. As with everything in aviation, and life for that matter, it's a trade-off.

The inner "Safety Ring," added electronically here, dramatically improves protection from stray body parts.

Weight

For backpack units intended to be foot launched, dry weight (paramotor without fuel) should be on the lighter and more powerful side of the Thrust vs Motor Weight Graph below. Weight is greater on electric-start machines since they require both a starter motor and battery but even those have lost weight by using newer battery technology.

How the machine hangs is another major concern. If it hangs low and cannot be raised on your back, or if the weight is far from your back, even a lightweight unit can feel awkward and heavy. If wearing the machine strains your stomach muscles after only a few minutes, it won't be comfortable on the ground.

You'll hear justification for heavy or uncomfortable machines by saying you'll only feel it briefly before launching. That might be true for experienced pilots, but for others it can be miserable. Plus, some pilots enjoy landing, messing around on the ground and taking off just for the fun of it.

Don't get an underpowered unit, though, in search of lightness. That can be equally frustrating.

The charts below can help determine desirable power and motor weight for your particular situation. When comparing manufacturer weights, be sure to find out if the prop and harness are included. Trike attachments will typically add between 30 and 45 pounds.

Thrust Vs. Motor Weight

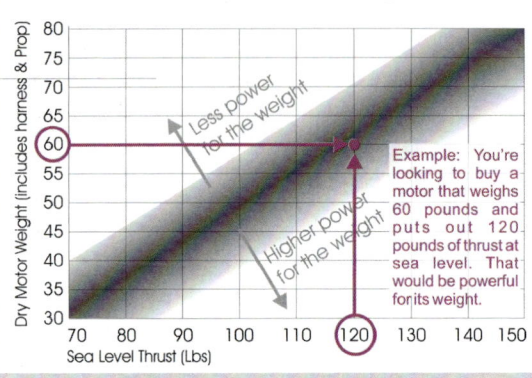

Example: You're looking to buy a motor that weighs 60 pounds and puts out 120 pounds of thrust at sea level. That would be powerful for its weight.

Thrust vs. Altitude

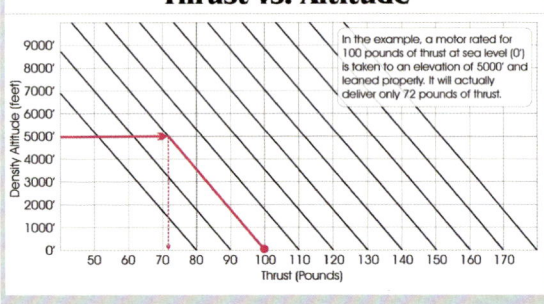

In the example, a motor rated for 100 pounds of thrust at sea level (0') is taken to an elevation of 5000' and leaned properly. It will actually deliver only 72 pounds of thrust.

How Much Thrust Is Enough?

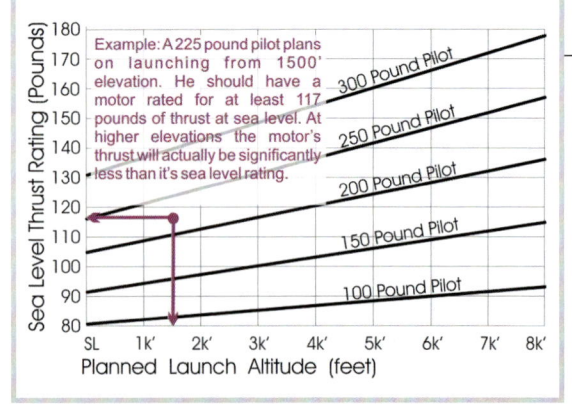

Example: A 225 pound pilot plans on launching from 1500' elevation. He should have a motor rated for at least 117 pounds of thrust at sea level. At higher elevations the motor's thrust will actually be significantly less than it's sea level rating.

Comfort

There are a many elements but, above all, it must be comfortable in flight. On some physiques, bars or straps may get in the way of either visibility or movement—you have to try it, at least in a simulator. The motor should balance on your back, be comfortable, not pull you backwards excessively or interfere with running.

Try to assess comfort only after adjustment by an instructor or other pilot who is intimately familiar with that model. Some machines will be completely underwhelming until you know how to adjust them.

It should be comfortable on the ground too. Can you stand up with it? Do you sit on the ground? Does that bother you? Talk to someone, preferably the dealer, about how it's intended to be used. Some motors can seem impossible to maneuver comfortably on the ground until you know the "trick."

Thrust

Generally, more thrust is better, up to a point. Beyond that point, too much thrust is dangerous. Thrust helps 1) power through the inflation during a *power forward*, 2) makes launch runs shorter, 3) improves climb and 4) allows flight at higher elevations. The downside is increased torque—high thrust machines can be dangerous for light pilots unless they are experienced at handling the torque. A lightweight pilot on a powerful machine may well wind up quickly twisting all the way around unless the machine is perfectly adjusted.

The chart at left gives a good indication of thrust required. All machines will advertise their sea-level thrust. Try to use numbers culled from published tests at fly-ins or by independent organizations. Balance them with advertised numbers and if there's a big discrepancy, ask why.

All motors lose thrust at higher elevations. If that's where you'll be flying, the sea level thrust rating must be greater. For each 1000 feet of elevation above sea level, increase the desired sea level thrust desired by 2%.

On carts, more power is almost always better. Up the thrust requirements by at least 10% if you plan on adding wheels. If you won't be foot launching then there is little penalty to having more power since weight won't be much of an issue.

Quality

Like anything built by humans, some machines are better made than others; most call it the "fit and finish."

Quality inhabits many forms. If things don't fit together, that's a sign of sloppy production. Well-made machines will interchange parts easily—the cage frame from one machine will fit fine on another like-model as long as neither has been damaged. It is rare, however, that a frame is not just a bit "tweaked" from transportation bumps or small falls.

Welds should look solid and be built to last without being overly heavy. Too much use of wire ties and hardware-store parts may be a bad sign although field-repairability is quite desirable. Hardware store parts are OK in places where they're not critical to structural integrity.

Powerplant Considerations

We want smooth, quiet power that's easy to start, has a linear throttle response, sips cheap gas without pollution and weighs nothing. As long as we're dreaming, it should be maintenance-free and cheap. Or how about electric power? Three hours of flight time on a 10 minute charge would be about right. Waking up, now, we find ourselves in the reality of two-strokeville and it's *many* trade-offs.

Electric Start vs. Pull Start

Pushing a button to start is nice; and doing so while wearing the motor lessens your exposure to starting injuries. But, as always, there are trade-offs.

Most models come with either electric or manual start but not usually both. Only a few models can charge the batteries in flight and even those will probably require some charging at home to really be ready.

Electric Start Pros: It's convenient, reduces some propeller/body contact risks associated with having to pull start, and enables easy in-flight restarts for soaring or aborting a landing.

Electric Start Cons: Having only electric start means that you could be grounded if the battery or starter dies and it can't be "jumped" with a car. Batteries and starters are heavier than pull-starters, up to 10 pounds more. It frequently costs more and will likely require extra maintenance, not that pull-start assemblies are maintenance free.

Reliability

"Why can't my paramotor be as reliable as my car?" you ask. Good question given that you probably don't work on your car and it starts thousands of times with nary a snivel.

There are three big reasons: weight, production quantity, and vibration.

1. We have to carry it on our back so we demand exceptional lightness for the push provided. Parts are built out of lighter material and in the lightest manner possible, narrowing strength margins.

2. Even the best selling motors see fewer than a thousand units per year. They're all essentially hand-built with minimal, if any, automation. There's just not enough volume to enable investment in mass production facilities like a car maker.

3. Even the best balanced motor is imparting a powerful torque pulse with every power stroke. There's just no way to eliminate its weld-rending vibration.

This unusual machine had an early Konig 3-cylinder radial mounted on it. Starting was unique — the pilot wrapped the pull cord around a protrusion at the prop hub and pulled. You hoped not to have to do that a lot.

Number of Cylinders & Displacement

Nearly all PPG motors have only one cylinder to minimize weight. Twin or multi cylinder motors may be smoother but will usually weigh more and offer more opportunity for mechanical problems.

Like motorcycles, displacement is measured in cubic centimeters and ranges from 80cc up to about 312cc. Beyond that, the human frame starts requiring more maintenance (think "back strain"). Larger sizes typically power tandem units, heavy pilots, trikes or those flying from high elevations.

Longevity & Reliability

Longevity is a measure of overall robustness. How many hours, how many cycles (start, fly, shut off) can you expect of the motor with no problems? It is notoriously difficult to predict. For one thing, it depends on how hard the motor is run. A small motor run constantly near its peak will wear out quicker than a larger one minimally tasked. Aviation is rife with examples of this; motors that run near their peak design limit have shorter recommended times between overhaul (TBO) than motors that are de-rated (max power artificially reduced).

Another aspect of longevity is support for the brand after the purchase. Obscure motors may be fine while everything works but finding replacement parts could be challenging. It's handy to have a common motor that enjoys good support.

Efficiency

Just like cars, small motors are more miserly. 80cc machines have won competitions where efficiency matters. It means you don't have to carry as much gas or can fly longer on the gas you have.

Efficiency is how much fuel is burned per hour, *at a given thrust*. For example, a big motor may burn 0.7 gallons per hour (gph) to generate 50 pounds of thrust while a small motor may only burn 0.5 gph to generate that same thrust.

Efficiency will also be impacted by the fuel/air mixture: running lean (less fuel per volume unit of air) will burn less fuel at the expense of higher temperatures. So any comparison should be done with the same relative fuel/air mixture.

Charging Ability

Some motors have the ability to output a current for charging batteries. This feature is nice if you plan to run other 12 volt accessories such as an aircraft strobe. Make sure the voltage and current capability works for your device.

Air Cooled vs. Water Cooled

The vast majority of motors are air cooled—it's simpler and there's no water to leak out. Some water-cooled models use convection transfer to eliminate the water pump, but that doesn't cool as well as its more complicated pump-driven brethren.

Water Cooling: The ability of a motor to produce power is tied significantly to its ability to dissipate heat, and water does that well. The improved cooling can be used to either increase power or increase longevity by letting it run cooler. That comes at some cost in complexity, weight, and cost.

Air Cooling: Some air-cooled models, especially the smaller ones (80-125cc), generally use a fan to improve cooling efficiency. If the fan breaks, it's just like losing

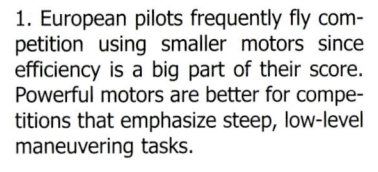

1. European pilots frequently fly competition using smaller motors since efficiency is a big part of their score. Powerful motors are better for competitions that emphasize steep, low-level maneuvering tasks.

2. The water cooling on this rare unit has no pump, rather it relies on convection. The pilot must keep tabs on temperature because, like the loss of a cooling fan, a leak in any of the water system would soon cook it.

water: the motor is headed for a meltdown.

Two Stroke vs. Four Stroke

Relatively simple two-stroke motors power the vast bulk of our fleet. They are popular for the same reasons they are used on weed-eaters and such: lightweight power makes them easy to carry.

Four stroke motors are quieter, cleaner burning and more efficient than their two-stroke counterparts. You don't have to mix oil since the motor carries its oil inside, just like a car. But they are also heavier (for the power) and more complicated.

On average, a four-stroke motor will burn between 10 and 15% less fuel than a two-stroke at the same thrust. The two-stroke is consuming fairly expensive oil with each gallon of gas burned while the four-stroke uses almost no oil. The four-stroke typically weighs about 15-25% more than a comparably powerful two-stroke but efficiency means you'll require less fuel weight be carried.

Ease of Launch

The paramotor design can have a significant affect on how easy it is to launch. A number of factors come into play with varying importance based on your location and experience.

All other things being equal, more thrust will make it easier to launch, up to a point. More thrust also means more torque, which must be managed. Excessive torque effects probably stem from poor adjustments (see Chapter 12), but when actual thrust exceeds about 70% of the pilot's body weight, torque effects become more problematic. Of course the pilot can learn to not use all the power which would eliminate this risk, but that takes practice.

Highly flexible cages can make launch somewhat more difficult if they prevent using power during initial inflation. You must get the wing nearly overhead by yourself before going to power—a technique recommended by some instructors regardless of cage type but generally more difficult than using power assistance.

Hang style, covered shortly, is likely the next most important element. A motor that sits higher on your back will be easier to manage and be less fatiguing while walking around with it. Motors that hang low tend to pull your shoulders back.

If a motor makes launching hard, it could be extremely frustrating. Flexible cages are a trade-off in launch ease since they require waiting until the wing is overhead before powering up.

On a forward launch, the lines should slide smoothly up the cage rim. If there's anything to snag on, it may sabotage the attempt.

Ease of Maintenance

Complicated or proprietary shapes and pieces may make repairs more difficult and expensive. What a shame to give up the simplicity of our machines with complicated access procedures.

Having pieces that can be readily replaced is valuable, too, especially when you're out in the field. The more parts that can be replaced or repaired by readily available hardware, the better. Consider what "dinging" the cage (fairly common) will entail. It may be worthwhile to ask what each cage and part costs if it damaged.

Fuel Tank Position

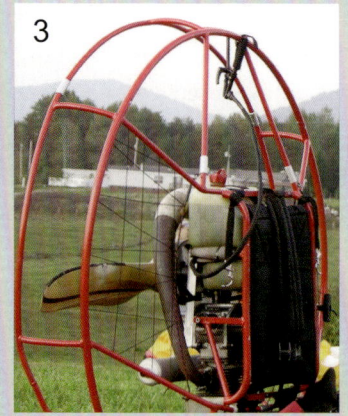

1. By far, the most common arrangement is with the tank below the motor. Care must be taken that the prop has sufficient clearance, at least 4 inches, to reduce the possibility of it hitting the tank in a crash or fall. Being able to remove the tank is handy.

2. Fuel is stored in the frame on this model which keeps the CG closer to the pilot. But fueling requires the machine to be present (not just the tank) and a sight tube is needed to tell quantity. Be mighty careful if you have to weld the frame!

3. On this one, the fuel tank is on top primarily to gravity feed the motor (no fuel pump required). History shows there is no more fire risk with this arrangement than in any other. Care must be taken to keep the muffler from contacting the fuel tank.

4. Another rare style: The fuel is in a tank against the pilot's back. One maker tried putting the gas in flexible bladder tanks and hanging them from the comfort bars. That did get the CG farther forward, a desirable trait, but was not popular.

Fuel Storage—Above, Below, or in the Frame

Almost all fuel tanks are made of a translucent white plastic that allows easy viewing of the level and easy removal. Aluminum tanks are expensive, require a "sight tube" or other means to tell quantity and are more difficult to repair because they can only be welded after thoroughly evacuating the tank.

History has shown that it doesn't matter a whit where the fuel is stored with regard to fire risk. Having the fuel tank above poses no extra risk for fire. Even on the rare occasions where fuel *has* dripped onto the motor it has not caused a fire.

Propeller Size and Style

In almost all cases, the largest prop will produce the most thrust with the least noise. But that might not be the most convenient for transport because it requires a proportionally large cage.

A three or four bladed prop is normally less efficient than a larger diameter two-blade prop. If the blades themselves are more efficiently shaped they will make more thrust. Carbon fiber or adjustable pitch props will be more expensive but tend to be more consistent. Powerful motors sometimes employ more blades to push out good thrust without needing a mammoth cage.

A few machines can accommodate a variety of prop sizes just by purchasing different cage pieces. This would be something to check on since, if you purchased it with the small prop but then needed more thrust, you could get it without buying a whole new machine. The trade-off is that such machines may not be ideally engineered for each size.

Attachment Points & Separation Bars

All motors try to keep the front portion of the harness from pressing against the pilot's chest, usually by incorporating some method of pushing the front webbing away from the back of the harness. J-Bars, distance bars or pivoting bars are different approaches to meeting the same objective.

A few machines have different options for hook-in points. At least one "floating J-bar" machine has the ability to also use under-arm distance bars so the pilot can choose what suits him best.

Low

Most motors with low attachments are trying to mimic a free-flight harness. They appeal to pilots who also own free-flight harnesses which nearly always have low hook-ins points for maximum weight-shift. Soaring wings typically have longer risers that work on low attachment machines without needing to adjust the brakes.

Some models, those with the lowest hang points and pivoting bars, are able to achieve significant weight shift. They allow moving the risers differentially about 6-8 inches by tilting the entire pilot/motor combination and moving the bars.

Low attachment machines that have no pivoting bars are probably trying to avoid weight shift and the looser feeling it invokes.

The hook-in is almost always onto a metal part of the frame with some kind of safety strap as a back-up.

Mid

Mid-attachment points are an effort to simplify matters by hooking directly to the harness webbing. Distance bars (underarm bars) of some sort, located beneath the pilot's arms, keep the front harness pushed away from the pilot.

These are actually just like high hook-ins since the hang point, when viewed in flight, is essentially identical. Weight shift, if offered, is via pivoting distance bars or a sliding strap arrangement. Pivoting arm units have the front left and right web segments attached to a free-moving pivot arm. Sliding strap types allow the front web segments to slide through a cutout as the pilot moves a leg up or down in the seat—it does not move quite as freely as a pivot bar, but gives a similar same amount of weight shift.

High

High attachment points come on machines with some form of over-the-shoulder J-Bar. Since weight is so far below the hang point, they tend to reduce the amount of turbulence transferred to the pilot. The smoother ride comes at some sacrifice in feel. This is due to the fact that the J-bars dampen out uneven pull from the risers as each side of the wing flies through slightly different air currents. Otherwise this uneven pull is transferred to the seat board and the pilot feels it.

Some older designs have fixed J-bars, which give almost no feedback from the wing—most modern units that use high J-bars have them "float" in some way. They either pivot up or down or are connected by a harness-like strap.

Low Hook-In

Like machine #1 on the next page, this low hook-in system attaches high enough to keep the thrust line below the pivot point. That allows good weight shift but with less fore-aft tilting than machines having lower attachment points. The bars are machined aluminum instead of tubes.

1. The secret sauce of this low hook-in machine is its pivoting arms' (highlighted) S-shape. They raise the tilt point enough to be on the thrustline instead of below it.

2. This high hook-in machine has geared pivoting comfort bars. When one bar goes down the other bar is forced up, making weight shift easier.

3. This is a fairly typical low hook-in machine with pivoting bars. Weight shift is done with bar movement and whole-machine tilting. Feel is more like a free flight harness but it transfers more wing movement to the pilot, giving a "busier" feel.

If the ground handling straps are not properly adjusted on these machines, the J-bars can ride uncomfortably on the pilot's shoulders.

Hybrid

At least one model (like the one pictured right) starts with high hook-in points during launch then mechanically moves them down and forward as the pilot pushes out on a bar. It gives a more laid-back posture in flight to more closely approximate free flight and improves weight shift at the expense of an increase in complexity and weight.

Weight Shift

The entire goal of allowing weight shift is to move one riser down while the other goes up (see Chapter 18). There are several ways to do this. Almost every design can achieve some weight shift, at least an inch, which is enough to effect very shallow turns.

Not everybody will like the active nature of the most weight-shiftable machines, especially the lowest hook-in styles. It gives a "busier" flight because you feel the wing's movement. Plus, those that hook in low on pivoting arms confer a fair amount of fore/aft tilting in turbulence in addition to the left/right motion.

Machines with good weight-shift will get over 6 inches of riser travel. Those that aren't designed for it will get less than two inches of travel with a fair amount of effort. Any fixed J-bar system with high hook-ins has almost none. Machines with low but fixed attachments will have some but not much.

Sliding strap

This system, described on the previous page, works well as long as it slides easily. Being able to weight shift is a by-product of the designs original goal which was to make getting in the seat easier.

Whole-Machine Tilt

On machines with low enough hook-in points, the pilot can tilt the entire machine right and left to accomplish the riser movement (see picture 3 at left). Just having low hook-ins is not enough, they must be *very* low. If intended to have weight shift, this arrangement will invariably have pivot bars even though each bar generally moves only a few inches in flight. These types will get over 6 inches of riser travel and are closest to the way free-flyers achieve weight shift.

Having the CG this low tends to make the machine feel "loose" since its pivot point is so close to the center of gravity. They tend to swing around in turbulence both fore/aft and left/right. Pilots acclimate to this feel, though it can be disconcerting at first.

If the machine has no pivot bar, it was probably not intended to have significant weight shift and will only get an inch or two of travel.

Pivot Arm Only

Machines with high or mid hook-ins can get good weight shift using a pivoting arm. Even better are models where the action of one arm going up makes the other arm go down. These "Wally Shifters," named after the original designer, can get over 6 inches of riser travel. Picture 2 on the opposite page shows this style.

Transportability

There are different requirements for transportability. For example, if you want to haul your motor around on airlines or ship it places, you want it to break down easily to a very small size. Some are made for this purpose—both the cage and frame pull apart easily, usually with poles for radial arms that pull out. While great for boxing, they take longer to disassemble for car transport. It's another trade-off.

The pole-type takes about 5 minutes to prepare for transport in a car and about 10 minutes to re-assemble. They'll realistically take about an hour to squeeze into the suitcase and the same to reassemble fully. Of course an experienced dealer can do it in much less time because he does it all the time.

If the machine only rides in the back of a van then having the cage's top half pop off with Velcro may be better. These can be disassembled or reassembled for car transport in about 3 minutes, especially if they stand upright in the car. They do, however, require larger boxes for shipping. Packing time to prepare for shipping is about the same for most models—about an hour is pretty realistic.

The smallest models are direct drives. These loud little buggers have small props and cages so they can usually be carried in cars (or airplanes or helicopters) without *any* disassembly at all. It depends on how you'll need to transport it. The one pictured at left fits, even if barely, inside a small helicopter.

Support—Parts and Expertise

Make sure you can get parts. Unless you're a tinkerer, you'll want support for your particular machine. Cages and frames can usually be fixed by local welding shops, but not the engine itself. The motor and its unique accessories are the important pieces that are not likely to be locally available. Check around to see if other pilots have had good luck getting support for the motor you're considering.

Having a popular engine means having expertise *and* parts availability. If lots of a particular motor are "out there", most of their problems have probably been identified and solutions found. Even if the manufacturer doesn't have the fixes, the pilot community probably will. More people are around to answer questions and there's a bigger market for dealers to profitably stock parts.

If you have a local school or shop that can support what they sell, consider the enormous value of their proximity. It may well be worth several times what you pay for the gear in frustration avoided.

1. Many motor's top cage half comes apart quickly. This may be more handy than having a style that breaks down farther but takes longer.

2. A motor that goes into a suitcase is great if you travel abroad a lot. Even though most airlines won't carry them as checked luggage (find out before you go), they're great for shipping. This is a safer way for transporting and certainly is the easiest to lug around. It takes a good hour, though, to prepare everything and shoehorn the machine in.

3. All motors can be shipped in boxes, some just need bigger boxes than others. They must be packed incredibly well to avoid damage. The smaller the box, the better, as long as there is at least 2 inches of stout padding around the motor.

This is a hybrid powered parachute (PPC) cart that uses a hand throttle and regular paraglider. See Chapter 6 for more about wheels.

The powerful engines used on these are too heavy for most foot launch applications. Even more powerful ultralight motors are sometimes used.

Desirable characteristics include a wide wheel base, both left/right and fore/aft, so as to reduce rollover tendency. Also, look for pilot protection.

You'll most likely need a trailer although some units fit in the confines of a full-sized pickup truck bed.

Whether wheeled or foot launched, buy your first motor from an instructor who you can work with. After learning the sport and gaining flight experience, your *second* motor will be a more informed choice. Plus you will have established what features are important to *you*.

Here is a label that would be fitting on every paramotor out there.

WARNING!
This machine has no brain
You must use your own

Safety

Hopefully equipment improvements will someday reduce our sport's biggest risk: The propeller. Getting a body part whacked is the most common serious injury and many of them could be prevented with a well-designed cage system (see below). Done properly, such a design would impose minimal penalty on performance and weight while adding little cost.

There are many other ideas out there to make our machines safer but it will ultimately be up to consumers to decide. Safety features are expensive, especially anything requiring electronics. They must be designed, built, tested, adjusted, etc. Then pilots have to buy them. First, however, consumers must ask for these features.

There is no perfectly safe machine nor will there ever be. Hopefully, passive safety will be improved but, in the meantime, it's up to us to be extremely vigilant when starting or loitering near running paramotors. More importantly, it's up to us to protect non-participants who may blunder into harms way.

A Better Paramotor (See Illustration Below)

One of paramotoring's worst injuries is getting a body part hit by the prop. Of course proper procedure can prevent it, but humans will be human, and if we can learn anything from airline safety success, it's that we must build better machines. Here are some (of many) design elements that could improve safety and comfort.

The cage, including its bottom area (4), should keep an open human hand (1) out of the prop at full rated thrust. Many won't. Ask about it. An inner hoop, roughly the same diameter as the prop, can be added to existing units for added strength. An auto-cutoff start system (5) could prevent the motor from going above idle for 5 seconds after start. Ergonomics of the pull starter (3) should help keep hands away from the prop and allow the motor to be well supported if it goes to full power. The prop should not stick out behind the cage (11) to help prevent it from snagging lines.

The harness and frame (7) should eliminate most torque twisting effects. That can be done by offsets, weight, hang points and other methods. The motor, specifically the prop, should be as close (10) to the pilot's back as possible. That improves comfort on the ground while reducing some torque twist tendencies during launch.

The frame and seat (8, 9) should provide protection in a vertical impact. By nature of their design, all paramotors provide some protection here.

Fuel tanks should be situated to reduce the chance of being hit by the prop (2) in a crash, or be forced against the exhaust. Bottom mounted tanks need at least 4 inches of clearance from short props (45 inches) and 6 inches for longer props (6).

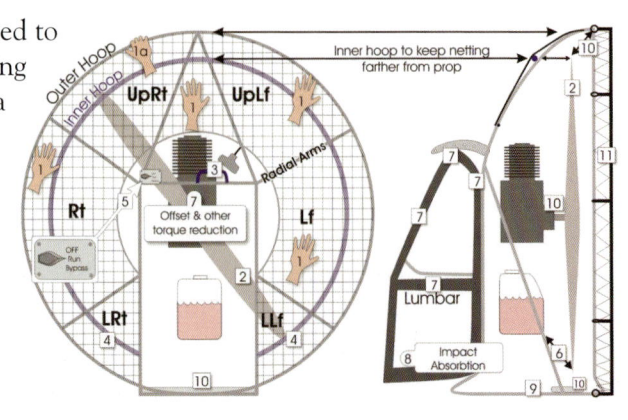

Accessories

CHAPTER 28

We've covered the basic accessories in Chapter 2, but this offers more detail on what pilots frequently add to a basic PPG package.

It's nice that you can accessorize with minimum fuss providing safety is minded. A lot can be attached, carried or used in conjunction with our craft but some goodies add more risk than utility. They cause distraction and yearn for the propeller. In fact, anything that can reach the prop eventually will. Accessorize carefully.

Reserve

A reserve (rescue) parachute can obviously be a lifesaver. This 8 pound accessory mounts on the machine, hooks in to the load bearing harness (see Chapter 12) and can be deployed successfully at very low altitudes (see Chapter 4 and 19). It is intended as a last resort for wing malfunctions that are unrecoverable.

The most popular reserve style is the *pulled apex* which achieves a slower descent rate on less diameter then the old round canopies. It deploys quickly and reliably. That quick deployment makes it completely unsuitable for use as a free-fall canopy—paraglider reserves are not intended for terminal velocity openings where you reach terminal velocity after a few hundred feet of falling.

Bigger is better, to a point. Landing under a reserve is like jumping from a 3 to 6 foot ladder. How high do you want to jump from? The larger size equates to the 3 foot height.

The primary factors affecting choice are size, reliability and opening speed. Sink rate will vary by

The PPG Bible: A complete Guide and Reference

size and you'll want to be within the weight range here. Unlike paragliders, where pilots frequently fly heavy on them, a reserve will not do it's job properly if improperly sized, especially if it's too small.

For any reserve to be used it must be mounted correctly. Improper mounting could make a situation worse than not having a reserve.

Adding Wheels

Chapter 6 covers most rolling options but here are some thoughts on wheels as accessories. If possible, choose a cart that's made for your motor—the mounts and balance will have already been optimized and tested for its frame. If you use a different motor or harness, do a thorough hang test.

The choice of wheels depends on where you fly. Balloon tires are great in sand and other soft surfaces but have more drag on the roll. Skinnier, larger diameter tires work well on firm surfaces but don't slide left and right as well, making them more tippy there. Plus tall wheels add height which further adds to tippyness.

Sitting close to the ground helps keeps the center of gravity low which helps resist toppling, but small wheels won't handle taller grass or rough ground. Having lower hook-in points reduces rollover tendency at the expense of wobbliness in flight.

A strong cage is a must to keep lines from flexing the hoop during inflation, possibly hitting the prop. There will always be some flex so you should not be able to bend the cage to within an inch of the prop tips using hand force alone.

The simplest add-ons don't have much occupant protection which is a safety tradeoff. However, if your motor's cage is strong and the mount stout, it will give some minimal protection. The comfort bars on most paramotors are *not* designed to support your seated weight during a bumpy roll so the trike should have some support under the pilot seat.

On tandem carts (check legalities), look for protection of the front seat occupant. There should be some structure extending beyond the front person's legs so that the frame absorbs a head-on impact instead of the passenger.

A functional trike is easy to build, but engineering good handling and crash protection takes thought. As always, there's more than meets the eye.

Stability

Stability, in this context, means resistance to tipping over sideways or backwards during launch and landing. In flight it refers to how much the cart moves around in turbulence and power changes. Here are some beneficial characteristics.

1. Widely spaced wheels dramatically reduce the tipping tendency. Quads with widely spaced wheels are the most stable but, if they have sled type steering, any bump that hits only one wheel will try to turn the cart in that direction.

2. Low center of gravity reduces the tendency to tip over sideways.

3. Moderately lower attachment points reduce the tipping tendency but increase the cart's wobbling around during turbulence.

4. Mass should be concentrated near the center to reduce rotational inertia so as to reduce cart movement in flight.

Above: A simple bolt-on cart. These do not fall under the U.S. *Sport Pilot* rule unless they have two seats or weigh over 254 pounds.

Right: Most carts use a trike configuration with single pivot steering where left pedal press turns right. Quads are the same although a few have incorporated dual pivot steering.

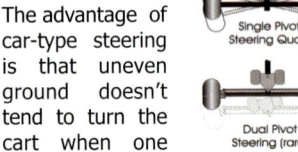

The advantage of car-type steering is that uneven ground doesn't tend to turn the cart when one side hits a rough spot and the other doesn't. The drawback is weight and complexity.

Some carts allow optional extra wheels to enhance stability. They greatly reduce the likelihood of either rolling over or flipping back on the cage (turtling).

The ultimate convertible. This trike accepts either a hang glider or paraglider wing but is powered by a paramotor.

5. The thrust line should be vertically close to, or below, the wing's pivot points so throttling up won't pitch the cart down. Thrust should also angle up enough to keep from ruffling the wing at idle.

Helmet, Hearing & Communications

A helmet should protect both your head and hearing while allowing easy radio communications. If it has no ear protection then use ear plugs with at least 25 db noise reduction to prevent permanent hearing loss. Even full face motorcycle helmets don't have enough hearing protection. Plus, they limit your peripheral vision and ability to see the wing overhead.

The more head and neck coverage the better since it must also protect from propeller shards.

Radio Compatibility

In the U.S., Family Radio Service (FRS) radios are common so most helmets can be made compatible with them but each brand is different. Make sure helmet and radio play together.

It's almost a given that helmets designed to work with FRS radios will not work with aviation radios. Some makers do allow this using special *pigtails* where different plugs can be hooked into an in-line connecter. But even these can have compatibility issues.

The key to a good sounding radio is it's microphone. A high quality dynamic, noise cancelling mic will make a huge difference. Not all microphones work with all radios, though. A dynamic mic requires power and expects the radio to provide it. Some do, some don't—you must check first. 2-meter radios, which are becoming more popular due to higher quality, usually do but they require a license to use.

Audio mixers can be had that allow music and radio communications to coexist. The music gets turned down when the radio sounds. Ideally this capability is built into the helmet because more connections are always bad for reliability. Another handy, but rare, feature is *sidetone*. It pipes your own voice into the headset so you hear yourself transmit. That helps keep you from shouting and lets you know that your microphone is working.

The ignition circuit on a paramotor generates enormous electronic noise that interferes with radio reception or other electronics. It causes static that you'll hear change with motor rpm. This noise can be reduced using a resister spark plug or a resister plug cap, but never combine the two—it will affect the motor's operation. A braided wrap around the spark plug wire (shield) will also reduce the noise.

Radios

U.S. Free flight pilots use VHF radios on specially designated channels in the 2-meter band. The Hang Gliding and Paragliding Association (USHPA) manages the licensing for the Federal Communications Commission (FCC). These radios are far more reliable, with better range and sound quality, but do cost more. The trick will be getting your flying buddies to use them.

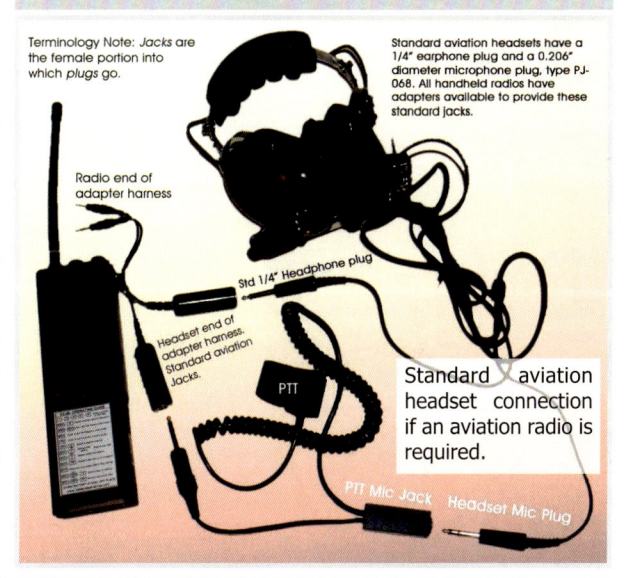

Terminology Note: *Jacks* are the female portion into which *plugs* go.

Standard aviation headsets have a 1/4" earphone plug and a 0.206" diameter microphone plug, type PJ-068. All handheld radios have adapters available to provide these standard jacks.

Standard aviation headset connection if an aviation radio is required.

Helmet Types

1. Motorcycle helmets work and this one includes a radio communications apparatus designed for motorcyclists. It's voice activated so that when the pilot talks it transmits using FRS (Family Radio Service) channels. That frequently doesn't work, however, in our higher noise environment. And these helmets usually don't have much hearing protection.

2. Purpose-built helmets such as this are expensive but work well. They'll work with most various radios (you may have to tell the seller what radio you use) and frequently allow for a music input. The transmit button is usually on the side of an ear cup.

3. A full face helmet offers the best protection. It can prevent injury in a face plant or other head-on mishap. This model is not designed for noise reduction so the wearer must wear ear plugs.

Music

Portable music devices are miraculous in their universal use of an 1/8th inch jack. Everything from MP3 to cassette players work fine although many modern players will require amplification to be loud enough.

Tachometer

A *tachometer* (tach) reads motor rpm. It's a great indicator of power since, with a fixed-pitch prop, maximum rpm means maximum power. It's especially useful for peaking the motor and knowing how it's performing. Propeller rpm will be lower depending on your reduction drive. A 9000 rpm indication through a 3:1 reduction drive means the propeller is spinning only 3000 rpm.

Most tachometers count sparks and, since some motors fire two sparks per revolution and others fire only once, you must have the correct tach (or setting) for your motor. If your tach reads half or twice of what you expect, it's the wrong type. Of course it will work fine; you just need to adjust the reading mentally.

Installation is simple, run the detector wire up to the spark plug wire and wrap it around 4 times or according to the instructions. The ground wire should be hooked to a ground although most tachs work without it connected to anything.

Optical tachometers are handy for working on motors that don't have a tach. You point it at the prop and read its rpm directly. Inexpensive units are available at model airplane (hobby) shops but these need to be held close to the prop. More expensive units, built for airplanes, can be held farther away.

Wind Indicators

You can be creative. An old fishing rod and surveyor's tape works almost as well as a windsock. Any lightweight plastic ribbon can be used for very sensitive tell-tales. Whatever you end up with, make sure it is discriminating in a light wind. It's not hard to tell direction in a stronger wind but is more difficult when the winds are light and variable; when you need it most, you'll want a sensitive sock.

Hand-held wind speed indicators (anemometers) are nice too, especially for learning to tell wind speed on the ground. With practice, you'll be able to estimate the winds within 10% or so.

EGT, CHT

Heat is the scourge of 2-stroke motors and our application can be particularly brutish, so it's valuable to know how much heat is building up.

As covered in Chapter 2, an EGT (Exhaust Gas Temperature) gauge responds quicker to temperature changes than a CHT (Cylinder Head Temperature) gauge. But EGT probes are more involved to install and lead a harsher, shorter life in the motor's hottest area.

There are two types, digital and analog. No battery is required on analog dial types since the probe generates its own voltage to run the gauge. Anything with an LCD-type display will require batteries. Multipurpose models can come bundled with other indicators that combine temperature, sink rate, rpm and more.

The Cylinder Head Temperature (CHT) is far more common since it just sits underneath the spark plug like a washer and is quite durable. It doesn't respond as quickly to temperature changes because the cylinder head must heat up; that makes unusable for adjusting the mixture.

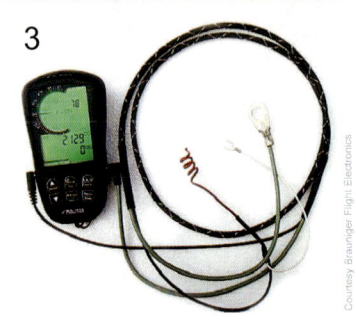

1. Hunter's Smoke is a fine powder that works great for telling wind direction when it's extremely light.

2. The wind sock at left is far more sensitive than the airport windsock to its right. Fortunately, these are also cheaper since they're not made for continuous use. Light wind indicators won't stand up to strong winds.

3. Soaring pilots will appreciate having a variometer to show instantaneous vertical speed. It's useful for finding the liftiest parts of thermals and averting their sinky siblings. Besides a display, it beeps in proportion to the climb rate or buzzes in proportion to the descent rate.

This model also includes a tachometer and Cylinder Head Temperature (CHT) readout.

Like the EGT, most CHT's generate their own voltage to move the needle (unless it is part of a digital readout).

Airspeed Indicator

An airspeed indicator tells how fast you're flying through the air. They are rarely found on PPG's because it's difficult to mount them clear of the motor's interfering thrust field. Wind speed indicators (anemometers) can be hand-carried to give an indication, at least while the motor is idling. Some variometers, made for soaring, have an airspeed probe that hangs below the pilot—beware of the prop.

GPS

Common among drivers, hikers and cruise missiles, the GPS tells far more than direction and distance to destination. Its most useful feature is displaying your speed and direction over the ground. That lets you get an idea of the wind aloft by turning a slow 360° circle to see where the wind is from. The direction of slowest groundspeed equates to the wind direction and the difference from slowest to fastest represents the wind speed.

Technology has improved such that they are accurate to within about 10 feet horizontally and within 50 feet of altitude—an amazing feat given that the signal comes from space. You'll prefer units that display altitude, groundspeed and direction simultaneously. Some include a barometric altimeter but accuracy of the GPS-generated altitude is usually sufficient.

Strapping it to your leg is ideal because you can see it easily and the antenna has a clear view of the sky.

Digging Deeper: Altimetry

We live underneath an ocean of air. Like liquid oceans, the pressure is highest at the bottom and decreases as you go up. That is what altimeters measure; how much pressure the air exerts on a small *diaphragm* which they display as feet (or meters).

Nearly all altimeters, including most of the wrist variety, have a way to set the current barometric pressure. It is called, appropriately, the altimeter setting. The advantage is that you don't have to know your elevation. By setting that barometric pressure, your altimeter will accurately display the altitude above sea level.

At sea level, the standard barometric pressure is 29.92 inches of mercury (abbreviated hg) and it decreases one inch for every 1000 ft altitude increase. Take a barometer that was reading 30.00 hg from it's sea level perch and drive it up to Atlanta, GA (about elevation 500 feet) and it will read 29.50 hg. When the weather men say the barometric pressure in Atlanta is 29.92, what they're really saying is that, *corrected for elevation,* the pressure is 29.92. The actual pressure is 29.42 but they account for the standard decrease of the higher elevation and call it 29.92 hg.

If you set an altimeter to the current field elevation and come back a few days later it will have changed, going up or down as the atmospheric pressure changes. A low pressure area will make it read higher and vice-versa for a high pressure area.

You may run into the terms QFE (Query Field Elevation) and QNH (Query Nautical Height). QFE is the pressure that results from setting your altimeter to zero. As you climb it reads height above field elevation. QNH is simply setting the barometric pressure. Your altimeter then reads altitude above sea level.

1. This very inexpensive GPS unit has all the necessary navigation functions and is well under the cost of a radio helmet.

2. Wearing GPS Nav on your wrist is convenient and they're just as accurate.

3. For a bit more money you can get a unit that plugs into your computer and has a rudimentary map. That's helpful when planning cross country trips. Besides, it's fun to download your flights and see them on Google Earth.

1. This self-extracting tree rescue kit incorporates a belay device that works with 105 feet of 6mm perlon rope and a sewn sling. You should get instruction and practice before needing it. And don't skimp on rope size—40% of the rated strength disappears with the first knot—heat and rough deceleration can eat up any remaining margin.

2. You can launch on frozen lakes but it's not for the faint of foot. Landing on them isn't so bad as long as the ice holds. Plan on being done after landing, though.

Emergency Kit

What you carry depends on where you'll be. A cell phone is your best defense in areas with coverage. Besides basic tools, consider a lighter, regular knife, and mosquito repellent if they're plentiful. For serious cross country flights there is a lot more that must be considered based on the terrain.

If you fly beyond reach of shore, then there is a lot to carry (See Chapter 19 for more.) First off, the whole machine must have flotation affixed in a way that won't leave your head submerged, should you ditch. The Agama, pictured here, is one approach—it inflates three seconds after being submerged; you don't have to do anything. Additionally, though, *you* need flotation. A thin life jacket is best because it's reliable and also requires nothing from you. A CO_2 powered life vest is more comfortable while you're but may require action on your part once submerged. Another option is a small, portable breathing system like that pictured above but you'll have to be able to reach it quickly and rehearse using it.

A tree rescue kit is essential if you spend much time over woodlands. There are two approaches. One is intended to help others get a rope up to you—that's basically 80 feet of dental floss (or similar) with a metal clasp at the end. The clasp is lowered so rescuers can tie a larger rope to. You haul up the larger rope then lower yourself down. The floss should bet at least as long as the highest trees in your area. The other approach, described at left, is for self rescuing—a much better plan if you go forest flying beyond cell phone or radio range.

Use common sense in equipping yourself for the mission and be prepared to handle being stranded by an engine failure.

Cold Weather Gear

Nothing saps the joy of flight quicker than being cold. Essential accessories include warm inside layers, a windproof outer layer, good gloves and face protection.

Full face motorcycle helmets with a visor are wonderful but make sure you can open the visor in flight to keep it from fogging up.

Every part of your body must be covered but scarves are a verboten—it's too easy to forget a loose end and have it stream prop-ward. Commercial flight suits are great but a cheaper option that also works are basic cold-weather overalls or snowmobile suits.

Big gloves are a necessary evil and a real pain to launch with—everything is difficult to feel. Some pilots have had luck with heated gloves and other garments but that entails more complexity. Chemical hand warmers, available from Walmart or sports stores, can also be helpful.

Home Building

CHAPTER 29

Jeff Baumgartner flying the prototype Skybolt. Its no-weld design was eventually turned into for-sale plans.

An entire organization, the Experimental Aircraft Association (EAA), has grown up around regular people building airplanes. There are, in fact, several thousand home-built airplanes plying the U.S. skies at speeds upwards of 500 mph. Burt Rutan, pioneer of the first private ride into space, started off as a home builder. So building your own paramotor is a viable option for some people.

But it's certainly not for everybody.

There is a *whole* lot more to it than meets the eye. For one, there is enormous risk for anyone not taking it seriously—your life depends on sound design and execution. Very, very few people that set out to build a paramotor on their own, from scratch and without previous aircraft building experience, ever get to fly it. On the other hand, those who build from respectable kits usually do succeed in flying their creation. You can see a list of reputable plans and kit makers on FootFlyer.com. Be extremely leary of buying anything not recommended, there are some scammers.

Don't build your *first* paramotor. For one thing, you'll be throwing away much of your ability to customize because you'll have no idea what you'll like. Buy an existing machine, learn on that, then build your masterpiece. It will allow forming ideas of what is *safe* to change along with what you'd *like* to change. The information in this book will help you know what *not* to change.

Build your own paramotor because you like to build, not because you want to save money. Even a well-implemented kit will take 50 hours depending on what comes assembled. If it has little or no pre-fab, expect up to 4 times that many hours.

As with any machine, make sure you have an instructor that is sufficiently familiar with it and is willing to teach you on it. Most will, provided they feel the

1. Welding aluminum is far more difficult than welding steel and should not be taken lightly. That's why almost all plans or kit machines do not require any welding. The machine above (see PPGPlans.com) uses fittings wherever tubes meet or cross and a very clever key-ring-through-hoop idea to secure the netting. Wheels pop on and off easily for hauling of the machine, wing, helmet etc.

2. This kit frame uses rivets and gussets to fasten the pieces together. Nearly the same technology is used in regular aircraft; it works well if done right and with plenty of rivets. These designs are both geared towards the home built market.

This is a case of modifying existing plans to suit a different suspension system. Notice the over-shoulder bars. Adding the safety ring dramatically reduces prop injury risk.

machine is reasonably safe and appropriate for your weight. The worst possible combination would be a marginally trained pilot trying to fly an un-tested, home-built motor.

Don't be fooled by the build-time estimates. They might be accurate for highly skilled mechanics but certainly don't include time for re-doing parts, multiple runs to the hardware store, or other surprises that invariably emerge.

Building Your Own Design

There's a lot more to paramotor design than meets the eye. The designing process should include an experienced paramotor pilots who understand the constructs, limitations and choices involved. It takes flight experience on different machines to know what ramifications each design feature will have. Experienced builders of other things will still need expert help or extensive paramotor flying experience to sort out paramotor design elements. Even long time designers get flummoxed when their great ideas don't always pan out, so don't be surprised when some super new feature you devised only makes matters worse. See the end of Chapter 27.

If you *do* have varied and significant experience, like to build, can work with simple tools and have time on your hands, then building your own design could be quite rewarding. The best approach is to model an existing machine as closely as possible. Find one that you like and learn why it's built that way. Look closely at how the harness attaches to the motor, where it hangs in a simulator and how the motor is mounted. Settle on the same type of motor to keep it balanced and stick with the same geometry. If you innovate, do so with great care.

Surprisingly small changes make big differences. For example, the weight shift bars common on high hook-in machines must be positioned just right. It was found, early on, that positioning the pivot point just 2 inches back (towards the propeller) made them far more effective.

There are many, many factors that likely went into a tried and true design, one that people are actually flying. Change them at your own peril. In the past, small changes to geometry or function have hobbled a machine to the point where it became unsafe. Pilots have been injured in such efforts. Be ready to deal with that and do lots of testing in the simulator before taking any new creation aloft.

After settling on a design—a time-consuming process that will probably involve many adjustments—the time and tools required to build a machine should be about the same as building from plans.

Building From Plans (Scratch)

If the plans are for a machine you've never seen fly, there's probably a reason. Find other plans that have been built and flown!

Buying plans from the back of a magazine or internet is a bad idea unless you've talked to a respected pilot who knows of its flying habits. It could save enormous heartache. Or seek out reviews from those who have flown the machines but are not selling the plans (like www.FootFlyer.com).

One of the biggest challenges will be acquiring all the parts. You'll need a harness, fuel tank, throttle, aluminum, motor mounts, fuel line, motor, netting material, throttle, etc. Good plans will have a current and thorough source list.

Tools: It depends on the design, but you may require aluminum welding which, unless you're quipped for it, adds difficulty and expense. You can expect to bend tubes, cut thick aluminum (fine tooth jigsaw can be used), rivet and/or fabricate various fittings. Anyone considering this should already have a normally-equipped shop with the skills to use it. Some reputable plans don't require welding or you can buy the welded parts separately.

Expect to take from **100 – 500 hours** total building time from start to first flight—more if the plans don't describe accurately what's needed. Visit FootFlyer.com to see what kits are recommended. Nearly worthless plans have been foisted on unsuspecting buyers for years; buy something that comes recommended.

Building From A Kit

This is, by far, the best way to build a machine for builder types. Even so, it should only be done with a proven kit that has examples flying in the field. Make sure you can watch or talk to pilots who have built the kit too. Any reputable seller will offer a list of customers to talk with. Even if they cherry pick the customer list it would be preferable to having no other information. Internet groups devoted to the machine provide another valuable resource.

Most kits do not require aluminum welding. Instead, they provide the welded pieces so the builder is mostly just assembling, riveting or bending tubes.

At least one kit makes extensive use of pop rivets and has no welded parts. The requisite rivet tool is inexpensive and, if done right, provides all the strength need-

1. As with all kits, the rivets and gussets of this machine must be done according to plan. In this case, it must be gusseted properly (the angled reinforcements).

2. Attaching cage netting is just as challenging for homebuilders as it is for manufacturers. On styles where the net is strung through frame members, it is cumbersome when a line breaks. The ingenious method shown below sidesteps that problem by riveting loops and having the netting line go through those. Restringing is a piece of cake.

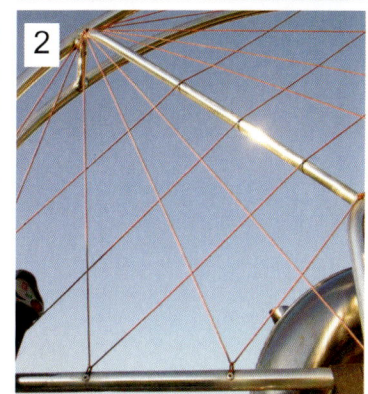

Since you build it, you can make it safer. This shows the safety ring drawn onto Jason's homebuilt, dramatically improving cage protection..

Test your creation thoroughly. Hang it in a simulator where an instructor can go through the completed assembly. Make sure you can get in the seat, reach all the controls, etc.

Dan Kriseler is pictured above working with a student using an unusual, but easily raised, simulator.

ed for a long life. Rivets work well provided no individual rivet supports too much load. Spreading out the load is how airplanes make use of rivets.

Tools: Generally you will already have what is needed: A drill, small hand tools, and a vice. The process is more assembly than fabrication which is especially good for the critical dimensions regarding motor mounting and frame alignment.

Time: Expect to take from **20 – 80 hours** total building time from start to flight. These times depend on the kit's level of completion.

Testing & Changes

There's always something. It may seem simple, but strange interactions and problems invariably show up during testing. Some are dangerous. Be ever mindful of the prop while going through the process. Some pilots (or would-be pilots) have been mangled after the briefest moment of inattentiveness.

Like any new machine, your preflight should make sure there's nothing within reach of the prop that could get sucked in. The cage must have good prop clearance and the fuel system be leak free with a good vent. These cautions go for changes to existing designs, too. Have an experienced pilot check it out for you.

Consider what would happen in a crash. Can components skewer the pilot? Will the prop flex down enough to slice through the fuel tank, spraying fuel around and potentially igniting a fireball?

Will the change allow the risers to come together, causing riser-twist in flight? Will the cage come forward on the risers and allow the brakes to go through the prop? These things have all happened and many other possibilities exist.

Hang the system by its carabiners to make sure you can get in and out of the seat easily. Install a kick-in strap and practice until it's second nature. Have an alternative (besides the kill switch) way to shut off the motor that doesn't involve reaching too close to the prop. When everything checks out, run it up on the simulator and see if any problems creep up.

Keep those first few flights close to home and check the condition of everything carefully after each flight. This is no different than buying a new machine or one that has recently been apart. Postflight is always a great time to inspect, but is even more important on a new machine or design.

Tinkering: Not all bright ideas in paramotoring come from manufacturers; many come from users, especially experienced pilots looking to get the most out of their gear.

Tinkerers have devised both doozies and duds. Wally Hines' counteracting weight shift, where one bar's upward travel pulls the other bar down, was a doozy as an aftermarket for certain brands.

Another Wally creation, pictured right, didn't go so far. While not a complete dud, this retractable foot rest never caught on. It stowed for launch or landing and could be extended whilst cruising. He soon decided that the weight didn't quite justify the comfort. But it sure was comfy once airborne!

Section VI

Getting the Most Out of Powered Paragliding

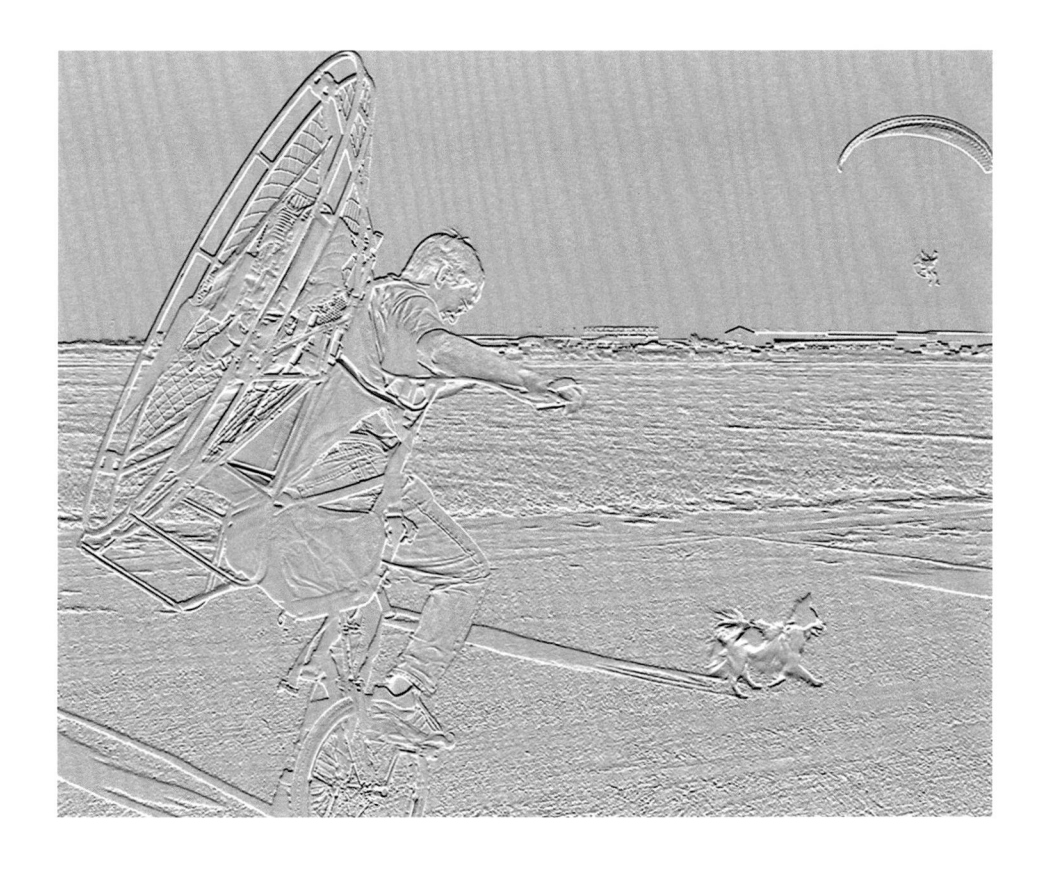

Section VI

Getting The Most Out of PPG

By Stacey Scholtes

Now that you're flying an aircraft that can travel with you, the list of possibilities is enormous. While a powered paraglider is wonderful for enjoying your *local* slice of heaven, there's a lot more heaven out there.

Being able to take the gear frees you from the road; family vacations can become a whole different experience. Business trips can become an excuse to explore from above, and family visits can include "demonstrations." And as you'll see, there are even more ways to enjoy this amazing craft.

Other Uses

CHAPTER 30

Stefan Obenauer actually did launch with these skis. In this case he just enjoyed cruising around. Be careful, falling is quite easy, and quite expensive (or worse), even as an accomplished skier!

What can be done with a paramotor is fun and surprising. It certainly is more amusing than practical but, who knows, one person's amusement may spawn another person's practical application. Be mindful of the risks; never forget that it's still an aircraft with that oh-so-effective spinning *fingerlator* on the back.

Using PPG for Transportation

The unfortunate catch phrase is: "Don't count on it." But exceptions may indeed allow using a paramotor to get somewhere. Fickle weather, limited conditions and slow speed generally conspire against us but, on those nice days, no locomotion scores higher on the intrigue scale.

Ideally, your launch is close to home (better yet, at home). The portability means that, after you get there, it can be folded up for the ride back. It's almost always better as a one-way trip and even better yet as a trip with a tailwind.

If you've got an airplane (you'd be surprised how many paramotor pilots do), this can be a great way to get back and forth to pick it up from maintenance. The same is true for cars if your shop has a nearby field. You may even need to choose your shop differently now.

Be leery of planning a round tip, though. If the paramotor is your only ride home it will be extremely tempting to push the limits and fly when you would otherwise pass. "Get-home-itis" has been the fatal flaw in many general aviation flights where visual-only pilots take on marginal conditions and lose.

If you've got good sites at both ends of a planned trip, the PPG is a fun way to get there. As always, stay clear of congested areas.

Planes, Lanes and Helicopters

Before discovering PPG, I had a helicopter (*Ellie*). It required yearly inspections at a shop some 35 miles away. Dropping it off involved an onerous drive through nasty traffic. Twice. Then along came paramotoring. In spite of living in a suburb, I had an uncongested air route from my house and, of course, the shop had a helipad (middle picture, below). The pad wasn't much, jutting out into a swamp and all, but it would do.

So when the next inspection came due, I loaded my paragear into the helicopter and headed out. Flying there was pretty quick—while helos are slow by aircraft standards, they're greased lightning by paramotor standards. After landing, Darryl Oliver, the shop owner, spirited *Ellie* into his repair lair. Then he got some friends to come over and watch the crazy PPG pilot (me) launch. He thought I was nuts.

With the swamp before me, and the wing laid out carefully behind, I was ready. Nervous, too; if the motor quit, or I couldn't climb well enough, that swamp would be no fun. So I psyched up, powered up and went for it. The edge came quickly; I lifted off just before the water and held my feet up to clear the longer shoots of swamp grass. Easing up on the brakes let me accelerate and climb. Whew! *That* was satisfying. Darryl later admitted that he half expected to fish me out of the muck.

Flying home was almost magical.

A couple weeks later I reversed the process—paramotoring up to the helipad and flying everything home. Boy did that beat driving. And landing at the helipad seemed brainless compared to launching there.

Another fun example of usefulness was retrieving a motorcycle after maintenance. How convenient it was that the shop had a field next door. I'm sure the employees got a kick out of that sight. And yes, a helmet *was* worn, both on the road and in the air.

Flags & Banners

Flags and banners can be fun to fly but do add some risk. Attaching anything to the wing adds drag which slightly increases the chance for parachutal stall and makes the wing that much more difficult to inflate. Attached stuff may also impede recovery from malfunctions. Risk has proven minimal but avoid rough weather, excessive brake usage and follow the connection guide below.

When connecting a banner or flag, you want to 1) minimize turning tendency, 2) keep it out of the lines and prop, and 3) make sure it flies fully.

There are several ways for attaching banners to the wing. Regardless of the method, put it near the center (to minimize turning pull). Since it can't be exactly centered, attach it on the opposite the side that your motor naturally torque turns. So if the motor makes you turn left, put the flag on the right side.

Use the most center brake line since that is the most rearward and will minimize turning tendency. You'll feel the flag flapping through your brake handle so some pilots will use a D-line (or C on 3-riser wings) instead.

You will have two lengths of 1/8" nylon strings that

are tied to the top and bottom of the banner's leading edge (2 & 3). The top line gets tied to where the brake line connects at the wing (1) and the bottom line connects where the brake line cascades from below (4). The length of each line, plus the flag's height should be slightly longer than the brake line distance between attach points. This will let the flag "bow" out without crumpling in the middle.

Put fishing clips (called snap swivels) on each end to make removing the flag easy.

Before launching, make sure the flag is on the ground and clear of the other lines. Generally just making sure it is on the ground and lines are on top of it is enough. After inflating make sure the flag is not hung up on anything before committing to flight—easy to do on a reverse inflation and a bit more challenging on a forward.

Hanging Banner

Hanging the banner works well if you want to fly somewhere before deploying it or if no-wind conditions make the inflation difficult.

Tie a weight (3 pounds should suffice, more for a bigger banner) to the banner's leading edge bottom (6) then tie a line to the top and secure that to a Velcro strap. Attach the Velcro to a low-hanging part of the frame or to your foot (5). It should attached so that a snagged banner would only peel the velcro off.

The pilot launches with the banner stowed and then, after reaching a safe altitude, throttles back and drops it. The banner could foul the propeller so be careful; it's better done with the prop stopped. Be over landable terrain in case of problems.

While flying, avoid flying close enough to people below who could get hurt if the banner dropped accidentally. Be mindful of how low it hangs, even with the Velcro, getting hooked on something could be ugly.

Before landing, either drop the banner or stow it back in a bag.

Cattle Herding

Don't laugh, a paramotor "round-up" has been done and the rancher loved it. In fact, he asks the pilots to help out regularly. Of course you can't get paid but you can earn another flying site, or at least a welcoming place to fly over.

Coordination is a must but it's mostly a matter of flying in such a way as to keep the cattle moving in a desired direction. Simply going out and finding strays helps a lot and the PPG, with its un-restricted view and slow speed, is perfect.

The coordination comes into play when two or more pilots are working one group of cattle. It also helps when working with people on the ground.

Be careful since it's easy to get so distracted by the mission that you fly right into wires, fences or the ground. It takes discipline to build a scan that regularly looks away from the "target" to ensure a clear flight path. Make no mistake, this adds risk; and doing it real low increases the risk dramatically.

Where cattle graze is usually landable terrain, but not everywhere. Be mindful of your engine-out options whenever spending attention away from flying. It's easy to get caught up in an activity and then be surprised by a motor failure. Surprise is decidedly unhelpful when only seconds remain before touchdown!

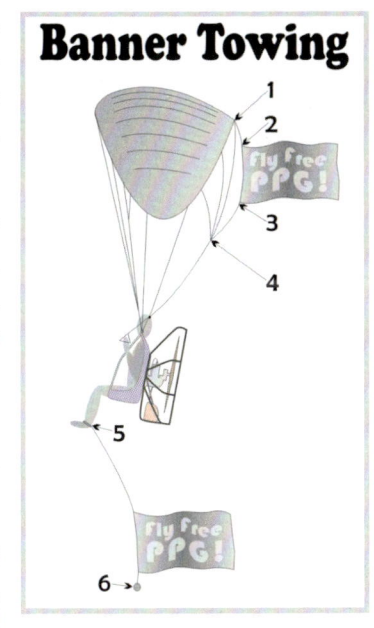

Top: This shows 2 ways to connect a banner, one on the wing and the other on your foot. Of course there are other ways, but these have proven reliable. The fishing tackle clip (middle) is a good way to fasten the banner line.

Above: The same New Mexico group that has pioneered rescue work has also been called on for cattle herding. This pilot is working a small band of separated cattle along the Rio Puerco, West of Albuquerque. Legally, these uses fall under allowed recreational use and there would probably be no question unless you were getting compensated in some way.

Search and Rescue

Our high perch is also useful for search and rescue. Although cell phones and GPS's have reduced the need for such efforts, people still get lost. While we can't do much if they're wandering the woods, we can certainly cover open areas, including difficult to inspect crop lands. This should only be pursued by experienced pilots who generally make launches on their first try.

Contact your state Search and Rescue director (if available) or the local fire and police departments to offer your services. It would be on a volunteer basis and is a great show of community support.

Be up front with them about your capabilities and limitations. The worst thing to do is exaggerate what you can do and then wind up needing a rescue yourself. Most important, explain the limited weather conditions you need to operate in and time of day constraints—don't expect to do this on mid-summer afternoons.

Finding Model Aircraft

A great way to befriend the local Radio Control flying club is offering your search services for their lost airplanes. Give them your telephone number and explain your capability.

When those planes go down they can be nearly impossible to find from the ground and they have quite a range. Tall grass is ideal to find planes by PPG—they're almost impossible to locate from below but frequently pop out from above.

The flying is obviously simple: Pick a pattern and fly it while scanning the ground. Pick different altitudes too. If the airplane is buried in deep grass, you might have to be nearly over it. Going up high puts your farther away but provides the vertical angle that may enable a better view.

Once the plane is located, identify nearby landmarks that you can find from the road (or hack a GPS). It is best if you go out personally to get the plane because you know where it is. The nuance of location can get lost in a translation.

Public Relations & Exhibition

Flying in airshows can be difficult. You may need a rating (PPG2 is required for insurance), approval by airshow management, and work with the "Air Boss" who's in charge of all flight operations. There are frequently exemptions from certain rules that the organizer obtains. Among other things, all pilots flying under that exemption must be specially qualified through the aviation authority (FAA in the U.S.) which can be a lengthy process that PPG ratings help with.

At smaller gatherings, or even some airshows, it can be great public relations to have your craft out there with some basic information brochures. They may even let you fly since it would keep up the audience interest.

1 & 2. Looking for lost models can be tedious. There's no guarantee they'll be immediately visible and you must fly a search grid from different altitudes. I spotted this one from 500 feet or so. Notice how very close to the road this model was and how nearly impossible it would have been to see from the ground. From above, though, it was pretty obvious in spite of blending in with other yellow vegetation.

3. On this occasion a model's remote control quit working and the pilotless plane wandered almost a mile away before crashing with little damage. It, too, proved easy to spot from the air while being impossibly hidden from ground searchers.

> **Motor Madness**
>
> The motor has turned up some surprising uses. For one, it is the monster of all leaf blowers. Of course a regular leaf blower won't cut your arm off but, for those willing to try it, there's no better way to move a big volume of air on very little gas. Only do this stuff wearing the motor on your back and don't let that cage near anything. The prop finds bystanders just as tasty as pilots. Be careful!

Traveling With Gear

CHAPTER 31

The ability to travel so readily with your aircraft is unique to powered paragliding. It's not always easy, but is almost always worth the effort. Free flyers have it even easier but, being able to motor to the where of your wishes, is an extraordinary capability. To see just how good this gets, watch the video "Why We Fly." You'll understand.

Shipping

PPG's can be boxed and shipped around the world using common consumer freight carriers. Other methods of transport abound, here are some tips to help.

Preparing the Motor

The machine must be completely free of fuel odors and packed well enough to endure rough handling.

First, make sure there is no fuel present, anywhere. Nearly all carriers, whether ground or air, prohibit carrying fuel or fuel vapors without calling it hazardous materials—a legal quagmire. You may luck out and not have your motor inspected but, for everybody's sake, don't risk it. Drain the tank into a gas can then run the motor to evacuate any residual fuel in the carburetor or fuel line.

Remove the harness and clean everything. Although fuel works well for cleaning, in this case use a sweet-smelling degreaser that doesn't harm aluminum. Spray-type carb cleaner gets rid of grime in hard-to-reach areas. Brake cleaner is good on clutches but brutal on paint.

If you have an air filter, now is a good time to replace it. Otherwise, double bag it and squeeze out excess air. Clean the airbox thoroughly. Wash the tank out with soapy water then deodorize it with a product like ZorbX (shown at right).

What a concept: Your entire wing fits in a small box or suitcase.

Avoid using the ruck sack supplied with some gliders—the straps catch on conveyer equipment. But a box works great and can even be made easy to carry with a strapping tape handle as shown below. This decidedly lowbrow method is very convenient. Put the wing in a stout bag before boxing—sometimes the boxes get punctured in transit.

Cardboard boxes must be well padded and taped securely. You still need at least 3 inches of foam or other packing material between protruding motor parts and the box's edge. Any parts that touch the box's wall will likely be broken or bent. Pet carriers and large plastic storage boxes work well—put a couple of cheap tie-down straps around them for strength.

"That's my aircraft you're carrying." A motor with removable poles is great for air travel or shipping. The motor and frame fit into the big box while the propeller and poles fit in the gun case.

If time permits, dry the fuel tank completely. When there is no fuel present it will be legal for transport but, as covered later, airlines still probably won't take it.

Remove as many attachments to the motor as possible—muffler, reduction drive and air filter. If the motor *can* be removed from the frame easily, it should be. Usually only the throttle, fuel line and battery line must be disconnected. Being compact is better for motor shipping and probably a lot cheaper. Plus, keeping the motor separate reduces the chance of a careless drop bending the frame.

Packaging

Using just one single hard-sided case makes packaging easier while giving the freight company less to lose. Pack it to survive a drop from several feet high. Moderately firm foam of at least 3 inches, including a softer layer next to the motor, should line the box. Foam can be purchased from fabric shops (and elsewhere) in sheets.

A few models break down enough to fit in an airline-legal hard-sided suitcase but all airline luggage is now screened in some way. So, unless you *know* the carrier will accept it, have another plan in case it's refused.

Another padding option is forming foam—a material that sprays out from a can and forms to your object (*Great Stuff Foam* is one brand) then hardens. It can be re-used in new boxes as the old ones wear out. Put your gear in a plastic garbage bag first.

Once the heavy pieces are secure then everything else can be added and packed in bubble wrap. Limit this box to necessary flight gear. Lighter is better. A good idea, for example, is to wrap the muffler and gear box (heavy items) in plastic wrap and put them in with the wing that you will check on the airline. That saves shipping costs but remember, the fewer boxes you need to have for an airworthy machine at the destination, the better your odds will be of getting airborne.

Propellers fit nicely in gun cases. Even the cheap ones from discount stores work well and accept two wooden props up to 50 inches long. *Puzzle props*, those that come apart at the hub, are great since they fit into your other boxes, negating the need for a separate prop container.

The wing conveniently squishes into a sleeping-bag sized, easily checked item. It can be good for packing other things with since the fabric serves as it's own protection. Just be sure that nothing sharp protrudes and that no fuel or oil can get on it.

Having more boxes may be easier to deal with for one person but every additional box is an additional chance of losing a required flight item. One big box is more likely to get there than several smaller ones. Find out about maximum weights, though, since some shippers may not take heavy or oversized boxes.

Airlines

Most airlines prohibit motors even though there is no federal regulation about it. There *are* regulations, for good reason, against carrying fuel and oil which are hazardous materials. You'd think that, since we don't have crankcase oil, our motors would be allowed. But they don't want to bother with differentiating types so they simply say "no motors." Some pilots have succeeded at getting motors on airlines but they're gambling that the agent doesn't know the airline's own rules. Non-U.S. carries my be more tolerant.

If an airline *does* allow your motor, remember all baggage is subject to search and so it probably *will* be inspected. If they smell any fuel odor at all it will **not go**! Don't think that plastic wrap will solve the problem; they will probably open it up. You should have a contingency plan.

If you really want to save money, remove the engine from its frame and ship it alone. Then check everything else on the airline. You'll end up checking one largish box containing the motorless frame, clean gas tank, harness, muffler, prop, redrive and other miscellaneous stuff. The long props may need their own box. Larger frames with rigid cage pieces will probably need two boxes which should be fairly lightweight to minimize damage potential. You may have to pay an oversize or excess baggage fee.

This method allows using a very small box for the motor which is cheaper and safer anyway. It's an issue of convenience as to how much hassle you want to tolerate at the airport for the savings.

Freight Carriers

Hazardous material requirements limit what cargo airlines can accept but they're more liberal than passenger lines. The box is still likely to be opened so don't leave fuel in anything—doing so endangers all involved. Plus, it's a federal offense and more shippers are inspecting contents, including removing gas tank lids.

Each shipping company has its own pricing structure. Some airlines have freight divisions but the cargo usually goes on passenger flights. If it's going to a foreign country, it must clear Customs and may be delayed up to three weeks while incurring steep customs fees (usually refundable once you take the gear back out of the country.) It can be quite the paper chase, too. These are reasons for taking the gear on your international passenger flight, if allowed.

Bus Lines

Some pilots have had good luck using commercial bus lines. You must drop the equipment off at the bus terminal and pick it up at a designated spot but sometimes arrangements can be made for delivery service. Check with the line to see if they'll take your gear.

Transporting via Road

Transporting by car is convenient, especially if you can avoid the teardown process. Plus, you can fly along the way if sites present themselves—an exhilarating way to add new perspective to your route.

Using the Platform

A platform lets you to carry the motor fully assembled outside your vehicle. It attaches to a receiver that you can get installed at many trailer stores (such as U-Haul). A two inch receiver is ideal since it's more common, but the 1 ¼ inch size works, too. You may need an adapter depending on your platform. Trailer lights are not required since the platforms are so minimal. Plus, they're easily removed.

When securing your motor, use at least two straps so that if one falls off or comes loose the other will hold. Secure free-spinning props (clutched units) to reduce bearing wear. Lock everything with a bicycle cable lock and cover it completely, if possible, to keep rain, prying eyes and dust away. But dust will still coat everything unless the cover is completely sealed. A large grill works but purpose built paramotor cov-

1. Platforms come in many sizes. This one fits two motors, most fit one.

2. Eric Sansli uses his motorcycle. A roadable trike negates the need for a platform—quite handy.

3 & 4. The two inch platform tongue (3) fits into the two inch receiver welded to the vehicles rear (4).

Check that the platform tongue actually does fit into your car's receiver. Sometimes the receiver's interior is too rounded and the platform's squared-off tongue won't fit. It can happen even though both are advertised as 2 inches.

There I Was...

Enough already. After flying morning and evening for the last week it was time for a break. Today would be that break.

I'd been flying some incredible scenery, including Meteor Crater and Flagstaff's volcanoes, motorhoming towards Phoenix and flying various places on the way.

Just before going down the big hill out of Flagstaff, I pulled into a scenic overlook. No flying, mind you, just admiring; my paramotorhome, the *Enterprise*, with its PPG signage and gear, rested.

Soon, a family parked next to me, got out and started in with the questions. "What is that? Do you really fly it?" So of course I got into the mode, explaining it all.

After describing how "You can launch with no wind but we'd rather have a bit." I walked to a small open area, hands spread out as if to catch the breeze: "This is about right—5 to 7 mph" I continued. "You don't need a lot of room but do want an 'out' in case of engine failure." I walked to the edge and was surprised to find a smooth, downsloping, grassy hill.

That was too much: "I'll tell you what," I concluded, "why don't I just show you!"

In a few steps I was off, climbing into an incredible skyscape east of Sedona, Arizona, with sweeping red hues, canyons and trees sprawling out below.

By the time I got back the family was long gone, probably scratching their heads at what they just watched. But I'll bet there was at least some wonderment at seeing a human run aloft to join the birds above, soaring through a beauty that they could only imagine.

What a capability—we don't need a "scenic overlook," we make our own!

---

ers are better and easier to use.

Be careful, gear gets damaged in transit more often than it gets damaged in flight for those who travel much. Plus, constant bouncing around is hard on everything. If possible, put hard foam on the bottom to absorb some of the jostling.

Gas & Oil

When traveling by air, you can't take a gas container so plan on buying one when you arrive and leaving it behind.

Unless you're flying a 4-stroke or electric, you'll need 2-stroke oil. Although it's not considered a hazardous material, most airlines still prohibit it, even in checked baggage. Motorcycle and go-cart racing shops usually have the best selection of oils. Hardware stores frequently carry it for chain saws and gas stations sometimes stock outboard blends—not ideal, but works in a pinch. In most cases you'll be OK since your motor is completely emptied on each end of your trip.

See Chapter 4 for more on choosing 2-stroke oil.

Customs

The problem here isn't fuel, it's taxes and tariffs. Registering your motor with an organization and having the documentation may help to show that it's yours. Some countries (not the US) require registration with the government. The border folks fear that you may be importing the motor for sale so it's more suspicious if you're traveling with more than one. They may also fear some nefarious use so having a picture of it in flight may be helpful.

If you're traveling with a group, it may be best to have the frame in a box with the prop separated. You'll attract less attention.

The most appropriate declaration is "Sporting Equipment" or "Paragliding Equipment" for personal use. It is helpful if you have a local person there to help deal with issues especially if you don't speak the foreign language.

In the U.S., anti-terror laws do not allow individuals to ship using airline cargo services—you must go through a *freight forwarder* who ships using the cheapest means, most likely a freight airline for rapid delivery. Otherwise, you must be certified as a *known shipper*. Your dealer may have already acquired that status and be able to help.

The large freight companies can be used (Fedex & UPS) but are expensive depending on the destination. They do handle the customs issues but don't be surprised if there is a very large charge at the end. Some countries can be "creative" with charges which is why it's good to enlist the help of a local. Some charges verge on extortion.

In any case, some of the best advice you get will come from other pilots who have already traveled to your intended destination. Seek them out on the Internet and give kudos to modern communications.

This high quality production, set brilliantly to music, documents an incredible journey. It has instructional value too, especially for those venturing into windy areas.

Follow the narrated drama of trying to PPG in a foreign, and strikingly beautiful land. "Why We Fly," by Phil Russman, will open your eyes to the surprising potential of paramotoring the planet. It's a flying film that even your non-flying friends might enjoy.

Photography

CHAPTER 32

What an amazing platform for capturing pictures and video—providing perspectives that just aren't practical with any other craft, especially since you can bring it along. Rules in most countries limit commercial use (see Chapter 8) but there's still a lot you can do with it.

Distraction is a major concern. It requires discipline to remain aware of your surroundings and insure a clear flight path—concentrating too much on the shot, especially while flying low, adds tremendous risk.

Always secure the camera with a long enough leash to allow movement without being long enough to foul the prop or engine. Looping the camera strap through a harness piece is better than looping it around a part of your body. Hanging the camera strap around your neck, for example, could allow it to get caught in the propeller or other moving parts. This has happened with almost dire results. If you *do* launch with anything around your neck make sure it is cinched up tight. Then, once in flight, you can re-attach it to some part of the machine if necessary.

Still Photography Basics

Photography merits its own book but these few tidbits will help you get great shots, even ones worthy of magazine covers.

Quality

There's lots more to quality than pixel counts; check out the Pixels and Pictures box on the next page. What matters most is lens and sensor size (bigger=better), sensor quality, image stabilization, rapid refresh and others.

Higher quality gear also does better in low light, like sunrise and sunset, which pro-

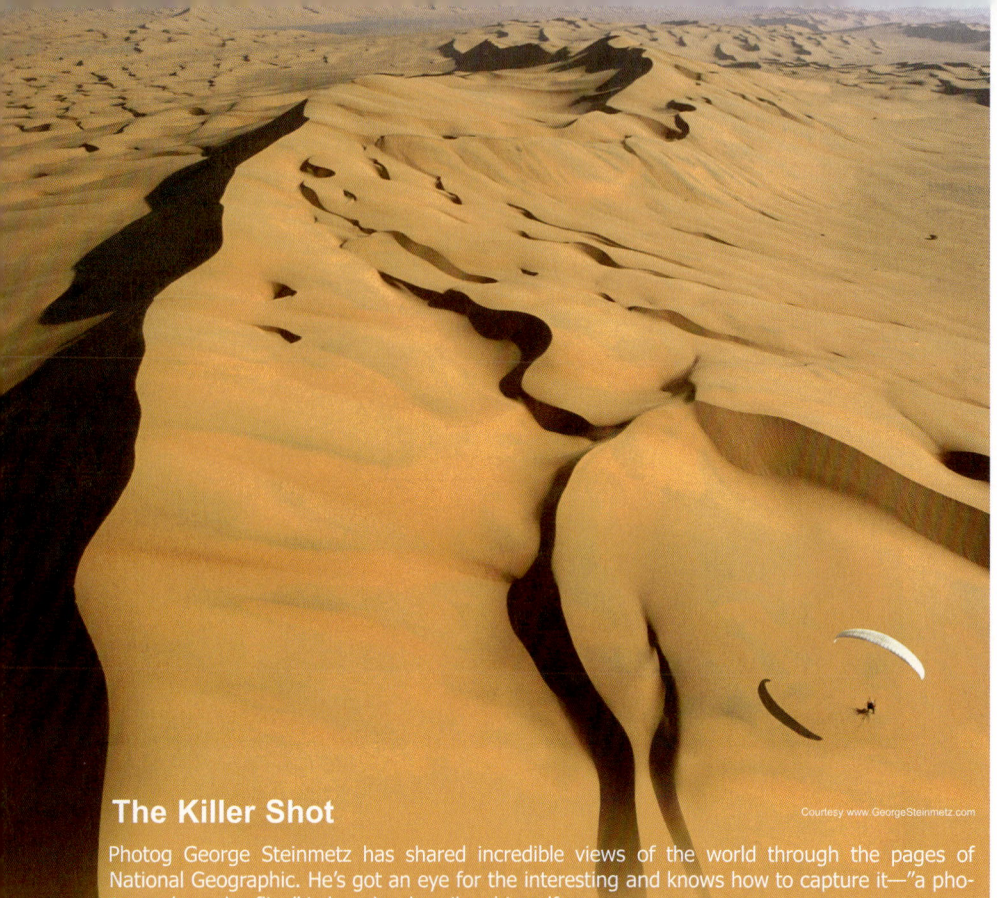

The Killer Shot

Photog George Steinmetz has shared incredible views of the world through the pages of National Geographic. He's got an eye for the interesting and knows how to capture it—"a photographer who flies" is how he describes himself.

His paramotor has become a tool that sometimes has no equal, especially in the lesser accessible places that he so frequently visits. It can easily be the only practical way aloft. And he gains access to flying sites the same way most of us do: asking politely for permission or, on occasion, forgiveness. He offers that being respectful is important; never be annoying or arrogant—advice that has served him well.

When asked to share some wisdom with aspiring photographers, he offers: "I do a lot of research before I go. But I always find interesting, unexpected things when I arrive. With close ground support, I can scout a lot by boat, car or camel, but it always looks different from above."

This shot of the Gobi Desert's "Empty Quarter" shows several principals at work. First, of course, you have to know it's there. Then get to the right place with the right equipment and finally, set up the shot. In this case, having the horizon in view adds greatly to the sense of size. Having an interesting foreground helps a lot too. Try shooting during the low sun of morning and evening—fortunately, our best times for flying, too.

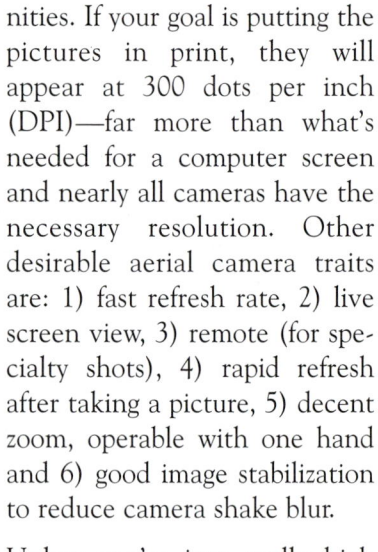

Courtesy www.GeorgeSteinmetz.com

vides some of our best opportunities. If your goal is putting the pictures in print, they will appear at 300 dots per inch (DPI)—far more than what's needed for a computer screen and nearly all cameras have the necessary resolution. Other desirable aerial camera traits are: 1) fast refresh rate, 2) live screen view, 3) remote (for specialty shots), 4) rapid refresh after taking a picture, 5) decent zoom, operable with one hand and 6) good image stabilization to reduce camera shake blur.

Unless you're into really high control, use the default compression format, JPEG (or JPG). These sacrifice some minor quality degradation (unnoticeable in most uses) for a significantly smaller file size. *Fineness* describes the level of compression—more *fine* means less compression.

If your pictures are intended for magazines or other published media, use the highest resolution and fineness available. Even though cheaper cameras tend to make bloated, grainy images at their highest resolutions, it's better to reduce later than to wish you had used higher settings. Only use a lower setting if memory is an issue.

The best cameras have removable lenses and fast refresh rates with optical stabilization. Single lens reflex (SLR) models let you see through the same lens that the camera uses to record images. These usually have the highest quality but choose one that also has an LCD display for when you're framing the shot while airborne.

Focus

Any picture is essentially worthless if the main subject is blurry. Most cameras have an autofocus that works well but it has limits, the worst of which is focusing on the wrong thing. Equally useless is a slow autofocus that balks when your subject moves into position and doesn't take the shot because it's "hunting" for focus. You may be able to reduce this by setting focus to "center spot." Then point to the center of the subject, press the button down halfway, reframe the shot then push the button all the way down to take the shot. That keeps the camera from focusing on something real close like your own risers or cage. As long as you're shooting with no zoom (the subject looks far away), you can set most cameras to remain on infinity where everything farther than about 8 feet is in focus. There's nothing worse then discovering that your perfect shot of a spiraling pilot is a perfectly focused shot of your leg.

In low light situations it gets harder for the camera to focus. On most models, holding the shutter down half-way makes the camera "calculate" the shot—setting shutter speed, focusing, and other parameters. Then when you press the button fully, it takes the picture right away. So if it won't focus on your subject, point it towards something with better contrast but the same distance, push the shutter button half-way, point it back to your subject and press the button all the way.

Sharp Subject, Blurry Background

Professional photographers value blurry backgrounds to make their subject stand out. There are two primary ways to do this:

1. **Panning**. Carefully track the moving subject so the background is zipping by, causing it to blur. The slower the shutter speed, the more dramatic the effect. Of course a slow shutter speed makes it harder to keep the subject sharp too.

2. Narrowing the **depth of field**. The in-focus distance range is called *depth of field* (*DoF*). A wide DoF means that most everything, distant and near, is in focus. A narrow DoF means that only objects at the focused distance are sharp, while closer or farther objects are blurry. Zooming in narrows the DoF; as you zoom in on the subject its background gets more blurry. Opening up the aperture also narrows the DoF. The wide aperture (smaller f-numbers mean larger aperture) lets in a lot of light which means that shutter speed will be quite high. A camera with a large lens, and more importantly a large pickup area behind it, will be able to achieve a narrower DoF. More expensive cameras usually have a larger pickup area.

1. Depth of field blur. Zoom and an open aperture help create this.

2. Motion Blur. To get this effect, zoom a bit, pan the subject and use the slowest shutter speed possible.

Other Settings & Tidbits

Fortunately the auto setting on most cameras does a decent job in our usual bright light conditions. Using auto leaves you free you to frame and fly.

Digging Deeper: Exposure, Getting the Light Right

Exposure tells a lot about a picture; underexposed is dark and over exposed is too light. Anytime you have to correct something later, information is lost so always try to have the best settings. Three notable attributes affecting exposure:

ISO or "film speed" is the pickup medium's sensitivity to light. The lower the ISO number the less the sensitivity. So ISO 100 is less sensitive than ISO 400. More sensitivity, though, means more noise—pictures are splotchy or grainy when enlarged so you'll have to choose.

Shutter speed is how long the shutter stays open. Longer times mean more light. So 1/60th of a second gathers more light than 1/250th but having the shutter open longer means more motion blur. A good minimum speed is about 1/125th.

Aperture is how big the opening is where light comes through and is expressed as "f stop" where larger numbers mean a smaller opening. So an f-stop of f1.8 is wide open (many cameras can't go that big) and f5.6 is a small opening. The bigger the aperture, the more light can pass. That allows shooting in lower light at faster shutter speeds.

Most cameras automatically choose aperture and f-stop based on lighting when you press the shutter button down halfway. Almost all models, beyond the most basic, let you change one setting while it adjusts the other. For example if you want to "stop" the action in a shot, you choose a faster shutter speed and let the camera chooses an optimum aperture (open it up to allow more light). ISO is usually set by the user and not adjusted in the auto process.

Use your camera's highest settings. The bulk of your effort was getting to this vantage point—don't waste it on suboptimal quality. Your magazine cover shot needs to be at least 2700 x 3300 pixels.

Here are some basic tips to help capture images from a PPG. There are no hard and fast rules so these are just general guidelines:

- Use the auto setting unless you really know what you're doing and the camera allows quick adjustments. One exception might be setting focus to infinity unless you're doing *very* close work.

- Have sufficient light. Once the sun gets too low you must be very steady for pictures to be sharp. In poor light it might be a good trade-off to set the camera's *ISO* to a higher number (or use higher speed film if not using digital). This increases the sensitivity of the capture surface (just like film) at some expense in *noise*. Noise is to digital photography what *grainy* was to film.

- Fill the picture with your subject—at least 50% of the shot should be occupied by your subject and more is usually better. Of course if there is something equally interesting in the background then adjust accordingly.

- Be leery of zoom. Autofocus confuses more easily if you're not centered on the subject and even slight movement of the camera will blur the shot. Good optical stabilization negates some of this.

- Use zoom when appropriate. You'll have to have bright light for a high shutter speed, but it is much better to zoom now then to crop later in your photo editing software.

- Skip *digital zoom* where the camera simply makes the pixels bigger but has fewer of them. Cropping later does the same thing but gives you more control.

- Try wide angle lenses, especially for self portraits. Positioning these on your frame or wing and shooting remotely can yield spectacular shots.

- Keep shooting to increase your odds of getting it right. But if the shot is obviously boring, skip it. Later on you'll quickly tire of reviewing boring shots.

- Be close and get your subject to banks and dives for added interest but, above all, keep flying the craft! This is extremely risky since you're not only flying close, you're thinking about the camera.

- Generally, try keeping your subject down sun. But sometimes cool effects can be had when shooting into the sun, especially in hazy conditions.

- It's usually more interesting to see the pilot's face, especially if he's looking at you. There are exceptions, of course, and experimenting is half the fun.

- Unless you have specific scenery in mind, try to get a human subject in the shot, especially another PPGer.

- Have something or someone of prominence in the foreground to add interest and scale.

1. Including part of yourself or frame in the shot can add interest. It gives perspective while letting the viewer know what it was taken from.

For air-to-air work, cameras with an external display are handy. If you are forced to look through a view finder, shots like this are difficult.

2. Self portraits can make for interesting angles. In this case, Red Bull acro pilot Chris Santacroce mugs for his "Hairy Leg Cam." Page 300 has ideas on where to mount cameras.

Video

One of the hardest things to get while flying is good video. Start off with appropriate equipment—essentially as good a quality camera as you can afford. Quality has improved so that consumer equipment is only about 5 years behind its professional predecessor. Bigger is better for lenses, too, and make sure the camera can accept a wide-angle adapter. A wide-angle lens, about 0.5x, captures the pilot and glider in the same shot without being too far away.

Steady is king. The absolute worst thing you can do is subject your viewer to jittery video. Everything else is secondary. Technology that reduces skaky images may be helpful but use it wisely; optical stabilization is remarkably effective but doesn't work well with certain types of shots (see your camera's manual).

The camera can be handheld but it tends to shake—using two hands helps but that leaves nobody minding the paraglider. Weight shift steering is a plus here.

Occasionally, use the widest angle lens that you can afford. You have to be very close (risky) to the subject, though, or they'll appear too far away.

A helmet with sighting viewfinder is a great tool. Besides freeing your hands up to fly, it can yield reasonably steady shots, especially with a wide angle lens. You must be able to see the shot you're framing, though. It can be as simple as bending a coat hangar for the sight and taping to the helmet. Also, skydiver accessory suppliers have helmets ready-made to accept a camera.

Hanging small cameras from your wing or other locations can add interest. Be careful launching—making sure you're balanced and the camera stays put. Page 300 has some ideas on placement.

When flying close, as required with a wide-angle lens, be aware of the extreme collision risk and include extra precautions. Plan to avoid wake turbulence, too, when working around other flyers.

Here are some tips to improve your in-flight video recording:

- Be smooth. If it wiggles, it won't likely make the cut. Choose smooth air whenever possible.
- Be leery of zoom. Even more than stills, video rarely looks good when zoomed because it's too jittery. Only zoom with calm conditions when you can hold the camera extremely steady. Even then be ready for throw-away footage.

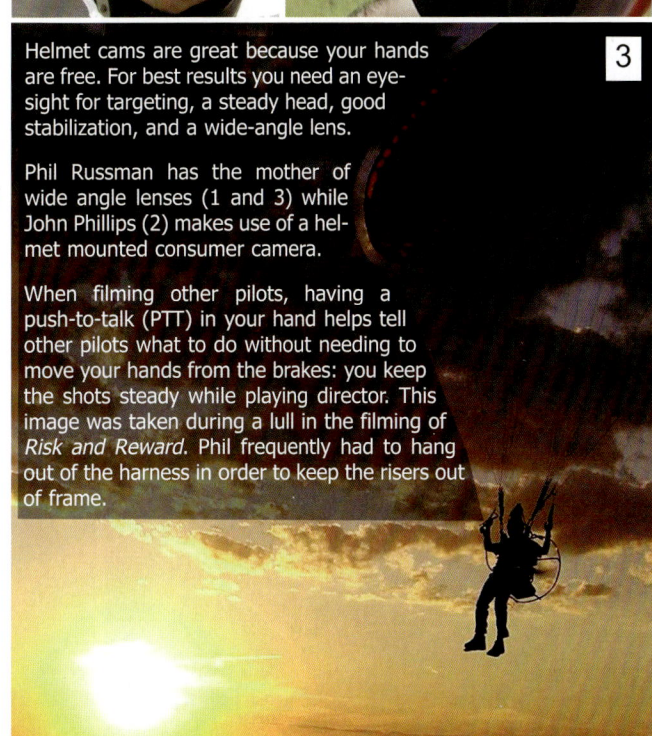

Helmet cams are great because your hands are free. For best results you need an eyesight for targeting, a steady head, good stabilization, and a wide-angle lens.

Phil Russman has the mother of wide angle lenses (1 and 3) while John Phillips (2) makes use of a helmet mounted consumer camera.

When filming other pilots, having a push-to-talk (PTT) in your hand helps tell other pilots what to do without needing to move your hands from the brakes: you keep the shots steady while playing director. This image was taken during a lull in the filming of *Risk and Reward*. Phil frequently had to hang out of the harness in order to keep the risers out of frame.

Digging Deeper: Pixels and Pictures

Pixels are the little colored dots recorded by your camera and displayed on monitors or printed pages. Resolution is the number of pixels horizontally and vertically. Generally, more is better. A one megapixel image has a resolution of 1200 by 800 (1200 dots across by 800 dots down). That fills up a monitor, which uses 72 dots per inch (DPI) but is only 4 inches wide when printed since print needs 300 DPI.

Your eye has amazing resolution—it would take a 25 megapixel camera to approach the quality available through an open human eyeball.

The PPG Bible: A Complete Guide and Reference

- Use the widest angle you can get if you're close enough to the subject.
- Frame your subject close. Little gliders, far away, are rarely interesting.
- Vary the shot. Vary the angle, the zoom, the background, the subject, bank angles, etc. Editing shots rarely last longer than 2 to 5 seconds.
- Try to always have something in the shot moving and have something else moving very little. For example, having the subject flying by from right to left may be more interesting if you don't follow him. Point the camera so that he flies into and out of frame where the background slides by at the same rate.

Mounting the camera in different places adds tremendous interest for both stills and video. (Above) Jeff Hamann using his unique line-mount setup. All shots done close like this need to use a very wide angle lens. The photo just below Jeff's was done for a newspaper. Such mounts are sure easier than flying close formation.

Right Pictures: Three great tools wielded expertly by Phil Russman: HD helmet cam with electronic eyepiece, quality communications with Push-To-Talk and a steady neck.

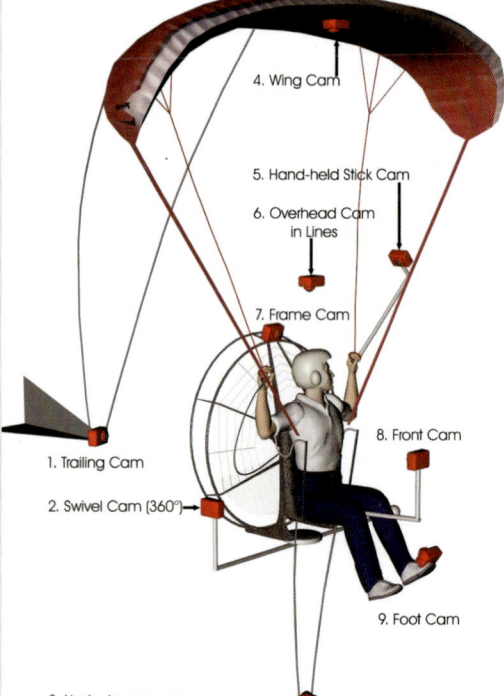

Some of the best PPG video is shot on the ground. It's not as much fun but the quality can be much better and it's a lot safer. You'll capture more launching and landing which is, after all, our sport's most entertaining action. Getting experienced pilots to play around on objects is also quite entertaining.

Have someone record your own flights for later review and critique. It's an invaluable tool for learning.

More than anything, though, capturing our passion in action is yet another great reason to exercise that passion. So go out, capture carefully, capture frequently, and revel in the fantastic freedom afforded by our incredible platform.

The coolest video usually comes from getting close. That's the riskiest way, too. Be extremely careful!

1. Trailing Cam
2. Swivel Cam (360°)
3. Under-harness cam
4. Wing Cam
5. Hand-held Stick Cam
6. Overhead Cam in Lines
7. Frame Cam
8. Front Cam
9. Foot Cam

Here are some places where pilots have mounted cameras in order to get different and interesting angles. Be careful anytime you're connecting something to you frame or wing since that may change its behavior. Also consider what would happen in an accident.

Section VI: Getting The Most Out Of PPG

Appendix - Checklists

Checklists are important tools that are well worth using. They should be compact and easy to remember which means brief—covering only the most important stuff and rolling easily off the tongue. It's useless if it's not used. The flight checklists below (Pre-Launch and Pre-Landing) have been designed with a "memory aid" sing-song cadence to improve recall.

Use a paper copy until you're thoroughly familiar with the routine. Refer back to the checklist after you've done a procedure to see if you've missed anything.

Items may be different based on your machine but these checklists give a good basic plan. If you do not recognize a part name then it probably doesn't apply to you. For the preflight, start with your carabiners and proceed around. Look for the most obvious items: loose, missing or damaged parts, broken safety wire, etc. If a machine has just been assembled, do a post-assembly inspection as well as a good once-over before flying. A paramotor preflight takes only a minute and you'll be surprised at what you'll find. Don't skimp on inspections when borrowing gear.

After flying, clean the machine and do a thorough postflight inspection. You'll appreciate finding problems *now*, so you can fix them before your next session.

These checklists are intended to help learn what to look for. Once you're familiar with the flow then the paper checklist can be used optionally.

Remember, more propeller-strike injuries happen while starting or test running a motor than at any other time, so treat the machine with enormous respect. And a helmet can protect you in case of a disintegrating prop while also providing ear protection.

Preflight Inspection Checklist

Item	Action
Carabiners	Attached properly, no damage, in correct hole for pilot weight/loading.
Lift web	No nicks, burns or other damage.
Harness	Attached properly, no damage (lift at carabiners to shape for inspection).
Attachments	Pouches zipped, GPS/Instruments/strobe/etc secure.
Reserve	Mounts secure, pin in, bridle run properly.
Kick-in strap & speedbar	Attached properly, no damage, stowed as needed.
Distance/comfort/J bars	Attached properly to frame and lift web.
Safety Strap (J-Bar)	Attached properly, no damage, motor release set (as installed).
Frame	General condition, velcro/fasteners in place.
Cage	Netting General condition, velcro/fasteners in place, secure.
Motor	Spark plug, muffler bolts, wires, head tightness, motor mounts secure.
Air filter/box	Secure, free.
Fuel Tank	Lid on, straps/bolts secure, vent free, fuel line in good condition.
Propeller	Main bolts, does not wiggle fore/aft, (center bolt tight), no cracks.
Redrive	Not loose, belt tensioned and on all groves.
Throttle	Free, undamaged, **full travel at the carburetor** when moved, at idle.
Battery	Secure, plugged in, master switch as required (on if about to start).

Before Start Checklist

Item	Action
Area	Look around to make sure the prop and blast area is clear of straps & debris.
Throttle	Idle, hold so that it is impossible to throttle up even if the motor pushes hard, kill switch accessible. Watch at throttle linkage.
Fuel Valve	On.
Choke or Prime	Set choke or Prime as required.
Master Switch	Brace in case starter engages, then On.
Brace	**Brace in case of full power!** If possible, start it on your back.
Clear	Yell, "Clear Prop," wait for 2 seconds.
Start	Pull or press the starter button until it starts.

These basic checklists cover most problems on launch or landing. Some, like "chin," may seem trivial, but pilots have inflated, looked back at the wing, and had their un-strapped helmet fly into the prop.

Pre-Launch Checklist

Item	Action	Memory aid
Leg strap left	Fastened and adjusted.	Leg,
Leg strap right	Fastened and adjusted.	Leg,
Chest straps	Fastened and adjusted.	Chest and
Helmet strap	Fastened and adjusted.	Chin;
Brakes	Correct hand, clr to pulley	Brakes and
Carabiners	Closed, locked	'Biners,
Trimmers	Adjusted for takeoff.	Trimmers and
Pouches, Extras	Secure and Zipped.	Zippers;
Run-up	Power & kill switch test.	Run-up,
Look	Weather & path clear	Look and
Launch	Go for it!	Launch.

Pre-Landing Checklist

Item	Action	Memory aid
Harness Straps	Adjusted for landing	Harness
Trimmers	Slow (or as required)	Trimmers and
Pouches, Extras	Secure and Zipped.	Zippers;
Wind	Insure landing into it.	Wind
Pattern	Establish flight path	Path and
Gear	Legs (gear) extended	Legs

Appendix - Resources

Fuel/Oil Mix Chart

Consult your engine maker for recommended types of gas, two-stroke oil, and desired mixes. There are different requirements for breaking in a motor (seating the rings properly) which is normally considered the first 5 hours. This table shows how to mix some common fuel/oil ratios (32:1, 40:1 and 50:1) using the markings on many oil and fuel containers. This may be helpful when the gas and oil container markings are not uniform.

For this many units of fuel	Add this many **ounces** of oil:			Add this many **milliliters** of oil:		
Ratio→	at 32:1	at 40:1	at 50:1	at 32:1	at 40:1	at 50:1
1 gal	4.0	3.2	2.6	118	95	76
2 gal	8.0	6.4	5.1	237	189	151
5 gal	20.0	16.0	12.8	591	473	379
1 ltr	1.1	0.8	0.7	31	25	20
2 ltr	2.1	1.7	1.4	63	50	40
5 ltr	5.3	4.2	3.4	156	125	100
10 ltr	10.6	8.5	6.8	313	250	200

Note the crazy English volume units: 1 US Gal = 4 quarts = 8 pints = 128 ounces = 3.785412 liters = 0.832 UK gallons
Metric units: 1 Liter = 1000 milliliters = 0.2641721 US gallon

Repair

The best resource for replacement or repair is the dealer where you bought the gear. It's likely that they know where to look, or what can be substituted. They will also know best whether replacement is necessary. Visit www.FootFlyer.com for updates to resources along with other new information relating to powered paragliding.

Instruction

A valuable resource is www.USPPA.org where it lists certified paramotor instructors. In the USA, solo pilot certification programs are run by the U.S. Powered Paragliding Association (USPPA) and U.S. Ultralight Association (USUA). Tandem exemption programs may be run by the USPPA or other organizations but check out their website. FootFlyer.com maintains a section on the current status of training exemptions under Educational, Chapter 1. Check with the organization for your country to find a certified instructor for solo or tandem training.

Welding

Aluminum welding is very specialized and not all shops do it. Even fewer will do it if they know it's for a flying machine. Look in the yellow pages under welding—even if they don't do aluminum they should know who to call.

When you do find someone to weld, avoid describing it's primary function unless it comes up. Some pilots have tried calling it by one of its auxiliary uses such glorified leaf blower, ski & skate power for the vertically challenged, etc.

Appendix - FAR 103

For convenience, here is the U.S. Federal Aviation Regulation (FAR) relating to Ultralights. The most recent version can be found at www.faa.gov using the title *FAR 103*. A related advisory circular (not included here) is AC 103-7 which details much of the process and intent of the regulation. Note that FAR 103.20 requires adherence to certain FAR part 91 rules that pertain mostly to airspace restrictions.

Subpart A—General

§ 103.1 Applicability.
This part prescribes rules governing the operation of ultralight vehicles in the United States.
For the purposes of this part, an ultralight vehicle is a vehicle that:

(a) Is used or intended to be used for manned operation in the air by a single occupant;
(b) Is used or intended to be used for recreation or sport purposes only;
(c) Does not have any U.S. or foreign airworthiness certificate; and
(d) If unpowered, weighs less than 155 pounds; or
(e) If powered:
  (1) Weighs less than 254 pounds empty weight, excluding floats and safety devices which are intended for deployment in a potentially catastrophic situation;
  (2) Has a fuel capacity not exceeding 5 U.S. gallons;
  (3) Is not capable of more than 55 knots calibrated airspeed at full power in level flight; and
  (4) Has a power—off stall speed which does not exceed 24 knots calibrated airspeed.

§ 103.3 Inspection requirements.
(a) Any person operating an ultralight vehicle under this part shall, upon request, allow the Administrator, or his designee, to inspect the vehicle to determine the applicability of this part.
(b) The pilot or operator of an ultralight vehicle must, upon request of the Administrator, furnish satisfactory evidence that the vehicle is subject only to the provisions of this part.

§ 103.5 Waivers.
No person may conduct operations that require a deviation from this part except under a written waiver issued by the Administrator.

§ 103.7 Certification and registration.
(a) Notwithstanding any other section pertaining to certification of aircraft or their parts or equipment, ultralight vehicles and their component parts and equipment are not required to meet the airworthiness certification standards specified for aircraft or to have certificates of airworthiness.
(b) Notwithstanding any other section pertaining to airman certification, operators of ultralight vehicles are not required to meet any aeronautical knowledge, age, or experience requirements to operate those vehicles or to have airman or medical certificates.
(c) Notwithstanding any other section pertaining to registration and marking of aircraft, ultralight vehicles are not required to be registered or to bear markings of any type.

Subpart B—Operating Rules

§ 103.9 Hazardous operations.
(a) No person may operate any ultralight vehicle in a manner that creates a hazard to other persons or property.
(b) No person may allow an object to be dropped from an ultralight vehicle if such action creates a hazard to other persons or property.

§ 103.11 Daylight operations.
(a) No person may operate an ultralight vehicle except between the hours of sunrise and sunset.
(b) Notwithstanding paragraph (a) of this section, ultralight vehicles may be operated during the twilight periods 30 minutes before official sunrise and 30 minutes after official sunset or, in Alaska, during the period of civil twilight as defined in the Air Almanac, if:
  (1) The vehicle is equipped with an operating anticollision light visible for at least 3 statute miles; and
  (2) All operations are conducted in uncontrolled airspace.

§ 103.13 Operation near aircraft; right-o-way rules.
(a) Each person operating an ultralight vehicle shall maintain vigilance so as to see and avoid aircraft and shall yield the right—of—way to all aircraft.
(b) No person may operate an ultralight vehicle in a manner that creates a collision hazard with respect to any aircraft.
(c) Powered ultralights shall yield the right—of—way to unpowered ultralights.

Appendix - FAR 103 (Continued)

§ 103.15 Operations over congested areas.
No person may operate an ultralight vehicle over any congested area of a city, town, or settlement, or over any open air assembly of persons.

§ 103.17 Operations in certain airspace.
No person may operate an ultralight vehicle within Class A, Class B, Class C, or Class D airspace or within the lateral boundaries of the surface area of Class E airspace designated for an airport unless that person has prior authorization from the ATC facility having jurisdiction over that airspace.

§ 103.19 Operations in prohibited or restricted areas.
No person may operate an ultralight vehicle in prohibited or restricted areas unless that person has permission from the using or controlling agency, as appropriate.

§ 103.20 Flight restrictions in the proximity of certain areas designated by notice to airmen.
No person may operate an ultralight vehicle in areas designated in a Notice to Airmen under §91.137, §91.138, §91.141, §91.143 or §91.145 of this chapter, unless authorized by:

(a) Air Traffic Control (ATC); or
(b) A Flight Standards Certificate of Waiver or Authorization issued for the demonstration or event.
[Doc. No. FAA-2000-8274, 66 FR 47378, Sept. 11, 2001]

§ 103.21 Visual reference with the surface.
No person may operate an ultralight vehicle except by visual reference with the surface.

§ 103.23 Flight visibility and cloud clearance requirements.
No person may operate an ultralight vehicle when the flight visibility or distance from clouds is less than that in the table found below. All operations in Class A, Class B, Class C, and Class D airspace or Class E airspace designated for an airport must receive prior ATC authorization as required in §103.17 of this part.

Airspace	Visibility Required	Distance From Clouds
Class A:	Not applicable	Not Applicable.
Class B:	3 statute miles	Clear of Clouds.
Class C:	3 statute miles	500 feet below, 1000 feet above, 2,000 feet horizontal.
Class D:	3 statute miles.	500 feet below, 1000 feet above, 2,000 feet horizontal.
Class E:		
Less than 10,000 feet MSL	3 statute miles	500 feet below, 1000 feet above, 2000 feet horizontal.
10,000 feet or higher MSL	5 statute miles	1000 feet below, 1000 feet above, 1 statute mile horizontal.
Class G:		
1200 feet or less above the surface (regardless of MSL altitude)	1 statute mile	Clear of clouds.
More than 1200 feet above the surface but less than 10,000 feet MSL	1 statute mile	500 feet below, 1000 feet above, 2,000 feet horizontal.
More than 1200 above the surface and at or above 10,000 MSL	5 statute miles	1000 feet below, 1000 feet above, 1 statute mile horizontal.

[Amdt. 103-17, 56 FR 65662, Dec. 17, 1991] Last updated: February 18, 2004 as of Jan, 2012

Glossary

2-Stroke—A valveless motor with a power stroke every time the piston goes down.

4-Stroke—A valved motor with a power stroke ever other time the piston goes down.

A Lines—The first row of paraglider lines; they go from the A riser to the leading edge of the wing.

Absolute Altitude—height above the terrain if you could measure it with a long tape measure.

Accelerator—System used to accelerate the wing using a foot bar connected to the risers, through the harness. The pilot activates it by pushing the bar out with both feet. Also called Speedbar.

Active Flying—The fine control inputs required to keep the wing exactly overhead in turbulence or maneuvering, damping both left/right oscillations and fore/aft surges.

AGL—Above Ground Level.

ACPUL—Association des Constructeurs de Parapente Ultra Legers. European association that developed test standards for paragliders later adopted by AFNOR.

AFNOR—Association Française de Normalisation, French organization that does certification of paragliders (among many other things).

ASL—Above Sea Level.

ATC—Air Traffic Control which consists of Approach Controls, Control Towers and Air Route Traffic Control Centers (just called "Center").

Airspeed—Speed through the air. A GPS reads ground speed, the pilot feels airspeed.

Aspect Ratio—Ratio of the wingspan (projected) to the average chord.

Asymmetrical Collapse—When one side of the wing deflates and not the other. It is the most common paraglider malady that results from turbulence.

Asymmetric Blade Thrust—see P-Factor.

Asymmetric Spiral—A spiral dive where the bank on one side of the circle is shallower than the other.

B Lines—The second row of paraglider lines; they go from the B riser to the wing.

B Line Stall—A condition where the wing is stalled by virtue of the pilot pulling the B-lines down to his chest. Descent rate is usually about 4 times normal.

Big Ears—A maneuver where the pilot pulls the outer A lines such that the tips of the wing fold downward to increase descent rate.

Brake Lines—Lines that go from the brake toggles, through a pulley or loop on the rear riser and up to the trailing edge of the wing.

Brake Toggles—The handles used by the pilot to control the craft. They attach to the brake lines.

C Lines—The third row of lines; goes from the C riser to the wing.

Canopy—Another name for the wing.

Carabiners—Metal fasteners that attach the wing, through its riser loops, to the harness.

Cart—Wheeled assembly that allows for a rolling launch.

Cascade—The split in a wing's lines where it spreads from one line to several as it goes up to the wing. This design feature reduces the total line count and resulting drag.

Cells—A single sewn section of a wing containing air that makes up the airfoil shape.

CEN—Comittee of the European standards organization that set certification standards for paragliders (among other things).

CHT—Cylinder Head Temperature.

CIMA—International Microlight Commission of FAI.

Clip-In Weight—The pilot weight plus motor, fuel and any accessories necessary to fly. Aka *hook-in weight*.

Chord—The distance from the leading edge to trailing edge at any point along the span.

Collapse—What happens when part or all of the wing deforms (aka fold or deflation) due to turbulence or pilot input.

Constant Stall—*see Parachutal Stall.*

Crab—Heading some amount into the wind to maintain a desired ground track.

Damping—The pilot action required to reduce any pendular or fore/aft oscillation.

Deck Angle—*see Pitch.*

Deflation—*see Collapse.*

Density Altitude—Altitude adjusted for pressure, temperature and humidity. Hot, humid air hurts aircraft performance—it is said to be at a higher density altitude. Aircraft performance is based on density altitude, not the actual altitude as read on an altimeter.

DHV—German Hanggliding and Paragliding Federation "Deutcher Hangeleiter Verband." They certify free-flight paragliders, harnesses and related equipment in Germany. This is the most common service used to certify paragliders.

DULV—German Ultralight Flight organization that certifies paramotors and paramotor wings designed for paramotoring.

Downwind Demon—Series of illusions that frequently lead to a pilot pulling too much brake when low to the ground and turning downwind.

EN—European Standards organization. See also CEN.

FAI—Fédération Aéronautique International. The world's Air Sports Federation. *See also CIMA.*

FAR—Federal Aviation Regulations; governing law for paramotor pilots in the USA.

Float Bowl Carburetor—A type of carburetor that uses a float to regulate fuel level in the bowl.

Fold—*See collapse.*

FPM—Feet Per Minute. A measure of climb or descent rate.

Full Stall—An extreme maneuver where the pilot pulls enough brake to deform the wing so much that slows dramatically and deforms the glider and is characterized with a very high descent rate.

Forward Inflation—Any inflation done while facing away from the wing and into the wind; usually done in light winds.

Front Tuck—*see frontal.*

Frontal—A wing deformation where the leading edge folds downward. Maintained in this state, the wing will descend about 3 times the normal rate.

Free Flyer—One who flies without a motor; a paraglider pilot. They generally seek out natural lift sources and launch from high places or get towed in aloft.

GA—General Aviation; all aviation that is not military, governmental or scheduled airlines.

Gyroscopic Precession—The characteristic of a any rotating mass whereby a force acting perpendicular to the direction of rotation will cause the reaction 90 degrees in the direction of rotation.

Harness—The combination of fabric and straps that holds the pilot up in flight through an attachment to the wing and also what the motor is attached to.

Page 305

Glossary

Helicopter—One of several aerobatic maneuvers where the pilot is spinning around an axis other than the center of the wing.

Lateral Axis—An imaginary left/right line around which the PPG pitches up or down. The extended arms of a seated pilot represent the lateral axis direction but the axis itself is between the pilot and wing.

Leading Edge—Front of the wing where the cell openings are.

Longitudinal Axis—An imaginary front-to-back line around which the PPG rolls (banks).

Horseshoe—When referring to a paraglider, the wing deformation where the wing tips come forward and may touch each other. Descent rate is usually about 4 times normal.

Loop—A high energy aerobatic maneuver where the pilot uses speed from a steep spiral to fly over the top of the glider.

Maillon—*see quick link.*

Membrane Carburetor—A type of carburetor that uses a membrane to regulate fuel flow.

Mechanical Turbulence—Random swirls of air downwind of a solid object (building, hill, mountain, etc.).

MSL—Mean Sea Level. Usually is used in reference to altitudes above sea level (ASL).

NOTAM—Notice To Airmen.

Over-The-Nose Spiral—A spiral dive where the wing is pointed nearly straight down. Recovery can be difficult.

P-Factor—Assymetric force caused by a prop that is not acting perpendicular to the relative wind.

Parablend—An expensive Nylon/Kevlar cocktail, stired by a paramotor prop, usually prepared after an aborted launch.

Parachutage—*see Parachutal Stall.*

Parachutal Stall—A stall where the fully-formed wing stops flying forward and descends like an old round parachute.

Parasite—Location where powered paragliding takes place.

Pendulum—The left right swinging action that occurs whenever the glider is upset laterally.

Pitch—Motion around the PPG's latitudinal axis. The pilot is said to *Pitch up* when power is added.

PLF—Parachute Landing Fall.

PPG—Powered Paraglider

Pressure Altitude—Pressure represented as an altitude, assuming a standard atmosphere. It is also the altitude indicated on your altimeter when set to 29.92 in Hg. *See also Density Altitude.*

Propeller—The long skinny blade that provides propulsion.

Quick Link—The steel ring that connect the wing's A, B, C or D lines to their respective riser. Also called Maillon Rapide (primarily in Europe). The distinction is they use screw-together gates.

Rear Riser—The aftmost riser. On 3-riser wings, it is the C riser. On 4-riser wings it is the D riser.

Reverse Inflation—Any Inflation started while facing the wing instead of the wind. Usually done in stronger wind.

Riser Loops—The loops at the very bottom of each riser where the carabiner goes through.

Riser Set—The combination of individual A, B, C and D risers and their corresponding loop for each side of the wing that connect to the harness through a carabiner and lines through quick links.

Roll—Motion around the PPG's longitudinal axis.

Rotor—The swirling air that results from wind blowing around an obstacle.

S.A.T.—"Safety Acrobatic Team's" maneuver where the glider and pilot appear to be rotating around each other.

SHV—Swiss paraglider certifying agency of the Swiss Hang gliding Association.

Speedbar—*see Accelerator.*

Spiral Dive—An extreme banked turn where the wing is angled towards the ground. *See also "Over-The-Nose" spiral dive.*

Stall—*see Full Stall.*

Surge—The characteristic of the wing to overfly the pilot under some conditions. It can be induced by pilot action or turbulence.

Stabilo Line—Line that goes to the very tip of the wing, usually a B line.

Tell Tale—A small wind indicator, usually a streamer of some sort.

Torque—The property of a motor/propeller that makes the motor, and its harnessed occupant, want to twist in the opposite direction of propeller spin.

Torque Induced Lockout—A condition where angled thrust pushes the pilot sideways, and into a bank the other way. Lockout is reached when brake pressure alone cannot compensate for the resulting turn.

Trailing Edge—The rearmost part of the wing when in flight.

Trimmers—Mechanism of some risers (usually on motoring wings) that allows changing the rear risers to increase speed. The pilot pulls a "Trim Tab" to effect the change.

Trim Speed—The speed that results when flying with no brakes applied, trimmers in their cruise setting and no speedbar.

True Airspeed—Actual speed through the air as opposed to what it feels like to the pilot. At high elevations, the pilot must move faster through the air to get the same feel as at lower elevations.

True Altitude—Altutude above sea level if you could memasure it with a long tape measure. *see also absolute altitude.*

Turtle—The occurrence when a pilot falls backwards such that he is lying on top of the motor, unable to move until un-clipping from the unit.

Vertical Axis—an imaginary top-to-bottom line around which the PPG yaws (twists left or right).

Virga—Precipitation that evaporates before reaching the ground.

VOR—Very High Frequency (VHF) Omni Directional Range used for navigation by airplane pilots and as reference points on charts.

Windmilling—The spinning of a prop due solely to the relative wind blowing through it.

Wind Shadow—A calm that exists downwind of obstructions.

Wing—The means to our magic.

Wing Fold—*see Collapse.*

Wing Over—A series of turns in concert with the natural pendular bank rate of the glider.

Yaw—Motion around the PPG's vertical axis. If the PPG rotates to the left without banking it is said to yaw to the left.

Index

2-meter 22, 214
2-stroke motor 230-234
4-stroke motor 230

A

A-helpers 65, 66
accessories 40, 275-280
accordian fold 35
active flying 47, 164, 180, 214, 299
adiabatic lapse rate 296
ADIZ 89
adjusting, motor *See harness, setup*
advertising 83
aerobatic wings 298
aerobatics 175
aerodynamics 219-228
AFNOR 300
Agama 280
AGL 86
agonic line 135
air cooled, motor 268
airbag harness 214
airflow, mountain 74
airfoil shape 224
airline pilot 11
airlines 185, 194, 292
airplane 58, 80, 87, 91, 94, 102-105, 133, 137, 287
See Powered Parachute
airport 58, 78, 87, 99, 101, 131
airport, controlled 107-112
airshow 191
airspace 77, 80, 86-98, 132, 133
airspeed 134, 159, 164, 174
airspeed indicator 279
airway 98
alert areas 86, 89
alphabet, phonetic 111
altimeter 20-21
altimetry 279
altitude 131, 137
altitude abbreviations 86
altitudes 58, 140
aluminum 115, 118, 119
anemometer 278
angle of attack 219, 223
angle of attack, prop 237
angle of incidence 225, 226
anhedral 224
animals 86
anti-torque strap 16, 114, 176
aperture 297
approach 59
arrogance 12
ARTCC (center) 92
aspect ratio 225
asymmetric blade thrust 242
asymmetric spiral 180
ATC 92, 107
ATIS 108, 109, 110
atmosphere 72
atmospheric pressure 168
attachment points 177, 271-272
authorities 82
aviation radios 277
aviation weather 77-78
avisory circular AC 103-7 83
AWOS 95, 109
axis of motion 221
latitudinal (pitch) 221
longitudinal (roll) 221
vertical (yaw) 221

B

B Line Stall 179

B-line stall 196
backwards flying 151
balance *See CG*
balloon 163
bank 159, 190, 220, 221, 226
Barish, David 254
base leg, pattern 60, 103-105
beach 157, 298
beach, weather 74
bearings 119-120, 235
belt drive 119, 120
distance 120
slipping 120
tension 120
belt tension, checking 119
Bernoulli 225
big air 216, 300
big ears 178, 216
bolts 118
boots 22
boxes 292
brake line length 24
brake lines 14, 126
brake positions/pressures 24, 159, 189
brake pulley 14
brakes, feel position 157
break-in, motor 38
bridles 22
brummel hooks *See sister clips*
bubbles, fuel line 119
bump scale 57, 142
bundling the wing 62
bunny hills 8
burns, line 145, 150
bus lines, transporting 293
buzzing 140

C

C-line deflation 34
cage 40, 162, 175, 269
flex 52
camber 127
carabiner 20
carbon deposits 118
carbon fiber prop 123
carburetor tuning 233
carburetors 231-234
carry strap *See Ground Handling Strap*
cart 276
carts 267, 274
cascade 14
cascade failure 127
cattle herding 289
cell openings 26
cell phone 280
CEN 300
center of lift 221, 223
centered, forward inflation 27
centripetal force 232
certification 7
certified aircraft 58, 80
certified wings 113, 178, 300
CG 65, 116, 177, 221, 238
chart 84
checklist 51, 52, 301
chest strap 176
choosing a motor unit 265-274
choosing the site 100-101
chord line 225, 226
CHT 21, **278**
CIMA 201
circuits, carburetor 234
city 81, 137

class A airspace 87
class B airspace 87, 93, 94, 95, 96
class C airspace 87
class D airspace 87, 92, 93, 97, 98, 107, 109, 112
class E airspace 85-98, 102-105
class E surface area 87, 88, 111
class F airspace 86
class G airspace 80, 85-98, 102-105
cleaning 62, 145, 291
clearing the lines 26
clearing the turn 57
cliff, launching from 215
climb 56, 141, 165, 169, 211
climb angle 100
climbout 139, 170, 171
cloud clearance 85, 87, 91, 304
cloud suck 298, 301
clouds 71, 91, 132, 133, 297, 300-302
cumuliform 301
cumulus 91, 132, 295
clutch 119, 120, 232
bell 120
pads 120
shoes 120
clutched units 52, 222-223
coastal weather 298
coatings 13-22
cold fronts 78, 302-303
cold weather gear 280
collapse 47, 54, 71, 141, 164, 177, 193, 225, 299, 298
asymmetric 182
frontal 182
collapse, how it happens 227
collapses, large 101
collision 80, 91, 140, 142, 191
collision hazard 102-105
comfort bars *See also J-bars*
commercial use 83
common sense 79, 80, 81, 83, 139
communications 142
communications, control tower 109, 111
compass 134, **135**
compass rose 77, 92
compensation 83, 84
competition 161-162, 176, 192, 201-208
circle and two lines 206
cloverleaf 202
endurance 207
engine failure 201
fair 202
flight precision 206
foot drag 204
ground precision 202-205
kiting war 207
scoring 208
speedbar 203
spot landing 205
touch and go 205
complaint 84
compression 118-119
compression release 234
concertina fold *see accordian*
conduction 296
congested 81, 84, 172
constant stall 183
control tower 87, 88, 89, 93, 95, 98, 107-112
convergence zone 75, 298
coordinated turn 176

coordinates 94
cost 296
courtesy 139-140
crabbing 67, 136
crankshaft 120
cravat 48, 179, 180, **181**, 184
critical angle of attack 219, 226, 228
crops 99, 101
cross country 131-138
cross-armed inflation 154
cross-section 225
crosswind 28, 59, 66, 135, 156, 162, 169
cruising 58
cumulonimbus
customs 294

D

daylight 72
daylight savings time 76
de-rated 268
dead reckoning 133
deck angle 226
decompression valve
See compression release
deflating 24, 33, 147, 153
demonstration 175, 185
density altitude 66, 168, 169
deploying 180
deployment 22
depth of field 298
descent techniques 178-181
desert weather 299
dewpoint 77, 296
DHV 300
diaphragm carburetor 232
dips and loops 25
direct drive 235, 273
directional control 100
disk, propeller 236
distance bars 271-272
distance, judging 100
distraction 22, 140, 191, 295
ditching 194
dog, as passenger 68
downhill, launching 101
downwind 169
downwind demon 190-191
downwind leg 59, 104
drag, aerodynamic 178, 219-221
center of 221, 223
form 220
induced 220
parasitic 220
drift 60, 106
dropping objects 82
DULV 300
dust devils 72, 299
Dyneema 127

E

E Surface Area *See class E surface area*
EAA 281, 302
efficiency 224
EGT 21, **278**
electric start 267
emergencies 43-50, 56
brake line failure or tangle 45-50
cravat 48-50
kill switch failure 48-50
motor failure 46-50
parachutal stall 50
PLF 50

Index

radio failure 45-50
reserve deployment 49-50
riser twist 48-50
severe asymmetric collapse 47-50
small wing collapse 47-50
throttle cable caught 44-50
throttle failure 48
unfastened leg straps 49-50
emergencies, situational 194-200
accidental reserve deployment 200
cloud suck 197
engine failure 198
fire 200
fogged in 199
gust front 195
impending collision 199
landing in power lines 197
landing in water 194
motor stuck at power 196
wing or connection failure 200
emergency kit 280
emergency landing site 99
emergency tool kit 128
EN certification 300
endurance 133
energy 160-161, 186
enforcement 82
engine failure 46-50, 100, 105, 132, 139, 165, 170, 171, 185, 186, 187
evaporation 298
exemption 83, 84
exhibition 290
exposure 297

F

f-stop 297
FAA 77, 79-84, 86, 90, 253
face plant 52
FAI 201
Fan Man 255
FAR 103 80, 81, 303
FCC 22
FCC test 278
federal funds, airport 102-105
federal lands 99
feel 171
final approach, pattern 103-105
fine, law enforcement 84
fire 119
flag 222-223
flag, on wing 288-289
flapping 174
flare 126, 165
flat area (wing) 260
flight path 59, 220
float bowl carburetor 232, 233
floating J-bars 115
fly-ins 81
folding 36, 62
foot drag 157, 162
foot-pound 118
footware 164
footwear 187, 193
forces, balance 219-221
forecast 71
forested areas 99
formation 140, 142, 163-164, 191
forward inflation 26, 52-55, 65, 210
forward kiting 28, 29
frangible prop 238
free flight, learn motoring 209-210
free flight, learn paragliding 213-214
frisbee 173
front tuck (frontal) 28, 31, 54, 147, 154, 177, 182
fronts 302-303
FRS 22, 277
FSS 78, 86, 89, 90, 92, 108
fuel 38-39, 133
fueling 38
mixture 38
preflight 40
selection and storage 38
weight 38
fuel lines 119

G

G force 49, 179, 193, 220
gasoline *See fuel*
gear, PPG 13-22
gear, reduction drive 119-120
general aviation 102-105
glide 61-62, 132, 172-174, 198
stretching 61, 198
glide ratio 58, 222-223, 228
gloves 25, 145, 150, 193, 280
GMRS 22
GPS 91, 94, 98, 131, 133, 138, 279
GPS groundspeed 106
gradient 131
grass 66, 100, 101, 105, 131
Greenwich, England 76
ground effect 224
ground handling 23
ground handling straps 17, 114, 115
ground track 59, 134
groundspeed 131, 134, 135, 136, 160, 168
gust 159-160, 166
gust front 73, 78, 301-302
gust front, handling 195
gusts 72
gyroscopic precession 240

H

hand signals 43
handling the wing 23-36
hands up, power off 44, 50, 141, 181, *See collapse, assymetric*
hang check 37
hang glider 11, 98
hang gliding 253
hang point 238
hang-back angle 116
harness 16-19, 25, 37, 72, 113-116, 175
adjusting 16, 37, 168
for kiting 20
free flight 175, 176, 177
height 16
mountain climbing harness 20
setup 113-116
hazardous material 293
heading 134
headset 108-112
headwind 61, 133, 173
hearing protection 277
helicopter 80, 90, 94, 104-105, 288 *See Powered Parachute*
helicopters 58
helicopters (maneuver) 175
helmet 21-22, 25, 108-112, 187, 193
helmets 277
high elevation 100, 101-102, 167-169, 170
high wind techniques 148-153
highway 102
hill, launching from 215
history of PPG 253-256
home building 281
hook knife 22, 194
hook turn 166
hook-in 221
hooking in, alternate 29
hooking in, forward 27
hooking in, reversed 29-35
horsepower (HP) 229-230, 238
horseshoe 179, 180, 227
hot conditions 100, 167-169
houses 82
humid 167-169
humidity 168
hurricane 299
hybrid 274
hybrid, PPC 64

I

ignition circuit noise 277
illusions, downwind
See downwind demon
inch-pound 119
inflation 26, 31-32, 168, 169
power forward 169
inflation, stronger winds 54
inspection 13-22, 156
inspection, postflight 62
inspection, wing 127
instructing, for pay 83
instruction 302
Instruments 20-21
intercepting 164
intermediate syndrome 188
inversion 74, 297
IR, instrument route 89
ISA 296
isogonic line 134, 135

J

J bar 176
J-bars 17, 114, 115, 116
comfort bars 18
shoulder J-Bars 17
underarm 18
James Watt 230
jet 185
jets 91, 104-105, 137
judging distance 100

K

Kevlar 127
kick-in bar 114, 115
kick-in strap 56
kill switch 34, **48**, 56, 60, 142
kit, building from 283
Kite Lines 200
kiting 11, 23, 48, 141, 145, 216
forward 29
high winds 148-153
light winds 153
reverse 29, 32-35
straight riser reversed 33
upside down 145
wars 154
without a harness 146
kiting harness 25, 145
kiting war 207
kiting, the wing 54
knot, brake line 126
Kodak Courage 191

L

L/D speed, best 222-223
landing 59-61, 101, 165, 172, 211
crosshill 101
crosswind 101
flare 61
in turbulence 172
one step 166
pattern 57, 59
power on 166
scoop 165
slider 165
spot 165
troubleshooting 61
uphill 101
landmarks 133
lapse rate 296, 299
latent heat 298
latitude, line of 87, 92, 134, 135
launch 51-55, 100, 170
distances 100
roads 168, 174
slope 101
steering 170
law, the 79-84
layout 26, 65
layout, wing 52
leading edge 27, 31, 40, 146
lee, of obstruction 74
leg drag 168
leg straps 114
letter of agreement 112
lettering the wing 84
license 2, 83
licensed pilots 102-105
lift, aerodynamic 219-221
lift, atmospheric 76
lifted index 300
liftoff 100
liftweb 113, 115
line chart 127
line over 25
line stretching 127
lines, paraglider 14
lipstick cameras 299
loaded 184
Loaded Riser Twist 48, 53, 227, 241
longitude, line of 87, 92, 134, 135
loops 175
lost 133
low flying 161-163

M

mach 235, 236
macrometeorology 302
magnetic course 134, 135
magnetic north 77, 135
maillon *See quick link*
maintenance, motor 113-130
flowchart 117
motor 118-119
troubleshooting 118
maintenance, wing 125-128
adjusting brake lines 126
brake line knot 125
cascade 127
fabric repair 127
inspection 127
ocean dunking 128
replacing risers 125
tape 127
maneuvers clinic 6
See SIV course
maneuvers, advanced 175-184
mechanical turbulence 75, 100, 303

Index

MEF *94*
membrane carburetor *232, 234*
Mercury, inches of *168*
meteorologist *295*
micro balloons *123*
microlight *201*
micrometeorology *295*
microphones *277*
mid-air *49*
military *86, 89*
Miller, James *255*
minimum sink speed *228*
minutes, degree *94*
mirror *66, 133*
mixture *234*
MOA's, airspace *89*
mode C *89*
model aircraft, finding *290*
monsoons *299*
motor failure *56, 57, 58*
motor induced lock out *48*
motor mount *40*
motor risers *301*
motor-induced lock-out *240*
motor-induced lockout *56*
motorcycle *288, 293*
mountain weather *74*
mountains *172*
MSL *86*
muffler *40, 79, 118*
multi line attachments *17*
music *191, 277*
mylar *36*

N

nature preserve
   See wilderness areas
nautical mile *87, 92, 138*
navigation *133*
negative G *219*
neighbors *101*
Newton, Isaac *220*
night *132*
noise *79, 81, 82, 103-105, 139, 237*
nosewheel *64*
NOTAM *77, 78, 92*
NTSB *84*

O

obstacles *170, 171*
obstructions *100, 101, 170*
ocean *194*
offset thrust *116, 239*
oil *132, 302*
   four-cycle 39
   mineral 39
   mixing 38, 302
   selection 38
   synthetic 39
   two-cycle oil 39
oil, buying *294*
oil, gear *119-120*
open air assembly *81*
orographic lift *77*
oscillation *29, 54, 58, 66, 67, 158, 159, 164, 165*
other uses *287-290*
over the nose spiral *180*
over-braking *58*
overfly *28, 33, 54, 62, 147, 150*
overheat *233*

P

P-factor *242*
packaging *292*
panning *297*
parablending *54, 55*
parachutal stall *50, 71, 164, 178, 183, 288*
parachute *See reserve*
parachute landing fall *See PLF*
parachute rigger *115, 130*
parachute, reserve *175, 193*
Paracommander **254**
paraglider, high performance *165*
paragliding *213-216*
parasailing *253*
parascending *254*
parks *86, 90, 99, 101, 171*
parts, availability *273-274*
patch *127*
pattern *42-43, 98, 103-105, 140, 171, 173*
pattern, airplane *93, 94, 96*
pendular control *183*
pendulum *14, 58, 60, 158, 159*
penetrate *173, 198*
penetration *188*
permission *101*
phonetic alphabet *111*
photography *83, 295-300*
   focus 297
   ISO 297
   noise 298
pictures *295*
pilotage *133, 136*
pipeline patrols *58*
piston rings *117*
pitch *219*
pitch, propeller *236*
pivoting bar *176, 177*
placard, wing *301*
plans, building from *283*
platform *293*
play, in prop *119-120*
PLF *50*
polar curve *223, 228*
pole standing *164*
police *79*
pop-off pressure *234*
porosity *127, 192*
postflight *62*
posture *168*
power *101, 160, 162, 169, 172, 177*
power band *230-234*
power band, wing *24*
power forward *52, 210-211, 266, 269*
power to weight ratio *256*
Powered Parachute *64*
PPC *141, 256, 274*
   See also Powered Parachute
precision flying *157-166, 176*
preflight choices *169*
preflight inspection *39-41, 301*
premix *See fueling*
preparing the wing *26*
preservation, wing *36*
preventative maintenance *118-119*
private pilots *83*
professional pilots *84*
prohibited area *82*
projected area (wing) *298*
pronunciation, alphabet *111*
prop blast *140*
prop disk *114*
prop tape *122*
prop wash *140*
propeller *37, 40, 120-122, 235-238, 270-271*
   aerodynamic balance 121
   balancers 121
   chordwise offset 121, 123
   efficiency 235
   impbalance, offset 123
   larger repairs 123
   leading edge tape 122
   mounting 120
   static balance 121, 123
   static balance, solder 123
   tip speed 235
   torsional stress 120
   tracking 122
propeller plane *140*
propeller repair *122*
   baking soda 123
   carbon fiber props 123
   caution 122
   fiberglass 123
   foam 124
   small divots 123
   wood props 123
property damage *101*
public property *99*
public relations *290*
pull start *232, 267*
pulley, brake *126*
pulleys *115-116, 119, 120, 126-128*
puzzle props *292*

Q

QFE *279*
QNH *279*
quad *276*
quick links *15, **17**, **18**, 41, 126*

R

radiant cooling *296*
radio *9-10, 22, 43, 142, 163, 214, 278*
radio compatibility *277*
radio, aviation *87, 88, 89, 92, 96, 97, 105, 107-112*
rain *71*
range *133*
ratings *2, 70, 214*
ratio, fuel/oil *117*
record, number aloft *78*
redrive *40*
reduction drive *119-120, 235-238*
   propside gear 120
   small gear 120
reed valve *234*
reflex *298, 301, 225*
reflex airfoil *226*
reflex risers *261*
registering your motor *294*
regulations *80-81, 84, 85*
rehearse *57*
reliability *267, 268*
repair *118, 121, 124 See propeller repair*
repair shops *118*
repairing, wing *127*
rescuing *141*
reserve parachute *22, 128-130*
   bridle routing 129-130
   deployment 49
   deployment bag 130
   installation 129
   maintenance 129-130
   mounting 129-130
   pins 40
   repacking 130
   setup 129-130
   skydiving reserves 130
resolution *299*
retrieval *137*
reverse inflation *29-35, 54, 55, 210*
reverse Inflation, cart *153*
rich fuel/air mixture *233*
rich of peak *233*
ridge lift *See lift, atmospheric*
ridge rules *213*
rigger, parachute *130*
right of way *80, 102*
right of way, soaring *213*
ripstop nylon *13-22*
riser shift *239, See weight shift*
riser twist *53, 56, 113, 116, 239-242*
   See collapse, assymetric
risers, reflex *see reflex risers*
risers *15-16, 25, 125, 126, 145, 301-302*
   changing 125
   spread 25, 113, 115
risk *viii, 144, 155, 161, 163, 165, 298, 299, 295*
Risk & Reward *9, 70*
risk management *185-200*
risks *140-141, 142*
risky *173, 175, 181*
rivers *135*
rivets *282*
roads *81, 94, 102, 132, 133, 135, 169, 174*
rocket launches *86*
Rogallo *254*
rollover *64*
rolls *175*
rosette the wing *35, 152*
rotor *57, 74, 75, 76, 198, 303*
RPM *235*
runway *91-94, 103-105, 131*
rust *120*

S

S-Turn *173*
safety strap *116*
safety wire *118*
salt water *128*
sand *101, 146, 158, 166, 169*
Santa Ana winds *299*
SAT's *175*
school *4-5, 106*
sea breeze *298*
search and rescue *290*
seat *56*
seat, getting into *37*
seatboard *56*
sectional chart *85, 87, 89, 91-94, 98, 107, 108, 138*
security airspace *86, 89*
segmented circle *103-105*
seize *233*
seized *39, 117*
self training *viii*
setup, harness *113*
setup, trike *64*
severe weather *74*
shadow *140*
Shatner, William *10*
shear zone *See wind shear*
sheath *14*
shipping *36, 291*
SHV *300*
sidetone *277*
simulator *7, 9, 37, 43, 57, 113, 114, 115, 130*

Index

single-point failure 192
sink 76, 101
sink rate 223
siphoning fuel PB 38
sister clips 115
sites 98, 99, 100-101, 105, 106, 170
    challenging 167-174
    tight 170-174
SIV course 186, 216
skis 287
sky divers 12
sky diving reserves 130
slider 166
slipstream 37
slow 161
soaring 13-22, 74, 76, 98, 176, 213, 300
soft J-bar 114
span 222-223
spare air 193
spark plug 40, 118, 128
sparsely populated 81, 82, 89
spectators 81, 139
Spectra 127
speed system 15
speedbar 18, 114, 115, 129, 164, 173, 222-223, 224, 228, 300
speedbar use 177
spin 50, 56, 173, 174, 176, 181-182
spiral dive 180
split A's 15, 52, 302
sport parachuting 253, 254
Sport Pilot 276
Sport Pilot regulation 84
sporting events 81
spot landing 172-174
    flare 173-174
    touchdown 172
spread 113
springs, safety wiring 118
stability 221, 226
stability, cart 276
stabilo line 48, 184
stall 24, 173, 174
stall, aerodynamics of 219, 228
stall, full 181
stall, parachutal
    See parachutal stall
standard atmosphere 296
standard temperature 168
starter, electric 42
starting 187
starting the motor 41
state change 298
state lands 99
statute mile 108, 138
steep turns 179
steering 276
steering lines See brake Lines
steering, launch run 102
sternum strap 115
storage, fuel See fueling
storing the wing 25, 35-36
straight riser kiting 33
straight-in, airports 104-105
stratiform 301
strength test, field 41
stretching, lines 127
strobe 80
structural failure 22
stuffing the wing 35
sublimation 298
suitcase, packing into 292
sunrise 80, 100, 297
sunset 80

surf 198
surface area of Class E 88, 92
surfaces 101, 166, 168, 169
    difficult 174
surge 151, 159, 160, 164
suspension lines
    See lines, paraglider
swinging arms 116
swoooping 165, 166
symmetrical 225
symmetrical airfoil 220, 225

T

Tachometer 278
tailwind 28, 61, 134, 159, 167
tandem 2, 5, 7, 8-9, 63, 68, 83, 141, 216, 265,
    foot-launched 265
tandem carts 8, 276
tangled 25, 62, 140, 175
target fixation 60
taxi 66
TBO 268
telephone, permission 107
telltale 167
temperature 168
tensile strength 14
Terminal Area Chart 85, 98
terminal velocity 130
terrain 101, 137, 181, 192
test, airspace 94
testing gear 188, 296, 284
TFR 91-94
thermaling 213
thermals 52, 72, 106, 132, 156, 227, 297, 299
throttle 54, 65, 130, 141, 160
throttle simulator 9, 27, 34
thrust 161-162, 167, 168, 169, 172, 269
thrust line 114, 116, 221, 224, 227, 238-242
thrust required 228
thrust vs. horsepower 229-230
thrust, choosing 266
thunderstorm 73, 75, 302
time, universal 76
tip line See stabilo
tires 276
toggle, brake 27, 163
toggles 14, 145, 150
tool kit, emergency 128
tools 118, 132, 169
topographical information 97
tornadoes 72, 73
torque 52, 56, 239-242, 266
torque wrench 118
torque, motor 114, 116
touchdown 50, 60-61, 165-166, 173
tow, boat 177
tower frequency 93
towing 6
towing, hand 8
town 81
track 135
traffic 59, 140
trailing edge 14, 31, 145
training 3-12, 187
transition areas 86, 87, 88, 97
transitioning to power 209
transmissions 109
transponder 89
transportability 273
transportation 287
traveling with gear 291-294

tree rescue kit 280
trees 100, 171
trespassing 99
trike 55
trim speed 159, 222-223
trimmers 15, 18, 41, 159, 164, 173, 177, 222-223, 224, 228, 300
true course 134, 135
true north 77
trying gear 188
tuned pipe 230-234
turbulence 47, 72, 101, 106, 141, 160, 164, 172, 175, 177, 181, 298
    landing in 172
turn 158
turning, aerodynamics of 226
turns 57, 100, 140, 161-162
turtle 55, 68
tweaking the A's 50
Tygon 119

U

U.S. Nationals 131
ultralight 71, 80, 85, 90, 98, 253, 304
ultralight types 296
uncontrolled airports 102-105
underarm bars 17
    See also comfort bars
unicom 97, 105
units 138
unloading 141, 193, 227
unstable atmosphere 300
untangling 25
updrafts See thermals
USHPA 214, 255, 278, 302
USHPA radio test 278
USPPA 7, 10, 70, 302
USUA 206, 302
UTC 78, See Zulu
UV 14, 62

V

variation 134, **135**
variation, line of 96
variometer 21
vector diagram 135
venturi 232-234
VFR 85
vibration 119, 121, 122, 123
video 83, 295, 299
visibility 58, 85-98, 304
VOR 78, 90, 91, 92, 94, 98, 107
vortices See wake turbulence
VR, visual route 89

W

waiver 11, 84
wake turbulence 58, 104-105, 112, 140, 141, 164, 193, 225
wall 146, 149, 152, 154
wall, building 30-31
warm fronts 302-303
water 141, 161, 171, 177, 194
water cooled, motor 268
weather 71-78, 295-304
webbing, harness 16
weight 13, 14, 16, 18, 19, 20, 265, 266
weight shift 57, 114, 140, 176-177, 178, 211, 214, 215, 239, 272-273
welding 282, 302
wheels 9, 63, 276
Why We Fly video 294

Wilbur Wright viii
wilderness 86, 90
wind 52, 71, 101, 131-138, 172, 295-304
    aloft 74, 75
    bow wave 74
    Coriolis effect 304
    direction 135
    drift 134, 136
    fronts 303
    gradient 75, 131-138, 172
    high pressure area 304
    hurricane 304
    indicators 52, 60
    jet stream 304
    land-breeze 75
    low pressure area 304
    mechanical turbulence 303
    mountain wave 304
    relative 219
    ridge 304
    rotor 303
    sea breeze 74
    shadow 57, 74, 101, 303
    shear 75
    surface 75, 106
    telling direction 106
    upslope 105
    VAD winds 78
    venturi effect 304
wind gradient 190
wind indicators 278
wind shadow 23
windmilling 178, 222-223
wing 41, 101, 169, 297
    area 223
    fast 169
    strength test 41
wing loading 216, 298
wingover 183-184, 227
wingtip vortices 220, 224
    See also wake turbulence
wire ties 119, 128, 129
wires 100, 132, 135, 142, 162, 187, 189
wraps 149
Wright Brothers 13

Y

yaw 219

Z

zoom 300
Zulu 76